FEDERAL RULES
OF APPELLATE PROCEDURE
2020

ANNOTATED

UNITED STATES
GOVERNMENT

Table of Contents

FEDERAL RULES OF CRIMINAL PROCEDURE
(As amended to December 1, 2019)

HISTORICAL NOTE

The original Federal Rules of Criminal Procedure were adopted by order of the Supreme Court on Dec. 26, 1944, transmitted to Congress by the Attorney General on Jan. 3, 1945, and became effective on Mar. 21, 1946.

The Rules have been amended Dec. 27, 1948, eff. Jan. 1, 1949; Dec. 27, 1948, eff. Oct. 20, 1949; Apr. 12, 1954, eff. July 1, 1954; Apr. 9, 1956, eff. July 8, 1956; Feb. 28, 1966, eff. July 1, 1966; Dec. 4, 1967, eff. July 1, 1968; Mar. 1, 1971, eff. July 1, 1971; Apr. 24, 1972, eff. Oct. 1, 1972; Nov. 20, 1972, eff. July 1, 1975, pursuant to Pub. L. 93–595; Mar. 18, 1974, eff. July 1, 1974; Apr. 22, 1974, eff. in part Aug. 1, 1975, and Dec. 1, 1975, pursuant to Pub. L. 93–361 and Pub. L. 94–64; Dec. 12, 1975, Pub. L. 94–149, §5, 89 Stat. 806; Apr. 26, 1976, eff. in part Aug. 1, 1976, and Oct. 1, 1977, pursuant to Pub. L. 94–349 and Pub. L. 95–78; Apr. 30, 1979, eff. in part Aug. 1, 1979, and Dec. 1, 1980, pursuant to Pub. L. 96–42; Apr. 28, 1982, eff. Aug. 1, 1982; Oct. 12, 1982, Pub. L. 97–291, §3, 96 Stat. 1249; Apr. 28, 1983, eff. Aug. 1, 1983; Oct. 12, 1984, Pub. L. 98–473, title II, §§209, 215, 404, 98 Stat. 1986, 2014, 2067; Oct. 30, 1984, Pub. L. 98–596, §11(a), (b), 98 Stat. 3138; Apr. 29, 1985, eff. Aug. 1, 1985; Oct. 27, 1986, Pub. L. 99–570, title I, §1009(a), 100 Stat. 3207–8; Nov. 10, 1986, Pub. L. 99–646, §§12(b), 24, 25(a), 54(a), 100 Stat. 3594, 3597, 3607; Mar. 9, 1987, eff. Aug. 1, 1987; Apr. 25, 1988, eff. Aug. 1, 1988; Nov. 18, 1988, Pub. L. 100–690, title VI, §6483, title VII, §§7076, 7089(c), 102 Stat. 4382, 4406, 4409; Apr. 25, 1989, eff. Dec. 1, 1989; May 1, 1990, eff. Dec. 1, 1990; Apr. 30, 1991, eff. Dec. 1, 1991; Apr. 22, 1993, eff. Dec. 1, 1993; Apr. 29, 1994, eff. Dec. 1, 1994; Sept. 13, 1994, Pub. L. 103–322, title XXIII, §230101(b), title XXXIII, §330003(h), 108 Stat. 2078, 2141; Apr. 27, 1995, eff. Dec. 1, 1995; Apr. 23, 1996, eff. Dec. 1, 1996; Apr. 24, 1996, Pub. L. 104–132, title II, §207(a), 110 Stat. 1236; Apr. 11, 1997, eff. Dec. 1, 1997; Apr. 24, 1998, eff. Dec. 1, 1998; Apr. 26, 1999, eff. Dec. 1, 1999; Apr. 17, 2000, eff. Dec. 1, 2000; Oct. 26, 2001, Pub. L. 107–56, title II, §§203(a), 219, 115 Stat. 278, 291; Apr. 29, 2002, eff. Dec. 1, 2002; Nov. 2, 2002, Pub. L. 107–273, div. C, title I, §11019(b), 116 Stat. 1825; Nov. 25, 2002, Pub. L. 107–296, title VIII, §895, 116 Stat. 2256; Apr. 30, 2003, Pub. L. 108–21, title VI, §610(b), 117 Stat. 692; Apr. 26, 2004, eff. Dec. 1, 2004; Pub. L. 108–458, title VI, §6501(a), Dec. 17, 2004, 118 Stat. 3760; Apr. 25, 2005, eff. Dec. 1, 2005; Apr. 12, 2006, eff. Dec. 1, 2006; Apr. 30, 2007, eff. Dec. 1, 2007; Apr. 23, 2008, eff. Dec. 1, 2008; Mar. 26, 2009, eff. Dec. 1, 2009; Apr. 28, 2010, eff. Dec. 1, 2010; Apr. 26, 2011, eff. Dec. 1, 2011; Apr. 23, 2012, eff. Dec. 1, 2012; Apr. 16, 2013, eff. Dec. 1, 2013; Apr. 25, 2014, eff. Dec. 1, 2014; Apr. 28, 2016, eff. Dec. 1, 2016; Pub. L. 114–324, §12(c), Dec. 16, 2016, 130 Stat. 1948; Apr. 26, 2018, eff. Dec. 1, 2018; Apr. 25, 2019, eff. Dec. 1, 2019.

TITLE VII. POST-CONVICTION PROCEDURES

TITLE VIII. SUPPLEMENTARY AND SPECIAL PROCEEDINGS

TITLE IX. GENERAL PROVISIONS

TITLE I. APPLICABILITY

Rule 1. Scope; Definitions

(a) Scope.

(1) In General. These rules govern the procedure in all criminal proceedings in the United States district courts, the United States courts of appeals, and the Supreme Court of the United States.

(2) State or Local Judicial Officer. When a rule so states, it applies to a proceeding before a state or local judicial officer.

(3) Territorial Courts. These rules also govern the procedure in all criminal proceedings in the following courts:

(A) the district court of Guam;

(B) the district court for the Northern Mariana Islands, except as otherwise provided by law; and

(C) the district court of the Virgin Islands, except that the prosecution of offenses in that court must be by indictment or information as otherwise provided by law.

(4) Removed Proceedings. Although these rules govern all proceedings after removal from a state court, state law governs a dismissal by the prosecution.

(5) Excluded Proceedings. Proceedings not governed by these rules include:

(A) the extradition and rendition of a fugitive;

(B) a civil property forfeiture for violating a federal statute;

(C) the collection of a fine or penalty;

(D) a proceeding under a statute governing juvenile delinquency to the extent the procedure is inconsistent with the statute, unless Rule 20(d) provides otherwise;

(E) a dispute between seamen under 22 U.S.C. §§256–258; and

(F) a proceeding against a witness in a foreign country under 28 U.S.C. §1784.

(b) Definitions. The following definitions apply to these rules:

(1) "Attorney for the government" means:

(A) the Attorney General or an authorized assistant;

(B) a United States attorney or an authorized assistant;

(C) when applicable to cases arising under Guam law, the Guam Attorney General or other person whom Guam law authorizes to act in the matter; and

(D) any other attorney authorized by law to conduct proceedings under these rules as a prosecutor.

(2) "Court" means a federal judge performing functions authorized by law.

(3) "Federal judge" means:

(A) a justice or judge of the United States as these terms are defined in 28 U.S.C. §451;

(B) a magistrate judge; and

(C) a judge confirmed by the United States Senate and empowered by statute in any commonwealth, territory, or possession to perform a function to which a particular rule relates.

(4) "Judge" means a federal judge or a state or local judicial officer.

(5) "Magistrate judge" means a United States magistrate judge as defined in 28 U.S.C. §§631–639.

(6) "Oath" includes an affirmation.

(7) "Organization" is defined in 18 U.S.C. §18.

(8) "Petty offense" is defined in 18 U.S.C. §19.

(9) "State" includes the District of Columbia, and any commonwealth, territory, or possession of the United States.

(10) "State or local judicial officer" means:

(A) a state or local officer authorized to act under 18 U.S.C. §3041; and

(B) a judicial officer empowered by statute in the District of Columbia or in any commonwealth, territory, or possession to perform a function to which a particular rule relates.

(11) "Telephone" means any technology for transmitting live electronic voice communication.

(12) "Victim" means a "crime victim" as defined in 18 U.S.C. §3771(e).[1]

(c) Authority of a Justice or Judge of the United States. When these rules authorize a magistrate judge to act, any other federal judge may also act.

(As amended Apr. 24, 1972, eff. Oct. 1, 1972; Apr. 28, 1982, eff. Aug. 1, 1982; Apr. 22, 1993, eff. Dec. 1, 1993; Apr. 29, 2002, eff. Dec. 1, 2002; Apr. 23, 2008, eff. Dec. 1, 2008; Apr. 26, 2011, eff. Dec. 1, 2011.)

NOTES OF ADVISORY COMMITTEE ON RULES——1944

1. These rules are prescribed under the authority of two acts of Congress, namely: the Act of June 29, 1940, c. 445, 18 U.S.C. 687 (Proceedings in criminal cases prior to and including verdict; power of Supreme Court to prescribe rules), and the Act of November 21, 1941, c. 492, 18 U.S.C. 689 (Proceedings to punish for criminal contempt of court; application to sections 687 and 688).

2. The courts of the United States covered by the rules are enumerated in Rule 54(a). In addition to Federal courts in the continental United States they include district courts in Alaska, Hawaii, Puerto Rico and the Virgin Islands. In the Canal Zone only the rules governing proceedings after verdict, finding or plea of guilty are applicable.

3. While the rules apply to proceedings before commissioners when acting as committing magistrates, they do not govern when a commissioner acts as a trial magistrate for the trial of petty offenses committed on Federal reservations. That procedure is governed by rules adopted by order promulgated by the Supreme Court on January 6, 1941 (311 U.S. 733), pursuant to the Act of October 9, 1940, c. 785, secs. 1–5. See 18 U.S.C. 576–576d [now 3401, 3402] (relating to trial of petty offenses on Federal reservations by United States commissioners).

NOTES OF ADVISORY COMMITTEE ON RULES——1972 AMENDMENT

The rule is amended to make clear that the rules are applicable to courts of the United States and, where the rule so provides, to proceedings before United States magistrates and state or local judicial officers.

Primarily these rules are intended to govern proceedings in criminal cases triable in the United States District Court. Special rules have been promulgated, pursuant to the authority set forth in 28 U.S.C. §636(c), for the trial of "minor offenses" before United States magistrates. (See Rules of Procedure for the Trial of Minor Offenses Before United States Magistrates (January 27, 1971).)

However, there is inevitably some overlap between the two sets of rules. The Rules of Criminal Procedure for the United States District Courts deal with preliminary, supplementary, and special proceedings which will often be conducted before United States magistrates. This is true, for example, with regard to rule 3—The Complaint; rule 4—Arrest Warrant or Summons Upon Complaint; rule 5—Initial Appearance Before the Magistrate; and rule 5.1—Preliminary Examination. It is also true, for example, of supplementary and special proceedings such as rule 40—Commitment to Another District, Removal; rule 41—Search and Seizure; and rule 46—Release from Custody. Other of these rules, where applicable, also apply to proceedings before United States magistrates. See Rules of Procedure for the Trial of Minor Offenses Before United States Magistrates, rule 1—Scope:

These rules govern the procedure and practice for the trial of minor offenses (including petty offenses) before United States magistrates under Title 18, U.S.C. §3401, and for appeals in such cases to judges of the district courts. To the extent that pretrial and trial procedure and practice are not specifically covered by these rules, the Federal Rules of Criminal Procedure apply as to minor offenses other than petty offenses. All other proceedings in criminal matters, other than petty offenses, before United States magistrates are governed by the Federal Rules of Criminal Procedure.

State and local judicial officers are governed by these rules, but only when the rule specifically so provides. This is the case of rule 3—The Complaint; rule 4—Arrest Warrant or Summons Upon Complaint; and rule 5—Initial Appearance Before the Magistrate. These rules confer authority upon the "magistrate," a term which is defined in new rule 54 as follows:

"Magistrate" includes a United States magistrate as defined in 28 U.S.C. §§631–639, a judge of the United States, another judge or judicial officer specifically empowered by statute in force in any territory or possession, the commonwealth of Puerto Rico, or the District of Columbia, to perform a function to which a particular rule relates, and a state or local judicial officer, authorized by 18 U.S.C. §3041 to perform the functions prescribed in rules 3, 4, and 5.

Rule 41 provides that a search warrant may be issued by "a judge of a state court of record" and thus confers that authority upon appropriate state judicial officers.

The scope of rules 1 and 54 is discussed in C. Wright, Federal Practice and Procedure: Criminal §§21, 871–874 (1969, Supp. 1971), and 8 and 8A J. Moore, Federal Practice chapters 1 and 54 (2d ed. Cipes 1970, Supp. 1971).

NOTES OF ADVISORY COMMITTEE ON RULES—1982 AMENDMENT

The amendment corrects an erroneous cross reference, from Rule 54(c) to Rule 54(a), and replaces the word "defined" with the more appropriate word "provided."

NOTES OF ADVISORY COMMITTEE ON RULES—1993 AMENDMENT

The Rule is amended to conform to the Judicial Improvements Act of 1990 [P.L. 101–650, Title III, Section 321] which provides that each United States magistrate appointed under section 631 of title 28, United States Code, shall be known as a United States magistrate judge.

COMMITTEE NOTES ON RULES—2002 AMENDMENT

Rule 1 is entirely revised and expanded to incorporate Rule 54, which deals with the application of the rules. Consistent with the title of the existing rule, the Committee believed that a statement of the scope of the rules should be placed at the beginning to show readers which proceedings are governed by these rules. The Committee also revised the rule to incorporate the definitions found in Rule 54(c) as a new Rule 1(b).

Rule 1(a) contains language from Rule 54(b). But language in current Rule 54(b)(2)–(4) has been deleted for several reasons: First, Rule 54(b)(2) refers to a venue statute that governs an offense committed on the high seas or somewhere outside the jurisdiction of a particular district; it is unnecessary and has been deleted because once venue has been established, the Rules of Criminal Procedure automatically apply. Second, Rule 54(b)(3) currently deals with peace bonds; that provision is inconsistent with the governing statute and has therefore been deleted. Finally, Rule 54(b)(4) references proceedings conducted before United States Magistrate Judges, a topic now covered in Rule 58.

Rule 1(a)(5) consists of material currently located in Rule 54(b)(5), with the exception of the references to the navigation laws and to fishery offenses. Those provisions were considered obsolete. But if those proceedings were to arise, they would be governed by the Rules of Criminal Procedure.

Rule 1(b) is composed of material currently located in Rule 54(c), with several exceptions. First, the reference to an "Act of Congress" has been deleted from the restyled rules; instead the rules use the self-explanatory term "federal statute." Second, the language concerning demurrers, pleas in abatement, etc., has been deleted as being anachronistic. Third, the definitions of "civil action" and "district court" have been deleted. Fourth, the term "attorney for the government" has been expanded to include reference to those attorneys who may serve as special or independent counsel under applicable federal statutes. The term "attorney for the government" contemplates an attorney of record in the case.

Fifth, the Committee added a definition for the term "court" in Rule 1(b)(2). Although that term originally was almost always synonymous with the term "district judge," the term might be misleading or unduly narrow because it may not cover the many functions performed by magistrate judges. See generally 28 U.S.C. §§132, 636. Additionally, the term does not cover circuit judges who may be authorized to hold a district court. See 28 U.S.C. §291. The proposed definition continues the traditional view that "court" means district judge, but also reflects the current understanding that magistrate judges act as the "court" in many proceedings. Finally, the Committee intends that the term "court" be used principally to describe a judicial officer, except where a rule uses the term in a spatial sense, such as describing proceedings in "open court."

Sixth, the term "Judge of the United States" has been replaced with the term "Federal judge." That term includes Article III judges and magistrate judges and, as noted in Rule 1(b)(3)(C), federal judges other than Article III judges who may be authorized by statute to perform a particular act specified in the Rules of Criminal Procedure. The term does not include local judges in the District of Columbia. Seventh, the definition of "Law" has been deleted as being superfluous and possibly misleading because it suggests that administrative regulations are excluded.

Eighth, the current rules include three definitions of "magistrate judge." The term used in amended Rule 1(b)(5) is limited to United States magistrate judges. In the current rules the term magistrate judge includes not only United States magistrate judges, but also district court judges, court of appeals judges, Supreme Court justices, and where authorized, state and local officers. The Committee believed that the rules should reflect current practice, i.e., the wider and almost exclusive use of United States magistrate judges, especially in preliminary matters. The definition, however, is not intended to restrict the use of other federal judicial officers to perform those functions. Thus, Rule 1(c) has been added to make it clear that where the rules authorize a magistrate judge to act, any other federal judge or justice may act.

Finally, the term "organization" has been added to the list of definitions.

The remainder of the rule has been amended as part of the general restyling of the rules to make them more easily understood. In addition to changes made to improve the clarity, the Committee has changed language to make style and terminology consistent throughout the Criminal Rules. These changes are intended to be stylistic only.

COMMITTEE NOTES ON RULES—2008 AMENDMENT

Subdivision (b)(11). This amendment incorporates the definition of the term "crime victim" found in the Crime Victims' Rights Act, codified at 18 U.S.C. §3771(e). It provides that "the term 'crime victim' means a person directly and proximately harmed as a result of the commission of a Federal offense or an offense in the District of Columbia."

Upon occasion, disputes may arise over the question whether a particular person is a victim. Although the rule makes no special provision for such cases, the courts have the authority to do any necessary fact finding and make any necessary legal rulings.

Changes Made to Proposed Amendment Released for Public Comment. The Committee revised the text of Rule 1(b)(11) in response to public comments by transferring portions of the subdivision relating to who may assert the rights of a victim to Rule 60(b)(2). The Committee Note was revised to reflect that change and to indicate that the Court has the power to decide any dispute as to who is a victim.

COMMITTEE NOTES ON RULES—2011 AMENDMENT

Subdivisions (b)(11) and (12). The added definition clarifies that the term "telephone" includes technologies enabling live voice conversations that have developed since the traditional "land line" telephone. Calls placed by cell phone or from a computer over the internet, for example, would be included. The definition is limited to live communication in order to ensure contemporaneous communication and excludes voice recordings. Live voice communication should include services for the hearing impaired, or other contemporaneous translation, where necessary.

Changes Made to Proposed Amendment Released for Public Comment. The text was rephrased by the Committee to describe the telephone as a "technology for transmitting electronic voice communication" rather than a "form" of communication.

18 U.S.C. §3771(e), referred to in subd. (b)(12), was redesignated 18 U.S.C. §3771(e)(2) by Pub. L. 114–22, title I, §113(a)(3)(A), May 29, 2015, 129 Stat. 240.

¹ See References in Text note below.

Rule 2. Interpretation

These rules are to be interpreted to provide for the just determination of every criminal proceeding, to secure simplicity in procedure and fairness in administration, and to eliminate unjustifiable expense and delay.

(As amended Apr. 29, 2002, eff. Dec. 1, 2002.)

NOTES OF ADVISORY COMMITTEE ON RULES—1944

Compare Federal Rules of Civil Procedure [28 U.S.C., Appendix], Rule 1 (Scope of Rules), last sentence: "They [the Federal Rules of Civil Procedure] shall be construed to secure the just, speedy, and inexpensive determination of every action."

COMMITTEE NOTES ON RULES—2002 AMENDMENT

The language of Rule 2 has been amended as part of the general restyling of the Criminal Rules to make them more easily understood and to make style and terminology consistent throughout the rules. These changes are intended to be stylistic. No substantive change is intended.

In particular, Rule 2 has been amended to clarify the purpose of the Rules of Criminal Procedure. The words "are intended" have been changed to read "are to be interpreted." The Committee believed that that was the original intent of the drafters and more accurately reflects the purpose of the rules.

TITLE II. PRELIMINARY PROCEEDINGS

Rule 3. The Complaint

The complaint is a written statement of the essential facts constituting the offense charged. Except as provided in Rule 4.1, it must be made under oath before a magistrate judge or, if none is reasonably available, before a state or local judicial officer.

(As amended Apr. 24, 1972, eff. Oct. 1, 1972; Apr. 22, 1993, eff. Dec. 1, 1993; Apr. 29, 2002, eff. Dec. 1, 2002; Apr. 26, 2011, eff. Dec. 1, 2011.)

NOTES OF ADVISORY COMMITTEE ON RULES—1944

The rule generally states existing law and practice, 18 U.S.C. 591 [now 3041] (Arrest and removal for trial); United States v. Simon (E.D.Pa.), 248 F. 980; United States v. Maresca (S.D.N.Y.), 266 F. 713, 719—721. It eliminates, however, the requirement of conformity to State law as to the form and sufficiency of the complaint. See, also, rule 57(b).

NOTES OF ADVISORY COMMITTEE ON RULES—1972 AMENDMENT

The amendment deletes the reference to "commissioner or other officer empowered to commit persons charged with offenses against the United States" and substitute therefor "magistrate."

The change is editorial in nature to conform the language of the rule to the recently enacted Federal Magistrates Act. The term "magistrate" is defined in rule 54.

NOTES OF ADVISORY COMMITTEE ON RULES—1993 AMENDMENT

The Rule is amended to conform to the Judicial Improvements Act of 1990 [P.L. 101–650, Title III, Section 321] which provides that each United States magistrate appointed under section 631 of title 28, United States Code, shall be known as a United States magistrate judge.

COMMITTEE NOTES ON RULES—2002 AMENDMENT

The language of Rule 3 is amended as part of the general restyling of the Criminal Rules to make them more easily understood and to make style and terminology consistent throughout the rules. These changes are intended to be stylistic and no substantive change is intended, except as described below.

The amendment makes one change in practice. Currently, Rule 3 requires the complaint to be sworn before a "magistrate judge," which under current Rule 54 could include a state or local judicial officer. Revised Rule 1 no longer includes state and local officers in the definition of magistrate judges for the purposes of these rules. Instead, the definition includes only United States magistrate judges. Rule 3 requires that the complaint be made before a United States magistrate judge or before a state or local officer. The revised rule does, however, make a change to reflect prevailing practice and the outcome desired by the Committee—that the procedure take place before a federal judicial officer if one is reasonably available. As noted in Rule 1(c), where the rules, such as Rule 3, authorize a magistrate judge to act, any other federal judge may act.

COMMITTEE NOTES ON RULES—2011 AMENDMENT

Under the amended rule, the complaint and supporting material may be submitted by telephone or reliable electronic means; however, the rule requires that the judicial officer administer the oath or affirmation in person or by telephone. The Committee concluded that the benefits of making it easier to obtain judicial oversight of the arrest decision and the increasing reliability and accessibility to electronic communication warranted amendment of the rule. The amendment makes clear that the submission of a complaint to a judicial officer need not be done in person and may instead be made by telephone or other reliable electronic means. The successful experiences with electronic applications under Rule 41, which permits electronic applications for search warrants, support a comparable process for arrests. The provisions in Rule 41 have been transferred to new Rule 4.1, which governs applications by telephone or other electronic means under Rules 3, 4, 9, and 41.

Changes Made to Proposed Amendment Released for Public Comment. No changes were made in the amendment as published.

Rule 4. Arrest Warrant or Summons on a Complaint

(a) Issuance. If the complaint or one or more affidavits filed with the complaint establish probable cause to believe that an offense has been committed and that the defendant committed it, the judge must issue an arrest warrant to an officer authorized to execute it. At the request of an attorney for the government, the judge must issue a summons, instead of a warrant, to a person authorized to serve it. A judge may issue more than one warrant or summons on the same complaint. If an individual defendant fails to appear in response to a summons, a judge may, and upon request of an attorney for the government must, issue a warrant. If an organizational defendant fails to appear in response to a summons, a judge may take any action authorized by United States law.

(b) Form.

(1) Warrant. A warrant must:

(A) contain the defendant's name or, if it is unknown, a name or description by which the defendant can be identified with reasonable certainty;

(B) describe the offense charged in the complaint;

(C) command that the defendant be arrested and brought without unnecessary delay before a magistrate judge or, if none is reasonably available, before a state or local judicial officer; and

(D) be signed by a judge.

(2) Summons. A summons must be in the same form as a warrant except that it must require the defendant to appear before a magistrate judge at a stated time and place.

(c) Execution or Service, and Return.

(1) By Whom. Only a marshal or other authorized officer may execute a warrant. Any person authorized to serve a summons in a federal civil action may serve a summons.

(2) Location. A warrant may be executed, or a summons served, within the jurisdiction of the United States or anywhere else a federal statute authorizes an arrest. A summons to an organization under Rule 4(c)(3)(D) may also be served at a place not within a judicial district of the United States.

(3) Manner.

(A) A warrant is executed by arresting the defendant. Upon arrest, an officer possessing the original or a duplicate original warrant must show it to the defendant. If the officer does not possess the warrant, the officer must inform the defendant of the warrant's existence and of the offense charged and, at the defendant's request, must show the original or a duplicate original warrant to the defendant as soon as possible.

(B) A summons is served on an individual defendant:

(i) by delivering a copy to the defendant personally; or

(ii) by leaving a copy at the defendant's residence or usual place of abode with a person of suitable age and discretion residing at that location and by mailing a copy to the defendant's last known address.

(C) A summons is served on an organization in a judicial district of the United States by delivering a copy to an officer, to a managing or general agent, or to another agent appointed or legally authorized to receive service of process. If the agent is one authorized by statute and the statute so requires, a copy must also be mailed to the organization.

(D) A summons is served on an organization not within a judicial district of the United States:

(i) by delivering a copy, in a manner authorized by the foreign jurisdiction's law, to an officer, to a managing or general agent, or to an agent appointed or legally authorized to receive service of process; or

(ii) by any other means that gives notice, including one that is:

(a) stipulated by the parties;

(b) undertaken by a foreign authority in response to a letter rogatory, a letter of request, or a request submitted under an applicable international agreement; or

(c) permitted by an applicable international agreement.

(4) Return.

(A) After executing a warrant, the officer must return it to the judge before whom the defendant is brought in accordance with Rule 5. The officer may do so by reliable electronic means. At the request of an attorney for the government, an unexecuted warrant must be brought back to and canceled by a magistrate judge or, if none is reasonably available, by a state or local judicial officer.

(B) The person to whom a summons was delivered for service must return it on or before the return day.

(C) At the request of an attorney for the government, a judge may deliver an unexecuted warrant, an unserved summons, or a copy of the warrant or summons to the marshal or other authorized person for execution or service.

(d) Warrant by Telephone or Other Reliable Electronic Means. In accordance with Rule 4.1, a magistrate judge may issue a warrant or summons based on information communicated by telephone or other reliable electronic means.

(As amended Feb. 28, 1966, eff. July 1, 1966; Apr. 24, 1972, eff. Oct. 1, 1972; Apr. 22, 1974, eff. Dec. 1, 1975; Pub. L. 94–64, §3(1)–(3), July 31, 1975, 89 Stat. 370; Mar. 9, 1987, eff. Aug. 1, 1987; Apr. 22, 1993, eff. Dec. 1, 1993; Apr. 29, 2002, eff. Dec. 1, 2002; Apr. 26, 2011, eff. Dec. 1, 2011; Apr. 28, 2016, eff. Dec. 1, 2016.)

NOTES OF ADVISORY COMMITTEE ON RULES—1944

Note to Subdivision (a). 1. The rule states the existing law relating to warrants issued by commissioner or other magistrate. United States Constitution, Amendment IV; 18 U.S.C. 591 [now 3041] (Arrest and removal for trial).

2. The provision for summons is new, although a summons has been customarily used against corporate defendants, 28 U.S.C. 377 [now 1651] (Power to issue writs); United States v. John Kelso Co., 86 F. 304 (N.D.Cal., 1898). See also, Albrecht v. United States, 273 U.S. 1, 8 (1927). The use of the summons in criminal cases is sanctioned by many States, among them Indiana, Maryland, Massachusetts, New York, New Jersey, Ohio, and others. See A.L.I. Code of Criminal Procedure (1931), Commentaries to secs. 12, 13, and 14. The use of the summons is permitted in England by 11 & 12 Vict., c. 42, sec. 1 (1848). More general use of a summons in place of

a warrant was recommended by the National Commission on Law Observance and Enforcement, Report on Criminal Procedure (1931) 47. The Uniform Arrest Act, proposed by the Interstate Commission on Crime, provides for a summons. Warner, 28 Va.L.R. 315. See also, Medalie, 4 Lawyers Guild, R. 1, 6.

3. The provision for the issuance of additional warrants on the same complaint embodies the practice heretofore followed in some districts. It is desirable from a practical standpoint, since when a complaint names several defendants, it may be preferable to issue a separate warrant as to each in order to facilitate service and return, especially if the defendants are apprehended at different times and places. Berge, 42 Mich.L.R. 353, 356.

4. Failure to respond to a summons is not a contempt of court, but is ground for issuing a warrant.

Note to Subdivision (b). Compare Rule 9(b) and forms of warrant and summons, Appendix of Forms.

Note to Subdivision (c)(2). This rule and Rule 9(c)(1) modify the existing practice under which a warrant may be served only within the district in which it is issued. Mitchell v. Dexter, 244 F. 926 (C.C.A. 1st, 1917); Palmer v. Thompson, 20 App. D.C. 273 (1902); but see In re Christian, 82 F. 885 (C.C.W.D.Ark., 1897); 2 Op.Atty.Gen. 564. When a defendant is apprehended in a district other than that in which the prosecution has been instituted, this change will eliminate some of the steps that are at present followed: the issuance of a warrant in the district where the prosecution is pending; the return of the warrant non est inventus; the filing of a complaint on the basis of the warrant and its return in the district in which the defendant is found; and the issuance of another warrant in the latter district. The warrant originally issued will have efficacy throughout the United States and will constitute authority for arresting the defendant wherever found. Waite, 27 Jour. of Am. Judicature Soc. 101, 103. The change will not modify or affect the rights of the defendant as to removal. See Rule 40. The authority of the marshal to serve process is not limited to the district for which he is appointed, 28 U.S.C. 503 [now 569].

Note to Subdivision (c)(3). 1. The provision that the arresting officer need not have the warrant in his possession at the time of the arrest is rendered necessary by the fact that a fugitive may be discovered and apprehended by any one of many officers. It is obviously impossible for a warrant to be in the possession of every officer who is searching for a fugitive or who unexpectedly might find himself in a position to apprehend the fugitive. The rule sets forth the customary practice in such matters, which has the sanction of the courts. "It would be a strong proposition in an ordinary felony case to say that a fugitive from justice for whom a capias or warrant was outstanding could not be apprehended until the apprehending officer had physical possession of the capias or the warrant. If such were the law, criminals could circulate freely from one end of the land to the other, because they could always keep ahead of an officer with the warrant." In re Kosopud (N.D. Ohio), 272 F. 330, 336. Waite, 27 Jour. of Am. Judicature Soc. 101, 103. The rule, however, safeguards the defendant's rights in such case.

2. Service of summons under the rule is substantially the same as in civil actions under Federal Rules of Civil Procedure, Rule 4(d)(1) [28 U.S.C., Appendix].

Note to Subdivision (c)(4). Return of a warrant or summons to the commissioner or other officer is provided by 18 U.S.C. 603 [now 4084] (Writs; copy as jailer's authority). The return of all "copies of process" by the commissioner to the clerk of the court is provided by 18 U.S.C. 591 [now 3041]; and see Rule 5(c), infra.

In Giordenello v. United States, 357 U.S. 480 (1958) it was held that to support the issuance of a warrant the complaint must contain in addition to a statement "of the essential facts constituting the offense" (Rule 3) a statement of the facts relied upon by the complainant to establish probable cause. The amendment permits the complainant to state the facts constituting probable cause in a separate affidavit in lieu of spelling them out in the complaint. See also Jaben v. United States, 381 U.S. 214 (1965).

Throughout the rule the term "magistrate" is substituted for the term "commissioner." Magistrate is defined in rule 54 to include a judge of the United States, a United States magistrate, and those state and local judicial officers specified in 18 U.S.C. §3041.

The amendments are designed to achieve several objectives: (1) to make explicit the fact that the determination of probable cause may be based upon hearsay evidence; (2) to make clear that probable cause is a prerequisite to the issuance of a summons; and (3) to give priority to the issuance of a summons rather than a warrant.

Subdivision (a) makes clear that the normal situation is to issue a summons.

Subdivision (b) provides for the issuance of an arrest warrant in lieu of or in addition to the issuance of a summons.

Subdivision (b)(1) restates the provision of the old rule mandating the issuance of a warrant when a defendant fails to appear in response to a summons.

Subdivision (b)(2) provides for the issuance of an arrest warrant rather than a summons whenever "a valid reason is shown" for the issuance of a warrant. The reason may be apparent from the face of the complaint or may be provided by the federal law enforcement officer or attorney for the government. See comparable provision in rule 9.

Subdivision (b)(3) deals with the situation in which conditions change after a summons has issued. It affords the government an opportunity to demonstrate the need for an arrest warrant. This may be done in the district in which the defendant is located if this is the convenient place to do so.

Subdivision (c) provides that a warrant or summons may issue on the basis of hearsay evidence. What constitutes probable cause is left to be dealt with on a case-to-case basis, taking account of the unlimited variations in source of information and in the opportunity of the informant to perceive accurately the factual data which he furnishes. See e.g., Giordenello v. United States, 357 U.S. 480, 78 S.Ct. 1245, 2 L.Ed.2d 1503 (1958); Aguilar v. Texas, 378 U.S. 108, 84 S.Ct. 1509, 12 L.Ed.2d 723 (1964); United States v. Ventresca, 380 U.S. 102, 85 S.Ct. 741, 13 L.Ed.2d 684 (1965); Jaben v. United States, 381 U.S. 214, 85 S.Ct. 1365, 14 L.Ed.2d 345 (1965); McCray v. Illinois, 386 U.S. 300, 87 S.Ct. 1056, 18 L.Ed.2d 62 (1967); Spinelli v. United States, 393 U.S. 410, 89 S.Ct. 584, 21 L.Ed.2d 637 (1969); United States v. Harris, 403 U.S. 573, 91 S.Ct. 2075, 29 L.Ed.2d 723 (1971); Note, The Informer's Tip as Probable Cause for Search or Arrest, 54 Cornell L.Rev. 958 (1969); C. Wright, Federal Practice and Procedure: Criminal §52 (1969, Supp. 1971); 8 S.J. Moore, Federal Practice 4.03 (2d ed. Cipes 1970, Supp. 1971).

A. Amendments Proposed by the Supreme Court. Rule 4 of the Federal Rules of Criminal Procedure deals with arrest procedures when a criminal complaint has been filed. It provides in pertinent part:

If it appears . . . that there is probable cause . . . a warrant for the arrest of the defendant shall issue to any officer authorized by law to execute it.
Upon the request of the attorney for the government a summons instead of a warrant shall issue. [emphasis added]
The Supreme Court's amendments make a basic change in Rule 4. As proposed to be amended, Rule 4 gives priority to the issuance of a summons instead of an arrest warrant. In order for the magistrate to issue an arrest warrant, the attorney for the government must show a "valid reason."

B. Committee Action. The Committee agrees with and approves the basic change in Rule 4. The decision to take a citizen into custody is a very important one with far-reaching consequences. That decision ought to be made by a neutral official (a magistrate) rather than by an interested party (the prosecutor).

It has been argued that undesirable consequences will result if this change is adopted—including an increase in the number of fugitives and the introduction of substantial delays in our system of criminal justice. [See testimony of Assistant Attorney General W. Vincent Rakestraw in Hearings on Proposed Amendments to Federal Rules of Criminal Procedure Before the Subcommittee on Criminal Justice of the House Committee on the Judiciary, 93d Cong., 2d Sess., Serial No. 61, at 41–43 (1974) [hereinafter cited as "Hearing I"].] The Committee has carefully considered these arguments and finds them to be wanting. [The Advisory Committee on Criminal Rules has thoroughly analyzed the arguments raised by Mr. Rakestraw and convincingly demonstrated that the undesirable consequences predicted will not necessarily result. See Hearings on Proposed Amendments to Federal Rules on Proposed Amendments to Federal Rules of Criminal Procedure Before the Subcommittee on Criminal Justice of the House Committee on the Judiciary, 94th Congress, 1st Session, Serial No. 6, at 208–09 (1975) [hereinafter cited "Hearings II"].] The present rule permits the use of a summons in lieu of a warrant. The major difference between the present rule and the proposed rule is that the present rule vests the decision to issue a summons or a warrant in the prosecutor, while the proposed rule vests that decision in a judicial officer. Thus, the basic premise underlying the arguments against the proposed rule is the notion that only the prosecutor can be trusted to act responsibly in deciding whether a summons or a warrant shall issue.

The Committee rejects the notion that the federal judiciary cannot be trusted to exercise discretion wisely and in the public interest.

The Committee recast the language of Rule 4(b). No change in substance is intended. The phrase "valid reason" was changed to "good cause," a phrase with which lawyers are more familiar. [Rule 4, both as proposed by the Supreme Court and as changed by the Committee, does not in any way authorize a magistrate to issue a summons or a warrant sua sponte, nor does it enlarge, limit or change in any way the law governing warrantless arrests.]

The Committee deleted two sentences from Rule 4(c). These sentences permitted a magistrate to question the complainant and other witnesses under oath and required the magistrate to keep a record or summary of such a proceeding. The Committee does not intend this change to discontinue or discourage the practice of having the complainant appear personally or the practice of making a record or summary of such an appearance. Rather, the Committee intended to leave Rule 4(c) neutral on this matter, neither encouraging nor discouraging these practices.

The Committee added a new section that provides that the determination of good cause for the issuance of a warrant in lieu of a summons shall not be grounds for a motion to suppress evidence. This provision does not apply when the issue is whether there was probable cause to believe an offense has been committed. This provision does not in any way expand or limit the so-called "exclusionary rule."

NOTES OF CONFERENCE COMMITTEE, HOUSE REPORT NO. 94–414; 1975 AMENDMENT

Rule 4(e)(3) deals with the manner in which warrants and summonses may be served. The House version provides two methods for serving a summons: (1) personal service upon the defendant, or (2) service by leaving it with someone of suitable age at the defendant's dwelling and by mailing it to the defendant's last known address. The Senate version provides three methods: (1) personal service, (2) service by leaving it with someone of suitable age at the defendant's dwelling, or (3) service by mailing it to defendant's last known address.

NOTES OF ADVISORY COMMITTEE ON RULES—1987 AMENDMENT

The amendments are technical. No substantive change is intended.

NOTES OF ADVISORY COMMITTEE ON RULES—1993 AMENDMENT

The Rule is amended to conform to the Judicial Improvements Act of 1990 [P.L. 101–650, Title III, Section 321] which provides that each United States magistrate appointed under section 631 of title 28, United States Code, shall be known as a United States magistrate judge.

COMMITTEE NOTES ON RULES—2002 AMENDMENT

The language of Rule 4 has been amended as part of the general restyling of the Criminal Rules to make them more easily understood and to make style and terminology consistent throughout the rules. These changes are intended to be stylistic, except as noted below.

The first non-stylistic change is in Rule 4(a), which has been amended to provide an element of discretion in those situations when the defendant fails to respond to a summons. Under the current rule, the judge must in all cases issue an arrest warrant. The revised rule provides discretion to the judge to issue an arrest warrant if the attorney for the government does not request that an arrest warrant be issued for a failure to appear.

Current Rule 4(b), which refers to the fact that hearsay evidence may be used to support probable cause, has been deleted. That language was added to the rule in 1974, apparently to reflect emerging federal case law. See Advisory Committee Note to 1974 Amendments to Rule 4 (citing cases). A similar amendment was made to Rule 41 in 1972. In the intervening years, however, the case law has become perfectly clear on that proposition. Thus, the Committee believed that the reference to hearsay was no longer necessary. Furthermore, the limited reference to hearsay evidence was misleading to the extent that it might have suggested that other forms of inadmissible evidence could not be considered. For example, the rule made no reference to considering a defendant's prior criminal record, which clearly may be considered in deciding whether probable cause exists. See, e.g., Brinegar v. United States, 338 U.S. 160 (1949) (officer's knowledge of defendant's prior criminal activity). Rather than address that issue, or any other similar issues, the Committee believed that the matter was best addressed in Rule 1101(d)(3), Federal Rules of Evidence. That rule explicitly provides that the Federal Rules of Evidence do not apply to "preliminary examinations in criminal cases, . . . issuance of warrants for arrest, criminal summonses, and search warrants." The Advisory Committee Note accompanying that rule recognizes that: "The nature of the proceedings makes application of the formal rules of evidence inappropriate and impracticable." The Committee did not intend to make any substantive changes in practice by deleting the reference to hearsay evidence.

New Rule 4(b), which is currently Rule 4(c), addresses the form of an arrest warrant and a summons and includes two non-stylistic changes. First, Rule 4(b)(1)(C) mandates that the warrant require that the defendant be brought "without unnecessary delay" before a judge. The Committee believed that this was a more appropriate standard than the current requirement that the defendant be brought before the "nearest available" magistrate judge. This new language accurately reflects the thrust of the original rule, that time is of the essence and that the defendant should be brought with dispatch before a judicial officer in the district. Second, the revised rule states a preference that the defendant be brought before a federal judicial officer.

Rule 4(b)(2) has been amended to require that if a summons is issued, the defendant must appear before a magistrate judge. The current rule requires the appearance before a "magistrate," which could include a state or local judicial officer. This change is consistent with the preference for requiring defendants to appear before federal judicial officers stated in revised Rule 4(b)(1).

Rule 4(c) (currently Rule 4(d)) includes three changes. First, current Rule 4(d)(2) states the traditional rule recognizing the territorial limits for executing warrants. Rule 4(c)(2) includes new language that reflects the recent enactment of the Military Extraterritorial Jurisdiction Act (Pub. L. No. 106–523, 114 Stat. 2488) that permits arrests of certain military and Department of Defense personnel overseas. See also 14 U.S.C. §89 (Coast Guard authority to effect arrests outside territorial limits of United States). Second, current Rule 4(d)(3) provides that the arresting officer is only required to inform the defendant of the offense charged and that a warrant exists if the officer does not have a copy of the warrant. As revised, Rule 4(c)(3)(A) explicitly requires the arresting officer in all instances to inform the defendant of the offense charged and of the fact that an arrest warrant exists. The new rule continues the current provision that the arresting officer need not have a copy of the warrant, but if the

14

defendant requests to see it, the officer must show the warrant to the defendant as soon as possible. The rule does not attempt to define any particular time limits for showing the warrant to the defendant.

Third, Rule 4(c)(3)(C) is taken from former Rule 9(c)(1). That provision specifies the manner of serving a summons on an organization. The Committee believed that Rule 4 was the more appropriate location for general provisions addressing the mechanics of arrest warrants and summonses. Revised Rule 9 liberally cross-references the basic provisions appearing in Rule 4. Under the amended rule, in all cases in which a summons is being served on an organization, a copy of the summons must be mailed to the organization.

Fourth, a change is made in Rule 4(c)(4). Currently, Rule 4(d)(4) requires that an unexecuted warrant must be returned to the judicial officer or judge who issued it. As amended, Rule 4(c)(4)(A) provides that after a warrant is executed, the officer must return it to the judge before whom the defendant will appear under Rule 5. At the government's request, however, an unexecuted warrant must be canceled by a magistrate judge. The change recognizes the possibility that at the time the warrant is returned, the issuing judicial officer may not be available.

Committee Notes on Rules—2011 Amendment

Rule 4 is amended in three respects to make the arrest warrant process more efficient through the use of technology.

Subdivision (c). First, Rule 4(c)(3)(A) authorizes a law enforcement officer to retain a duplicate original arrest warrant, consistent with the change to subdivision (d), which permits a court to issue an arrest warrant electronically rather than by physical delivery. The duplicate original warrant may be used in lieu of the original warrant signed by the magistrate judge to satisfy the requirement that the defendant be shown the warrant at or soon after an arrest. Cf. Rule 4.1(b)(5) (providing for a duplicate original search warrant).

Second, consistent with the amendment to Rule 41(f), Rule 4(c)(4)(A) permits an officer to make a return of the arrest warrant electronically. Requiring an in-person return can be burdensome on law enforcement, particularly in large districts when the return can require a great deal of time and travel. In contrast, no interest of the accused is affected by allowing what is normally a ministerial act to be done electronically.

Subdivision (d). Rule 4(d) provides that a magistrate judge may issue an arrest warrant or summons based on information submitted electronically rather than in person. This change works in conjunction with the amendment to Rule 3, which permits a magistrate judge to consider a criminal complaint and accompanying documents that are submitted electronically. Subdivision (d) also incorporates the procedures for applying for and issuing electronic warrants set forth in Rule 4.1.

Changes Made to Proposed Amendment Released for Public Comment. No changes were made in the amendment as published.

Committee Notes on Rules—2016 Amendment

Subdivision (a). The amendment addresses a gap in the current rule, which makes no provision for organizational defendants who fail to appear in response to a criminal summons. The amendment explicitly limits the issuance of a warrant to individual defendants who fail to appear, and provides that the judge may take whatever action is authorized by law when an organizational defendant fails to appear. The rule does not attempt to specify the remedial actions a court may take when an organizational defendant fails to appear.

Subdivision (c)(2). The amendment authorizes service of a criminal summons on an organization outside a judicial district of the United States.

Subdivision (c)(3)(C). The amendment makes two changes to subdivision (c)(3)(C) governing service of a summons on an organization. First, like Civil Rule 4(h), the amended provision does not require a separate mailing to the organization when delivery has been made in the United States to an officer or to a managing or general agent. Service of process on an officer or a managing or general agent is in effect service on the principal. Mailing is required when delivery has been made on an agent authorized by statute, if the statute itself requires mailing to the entity.

Second, also like Civil Rule 4(h), the amendment recognizes that service outside the United States requires separate consideration, and it restricts Rule 4(c)(3)(C) and its modified mailing requirement to service on organizations within the United States. Service upon organizations outside the United States is governed by new subdivision (c)(3)(D).

These two modifications of the mailing requirement remove an unnecessary impediment to the initiation of criminal proceedings against organizations that commit domestic offenses but have no place of business or mailing address within the United States. Given the realities of today's global economy, electronic communication, and federal criminal practice, the mailing requirement should not shield a defendant organization when the Rule's core objective—notice of pending criminal proceedings—is accomplished.

Subdivision (c)(3)(D). This new subdivision states that a criminal summons may be served on an organizational defendant outside the United States and enumerates a non-exhaustive list of permissible means of service that provide notice to that defendant.

Although it is presumed that the enumerated means will provide notice, whether actual notice has been provided may be challenged in an individual case.

Subdivision (c)(3)(D)(i). Subdivision (i) notes that a foreign jurisdiction's law may authorize delivery of a copy of the criminal summons to an officer, or to a managing or general agent. This is a permissible means for serving an organization outside of the United States, just as it is for organizations within the United States. The subdivision also recognizes that a foreign jurisdiction's law may provide for service of a criminal summons by delivery to an appointed or legally authorized agent in a manner that provides notice to the entity, and states that this is an acceptable means of service.

Subdivision (c)(3)(D)(ii). Subdivision (ii) provides a non-exhaustive list illustrating other permissible means of giving service on organizations outside the United States, all of which must be carried out in a manner that "gives notice."

Paragraph (a) recognizes that service may be made by a means stipulated by the parties.

Paragraph (b) recognizes that service may be made by the diplomatic methods of letters rogatory and letters of request, and the last clause of the paragraph provides for service under international agreements that obligate the parties to provide broad measures of assistance, including the service of judicial documents. These include crime-specific multilateral agreements (e.g., the United Nations Convention Against Corruption (UNCAC), S. Treaty Doc. No. 109–6 (2003)), regional agreements (e.g., the Inter-American Convention on Mutual Assistance in Criminal Matters (OAS MLAT), S. Treaty Doc. No. 105–25 (1995)), and bilateral agreements.

Paragraph (c) recognizes that other means of service that provide notice and are permitted by an applicable international agreement are also acceptable when serving organizations outside the United States.

As used in this rule, the phrase "applicable international agreement" refers to an agreement that has been ratified by the United States and the foreign jurisdiction and is in force.

1975—Pub. L. 94–64 struck out subds. (a), (b), and (c) and inserted in lieu new subds. (a) and (b); redesignated subd. (d) as (c); and redesignated subd. (e) as (d) and amended par. (3) thereof generally.

APPROVAL AND EFFECTIVE DATE OF AMENDMENTS PROPOSED APRIL 22, 1974; EFFECTIVE DATE OF 1975 AMENDMENTS

Pub. L. 94–64, §2, July 31, 1975, 89 Stat. 370, provided that: "The amendments proposed by the United States Supreme Court to the Federal Rules of Criminal Procedure [adding rules 12.1, 12.2 and 29.1 and amending rules 4, 9, 11, 12, 15, 16, 17, 20, 32, and 43 of these rules] which are embraced in the order of that Court on April 22, 1974, are approved except as otherwise provided in this Act and shall take effect on December 1, 1975. Except with respect to the amendment to Rule 11, insofar as it adds Rule 11(e)(6), which shall take effect on August 1, 1975, the amendments made by section 3 of this Act [to rules 4, 9, 11, 12, 12.1, 12.2, 15, 16, 17, 20, 32, and 43 of these rules] shall also take effect on December 1, 1975."

Rule 4.1. Complaint, Warrant, or Summons by Telephone or Other Reliable Electronic Means

(a) In General. A magistrate judge may consider information communicated by telephone or other reliable electronic means when reviewing a complaint or deciding whether to issue a warrant or summons.

(b) Procedures. If a magistrate judge decides to proceed under this rule, the following procedures apply:

(1) Taking Testimony Under Oath. The judge must place under oath—and may examine—the applicant and any person on whose testimony the application is based.

(2) Creating a Record of the Testimony and Exhibits.

(A) Testimony Limited to Attestation. If the applicant does no more than attest to the contents of a written affidavit submitted by reliable electronic means, the judge must acknowledge the attestation in writing on the affidavit.

(B) Additional Testimony or Exhibits. If the judge considers additional testimony or exhibits, the judge must:

(i) have the testimony recorded verbatim by an electronic recording device, by a court reporter, or in writing;

(ii) have any recording or reporter's notes transcribed, have the transcription certified as accurate, and file it;

(iii) sign any other written record, certify its accuracy, and file it; and

(iv) make sure that the exhibits are filed.

(3) Preparing a Proposed Duplicate Original of a Complaint, Warrant, or Summons. The applicant must prepare a proposed duplicate original of a complaint, warrant, or summons, and must read or otherwise transmit its contents verbatim to the judge.

(4) Preparing an Original Complaint, Warrant, or Summons. If the applicant reads the contents of the proposed duplicate original, the judge must enter those contents into an original complaint, warrant, or summons. If the applicant transmits the contents by reliable electronic means, the transmission received by the judge may serve as the original.

(5) Modification. The judge may modify the complaint, warrant, or summons. The judge must then:

(A) transmit the modified version to the applicant by reliable electronic means; or

(B) file the modified original and direct the applicant to modify the proposed duplicate original accordingly.

(6) Issuance. To issue the warrant or summons, the judge must:

(A) sign the original documents;

(B) enter the date and time of issuance on the warrant or summons; and

(C) transmit the warrant or summons by reliable electronic means to the applicant or direct the applicant to sign the judge's name and enter the date and time on the duplicate original.

(c) Suppression Limited. Absent a finding of bad faith, evidence obtained from a warrant issued under this rule is not subject to suppression on the ground that issuing the warrant in this manner was unreasonable under the circumstances.

(Added Apr. 26, 2011, eff. Dec. 1, 2011.)

COMMITTEE NOTES ON RULES——2011

New Rule 4.1 brings together in one rule the procedures for using a telephone or other reliable electronic means for reviewing complaints and applying for and issuing warrants and summonses. In drafting Rule 4.1, the Committee recognized that modern technological developments have improved access to judicial officers, thereby reducing the necessity of government action without prior judicial approval. Rule 4.1 prescribes uniform procedures and ensures an accurate record.

The procedures that have governed search warrants "by telephonic or other means," formerly in Rule 41(d)(3) and (e)(3), have been relocated to this rule, reordered for easier application, and extended to arrest warrants, complaints, and summonses. Successful experience using electronic applications for search warrants under Rule 41, combined with increased access to reliable electronic communication, support the extension of these procedures to arrest warrants, complaints, and summonses.

With one exception noted in the next paragraph, the new rule preserves the procedures formerly in Rule 41 without change. By using the term "magistrate judge," the rule continues to require, as did former Rule 41(d)(3) and (e)(3), that a federal judge (and not a state judge) handle electronic applications, approvals, and issuances. The rule continues to require that the judge place an applicant under oath over the telephone, and permits the judge to examine the applicant, as Rule 41 had provided. Rule 4.1(b) continues to require that when electronic means are used to issue the warrant, the magistrate judge retain the original warrant. Minor changes in wording and reorganization of the language formerly in Rule 41 were made to aid in application of the rules, with no intended change in meaning.

The only substantive change to the procedures formerly in Rule 41(d)(3) and (e)(3) appears in new Rule 4.1(b)(2)(A). Former Rule 41(d)(3)(B)(ii) required the magistrate judge to make a verbatim record of the entire conversation with the applicant. New Rule 4.1(b)(2)(A) provides that when a warrant application and affidavit are sent electronically to the magistrate judge and the telephone conversation between the magistrate judge and affiant is limited to attesting to those written documents, a verbatim record of the entire conversation is no longer required. Rather, the magistrate judge should simply acknowledge in writing the attestation on the affidavit. This may be done, for example, by signing the jurat included on the Administrative Office of U.S. Courts form. Rule 4.1(b)(2)(B) carries forward the requirements formerly in Rule 41 to cases in which the magistrate judge considers testimony or exhibits in addition to the affidavit. In addition, Rule 4.1(b)(6) specifies that in order to issue a warrant or summons the magistrate judge must sign all of the original documents and enter the date and time of issuance on the warrant or summons. This procedure will create and maintain a complete record of the warrant application process.

Changes Made to Proposed Amendment Released for Public Comment. Published subdivision (a) referred to the action of a magistrate judge as "deciding whether to approve a complaint." To accurately describe the judge's action, it was rephrased to refer to the judge "reviewing a complaint."

Subdivisions (b)(2) and (3) were combined into subdivisions (b)(2)(A) and (B) to clarify the procedures applicable when the applicant does no more than attest to the contents of a written affidavit and those applicable when additional testimony or exhibits are presented. The clauses in subparagraph (B) were reordered and further divided into items (i) through (iv). Subsequent subdivisions were renumbered because of the merger of (b)(2) and (3).

In subdivision (b)(5), language was added requiring the judge to file the modified original if the judge has directed an applicant to modify a duplicate original. This will ensure that a complete record is preserved. Additionally, the clauses in this subdivision were broken out into subparagraphs (A) and (B).

In subdivision (b)(6), introductory language erroneously referring to a judge's approval of a complaint was deleted, and the rule was revised to refer only to the steps necessary to issue a warrant or summons, which are the actions taken by the judicial officer.

In subdivision (b)(6)(A), the requirement that the judge "sign the original" was amended to require signing of "the original documents." This is broad enough to encompass signing a summons, an arrest or search warrant, and the current practice of the judge signing the jurat on complaint forms. Depending on the nature of the case, it might also include many other kinds of documents, such as the jurat on affidavits, the certifications of written records supplementing the transmitted affidavit, or papers that correct or modify affidavits or complaints.

In subdivision (b)(6)(B), the superfluous and anachronistic reference to the "face" of a document was deleted, and rephrasing clarified that the action is the entry of the date and time of "the approval of a warrant or summons." Additionally, subdivision (b)(6)(C) was modified to require that the judge must direct the applicant not only to sign the duplicate original with the judge's name, but also to note the date and time.

Rule 5. Initial Appearance

(a) In General.
    (1) Appearance Upon an Arrest.
        (A) A person making an arrest within the United States must take the defendant without unnecessary delay before a magistrate judge, or before a state or local judicial officer as Rule 5(c) provides, unless a statute provides otherwise.
        (B) A person making an arrest outside the United States must take the defendant without unnecessary delay before a magistrate judge, unless a statute provides otherwise.

    (2) Exceptions.
        (A) An officer making an arrest under a warrant issued upon a complaint charging solely a violation of 18 U.S.C. §1073 need not comply with this rule if:
            (i) the person arrested is transferred without unnecessary delay to the custody of appropriate state or local authorities in the district of arrest; and
            (ii) an attorney for the government moves promptly, in the district where the warrant was issued, to dismiss the complaint.

        (B) If a defendant is arrested for violating probation or supervised release, Rule 32.1 applies.
        (C) If a defendant is arrested for failing to appear in another district, Rule 40 applies.

    (3) Appearance Upon a Summons. When a defendant appears in response to a summons under Rule 4, a magistrate judge must proceed under Rule 5(d) or (e), as applicable.

(b) Arrest Without a Warrant. If a defendant is arrested without a warrant, a complaint meeting Rule 4(a)'s requirement of probable cause must be promptly filed in the district where the offense was allegedly committed.

(c) Place of Initial Appearance; Transfer to Another District.
    (1) Arrest in the District Where the Offense Was Allegedly Committed. If the defendant is arrested in the district where the offense was allegedly committed:
        (A) the initial appearance must be in that district; and
        (B) if a magistrate judge is not reasonably available, the initial appearance may be before a state or local judicial officer.

    (2) Arrest in a District Other Than Where the Offense Was Allegedly Committed. If the defendant was arrested in a district other than where the offense was allegedly committed, the initial appearance must be:
        (A) in the district of arrest; or
        (B) in an adjacent district if:
            (i) the appearance can occur more promptly there; or
            (ii) the offense was allegedly committed there and the initial appearance will occur on the day of arrest.

    (3) Procedures in a District Other Than Where the Offense Was Allegedly Committed. If the initial appearance occurs in a district other than where the offense was allegedly committed, the following procedures apply:
        (A) the magistrate judge must inform the defendant about the provisions of Rule 20;
        (B) if the defendant was arrested without a warrant, the district court where the offense was allegedly committed must first issue a warrant before the magistrate judge transfers the defendant to that district;
        (C) the magistrate judge must conduct a preliminary hearing if required by Rule 5.1;
        (D) the magistrate judge must transfer the defendant to the district where the offense was allegedly committed if:
            (i) the government produces the warrant, a certified copy of the warrant, or a reliable electronic form of either; and
            (ii) the judge finds that the defendant is the same person named in the indictment, information, or warrant; and

        (E) when a defendant is transferred and discharged, the clerk must promptly transmit the papers and any bail to the clerk in the district where the offense was allegedly committed.

    (4) Procedure for Persons Extradited to the United States. If the defendant is surrendered to the United States in accordance with a request for the defendant's extradition, the initial appearance must be in the district (or one of the districts) where the offense is charged.

(d) Procedure in a Felony Case.
    (1) Advice. If the defendant is charged with a felony, the judge must inform the defendant of the following:
        (A) the complaint against the defendant, and any affidavit filed with it;
        (B) the defendant's right to retain counsel or to request that counsel be appointed if the defendant cannot obtain counsel;
        (C) the circumstances, if any, under which the defendant may secure pretrial release;
        (D) any right to a preliminary hearing;
        (E) the defendant's right not to make a statement, and that any statement made may be used against the defendant; and
        (F) that a defendant who is not a United States citizen may request that an attorney for the government or a federal law enforcement official notify a consular officer from the defendant's country of nationality that the defendant has been arrested—but that even without the defendant's request, a treaty or other international agreement may require consular notification.

    (2) Consulting with Counsel. The judge must allow the defendant reasonable opportunity to consult with counsel.
    (3) Detention or Release. The judge must detain or release the defendant as provided by statute or these rules.
    (4) Plea. A defendant may be asked to plead only under Rule 10.

(e) Procedure in a Misdemeanor Case. If the defendant is charged with a misdemeanor only, the judge must inform the defendant in accordance with Rule 58(b)(2).

(f) Video Teleconferencing. Video teleconferencing may be used to conduct an appearance under this rule if the defendant consents.

(As amended Feb. 28, 1966, eff. July 1, 1966; Apr. 24, 1972, eff. Oct. 1, 1972; Apr. 28, 1982, eff. Aug. 1, 1982; Pub. L. 98–473, title II, §209(a), Oct. 12, 1984, 98 Stat. 1986; Mar. 9, 1987, eff. Aug. 1, 1987; May 1, 1990, eff. Dec. 1, 1990; Apr. 22, 1993, eff. Dec. 1, 1993; Apr. 27, 1995, eff. Dec. 1, 1995; Apr. 29, 2002, eff. Dec. 1, 2002; Apr. 12, 2006, eff. Dec. 1, 2006; Apr. 23, 2012, eff. Dec. 1, 2012; Apr. 25, 2014, eff. Dec. 1, 2014.)

NOTES OF ADVISORY COMMITTEE ON RULES——1944

Note to Subdivision (a). 1. The time within which a prisoner must be brought before a committing magistrate is defined differently in different statutes. The rule supersedes all statutory provisions on this point and fixes a single standard, i.e., "without unnecessary delay", 18 U.S.C. [former] 593 (Operating illicit distillery; arrest; bail); sec. [former] 595 (Persons arrested taken before nearest officer for hearing); 5 U.S.C. 300a [now 18 U.S.C. 3052, 3107] (Division of Investigation; authority of officers to serve warrants and make arrests); 16 U.S.C. 10 (Arrests by employees of park service for violations of laws and regulations); sec. 706 (Migratory Bird Treaty Act; arrests; search warrants); D.C. Code (1940), Title 4, sec. 140 (Arrests without warrant); see, also, 33 U.S.C. 436, 446, 452; 46 U.S.C. 708 [now 18 U.S.C. 2279]. What constitutes "unnecessary delay", i.e., reasonable time within which the prisoner should be brought before a committing magistrate, must be determined in the light of all the facts and circumstances of the case. The following authorities discuss the question what constitutes reasonable time for this purpose in various situations: Carroll v. Parry, 48 App.D.C. 453; Janus v. United States, 38 F.2d 431 (C.C.A. 9th); Commonwealth v. Di Stasio, 294 Mass. 273; State v. Freeman, 86 N.C. 683; Peloquin v. Hibner, 231 Wis. 77; see, also, Warner, 28 Va.L.R. 315, 339–341.

2. The rule also states the prevailing state practice, A.L.I. Code of Criminal Procedure (1931), Commentaries to secs. 35, 36.

Note to Subdivisions (b) and (c). 1. These rules prescribe a uniform procedure to be followed at preliminary hearings before a commissioner. They supersede the general provisions of 18 U.S.C. 591 [now 3041] (Arrest and removal for trial). The procedure prescribed by the rules is that generally prevailing. See Wood v. United States, 128 F.2d 265, 271–272 (App. D.C.); A.L.I. Code of Criminal Procedure (1931), secs. 39–60 and Commentaries thereto; Manual for United States Commissioners, pp. 6–10, published by Administrative Office of the United States Courts.

2. Pleas before a commissioner are excluded, as a plea of guilty at this stage has no legal status or function except to serve as a waiver of preliminary examination. It has been held inadmissible in evidence at the trial, if the defendant was not represented by counsel when the plea was entered. Wood v. United States, 128 F.2d 265 (App. D.C.) The rule expressly provides for a waiver of examination, thereby eliminating any necessity for a provision as to plea.

NOTES OF ADVISORY COMMITTEE ON RULES——1966 AMENDMENT

The first change is designed to insure that under the revision made in Rule 4(a) the defendant arrested on a warrant will receive the same information concerning the basis for the issuance of the warrant as would previously have been given him by the complaint itself.

The second change obligates the commissioner to inform the defendant of his right to request the assignment of counsel if he is unable to obtain counsel. Cf. the amendment to Rule 44, and the Advisory Committee's Note thereon.

NOTES OF ADVISORY COMMITTEE ON RULES——1972 AMENDMENT

There are a number of changes made in rule 5 which are designed to improve the editorial clarity of the rule; to conform the rule to the Federal Magistrates Act; and to deal explicitly in the rule with issues as to which the rule was silent and the law uncertain.

The principal editorial change is to deal separately with the initial appearance before the magistrate and the preliminary examination. They are dealt with together in old rule 5. They are separated in order to prevent confusion as to whether they constitute a single or two separate proceedings. Although the preliminary examination can be held at the time of the initial appearance, in practice this ordinarily does not occur. Usually counsel need time to prepare for the preliminary examination and as a consequence a separate date is typically set for the preliminary examination.

Because federal magistrates are reasonably available to conduct initial appearances, the rule is drafted on the assumption that the initial appearance is before a federal magistrate. If experience under the act indicates that there must be frequent appearances before state or local judicial officers it may be desirable to draft an additional rule, such as the following, detailing the procedure for an initial appearance before a state or local judicial officer:

Initial Appearance Before a State or Local Judicial Officer. If a United States magistrate is not reasonably available under rule 5(a), the arrested person shall be brought before a state or local judicial officer authorized by 18 U.S.C. §3041, and such officer shall inform the person of the rights specified in rule 5(c) and shall authorize the release of the arrested person under the terms provided for by these rules and by 18 U.S.C. §3146. The judicial officer shall immediately transmit any written order of release and any papers filed before him to the appropriate United States magistrate of the district and order the arrested person to appear before such United States magistrate within three days if not in custody or at the next regular hour of business of the United States magistrate if the arrested person is retained in custody. Upon his appearance before the United States magistrate, the procedure shall be that prescribed in rule 5.

Several changes are made to conform the language of the rule to the Federal Magistrates Act.

(1) The term "magistrate," which is defined in new rule 54, is substituted for the term "commissioner." As defined, "magistrate" includes those state and local judicial officers specified in 18 U.S.C. §3041, and thus the initial appearance may be before a state or local judicial officer when a federal magistrate is not reasonably available. This is made explicit in subdivision (a).

(2) Subdivision (b) conforms the rule to the procedure prescribed in the Federal Magistrate Act when a defendant appears before a magistrate charged with a "minor offense" as defined in 18 U.S.C. §3401(f):

"misdemeanors punishable under the laws of the United States, the penalty for which does not exceed imprisonment for a period of one year, or a fine of not more than $1,000, or both, except that such term does not include . . . [specified exceptions]."
If the "minor offense" is tried before a United States magistrate, the procedure must be in accordance with the Rules of Procedure for the Trial of Minor Offenses Before United States Magistrates, (January 27, 1971).

(3) Subdivision (d) makes clear that a defendant is not entitled to a preliminary examination if he has been indicted by a grand jury prior to the date set for the preliminary examination or, in appropriate cases, if any information is filed in the district court prior to that date. See C. Wright, Federal Practice and Procedure: Criminal §80, pp. 137–140 (1969, Supp. 1971). This is also provided in the Federal Magistrates Act, 18 U.S.C. §3060(e).

Rule 5 is also amended to deal with several issues not dealt with in old rule 5:

Subdivision (a) is amended to make clear that a complaint, complying with the requirements of rule 4(a), must be filed whenever a person has been arrested without a warrant. This means that the complaint, or an affidavit or affidavits filed with the complaint, must show probable cause. As provided in rule 4(a) the showing of probable cause "may be based upon hearsay evidence in whole or in part."

Subdivision (c) provides that defendant should be notified of the general circumstances under which he is entitled to pretrial release under the Bail Reform Act of 1966 (18 U.S.C. §§3141–3152). Defendants often do not in fact have counsel at the initial appearance and thus, unless told by the magistrate, may be unaware of their right to pretrial release. See C. Wright, Federal Practice and Procedure: Criminal §78 N. 61 (1969).

Subdivision (c) makes clear that a defendant who does not waive his right to trial before a judge of the district court is entitled to a preliminary examination to determine probable cause for any offense except a petty offense. It also, by necessary implication, makes clear that a defendant is not entitled to a preliminary examination if he consents to be tried on the issue of guilt or innocence by the United States magistrate, even though the offense may be one not heretofore triable by the United States commissioner and therefore one as to which the defendant had a right to a preliminary examination. The rationale is that the preliminary examination serves only to justify holding the defendant in custody or on bail during the period of time it takes to bind the defendant over to the district court for trial. See State v. Solomon, 158 Wis. 146, 147 N.W. 640 (1914). A similar conclusion is reached in the New York Proposed Criminal Procedure Law. See McKinney's Session Law News, April 10, 1969, at p. A–119.

Subdivision (c) also contains time limits within which the preliminary examination must be held. These are taken from 18 U.S.C. §3060. The provisions for the extension of the prescribed time limits are the same as the provisions of 18 U.S.C. §3060 with two exceptions: The new language allows delay consented to by the defendant only if there is "a showing of good cause, taking into account the public interest in the prompt disposition of criminal cases." This reflects the view of the Advisory Committee that delay, whether prosecution or defense induced, ought to be avoided whenever possible. The second difference between the new rule and 18 U.S.C. §3060 is that the rule allows the decision to grant a continuance to be made by a United States magistrate as well as by a judge of the United States. This reflects the view of the Advisory Committee that the United States magistrate should have sufficient judicial competence to make decisions such as that contemplated in subdivision (c).

NOTES OF ADVISORY COMMITTEE ON RULES——1982 AMENDMENT

The amendment of subdivision (b) reflects the recent amendment of 18 U.S.C. §3401(a), by the Federal Magistrate Act of 1979, to read: "When specially designated to exercise such jurisdiction by the district court or courts he serves, any United States magistrate shall have jurisdiction to try persons accused of, and sentence persons convicted of, misdemeanors committed within that judicial district."

NOTES OF ADVISORY COMMITTEE ON RULES——1987 AMENDMENT

The amendments are technical. No substantive change is intended.

NOTES OF ADVISORY COMMITTEE ON RULES——1990 AMENDMENT

Rule 5(b) is amended to conform the rule to Rule 58.

NOTES OF ADVISORY COMMITTEE ON RULES——1993 AMENDMENT

The Rule is amended to conform to the Judicial Improvements Act of 1990 [P.L. 101–650, Title III, Section 321] which provides that each United States magistrate appointed under section 631 of title 28, United States Code, shall be known as a United States magistrate judge.

NOTES OF ADVISORY COMMITTEE ON RULES——1995 AMENDMENT

The amendment to Rule 5 is intended to address the interplay between the requirements for a prompt appearance before a magistrate judge and the processing of persons arrested for the offense of unlawfully fleeing to avoid prosecution under 18 U.S.C. §1073, when no federal prosecution is intended. Title 18 U.S.C. §1073 provides in part:

Whoever moves or travels in interstate or foreign commerce with intent . . . to avoid prosecution, or custody or confinement after conviction, under the laws of the place from which he flees . . . shall be fined not more than $5,000 or imprisoned not more than five years, or both.

Violations of this section may be prosecuted . . . only upon formal approval in writing by the Attorney General, the Deputy Attorney General, the Associate Attorney General, or an Assistant Attorney General of the United States, which function of approving prosecutions may not be delegated.

In enacting §1073, Congress apparently intended to provide assistance to state criminal justice authorities in an effort to apprehend and prosecute state offenders. It also appears that by requiring permission of high ranking officials, Congress intended that prosecutions be limited in number. In fact, prosecutions under this section have been rare. The purpose of the statute is fulfilled when the person is apprehended and turned over to state or local authorities. In such cases the requirement of Rule 5 that any person arrested under a federal warrant must be brought before a federal magistrate judge becomes a largely meaningless exercise and a needless demand upon federal judicial resources.

In addressing this problem, several options are available to federal authorities when no federal prosecution is intended to ensue after the arrest. First, once federal authorities locate a fugitive, they may contact local law enforcement officials who make the arrest based upon the underlying out-of-state warrant. In that instance, Rule 5 is not implicated and the United States Attorney in the district issuing the §1073 complaint and warrant can take action to dismiss both. In a second scenario, the fugitive is arrested by federal authorities who, in compliance with Rule 5, bring the person before a federal magistrate judge. If local law enforcement officers are present, they can take custody, once the United States Attorney informs the magistrate judge that there will be no prosecution under §1073. Depending on the availability of state or local officers, there may be some delay in the Rule 5 proceedings; any delays following release to local officials, however, would not be a function of Rule 5. In a third situation, federal authorities arrest the fugitive but local law enforcement authorities are not present at the Rule 5 appearance. Depending on a variety of practices, the magistrate judge may calendar a removal hearing under Rule 40, or order that the person be held in federal custody pending further action by the local authorities.

Under the amendment, officers arresting a fugitive charged only with violating §1073 need not bring the person before a magistrate judge under Rule 5(a) if there is no intent to actually prosecute the person under that charge. Two requirements, however, must be met. First, the arrested fugitive must be transferred without unnecessary delay to the custody of state officials. Second, steps must be taken in the appropriate district to dismiss the complaint alleging a violation of §1073. The rule continues to contemplate that persons arrested by federal officials are entitled to prompt handling of federal charges, if prosecution is intended, and prompt transfer to state custody if federal prosecution is not contemplated.

COMMITTEE NOTES ON RULES——2002 AMENDMENT

The language of Rule 5 has been amended as part of the general restyling of the Criminal Rules to make them more easily understood and to make style and terminology consistent throughout the rules. These changes are intended to be stylistic, except as noted below.

Rule 5 has been completely revised to more clearly set out the procedures for initial appearances and to recognize that such appearances may be required at various stages of a criminal proceeding, for example, where a defendant has been arrested for violating the terms of probation.

Rule 5(a), which governs initial appearances by an arrested defendant before a magistrate judge, includes several changes. The first is a clarifying change; revised Rule 5(a)(1) provides that a person making the arrest must bring the defendant "without unnecessary delay" before a magistrate judge, instead of the current reference to "nearest available" magistrate judge. This language parallels changes in Rule 4 and reflects the view that time is of the essence. The Committee intends no change in practice. In using the term, the Committee recognizes that on occasion there may be necessary delay in presenting the defendant, for example, due to weather conditions or other natural causes. A second change is non-stylistic, and reflects the stated preference (as in other provisions throughout the rules) that the defendant be brought before a federal judicial officer. Only if a magistrate judge is not available should the defendant be taken before a state or local officer.

The third sentence in current Rule 5(a), which states that a magistrate judge must proceed in accordance with the rule where a defendant is arrested without a warrant or given a summons, has been deleted because it is unnecessary.

Rule 5(a)(1)(B) codifies the caselaw reflecting that the right to an initial appearance applies not only when a person is arrested within the United States but also when an arrest occurs outside the United States. See, e.g., United States v. Purvis, 768 F.2d 1237 (11th Cir. 1985); United States v. Yunis, 859 F.2d 953 (D.C. Cir. 1988). In these circumstances, the Committee believes—and the rule so provides—that the initial appearance should be before a federal magistrate judge rather than a state or local judicial officer. Rule 5(a)(1)(B) has also been amended by adding the words, "unless a federal statute provides otherwise," to reflect recent enactment of the Military Extraterritorial Jurisdiction Act (Pub. L. No. 106–523, 114 Stat. 2488) that permits certain persons overseas to appear before a magistrate judge by telephonic communication.

Rule 5(a)(2)(A) consists of language currently located in Rule 5 that addresses the procedure to be followed where a defendant has been arrested under a warrant issued on a complaint charging solely a violation of 18 U.S.C. §1073 (unlawful flight to avoid prosecution). Rule 5(a)(2)(B) and 5(a)(2)(C) are new provisions. They are intended to make it clear that when a defendant is arrested for violating probation or supervised release, or for failing to appear in another district, Rules 32.1 or 40 apply. No change in practice is intended.

Rule 5(a)(3) is new and fills a perceived gap in the rules. It recognizes that a defendant may be subjected to an initial appearance under this rule if a summons was issued under Rule 4, instead of an arrest warrant. If the defendant is appearing pursuant to a summons in a felony case, Rule 5(d) applies, and if the defendant is appearing in a misdemeanor case, Rule 5(e) applies.

Rule 5(b) carries forward the requirement in former Rule 5(a) that if the defendant is arrested without a warrant, a complaint must be promptly filed.

Rule 5(c) is a new provision and sets out where an initial appearance is to take place. If the defendant is arrested in the district where the offense was allegedly committed, under Rule 5(c)(1) the defendant must be taken to a magistrate judge in that district. If no magistrate judge is reasonably available, a state or local judicial officer may conduct the initial appearance. On the other hand, if the defendant is arrested in a district other than the district where the offense was allegedly committed, Rule 5(c)(2) governs. In those instances, the defendant must be taken to a magistrate judge within the district of arrest, unless the appearance can take place more promptly in an adjacent district. The Committee recognized that in some cases, the nearest magistrate judge may actually be across a district's lines. The remainder of Rule 5(c)(2) includes material formerly located in Rule 40.

Rule 5(d), derived from current Rule 5(c), has been retitled to more clearly reflect the subject of that subdivision and the procedure to be used if the defendant is charged with a felony. Rule 5(d)(4) has been added to make clear that a defendant may only be called upon to enter a plea under the provisions of Rule 10. That language is intended to reflect and reaffirm current practice.

The remaining portions of current Rule 5(c) have been moved to Rule 5.1, which deals with preliminary hearings in felony cases.

The major substantive change is in new Rule 5(f), which permits video teleconferencing for an appearance under this rule if the defendant consents. This change reflects the growing practice among state courts to use video teleconferencing to conduct initial proceedings. A similar amendment has been made to Rule 10 concerning arraignments.

In amending Rules 5, 10, and 43 (which generally requires the defendant's presence at all proceedings), the Committee carefully considered the argument that permitting a defendant to appear by video teleconferencing might be considered an erosion of an important element of the judicial process. Much can be lost when video teleconferencing occurs. First, the setting itself may not promote the public's confidence in the integrity and solemnity of a federal criminal proceeding; that is the view of some who have witnessed the use of such proceedings in some state jurisdictions. While it is difficult to quantify the intangible benefits and impact of requiring a defendant to be brought before a federal judicial officer in a federal courtroom, the Committee realizes that something is lost when a defendant is not required to make a personal appearance. A related consideration is that the defendant may be located in a room that bears no resemblance whatsoever to a judicial forum and the equipment may be inadequate for high-quality transmissions. Second, using video teleconferencing can interfere with counsel's ability to meet personally with his or her client at what, at least in that jurisdiction, might be an important appearance before a magistrate judge. Third, the defendant may miss an opportunity to meet with family or friends, and others who might be able to assist the defendant, especially in any attempts to obtain bail. Finally, the magistrate judge may miss an opportunity to accurately assess the physical, emotional, and mental condition of a defendant—a factor that may weigh on pretrial decisions, such as release from detention.

On the other hand, the Committee considered that in some jurisdictions, the court systems face a high volume of criminal proceedings. In other jurisdictions, counsel may not be appointed until after the initial appearance and thus there is no real problem with a defendant being able to consult with counsel before or during that proceeding. The Committee was also persuaded to adopt the amendment because in some jurisdictions delays may occur in travel time from one location to another—in some cases requiring either the magistrate judge or the participants to travel long distances. In those instances, it is not unusual for a defense counsel to recognize the benefit of conducting a video teleconferenced proceeding, which will eliminate lengthy and sometimes expensive travel or permit the initial appearance to be conducted much sooner. Finally, the Committee was aware that in some jurisdictions, courtrooms now contain high quality technology for conducting such procedures, and that some courts are already using video teleconferencing—with the consent of the parties.

The Committee believed that, on balance and in appropriate circumstances, the court and the defendant should have the option of using video teleconferencing, as long as the defendant consents to that procedure. The question of when it would be appropriate for a defendant to consent is not spelled out in the rule. That is left to the defendant and the court in each case. Although the rule does not specify any particular technical requirements regarding the system to be used, if the equipment or technology is deficient, the public may lose confidence in the integrity and dignity of the proceedings.

The amendment does not require a court to adopt or use video teleconferencing. In deciding whether to use such procedures, a court may wish to consider establishing clearly articulated standards and procedures. For example, the court would normally want to insure that the location used for televising the video teleconferencing is conducive to the solemnity of a federal criminal proceeding. That might require additional coordination, for example, with the detention facility to insure that the room, furniture, and furnishings reflect the dignity associated with a federal courtroom. Provision should also be made to insure that the judge, or a surrogate, is in a position to carefully assess the defendant's condition. And the court should also consider establishing procedures for insuring that counsel and the defendant (and even the defendant's immediate family) are provided an ample opportunity to confer in private.

COMMITTEE NOTES ON RULES—2006 AMENDMENT

Subdivisions (c)(3)(C) and (D). The amendment to Rule 5(c)(3)(C) parallels an amendment to Rule 58(b)(2)(G), which in turn has been amended to remove a conflict between that rule and Rule 5.1(a), concerning the right to a preliminary hearing.

Rule 5(c)(3)(D) has been amended to permit the magistrate judge to accept a warrant by reliable electronic means. Currently, the rule requires the government to produce the original warrant, a certified copy of the warrant, or a facsimile copy of either of those documents. This amendment parallels similar changes to Rules 32.1(a)(5)(B)(i) and 41. The reference to a facsimile version of the warrant was removed because the Committee believed that the broader term "electronic form" includes facsimiles.

The amendment reflects a number of significant improvements in technology. First, more courts are now equipped to receive filings by electronic means, and indeed, some courts encourage or require that certain documents be filed by electronic means. Second, the technology has advanced to the state where such filings could be sent from, and received at, locations outside the courthouse. Third, electronic media can now provide improved quality of transmission and security measures. In short, in a particular case, using electronic media to transmit a document might be just as reliable and efficient as using a facsimile.

The term "electronic" is used to provide some flexibility to the rule and make allowance for further technological advances in transmitting data.

The rule requires that if electronic means are to be used to transmit a warrant to the magistrate judge, that the means used be "reliable." While the rule does not further define that term, the Committee envisions that a court or magistrate judge would make that determination as a local matter. In deciding whether a particular electronic means, or media, would be reliable, the court might consider first, the expected quality and clarity of the transmission. For example, is it possible to read the contents of the warrant in its entirety, as though it were the original or a clean photocopy? Second, the court may consider whether security measures are available to insure that the transmission is not compromised. In this regard, most courts are now equipped to require that certain documents contain a digital signature, or some other similar system for restricting access. Third, the court may consider whether there are reliable means of preserving the document for later use.

Changes Made After Publication and Comment. The Committee made no changes in the Rule and Committee Note as published. It considered and rejected the suggestion that the rule should refer specifically to non-certified photocopies, believing it preferable to allow the definition of reliability to be resolved at the local level. The Committee Note provides examples of the factors that would bear on reliability.

COMMITTEE NOTES ON RULES—2012 AMENDMENT

Subdivision (c)(4). The amendment codifies the longstanding practice that persons who are charged with criminal offenses in the United States and surrendered to the United States following extradition in a foreign country make their initial appearance in the jurisdiction that sought their extradition.

This rule is applicable even if the defendant arrives first in another district. The earlier stages of the extradition process have already fulfilled some of the functions of the initial appearance. During foreign extradition proceedings, the extradited person, assisted by counsel, is afforded an opportunity to review the charging document, U.S. arrest warrant, and supporting evidence. Rule 5(a)(1)(B) requires the person be taken before a magistrate judge without unnecessary delay. Consistent with this obligation, it is preferable not to delay an extradited person's transportation to hold an initial appearance in the district of arrival, even if the person will be present in that district for some time as a result of connecting flights or logistical difficulties. Interrupting an extradited defendant's transportation at this point can impair his or her ability to obtain and consult with trial counsel and to prepare his or her defense in the district where the charges are pending.

Changes Made to Proposed Amendment Released for Public Comment. No changes were made in the amendment as published.

COMMITTEE NOTES ON RULES—2014 AMENDMENT

Rule 5(d)(1)(F). Article 36 of the Vienna Convention on Consular Relations provides that detained foreign nationals shall be advised that they may have the consulate of their home country notified of their arrest and detention, and bilateral agreements with numerous countries require consular notification whether or not the detained foreign national requests it. Article 36 requires consular notification advice to be given "without delay," and arresting officers are primarily responsible for providing this advice.

Providing this advice at the initial appearance is designed, not to relieve law enforcement officers of that responsibility, but to provide additional assurance that U.S. treaty obligations are fulfilled, and to create a judicial record of that action. The Committee concluded that the most effective and efficient method of conveying this information is to provide it to every defendant, without attempting to determine the defendant's citizenship.

At the time of this amendment, many questions remain unresolved by the courts concerning Article 36, including whether it creates individual rights that may be invoked in a judicial proceeding and what, if any, remedy may exist for a violation of Article 36. Sanchez-Llamas v. Oregon, 548 U.S. 331 (2006). This amendment does not address those questions. More particularly, it does not create any such rights or remedies.

Changes Made After Publication and Comment. In response to public comments the amendment was rephrased to state that the information regarding consular notification should be provided to all defendants who are arraigned. Although it is anticipated that ordinarily only defendants who are held in custody will ask the government to notify a consular official of their arrest, it is appropriate to provide this information to all defendants at their initial appearance. The new phrasing also makes it clear that the advice should be provided to every defendant, without any attempt to determine the defendant's citizenship. A conforming change was made to the Committee Note.

AMENDMENT BY PUBLIC LAW

1984—Subd. (c). Pub. L. 98–473 substituted "shall detain or conditionally release the defendant" for "shall admit the defendant to bail".

Rule 5.1. Preliminary Hearing

(a) In General. If a defendant is charged with an offense other than a petty offense, a magistrate judge must conduct a preliminary hearing unless:
    (1) the defendant waives the hearing;
    (2) the defendant is indicted;
    (3) the government files an information under Rule 7(b) charging the defendant with a felony;
    (4) the government files an information charging the defendant with a misdemeanor; or
    (5) the defendant is charged with a misdemeanor and consents to trial before a magistrate judge.

(b) Selecting a District. A defendant arrested in a district other than where the offense was allegedly committed may elect to have the preliminary hearing conducted in the district where the prosecution is pending.

(c) Scheduling. The magistrate judge must hold the preliminary hearing within a reasonable time, but no later than 14 days after the initial appearance if the defendant is in custody and no later than 21 days if not in custody.

(d) Extending the Time. With the defendant's consent and upon a showing of good cause—taking into account the public interest in the prompt disposition of criminal cases—a magistrate judge may extend the time limits in Rule 5.1(c) one or more times. If the defendant does not consent, the magistrate judge may extend the time limits only on a showing that extraordinary circumstances exist and justice requires the delay.

(e) Hearing and Finding. At the preliminary hearing, the defendant may cross-examine adverse witnesses and may introduce evidence but may not object to evidence on the ground that it was unlawfully acquired. If the magistrate judge finds probable cause to believe an offense has been committed and the defendant committed it, the magistrate judge must promptly require the defendant to appear for further proceedings.

(f) Discharging the Defendant. If the magistrate judge finds no probable cause to believe an offense has been committed or the defendant committed it, the magistrate judge must dismiss the complaint and discharge the defendant. A discharge does not preclude the government from later prosecuting the defendant for the same offense.

(g) Recording the Proceedings. The preliminary hearing must be recorded by a court reporter or by a suitable recording device. A recording of the proceeding may be made available to any party upon request. A copy of the recording and a transcript may be provided to any party upon request and upon any payment required by applicable Judicial Conference regulations.

(h) Producing a Statement.

(1) In General. Rule 26.2(a)–(d) and (f) applies at any hearing under this rule, unless the magistrate judge for good cause rules otherwise in a particular case.

(2) Sanctions for Not Producing a Statement. If a party disobeys a Rule 26.2 order to deliver a statement to the moving party, the magistrate judge must not consider the testimony of a witness whose statement is withheld.

(Added Apr. 24, 1972, eff. Oct. 1, 1972; amended Mar. 9, 1987, eff. Aug. 1, 1987; Apr. 22, 1993, eff. Dec. 1, 1993; Apr. 24, 1998, eff. Dec. 1, 1998; Apr. 29, 2002, eff. Dec. 1, 2002; Mar. 26, 2009, eff. Dec. 1, 2009.)

NOTES OF ADVISORY COMMITTEE ON RULES—1972

Rule 5.1 is, for the most part, a clarification of old rule 5(c).

Under the new rule, the preliminary examination must be conducted before a "federal magistrate" as defined in rule 54. Giving state or local judicial officers authority to conduct a preliminary examination does not seem necessary. There are not likely to be situations in which a "federal magistrate" is not "reasonably available" to conduct the preliminary examination, which is usually not held until several days after the initial appearance provided for in rule 5.

Subdivision (a) makes clear that a finding of probable cause may be based on "hearsay evidence in whole or in part." The propriety of relying upon hearsay at the preliminary examination has been a matter of some uncertainty in the federal system. See C. Wright, Federal Practice and Procedure: Criminal §80 (1969, Supp. 1971); 8 J. Moore, Federal Practice 504[4] (2d ed. Cipes 1970, Supp. 1971); Washington v. Clemmer, 339 F.2d 715, 719 (D.C. Cir. 1964); Washington v. Clemmer, 339 F.2d 725, 728 (D.C. Cir. 1964); Ross v. Sirica, 380 F.2d 557, 565 (D.C. Cir. 1967); Howard v. United States, 389 F.2d 287, 292 (D.C. Cir. 1967); Weinberg and Weinberg, The Congressional Invitation to Avoid the Preliminary Hearing: An Analysis of Section 303 of the Federal Magistrates Act of 1968, 67 Mich.L.Rev. 1361, especially n. 92 at 1383 (1969); D. Wright, The Rules of Evidence Applicable to Hearings in Probable Cause, 37 Conn.B.J. 561 (1963); Comment, Preliminary Examination—Evidence and Due Process, 15 Kan.L.Rev. 374, 379–381 (1967).

A grand jury indictment may properly be based upon hearsay evidence. Costello v. United States, 350 U.S. 359 (1956); 8 J. Moore, Federal Practice 6.03[2] (2d ed. Cipes 1970, Supp. 1971). This being so, there is practical advantage in making the evidentiary requirements for the preliminary examination as flexible as they are for the grand jury. Otherwise there will be increased pressure upon United States Attorneys to abandon the preliminary examination in favor of the grand jury indictment. See C. Wright, Federal Practice and Procedure: Criminal §80 at p. 143 (1969). New York State, which also utilizes both the preliminary examination and the grand jury, has under consideration a new Code of Criminal Procedure which would allow the use of hearsay at the preliminary examination. See McKinney's Session Law News, April 10, 1969, pp. A119–A120.

For the same reason, subdivision (a) also provides that the preliminary examination is not the proper place to raise the issue of illegally obtained evidence. This is current law. In Giordenello v. United States, 357 U.S. 480, 484 (1958), the Supreme Court said:

[T]he Commissioner here had no authority to adjudicate the admissibility at petitioner's later trial of the heroin taken from his person. That issue was for the trial court. This is specifically recognized by Rule 41(e) of the Criminal Rules, which provides that a defendant aggrieved by an unlawful search and seizure may "* * * move the district court * * * to suppress for use as evidence anything so obtained on the ground that * * *" the arrest warrant was defective on any of several grounds.

Dicta in Costello v. United States, 350 U.S. 359, 363–364 (1956), and United States v. Blue, 384 U.S. 251, 255 (1966), also support the proposed rule. In United States ex rel. Almeida v. Rundle, 383 F.2d 421, 424 (3d Cir. 1967), the court, in considering the adequacy of an indictment said:

On this score, it is settled law that (1) "[an] indictment returned by a legally constituted nonbiased grand jury, * * * is enough to call for a trial of the charge on the merits and satisfies the requirements of the Fifth Amendment.", Lawn v. United States, 355 U.S. 399, 349, 78 S.Ct. 311, 317, 2 L.Ed.2d 321 (1958); (2) an indictment cannot be challenged "on the ground that there was inadequate or incompetent evidence before the grand jury", Costello v. United States, 350 U.S. 359, 363, 76 S.Ct. 406, 408, 100 L.Ed. 397 (1956); and (3) a prosecution is not abated, nor barred, even where "tainted evidence" has been submitted to a grand jury, United States v. Blue, 384 U.S. 251, 86 S.Ct. 1416, 16 L.Ed.2d 510 (1966).

See also C. Wright, Federal Practice and Procedure: Criminal §80 at 143 n. 5 (1969, Supp. 1971) 8 J. Moore, Federal Practice 6.03[3] (2d ed. Cipes 1970, Supp. 1971). The Manual for United States Commissioners (Administrative Office of United States Courts, 1948) provides at pp. 24–25: "Motions for this purpose [to suppress illegally obtained evidence] may be made and heard only before a district judge. Commissioners are not empowered to consider or act upon such motions."

It has been urged that the rules of evidence at the preliminary examination should be those applicable at the trial because the purpose of the preliminary examination should be, not to review the propriety of the arrest or prior detention, but rather to determine whether there is evidence sufficient to justify subjecting the defendant to the expense and inconvenience of trial. See Weinberg and Weinberg, The Congressional Invitation to Avoid the Preliminary Hearing: An Analysis of Section 303 of the Federal Magistrates Act of 1968, 67 Mich. L. Rev. 1361, 1396–1399 (1969). The rule rejects this view for reasons largely of administrative necessity and the efficient administration of justice. The Congress has decided that a preliminary examination shall not be required when there is a grand jury indictment (18 U.S.C. §3060). Increasing the procedural and evidentiary requirements applicable to the preliminary examination will therefore add to the administrative pressure to avoid the preliminary examination. Allowing objections to evidence on the ground that evidence has been illegally obtained would require two determinations of admissibility, one before the United States magistrate and one in the district court. The objective is to reduce, not increase, the number of preliminary motions.

To provide that a probable cause finding may be based upon hearsay does not preclude the magistrate from requiring a showing that admissible evidence will be available at the time of trial. See Comment, Criminal Procedure—Grand Jury—Validity of Indictment Based Solely on Hearsay Questioned When Direct Testimony Is Readily Available, 43 N.Y.U. L. Rev. 578 (1968); United States v. Umans, 368 F.2d 725 (2d Cir. 1966), cert. dismissed as improvidently granted 389 U.S. 80 (1967); United States v. Andrews, 381 F.2d 377, 378 (2d Cir. 1967); United States v. Messina, 388 F.2d 393, 394 n. 1 (2d Cir. 1968); and United States v. Beltram. 388 F.2d 449 (2d Cir. 1968); and United States v. Arcuri, 282 F.Supp. 347 (E.D.N.Y. 1968). The fact that a defendant is not entitled to object to evidence alleged to have been illegally obtained does not deprive him of an opportunity for a pretrial determination of the admissibility of evidence. He can raise such an objection prior to trial in accordance with the provisions of rule 12.

Subdivision (b) makes it clear that the United States magistrate may not only discharge the defendant but may also dismiss the complaint. Current federal law authorizes the magistrate to discharge the defendant but he must await authorization from the United States Attorney before he can close his records on the case by dismissing the complaint. Making dismissal of the complaint a separate procedure accomplishes no worthwhile objective, and the new rule makes it clear that the magistrate can both discharge the defendant and file the record with the clerk.

Subdivision (b) also deals with the legal effect of a discharge of a defendant at a preliminary examination. This issue is not dealt with explicitly in the old rule. Existing federal case law is limited. What cases there are seem to support the right of the government to issue a new complaint and start over. See e.q., Collins v. Loisel, 262 U.S. 426 (1923); Morse v. United States, 267 U.S. 80 (1925). State law is similar. See People v. Dillon, 197 N.Y. 254, 90 N.E. 820 (1910; Tell v. Wolke, 21 Wis.2d 613, 124 N.W.2d 655 (1963). In the Tell case the Wisconsin court stated the common rationale for allowing the prosecutor to issue a new complaint and start over:

The state has no appeal from errors of law committed by a magistrate upon preliminary examination and the discharge on a preliminary would operate as an unchallengeable acquittal. * * * The only way an error of law committed on the preliminary examination prejudicial to the state may be challenged or corrected is by a preliminary examination on a second complaint. (21 Wis. 2d at 619–620.)

Subdivision (c) is based upon old rule 5(c) and upon the Federal Magistrates Act, 18 U.S.C. §3060(f). It provides methods for making available to counsel the record of the preliminary examination. See C. Wright, Federal Practice and Procedure: Criminal §82 (1969, Supp. 1971). The new rule is designed to eliminate delay and expense occasioned by preparation of transcripts where listening to the tape recording would be sufficient. Ordinarily the recording should be made available pursuant to subdivision (c)(1). A written transcript may be provided under subdivision (c)(2) at the discretion of the court, a discretion which must be exercised in accordance with Britt v. North Carolina, 404 U.S. 226, 30 L.Ed.2d 400, 405 (1971):

A defendant who claims the right to a free transcript does not, under our cases, bear the burden of proving inadequate such alternatives as may be suggested by the State or conjured up by a court in hindsight. In this case, however, petitioner has conceded that he had available an informal alternative which appears to be substantially equivalent to a transcript. Accordingly, we cannot conclude that the court below was in error in rejecting his claim.

NOTES OF ADVISORY COMMITTEE ON RULES——1987 AMENDMENT

The amendments are technical. No substantive change is intended.

NOTES OF ADVISORY COMMITTEE ON RULES——1993 AMENDMENT

The Rule is amended to conform to the Judicial Improvements Act of 1990 [P.L. 101–650, Title III, Section 321] which provides that each United States magistrate appointed under section 631 of title 28, United States Code, shall be known as a United States magistrate judge.

COMMITTEE NOTES ON RULES——1998 AMENDMENT

The addition of subdivision (d) mirrors similar amendments made in 1993 which extended the scope of Rule 26.2 to Rules 32, 32.1, 46 and Rule 8 of the Rules Governing Proceedings under 28 U.S.C. §2255. As indicated in the Committee Notes accompanying those amendments, the primary reason for extending the coverage of Rule 26.2 rested heavily upon the compelling need for accurate information affecting a witness' credibility. That need, the Committee believes, extends to a preliminary examination under this rule where both the prosecution and the defense have high interests at stake.

A witness' statement must be produced only after the witness has personally testified.

Changes Made to Rule 5.1 After Publication ("GAP Report"). The Committee made no changes to the published draft.

COMMITTEE NOTES ON RULES——2002 AMENDMENT

The language of Rule 5.1 has been amended as part of the general restyling of the Criminal Rules to make them more easily understood and to make style and terminology consistent throughout the rules. These changes are intended to be stylistic, except as noted below.

First, the title of the rule has been changed. Although the underlying statute, 18 U.S.C. §3060, uses the phrase preliminary examination, the Committee believes that the phrase preliminary hearing is more accurate. What happens at this proceeding is more than just an examination; it includes an evidentiary hearing, argument, and a judicial ruling. Further, the phrase preliminary hearing predominates in actual usage.

Rule 5.1(a) is composed of the first sentence of the second paragraph of current Rule 5(c). Rule 5.1(b) addresses the ability of a defendant to elect where a preliminary hearing will be held. That provision is taken from current Rule 40(a).

Rule 5.1(c) and (d) include material currently located in Rule 5(c): scheduling and extending the time limits for the hearing. The Committee is aware that in most districts, magistrate judges perform these functions. That point is also reflected in the definition of "court" in Rule 1(b), which in turn recognizes that magistrate judges may be authorized to act.

Rule 5.1(d) contains a significant change in practice. The revised rule includes language that expands the authority of a United States magistrate judge to grant a continuance for a preliminary hearing conducted under the rule. Currently, the rule authorizes a magistrate judge to grant a continuance only in those cases in which the defendant has consented to the continuance. If the defendant does not consent, then the government must present the matter to a district judge, usually on the same day. The proposed amendment conflicts with 18 U.S.C. §3060, which tracks the original language of the rule and permits only district judges to grant continuances when the defendant objects. The Committee believes that this restriction is an anomaly and that it can lead to needless consumption of judicial and other resources. Magistrate judges are routinely required to make probable cause determinations and other difficult decisions regarding the defendant's liberty interests, reflecting that the magistrate judge's role has developed toward a higher level of responsibility for pre-indictment matters. The Committee believes that the change in the rule will provide greater judicial economy and that it is entirely appropriate to seek this change to the rule through the Rules Enabling Act procedures. See 28 U.S.C. §2072(b). Under those procedures, approval by Congress of this rule change would supersede the parallel provisions in 18 U.S.C. §3060.

Rule 5.1(e), addressing the issue of probable cause, contains the language currently located in Rule 5.1(a), with the exception of the sentence, "The finding of probable cause may be based upon hearsay evidence in whole or in part." That language was included in the original promulgation of the rule in 1972. Similar language was added to Rule 4 in 1974. In the Committee Note on the 1974 amendment, the Advisory Committee explained that the language was included to make it clear that a finding of probable cause may be based upon hearsay, noting that there had been some uncertainty in the federal system about the propriety of relying upon hearsay at the preliminary hearing. See Advisory Committee Note to Rule 5.1 (citing cases and commentary). Federal law is now clear on that proposition. Thus, the Committee believed that the reference to hearsay was no longer necessary. Further, the Committee believed that the matter was best addressed in Rule 1101(d)(3), Federal Rules of Evidence. That rule explicitly states that the Federal Rules of Evidence do not apply to "preliminary examinations in criminal cases, . . . issuance of warrants for arrest, criminal summonses, and search warrants." The Advisory Committee Note accompanying that rule recognizes that: "The nature of the proceedings makes application of the formal rules of evidence inappropriate and impracticable." The Committee did not intend to make any substantive changes in practice by deleting the reference to hearsay evidence.

Rule 5.1(f), which deals with the discharge of a defendant, consists of former Rule 5.1(b).

Rule 5.1(g) is a revised version of the material in current Rule 5.1(c). Instead of including detailed information in the rule itself concerning records of preliminary hearings, the Committee opted simply to direct the reader to the applicable Judicial Conference regulations governing records. The Committee did not intend to make any substantive changes in the way in which those records are currently made available.

Finally, although the rule speaks in terms of initial appearances being conducted before a magistrate judge, Rule 1(c) makes clear that a district judge may perform any function in these rules that a magistrate judge may perform.

COMMITTEE NOTES ON RULES——2009 AMENDMENT

The times set in the former rule at 10 or 20 days have been revised to 14 or 21 days. See the Committee Note to Rule 45(a).

TITLE III. THE GRAND JURY, THE INDICTMENT, AND THE INFORMATION

Rule 6. The Grand Jury

(a) Summoning a Grand Jury.

(1) In General. When the public interest so requires, the court must order that one or more grand juries be summoned. A grand jury must have 16 to 23 members, and the court must order that enough legally qualified persons be summoned to meet this requirement.

(2) Alternate Jurors. When a grand jury is selected, the court may also select alternate jurors. Alternate jurors must have the same qualifications and be selected in the same manner as any other juror. Alternate jurors replace jurors in the same sequence in which the alternates were selected. An alternate juror who replaces a juror is subject to the same challenges, takes the same oath, and has the same authority as the other jurors.

(b) Objection to the Grand Jury or to a Grand Juror.

(1) Challenges. Either the government or a defendant may challenge the grand jury on the ground that it was not lawfully drawn, summoned, or selected, and may challenge an individual juror on the ground that the juror is not legally qualified.

(2) Motion to Dismiss an Indictment. A party may move to dismiss the indictment based on an objection to the grand jury or on an individual juror's lack of legal qualification, unless the court has previously ruled on the same objection under Rule 6(b)(1). The motion to dismiss is governed by 28 U.S.C. §1867(e). The court must not dismiss the indictment on the ground that a grand juror was not legally qualified if the record shows that at least 12 qualified jurors concurred in the indictment.

(c) Foreperson and Deputy Foreperson. The court will appoint one juror as the foreperson and another as the deputy foreperson. In the foreperson's absence, the deputy foreperson will act as the foreperson. The foreperson may administer oaths and affirmations and will sign all indictments. The foreperson—or another juror designated by the foreperson—will record the number of jurors concurring in every indictment and will file the record with the clerk, but the record may not be made public unless the court so orders.

(d) Who May Be Present.

(1) While the Grand Jury Is in Session. The following persons may be present while the grand jury is in session: attorneys for the government, the witness being questioned, interpreters when needed, and a court reporter or an operator of a recording device.

(2) During Deliberations and Voting. No person other than the jurors, and any interpreter needed to assist a hearing-impaired or speech-impaired juror, may be present while the grand jury is deliberating or voting.

(e) Recording and Disclosing the Proceedings.

(1) Recording the Proceedings. Except while the grand jury is deliberating or voting, all proceedings must be recorded by a court reporter or by a suitable recording device. But the validity of a prosecution is not affected by the unintentional failure to make a recording. Unless the court orders otherwise, an attorney for the government will retain control of the recording, the reporter's notes, and any transcript prepared from those notes.

(2) Secrecy.

(A) No obligation of secrecy may be imposed on any person except in accordance with Rule 6(e)(2)(B).

(B) Unless these rules provide otherwise, the following persons must not disclose a matter occurring before the grand jury:

(i) a grand juror;

(ii) an interpreter;

(iii) a court reporter;

(iv) an operator of a recording device;

(v) a person who transcribes recorded testimony;

(vi) an attorney for the government; or

(vii) a person to whom disclosure is made under Rule 6(e)(3)(A)(ii) or (iii).

(3) Exceptions.

(A) Disclosure of a grand-jury matter—other than the grand jury's deliberations or any grand juror's vote—may be made to:

(i) an attorney for the government for use in performing that attorney's duty;

(ii) any government personnel—including those of a state, state subdivision, Indian tribe, or foreign government—that an attorney for the government considers necessary to assist in performing that attorney's duty to enforce federal criminal law; or

(iii) a person authorized by 18 U.S.C. §3322.

(B) A person to whom information is disclosed under Rule 6(e)(3)(A)(ii) may use that information only to assist an attorney for the government in performing that attorney's duty to enforce federal criminal law. An attorney for the government must promptly provide the court that impaneled the grand jury with the names of all persons to whom a disclosure has been made, and must certify that the attorney has advised those persons of their obligation of secrecy under this rule.

(C) An attorney for the government may disclose any grand-jury matter to another federal grand jury.

(D) An attorney for the government may disclose any grand-jury matter involving foreign intelligence, counterintelligence (as defined in 50 U.S.C. §3003), or foreign intelligence information (as defined in Rule 6(e)(3)(D)(iii)) to any federal law enforcement, intelligence, protective, immigration, national defense, or national security official to assist the official receiving the information in the performance of that official's duties. An attorney for the government may also disclose any grand-jury matter involving, within the United States or elsewhere, a threat of attack or other grave hostile acts of a foreign power or its agent, a threat of domestic or international sabotage or terrorism, or clandestine intelligence gathering activities by an intelligence service or network of a foreign power or by its agent, to any appropriate federal, state, state subdivision, Indian tribal, or foreign government official, for the purpose of preventing or responding to such threat or activities.

(i) Any official who receives information under Rule 6(e)(3)(D) may use the information only as necessary in the conduct of that person's official duties subject to any limitations on the unauthorized disclosure of such information. Any state, state subdivision, Indian tribal, or foreign government official who receives information under Rule 6(e)(3)(D) may use the information only in a manner consistent with any guidelines issued by the Attorney General and the Director of National Intelligence.

(ii) Within a reasonable time after disclosure is made under Rule 6(e)(3)(D), an attorney for the government must file, under seal, a notice with the court in the district where the grand jury convened stating that such information was disclosed and the departments, agencies, or entities to which the disclosure was made.

(iii) As used in Rule 6(e)(3)(D), the term "foreign intelligence information" means:

(a) information, whether or not it concerns a United States person, that relates to the ability of the United States to protect against—
• actual or potential attack or other grave hostile acts of a foreign power or its agent;
• sabotage or international terrorism by a foreign power or its agent; or
• clandestine intelligence activities by an intelligence service or network of a foreign power or by its agent; or

(b) information, whether or not it concerns a United States person, with respect to a foreign power or foreign territory that relates to—
• the national defense or the security of the United States; or
• the conduct of the foreign affairs of the United States.

(E) The court may authorize disclosure—at a time, in a manner, and subject to any other conditions that it directs—of a grand-jury matter:

(i) preliminarily to or in connection with a judicial proceeding;

(ii) at the request of a defendant who shows that a ground may exist to dismiss the indictment because of a matter that occurred before the grand jury;

(iii) at the request of the government, when sought by a foreign court or prosecutor for use in an official criminal investigation;

(iv) at the request of the government if it shows that the matter may disclose a violation of State, Indian tribal, or foreign criminal law, as long as the disclosure is to an appropriate state, state-subdivision, Indian tribal, or foreign government official for the purpose of enforcing that law; or

(v) at the request of the government if it shows that the matter may disclose a violation of military criminal law under the Uniform Code of Military Justice, as long as the disclosure is to an appropriate military official for the purpose of enforcing that law.

(F) A petition to disclose a grand-jury matter under Rule 6(e)(3)(E)(i) must be filed in the district where the grand jury convened. Unless the hearing is ex parte—as it may be when the government is the petitioner—the petitioner must serve the petition on, and the court must afford a reasonable opportunity to appear and be heard to:

(i) an attorney for the government;

(ii) the parties to the judicial proceeding; and

(iii) any other person whom the court may designate.

(G) If the petition to disclose arises out of a judicial proceeding in another district, the petitioned court must transfer the petition to the other court unless the petitioned court can reasonably determine whether disclosure is proper. If the petitioned court decides to transfer, it must send to the transferee court the material sought to be disclosed, if feasible, and a written evaluation of the need for continued grand-jury secrecy. The transferee court must afford those persons identified in Rule 6(e)(3)(F) a reasonable opportunity to appear and be heard.

(4) Sealed Indictment. The magistrate judge to whom an indictment is returned may direct that the indictment be kept secret until the defendant is in custody or has been released pending trial. The clerk must then seal the indictment, and no person may disclose the indictment's existence except as necessary to issue or execute a warrant or summons.

(5) Closed Hearing. Subject to any right to an open hearing in a contempt proceeding, the court must close any hearing to the extent necessary to prevent disclosure of a matter occurring before a grand jury.

(6) Sealed Records. Records, orders, and subpoenas relating to grand-jury proceedings must be kept under seal to the extent and as long as necessary to prevent the unauthorized disclosure of a matter occurring before a grand jury.

(7) Contempt. A knowing violation of Rule 6, or of any guidelines jointly issued by the Attorney General and the Director of National Intelligence under Rule 6, may be punished as a contempt of court.

(f) Indictment and Return. A grand jury may indict only if at least 12 jurors concur. The grand jury—or its foreperson or deputy foreperson—must return the indictment to a magistrate judge in open court. To avoid unnecessary cost or delay, the magistrate judge may take the return by video teleconference from the court where the grand jury sits. If a complaint or information is pending against the defendant and 12 jurors do not concur in the indictment, the foreperson must promptly and in writing report the lack of concurrence to the magistrate judge.

(g) Discharging the Grand Jury. A grand jury must serve until the court discharges it, but it may serve more than 18 months only if the court, having determined that an extension is in the public interest, extends the grand jury's service. An extension may be granted for no more than 6 months, except as otherwise provided by statute.

(h) Excusing a Juror. At any time, for good cause, the court may excuse a juror either temporarily or permanently, and if permanently, the court may impanel an alternate juror in place of the excused juror.

(i) "Indian Tribe" Defined. "Indian tribe" means an Indian tribe recognized by the Secretary of the Interior on a list published in the Federal Register under 25 U.S.C. §479a–1.[1]

(As amended Feb. 28, 1966, eff. July 1, 1966; Apr. 24, 1972, eff. Oct. 1, 1972; Apr. 26 and July 8, 1976, eff. Aug. 1, 1976; Pub. L. 95–78, §2(a), July 30, 1977, 91 Stat. 319; Apr. 30, 1979, eff. Aug. 1, 1979; Apr. 28, 1983, eff. Aug. 1, 1983; Pub. L. 98–473, title II, §215(f), Oct. 12, 1984, 98 Stat. 2016; Apr. 29, 1985, eff. Aug. 1, 1985; Mar. 9, 1987, eff. Aug. 1, 1987; Apr. 22, 1993, eff. Dec. 1, 1993; Apr. 26, 1999, eff. Dec. 1, 1999; Pub. L. 107–56, title II, §203(a), Oct. 26, 2001, 115 Stat. 278; Apr. 29, 2002, eff. Dec. 1, 2002; Pub. L. 107–296, title VIII, §895, Nov. 25, 2002, 116 Stat. 2256; Pub. L. 108–458, title VI, §6501(a), Dec. 17, 2004, 118 Stat. 3760; Apr. 12, 2006, eff. Dec. 1, 2006; Apr. 26, 2011, eff. Dec. 1, 2011; Apr. 25, 2014, eff. Dec. 1, 2014.)

NOTES OF ADVISORY COMMITTEE ON RULES——1944

Note to Subdivision (a). 1. The first sentence of this rule vests in the court full discretion as to the number of grand juries to be summoned and as to the times when they should be convened. This provision supersedes the existing law, which limits the authority of the court to summon more than one grand jury at the same time. At present two grand juries may be convened simultaneously only in a district which has a city or borough of at least 300,000 inhabitants, and three grand juries only in the Southern District of New York, 28 U.S.C. [former] 421 (Grand juries; when, how and by whom summoned; length of service). This statute has been construed, however, as only limiting the authority of the court to summon more than one grand jury for a single place of holding court, and as not circumscribing the power to convene simultaneously several grand juries at different points within the same district, Morris v. United States, 128 F.2d 912 (C.C.A. 5th); United States v. Perlstein, 39 F.Supp. 965 (D.N.J.).

2. The provision that the grand jury shall consist of not less than 16 and not more than 23 members continues existing law, 28 U.S.C. 419 [now 18 U.S.C. 3321] (Grand jurors; number when less than required number).

3. The rule does not affect or deal with the method of summoning and selecting grand juries. Existing statutes on the subjects are not superseded. See 28 U.S.C. 411–426 [now 1861–1870]. As these provisions of law relate to jurors for both criminal and civil cases, it seemed best not to deal with this subject.

Note to Subdivision (b)(1). Challenges to the array and to individual jurors, although rarely invoked in connection with the selection of grand juries, are nevertheless permitted in the Federal courts and are continued by this rule, United States v. Gale, 109 U.S. 65, 69–70; Clawson v. United States, 114 U.S. 477; Agnew v. United States, 165 U.S. 36, 44. It is not contemplated, however, that defendants held for action of the grand jury shall receive notice of the time and place of the impaneling of a grand jury, or that defendants in custody shall be brought to court to attend at the selection of the grand jury. Failure to challenge is not a waiver of any objection. The objection may still be interposed by motion under Rule 6(b)(2).

Note to Subdivision (b)(2). 1. The motion provided by this rule takes the place of a plea in abatement, or motion to quash. Crowley v. United States, 194 U.S. 461, 469–474; United States v. Gale, supra.

2. The second sentence of the rule is a restatement of 18 U.S.C. [former] 554(a) (Indictments and presentments; objection on ground of unqualified juror barred where twelve qualified jurors concurred; record of number concurring), and introduces no change in existing law.

Note to Subdivision (c). 1. This rule generally is a restatement of existing law, 18 U.S.C. [former] 554(a) and 28 U.S.C. [former] 420. Failure of the foreman to sign or endorse the indictment is an irregularity and is not fatal, Frisbie v. United States, 157 U.S. 160, 163–165.

2. The provision for the appointment of a deputy foreman is new. Its purpose is to facilitate the transaction of business if the foreman is absent. Such a provision is found in the law of at least one State, N.Y. Code Criminal Procedure, sec. 244.

Note to Subdivision (d). This rule generally continues existing law. See 18 U.S.C. [former] 556 (Indictments and presentments; defects of form); and 5 U.S.C. 310 [now 28 U.S.C. 515(a)] (Conduct of legal proceedings).

Note to Subdivision (e). 1. This rule continues the traditional practice of secrecy on the party of members of the grand jury, except when the court permits a disclosure, Schmidt v. United States, 115 F.2d 394 (C.C.A. 6th); United States v. American Medical Association, 26 F.Supp. 429 (D.C.); Cf. Atwell v. United States, 162 F. 97 (C.C.A. 4th); and see 18 U.S.C. [former] 554(a) (Indictments and presentments; objection on ground of unqualified juror barred where twelve qualified jurors concurred; record of number concurring). Government attorneys are entitled to disclosure of grand jury proceedings, other than the deliberations and the votes of the jurors, inasmuch as they may be present in the grand jury room during the presentation of evidence. The rule continues this practice.

2. The rule does not impose any obligation of secrecy on witnesses. The existing practice on this point varies among the districts. The seal of secrecy on witnesses seems an unnecessary hardship and may lead to injustice if a witness is not permitted to make a disclosure to counsel or to an associate.

3. The last sentence authorizing the court to seal indictments continues present practice.

Note to Subdivision (f). This rule continues existing law, 18 U.S.C. [former] 554 (Indictments and presentments; by twelve grand jurors). The purpose of the last sentence is to provide means for a prompt release of a defendant if in custody, or exoneration of bail if he is on bail, in the event that the grand jury considers the case of a defendant held for its action and finds no indictment.

Note to Subdivision (g). Under existing law a grand jury serves only during the term for which it is summoned, but the court may extend its period of service for as long as 18 months, 28 U.S.C. [former] 421. During the extended period, however, a grand jury may conduct only investigations commenced during the original term. The rule continues the 18 months' maximum for the period of service of a grand jury, but provides for such service as a matter of course, unless the court terminates it at an earlier date. The matter is left in the discretion of the court, as it is under existing law. The expiration of a term of court as a time limitation is elsewhere entirely eliminated (Rule 45(c)) and specific time limitations are substituted therefor. This was previously done by the Federal Rules of Civil Procedure for the civil side of the courts (Federal Rules of Civil Procedure, Rule 6(c) [28 U.S.C., Appendix]). The elimination of the requirement that at an extended period the grand jury may continue only investigations previously commenced, will obviate such a controversy as was presented in United States v. Johnson, 319 U.S. 503.

NOTES OF ADVISORY COMMITTEE ON RULES——1966 AMENDMENT

Subdivision (d).——The amendment makes it clear that recording devices may be used to take evidence at grand jury sessions.

Subdivision (e).——The amendment makes it clear that the operator of a recording device and a typist who transcribes recorded testimony are bound to the obligation of secrecy.

Subdivision (f).——A minor change conforms the language to what doubtless is the practice. The need for a report to the court that no indictment has been found may be present even though the defendant has not been "held to answer." If the defendant is in custody or has given bail, some official record should be made of the grand jury action so that the defendant can be released or his bail exonerated.

NOTES OF ADVISORY COMMITTEE ON RULES——1972 AMENDMENT

Subdivision (b)(2) is amended to incorporate by express reference the provisions of the Jury Selection and Service Act of 1968. That act provides in part:

The procedures prescribed by this section shall be the exclusive means by which a person accused of a Federal crime [or] the Attorney General of the United States * * * may challenge any jury on the ground that such jury was not selected in conformity with the provisions of this title. [28 U.S.C. §1867(c)]

Under rule 12(e) the judge shall decide the motion before trial or order it deferred until after verdict. The authority which the judge has to delay his ruling until after verdict gives him an option which can be exercised to prevent the unnecessary delay of a trial in the event that a motion attacking a grand jury is made on the eve of the trial. In addition, rule 12(c) gives the judge authority to fix the time at which pretrial motions must be made. Failure to make a pretrial motion at the appropriate time may constitute a waiver under rule 12(f).

NOTES OF ADVISORY COMMITTEE ON RULES——1976 AMENDMENT

Under the proposed amendment to rule 6(f), an indictment may be returned to a federal magistrate. ("Federal magistrate" is defined in rule 54(c) as including a United States magistrate as defined in 28 U.S.C. §§631—639 and a judge of the United States.) This change will foreclose the possibility of noncompliance with the Speedy Trial Act timetable because of the nonavailability of a judge. Upon the effective date of certain provisions of the Speedy Trial Act of 1974, the timely return of indictments will become a matter of critical importance; for the year commencing July 1, 1976, indictments must be returned within 60 days of arrest or summons, for the year following within 45 days, and thereafter within 30 days. 18 U.S.C. §§3161(b) and (f), 3163(a). The problem is acute in a one-judge district where, if the judge is holding court in another part of the district, or is otherwise absent, the return of the indictment must await the later reappearance of the judge at the place where the grand jury is sitting.

A corresponding change has been made to that part of subdivision (f) which concerns the reporting of a "no bill," and to that part of subdivision (e) which concerns keeping an indictment secret.

The change in the third sentence of rule 6(f) is made so as to cover all situations in which by virtue of a pending complaint or information the defendant is in custody or released under some form of conditional release.

NOTES OF ADVISORY COMMITTEE ON RULES——1977 AMENDMENT

The proposed definition of "attorneys for the government" in subdivision (e) is designed to facilitate an increasing need, on the part of government attorneys, to make use of outside expertise in complex litigation. The phrase "other government personnel" includes, but is not limited to, employees of administrative agencies and government departments.

Present subdivision (e) provides for disclosure "to the attorneys for the government for use in the performance of their duties." This limitation is designed to further "the long established policy that maintains the secrecy of the grand jury in federal courts." United States v. Procter and Gamble Co., 356 U.S. 677 (1958).

As defined in rule 54(c), " 'Attorney for the government' means the Attorney General, an authorized assistant of the Attorney General, a United States Attorney, an authorized assistant of a United States Attorney and when applicable to cases arising under the laws of Guam * * *." The limited nature of this definition is pointed out in In re Grand Jury Proceedings, 309 F.2d 440 (3d Cir. 1962) at 443:

The term attorneys for the government is restrictive in its application. * * * If it had been intended that the attorneys for the administrative agencies were to have free access to matters occurring before a grand jury, the rule would have so provided.

The proposed amendment reflects the fact that there is often government personnel assisting the Justice Department in grand jury proceedings. In In re Grand Jury Investigation of William H. Pflaumer & Sons, Inc., 53 F.R.D. 464 (E.D.Pa. 1971), the opinion quoted the United States Attorney:

It is absolutely necessary in grand jury investigations involving analysis of books and records, for the government attorneys to rely upon investigative personnel (from the government agencies) for assistance.

See also 8 J. Moore, Federal Practice 6.05 at 6–28 (2d ed. Cipes, 1969):

The rule [6(e)] has presented a problem, however, with respect to attorneys and nonattorneys who are assisting in preparation of a case for the grand jury. * * * These assistants often cannot properly perform their work without having access to grand jury minutes.

Although case law is limited, the trend seems to be in the direction of allowing disclosure to government personnel who assist attorneys for the government in situations where their expertise is required. This is subject to the qualification that the matters disclosed be used only for the purposes of the grand jury investigation. The court may inquire as to the good faith of the assisting personnel, to ensure that access to material is not merely a subterfuge to gather evidence unattainable by means other than the grand jury. This approach was taken in In re Grand Jury Investigation of William H. Pflaumer & Sons, Inc., 53 F.R.D. 464 (E.D.Pa. 1971); In re April 1956 Term Grand Jury, 239 F.2d 263 (7th Cir. 1956); United States v. Anzelimo, 319 F.Supp. 1106 (D.C.La. 1970). Another case, Application of Kelly, 19 F.R.D. 269 (S.D.N.Y. 1956), assumed, without deciding, that assistance given the attorney for the government by IRS and FBI agents was authorized.

The change at line 27 reflects the fact that under the Bail Reform Act of 1966 some persons will be released without requiring bail. See 18 U.S.C. §§3146, 3148.

Under the proposed amendment to rule 6(f), an indictment may be returned to a federal magistrate. ("Federal magistrate" is defined in rule 54(c) as including a United States magistrate as defined in 28 U.S.C. §631–639 and a judge of the United States.) This change will foreclose the possibility of noncompliance with the Speedy Trial Act timetable because of the nonavailability of a judge. Upon the effective date of certain provisions of the Speedy Trial Act of 1974, the timely return of indictments will become a matter of critical importance; for the year commencing July 1, 1976, indictments must be returned within 60 days of arrest or summons, for the year following within 45 days, and thereafter within 30 days. 18 U.S.C. §§3161(b) and (f), 3163(a). The problem is acute in a one-judge district where, if the judge is holding court in another part of the district, or is otherwise absent, the return of the indictment must await the later reappearance of the judge at the place where the grand jury is sitting.

A corresponding change has been made to that part of subdivision (f) which concerns the reporting of a "no bill," and to that part of subdivision (e) which concerns keeping an indictment secret.

The change in the third sentence of rule 6(f) is made so as to cover all situations in which by virtue of a pending complaint or information the defendant is in custody or released under some form of conditional release.

NOTES OF COMMITTEE ON THE JUDICIARY, SENATE REPORT NO. 95–354; 1977 AMENDMENTS PROPOSED BY THE SUPREME COURT

Rule 6(e) currently provides that "disclosure of matters occurring before the grand jury other than its deliberations and the vote of any juror may be made to the attorneys for the government for use in the performance of their duties." Rule 54(c) defines attorneys for the government to mean "the Attorney General, an authorized assistant to the Attorney General, a United States attorney, and an authorized assistant of the United States attorney, and when applicable to cases arising under the laws of Guam, means the Attorney General of Guam. . . ."

The Supreme Court proposal would change Rule 6(e) by adding the following new language:

For purposes of this subdivision, "attorneys for the government" includes those enumerated in Rule 54(c); it also includes such other government personnel as are necessary to assist the attorneys for the government in the performance of their duties.

It would also make a series of changes in the rule designed to make its provisions consistent with other provisions in the Rules and the Bail Reform Act of 1966.

The Advisory Committee note states that the proposed amendment is intended "to facilitate an increasing need, on the part of Government attorneys to make use of outside expertise in complex litigation". The note indicated that:

Although case law is limited, the trend seems to be in the direction of allowing disclosure to Government personnel who assist attorneys for the Government in situations where their expertise is required. This is subject to the qualification that the matter disclosed be used only for the purposes of the grand jury investigation.

It is past history at this point that the Supreme Court proposal attracted substantial criticism, which seemed to stem more from the lack of precision in defining, and consequent confusion and uncertainty concerning, the intended scope of the proposed change than from a fundamental disagreement with the objective.

Attorneys for the Government in the performance of their duties with a grand jury must possess the authority to utilize the services of other government employees. Federal crimes are "investigated" by the FBI, the IRS, or by Treasury agents and not by government prosecutors or the citizens who sit on grand juries. Federal agents gather and present information relating to criminal behavior to prosecutors who analyze and evaluate it and present it to grand juries. Often the prosecutors need the assistance of the agents in evaluating evidence. Also, if further investigation is required during or after grand jury proceedings, or even during the course of criminal trials, the Federal agents must do it. There is no reason for a barrier of secrecy to exist between the facets of the criminal justice system upon which we all depend to enforce the criminal laws.

The parameters of the authority of an attorney for the government to disclose grand jury information in the course of performing his own duties is not defined by Rule 6. However, a commonsense interpretation prevails, permitting "Representatives of other government agencies actively assisting United States attorneys in a grand jury investigation . . . access to grand jury material in the performance of their duties." Yet projected against this current practice, and the weight of case law, is the anomalous language of Rule 6(e) itself, which, in its present state of uncertainty, is spawning some judicial decisions highly restrictive of the use of government experts that require the government to "show the necessity (to the Court) for each particular person's aid rather than showing merely a general necessity for assistance, expert or otherwise" and that make Rule 6(e) orders subject to interlocutory appeal.

In this state of uncertainty, the Committee believes it is timely to redraft subdivision (e) of Rule 6 to make it clear.

Paragraph (1) as proposed by the Committee states the general rule that a grand jury, an interpreter, a stenographer, an operator of a recording device, a typist who transcribes recorded testimony, an attorney for the government, or government personnel to whom disclosure is made under paragraph (2)(A)(ii) shall not disclose matters occurring before the grand jury, except as otherwise provided in these rules. It also expressly provides that a knowing violation of Rule 6 may be punished as a contempt of court. In addition, it carries forward the current provision that no obligation of secrecy may be imposed on any person except in accordance with this Rule.

Having stated the general rule of nondisclosure, paragraph (2) sets forth exemptions from nondisclosure. Subparagraph (A) of paragraph (2) provides that disclosure otherwise prohibited, other than the grand jury deliberations and the vote of any grand juror, may be made to an attorney for the government for use in the performance of his duty and to such personnel as are deemed necessary by an attorney for the government to assist an attorney for the government in the performance of such attorney's duty to enforce Federal criminal law. In order to facilitate resolution of subsequent claims of improper disclosure, subparagraph (B) further provides that the names of government personnel designated to assist the attorney for the government shall be promptly provided to the district court and such personnel shall not utilize grand jury material for any purpose other than assisting the attorney for the government in the performance of such attorney's duty to enforce Federal criminal law. Although not expressly required by the rule, the Committee contemplates that the names of such personnel will generally be furnished to the court before disclosure is made to them. Subparagraph (C) permits disclosure as directed by a court preliminarily to or in connection with a judicial proceeding or, at the request of the defendant, upon a showing that grounds may exist for dismissing the indictment because of matters occurring before the grand jury. Paragraph (3) carries forward the last sentence of current Rule 6(e) with the technical changes recommended by the Supreme Court.

The Rule as redrafted is designed to accommodate the belief on the one hand that Federal prosecutors should be able, without the time-consuming requirement of prior judicial interposition, to make such disclosures of grand jury information to other government personnel as they deem necessary to facilitate the performance of their duties relating to criminal law enforcement. On the other hand, the Rule seeks to allay the concerns of those who fear that such prosecutorial power will lead to misuse of the grand jury to enforce non-criminal Federal laws by (1) providing a clear prohibition, subject to the penalty of contempt and (2) requiring that a court order under paragraph (C) be obtained to authorize such a disclosure. There is, however, no intent to preclude the use of grand jury-developed evidence for civil law enforcement purposes. On the contrary, there is no reason why such use is improper, assuming that the grand jury was utilized for the legitimate purpose of a criminal investigation. Accordingly, the Committee believes and intends that the basis for a court's refusal to issue an order under paragraph (C) to enable the government to disclose grand jury information in a non-criminal proceeding should be no more restrictive than is the case today under prevailing court decisions. It is contemplated that the judicial hearing in connection with an application for a court order by the government under subparagraph (3)(C)(i) should be ex parte so as to preserve, to the maximum extent possible, grand jury secrecy.

CONGRESSIONAL MODIFICATION OF PROPOSED 1977 AMENDMENT

Pub. L. 95–78, §2(a), July 30, 1977, 91 Stat. 319, provided in part that the amendment proposed by the Supreme Court [in its order of Apr. 26, 1977] to subdivision (e) of rule 6 of the Federal Rules of Criminal Procedure [subd. (e) of this rule] is approved in a modified form.

NOTES OF ADVISORY COMMITTEE ON RULES—1979 AMENDMENT

Note to Subdivision (e)(1). Proposed subdivision (e)(1) requires that all proceedings, except when the grand jury is deliberating or voting, be recorded. The existing rule does not require that grand jury proceedings be recorded. The provision in rule 6(d) that "a stenographer or operator of a recording device may be present while the grand jury is in session" has been taken to mean that recordation is permissive and not mandatory; see United States v. Aloisio, 440 F.2d 705 (7th Cir. 1971), collecting the cases. However, the cases rather frequently state that recordation of the proceedings is the better practice; see United States v. Aloisio, supra; United States v. Cramer, 447 F.2d 210 (2d Cir. 1971), Schlinsky v. United States, 379 F.2d 735 (1st Cir. 1967); and some cases require the district court, after a demand to exercise discretion as to whether the proceedings should be recorded. United States v. Price, 474 F.2d 1223 (9th Cir. 1973); United States v. Thoresen, 428 F.2d 654 (9th Cir. 1970). Some district courts have adopted a recording requirement. See e.g. United States v. Aloisio, supra; United States v. Gramolini, 301 F.Supp. 39 (D.R.I. 1969). Recording of grand jury proceedings is currently a requirement in a number of states. See, e.g., Cal.Pen.Code §§938–938.3; Iowa Code Ann. §772.4; Ky.Rev.Stat.Ann. §28.460; and Ky.R.Crim.P. §5.16(2).

The assumption underlying the proposal is that the cost of such recording is justified by the contribution made to the improved administration of criminal justice. See United States v. Gramolini, supra, noting: "Nor can it be claimed that the cost of recordation is prohibitive; in an electronic age, the cost of recordation must be categorized as miniscule." For a discussion of the success of electronic recording in Alaska, see Reynolds, Alaska's Ten Years of Electronic Reporting, 56 A.B.A.J. 1080 (1970).

Among the benefits to be derived from a recordation requirement are the following:

(1) Ensuring that the defendant may impeach a prosecution witness on the basis of his prior inconsistent statements before the grand jury. As noted in the opinion of Oakes, J., in United States v. Cramer: "First since Dennis v. United States, 384 U.S. 855, 86 S.Ct. 1840, 16 L.Ed.2d 973 (1966), a defendant has been entitled to examine the grand jury testimony of witnesses against him. On this point, the Court was unanimous, holding that there was 'no justification' for the District of Columbia Court of Appeals' relying upon [the] "assumption" ' that 'no inconsistencies would have come to light.' The Court's decision was based on the general proposition that '[i]n our adversary system for determining guilt or innocence, it is rarely justifiable for the prosecution to have exclusive access to a storehouse of relevant facts.' In the case at bar the prosecution did have exclusive access to the grand jury testimony of the witness Sager, by virtue of being present, and the defense had none—to determine whether there were any inconsistencies with, say, his subsequent testimony as to damaging admissions by the defendant and his attorney Richard Thaler. The Government claims, and it is supported by the majority here, that there is no problem since defendants were given the benefit of Sager's subsequent statements including these admissions as Jencks Act materials. But assuming this to be true, it does not cure the basic infirmity that the defense could not know whether the witness testified inconsistently before the grand jury."

(2) Ensuring that the testimony received by the grand jury is trustworthy. In United States v. Cramer, Oakes, J., also observed: "The recording of testimony is in a very real sense a circumstantial guaranty of trustworthiness. Without the restraint of being subject to prosecution for perjury, a restraint which is wholly meaningless or nonexistent if the testimony is unrecorded, a witness may make baseless accusations founded on hearsay or false accusations, all resulting in the indictment of a fellow citizen for a crime."

(3) Restraining prosecutorial abuses before the grand jury. As noted in United States v. Gramolini: "In no way does recordation inhibit the grand jury's investigation. True, recordation restrains certain prosecutorial practices which might, in its absence be used, but that is no reason not to record. Indeed, a sophisticated prosecutor must acknowledge that there develops between a grand jury and the prosecutor with whom the jury is closeted a rapport—a dependency relationship—which can easily be turned into an instrument of influence on grand jury deliberations. Recordation is the most effective restraint upon such potential abuses."

(4) Supporting the case made by the prosecution at trial. Oakes, J., observed in United States v. Cramer: "The benefits of having grand jury testimony recorded do not all inure to the defense. See, e.g., United States v. DeSisto, 329 F.2d 929, 934: (2nd Cir.), cert. denied, 377 U.S. 979, 84 S.Ct. 1885, 12 L.Ed.2d 747 (1964) (conviction sustained in part on basis of witnesses's prior sworn testimony before grand jury)." Fed.R.Evid. 801(d)(1)(A) excludes from the category of hearsay the prior inconsistent testimony of a witness given before a grand jury. United States v. Morgan, 555 F.2d 238 (9th Cir. 1977). See also United States v. Carlson, 547 F.2d 1346 (8th Cir. 1976), admitting under Fed.R.Evid. 804(b)(5) the grand jury testimony of a witness who refused to testify at trial because of threats by the defendant.

Commentators have also supported a recording requirement. 8 Moore, Federal Practice par. 6.02[2][d] (2d ed. 1972) states: "Fairness to the defendant would seem to compel a change in the practice, particularly in view of the 1970 amendment to 18 USC §3500 making grand jury testimony of government witnesses available at trial for purposes of impeachment. The requirement of a record may also prove salutary in controlling overreaching or improper examination of witnesses by the prosecutor." Similarly, 1 Wright, Federal Practice and Procedure—Criminal §103 (1969), states that the present rule "ought to be changed, either by amendment or by judicial construction. The Supreme Court has emphasized the importance to the defense of access to the transcript of the grand jury proceedings [citing Dennis]. A defendant cannot have that advantage if the proceedings go unrecorded." American Bar Association, Report of the Special Committee on Federal Rules of Procedure, 52 F.R.D. 87, 94–95 (1971), renews the committee's 1965 recommendation "that all accusatorial grand jury proceedings either be transcribed by a reporter or recorded by electronic means."

Under proposed subdivision (e)(1), if the failure to record is unintentional, the failure to record would not invalidate subsequent judicial proceedings. Under present law, the failure to compel production of grand jury testimony where there is no record is not reversible error. See Wyatt v. United States, 388 F.2d 395 (10th Cir. 1968).

The provision that the recording or reporter's notes or any transcript prepared therefrom are to remain in the custody or control (as where the notes are in the immediate possession of a contract reporter employed by the Department of Justice) of the attorney for the government is in accord with present practice. It is specifically recognized, however, that the court in a particular case may have reason to order otherwise.

It must be emphasized that the proposed changes in rule 6(e) deal only with the recording requirement, and in no way expand the circumstances in which disclosure of the grand jury proceedings is permitted or required. "Secrecy of grand jury proceedings is not jeopardized by recordation. The making of a record cannot be equated with disclosure of its contents, and disclosure is controlled by other means." United States v. Price, 474 F.2d 1223 (9th Cir. 1973). Specifically, the proposed changes do not provide for copies of the grand jury minutes to defendants as a matter of right, as is the case in some states. See, e.g., Cal.Pen.Code §938.1; Iowa Code Ann. §772.4. The matter of disclosure continues to be governed by other provisions, such as rule 16(a) (recorded statements of the defendant), 18 U.S.C. §3500 (statements of government witnesses), and the unchanged portions of rule 6(e), and the cases interpreting these provisions. See e.g., United States v. Howard, 433 F.2d 1 (5th Cir. 1970), and Beatrice Foods Co. v. United States, 312 F.2d 29 (8th Cir. 1963), concerning the showing which must be made of improper matters occurring before the grand jury before disclosure is required.

Likewise, the proposed changes in rule 6(e) are not intended to make any change regarding whether a defendant may challenge a grand jury indictment. The Supreme Court has declined to hold that defendants may challenge indictments on the ground that they are not supported by sufficient or competent evidence. Costello v. United States, 350 U.S. 359 (1956); Lawn v. United States, 355 U.S. 339 (1958); United States v. Blue, 384 U.S. 251 (1966). Nor are the changes intended to permit the defendant to challenge the conduct of the attorney for the government before the grand jury absent a preliminary factual showing of serious misconduct.

Note to Subdivision (e)(3)(C). The sentence added to subdivision (e)(3)(C) gives express recognition to the fact that if the court orders disclosure, it may determine the circumstances of the disclosure. For example, if the proceedings are electronically recorded, the court would have discretion in an appropriate case to deny defendant the right to a transcript at government expense. While it takes special skills to make a stenographic record understandable, an electronic recording can be understood by merely listening to it, thus avoiding the expense of transcription.

NOTES OF ADVISORY COMMITTEE ON RULES—1983 AMENDMENT

Note to Subdivision (e)(3)(C). New subdivision (e)(3)(C)(iii) recognizes that it is permissible for the attorney for the government to make disclosure of matters occurring before one grand jury to another federal grand jury. Even absent a specific provision to that effect, the courts have permitted such disclosure in some circumstances. See, e.g., United States v. Socony-Vacuum Oil Co. 310 U.S. 150 (1940); United States v. Garcia, 420 F.2d 309 (2d Cir. 1970). In this kind of situation, "[s]ecrecy of grand jury materials should be protected almost as well by the safeguards at the second grand jury proceeding, including the oath of the jurors, as by judicial supervision of the disclosure of such materials." United States v. Malatesta, 583 F.2d 748 (5th Cir. 1978).

Note to Subdivision (e)(3)(D). In Douglas Oil Co. v. Petrol Stops Northwest, 441 U.S. 211 (1979), the Court held on the facts there presented that it was an abuse of discretion for the district judge to order disclosure of grand jury transcripts for use in civil proceedings in another district where that judge had insufficient knowledge of those proceedings to make a determination of the need for disclosure. The Court suggested a "better practice" on those facts, but declared that "procedures to deal with the many variations are best left to the rulemaking procedures established by Congress."

The first sentence of subdivision (e)(3)(D) makes it clear that when disclosure is sought under subdivision (e)(2)(C)(i), the petition is to be filed in the district where the grand jury was convened, whether or not it is the district of the "judicial proceeding" giving rise to the petition. Courts which have addressed the question have generally taken this view, e.g., Illinois v. Sarbaugh, 522 F.2d 768 (7th Cir. 1977). As stated in Douglas Oil,

those who seek grand jury transcripts have little choice other than to file a request with the court that supervised the grand jury, as it is the only court with control over the transcripts.

Quite apart from the practical necessity, the policies underlying Rule 6(e) dictate that the grand jury's supervisory court participate in reviewing such requests, as it is in the best position to determine the continuing need for grand jury secrecy. Ideally, the judge who supervised the grand jury should review the request for disclosure, as he will have firsthand knowledge of the grand jury's activities. But even other judges of the district where the grand jury sat may be able to discover facts affecting the need for secrecy more easily than would judges from elsewhere around the country. The records are in the custody of the District Court, and therefore are readily available for references. Moreover, the personnel of that court—particularly those of the United States Attorney's Office who worked with the grand jury—are more likely to be informed about the grand jury proceedings than those in a district that had no prior experience with the subject of the request.

The second sentence requires the petitioner to serve notice of his petition upon several persons who, by the third sentence, are recognized as entitled to appear and be heard on the matter. The notice requirement ensures that all interested parties, if they wish, may make a timely appearance. Absent such notice, these persons, who then might only learn of the order made in response to the motion after it was entered, have had to resort to the cumbersome and inefficient procedure of a motion to vacate the order. In re Special February 1971 Grand Jury v. Conlisk, 490 F.2d 894 (7th Cir. 1973).

Though some authority is to be found that parties to the judicial proceeding giving rise to the motion are not entitled to intervene, in that "the order to produce was not directed to" them, United States v. American Oil Co., 456 F.2d 1043 (3d Cir. 1972), that position was rejected in Douglas Oil, where it was noted that such persons have standing "to object to the disclosure order, as release of the transcripts to their civil adversaries could result in substantial injury to them." As noted in Illinois v. Sarbaugh, supra, while present rule 6(e) "omits to state whether any one is entitled to object to disclosure," the rule

seems to contemplate a proceeding of some kind, judicial proceedings are not normally ex parte, and persons in the situation of the intervenors [parties to the civil proceeding] are likely to be the only ones to object to an order for disclosure. If they are not allowed to appear, the advantages of an adversary proceeding are lost.

If the judicial proceeding is a class action, notice to the representative is sufficient.

The amendment also recognizes that the attorney for the government in the district where the grand jury convened also has an interest in the matter and should be allowed to be heard. It may sometimes be the case, as in Douglas Oil, that the prosecutor will have relatively little concern for secrecy, at least as compared with certain parties to the civil proceeding. Nonetheless, it is appropriate to recognize that generally the attorney for the government is entitled to be heard so that he may represent what Douglas Oil characterizes as "the public interest in secrecy," including the government's legitimate concern about "the possible effect upon the functioning of future grand juries" of unduly liberal disclosure.

The second sentence leaves it to the court to decide whether any other persons should receive notice and be allowed to intervene. This is appropriate, for the necessity for and feasibility of involving others may vary substantially from case to case. In Douglas Oil, it was noted that the individual who produced before the grand jury the information now sought has an interest in the matter:

Fear of future retribution or social stigma may act as powerful deterrents to those who would come forward and aid the grand jury in the performance of its duties. Concern as to the future consequences of frank and full testimony is heightened where the witness is an employee of a company under investigation.

Notice to such persons, however is by no means inevitably necessary, and in some cases the information sought may have reached the grand jury from such a variety of sources that it is not practicable to involve these sources in the disclosure proceeding. Similarly, while Douglas Oil notes that rule 6(e) secrecy affords "protection of the innocent accused from disclosure of the accusation made against him before the grand jury," it is appropriate to leave to the court whether that interest requires representation directly by the grand jury target at this time. When deemed necessary to protect the identity of such other persons, it would be a permissible alternative for the government or the court directly to give notice to these other persons, and thus the rule does not foreclose such action.

The notice requirement in the second sentence is inapplicable if the hearing is to be ex parte. The legislative history of rule 6(e) states: "It is contemplated that the judicial hearing in connection with an application for a court order by the government, under subparagraph (3)(C)(i) should be ex parte so as to preserve, to the maximum extent possible, grand jury secrecy." S.Rep. No. 95–354, 1977 U.S. Code Cong. & Admin. News p. 532. Although such cases are distinguishable from other cases arising under this subdivision because internal regulations limit further disclosure of information disclosed to the government, the rule provides only that the hearing "may" be ex parte when the petitioner is the government. This allows the court to decide that matter based upon the circumstances of the particular case. For example, an ex parte proceeding is much less likely to be appropriate if the government acts as petitioner as an accommodation to, e.g., a state agency.

Note to Subdivision (e)(3)(E). Under the first sentence in new subdivision (e)(3)(E), the petitioner or any intervenor might seek to have the matter transferred to the federal district court where the judicial proceeding giving rise to the petition is pending. Usually, it will be the petitioner, who is seeking disclosure, who will desire the transfer, but this is not inevitably the case. An intervenor might seek transfer on the ground that the other court, with greater knowledge of the extent of the need, would be less likely to conclude "that the material * * * is needed to avoid a possible injustice" (the test under Douglas Oil). The court may transfer on its own motion, for as noted in Douglas Oil, if transfer is the better course of action it should not be foreclosed "merely because the parties have failed to specify the relief to which they are entitled."

It must be emphasized that transfer is proper only if the proceeding giving rise to the petition "is in federal district court in another district." If, for example, the proceeding is located in another district but is at the state level, a situation encompassed within rule 6(e)(3)(C)(i), In re Special February 1971 Grand Jury v. Conlisk, supra, there is no occasion to transfer. Ultimate resolution of the matter cannot be placed in the hands of the state court, and in such a case the federal court in that place would lack what Douglas Oil recognizes as the benefit to be derived from transfer: "first-hand knowledge of the litigation in which the transcripts allegedly are needed." Formal transfer is unnecessary in intradistrict cases, even when the grand jury court and judicial proceeding court are not in the same division.

As stated in the first sentence, transfer by the court is appropriate "unless it can reasonably obtain sufficient knowledge of the proceeding to determine whether disclosure is proper." (As reflected by the "whether disclosure is proper" language, the amendment makes no effort to define the disclosure standard; that matter is currently governed by Douglas Oil and the authorities cited therein, and is best left to elaboration by future case law.) The amendment expresses a preference for having the disclosure issue decided by the grand jury court. Yet, it must be recognized, as stated in Douglas Oil, that often this will not be possible because

the judges of the court having custody of the grand jury transcripts will have no first-hand knowledge of the litigation in which the transcripts allegedly are needed, and no practical means by which such knowledge can be obtained. In such a case, a judge in the district of the grand jury cannot weigh in an informed manner the need for disclosure against the need for maintaining grand jury secrecy.

The penultimate sentence provides that upon transfer the transferring court shall order transmitted the material sought to be disclosed and also a written evaluation of the need for continuing grand jury secrecy. Because the transferring court is in the best position to assess the interest in continued grand jury secrecy in the particular instance, it is important that the court which will now have to balance that interest against the need for disclosure receive the benefit of the transferring court's assessment. Transmittal of the material sought to be disclosed will not only facilitate timely disclosure if it is thereafter ordered, but will also assist the other court in deciding how great the need for disclosure actually is. For example, with that material at hand the other court will be able to determine if there is any inconsistency between certain grand jury testimony and testimony received in the other judicial proceeding. The rule recognizes, however, that there may be instances in which transfer of everything sought to be disclosed is not feasible. See, e.g., In re 1975–2 Grand Jury Investigation, 566 F.2d 1293 (5th Cir. 1978) (court ordered transmittal of "an inventory of the grand jury subpoenas, transcripts, and documents," as the materials in question were "exceedingly voluminous, filling no less than 55 large file boxes and one metal filing cabinet").

The last sentence makes it clear that in a case in which the matter is transferred to another court, that court should permit the various interested parties specified in the rule to be heard. Even if those persons were previously heard before the court which ordered the transfer, this will not suffice. The order of transfer did not decide the ultimate issue of "whether a particularized need for disclosure outweighs the interest in continued grand jury secrecy," Douglas Oil, supra, which is what now remains to be resolved by the court to which transfer was made. Cf. In re 1975–2 Grand Jury Investigation, supra, holding that a transfer order is not appealable because it does not determine the ultimate question of disclosure, and thus "[n]o one has yet been aggrieved and no one will become aggrieved until [the court to which the matter was transferred] acts."

Note to Subdivision (e)(5). This addition to rule 6 would make it clear that certain hearings which would reveal matters which have previously occurred before a grand jury or are likely to occur before a grand jury with respect to a pending or ongoing investigation must be conducted in camera in whole or in part in order to prevent public disclosure of such secret information. One such hearing is that conducted under subdivision (e)(3)(D), for it will at least sometimes be necessary to consider and assess some of the "matters occurring before the grand jury" in order to decide the disclosure issue. Two other kinds of hearings at which information about a particular grand jury investigation might need to be discussed are those at which the question is whether to grant a grand jury witness immunity or whether to order a grand jury witness to comply fully with the terms of a subpoena directed to him.

A recent GAO study established that there is considerable variety in the practice as to whether such hearings are closed or open, and that open hearings often seriously jeopardize grand jury secrecy:

For judges to decide these matters, the witness' relationship to the case under investigation must be discussed. Accordingly, the identities of witnesses and targets, the nature of expected testimony, and the extent to which the witness is cooperating are often revealed during preindictment proceedings. Because the matters discussed can compromise the purposes of grand jury secrecy, some judges close the preindictment proceedings to the public and the press; others do not. When the proceeding is open, information that may otherwise be kept secret under rule 6(e) becomes available to the public and the press . . . .

Open preindictment proceedings are a major source of information which can compromise the purposes of grand jury secrecy. In 25 cases we were able to establish links between open proceedings and later newspaper articles containing information about the identities of witnesses and targets and the nature of grand jury investigations.

Comptroller General, More Guidance and Supervision Needed over Federal Grand Jury Proceedings 8–9 (Oct. 16, 1980).

The provisions of rule 6(e)(5) do not violate any constitutional right of the public or media to attend such pretrial hearings. There is no Sixth Amendment right in the public to attend pretrial proceedings, Gannett Co., Inc. v. DePasquale, 443 U.S. 368 (1979), and Richmond Newspapers, Inc. v. Virginia, 448 U.S. 555, (1980), only recognizes a First Amendment "right to attend criminal trials." Richmond Newspapers was based largely upon the "unbroken, uncontradicted history" of public trials, while in Gannett it was noted "there exists no persuasive evidence that at common law members of the public had any right to attend pretrial proceedings." Moreover, even assuming some public right to attend certain pretrial proceedings, see United States v. Criden, 675 U.S. 550 (3d Cir. 1982), that right is not absolute; it must give way, as stated in Richmond Newspapers, to "an overriding interest" in a particular case in favor of a closed proceeding. By permitting closure only "to the extent necessary to prevent disclosure of matters occurring before a grand jury," rule 6(e)(5) recognizes the longstanding interest in the secrecy of grand jury proceedings. Counsel or others allowed to be present at the closed hearing may be put under a protective order by the court.

Subdivision (e)(5) is expressly made "subject to any right to an open hearing in contempt proceedings." This will accommodate any First Amendment right which might be deemed applicable in that context because of the proceedings' similarities to a criminal trial, cf. United States v. Criden, supra, and also any Fifth or Sixth Amendment right of the contemnor. The latter right clearly exists as to a criminal contempt proceeding, In re Oliver, 333 U.S. 257 (1948), and some authority is to be found recognizing such a right in civil contempt proceedings as well. In re Rosahn, 671 F.2d 690 (2d Cir. 1982). This right of the contemnor must be requested by him and, in any event, does not require that the entire contempt proceedings, including recitation of the substance of the questions he has refused to answer, be public. Levine v. United States, 362 U.S. 610 (1960).

Note to Subdivision (e)(6). Subdivision (e)(6) provides that records, orders and subpoenas relating to grand jury proceedings shall be kept under seal to the extent and for so long as is necessary to prevent disclosure of matters occurring before a grand jury. By permitting such documents as grand jury subpoenas and immunity orders to be kept under seal, this provision addresses a serious problem of grand jury secrecy and expressly authorizes a procedure now in use in many but not all districts. As reported in Comptroller General, More Guidance and Supervision Needed over Federal Grand Jury Proceedings 10, 14 (Oct. 16, 1980):

> In 262 cases, documents presented at open preindictment proceedings and filed in public files revealed details of grand jury investigations. These documents are, of course, available to anyone who wants them, including targets of investigations. [There are] two documents commonly found in public files which usually reveal the identities of witnesses and targets. The first document is a Department of Justice authorization to a U.S. attorney to apply to the court for a grant of immunity for a witness. The second document is the court's order granting the witness immunity from prosecution and compelling him to testify and produce requested information. * * *

> Subpoenas are the fundamental documents used during a grand jury's investigation because through subpoenas, grand juries can require witnesses to testify and produce documentary evidence for their consideration. Subpoenas can identify witnesses, potential targets, and the nature of an investigation. Rule 6(e) does not provide specific guidance on whether a grand jury's subpoena should be kept secret. Additionally, case law has not consistently stated whether the subpoenas are protected by rule 6(e).

> District courts still have different opinions about whether grand jury subpoenas should be kept secret. Out of 40 Federal District Courts we contacted, 36 consider these documents to be secret. However, 4 districts do make them available to the public.

Note to Subdivision (g). In its present form, subdivision 6(g) permits a grand jury to serve no more than 18 months after its members have been sworn, and absolutely no exceptions are permitted. (By comparison, under the Organized Crime Control Act of 1970, Title I, 18 U.S.C. §§3331–3334, special grand juries may be extended beyond their basic terms of 18 months if their business has not been completed.) The purpose of the amendment is to permit some degree of flexibility as to the discharge of grand juries where the public interest would be served by an extension.

As noted in United States v. Fein, 504 F.2d 1170 (2d Cir. 1974), upholding the dismissal of an indictment returned 9 days after the expiration of the 18–month period but during an attempted extension, under the present inflexible rule "it may well be that criminal proceedings which would be in the public interest will be frustrated and that those who might be found guilty will escape trial and conviction." The present inflexible rule can produce several undesirable consequences, especially when complex fraud, organized crime, tax or antitrust cases are under investigation: (i) wastage of a significant amount of time and resources by the necessity of presenting the case once again to a successor grand jury simply because the matter could not be concluded before the term of the first grand jury expired; (ii) precipitous action to conclude the investigation before the expiration date of the grand jury; and (iii) potential defendants may be kept under investigation for a longer time because of the necessity to present the matter again to another grand jury.

The amendment to subdivision 6(g) permits extension of a regular grand jury only "upon a determination that such extension is in the public interest." This permits some flexibility, but reflects the fact that extension of regular grand juries beyond 18 months is to be the exception and not the norm. The intention of the amendment is to make it possible for a grand jury to have sufficient extra time to wind up an investigation when, for example, such extension becomes necessary because of the unusual nature of the case or unforeseen developments.

Because terms of court have been abolished, 28 U.S.C. §138, the second sentence of subdivision 6(g) has been deleted.

NOTES OF ADVISORY COMMITTEE ON RULES——1985 AMENDMENT

Note to Subdivision (e)(3)(A)(ii). Rule 6(e)(3)(A)(ii) currently provides that an attorney for the government may disclose grand jury information, without prior judicial approval, to other government personnel whose assistance the attorney for the government deems necessary in conducting the grand jury investigation. Courts have differed over whether employees of state and local governments are "government personnel" within the meaning of the rule. Compare In re Miami Federal Grand Jury No. 79–9, 478 F.Supp. 490 (S.D.Fla. 1979), and In re Grand Jury Proceedings, 445 F.Supp. 349 (D.R.I. 1978) (state and local personnel not included); with In re 1979 Grand Jury Proceedings, 479 F.Supp. 93 (E.D.N.Y. 1979) (state and local personnel included). The amendment clarifies the rule to include state and local personnel.

It is clearly desirable that federal and state authorities cooperate, as they often do, in organized crime and racketeering investigations, in public corruption and major fraud cases, and in various other situations where federal and state criminal jurisdictions overlap. Because of such cooperation, government attorneys in complex grand jury investigations frequently find it necessary to enlist the help of a team of government agents. While the agents are usually federal personnel, it is not uncommon in certain types of investigations that federal prosecutors wish to obtain the assistance of state law enforcement personnel, which could be uniquely beneficial. The amendment permits disclosure to those personnel in the circumstances stated.

It must be emphasized that the disclosure permitted is limited. The disclosure under this subdivision is permissible only in connection with the attorney for the government's "duty to enforce federal criminal law" and only to those personnel "deemed necessary . . . to assist" in the performance of that duty. Under subdivision (e)(3)(B), the material disclosed may not be used for any other purpose, and the names of persons to whom disclosure is made must be promptly provided to the court.

Note to Subdivision (e)(3)(B). The amendment to subdivision (e)(3)(B) imposes upon the attorney for the government the responsibility to certify to the district court that he has advised those persons to whom disclosure was made under subdivision (e)(3)(A)(ii) of their obligation of secrecy under Rule 6. Especially with the amendment of subdivision (e)(3)(A)(ii) to include personnel of a state or subdivision of a state, who otherwise would likely be unaware of this obligation of secrecy, the giving of such advice is an important step in ensuring against inadvertent breach of grand jury secrecy. But because not all federal government personnel will otherwise know of this obligation, the giving of the advice and certification thereof is required as to all persons receiving disclosure under subdivision (e)(3)(A)(ii).

Note to Subdivision (e)(3)(C). It sometimes happens that during a federal grand jury investigation evidence will be developed tending to show a violation of state law. When this occurs, it is very frequently the case that this evidence cannot be communicated to the appropriate state officials for further investigation. For one thing, any state officials who might seek this information must show particularized need. Illinois v. Abbott & Associates, 103 S.Ct. 1356 (1983). For another, and more significant, it is often the case that the information relates to a state crime outside the context of any pending or even contemplated state judicial proceeding, so that the "preliminarily to or in connection with a judicial proceeding" requirement of subdivision (e)(3)(C)(i) cannot be met.

This inability lawfully to disclose evidence of a state criminal violation——evidence legitimately obtained by the grand jury——constitutes an unreasonable barrier to the effective enforcement of our two-tiered system of criminal laws. It would be removed by new subdivision (e)(3)(C)(iv), which would allow a court to permit disclosure to a state or local official for the purpose of enforcing state law when an attorney for the government so requests and makes the requisite showing.

The federal court has been given control over any disclosure which is authorized, for subdivision (e)(3)(C) presently states that "the disclosure shall be made in such manner, at such time, and under such conditions as the court may direct." The Committee is advised that it will be the policy of the Department of Justice under this amendment to seek such disclosure only upon approval of the Assistant Attorney General in charge of the Criminal Division. There is no intention, by virtue of this amendment, to have federal grand juries act as an arm of the state.

NOTES OF ADVISORY COMMITTEE ON RULES——1987 AMENDMENT

New subdivision (a)(2) gives express recognition to a practice now followed in some district courts, namely, that of designating alternate grand jurors at the time the grand jury is selected. (A person so designated does not attend court and is not paid the jury attendance fees and expenses authorized by 28 U.S.C. §1871 unless subsequently impanelled pursuant to Rule 6(g).) Because such designation may be a more efficient procedure than election of additional grand jurors later as need arises under subdivision (g), the amendment makes it clear that it is a permissible step in the grand jury selection process.

This amendment is not intended to work any change in subdivision (g). In particular, the fact that one or more alternate jurors either have or have not been previously designated does not limit the district court's discretion under subdivision (g) to decide whether, if a juror is excused temporarily or permanently, another person should replace him to assure the continuity of the grand jury and its ability to obtain a quorum in order to complete its business.

The amendments [subdivisions (c) and (f)] are technical. No substantive change is intended.

Notes of Advisory Committee on Rules—1993 Amendment

The Rule is amended to conform to the Judicial Improvements Act of 1990 [P.L. 101–650, Title III, Section 321] which provides that each United States magistrate appointed under section 631 of title 28, United States Code, shall be known as a United States magistrate judge.

Committee Notes on Rules—1999 Amendment

Subdivision 6(d). As currently written, Rule 6(d) absolutely bars any person, other than the jurors themselves, from being present during the jury's deliberations and voting. Accordingly, interpreters are barred from attending the deliberations and voting by the grand jury, even though they may have been present during the taking of testimony. The amendment is intended to permit interpreters to assist persons who are speech or hearing impaired and are serving on a grand jury. Although the Committee believes that the need for secrecy of grand jury deliberations and voting is paramount, permitting interpreters to assist hearing and speech impaired jurors in the process seems a reasonable accommodation. See also United States v. Dempsey, 830 F.2d 1084 (10th Cir. 1987) (constitutionally rooted prohibition of non-jurors being present during deliberations was not violated by interpreter for deaf petit jury member).

The subdivision has also been restyled and reorganized.

Subdivision 6(f). The amendment to Rule 6(f) is intended to avoid the problems associated with bringing the entire jury to the court for the purpose of returning an indictment. Although the practice is long-standing, in Breese v. United States, 226 U.S. 1 (1912), the Court rejected the argument that the requirement was rooted in the Constitution and observed that if there were ever any strong reasons for the requirement, "they have disappeared, at least in part." 226 U.S. at 9. The Court added that grand jury's presence at the time the indictment was presented was a defect, if at all, in form only. Id. at 11. Given the problems of space, in some jurisdictions the grand jury sits in a building completely separated from the courtrooms. In those cases, moving the entire jury to the courtroom for the simple process of presenting the indictment may prove difficult and time consuming. Even where the jury is in the same location, having all of the jurors present can be unnecessarily cumbersome in light of the fact that filing of the indictment requires a certification as to how the jurors voted.

The amendment provides that the indictment must be presented either by the jurors themselves, as currently provided for in the rule, or by the foreperson or the deputy foreperson, acting on behalf of the jurors. In an appropriate case, the court might require all of the jurors to be present if it had inquiries about the indictment.

GAP Report—Rule 6. The Committee modified Rule 6(d) to permit only interpreters assisting hearing or speech impaired grand jurors to be present during deliberations and voting.

Committee Notes on Rules—2002 Amendment

The language of Rule 6 has been amended as part of the general restyling of the Criminal Rules to make them more easily understood and to make style and terminology consistent throughout the rules. These changes are intended to be stylistic, except as noted below.

The first change is in Rule 6(b)(1). The last sentence of current Rule 6(b)(1) provides that "Challenges shall be made before the administration of the oath to the jurors and shall be tried by the court." That language has been deleted from the amended rule. The remainder of this subdivision rests on the assumption that formal proceedings have begun against a person, i.e., an indictment has been returned. The Committee believed that although the first sentence reflects current practice of a defendant being able to challenge the composition or qualifications of the grand jurors after the indictment is returned, the second sentence does not comport with modern practice. That is, a defendant will normally not know the composition of the grand jury or identity of the grand jurors before they are administered their oath. Thus, there is no opportunity to challenge them and have the court decide the issue before the oath is given.

In Rule 6(d)(1), the term "court stenographer" has been changed to "court reporter." Similar changes have been made in Rule 6(e)(1) and (2).

Rule 6(e) continues to spell out the general rule of secrecy of grand-jury proceedings and the exceptions to that general rule. The last sentence in current Rule 6(e)(2), concerning contempt for violating Rule 6, now appears in Rule 6(e)(7). No change in substance is intended.

Rule 6(e)(3)(A)(ii) includes a new provision recognizing the sovereignty of Indian Tribes and the possibility that it would be necessary to disclose grand-jury information to appropriate tribal officials in order to enforce federal law. Similar language has been added to Rule 6(e)(3)(D)(iii).

Rule 6(e)(3)(A)(iii) is a new provision that recognizes that disclosure may be made to a person under 18 U.S.C. §3322 (authorizing disclosures to an attorney for the government and banking regulators for enforcing civil forfeiture and civil banking laws). This reference was added to avoid the possibility of the amendments to Rule 6 superseding that particular statute.

Rule 6(e)(3)(C) consists of language located in current Rule 6(e)(3)(C)(iii). The Committee believed that this provision, which recognizes that prior court approval is not required for disclosure of a grand-jury matter to another grand jury, should be treated as a separate subdivision in revised Rule 6(e)(3). No change in practice is intended.

Rule 6(e)(3)(D) is new and reflects changes made to Rule 6 in the Uniting and Strengthening America by Providing Appropriate Tools Required to Intercept and Obstruct Terrorism (USA PATRIOT ACT) Act of 2001. The new provision permits an attorney for the government to disclose grand-jury matters involving foreign intelligence or counterintelligence to other Federal officials, in order to assist those officials in performing their duties. Under Rule 6(e)(3)(D)(i), the federal official receiving the information may only use the information as necessary and may be otherwise limited in making further disclosures. Any disclosures made under this provision must be reported under seal, within a reasonable time, to the court. The term "foreign intelligence information" is defined in Rule 6(e)(3)(D)(iii).

Rule 6(e)(3)(E)(iv) is a new provision that addresses disclosure of grand-jury information to armed forces personnel where the disclosure is for the purpose of enforcing military criminal law under the Uniform Code of Military Justice, 10 U.S.C. §§801–946. See, e.g., Department of Defense Directive 5525.7 (January 22, 1985); 1984 Memorandum of Understanding Between Department of Justice and the Department of Defense Relating to the Investigation and Prosecution of Certain Crimes; Memorandum of Understanding Between the Departments of Justice and Transportation (Coast Guard) Relating to the Investigations and Prosecution of Crimes Over Which the Two Departments Have Concurrent Jurisdiction (October 9, 1967).

32

In Rule 6(e)(3)(F)(ii), the Committee considered whether to amend the language relating to "parties to the judicial proceeding" and determined that in the context of the rule it is understood that the parties referred to are the parties in the same judicial proceeding identified in Rule 6(e)(3)(E)(i).

The Committee decided to leave in subdivision (e) the provision stating that a "knowing violation of Rule 6" may be punished by contempt notwithstanding that, due to its apparent application to the entirety of the Rule, the provision seemingly is misplaced in subdivision (e). Research shows that Congress added the provision in 1977 and that it was crafted solely to deal with violations of the secrecy prohibitions in subdivision (e). See S. Rep. No. 95–354, p. 8 (1977). Supporting this narrow construction, the Committee found no reported decision involving an application or attempted use of the contempt sanction to a violation other than of the disclosure restrictions in subdivision (e). On the other hand, the Supreme Court in dicta did indicate on one occasion its arguable understanding that the contempt sanction would be available also for a violation of Rule 6(d) relating to who may be present during the grand jury's deliberations. Bank of Nova Scotia v. United States, 487 U.S. 250, 263 (1988).

In sum, it appears that the scope of the contempt sanction in Rule 6 is unsettled. Because the provision creates an offense, altering its scope may be beyond the authority bestowed by the Rules Enabling Act, 28 U.S.C. §§2071 et seq. See 28 U.S.C. §2072(b) (Rules must not "abridge, enlarge, or modify any substantive right"). The Committee decided to leave the contempt provision in its present location in subdivision (e), because breaking it out into a separate subdivision could be construed to support the interpretation that the sanction may be applied to a knowing violation of any of the Rule's provisions rather than just those in subdivision (e). Whether or not that is a correct interpretation of the provision—a matter on which the Committee takes no position—must be determined by case law, or resolved by Congress.

Current Rule 6(g) has been divided into two new subdivisions, Rule 6(g), Discharge, and Rule 6(h), Excuse. The Committee added the phrase in Rule 6(g) "except as otherwise provided by statute," to recognize the provisions of 18 U.S.C. §3331 relating to special grand juries.

Rule 6(i) is a new provision defining the term "Indian Tribe," a term used only in this rule.

COMMITTEE NOTES ON RULES—2006 AMENDMENT

Subdivision (e)(3) and (7). This amendment makes technical changes to the language added to Rule 6 by the Intelligence Reform and Terrorism Prevention Act of 2004, Pub. L. 108–458, Title VI, §6501(a), 118 Stat. 3760, in order to bring the new language into conformity with the conventions introduced in the general restyling of the Criminal Rules. No substantive change is intended.

COMMITTEE NOTES ON RULES—2011 AMENDMENT

Subdivision (f). The amendment expressly allows a judge to take a grand jury return by video teleconference. Having the judge in the same courtroom remains the preferred practice because it promotes the public's confidence in the integrity and solemnity of a federal criminal proceeding. But there are situations when no judge is present in the courthouse where the grand jury sits, and a judge would be required to travel long distances to take the return. Avoiding delay is also a factor, since the Speedy Trial Act, 18 U.S.C. §3161(b), requires that an indictment be returned within thirty days of the arrest of an individual to avoid dismissal of the case. The amendment is particularly helpful when there is no judge present at a courthouse where the grand jury sits and the nearest judge is hundreds of miles away.

Under the amendment, the grand jury (or the foreperson) would appear in a courtroom in the United States courthouse where the grand jury sits. Utilizing video teleconference, the judge could participate by video from a remote location, convene court, and take the return. Indictments could be transmitted in advance to the judge for review by reliable electronic means. This process accommodates the Speedy Trial Act, 18 U.S.C. §3161(b), and preserves the judge's time and safety.

Changes Made to Proposed Amendment Released for Public Comment. No changes were made in the amendment as published.

COMMITTEE NOTES ON RULES—2014 AMENDMENT

Rule 6(e)(3)(D). This technical and conforming amendment updates a citation affected by the editorial reclassification of chapter 15 of title 50, United States Code. The amendment replaces the citation to 50 U.S.C. §401a with a citation to 50 U.S.C. §3003. No substantive change is intended.

REFERENCES IN TEXT

The Uniform Code of Military Justice, referred to in subd. (e)(3)(E)(v), is classified to chapter 47 (§801 et seq.) of Title 10, Armed Forces.

25 U.S.C. §479a–1, referred to in subd. (i), was editorially reclassified as 25 U.S.C. 5131.

AMENDMENT BY PUBLIC LAW

2004—Subd. (e)(3)(A)(ii). Pub. L. 108–458, §6501(a)(1)(A), substituted ", state subdivision, Indian tribe, or foreign government" for "or state subdivision or of an Indian tribe".

Subd. (e)(3)(D). Pub. L. 108–458, §6501(a)(1)(B)(i), inserted after first sentence "An attorney for the government may also disclose any grand jury matter involving, within the United States or elsewhere, a threat of attack or other grave hostile acts of a foreign power or its agent, a threat of domestic or international sabotage or terrorism, or clandestine intelligence gathering activities by an intelligence service or network of a foreign power or by its agent, to any appropriate Federal, State, State subdivision, Indian tribal, or foreign government official, for the purpose of preventing or responding to such threat or activities."

Subd. (e)(3)(D)(i). Pub. L. 108–458, §6501(a)(1)(B)(ii), struck out "federal" before "official who" in first sentence and inserted at end "Any State, State subdivision, Indian tribal, or foreign government official who receives information under Rule 6(e)(3)(D) may use the information only consistent with such guidelines as the Attorney General and the Director of National Intelligence shall jointly issue."

Subd. (e)(3)(E)(iii). Pub. L. 108–458, §6501(a)(1)(C)(ii), added cl. (iii). Former cl. (iii) redesignated (iv).

Subd. (e)(3)(E)(iv). Pub. L. 108–458, §6501(a)(1)(C)(iii), substituted "State, Indian tribal, or foreign" for "state or Indian tribal" and "Indian tribal, or foreign government official" for "or Indian tribal official".

Pub. L. 108–458, §6501(a)(1)(C)(i), redesignated cl. (iii) as (iv). Former cl. (iv) redesignated (v).

Subd. (e)(3)(E)(v). Pub. L. 108–458, §6501(a)(1)(C)(i), redesignated cl. (iv) as (v).

Subd. (e)(7). Pub. L. 108–458, §6501(a)(2), inserted ", or of guidelines jointly issued by the Attorney General and the Director of National Intelligence pursuant to Rule 6," after "violation of Rule 6".

2002—Subd. (e). Pub. L. 107–296, §895, which directed certain amendments to subdiv. (e), could not be executed because of the amendment by the Court by order dated Apr. 29, 2002, eff. Dec. 1, 2002. Section 895 of Pub. L. 107–296 provided:

"Rule 6(e) of the Federal Rules of Criminal Procedure is amended—

"(1) in paragraph (2), by inserting ', or of guidelines jointly issued by the Attorney General and Director of Central Intelligence pursuant to Rule 6,' after 'Rule 6'; and

"(2) in paragraph (3)—

"(A) in subparagraph (A)(ii), by inserting 'or of a foreign government' after '(including personnel of a state or subdivision of a state';
"(B) in subparagraph (C)(i)—

"(i) in subclause (I), by inserting before the semicolon the following: 'or, upon a request by an attorney for the government, when sought by a foreign court or prosecutor for use in an official criminal investigation';
"(ii) in subclause (IV)—

"(I) by inserting 'or foreign' after 'may disclose a violation of State';
"(II) by inserting 'or of a foreign government' after 'to an appropriate official of a State or subdivision of a State'; and
"(III) by striking 'or' at the end;

"(iii) by striking the period at the end of subclause (V) and inserting '; or'; and
"(iv) by adding at the end the following:
" '(VI) when matters involve a threat of actual or potential attack or other grave hostile acts of a foreign power or an agent of a foreign power, domestic or international sabotage, domestic or international terrorism, or clandestine intelligence gathering activities by an intelligence service or network of a foreign power or by an agent of a foreign power, within the United States or elsewhere, to any appropriate federal, state, local, or foreign government official for the purpose of preventing or responding to such a threat.'; and
"(C) in subparagraph (C)(iii)—
"(i) by striking 'Federal';
"(ii) by inserting 'or clause (i)(VI)' after 'clause (i)(V)'; and
"(iii) by adding at the end the following: 'Any state, local, or foreign official who receives information pursuant to clause (i)(VI) shall use that information only consistent with such guidelines as the Attorney General and Director of Central Intelligence shall jointly issue.'."

2001—Subd. (e)(3)(C). Pub. L. 107–56, §203(a)(1), amended subpar. (C) generally. Prior to amendment, subpar. (C) read as follows: "Disclosure otherwise prohibited by this rule of matters occurring before the grand jury may also be made—

"(i) when so directed by a court preliminarily to or in connection with a judicial proceeding;

"(ii) when permitted by a court at the request of the defendant, upon a showing that grounds may exist for a motion to dismiss the indictment because of matters occurring before the grand jury;

"(iii) when the disclosure is made by an attorney for the government to another federal grand jury; or

"(iv) when permitted by a court at the request of an attorney for the government, upon a showing that such matters may disclose a violation of state criminal law, to an appropriate official of a state or subdivision of a state for the purpose of enforcing such law.

If the court orders disclosure of matters occurring before the grand jury, the disclosure shall be made in such manner, at such time, and under such conditions as the court may direct."

Subd. (e)(3)(D). Pub. L. 107–56, §203(a)(2), substituted "subdivision (e)(3)(C)(i)(I)" for "subdivision (e)(3)(C)(i)".

1984—Subd. (e)(3)(C)(iv). Pub. L. 98–473, eff. Nov. 1, 1987, added subcl. (iv), identical to subcl. (iv) which had been previously added by Order of the Supreme Court dated Apr. 29, 1985, eff. Aug. 1, 1985, thereby requiring no change in text.

EFFECTIVE DATE OF 1984 AMENDMENT

Amendment by Pub. L. 98–473 effective Nov. 1, 1987, and applicable only to offenses committed after the taking effect of such amendment, see section 235(a)(1) of Pub. L. 98–473, set out as an Effective Date note under section 3551 of this title.

EFFECTIVE DATE OF 1977 AMENDMENT

Amendment of this rule by order of the United States Supreme Court on Apr. 26, 1977, modified and approved by Pub. L. 95–78, effective Oct. 1, 1977, see section 4 of Pub. L. 95–78, set out as an Effective Date of Pub. L. 95–78 note under section 2074 of Title 28, Judiciary and Judicial Procedure.

EFFECTIVE DATE OF 1976 AMENDMENT

Amendment of subd. (f) by the order of the United States Supreme Court of Apr. 26, 1976, effective Aug. 1, 1976, see section 1 of Pub. L. 94–349, July 8, 1976, 90 Stat. 822, set out as a note under section 2074 of Title 28, Judiciary and Judicial Procedure.

¹ See References in Text note below.

Rule 7. The Indictment and the Information

(a) When Used.
(1) Felony. An offense (other than criminal contempt) must be prosecuted by an indictment if it is punishable:
(A) by death; or
(B) by imprisonment for more than one year.

(2) Misdemeanor. An offense punishable by imprisonment for one year or less may be prosecuted in accordance with Rule 58(b)(1).

(b) Waiving Indictment. An offense punishable by imprisonment for more than one year may be prosecuted by information if the defendant—in open court and after being advised of the nature of the charge and of the defendant's rights—waives prosecution by indictment.
(c) Nature and Contents.
(1) In General. The indictment or information must be a plain, concise, and definite written statement of the essential facts constituting the offense charged and must be signed by an attorney for the government. It need not contain a formal introduction or conclusion. A count may incorporate by reference an allegation made in another count. A count may allege that the means by which the defendant committed the offense are unknown or that the defendant committed it by one or more specified means. For each count, the indictment or information must give the official or customary citation of the statute, rule, regulation, or other provision of law that the defendant is alleged to have violated. For purposes of an indictment referred to in section 3282 of title 18, United States Code, for which the identity of the defendant is unknown, it shall be sufficient for the indictment to describe the defendant as an individual whose name is unknown, but who has a particular DNA profile, as that term is defined in that section 3282.

(2) Citation Error. Unless the defendant was misled and thereby prejudiced, neither an error in a citation nor a citation's omission is a ground to dismiss the indictment or information or to reverse a conviction.

(d) Surplusage. Upon the defendant's motion, the court may strike surplusage from the indictment or information.

(e) Amending an Information. Unless an additional or different offense is charged or a substantial right of the defendant is prejudiced, the court may permit an information to be amended at any time before the verdict or finding.

(f) Bill of Particulars. The court may direct the government to file a bill of particulars. The defendant may move for a bill of particulars before or within 14 days after arraignment or at a later time if the court permits. The government may amend a bill of particulars subject to such conditions as justice requires.

(As amended Feb. 28, 1966, eff. July 1, 1966; Apr. 24, 1972, eff. Oct. 1, 1972; Apr. 30, 1979, eff. Aug. 1, 1979; Mar. 9, 1987, eff. Aug. 1, 1987; Apr. 17, 2000, eff. Dec. 1, 2000; Apr. 29, 2002, eff. Dec. 1, 2002; Pub. L. 108–21, title VI, §610(b), Apr. 30, 2003, 117 Stat. 692; Mar. 26, 2009, eff. Dec. 1, 2009.)

NOTES OF ADVISORY COMMITTEE ON RULES——1944

Note to Subdivision (a). 1. This rule gives effect to the following provision of the Fifth Amendment to the Constitution of the United States: "No person shall be held to answer for a capital, or otherwise infamous crime, unless on a presentment or indictment of a Grand Jury * * *". An infamous crime has been defined as a crime punishable by death or by imprisonment in a penitentiary or at hard labor, Ex parte Wilson, 114 U.S. 417, 427; United States v. Moreland, 258 U.S. 433. Any sentence of imprisonment for a term of over one year may be served in a penitentiary, if so directed by the Attorney General, 18 U.S.C. 753f [now 4082, 4083] (Commitment of persons by any court of the United States and the juvenile court of the District of Columbia; place of confinement; transfers). Consequently any offense punishable by imprisonment for a term of over one year is an infamous crime.

2. Petty offenses and misdemeanors for which no infamous punishment is prescribed may now be prosecuted by information, 18 U.S.C. 541 [see 1] (Felonies and misdemeanors); Duke v. United States, 301 U.S. 492.

3. For a discussion of the provision for waiver of indictment, see Note to Rule 7(b), infra.

4. Presentment is not included as an additional type of formal accusation, since presentments as a method of instituting prosecutions are obsolete, at least as concerns the Federal courts.

Note to Subdivision (b). 1. Opportunity to waive indictment and to consent to prosecution by information will be a substantial aid to defendants, especially those who, because of inability to give bail, are incarcerated pending action of the grand jury, but desire to plead guilty. This rule is particularly important in those districts in which considerable intervals occur between sessions of the grand jury. In many districts where the grand jury meets infrequently a defendant unable to give bail and desiring to plead guilty is compelled to spend many days, and sometimes many weeks, and even months, in jail before he can begin the service of his sentence, whatever it may be, awaiting the action of a grand jury. Homer Cummings, 29 A.B.A.Jour. 654–655; Vanderbilt, 29 A.B.A.Jour. 376, 377; Robinson, 27 Jour. of the Am. Judicature Soc. 38, 45; Medalie, 4 Lawyers Guild R. (3)1, 3. The rule contains safeguards against improvident waivers.

The Judicial Conference of Senior Circuit Judges, in September 1941, recommended that "existing law or established procedure be so changed, that a defendant may waive indictment and plead guilty to an information filed by a United States attorney in all cases except capital felonies." Report of the Judicial Conference of Senior Circuit Judges (1941) 13. In September 1942 the Judicial Conference recommended that provision be made "for waiver of indictment and jury trial, so that persons accused of crime may not be held in jail needlessly pending trial." Id. (1942) 8.

Attorneys General of the United States have from time to time recommended legislation to permit defendants to waive indictment and to consent to prosecution by information. See Annual Report of the Attorney General of the United States (Mitchell) (1931) 3; Id. (Mitchell) (1932) 6; Id. (Cummings) (1933) 1, (1936) 2, (1937) 11, (1938) 9; Id. (Murphy) (1939) 7.

The Federal Juvenile Delinquency Act [now 18 U.S.C. 5031–5037], now permits a juvenile charged with an offense not punishable by death or life imprisonment to consent to prosecution by information on a charge of juvenile delinquency, 18 U.S.C. 922 [now 5032, 5033].

2. On the constitutionality of this rule, see United States v. Gill, 55 F.2d 399 (D.N.M.), holding that the constitutional guaranty of indictment by grand jury may be waived by defendant. It has also been held that other constitutional guaranties may be waived by the defendant, e. g., Patton v. United States, 281 U.S. 276 (trial by jury); Johnson v. Zerbst, 304 U.S. 458, 465 (right of counsel); Trono v. United States, 199 U.S. 521, 534 (protection against double jeopardy); United States v. Murdock, 284 U.S. 141, 148 (privilege against self-incrimination); Diaz v. United States, 223 U.S. 442, 450 (right of confrontation).

Note to Subdivision (c). 1. This rule introduces a simple form of indictment, illustrated by Forms 1 to 11 in the Appendix of Forms. Cf. Rule 8(a) of the Federal Rules of Civil Procedure [28 U.S.C., Appendix]. For discussion of the effect of this rule and a comparison between the present form of indictment and the simple form introduced by this rule, see Vanderbilt, 29 A.B.A.Jour. 376, 377; Homer Cummings, 29 A.B.A.Jour. 654, 655; Holtzoff, 3 F.R.D. 445, 448–449; Holtzoff, 12 Geo. Washington L.R. 119, 123–126; Medalie, 4 Lawyers Guild R. (3)1, 3.

2. The provision contained in the fifth sentence that it may be alleged in a single count that the means by which the defendant committed the offense are unknown, or that he committed it by one or more specified means, is intended to eliminate the use of multiple counts for the purpose of alleging the commission of the offense by different means or in different ways. Cf. Federal Rules of Civil Procedure, Rule 8(e)(2) [28 U.S.C., Appendix].

3. The law at present regards citations to statutes or regulations as not a part of the indictment. A conviction may be sustained on the basis of a statute or regulation other than that cited. Williams v. United States, 168 U.S. 382, 389; United States v. Hutcheson, 312 U.S. 219, 229. The provision of the rule, in view of the many statutes and regulations, is for the benefit of the defendant and is not intended to cause a dismissal of the indictment, but simply to provide a means by which he can be properly informed without danger to the prosecution.

Note to Subdivision (d). This rule introduces a means of protecting the defendant against immaterial or irrelevant allegations in an indictment or information, which may, however, be prejudicial. The authority of the court to strike such surplusage is to be limited to doing so on defendant's motion, in the light of the rule that the guaranty of indictment by a grand jury implies that an indictment may not be amended, Ex parte Bain, 121 U.S. 1. By making such a motion, the defendant would, however, waive his rights in this respect.

Note to Subdivision (e). This rule continues the existing law that, unlike an indictment, an information may be amended, Muncy v. United States, 289 F. 780 (C.C.A. 4th).

Note to Subdivision (f). This rule is substantially a restatement of existing law on bills of particulars.

NOTES OF ADVISORY COMMITTEE ON RULES——1966 AMENDMENT

35

The amendment to the first sentence eliminating the requirement of a showing of cause is designed to encourage a more liberal attitude by the courts toward bills of particulars without taking away the discretion which courts must have in dealing with such motions in individual cases. For an illustration of wise use of this discretion see the opinion by Justice Whittaker written when he was a district judge in United States v. Smith, 16 F.R.D. 372 (W.D.Mo. 1954).

The amendment to the second sentence gives discretion to the court to permit late filing of motions for bills of particulars in meritorious cases. Use of late motions for the purpose of delaying trial should not, of course, be permitted. The courts have not been agreed as to their power to accept late motions in the absence of a local rule or a previous order. See United States v. Miller, 217 F.Supp. 760 (E.D.Pa. 1963); United States v. Taylor, 25 F.R.D. 225 (E.D.N.Y. 1960); United States v. Sterling, 122 F.Supp. 81 (E.D.Pa. 1954) (all taking a limited view of the power of the court). But cf. United States v. Brown, 179 F.Supp. 893 (E.D.N.Y. 1959) (exercising discretion to permit an out of time motion).

NOTES OF ADVISORY COMMITTEE ON RULES——1972 AMENDMENT

Subdivision (c)(2) is new. It is intended to provide procedural implementation of the recently enacted criminal forfeiture provision of the Organized Crime Control Act of 1970, Title IX, §1963, and the Comprehensive Drug Abuse Prevention and Control Act of 1970, Title II, §408(a)(2).

The Congress viewed the provisions of the Organized Crime Control Act of 1970 as reestablishing a limited common law criminal forfeiture. S. Rep. No. 91–617, 91st Cong., 1st Sess. 79–80 (1969). The legislative history of the Comprehensive Drug Abuse Prevention and Control Act of 1970 indicates a congressional purpose to have similar procedures apply to the forfeiture of profits or interests under that act. H. Rep. No. 91–1444 (part I), 91st Cong., 2d Sess. 81–85 (1970).

Under the common law, in a criminal forfeiture proceeding the defendant was apparently entitled to notice, trial, and a special jury finding on the factual issues surrounding the declaration of forfeiture which followed his criminal conviction. Subdivision (c)(2) provides for notice. Changes in rules 31 and 32 provide for a special jury finding and for a judgment authorizing the Attorney General to seize the interest or property forfeited.

NOTES OF ADVISORY COMMITTEE ON RULES——1979 AMENDMENT

The amendment to rule 7(c)(2) is intended to clarify its meaning. Subdivision (c)(2) was added in 1972, and, as noted in the Advisory Committee Note thereto, was "intended to provide procedural implementation of the recently enacted criminal forfeiture provision of the Organized Crime Control Act of 1970, Title IX, §1963, and the Comprehensive Drug Abuse Prevention and Control Act of 1970, Title II, §408(a)(2)." These provisions reestablished a limited common law criminal forfeiture, necessitating the addition of subdivision (c)(2) and corresponding changes in rules 31 and 32, for at common law the defendant in a criminal forfeiture proceeding was entitled to notice, trial, and a special jury finding on the factual issues surrounding the declaration of forfeiture which followed his criminal conviction.

Although there is some doubt as to what forfeitures should be characterized as "punitive" rather than "remedial," see Note, 62 Cornell L.Rev. 768 (1977), subdivision (c)(2) is intended to apply to those forfeitures which are criminal in the sense that they result from a special verdict under rule 31(e) and a judgment under rule 32(b)(2), and not to those resulting from a separate in rem proceeding. Because some confusion in this regard has resulted from the present wording of subdivision (c)(2), United States v. Hall, 521 F.2d 406 (9th Cir. 1975), a clarifying amendment is in order.

NOTES OF ADVISORY COMMITTEE ON RULES——1987 AMENDMENT

The amendments are technical. No substantive change is intended.

COMMITTEE NOTES ON RULES——2000 AMENDMENT

The rule is amended to reflect new Rule 32.2, which now governs criminal forfeiture procedures.

GAP Report—Rule 7. The Committee initially made no changes to the published draft of the Rule 7 amendment. However, because of changes to Rule 32.2(a), discussed infra, the proposed language has been changed to reflect that the indictment must provide notice of an intent to seek forfeiture.

COMMITTEE NOTES ON RULES——2002 AMENDMENT

The language of Rule 7 has been amended as part of the general restyling of the Criminal Rules to make them more easily understood and to make style and terminology consistent throughout the rules. These changes are intended to be stylistic.

The Committee has deleted the references to "hard labor" in the rule. This punishment is not found in current federal statutes.

The Committee added an exception for criminal contempt to the requirement in Rule 7(a)(1) that a prosecution for felony must be initiated by indictment. This is consistent with case law, e.g., United States v. Eichhorst, 544 F.2d 1383 (7th Cir. 1976), which has sustained the use of the special procedures for instituting criminal contempt proceedings found in Rule 42. While indictment is not a required method of bringing felony criminal contempt charges, however, it is a permissible one. See United States v. Williams, 622 F.2d 830 (5th Cir. 1980). No change in practice is intended.

The title of Rule 7(c)(3) has been amended. The Committee believed that potential confusion could arise with the use of the term "harmless error." Rule 52, which deals with the issues of harmless error and plain error, is sufficient to address the topic. Potentially, the topic of harmless error could arise with regard to any of the other rules and there is insufficient need to highlight the term in Rule 7. Rule 7(c)(3), on the other hand, focuses specifically on the effect of an error in the citation of authority in the indictment. That material remains but without any reference to harmless error.

COMMITTEE NOTES ON RULES——2009 AMENDMENT

The time set in the former rule at 10 days has been revised to 14 days. See the Committee Note to Rule 45(a).

Subdivision (c). The provision regarding forfeiture is obsolete. In 2000 the same language was repeated in subdivision (a) of Rule 32.2, which was intended to consolidate the rules dealing with forfeiture.

AMENDMENT BY PUBLIC LAW

2003—Subd. (c)(1). Pub. L. 108–21 inserted at end "For purposes of an indictment referred to in section 3282 of title 18, United States Code, for which the identity of the defendant is unknown, it shall be sufficient for the indictment to describe the defendant as an individual whose name is unknown, but who has a particular DNA profile, as that term is defined in that section 3282."

Rule 8. Joinder of Offenses or Defendants

(a) Joinder of Offenses. The indictment or information may charge a defendant in separate counts with 2 or more offenses if the offenses charged—whether felonies or misdemeanors or both—are of the same or similar character, or are based on the same act or transaction, or are connected with or constitute parts of a common scheme or plan.

(b) Joinder of Defendants. The indictment or information may charge 2 or more defendants if they are alleged to have participated in the same act or transaction, or in the same series of acts or transactions, constituting an offense or offenses. The defendants may be charged in one or more counts together or separately. All defendants need not be charged in each count.

(As amended Apr. 29, 2002, eff. Dec. 1, 2002.)

NOTES OF ADVISORY COMMITTEE ON RULES——1944

Note to Subdivision (a). This rule is substantially a restatement of existing law, 18 U.S.C. [former] 557 (Indictments and presentments; joinder of charges).

Note to Subdivision (b). The first sentence of the rule is substantially a restatement of existing law, 9 Edmunds, Cyclopedia of Federal Procedure (2d Ed.) 4116. The second sentence formulates a practice now approved in some circuits. Caringella v. United States, 78 F.2d 563, 567 (C.C.A. 7th).

COMMITTEE NOTES ON RULES——2002 AMENDMENT

The language of Rule 8 has been amended as part of the general restyling of the Criminal Rules to make them more easily understood and to make style and terminology consistent throughout the rules. These changes are intended to be stylistic only.

Rule 9. Arrest Warrant or Summons on an Indictment or Information

(a) Issuance. The court must issue a warrant—or at the government's request, a summons—for each defendant named in an indictment or named in an information if one or more affidavits accompanying the information establish probable cause to believe that an offense has been committed and that the defendant committed it. The court may issue more than one warrant or summons for the same defendant. If a defendant fails to appear in response to a summons, the court may, and upon request of an attorney for the government must, issue a warrant. The court must issue the arrest warrant to an officer authorized to execute it or the summons to a person authorized to serve it.

(b) Form.

(1) Warrant. The warrant must conform to Rule 4(b)(1) except that it must be signed by the clerk and must describe the offense charged in the indictment or information.

(2) Summons. The summons must be in the same form as a warrant except that it must require the defendant to appear before the court at a stated time and place.

(c) Execution or Service; Return; Initial Appearance.

(1) Execution or Service.

(A) The warrant must be executed or the summons served as provided in Rule 4(c)(1), (2), and (3).

(B) The officer executing the warrant must proceed in accordance with Rule 5(a)(1).

(2) Return. A warrant or summons must be returned in accordance with Rule 4(c)(4).

(3) Initial Appearance. When an arrested or summoned defendant first appears before the court, the judge must proceed under Rule 5.

(d) Warrant by Telephone or Other Means. In accordance with Rule 4.1, a magistrate judge may issue an arrest warrant or summons based on information communicated by telephone or other reliable electronic means.

(As amended Apr. 24, 1972, eff. Oct. 1, 1972; Apr. 22, 1974, eff. Dec. 1, 1975; Pub. L. 94–64, §3(4), July 31, 1975, 89 Stat. 370; Pub. L. 94–149, §5, Dec. 12, 1975, 89 Stat. 806; Apr. 30, 1979, eff. Aug. 1, 1979; Apr. 28, 1982, eff. Aug. 1, 1982; Apr. 22, 1993, eff. Dec. 1, 1993; Apr. 29, 2002, eff. Dec. 1, 2002; Apr. 26, 2011, eff. Dec. 1, 2011.)

NOTES OF ADVISORY COMMITTEE ON RULES——1944

1. See Note to Rule 4, supra.

2. The provision of Rule 9(a) that a warrant may be issued on the basis of an information only if the latter is supported by oath is necessitated by the Fourth Amendment to the Constitution of the United States. See Albrecht v. United States, 273 U.S. 1, 5.

3. The provision of Rule 9(b)(1) that the amount of bail may be fixed by the court and endorsed on the warrant states a practice now prevailing in many districts and is intended to facilitate the giving of bail by the defendant and eliminate delays between the arrest and the giving of bail, which might ensue if bail cannot be fixed until after arrest.

NOTES OF ADVISORY COMMITTEE ON RULES——1972 AMENDMENT

Subdivision (b) is amended to make clear that the person arrested shall be brought before a United States magistrate if the information or indictment charges a "minor offense" triable by the United States magistrate.

Subdivision (c) is amended to reflect the office of United States magistrate.

Subdivision (d) is new. It provides for a remand to the United States magistrate of cases in which the person is charged with a "minor offense." The magistrate can then proceed in accordance with rule 5 to try the case if the right to trial before a judge of the district court is waived.

NOTES OF ADVISORY COMMITTEE ON RULES——1974 AMENDMENT

Rule 9 is revised to give high priority to the issuance of a summons unless a "valid reason" is given for the issuance of an arrest warrant. See a comparable provision in rule 4.

Under the rule, a summons will issue by the clerk unless the attorney for the government presents a valid reason for the issuance of an arrest warrant. Under the old rule, it has been argued that the court must issue an arrest warrant if one is desired by the attorney for the government. See authorities listed in Frankel, Bench Warrants Upon the Prosecutor's Demand: A View From the Bench, 71 Colum.L.Rev. 403, 410 n. 25 (1971). For an expression of the view that this is undesirable policy, see Frankel, supra, pp. 410–415.

A summons may issue if there is an information supported by oath. The indictment itself is sufficient to establish the existence of probable cause. See C. Wright, Federal Practice and Procedure: Criminal §151 (1969); 8 J. Moore, Federal Practice 9.02[2] at p. 9–4 (2d ed.) Cipes (1969); Giordenello v. United States, 357 U.S. 480, 78 S.Ct. 1245, 2 L.Ed. 2d 1503 (1958). This is not necessarily true in the case of an information. See C. Wright, supra, §151; 8 J. Moore, supra, 9.02. If the government requests a warrant rather than a summons, good practice would obviously require the judge to satisfy himself that there is probable cause. This may appear from the information or from an affidavit filed with the information. Also a defendant can, at a proper time, challenge an information issued without probable cause.

NOTES OF COMMITTEE ON THE JUDICIARY, HOUSE REPORT NO. 94–247; 1975 AMENDMENT

A. Amendments Proposed by the Supreme Court. Rule 9 of the Federal Rules of Criminal Procedure is closely related to Rule 4. Rule 9 deals with arrest procedures after an information has been filed or an indictment returned. The present rule gives the prosecutor the authority to decide whether a summons or a warrant shall issue.

The Supreme Court's amendments to Rule 9 parallel its amendments to Rule 4. The basic change made in Rule 4 is also made in Rule 9.

B. Committee Action. For the reasons set forth above in connection with Rule 4, the Committee endorses and accepts the basic change in Rule 9. The Committee made changes in Rule 9 similar to the changes it made in Rule 4.

NOTES OF ADVISORY COMMITTEE ON RULES—1979 AMENDMENT

Subdivision (a) is amended to make explicit the fact that a warrant may issue upon the basis of an information only if the information or an affidavit filed with the information shows probable cause for the arrest. This has generally been assumed to be the state of the law even though not specifically set out in rule 9; see C. Wright, Federal Practice and Procedure: Criminal §151 (1969); 8 J. Moore, Federal Practice par. 9.02[2] (2d ed. 1976).

In Gerstein v. Pugh, 420 U.S. 103 (1975), the Supreme Court rejected the contention "that the prosecutor's decision to file an information is itself a determination of probable cause that furnishes sufficient reason to detain a defendant pending trial," commenting:

Although a conscientious decision that the evidence warrants prosecution affords a measure of protection against unfounded detention, we do not think prosecutorial judgment standing alone meets the requirements of the Fourth Amendment. Indeed, we think the Court's previous decisions compel disapproval of [such] procedure. In Albrecht v. United States, 273 U.S. 1, 5, 47 S.Ct. 250, 251, 71 L.Ed. 505 (1927), the Court held that an arrest warrant issued solely upon a United States Attorney's information was invalid because the accompanying affidavits were defective. Although the Court's opinion did not explicitly state that the prosecutor's official oath could not furnish probable cause, that conclusion was implicit in the judgment that the arrest was illegal under the Fourth Amendment.

No change is made in the rule with respect to warrants issuing upon indictments. In Gerstein, the Court indicated it was not disturbing the prior rule that "an indictment, 'fair upon its face,' and returned by a 'properly constituted grand jury' conclusively determines the existence of probable cause and requires issuance of an arrest warrant without further inquiry." See Ex parte United States, 287 U.S. 241, 250 (1932).

The provision to the effect that a summons shall issue "by direction of the court" has been eliminated because it conflicts with the first sentence of the rule, which states that a warrant "shall" issue when requested by the attorney for the government, if properly supported. However, an addition has been made providing that if the attorney for the government does not make a request for either a warrant or summons, then the court may in its discretion issue either one. Other stylistic changes ensure greater consistency with comparable provisions in rule 4.

NOTES OF ADVISORY COMMITTEE ON RULES—1982 AMENDMENT

Note to Subdivision (a). The amendment of subdivision (a), by reference to Rule 5, clarifies what is to be done once the defendant is brought before the magistrate. This means, among other things, that no preliminary hearing is to be held in a Rule 9 case, as Rule 5(c) provides that no such hearing is to be had "if the defendant is indicted or if an information against the defendant is filed."

Note to Subdivision (b). The amendment of subdivision (b) conforms Rule 9 to the comparable provisions in Rule 4(c)(1) and (2).

Note to Subdivision (c). The amendment of subdivision (c) conforms Rule 9 to the comparable provisions in Rules 4(d)(4) and 5(a) concerning return of the warrant.

Note to Subdivision (d). This subdivision, incorrect in its present form in light of the recent amendment of 18 U.S.C. §3401(a), has been abrogated as unnecessary in light of the change to subdivision (a).

NOTES OF ADVISORY COMMITTEE ON RULES—1993 AMENDMENT

The Rule is amended to conform to the Judicial Improvements Act of 1990 [P.L. 101–650, Title III, Section 321] which provides that each United States magistrate appointed under section 631 of title 28, United States Code, shall be known as a United States magistrate judge.

COMMITTEE NOTES ON RULES—2002 AMENDMENT

The language of Rule 9 has been amended as part of the general restyling of the Criminal Rules to make them more easily understood and to make style and terminology consistent throughout the rules. These changes are intended to be stylistic only, except as noted below.

Rule 9 has been changed to reflect its relationship to Rule 4 procedures for obtaining an arrest warrant or summons. Thus, rather than simply repeating material that is already located in Rule 4, the Committee determined that where appropriate, Rule 9 should simply direct the reader to the procedures specified in Rule 4.

Rule 9(a) has been amended to permit a judge discretion whether to issue an arrest warrant when a defendant fails to respond to a summons on a complaint. Under the current language of the rule, if the defendant fails to appear, the judge must issue a warrant. Under the amended version, if the defendant fails to appear and the government requests that a warrant be issued, the judge must issue one. In the absence of such a request, the judge has the discretion to do so. This change mirrors language in amended Rule 4(a).

A second amendment has been made in Rule 9(b)(1). The rule has been amended to delete language permitting the court to set the amount of bail on the warrant. The Committee believes that this language is inconsistent with the 1984 Bail Reform Act. See United States v. Thomas, 992 F. Supp. 782 (D.V.I. 1998) (bail amount endorsed on warrant that has not been determined in proceedings conducted under Bail Reform Act has no bearing on decision by judge conducting Rule 40 hearing).

The language in current Rule 9(c)(1), concerning service of a summons on an organization, has been moved to Rule 4.

COMMITTEE NOTES ON RULES—2011 AMENDMENT

Subdivision (d). Rule 9(d) authorizes a court to issue an arrest warrant or summons electronically on the return of an indictment or the filing of an information. In large judicial districts the need to travel to the courthouse to obtain an arrest warrant in person can be burdensome, and advances in technology make the secure transmission of a reliable version of the warrant or summons possible. This change works in conjunction with the amendment to Rule 6 that permits the electronic return of an indictment, which similarly eliminates the need to travel to the courthouse.

Changes Made to Proposed Amendment Released for Public Comment. No changes were made in the amendment as published.

AMENDMENT BY PUBLIC LAW

1975—Subd. (a). Pub. L. 94–64 amended subd. (a) generally.

Subd. (b)(1). Pub. L. 94–149 substituted reference to "rule 4(c)(1)" for "rule 4(b)(1)".

Subd. (c)(1). Pub. L. 94–149 substituted reference to "rule 4(d)(1), (2), and (3)" for "rule 4(c)(1), (2), and (3)".

EFFECTIVE DATE OF AMENDMENTS PROPOSED APRIL 22, 1974; EFFECTIVE DATE OF 1975 AMENDMENTS

Amendments of this rule embraced in the order of the United States Supreme Court on Apr. 22, 1974, and the amendments of this rule made by section 3 of Pub. L. 94–64, effective Dec. 1, 1975, see section 2 of Pub. L. 94–64, set out as a note under rule 4 of these rules.

TITLE IV. ARRAIGNMENT AND PREPARATION FOR TRIAL

Rule 10. Arraignment

(a) In General. An arraignment must be conducted in open court and must consist of:

(1) ensuring that the defendant has a copy of the indictment or information;

(2) reading the indictment or information to the defendant or stating to the defendant the substance of the charge; and then

(3) asking the defendant to plead to the indictment or information.

(b) Waiving Appearance. A defendant need not be present for the arraignment if:

(1) the defendant has been charged by indictment or misdemeanor information;

(2) the defendant, in a written waiver signed by both the defendant and defense counsel, has waived appearance and has affirmed that the defendant received a copy of the indictment or information and that the plea is not guilty; and

(3) the court accepts the waiver.

(c) Video Teleconferencing. Video teleconferencing may be used to arraign a defendant if the defendant consents.

(As amended Mar. 9, 1987, eff. Aug. 1, 1987; Apr. 29, 2002, eff. Dec. 1, 2002.)

NOTES OF ADVISORY COMMITTEE ON RULES—1944

1. The first sentence states the prevailing practice.

2. The requirement that the defendant shall be given a copy of the indictment or information before he is called upon to plead, contained in the second sentence, is new.

3. Failure to comply with arraignment requirements has been held not to be jurisdictional, but a mere technical irregularity not warranting a reversal of a conviction, if not raised before trial, Garland v. State of Washington, 232 U.S. 642.

NOTES OF ADVISORY COMMITTEE ON RULES—1987 AMENDMENT

The amendments are technical. No substantive change is intended.

COMMITTEE NOTES ON RULES—2002 AMENDMENT

The language of Rule 10 has been amended as part of the general restyling of the Criminal Rules to make them more easily understood and to make style and terminology consistent throughout the rules. These changes are intended to be stylistic only, except as noted below.

Read together, Rules 10 and 43 require the defendant to be physically present in court for the arraignment. See, e.g., Valenzuela-Gonzales v. United States, 915 F.2d 1276, 1280 (9th Cir. 1990) (Rules 10 and 43 are broader in protection than the Constitution). The amendments to Rule 10 create two exceptions to that requirement. The first provides that the court may hold an arraignment in the defendant's absence when the defendant has waived the right to be present in writing and the court consents to that waiver. The second permits the court to hold arraignments by video teleconferencing when the defendant is at a different location. A conforming amendment has also been made to Rule 43.

In amending Rule 10 and Rule 43, the Committee was concerned that permitting a defendant to be absent from the arraignment could be viewed as an erosion of an important element of the judicial process. First, it may be important for a defendant to see and experience first-hand the formal impact of the reading of the charge. Second, it may be necessary for the court to personally see and speak with the defendant at the arraignment, especially when there is a real question whether the defendant actually understands the gravity of the proceedings. And third, there may be difficulties in providing the defendant with effective and confidential assistance of counsel if counsel, but not the defendant, appears at the arraignment.

The Committee nonetheless believed that in appropriate circumstances the court, and the defendant, should have the option of conducting the arraignment in the defendant's absence. The question of when it would be appropriate for a defendant to waive an appearance is not spelled out in the rule. That is left to the defendant and the court in each case.

A critical element to the amendment is that no matter how convenient or cost effective a defendant's absence might be, the defendant's right to be present in court stands unless he or she waives that right in writing. Under the amendment, both the defendant and the defendant's attorney must sign the waiver. Further, the amendment requires that the waiver specifically state that the defendant has received a copy of the charging instrument.

If the trial court has reason to believe that in a particular case the defendant should not be permitted to waive the right, the court may reject the waiver and require that the defendant actually appear in court. That might be particularly appropriate when the court wishes to discuss substantive or procedural matters in conjunction with the arraignment and the court believes that the defendant's presence is important in resolving those matters. It might also be appropriate to reject a requested waiver where an attorney for the government presents reasons for requiring the defendant to appear personally.

The amendment does not permit waiver of an appearance when the defendant is charged with a felony information. In that instance, the defendant is required by Rule 7(b) to be present in court to waive the indictment. Nor does the amendment permit a waiver of appearance when the defendant is standing mute (see Rule 11(a)(4)), or entering a conditional plea (see Rule 11(a)(2)), a nolo contendere plea (see Rule 11(a)(3)), or a guilty plea (see Rule 11(a)(1)). In each of those instances the Committee believed that it was more appropriate for the defendant to appear personally before the court.

It is important to note that the amendment does not permit the defendant to waive the arraignment itself, which may be a triggering mechanism for other rules.

Rule 10(c) addresses the second substantive change in the rule. That provision permits the court to conduct arraignments through video teleconferencing, if the defendant waives the right to be arraigned in court. Although the practice is now used in state courts and in some federal courts, Rules 10 and 43 have generally prevented federal courts from using that method for arraignments in criminal cases. See, e.g., Valenzuela-Gonzales v. United States, supra (Rules 10 and 43 mandate physical presence of defendant at arraignment and that arraignment take place in open court). A similar amendment was proposed by the Committee in 1993 and published for public comment. The amendment was later withdrawn from consideration in order to consider the results of several planned pilot programs. Upon further consideration, the

Committee believed that the benefits of using video teleconferencing outweighed the costs of doing so. This amendment also parallels an amendment in Rule 5(f) that would permit initial appearances to be conducted by video teleconferencing.

In amending Rules 5, 10, and 43 (which generally requires the defendant's presence at all proceedings), the Committee carefully considered the argument that permitting a defendant to appear by video teleconferencing might be considered an erosion of an important element of the judicial process. Much can be lost when video teleconferencing occurs. First, the setting itself may not promote the public's confidence in the integrity and solemnity of a federal criminal proceeding; that is the view of some who have witnessed the use of such proceedings in some state jurisdictions. While it is difficult to quantify the intangible benefits and impact of requiring a defendant to be brought before a federal judicial officer in a federal courtroom, the Committee realizes that something is lost when a defendant is not required to make a personal appearance. A related consideration is that the defendant may be located in a room that bears no resemblance whatsoever to a judicial forum and the equipment may be inadequate for high-quality transmissions. Second, using video teleconferencing can interfere with counsel's ability to meet personally with his or her client at what, at least in that jurisdiction, might be an important appearance before a magistrate judge. Third, the defendant may miss an opportunity to meet with family or friends, and others who might be able to assist the defendant, especially in any attempts to obtain bail. Finally, the magistrate judge may miss an opportunity to accurately assess the physical, emotional, and mental condition of a defendant—a factor that may weigh on pretrial decisions, such as release from detention.

On the other hand, the Committee considered that in some jurisdictions, the courts face a high volume of criminal proceedings. The Committee was also persuaded to adopt the amendment because in some jurisdictions delays may occur in travel time from one location to another—in some cases requiring either the magistrate judge or the participants to travel long distances. In those instances, it is not unusual for a defense counsel to recognize the benefit of conducting a video teleconferenced proceeding, which will eliminate lengthy and sometimes expensive travel or permit the arraignment to be conducted much sooner. Finally, the Committee was aware that in some jurisdictions, courtrooms now contain high quality technology for conducting such procedures, and that some courts are already using video teleconferencing—with the consent of the parties.

The Committee believed that, on balance and in appropriate circumstances, the court and the defendant should have the option of using video teleconferencing for arraignments, as long as the defendant consents to that procedure. The question of when it would be appropriate for a defendant to consent is not spelled out in the rule. That is left to the defendant and the court in each case. Although the rule does not specify any particular technical requirements regarding the system to be used, if the equipment or technology is deficient, the public may lose confidence in the integrity and dignity of the proceedings.

The amendment does not require a court to adopt or use video teleconferencing. In deciding whether to use such procedures, a court may wish to consider establishing clearly articulated standards and procedures. For example, the court would normally want to insure that the location used for televising the video teleconferencing is conducive to the solemnity of a federal criminal proceeding. That might require additional coordination, for example, with the detention facility to insure that the room, furniture, and furnishings reflect the dignity associated with a federal courtroom. Provision should also be made to insure that the judge, or a surrogate, is in a position to carefully assess the condition of the defendant. And the court should also consider establishing procedures for insuring that counsel and the defendant (and even the defendant's immediate family) are provided an ample opportunity to confer in private.

Although the rule requires the defendant to waive a personal appearance for an arraignment, the rule does not require that the waiver for video teleconferencing be in writing. Nor does it require that the defendant waive that appearance in person, in open court. It would normally be sufficient for the defendant to waive an appearance while participating through a video teleconference.

The amendment leaves to the courts the decision first, whether to permit video arraignments, and second, the procedures to be used. The Committee was satisfied that the technology has progressed to the point that video teleconferencing can address the concerns raised in the past about the ability of the court and the defendant to see each other and for the defendant and counsel to be in contact with each other, either at the same location or by a secure remote connection.

Rule 11. Pleas
    (a) Entering a Plea.
        (1) In General. A defendant may plead not guilty, guilty, or (with the court's consent) nolo contendere.
        (2) Conditional Plea. With the consent of the court and the government, a defendant may enter a conditional plea of guilty or nolo contendere, reserving in writing the right to have an appellate court review an adverse determination of a specified pretrial motion. A defendant who prevails on appeal may then withdraw the plea.
        (3) Nolo Contendere Plea. Before accepting a plea of nolo contendere, the court must consider the parties' views and the public interest in the effective administration of justice.
        (4) Failure to Enter a Plea. If a defendant refuses to enter a plea or if a defendant organization fails to appear, the court must enter a plea of not guilty.

    (b) Considering and Accepting a Guilty or Nolo Contendere Plea.
        (1) Advising and Questioning the Defendant. Before the court accepts a plea of guilty or nolo contendere, the defendant may be placed under oath, and the court must address the defendant personally in open court. During this address, the court must inform the defendant of, and determine that the defendant understands, the following:
            (A) the government's right, in a prosecution for perjury or false statement, to use against the defendant any statement that the defendant gives under oath;
            (B) the right to plead not guilty, or having already so pleaded, to persist in that plea;
            (C) the right to a jury trial;
            (D) the right to be represented by counsel—and if necessary have the court appoint counsel—at trial and at every other stage of the proceeding;
            (E) the right at trial to confront and cross-examine adverse witnesses, to be protected from compelled self-incrimination, to testify and present evidence, and to compel the attendance of witnesses;
            (F) the defendant's waiver of these trial rights if the court accepts a plea of guilty or nolo contendere;
            (G) the nature of each charge to which the defendant is pleading;
            (H) any maximum possible penalty, including imprisonment, fine, and term of supervised release;
            (I) any mandatory minimum penalty;
            (J) any applicable forfeiture;
            (K) the court's authority to order restitution;
            (L) the court's obligation to impose a special assessment;
            (M) in determining a sentence, the court's obligation to calculate the applicable sentencing-guideline range and to consider that range, possible departures under the Sentencing Guidelines, and other sentencing factors under 18 U.S.C. §3553(a);
            (N) the terms of any plea-agreement provision waiving the right to appeal or to collaterally attack the sentence; and
            (O) that, if convicted, a defendant who is not a United States citizen may be removed from the United States, denied citizenship, and denied admission to the United States in the future.

        (2) Ensuring That a Plea Is Voluntary. Before accepting a plea of guilty or nolo contendere, the court must address the defendant personally in open court and determine that the plea is voluntary and did not result from force, threats, or promises (other than promises in a plea agreement).
        (3) Determining the Factual Basis for a Plea. Before entering judgment on a guilty plea, the court must determine that there is a factual basis for the plea.

    (c) Plea Agreement Procedure.

(1) In General. An attorney for the government and the defendant's attorney, or the defendant when proceeding pro se, may discuss and reach a plea agreement. The court must not participate in these discussions. If the defendant pleads guilty or nolo contendere to either a charged offense or a lesser or related offense, the plea agreement may specify that an attorney for the government will:

    (A) not bring, or will move to dismiss, other charges;

    (B) recommend, or agree not to oppose the defendant's request, that a particular sentence or sentencing range is appropriate or that a particular provision of the Sentencing Guidelines, or policy statement, or sentencing factor does or does not apply (such a recommendation or request does not bind the court); or

    (C) agree that a specific sentence or sentencing range is the appropriate disposition of the case, or that a particular provision of the Sentencing Guidelines, or policy statement, or sentencing factor does or does not apply (such a recommendation or request binds the court once the court accepts the plea agreement).

(2) Disclosing a Plea Agreement. The parties must disclose the plea agreement in open court when the plea is offered, unless the court for good cause allows the parties to disclose the plea agreement in camera.

(3) Judicial Consideration of a Plea Agreement.

    (A) To the extent the plea agreement is of the type specified in Rule 11(c)(1)(A) or (C), the court may accept the agreement, reject it, or defer a decision until the court has reviewed the presentence report.

    (B) To the extent the plea agreement is of the type specified in Rule 11(c)(1)(B), the court must advise the defendant that the defendant has no right to withdraw the plea if the court does not follow the recommendation or request.

(4) Accepting a Plea Agreement. If the court accepts the plea agreement, it must inform the defendant that to the extent the plea agreement is of the type specified in Rule 11(c)(1)(A) or (C), the agreed disposition will be included in the judgment.

(5) Rejecting a Plea Agreement. If the court rejects a plea agreement containing provisions of the type specified in Rule 11(c)(1)(A) or (C), the court must do the following on the record and in open court (or, for good cause, in camera):

    (A) inform the parties that the court rejects the plea agreement;

    (B) advise the defendant personally that the court is not required to follow the plea agreement and give the defendant an opportunity to withdraw the plea; and

    (C) advise the defendant personally that if the plea is not withdrawn, the court may dispose of the case less favorably toward the defendant than the plea agreement contemplated.

(d) Withdrawing a Guilty or Nolo Contendere Plea. A defendant may withdraw a plea of guilty or nolo contendere:

    (1) before the court accepts the plea, for any reason or no reason; or

    (2) after the court accepts the plea, but before it imposes sentence if:

        (A) the court rejects a plea agreement under Rule 11(c)(5); or

        (B) the defendant can show a fair and just reason for requesting the withdrawal.

(e) Finality of a Guilty or Nolo Contendere Plea. After the court imposes sentence, the defendant may not withdraw a plea of guilty or nolo contendere, and the plea may be set aside only on direct appeal or collateral attack.

(f) Admissibility or Inadmissibility of a Plea, Plea Discussions, and Related Statements. The admissibility or inadmissibility of a plea, a plea discussion, and any related statement is governed by Federal Rule of Evidence 410.

(g) Recording the Proceedings. The proceedings during which the defendant enters a plea must be recorded by a court reporter or by a suitable recording device. If there is a guilty plea or a nolo contendere plea, the record must include the inquiries and advice to the defendant required under Rule 11(b) and (c).

(h) Harmless Error. A variance from the requirements of this rule is harmless error if it does not affect substantial rights.

(As amended Feb. 28, 1966, eff. July 1, 1966; Apr. 22, 1974, eff. Dec. 1, 1975; Pub. L. 94–64, §3(5)–(10), July 31, 1975, 89 Stat. 371, 372; Apr. 30, 1979, eff. Aug. 1, 1979, and Dec. 1, 1980; Apr. 28, 1982, eff. Aug. 1, 1982; Apr. 28, 1983, eff. Aug. 1, 1983; Apr. 29, 1985, eff. Aug. 1, 1985; Mar. 9, 1987, eff. Aug. 1, 1987; Pub. L. 100–690, title VII, §7076, Nov. 18, 1988, 102 Stat. 4406; Apr. 25, 1989, eff. Dec. 1, 1989; Apr. 26, 1999, eff. Dec. 1, 1999; Apr. 29, 2002, eff. Dec. 1, 2002; Apr. 30, 2007, eff. Dec. 1, 2007; Apr. 16, 2013, eff. Dec. 1, 2013.)

NOTES OF ADVISORY COMMITTEE ON RULES—1944

1. This rule is substantially a restatement of existing law and practice, 18 U.S.C. [former] 564 (Standing mute); Fogus v. United States, 34 F.2d 97 (C.C.A. 4th) (duty of court to ascertain that plea of guilty is intelligently and voluntarily made).

2. The plea of nolo contendere has always existed in the Federal courts, Hudson v. United States, 272 U.S. 451; United States v. Norris, 281 U.S. 619. The use of the plea is recognized by the Probation Act, 18 U.S.C. 724 [now 3651]. While at times criticized as theoretically lacking in logical basis, experience has shown that it performs a useful function from a practical standpoint.

NOTES OF ADVISORY COMMITTEE ON RULES—1966 AMENDMENT

The great majority of all defendants against whom indictments or informations are filed in the federal courts plead guilty. Only a comparatively small number go to trial. See United States Attorneys Statistical Report, Fiscal Year 1964, p. 1. The fairness and adequacy of the procedures on acceptance of pleas of guilty are of vital importance in according equal justice to all in the federal courts.

Three changes are made in the second sentence. The first change makes it clear that before accepting either a plea of guilty or nolo contendere the court must determine that the plea is made voluntarily with understanding of the nature of the charge. The second change expressly requires the court to address the defendant personally in the course of determining that the plea is made voluntarily and with understanding of the nature of the charge. The reported cases reflect some confusion over this matter. Compare United States v. Diggs, 304 F.2d 929 (6th Cir. 1962); Domenica v. United States, 292 F.2d 483 (1st Cir. 1961); Gundlach v. United States, 262 F.2d 72 (4th Cir. 1958), cert. den., 360 U.S. 904 (1959); and Julian v. United States, 236 F.2d 155 (6th Cir. 1956), which contain the implication that personal interrogation of the defendant is the better practice even when he is represented by counsel, with Meeks v. United States, 298 F.2d 204 (5th Cir. 1962); Nunley v. United States, 294 F.2d 579 (10th Cir. 1961), cert. den., 368 U.S. 991 (1962); and United States v. Von der Heide, 169 F.Supp. 560 (D.D.C. 1959).

The third change in the second sentence adds the words "and the consequences of his plea" to state what clearly is the law. See, e.g., Von Moltke v. Gillies, 332 U.S. 708, 724 (1948); Kercheval v. United States, 274 U.S. 220, 223 (1927); Munich v. United States, 337 F.2d 356 (9th Cir. 1964); Pilkington v. United States, 315 F.2d 204 (4th Cir. 1963); Smith v. United States, 324 F.2d 436 (D.C. Cir. 1963); but cf. Marvel v. United States, 335 F.2d 101 (5th Cir. 1964).

A new sentence is added at the end of the rule to impose a duty on the court in cases where the defendant pleads guilty to satisfy itself that there is a factual basis for the plea before entering judgment. The court should satisfy itself, by inquiry of the defendant or the attorney for the government, or by examining the presentence report, or otherwise, that the conduct which the defendant admits constitutes the offense charged in the indictment or information or an offense included therein to which the defendant has pleaded guilty. Such inquiry should, e.g., protect a defendant who is in the position of pleading voluntarily with an understanding of the nature of the charge but without realizing that his conduct does not actually fall within the charge. For a similar requirement see Mich. Stat. Ann. §28.1058 (1954); Mich. Sup. Ct. Rule 35A; In re Valle, 364 Mich. 471, 110 N.W.2d 673 (1961); People v. Barrows, 358 Mich. 267, 99 N.W.2d 347 (1959); People v. Bumpus, 355 Mich. 374, 94 N.W.2d 854 (1959); People v. Coates, 337 Mich. 56, 59 N.W.2d 83 (1953). See also Stinson v. United States, 316 F.2d 554 (5th Cir. 1963). The normal consequence of a determination that there is not a factual basis for the plea would be for the court to set aside the plea and enter a plea of not guilty.

41

For a variety of reasons it is desirable in some cases to permit entry of judgment upon a plea of nolo contendere without inquiry into the factual basis for the plea. The new third sentence is not, therefore, made applicable to pleas of nolo contendere. It is not intended by this omission to reflect any view upon the effect of a plea of nolo contendere in relation to a plea of guilty. That problem has been dealt with by the courts. See e.g., Lott v. United States, 367 U.S. 421, 426 (1961).

NOTES OF ADVISORY COMMITTEE ON RULES—1974 AMENDMENT

The amendments to rule 11 are designed to achieve two principal objectives:

(1) Subdivision (c) prescribes the advice which the court must give to insure that the defendant who pleads guilty has made an informed plea.

(2) Subdivision (e) provides a plea agreement procedure designed to give recognition to the propriety of plea discussions; to bring the existence of a plea agreement out into the open in court; and to provide methods for court acceptance or rejection of a plea agreement.

Other less basic changes are also made. The changes are discussed in the order in which they appear in the rule.

Subdivision (b) retains the requirement that the defendant obtain the consent of the court in order to plead nolo contendere. It adds that the court shall, in deciding whether to accept the plea, consider the views of the prosecution and of the defense and also the larger public interest in the administration of criminal justice.

Although the plea of nolo contendere has long existed in the federal courts, Hudson v. United States, 272 U.S. 451, 47 S.Ct. 127, 71 L.Ed. 347 (1926), the desirability of the plea has been a subject of disagreement. Compare Lane-Reticker, Nolo Contendere in North Carolina, 34 N.C.L.Rev. 280, 290–291 (1956), with Note. The Nature and Consequences of the Plea of Nolo Contendere, 33 Neb.L.Rev. 428, 434 (1954), favoring the plea. The American Bar Association Project on Standards for Criminal Justice takes the position that "the case for the nolo plea is not strong enough to justify a minimum standard supporting its use," but because "use of the plea contributes in some degree to the avoidance of unnecessary trials" it does not proscribe use of the plea. ABA, Standards Relating to Pleas of Guilty §1.1(a) Commentary at 16 (Approved Draft, 1968).

A plea of nolo contendere is, for purposes of punishment, the same as the plea of guilty. See discussion of the history of the nolo plea in North Carolina v. Alford, 400 U.S. 25, 35–36 n. 8, 91 S.Ct. 160, 27 L.Ed.2d 162 (1970). Note, The Nature and Consequences of the Plea of Nolo Contendere, 33 Neb.L.Rev. 428, 430 (1954). A judgment upon the plea is a conviction and may be used to apply multiple offender statutes. Lenvin and Meyers, Nolo Contendere: Its Nature and Implications, 51 Yale L.J. 1255, 1265 (1942). Unlike a plea of guilty, however, it cannot be used against a defendant as an admission in a subsequent criminal or civil case. 4 Wigmore §1066(4), at 58 (3d ed. 1940, Supp. 1970); Rules of Evidence for United States Courts and Magistrates, rule 803(22) (Nov. 1971). See Lenvin and Meyers, Nolo Contendere: Its Nature and Implications, 51 Yale L.J. 1255 (1942); ABA Standards Relating to Pleas of Guilty §§1.1(a) and (b), Commentary at 15–18 (Approved Draft, 1968).

The factors considered relevant by particular courts in determining whether to permit the plea of nolo contendere vary. Compare United States v. Bagliore, 182 F.Supp. 714, 716 (E.D.N.Y. 1960), where the view is taken that the plea should be rejected unless a compelling reason for acceptance is established, with United States v. Jones, 119 F.Supp. 288, 290 (S.D.Cal. 1954), where the view is taken that the plea should be accepted in the absence of a compelling reason to the contrary.

A defendant who desires to plead nolo contendere will commonly want to avoid pleading guilty because the plea of guilty can be introduced as an admission in subsequent civil litigation. The prosecution may oppose the plea of nolo contendere because it wants a definite resolution of the defendant's guilt or innocence either for correctional purposes or for reasons of subsequent litigation. ABA Standards Relating to Pleas of Guilty §1.1(b) Commentary at 16–18 (Approved Draft, 1968). Under subdivision (b) of the new rule the balancing of the interests is left to the trial judge, who is mandated to take into account the larger public interest in the effective administration of justice.

Subdivision (c) prescribes the advice which the court must give to the defendant as a prerequisite to the acceptance of a plea of guilty. The former rule required that the court determine that the plea was made with "understanding of the nature of the charge and the consequences of the plea." The amendment identifies more specifically what must be explained to the defendant and also codifies, in the rule, the requirements of Boykin v. Alabama, 395 U.S. 238, 89 S.Ct. 1709, 23 L.Ed.2d 274 (1969), which held that a defendant must be apprised of the fact that he relinquishes certain constitutional rights by pleading guilty.

Subdivision (c) retains the requirement that the court address the defendant personally. See McCarthy v. United States, 394 U.S. 459, 466, 89 S.Ct. 1166, 22 L.Ed.2d 418 (1969). There is also an amendment to rule 43 to make clear that a defendant must be in court at the time of the plea.

Subdivision (c)(1) retains the current requirement that the court determine that the defendant understands the nature of the charge. This is a common requirement. See ABA Standards Relating to Pleas of Guilty §1.4(a) (Approved Draft, 1968); Illinois Supreme Court Rule 402(a)(1) (1970), Ill.Rev.Stat. 1973, ch. 110A, §402(a)(1). The method by which the defendant's understanding of the nature of the charge is determined may vary from case to case, depending on the complexity of the circumstances and the particular defendant. In some cases, a judge may do this by reading the indictment and by explaining the elements of the offense to the defendants. Thompson, The Judge's Responsibility on a Plea of Guilty 62 W.Va.L.Rev. 213, 220 (1960); Resolution of Judges of U.S. District Court for D.C., June 24, 1959.

Former rule 11 required the court to inform the defendant of the "consequences of the plea." Subdivision (c)(2) changes this and requires instead that the court inform the defendant of and determine that he understands "the mandatory minimum penalty provided by law, if any, and the maximum possible penalty provided by law for the offense to which the plea is offered." The objective is to insure that a defendant knows what minimum sentence the judge must impose and what maximum sentence the judge may impose. This information is usually readily ascertainable from the face of the statute defining the crime, and thus it is feasible for the judge to know specifically what to tell the defendant. Giving this advice tells a defendant the shortest mandatory sentence and also the longest possible sentence for the offense to which he is pleading guilty.

It has been suggested that it is desirable to inform a defendant of additional consequences which might follow from his plea of guilty. Durant v. United States, 410 F.2d 689 (1st Cir. 1969), held that a defendant must be informed of his ineligibility for parole. Trujillo v. United States, 377 F.2d 266 (5th Cir. 1967), cert. denied 389 U.S. 899, 88 S.Ct. 224, 19 L.Ed.2d 221 (1967), held that advice about eligibility for parole is not required. It has been suggested that a defendant be advised that a jury might find him guilty only of a lesser included offense. C. Wright, Federal Practice and Procedure: Criminal §173 at 374 (1969). See contra Dorrough v. United States, 385 F.2d 887 (5th Cir. 1967). The ABA Standards Relating to Pleas of Guilty §1.4(c)(iii) (Approved Draft, 1968) recommend that the defendant be informed that he may be subject to additional punishment if the offense charged is one for which a different or additional punishment is authorized by reason of the defendant's previous conviction.

Under the rule the judge is not required to inform a defendant about these matters, though a judge is free to do so if he feels a consequence of a plea of guilty in a particular case is likely to be of real significance to the defendant. Currently, certain consequences of a plea of guilty, such as parole eligibility, may be so complicated that it is not feasible to expect a judge to clearly advise the defendant. For example, the judge may impose a sentence under 18 U.S.C. §4202 making the defendant eligible for parole when he has served one third of the judicially imposed maximum; or, under 18 U.S.C. §4208(a)(1), making parole eligibility after a specified period of time less than one third of the maximum; or, under 18 U.S.C. §4208(a)(2), leaving eligibility to the discretion of the parole board. At the time the judge is required to advise the defendant of the consequences of his plea, the judge will usually not have seen the presentence report and thus will have no basis for giving a defendant any very realistic advice as to when he might be eligible for parole. Similar complications exist with regard to other, particularly collateral, consequences of a plea of guilty in a given case.

Subdivisions (c)(3) and (4) specify the constitutional rights that the defendant waives by a plea of guilty or nolo contendere. These subdivisions are designed to satisfy the requirements of understanding waiver set forth in Boykin v. Alabama, 395 U.S. 238, 89 S.Ct. 1709, 23 L.Ed.2d 274 (1969). Subdivision (c)(3) is intended to require

42

that the judge inform the defendant and determine that he understands that he waives his fifth amendment rights. The rule takes the position that the defendant's right not to incriminate himself is best explained in terms of his right to plead not guilty and to persist in that plea if it has already been made. This is language identical to that adopted in Illinois for the same purpose. See Illinois Supreme Court Rule 402(a)(3) (1970), Ill.Rev.Stat. 1973, ch. 110A, §402(a)(3).

Subdivision (c)(4) assumes that a defendant's right to have his guilt proved beyond a reasonable doubt and the right to confront his accusers are best explained by indicating that the right to trial is waived. Specifying that there will be no future trial of any kind makes this fact clear to those defendants who, though knowing they have waived trial by jury, are under the mistaken impression that some kind of trial will follow. Illinois has recently adopted similar language. Illinois Supreme Court Rule 402(a)(4) (1970), Ill.Rev.Stat. 1973, ch. 110A, §402(a)(4). In explaining to a defendant that he waives his right to trial, the judge may want to explain some of the aspects of trial such as the right to confront witnesses, to subpoena witnesses, to testify in his own behalf, or, if he chooses, not to testify. What is required, in this respect, to conform to Boykin is left to future case-law development.

Subdivision (d) retains the requirement that the court determine that a plea of guilty or nolo contendere is voluntary before accepting it. It adds the requirement that the court also inquire whether the defendant's willingness to plead guilty or nolo contendere results from prior plea discussions between the attorney for the government and the defendant or his attorney. See Santobello v. New York, 404 U.S. 257, 261–262, 92 S.Ct. 495, 30 L.Ed.2d 427 (1971): "The plea must, of course, be voluntary and knowing and if it was induced by promises, the essence of those promises must in some way be made known." Subdivisions (d) and (e) afford the court adequate basis for rejecting an improper plea agreement induced by threats or inappropriate promises.

The new rule specifies that the court personally address the defendant in determining the voluntariness of the plea.

By personally interrogating the defendant, not only will the judge be better able to ascertain the plea's voluntariness, but he will also develop a more complete record to support his determination in a subsequent post-conviction attack. * * * Both of these goals are undermined in proportion to the degree the district judge resorts to "assumptions" not based upon recorded responses to his inquiries. McCarthy v. United States, 394 U.S. 459, 466, 467, 89 S.Ct. 1166, 22 L.Ed.2d 418 (1969).

Subdivision (e) provides a plea agreement procedure. In doing so it gives recognition to the propriety of plea discussions and plea agreements provided that they are disclosed in open court and subject to acceptance or rejection by the trial judge.

Although reliable statistical information is limited, one recent estimate indicated that guilty pleas account for the disposition of as many as 95% of all criminal cases. ABA Standards Relating to Pleas of Guilty, pp. 1–2 (Approved Draft, 1968). A substantial number of these are the result of plea discussions. The President's Commission on Law Enforcement and Administration of Justice, Task Force Report: The Courts 9 (1967); D. Newman, Conviction: The Determination of Guilt or Innocence Without Trial 3 (1966); L. Weinreb, Criminal Process 437 (1969); Note, Guilty Plea Bargaining: Compromises by Prosecutors To Secure Guilty Pleas, 112 U.Pa.L.Rev. 865 (1964).

There is increasing acknowledgement of both the inevitability and the propriety of plea agreements. See, e.g., ABA Standards Relating to Pleas of Guilty §3.1 (Approved Draft, 1968); Illinois Supreme Court Rule 402 (1970), Ill.Rev.Stat. 1973, ch. 110A, §402.

In Brady v. United States, 397 U.S. 742, 752–753, 90 S.Ct. 1463, 25 L.Ed.2d 747 (1970), the court said:

Of course, that the prevalence of guilty pleas is explainable does not necessarily validate those pleas or the system which produces them. But we cannot hold that it is unconstitutional for the State to extend a benefit to a defendant who in turn extends a substantial benefit to the State and who demonstrates by his plea that he is ready and willing to admit his crime and to enter the correctional system in a frame of mind that affords hope for success in rehabilitation over a shorter period of time than might otherwise be necessary.

In Santobello v. New York, 404 U.S. 257, 260, 92 S.Ct. 495, 498, 30 L.Ed.2d 427 (1971), the court said:

The disposition of criminal charges by agreement between the prosecutor and the accused, sometimes loosely called "plea bargaining," is an essential component of the administration of justice. Properly administered, it is to be encouraged.

Administratively, the criminal justice system has come to depend upon pleas of guilty and, hence, upon plea discussions. See, e.g., President's Commission on Law Enforcement and Administration of Justice, Task Force Report. The Courts 9 (1967); Note, Guilty Plea Bargaining: Compromises By Prosecutors To Secure Guilty Pleas, 112 U.Pa.L.Rev. 865 (1964). But expediency is not the basis for recognizing the propriety of a plea agreement practice. Properly implemented, a plea agreement procedure is consistent with both effective and just administration of the criminal law. Santobello v. New York, 404 U.S. 257, 92 S.Ct. 495, 30 L.Ed.2d 427. This is the conclusion reached in the ABA Standards Relating to Pleas of Guilty §1.8 (Approved Draft, 1968); the ABA Standards Relating to The Prosecution Function and The Defense Function pp. 243–253 (Approved Draft, 1971); and the ABA Standards Relating to the Function of the Trial Judge, §4.1 (App.Draft, 1972). The Supreme Court of California recently recognized the propriety of plea bargaining. See People v. West, 3 Cal.3d 595, 91 Cal.Rptr. 385, 477 P.2d 409 (1970). A plea agreement procedure has recently been decided in the District of Columbia Court of General Sessions upon the recommendation of the United States Attorney. See 51 F.R.D. 109 (1971).

Where the defendant by his plea aids in insuring prompt and certain application of correctional measures, the proper ends of the criminal justice system are furthered because swift and certain punishment serves the ends of both general deterrence and the rehabilitation of the individual defendant. Cf. Note, The Influence of the Defendant's Plea on Judicial Determination of Sentence, 66 Yale L.J. 204, 211 (1956). Where the defendant has acknowledged his guilt and shown a willingness to assume responsibility for his conduct, it has been thought proper to recognize this in sentencing. See also ALI, Model Penal Code §7.01 (P.O.D. 1962); NPPA Guides for Sentencing (1957). Granting a charge reduction in return for a plea of guilty may give the sentencing judge needed discretion, particularly where the facts of a case do not warrant the harsh consequences of a long mandatory sentence or collateral consequences which are unduly severe. A plea of guilty avoids the necessity of a public trial and may protect the innocent victim of a crime against the trauma of direct and cross-examination.

Finally, a plea agreement may also contribute to the successful prosecution of other more serious offenders. See D. Newman, Conviction: The Determination of Guilt or Innocence Without Trial, chs. 2 and 3 (1966); Note, Guilty Plea Bargaining: Compromises By Prosecutors To Secure Guilty Pleas, 112 U.Pa.L.Rev. 865, 881 (1964).

Where plea discussions and agreements are viewed as proper, it is generally agreed that it is preferable that the fact of the plea agreement be disclosed in open court and its propriety be reviewed by the trial judge.

We have previously recognized plea bargaining as an ineradicable fact. Failure to recognize it tends not to destroy it but to drive it underground. We reiterate what we have said before: that when plea bargaining occurs it ought to be spread on the record [The Bench Book prepared by the Federal Judicial Center for use by United States District Judges now suggests that the defendant be asked by the court "if he believes there is any understanding or if any predictions have been made to him concerning the sentence he will receive." Bench Book for United States District Judges, Federal Judicial Center (1969) at 1.05.3.] and publicly disclosed. United States v. Williams, 407 F.2d 940 (4th Cir. 1969). * * * In the future we think that the district judges should not only make the general inquiry under Rule 11 as to whether the plea of guilty has been coerced or induced by promises, but should specifically inquire of counsel whether plea bargaining has occurred. Logically the general inquiry should elicit information about plea bargaining, but it seldom has in the past. Raines v. United States, 423 F.2d 526, 530 (4th Cir. 1970).

In the past, plea discussions and agreements have occurred in an informal and largely invisible manner. Enker, Perspectives on Plea Bargaining, in President's Commission on Law Enforcement and Administration of Justice, Task Force Report: The Courts 108, 115 (1967). There has often been a ritual of denial that any promises have been made, a ritual in which judges, prosecutors, and defense counsel have participated. ABA Standards Relating to Pleas of Guilty §3.1, Commentary at 60–69 (Approved Draft 1968); Task Force Report: The Courts 9. Consequently, there has been a lack of effective judicial review of the propriety of the agreements, thus increasing the risk of real or apparent unfairness. See ABA Standards Relating to Pleas of Guilty §3.1, Commentary at 60 et seq.; Task Force Report: The Courts 9–13.

The procedure described in subdivision (e) is designed to prevent abuse of plea discussions and agreements by providing appropriate and adequate safeguards.

Subdivision (e)(1) specifies that the "attorney for the government and the attorney for the defendant or the defendant when acting pro se may" participate in plea discussions. The inclusion of "the defendant when acting pro se" is intended to reflect the fact that there are situations in which a defendant insists upon representing himself. It may be desirable that an attorney for the government not enter plea discussions with a defendant personally. If necessary, counsel can be appointed for purposes of plea discussions. (Subdivision (d) makes it mandatory that the court inquire of the defendant whether his plea is the result of plea discussions between him and the attorney for the government. This is intended to enable the court to reject an agreement reached by an unrepresented defendant unless the court is satisfied that acceptance of the agreement adequately protects the rights of the defendant and the interests of justice.) This is substantially the position of the ABA Standards Relating to Pleas of Guilty §3.1(a), Commentary at 65–66 (Approved Draft, 1968). Apparently, it is the practice of most prosecuting attorneys to enter plea discussions only with defendant's counsel. Note, Guilty Plea Bargaining: Compromises By Prosecutors To Secure Guilty Pleas, 112 U.Pa.L.Rev. 865, 904 (1964). Discussions without benefit of counsel increase the likelihood that such discussions may be unfair. Some courts have indicated that plea discussions in the absence of defendant's attorney may be constitutionally prohibited. See Anderson v. North Carolina, 221 F.Supp. 930, 935 (W.D.N.C.1963); Shape v. Sigler, 230 F.Supp. 601, 606 (D.Neb. 1964).

Subdivision (e)(1) is intended to make clear that there are four possible concessions that may be made in a plea agreement. First, the charge may be reduced to a lesser or related offense. Second, the attorney for the government may promise to move for dismissal of other charges. Third, the attorney for the government may agree to recommend or not oppose the imposition of a particular sentence. Fourth, the attorneys for the government and the defense may agree that a given sentence is an appropriate disposition of the case. This is made explicit in subdivision (e)(2) where reference is made to an agreement made "in the expectation that a specific sentence will be imposed." See Note, Guilty Plea Bargaining: Compromises By Prosecutors To Secure Guilty Pleas, 112 U.Pa.L.Rev. 865, 898 (1964).

Subdivision (e)(1) prohibits the court from participating in plea discussions. This is the position of the ABA Standards Relating to Pleas of Guilty §3.3(a) (Approved Draft, 1968).

It has been stated that it is common practice for a judge to participate in plea discussions. See D. Newman, Conviction: The Determination of Guilt or Innocence Without Trial 32–52, 78–104 (1966); Note, Guilty Plea Bargaining: Compromises By Prosecutors To Secure Guilty Pleas, 112 U.Pa.L.Rev. 865, 891, 905 (1964).

There are valid reasons for a judge to avoid involvement in plea discussions. It might lead the defendant to believe that he would not receive a fair trial, were there a trial before the same judge. The risk of not going along with the disposition apparently desired by the judge might induce the defendant to plead guilty, even if innocent. Such involvement makes it difficult for a judge to objectively assess the voluntariness of the plea. See ABA Standards Relating to Pleas of Guilty §3.3(a), Commentary at 72–74 (Approved Draft, 1968); Note, Guilty Plea Bargaining: Compromises By Prosecutors To Secure Guilty Pleas, 112 U.Pa.L.Rev. 865, 891–892 (1964); Comment, Official Inducements to Plead Guilty: Suggested Morals for a Marketplace, 32 U.Chi.L.Rev. 167, 180–183 (1964); Informal Opinion No. 779 ABA Professional Ethics Committee ("A judge should not be a party to advance arrangements for the determination of sentence, whether as a result of a guilty plea or a finding of guilt based on proof."), 51 A.B.A.J. 444 (1965). As has been recently pointed out:

The unequal positions of the judge and the accused, one with the power to commit to prison and the other deeply concerned to avoid prison, as once raise a question of fundamental fairness. When a judge becomes a participant in plea bargaining he brings to bear the full force and majesty of his office. His awesome power to impose a substantially longer or even maximum sentence in excess of that proposed is present whether referred to or not. A defendant needs no reminder that if he rejects the proposal, stands upon his right to trial and is convicted, he faces a significantly longer sentence. United States ex rel. Elksnis v. Gilligan, 256 F.Supp. 244, 254 (S.D.N.Y. 1966).

On the other hand, one commentator has taken the position that the judge may be involved in discussions either after the agreement is reached or to help elicit facts and an agreement. Enker, Perspectives on Plea Bargaining, in President's Commission on Law Enforcement and Administration of Justice, Task Force Report: The Courts 108, 117–118 (1967).

The amendment makes clear that the judge should not participate in plea discussions leading to a plea agreement. It is contemplated that the judge may participate in such discussions as may occur when the plea agreement is disclosed in open court. This is the position of the recently adopted Illinois Supreme Court Rule 402(d)(1) (1970), Ill.Rev.Stat. 1973, ch. 110A, §402(d)(1). As to what may constitute "participation," contrast People v. Earegood, 12 Mich.App. 256, 268–269, 162 N.W.2d 802, 809–810 (1968), with Kruse v. State, 47 Wis.2d 460, 177 N.W.2d 322 (1970).

Subdivision (e)(2) provides that the judge shall require the disclosure of any plea agreement in open court. In People v. West, 3 Cal.3d 595, 91 Cal.Rptr. 385, 477 P.2d 409 (1970), the court said:

[T]he basis of the bargain should be disclosed to the court and incorporated in the record. * * *

Without limiting that court to those we set forth, we note four possible methods of incorporation: (1) the bargain could be stated orally and recorded by the court reporter, whose notes then must be preserved or transcribed; (2) the bargain could be set forth by the clerk in the minutes of the court; (3) the parties could file a written stipulation stating the terms of the bargain; (4) finally, counsel or the court itself may find it useful to prepare and utilize forms for the recordation of plea bargains. 91 Cal.Rptr. 393, 394, 477 P.2d at 417, 418.

The District of Columbia Court of General Sessions is using a "Sentence-Recommendation Agreement" form.

Upon notice of the plea agreement, the court is given the option to accept or reject the agreement or defer its decision until receipt of the presentence report.

The judge may, and often should, defer his decision until he examines the presentence report. This is made possible by rule 32 which allows a judge, with the defendant's consent, to inspect a presentence report to determine whether a plea agreement should be accepted. For a discussion of the use of conditional plea acceptance, see ABA Standards Relating to Pleas of Guilty §3.3(b), Commentary at 74–76, and Supplement, Proposed Revisions §3.3(b) at 2–3 (Approved Draft, 1968); Illinois Supreme Court Rule 402(d)(2) (1970), Ill.Rev.Stat. 1973, ch. 110A, §402(d)(2).

The plea agreement procedure does not attempt to define criteria for the acceptance or rejection of a plea agreement. Such a decision is left to the discretion of the individual trial judge.

Subdivision (e)(3) makes is mandatory, if the court decides to accept the plea agreement, that it inform the defendant that it will embody in the judgment and sentence the disposition provided in the plea agreement, or one more favorable to the defendant. This serves the purpose of informing the defendant immediately that the agreement will be implemented.

Subdivision (e)(4) requires the court, if it rejects the plea agreement, to inform the defendant of this fact and to advise the defendant personally, in open court, that the court is not bound by the plea agreement. The defendant must be afforded an opportunity to withdraw his plea and must be advised that if he persists in his guilty plea or plea of nolo contendere, the disposition of the case may be less favorable to him than that contemplated by the plea agreement. That the defendant should have the opportunity to withdraw his plea if the court rejects the plea agreement is the position taken in ABA Standards Relating to Pleas of Guilty, Supplement, Proposed Revisions §2.1(a)(ii)(5) (Approved Draft, 1968). Such a rule has been adopted in Illinois. Illinois Supreme Court Rule 402(d)(2) (1970), Ill.Rev.Stat. 1973, ch. 110A, §402(d)(2).

If the court rejects the plea agreement and affords the defendant the opportunity to withdraw the plea, the court is not precluded from accepting a guilty plea from the same defendant at a later time, when such plea conforms to the requirements of rule 11.

Subdivision (e)(5) makes it mandatory that, except for good cause shown, the court be notified of the existence of a plea agreement at the arraignment or at another time prior to trial fixed by the court. Having a plea entered at this stage provides a reasonable time for the defendant to consult with counsel and for counsel to complete any plea discussions with the attorney for the government. ABA Standards Relating to Pleas of Guilty §1.3 (Approved Draft, 1968). The objective of the provision is to make clear that the court has authority to require a plea agreement to be disclosed sufficiently in advance of trial so as not to interfere with the efficient scheduling of criminal cases.

Subdivision (e)(6) is taken from rule 410, Rules of Evidence for United States Courts and Magistrates (Nov. 1971). See Advisory Committee Note thereto. See also the ABA Standards Relating to Pleas of Guilty §2.2 (Approved Draft, 1968); Illinois Supreme Court Rule 402(f) (1970), Ill.Rev.Stat. 1973, ch. 110A, §402(f).

Subdivision (f) retains the requirement of old rule 11 that the court should not enter judgment upon a plea of guilty without making such an inquiry as will satisfy it that there is a factual basis for the plea. The draft does not specify that any particular type of inquiry be made. See Santobello v. New York, 404 U.S. 257, 261, 92 S.Ct. 495, 30 L.Ed.2d 427 (1971); "Fed.Rule Crim.Proc. 11, governing pleas in federal courts, now makes clear that the sentencing judge must develop, on the record, the factual basis for the plea, as, for example, by having the accused describe the conduct that gave rise to the charge." An inquiry might be made of the defendant, of the attorneys for the government and the defense, of the presentence report when one is available, or by whatever means is appropriate in a specific case. This is the position of the ABA Standards Relating to Pleas of Guilty §1.6 (Approved Draft, 1968). Where inquiry is made of the defendant himself it may be desirable practice to place the defendant under oath. With regard to a determination that there is a factual basis for a plea of guilty to a "lessor or related offense," compare ABA Standards Relating to Pleas of Guilty §3.1(b)(ii), Commentary at 67–68 (Approved Draft, 1968), with ALI, Model Penal Code §1.07(5) (P.O.D. 1962). The rule does not speak directly to the issue of whether a judge may accept a plea of guilty where there is a factual basis for the plea but the defendant asserts his innocence. North Carolina v. Alford, 400 U.S. 25, 91 S.Ct. 160, 27 L.Ed.2d 162 (1970). The procedure in such case would seem to be to deal with this as a plea of nolo contendere, the acceptance of which would depend upon the judge's decision as to whether acceptance of the plea is consistent with "the interest of the public in the effective administration of justice" [new rule 11(b)]. The defendant who asserts his innocence while pleading guilty or nolo contendere is often difficult to deal with in a correctional setting, and it may therefore be preferable to resolve the issue of guilt or innocence at the trial stage rather than leaving that issue unresolved, thus complicating subsequent correctional decisions. The rule is intended to make clear that a judge may reject a plea of nolo contendere and require the defendant either to plead not guilty or to plead guilty under circumstances in which the judge is able to determine that the defendant is in fact guilty of the crime to which he is pleading guilty.

Subdivision (g) requires that a verbatim record be kept of the proceedings. If there is a plea of guilty or nolo contendere, the record must include, without limitation, the court's advice to the defendant, the inquiry into the voluntariness of the plea and the plea agreement, and the inquiry into the accuracy of the plea. Such a record is important in the event of a postconviction attack. ABA Standards Relating to Pleas of Guilty §1.7 (Approved Draft, 1968). A similar requirement was adopted in Illinois: Illinois Supreme Court Rule 402(e) (1970), Ill.Rev.Stat. 1973, ch. 110A, §402(e).

NOTES OF COMMITTEE ON THE JUDICIARY, HOUSE REPORT NO. 94-247; 1975 AMENDMENT

A. Amendments Proposed by the Supreme Court. Rule 11 of the Federal Rules of Criminal Procedure deals with pleas. The Supreme Court has proposed to amend this rule extensively.

Rule 11 provides that a defendant may plead guilty, not guilty, or nolo contendere. The Supreme Court's amendments to Rule 11(b) provide that a nolo contendere plea "shall be accepted by the court only after due consideration of the views of the parties and the interest of the public in the effective administration of justice."

The Supreme Court amendments to Rule 11(c) spell out the advise that the court must give to the defendant before accepting the defendant's plea of guilty or nolo contendere. The Supreme Court amendments to Rule 11(d) set forth the steps that the court must take to insure that a guilty or nolo contendere plea has been voluntarily made.

The Supreme Court amendments to Rule 11(e) establish a plea agreement procedure. This procedure permits the parties to discuss disposing of a case without a trial and sets forth the type of agreements that the parties can reach concerning the disposition of the case. The procedure is not mandatory; a court is free not to permit the parties to present plea agreements to it.

The Supreme Court amendments to Rule 11(f) require that the court, before entering judgment upon a plea of guilty, satisfy itself that "there is a factual basis for the plea." The Supreme Court amendments to Rule 11(g) require that a verbatim record be kept of the proceedings at which the defendant enters a plea.

B. Committee Action. The proposed amendments to Rule 11, particularly those relating to the plea negotiating procedure, have generated much comment and criticism. No observer is entirely happy that our criminal justice system must rely to the extent it does on negotiated dispositions of cases. However, crowded court dockets make plea negotiating a fact that the Federal Rules of Criminal Procedure should contend with. The Committee accepts the basic structure and provisions of Rule 11(e).

Rule 11(e) as proposed permits each federal court to decide for itself the extent to which it will permit plea negotiations to be carried on within its own jurisdiction. No court is compelled to permit any plea negotiations at all. Proposed Rule 11(e) regulates plea negotiations and agreements if, and to the extent that, the court permits such negotiations and agreements. [Proposed Rule 11(e) has been criticized by some federal judges who read it to mandate the court to permit plea negotiations and the reaching of plea agreements. The Advisory Committee stressed during its testimony that the rule does not mandate that a court permit any form of plea agreement to be presented to it. See, e.g., the remarks of United States Circuit Judge William H. Webster in Hearings II, at 196. See also the exchange of correspondence between Judge Webster and United States District Judge Frank A. Kaufman in Hearings II, at 289–90.]

Proposed Rule 11(e) contemplates 4 different types of plea agreements. First, the defendant can plead guilty or nolo contendere in return for the prosecutor's reducing the charge to a less serious offense. Second, the defendant can plead guilty or nolo contendere in return for the prosecutor dropping, or not bringing, a charge or charges relating to other offenses. Third, the defendant can plead guilty or nolo contendere in return for the prosecutor's recommending a sentence. Fourth, the defendant and prosecutor can agree that a particular sentence is the appropriate disposition of the case. [It is apparent, though not explicitly stated, that Rule 11(e) contemplates that the plea agreement may bind the defendant to do more than just plead guilty or nolo contendere. For example, the plea agreement may bind the defendant to cooperate with the prosecution in a different investigation. The Committee intends by its approval of Rule 11(e) to permit the parties to agree on such terms in a plea agreement.]

The Committee added language in subdivisions (e)(2) and (e)(4) to permit a plea agreement to be disclosed to the court, or rejected by it, in camera. There must be a showing of good cause before the court can conduct such proceedings in camera. The language does not address itself to whether the showing of good cause may be made in open court or in camera. That issue is left for the courts to resolve on a case-by-case basis. These changes in subdivisions (e)(2) and (e)(4) will permit a fair trial when there is substantial media interest in a case and the court is rejecting a plea agreement.

The Committee added an exception to subdivision (e)(6). That subdivision provides:

> Evidence of a plea of guilty, later withdrawn, or a plea of nolo contendere, or of an offer to plead guilty or nolo contendere to the crime charged or any other crime, or of statements made in connection with any of the foregoing pleas or offers, is not admissible in any civil or criminal proceeding against the person who made the plea or offer.

The Committee's exception permits the use of such evidence in a perjury or false statement prosecution where the plea, offer, or related statement was made by the defendant on the record, under oath and in the presence of counsel. The Committee recognizes that even this limited exception may discourage defendants from being completely candid and open during plea negotiations and may even result in discouraging the reaching of plea agreements. However, the Committee believes that, on balance, it is more important to protect the integrity of the judicial process from willful deceit and untruthfulness. [The Committee does not intend its language to be construed as mandating or encouraging the swearing-in of the defendant during proceedings in connection with the disclosure and acceptance or rejection of a plea agreement.]

The Committee recast the language of Rule 11(c), which deals with the advice given to a defendant before the court can accept his plea of guilty or nolo contendere. The Committee acted in part because it believed that the warnings given to the defendant ought to include those that Boykin v. Alabama, 395 U.S. 238 (1969), said were constitutionally required. In addition, and as a result of its change in subdivision (e)(6), the Committee thought if only fair that the defendant be warned that his plea of guilty (later withdrawn) or nolo contendere, or his offer of either plea, or his statements made in connection with such pleas or offers, could later be used against him in a perjury trial if made under oath, on the record, and in the presence of counsel.

NOTES OF CONFERENCE COMMITTEE, HOUSE REPORT NO. 94–414; 1975 AMENDMENT

Note to subdivision (c). Rule 11(c) enumerates certain things that a judge must tell a defendant before the judge can accept that defendant's plea of guilty or nolo contendere. The House version expands upon the list originally proposed by the Supreme Court. The Senate version adopts the Supreme Court's proposal.

The Conference adopts the House provision.

Note to subdivision (e)(1). Rule 11(e)(1) outlines some general considerations concerning the plea agreement procedure. The Senate version makes nonsubstantive change in the House version.

The Conference adopts the Senate provision.

Note to subdivision (e)(6). Rule 11(e)(6) deals with the use of statements made in connection with plea agreements. The House version permits a limited use of pleas of guilty, later withdrawn, or nolo contendere, offers of such pleas, and statements made in connection with such pleas or offers. Such evidence can be used in a perjury or false statement prosecution if the plea, offer, or related statement was made under oath, on the record, and in the presence of counsel. The Senate version permits evidence of voluntary and reliable statements made in court on the record to be used for the purpose of impeaching the credibility of the declarant or in a perjury or false statement prosecution.

The Conference adopts the House version with changes. The Conference agrees that neither a plea nor the offer of a plea ought to be admissible for any purpose. The Conference-adopted provision, therefore, like the Senate provision, permits only the use of statements made in connection with a plea of guilty, later withdrawn, or a plea of nolo contendere, or in connection with an offer of a guilty or nolo contendere plea.

NOTES OF ADVISORY COMMITTEE ON RULES——1979 AMENDMENT

Note to Subdivision (e)(2). The amendment to rule 11(e)(2) is intended to clarify the circumstances in which the court may accept or reject a plea agreement, with the consequences specified in subdivision (e)(3) and (4). The present language has been the cause of some confusion and has led to results which are not entirely consistent. Compare United States v. Sarubbi, 416 F.Supp. 633 (D. N.J. 1976); with United States v. Hull, 413 F.Supp. 145 (E.D. Tenn. 1976).

Rule 11(e)(1) specifies three types of plea agreements, namely, those in which the attorney for the government might

(A) move for dismissal of other charges; or

(B) make a recommendation, or agree not to oppose the defendant's request, for a particular sentence, with the understanding that such recommendation or request shall not be binding upon the court; or

(C) agree that a specific sentence is the appropriate disposition of the case.

A (B) type of plea agreement is clearly of a different order than the other two, for an agreement to recommend or not to oppose is discharged when the prosecutor performs as he agreed to do. By comparison, critical to a type (A) or (C) agreement is that the defendant receive the contemplated charge dismissal or agreed-to sentence. Consequently, there must ultimately be an acceptance or rejection by the court of a type (A) or (C) agreement so that it may be determined whether the defendant shall receive the bargained-for concessions or shall instead be afforded an opportunity to withdraw his plea. But this is not so as to a type (B) agreement; there is no "disposition provided for" in such a plea agreement so as to make the acceptance provisions of subdivision (e)(3) applicable, nor is there a need for rejection with opportunity for withdrawal under subdivision (e)(4) in light of the fact that the defendant knew the nonbinding character of the recommendation or request. United States v. Henderson, 565 F.2d 1119 (9th Cir. 1977); United States v. Savage, 561 F.2d 554 (4th Cir. 1977).

Because a type (B) agreement is distinguishable from the others in that it involves only a recommendation or request not binding upon the court, it is important that the defendant be aware that this is the nature of the agreement into which he has entered. The procedure contemplated by the last sentence of amended subdivision (e)(2) will establish for the record that there is such awareness. This provision conforms to ABA Standards Relating to Pleas of Guilty §1.5 (Approved Draft, 1968), which provides that "the court must advise the defendant personally that the recommendations of the prosecuting attorney are not binding on the court."

Sometimes a plea agreement will be partially but not entirely of the (B) type, as where a defendant, charged with counts 1, 2 and 3, enters into an agreement with the attorney for the government wherein it is agreed that if defendant pleads guilty to count 1, the prosecutor will recommend a certain sentence as to that count and will move for dismissal of counts 2 and 3. In such a case, the court must take particular care to ensure that the defendant understands which components of the agreement involve only a (B) type recommendation and which do not. In the above illustration, that part of the agreement which contemplates the dismissal of counts 2 and 3 is an (A) type agreement, and thus under rule 11(e) the court must either accept the agreement to dismiss these counts or else reject it and allow the defendant to withdraw his plea. If rejected, the defendant must be allowed to withdraw the plea on count 1 even if the type (B) promise to recommend a certain sentence on that count is kept, for a multi-faceted plea agreement is nonetheless a single agreement. On the other hand, if counts 2 and 3 are dismissed and the sentence recommendation is made, then the defendant is not entitled to withdraw his plea even if the sentence recommendation is not accepted by the court, for the defendant received all he was entitled to under the various components of the plea agreement.

Note to Subdivision (e)(6). The major objective of the amendment to rule 11(e)(6) is to describe more precisely, consistent with the original purpose of the provision, what evidence relating to pleas or plea discussions is inadmissible. The present language is susceptible to interpretation which would make it applicable to a wide variety of statements made under various circumstances other than within the context of those plea discussions authorized by rule 11(e) and intended to be protected by subdivision (e)(6) of the rule. See United States v. Herman, 544 F.2d 791 (5th Cir. 1977), discussed herein.

Fed.R.Ev. 410, as originally adopted by Pub. L. 93–595, provided in part that "evidence of a plea of guilty, later withdrawn, or a plea of nolo contendere, or of an offer to plead guilty or nolo contendere to the crime charged or any other crime, or of statements made in connection with any of the foregoing pleas or offers, is not admissible in any civil or criminal action, case, or proceeding against the person who made the plea or offer." (This rule was adopted with the proviso that it "shall be superseded by any amendment to the Federal Rules of Criminal Procedure which is inconsistent with this rule.") As the Advisory Committee Note explained: "Exclusion of offers to plead guilty or nolo has as its purpose the promotion of disposition of criminal cases by compromise." The amendment of Fed.R.Crim.P. 11, transmitted to Congress by the Supreme Court in April 1974, contained a subdivision (e)(6) essentially identical to the rule 410 language quoted above, as a part of a substantial revision of rule 11. The most significant feature of this revision was the express recognition given to the fact that the "attorney for the government and the attorney for the defendant or the defendant when acting pro se may engage in discussions with a view toward reaching" a plea agreement. Subdivision (e)(6) was intended to encourage such discussions. As noted in H.R.Rep. No. 94–247, 94th Cong., 1st Sess. 7 (1975), the purpose of subdivision (e)(6) is to not "discourage defendants from being completely candid and open during plea negotiations." Similarly, H.R.Rep. No. 94–414, 94th Cong., 1st Sess. 10 (1975), states that "Rule 11(e)(6) deals with the use of statements made in connection with plea agreements." (Rule 11(e)(6) was thereafter enacted, with the addition of the proviso allowing use of statements in a prosecution for perjury, and with the qualification that the inadmissible statements must also be "relevant to" the inadmissible pleas or offers. Pub. L. 94–64; Fed.R.Ev. 410 was then amended to conform. Pub. L. 94–149.)

While this history shows that the purpose of Fed.R.Ev. 410 and Fed.R.Crim.P. 11(e)(6) is to permit the unrestrained candor which produces effective plea discussions between the "attorney for the government and the attorney for the defendant or the defendant when acting pro se," given visibility and sanction in rule 11(e), a literal reading of the language of these two rules could reasonably lead to the conclusion that a broader rule of inadmissibility obtains. That is, because "statements" are generally inadmissible if "made in connection with, and relevant to" an "offer to plead guilty," it might be thought that an otherwise voluntary admission to law enforcement officials is rendered inadmissible merely because it was made in the hope of obtaining leniency by a plea. Some decisions interpreting rule 11(e)(6) point in this direction. See United States v. Herman, 544 F.2d 791 (5th Cir. 1977) (defendant in custody of two postal inspectors during continuance of removal hearing instigated conversation with them and at some point said he would plead guilty to armed robbery if the murder charge was dropped; one inspector stated they were not "in position" to make any deals in this regard; held, defendant's statement inadmissible under rule 11(e)(6) because the defendant "made the statements during the course of a conversation in which he sought concessions from the government in return for a guilty plea"); United States v. Brooks, 536 F.2d 1137 (6th Cir. 1976) (defendant telephoned postal inspector and offered to plead guilty if he got 2-year maximum; statement inadmissible).

The amendment makes inadmissible statements made "in the course of any proceedings under this rule regarding" either a plea of guilty later withdrawn or a plea of nolo contendere, and also statements "made in the course of plea discussions with an attorney for the government which do not result in a plea of guilty or which result in a plea of guilty later withdrawn." It is not limited to statements by the defendant himself, and thus would cover statements by defense counsel regarding defendant's incriminating admissions to him. It thus fully protects the plea discussion process authorized by rule 11 without attempting to deal with confrontations between suspects and law enforcement agents, which involve problems of quite different dimensions. See, e.g., ALI Model Code of Pre-Arraignment Procedure, art. 140 and §150.2(8) (Proposed Official Draft, 1975) (latter section requires exclusion if "a law enforcement officer induces any person to make a statement by promising leniency"). This change, it must be emphasized, does not compel the conclusion that statements made to law enforcement agents, especially when the agents purport to have authority to bargain, are inevitably admissible. Rather, the point is that such cases are not covered by the per se rule of 11(e)(6) and thus must be resolved by that body of law dealing with police interrogations.

If there has been a plea of guilty later withdrawn or a plea of nolo contendere, subdivision (e)(6)(C) makes inadmissible statements made "in the course of any proceedings under this rule" regarding such pleas. This includes, for example, admissions by the defendant when he makes his plea in court pursuant to rule 11 and also admissions made to provide the factual basis pursuant to subdivision (f). However, subdivision (e)(6)(C) is not limited to statements made in court. If the court were to defer its decision on a plea agreement pending examination of the presentence report, as authorized by subdivision (e)(2), statements made to the probation officer in connection with the preparation of that report would come within this provision.

This amendment is fully consistent with all recent and major law reform efforts on this subject. ALI Model Code of Pre-Arraignment Procedure §350.7 (Proposed Official Draft, 1975), and ABA Standards Relating to Pleas of Guilty §3.4 (Approved Draft, 1968) both provide:

Unless the defendant subsequently enters a plea of guilty or nolo contendere which is not withdrawn, the fact that the defendant or his counsel and the prosecuting attorney engaged in plea discussions or made a plea agreement should not be received in evidence against or in favor of the defendant in any criminal or civil action or administrative proceedings.

The Commentary to the latter states:

The above standard is limited to discussions and agreements with the prosecuting attorney. Sometimes defendants will indicate to the police their willingness to bargain, and in such instances these statements are sometimes admitted in court against the defendant. State v. Christian, 245 S.W.2d 895 (Mo.1952). If the police initiate this kind of discussion, this may have some bearing on the admissibility of the defendant's statement. However, the policy considerations relevant to this issue are better dealt with in the context of standards governing in-custody interrogation by the police.

Similarly, Unif.R.Crim.P. 441(d) (Approved Draft, 1974), provides that except under limited circumstances "no discussion between the parties or statement by the defendant or his lawyer under this Rule," i.e., the rule providing "the parties may meet to discuss the possibility of pretrial diversion * * * or of a plea agreement," are admissible. The amendment is likewise consistent with the typical state provision on this subject; see, e.g., Ill.S.Ct. Rule 402(f).

The language of the amendment identifies with more precision than the present language the necessary relationship between the statements and the plea or discussion. See the dispute between the majority and concurring opinions in United States v. Herman, 544 F.2d 791 (5th Cir. 1977), concerning the meanings and effect of the phrases "connection to" and "relevant to" in the present rule. Moreover, by relating the statements to "plea discussions" rather than "an offer to plead," the amendment ensures "that even an attempt to open plea bargaining [is] covered under the same rule of inadmissibility." United States v. Brooks, 536 F.2d 1137 (6th Cir. 1976).

The last sentence of Rule 11(e)(6) is amended to provide a second exception to the general rule of nonadmissibility of the described statements. Under the amendment, such a statement is also admissible "in any proceeding wherein another statement made in the course of the same plea or plea discussions has been introduced and the statement ought in fairness be considered contemporaneously with it." This change is necessary so that, when evidence of statements made in the course of or as a consequence of a certain plea or plea discussions are introduced under circumstances not prohibited by this rule (e.g., not "against" the person who made the plea), other statements relating to the same plea or plea discussions may also be admitted when relevant to the matter at issue. For example, if a defendant upon a motion to dismiss a prosecution on some ground were able to admit certain statements made in aborted plea discussions in his favor, then other relevant statements made in the same plea discussions should be admissible against the defendant in the interest of determining the truth of the matter at issue. The language of the amendment follows closely that in Fed.R.Evid. 106, as the considerations involved are very similar.

The phrase "in any civil or criminal proceeding" has been moved from its present position, following the word "against," for purposes of clarity. An ambiguity presently exists because the word "against" may be read as referring either to the kind of proceeding in which the evidence is offered or the purpose for which it is offered. The change makes it clear that the latter construction is correct. No change is intended with respect to provisions making evidence rules inapplicable in certain situations. See, e.g., Fed.R.Evid. 104(a) and 1101(d).

Unlike ABA Standards Relating to Pleas of Guilty §3.4 (Approved Draft, 1968), and ALI Model Code of Pre-Arraignment Procedure §350.7 (Proposed Official Draft, 1975), rule 11(e)(6) does not also provide that the described evidence is inadmissible "in favor of" the defendant. This is not intended to suggest, however, that such evidence will inevitably be admissible in the defendant's favor. Specifically, no disapproval is intended of such decisions as United States v. Verdoorn, 528 F.2d 103 (8th Cir. 1976), holding that the trial judge properly refused to permit the defendants to put into evidence at their trial the fact the prosecution had attempted to plea bargain with them, as "meaningful dialogue between the parties would, as a practical matter, be impossible if either party had to assume the risk that plea offers would be admissible in evidence."

NOTES OF ADVISORY COMMITTEE ON RULES——1982 AMENDMENT

Note to Subdivision (c)(1). Subdivision (c)(1) has been amended by specifying "the effect of any special parole term" as one of the matters about which a defendant who has tendered a plea of guilty or nolo contendere is to be advised by the court. This amendment does not make any change in the law, as the courts are in agreement that such advice is presently required by Rule 11. See, e.g., Moore v. United States, 592 F.2d 753 (4th Cir. 1979); United States v. Eaton, 579 F.2d 1181 (10th Cir. 1978); Richardson v. United States, 577 F.2d 447 (8th Cir. 1978); United States v. Del Prete, 567 F.2d 928 (9th Cir. 1978); United States v. Watson, 548 F.2d 1058 (D.C.Cir. 1977); United States v. Crusco, 536 F.2d 21 (2d Cir. 1976); United States v. Yazbeck, 524 F.2d 641 (1st Cir. 1975); United States v. Wolak, 510 F.2d 164 (6th Cir. 1975). In United States v. Timmreck, 441 U.S. 780 (1979), 99 S.Ct. 2085, 60 L.Ed.2d 634 (1979), the Supreme Court assumed that the judge's failure in that case to describe the mandatory special parole term constituted "a failure to comply with the formal requirements of the Rule."

The purpose of the amendment is to draw more specific attention to the fact that advice concerning special parole terms is a necessary part of Rule 11 procedure. As noted in Moore v. United States, supra:

Special parole is a significant penalty. * * * Unlike ordinary parole, which does not involve supervision beyond the original prison term set by the court and the violation of which cannot lead to confinement beyond that sentence, special parole increases the possible period of confinement. It entails the possibility that a defendant may have to serve his original sentence plus a substantial additional period, without credit for time spent on parole. Explanation of special parole in open court is therefore essential to comply with the Rule's mandate that the defendant be informed of "the maximum possible penalty provided by law."

As the aforecited cases indicate, in the absence of specification of the requirement in the rule it has sometimes happened that such advice has been inadvertently omitted from Rule 11 warnings.

The amendment does not attempt to enumerate all of the characteristics of the special parole term which the judge ought to bring to the defendant's attention. Some flexibility in this respect must be preserved although it is well to note that the unique characteristics of this kind of parole are such that they may not be readily perceived by laymen. Moore v. United States supra, recommends that in an appropriate case the judge

inform the defendant and determine that he understands the following:
> (1) that a special parole term will be added to any prison sentence he receives;
> (2) the minimum length of the special parole term that must be imposed and the absence of a statutory maximum;
> (3) that special parole is entirely different from——and in addition to——ordinary parole; and
> (4) that if the special parole is violated, the defendant can be returned to prison for the remainder of his sentence and the full length of his special parole term.

The amendment should not be read as meaning that a failure to comply with this particular requirement will inevitably entitle the defendant to relief. See United States v. Timmreck, supra. Likewise, the amendment makes no change in the existing law to the effect

that many aspects of traditional parole need not be communicated to the defendant by the trial judge under the umbrella of Rule 11. For example, a defendant need not be advised of all conceivable consequences such as when he may be considered for parole or that, if he violates his parole, he will again be imprisoned. Bunker v. Wise, 550 F.2d 1155, 1158 (9th Cir. 1977).

Note to Subdivision (c)(4). The amendment to subdivision (c)(4) is intended to overcome the present conflict between the introductory language of subdivision (c), which contemplates the advice being given "[b]efore accepting a plea of guilty or nolo contendere," and thus presumably after the plea has been tendered, and the "if he pleads" language of subdivision (c)(4) which suggests the plea has not been tendered.

As noted by Judge Doyle in United States v. Sinagub, 468 F.Supp. 353 (W.D.Wis.1979):

Taken literally, this wording of subsection (4) of 11(c) suggests that before eliciting any plea at an arraignment, the court is required to insure that a defendant understands that if he or she pleads guilty or nolo contendere, the defendant will be waiving the right to trial. Under subsection (3) of 11(c), however, there is no requirement that at this pre-plea stage, the court must insure that the defendant understands that he or she enjoys the right to a trial and, at trial, the right to the assistance of counsel, the right to confront and cross-examine witnesses against him or her, and the right not to be compelled to incriminate himself or herself. It would be incongruous to require that at the pre-plea stage the court insure that the defendant understands that if he enters a plea of guilty or nolo contendere he will be waiving a right, the existence and nature of which need not be explained until after such a plea has been entered. I conclude that the insertion of the words "that if he pleads guilty or nolo contendere," as they appear in subsection (4) of 11(c), was an accident of draftsmanship which occurred in the course of Congressional rewriting of 11(c) as it has been approved by the Supreme Court. Those words are to be construed consistently with the words "Before accepting a plea of guilty or nolo contendere," as they appear in the opening language of 11(c), and consistently with the omission of the words "that if he pleads" from subsections (1), (2), and (3) of 11(c). That is, as they appear in subsection (4) of 11(c), the words, "that if he pleads guilty or nolo contendere" should be construed to mean "that if his plea of guilty or nolo contendere is accepted by the court."

Although this is a very logical interpretation of the present language, the amendment will avoid the necessity to engage in such analysis in order to determine the true meaning of subdivision (c)(4).

Note to Subdivision (c)(5). Subdivision (c)(5), in its present form, may easily be read as contemplating that in every case in which a plea of guilty or nolo contendere is tendered, warnings must be given about the possible use of defendant's statements, obtained under oath, on the record and in the presence of counsel, in a later prosecution for perjury or false statement. The language has prompted some courts to reach the remarkable result that a defendant who pleads guilty or nolo contendere without receiving those warnings must be allowed to overturn his plea on appeal even though he was never questioned under oath, on the record, in the presence of counsel about the offense to which he pleaded. United States v. Artis, No. 78–5012 (4th Cir. March 12, 1979); United States v. Boone, 543 F.2d 1090 (4th Cir. 1976). Compare United States v. Michaelson, 552 F.2d 472 (2d Cir. 1977) (failure to give subdivision (c)(5) warnings not a basis for reversal, "at least when, as here, defendant was not put under oath before questioning about his guilty plea"). The present language of subdivision (c)(5) may also have contributed to the conclusion, not otherwise supported by the rule, that "Rule 11 requires that the defendant be under oath for the entirety of the proceedings" conducted pursuant to that rule and that failure to place the defendant under oath would itself make necessary overturning the plea on appeal. United States v. Aldridge, 553 F.2d 922 (5th Cir. 1977).

When questioning of the kind described in subdivision (c)(5) is not contemplated by the judge who is receiving the plea, no purpose is served by giving the (c)(5) warnings, which in such circumstances can only confuse the defendant and detract from the force of the other warnings required by Rule 11. As correctly noted in United States v. Sinagub, supra,

subsection (5) of section (c) of Rule 11 is qualitatively distinct from the other sections of the Rule. It does not go to whether the plea is knowingly or voluntarily made, nor to whether the plea should be accepted and judgment entered. Rather, it does go to the possible consequences of an event which may or may not occur during the course of the arraignment hearing itself, namely, the administration of an oath to the defendant. Whether this event is to occur is wholly within the control of the presiding judge. If the event is not to occur, it is pointless to inform the defendant of its consequences. If a presiding judge intends that an oath not be administered to a defendant during an arraignment hearing, but alters that intention at some point, only then would the need arise to inform the defendant of the possible consequences of the administration of the oath.

The amendment to subdivision (c)(5) is intended to make it clear that this is the case.

The amendment limits the circumstances in which the warnings must be given, but does not change the fact, as noted in Sinagub that these warnings are "qualitatively distinct" from the other advice required by Rule 11(c). This being the case, a failure to give the subdivision (c)(5) warnings even when the defendant was questioned under oath, on the record and in the presence of counsel would in no way affect the validity of the defendant's plea. Rather, this failure bears upon the admissibility of defendant's answers pursuant to subdivision (e)(6) in a later prosecution for perjury or false statement.

NOTES OF ADVISORY COMMITTEE ON RULES——1983 AMENDMENT

Note to Subdivision (a). There are many defenses, objections and requests which a defendant must ordinarily raise by pretrial motion. See, e.g., 18 U.S.C. §3162(a)(2); Fed.R.Crim.P.12(b). Should that motion be denied, interlocutory appeal of the ruling by the defendant is seldom permitted. See United States v. MacDonald, 435 U.S. 850 (1978) (defendant may not appeal denial of his motion to dismiss based upon Sixth Amendment speedy trial grounds); DiBella v. United States, 369 U.S. 121 (1962) (defendant may not appeal denial of pretrial motion to suppress evidence); compare Abney v. United States, 431 U.S. 651 (1977) (interlocutory appeal of denial of motion to dismiss on double jeopardy grounds permissible). Moreover, should the defendant thereafter plead guilty or nolo contendere, this will usually foreclose later appeal with respect to denial of the pretrial motion "When a criminal defendant has solemnly admitted in open court that he is in fact guilty of the offense with which he is charged, he may not thereafter raise independent claims relating to the deprivation of constitutional rights that occurred prior to the entry of the guilty plea." Tollett v. Henderson, 411 U.S. 258, (1973). Though a nolo plea differs from a guilty plea in other respects, it is clear that it also constitutes a waiver of all nonjurisdictional defects in a manner equivalent to a guilty plea. Lott v. United States, 367 U.S. 421 (1961).

As a consequence, a defendant who has lost one or more pretrial motions will often go through an entire trial simply to preserve the pretrial issues for later appellate review. This results in a waste of prosecutorial and judicial resources, and causes delay in the trial of other cases, contrary to the objectives underlying the Speedy Trial Act of 1974, 18 U.S.C. §3161 et seq. These unfortunate consequences may be avoided by the conditional plea device expressly authorized by new subdivision (a)(2).

The development of procedures to avoid the necessity for trials which are undertaken for the sole purpose of preserving pretrial objections has been consistently favored by the commentators. See ABA Standards Relating to the Administration of Criminal Justice, standard 21—1.3(c) (2d ed. 1978); Model Code of Pre-Arraignment Procedure §SS 290.1(4)(b) (1975); Uniform Rules of Criminal Procedure, rule 444(d) (Approved Draft, 1974); 1 C. Wright, Federal Practice and Procedure — Criminal §175 (1969); 3 W. LaFave, Search and Seizure §11.1 (1978). The Supreme Court has characterized the New York practice, whereby appeals from suppression motions may be appealed notwithstanding a guilty plea, as a "commendable effort to relieve the problem of congested trial calendars in a manner that does not diminish the opportunity for the assertion of rights guaranteed by the Constitution." Lefkowitz v. Newsome, 420 U.S. 283, 293 (1975). That Court has never discussed conditional pleas as such, but has permitted without comment a federal appeal on issues preserved by a conditional plea. Jaben v. United States, 381 U.S. 214 (1965).

In the absence of specific authorization by statute or rule for a conditional plea, the circuits have divided on the permissibility of the practice. Two circuits have actually approved the entry of conditional pleas, United States v. Burke, 517 F.2d 377 (2d Cir. 1975); United States v. Moskow, 588 F.2d 882 (3d Cir. 1978); and two others have praised the conditional plea concept, United States v. Clark, 459 F.2d 977 (8th Cir. 1972); United States v. Dorsey, 449 F.2d 1104 (D.C.Cir. 1971). Three circuits have expressed the view that a conditional plea is logically inconsistent and thus improper, United States v. Brown, 499 F.2d 829 (7th Cir. 1974); United States v. Sepe, 472 F.2d 784, aff'd en banc, 486 F.2d 1044 (5th Cir. 1973); United States v. Cox, 464 F.2d 937 (6th Cir. 1972); three others have determined only that conditional pleas are not now authorized in the federal system, United States v. Benson, 579 F.2d 508 (9th Cir. 1978); United States v. Nooner, 565 F.2d 633 (10th Cir. 1977); United States v. Matthews, 472 F.2d 1173 (4th Cir. 1973); while one circuit has reserved judgment on the issue, United States v. Warwar, 478 F.2d 1183 (1st Cir. 1973). (At the state level, a few jurisdictions by statute allow appeal from denial of a motion to suppress notwithstanding a subsequent guilty plea, Cal. Penal Code §1538.5(m); N.Y.Crim. Proc. Law §710.20(1); Wis.Stat.Ann. §971.31(10), but in the absence of such a provision the state courts are also in disagreement as to whether a conditional plea is permissible; see cases collected in Comment, 26 U.C.L.A. L.Rev. 360, 373 (1978).)

The conditional plea procedure provided for in subdivision (a)(2) will, as previously noted, serve to conserve prosecutorial and judicial resources and advance speedy trial objectives. It will also produce much needed uniformity in the federal system on this matter; see United States v. Clark, supra, noting the split of authority and urging resolution by statute or rule. Also, the availability of a conditional plea under specified circumstances will aid in clarifying the fact that traditional, unqualified pleas do constitute a waiver of nonjurisdictional defects. See United States v. Nooner, supra (defendant sought appellate review of denial of pretrial suppression motion, despite his prior unqualified guilty plea, claiming the Second Circuit conditional plea practice led him to believe a guilty plea did not bar appeal of pretrial issues).

The obvious advantages of the conditional plea procedure authorized by subdivision (a)(2) are not outweighed by any significant or compelling disadvantages. As noted in Comment, supra, at 375: "Four major arguments have been raised by courts disapproving of conditioned pleas. The objections are that the procedure encourages a flood of appellate litigation, militates against achieving finality in the criminal process, reduces effectiveness of appellate review due to the lack of a full trial record, and forces decision on constitutional questions that could otherwise be avoided by invoking the harmless error doctrine." But, as concluded therein, those "arguments do not withstand close analysis." Ibid.

As for the first of those arguments, experience in states which have permitted appeals of suppression motions notwithstanding a subsequent plea of guilty is most relevant, as conditional pleas are likely to be most common when the objective is to appeal that kind of pretrial ruling. That experience has shown that the number of appeals has not increased substantially. See Comment, 9 Hous.L.Rev. 305, 315–19 (1971). The minimal added burden at the appellate level is certainly a small price to pay for avoiding otherwise unnecessary trials.

As for the objection that conditional pleas conflict with the government's interest in achieving finality, it is likewise without force. While it is true that the conditional plea does not have the complete finality of the traditional plea of guilty or nolo contendere because "the essence of the agreement is that the legal guilt of the defendant exists only if the prosecution's case" survives on appeal, the plea

continues to serve a partial state interest in finality, however, by establishing admission of the defendant's factual guilt. The defendant stands guilty and the proceedings come to an end if the reserved issue is ultimately decided in the government's favor.
Comment, 26 U.C.L.A. L.Rev. 360, 378 (1978).

The claim that the lack of a full trial record precludes effective appellate review may on occasion be relevant. Cf. United States v. MacDonald, supra (holding interlocutory appeal not available for denial of defendant's pretrial motion to dismiss, on speedy trial grounds, and noting that "most speedy trial claims * * * are best considered only after the relevant facts have been developed at trial"). However, most of the objections which would likely be raised by pretrial motion and preserved for appellate review by a conditional plea are subject to appellate resolution without a trial record. Certainly this is true as to the very common motion to suppress evidence, as is indicated by the fact that appellate courts presently decide such issues upon interlocutory appeal by the government.

With respect to the objection that conditional pleas circumvent application of the harmless error doctrine, it must be acknowledged that "[a]bsent a full trial record, containing all the government's evidence against the defendant, invocation of the harmless error rule is arguably impossible." Comment, supra, at 380. But, the harmless error standard with respect to constitutional objections is sufficiently high, see Chapman v. California, 386 U.S. 18 (1967), that relatively few appellate decisions result in affirmance upon that basis. Thus it will only rarely be true that the conditional plea device will cause an appellate court to consider constitutional questions which could otherwise have been avoided by invocation of the doctrine of harmless error.

To the extent that these or related objections would otherwise have some substance, they are overcome by the provision in Rule 11(a)(2) that the defendant may enter a conditional plea only "with the approval of the court and the consent of the government." (In this respect, the rule adopts the practice now found in the Second Circuit.) The requirement of approval by the court is most appropriate, as it ensures, for example, that the defendant is not allowed to take an appeal on a matter which can only be fully developed by proceeding to trial; cf. United States v. MacDonald, supra. As for consent by the government, it will ensure that conditional pleas will be allowed only when the decision of the court of appeals will dispose of the case either by allowing the plea to stand or by such action as compelling dismissal of the indictment or suppressing essential evidence. Absent such circumstances, the conditional plea might only serve to postpone the trial and require the government to try the case after substantial delay, during which time witnesses may be lost, memories dimmed, and the offense grown so stale as to lose jury appeal. The government is in a unique position to determine whether the matter at issue will be case-dispositive, and, as a party to the litigation, should have an absolute right to refuse to consent to potentially prejudicial delay. Although it was suggested in United States v. Moskow, supra, that the government should have no right to prevent the entry of a conditional plea because a defendant has no comparable right to block government appeal of a pretrial ruling pursuant to 18 U.S.C. §3731, that analogy is unconvincing. That statute requires the government to certify that the appeal is not taken for purposes of delay. Moreover, where the pretrial ruling is case-dispositive, §3731 is the only mechanism by which the government can obtain appellate review, but a defendant may always obtain review by pleading not guilty.

Unlike the state statutes cited earlier, Rule 11(a)(2) is not limited to instances in which the pretrial ruling the defendant wishes to appeal was in response to defendant's motion to suppress evidence. Though it may be true that the conditional plea device will be most commonly employed as to such rulings, the objectives of the rule are well served by extending it to other pretrial rulings as well. See, e.g., ABA Standards, supra (declaring the New York provision "should be enlarged to include other pretrial defenses"); Uniform Rules of Criminal Procedure, rule 444(d) (Approved Draft, 1974) ("any pretrial motion which, if granted, would be dispositive of the case").

The requirement that the conditional plea be made by the defendant "reserving in writing the right to appeal from the adverse determination of any specified pretrial motion," though extending beyond the Second Circuit practice, will ensure careful attention to any conditional plea. It will document that a particular plea was in fact conditional, and will identify precisely what pretrial issues have been preserved for appellate review. By requiring this added step, it will be possible to avoid entry of a conditional plea without the considered acquiescence of the government (see United States v. Burke, supra, holding that failure of the government to object to entry of a conditional plea constituted consent) and post-plea claims by the defendant that his plea should be deemed conditional merely because it occurred after denial of his pretrial motions (see United States v. Nooner, supra).

It must be emphasized that the only avenue of review of the specified pretrial ruling permitted under a rule 11(a)(2) conditional plea is an appeal, which must be brought in compliance with Fed.R.App.P. 4(b). Relief via 28 U.S.C. §2255 is not available for this purpose.

The Supreme Court has held that certain kinds of constitutional objections may be raised after a plea of guilty. Menna v. New York, 423 U.S. 61 (1975) (double jeopardy violation); Blackledge v. Perry, 417 U.S. 21 (1974) (due process violation by charge enhancement following defendant's exercise of right to trial de novo). Subdivision 11(a)(2) has no application to such situations, and should not be interpreted as either broadening or narrowing the Menna-Blackledge doctrine or as establishing procedures for its application.

Note to Subdivision (h). Subdivision (h) makes clear that the harmless error rule of Rule 52(a) is applicable to Rule 11. The provision does not, however, attempt to define the meaning of "harmless error," which is left to the case law. Prior to the amendments which took effect on Dec. 1, 1975, Rule 11 was very brief; it consisted of but four sentences. The 1975 amendments increased significantly the procedures which must be undertaken when a defendant tenders a plea of guilty or nolo contendere, but this change was warranted by the "two principal objectives" then identified in the Advisory Committee Note: (1) ensuring that the defendant has made an informed plea; and (2) ensuring that plea agreements are brought out into the open in court. An inevitable consequence of the 1975 amendments was some increase in the risk that a trial judge, in a particular case, might inadvertently deviate to some degree from the procedure which a very literal reading of Rule 11 would appear to require.

This being so, it became more apparent than ever that Rule 11 should not be given such a crabbed interpretation that ceremony was exalted over substance. As stated in United States v. Scarf, 551 F.2d 1124 (8th Cir. 1977), concerning amended Rule 11: "It is a salutary rule, and district courts are required to act in substantial compliance with it although * * * ritualistic compliance is not required." As similarly pointed out in United States v. Saft, 558 F.2d 1073 (2d Cir. 1977),

the Rule does note say that compliance can be achieved only by reading the specified items in haec verba. Congress meant to strip district judges of freedom to decide what they must explain to a defendant who wishes to plead guilty, not to tell them precisely how to perform this important task in the great variety of cases that would come before them. While a judge who contents himself with literal application of the Rule will hardly be reversed, it cannot be supposed that Congress preferred this to a more meaningful explanation, provided that all the specified elements were covered.

Two important points logically flow from these sound observations. One concerns the matter of construing Rule 11: it is not to be read as requiring a litany or other ritual which can be carried out only by word-for-word adherence to a set "script." The other, specifically addressed in new subdivision (h), is that even when it may be concluded Rule 11 has not been complied with in all respects, it does not inevitably follow that the defendant's plea of guilty or nolo contendere is invalid and subject to being overturned by any remedial device then available to the defendant.

Notwithstanding the declaration in Rule 52(a) that "[a]ny error, defect, irregularity or variance which does not affect substantial rights shall be disregarded," there has existed for some years considerable disagreement concerning the applicability of the harmless error doctrine to Rule 11 violations. In large part, this is attributable to uncertainty as to the continued vitality and the reach of McCarthy v. United States, 394 U.S. 459 (1969). In McCarthy, involving a direct appeal from a plea of guilty because of noncompliance with Rule 11, the Court concluded

that prejudice inheres in a failure to comply with Rule 11, for noncompliance deprives the defendant of the Rule's procedural safeguards, which are designed to facilitate a more accurate determination of the voluntariness of his plea. Our holding [is] that a defendant whose plea has been accepted in violation of Rule 11 should be afforded the opportunity to plead anew * * *.

McCarthy has been most frequently relied upon in cases where, as in that case, the defendant sought relief because of a Rule 11 violation by the avenue of direct appeal. It has been held that in such circumstances a defendant's conviction must be reversed whenever the "district court accepts his guilty plea without fully adhering to the procedure provided for in Rule 11," United States v. Boone, 543 F.2d 1090 (4th Cir. 1976), and that in this context any reliance by the government on the Rule 52(a) harmless error concept "must be rejected." United States v. Journet, 544 F.2d 633 (2d Cir. 1976). On the other hand, decisions are to be found taking a harmless error approach on direct appeal where it appeared the nature and extent of the deviation from Rule 11 was such that it could not have had any impact on the defendant's decision to plead or the fairness in now holding him to his plea. United States v. Peters, No. 77-1700 (4th Cir., Dec. 22, 1978) (where judge failed to comply fully with Rule 11(c)(1), in that defendant not correctly advised of maximum years of special parole term but was told it is at least 3 years, and defendant thereafter sentenced to 15 years plus 3-year special parole term, government's motion for summary affirmance granted, as "the error was harmless"); United States v. Coronado, 554 F.2d 166 (5th Cir. 1977) (court first holds that charge of conspiracy requires some explanation of what conspiracy means to comply with Rule 11(c)(1), but then finds no reversible error "because the rule 11 proceeding on its face discloses, despite the trial court's failure sufficiently to make the required explicitation of the charges, that Coronado understood them").

But this conflict has not been limited to cases involving nothing more than a direct appeal following defendant's plea. For example, another type of case is that in which the defendant has based a post-sentence motion to withdraw his plea on a Rule 11 violation. Rule 32(d) says that such a motion may be granted "to correct manifest injustice," and some courts have relied upon this latter provision in holding that post-sentence plea withdrawal need not be permitted merely because Rule 11 was not fully complied with and that instead the district court should hold an evidentiary hearing to determine "whether manifest injustice will result if the conviction based on the guilty plea is permitted to stand." United States v. Scarf, 551 F.2d 1124 (8th Cir. 1977). Others, however, have held that McCarthy applies and prevails over the language of Rule

32(d), so that "a failure to scrupulously comply with Rule 11 will invalidate a plea without a showing of manifest injustice." United States v. Cantor, 469 F.2d 435 (3d Cir. 1972).

Disagreement has also existed in the context of collateral attack upon pleas pursuant to 28 U.S.C. §2255. On the one hand, it has been concluded that "[n]ot every violation of Rule 11 requires that the plea be set aside" in a §2255 proceeding, and that "a guilty plea will be set aside on collateral attack only where to not do so would result in a miscarriage of justice, or where there exists exceptional circumstances justifying such relief." Evers v. United States, 579 F.2d 71 (10th Cir. 1978). The contrary view was that McCarthy governed in §2255 proceedings because "the Supreme Court hinted at no exceptions to its policy of strict enforcement of Rule 11." Timmreck v. United States, 577 F.2d 377 (6th Cir. 1978). But a unanimous Supreme Court resolved this conflict in United States v. Timmreck, 441 U.S. 780 (1979), where the Court concluded that the reasoning of Hill v. United States, 368 U.S. 424 (1962) (ruling a collateral attack could not be predicated on a violation of Rule 32(a))

is equally applicable to a formal violation of Rule 11.* * *

Indeed, if anything, this case may be a stronger one for foreclosing collateral relief than the Hill case. For the concern with finality served by the limitation on collateral attack has special force with respect to convictions based on guilty pleas.

"Every inroad on the concept of finality undermines confidence in the integrity of our procedures; and, by increasing the volume of judicial work, inevitably delays and impairs the orderly administration of justice. The impact is greatest when new grounds for setting aside guilty pleas are approved because the vast majority of criminal convictions result from such pleas. Moreover, the concern that unfair procedures may have resulted in the conviction of an innocent defendant is only rarely raised by a petition to set aside a guilty plea."

This interest in finality is strongest in the collateral attack context the Court was dealing with in Timmreck, which explains why the Court there adopted the Hill requirement that in a §2255 proceeding the rule violation must amount to "a fundamental defect which inherently results in a complete miscarriage of justice" or "an omission inconsistent with the rudimentary demands of fair procedure." The interest in finality of guilty pleas described in Timmreck is of somewhat lesser weight when a direct appeal is involved (so that the Hill standard is obviously inappropriate in that setting), but yet is sufficiently compelling to make unsound the proposition that reversal is required even where it is apparent that the Rule 11 violation was of the harmless error variety.

Though the McCarthy per se rule may have been justified at the time and in the circumstances which obtained when the plea in that case was taken, this is no longer the case. For one thing, it is important to recall that McCarthy dealt only with the much simpler pre-1975 version of Rule 11, which required only a brief procedure during which the chances of a minor, insignificant and inadvertent deviation were relatively slight. This means that the chances of a truly harmless error (which was not involved in McCarthy in any event, as the judge made no inquiry into the defendant's understanding of the nature of the charge, and the government had presented only the extreme argument that a court "could properly assume that petitioner was entering that plea with a complete understanding of the charge against him" merely from the fact he had stated he desired to plead guilty) are much greater under present Rule 11 than under the version before the Court in McCarthy. It also means that the more elaborate and lengthy procedures of present Rule 11, again as compared with the version applied in McCarthy, make it more apparent than ever that a guilty plea is not "a mere gesture, a temporary and meaningless formality reversible at the defendant's whim," but rather " 'a grave and solemn act,' which is 'accepted only with care and discernment.' " United States v. Barker, 514 F.2d 208 (D.C.Cir.1975), quoting from Brady v. United States, 397 U.S. 742 (1970). A plea of that character should not be overturned, even on direct appeal, when there has been a minor and technical violation of Rule 11 which amounts to harmless error.

Secondly, while McCarthy involved a situation in which the defendant's plea of guilty was before the court of appeals on direct appeal, the Supreme Court appears to have been primarily concerned with §2255-type cases, for the Court referred exclusively to cases of that kind in the course of concluding that a per se rule was justified as to Rule 11 violations because of "the difficulty of achieving [rule 11's] purposes through a post-conviction voluntariness hearing." But that reasoning has now been substantially undercut by United States v. Timmreck, supra, for the Court there concluded §2255 relief "is not available when all that is shown is a failure to comply with the formal requirements of the Rule," at least absent "other aggravating circumstances," which presumably could often only be developed in the course of a later evidentiary hearing.

Although all of the aforementioned considerations support the policy expressed in new subdivision (h), the Advisory Committee does wish to emphasize two important cautionary notes. The first is that subdivision (h) should not be read as supporting extreme or speculative harmless error claims or as, in effect, nullifying important Rule 11 safeguards. There would not be harmless error under subdivision (h) where, for example, as in McCarthy, there had been absolutely no inquiry by the judge into defendant's understanding of the nature of the charge and the harmless error claim of the government rests upon nothing more than the assertion that it may be "assumed" defendant possessed such understanding merely because he expressed a desire to plead guilty. Likewise, it would not be harmless error if the trial judge totally abdicated to the prosecutor the responsibility for giving to the defendant the various Rule 11 warnings, as this "results in the creation of an atmosphere of subtle coercion that clearly contravenes the policy behind Rule 11." United States v. Crook, 526 F.2d 708 (5th Cir. 1976).

Indeed, it is fair to say that the kinds of Rule 11 violations which might be found to constitute harmless error upon direct appeal are fairly limited, as in such instances the matter "must be resolved solely on the basis of the Rule 11 transcript" and the other portions (e.g., sentencing hearing) of the limited record made in such cases. United States v. Coronado, supra. Illustrative are: where the judge's compliance with subdivision (c)(1) was not absolutely complete, in that some essential element of the crime was not mentioned, but the defendant's responses clearly indicate his awareness of that element, see United States v. Coronado, supra; where the judge's compliance with subdivision (c)(2) was erroneous in part in that the judge understated the maximum penalty somewhat, but the penalty actually imposed did not exceed that indicated in the warnings, see United States v. Peters, supra; and where the judge completely failed to comply with subdivision (c)(5), which of course has no bearing on the validity of the plea itself, cf. United States v. Sinagub, supra.

The second cautionary note is that subdivision (h) should not be read as an invitation to trial judges to take a more casual approach to Rule 11 proceedings. It is still true, as the Supreme Court pointed out in McCarthy, that thoughtful and careful compliance with Rule 11 best serves the cause of fair and efficient administration of criminal justice, as it

will help reduce the great waste of judicial resources required to process the frivolous attacks on guilty plea convictions that are encouraged, and are more difficult to dispose of, when the original record is inadequate. It is, therefore, not too much to require that, before sentencing defendants to years of imprisonment, district judges take the few minutes necessary to inform them of their rights and to determine whether they understand the action they are taking.

Subdivision (h) makes no change in the responsibilities of the judge at Rule 11 proceedings, but instead merely rejects the extreme sanction of automatic reversal.

It must also be emphasized that a harmless error provision has been added to Rule 11 because some courts have read McCarthy as meaning that the general harmless error provision in Rule 52(a) cannot be utilized with respect to Rule 11 proceedings. Thus, the addition of subdivision (h) should not be read as suggesting that Rule 52(a) does not apply in other circumstances because of the absence of a provision comparable to subdivision (h) attached to other rules.

NOTES OF ADVISORY COMMITTEE ON RULES—1985 AMENDMENT

Note to Subdivision (c)(1). Section 5 of the Victim and Witness Protection Act of 1982, Pub. L. No. 97–291, 96 Stat. 1248 (1982), adds 18 U.S.C. §3579, providing that when sentencing a defendant convicted of a Title 18 offense or of violating various subsections of the Federal Aviation Act of 1958, the court "may order, in addition to or in lieu of any other penalty authorized by law, that the defendant make restitution to any victim of the offense." Under this law restitution is favored; if the court "does not order restitution, or orders only partial restitution, . . . the court shall state on the record the reasons therefor." Because this restitution is deemed an aspect of the defendant's sentence, S. Rept. No. 97–532, 97th Cong., 2d Sess., 30–33 (1982), it is a matter about which a defendant tendering a plea of guilty or nolo contendere should be advised.

Because this new legislation contemplates that the amount of the restitution to be ordered will be ascertained later in the sentencing process, this amendment to Rule 11(c)(1) merely requires that the defendant be told of the court's power to order restitution. The exact amount or upper limit cannot and need not be stated at the time of the plea. Failure of a court to advise a defendant of the possibility of a restitution order would constitute harmless error under subdivision (h) if no restitution were thereafter ordered.

NOTES OF ADVISORY COMMITTEE ON RULES—1987 AMENDMENT

The amendments are technical. No substantive change is intended.

NOTES OF ADVISORY COMMITTEE ON RULES—1989 AMENDMENT

The amendment mandates that the district court inform a defendant that the court is required to consider any applicable guidelines but may depart from them under some circumstances. This requirement assures that the existence of guidelines will be known to a defendant before a plea of guilty or nolo contendere is accepted. Since it will be impracticable, if not impossible, to know which guidelines will be relevant prior to the formulation of a presentence report and resolution of disputed facts, the amendment does not require the court to specify which guidelines will be important or which grounds for departure might prove to be significant. The advice that the court is required to give cannot guarantee that a defendant who pleads guilty will not later claim a lack of understanding as to the importance of guidelines at the time of the plea. No advice is likely to serve as a complete protection against post-plea claims of ignorance or confusion. By giving the advice, the court places the defendant and defense counsel on notice of the importance that guidelines may play in sentencing and of the possibility of a departure from those guidelines. A defendant represented by competent counsel will be in a position to enter an intelligent plea.

The amended rule does not limit the district court's discretion to engage in a more extended colloquy with the defendant in order to impart additional information about sentencing guidelines or to inquire into the defendant's knowledge concerning guidelines. The amended rule sets forth only the minimum advice that must be provided to the defendant by the court.

COMMITTEE NOTES ON RULES—1999 AMENDMENT

Subdivision (a). The amendment deletes use of the term "corporation" and substitutes in its place the term "organization," with a reference to the definition of that term in 18 U.S.C. §18.

Subdivision (c)(6). Rule 11(c) has been amended specifically to reflect the increasing practice of including provisions in plea agreements which require the defendant to waive certain appellate rights. The increased use of such provisions is due in part to the increasing number of direct appeals and collateral reviews challenging sentencing decisions. Given the increased use of such provisions, the Committee believed it was important to insure that first, a complete record exists regarding any waiver provisions, and second, that the waiver was voluntarily and knowingly made by the defendant. Although a number of federal courts have approved the ability of a defendant to enter into such waiver agreements, the Committee takes no position on the underlying validity of such waivers.

Subdivision (e). Amendments have been made to Rule 11(e)(1)(B) and (C) to reflect the impact of the Sentencing Guidelines on guilty pleas. Although Rule 11 is generally silent on the subject, it has become clear that the courts have struggled with the subject of guideline sentencing vis a vis plea agreements, entry and timing of guilty pleas, and the ability of the defendant to withdraw a plea of guilty. The amendments are intended to address two specific issues.

First, both subdivisions (e)(1)(B) and (e)(1)(C) have been amended to recognize that a plea agreement may specifically address not only what amounts to an appropriate sentence, but also a sentencing guideline, a sentencing factor, or a policy statement accompanying a sentencing guideline or factor. Under an (e)(1)(B) agreement, the government, as before, simply agrees to make a recommendation to the court, or agrees not to oppose a defense request concerning a particular sentence or consideration of a sentencing guideline, factor, or policy statement. The amendment makes it clear that this type of agreement is not binding on the court. Second, under an (e)(1)(C) agreement, the government and defense have actually agreed on what amounts to an appropriate sentence or have agreed to one of the specified components. The amendment also makes it clear that this agreement is binding on the court once the court accepts it. As is the situation under the current Rule, the court retains absolute discretion whether to accept a plea agreement.

GAP Report—Rule 11. The Committee made no changes to the published draft amendments to Rule 11. But it did add language to the Committee Note which reflects the view that the amendment is not intended to signal its approval of the underlying practice of including waiver provisions in pretrial agreements.

COMMITTEE NOTES ON RULES—2002 AMENDMENT

The language of Rule 11 has been amended and reorganized as part of the general restyling of the Criminal Rules to make them more easily understood and to make style and terminology consistent throughout the rules. These changes are intended to be stylistic only, except as noted below.

Amended Rule 11(b)(1) requires the court to apprise the defendant of his or her rights before accepting a plea of guilty or nolo contendere. The Committee determined to expand upon the incomplete listing in the current rule of the elements of the "maximum possible penalty" and any "mandatory minimum" penalty to include advice as to the maximum or minimum term of imprisonment, forfeiture, fine, and special assessment, in addition to the two types of maximum and minimum penalties presently enumerated: restitution and supervised release. The outmoded reference to a term of "special parole" has been eliminated.

Amended Rule 11(b)(2), formerly Rule 11(d), covers the issue of determining that the plea is voluntary, and not the result of force, threats, or promises (other than those in a plea agreement). The reference to an inquiry in current Rule 11(d) whether the plea has resulted from plea discussions with the government has been deleted. That reference, which was often a source of confusion to defendants who were clearly pleading guilty as part of a plea agreement with the government, was considered unnecessary.

Rule 11(c)(1)(A) includes a change, which recognizes a common type of plea agreement—that the government will "not bring" other charges.

The Committee considered whether to address the practice in some courts of using judges to facilitate plea agreements. The current rule states that "the court shall not participate in any discussions between the parties concerning such plea agreement." Some courts apparently believe that that language acts as a limitation only upon the judge taking the defendant's plea and thus permits other judges to serve as facilitators for reaching a plea agreement between the government and the defendant. See, e.g., United States v. Torres, 999 F.2d 376, 378 (9th Cir. 1993) (noting practice and concluding that presiding judge had not participated in a plea agreement that had resulted from discussions involving another judge). The Committee decided to leave the Rule as it is with the understanding that doing so was in no way intended either to approve or disapprove the existing law interpreting that provision.

Amended Rules 11(c)(3) to (5) address the topics of consideration, acceptance, and rejection of a plea agreement. The amendments are not intended to make any change in practice. The topics are discussed separately because in the past there has been some question about the possible interplay between the court's consideration of the guilty plea in conjunction with a plea agreement and sentencing and the ability of the defendant to withdraw a plea. See United States v. Hyde, 520 U.S. 670 (1997) (holding that plea and plea agreement need not be accepted or rejected as a single unit; "guilty pleas can be accepted while plea agreements are deferred, and the acceptance of the two can be separated in time."). Similarly, the Committee decided to more clearly spell out in Rule 11(d) and 11(e) the ability of the defendant to withdraw a plea. See United States v. Hyde, supra.

Amended Rule 11(e) is a new provision, taken from current Rule 32(e), that addresses the finality of a guilty or nolo contendere plea after the court imposes sentence. The provision makes it clear that it is not possible for a defendant to withdraw a plea after sentence is imposed.

The reference to a "motion under 28 U.S.C. §2255" has been changed to the broader term "collateral attack" to recognize that in some instances a court may grant collateral relief under provisions other than §2255. See United States v. Jeffers, 234 F.3d 277 (5th Cir. 2000) (petition under §2241 may be appropriate where remedy under §2255 is ineffective or inadequate).

Currently, Rule 11(e)(5) requires that unless good cause is shown, the parties are to give pretrial notice to the court that a plea agreement exists. That provision has been deleted. First, the Committee believed that although the provision was originally drafted to assist judges, under current practice few counsel would risk the consequences in the ordinary case of not informing the court that an agreement exists. Secondly, the Committee was concerned that there might be rare cases where the parties might agree that informing the court of the existence of an agreement might endanger a defendant or compromise an ongoing investigation in a related case. In the end, the Committee believed that, on balance, it would be preferable to remove the provision and reduce the risk of pretrial disclosure.

Finally, revised Rule 11(f), which addresses the issue of admissibility or inadmissibility of pleas and statements made during the plea inquiry, cross references Federal Rule of Evidence 410.

COMMITTEE NOTES ON RULES—2007 AMENDMENT

Subdivision (b)(1)(M). The amendment conforms Rule 11 to the Supreme Court's decision in United States v. Booker, 543 U.S. 220 (2005). Booker held that the provision of the federal sentencing statute that makes the Guidelines mandatory, 18 U.S.C. §3553(b)(1), violates the Sixth Amendment right to jury trial. With this provision severed and excised, the Court held, the Sentencing Reform Act "makes the Guidelines effectively advisory," and "requires a sentencing court to consider Guidelines ranges, see 18 U.S.C.A. §3553(a)(4) (Supp. 2004), but it permits the court to tailor the sentence in light of other statutory concerns as well, see §3553(a) (Supp. 2004)." Id. at 245–46. Rule 11(b)(M) incorporates this analysis into the information provided to the defendant at the time of a plea of guilty or nolo contendere.

Changes Made to Proposed Amendment Released for Public Comment. No changes were made to the text of the proposed amendment as released for public comment. One change was made to the Committee note. The reference to the Fifth Amendment was deleted from the description of the Supreme Court's decision in Booker.

COMMITTEE NOTES ON RULES—2013 AMENDMENT

Subdivision (b)(1)(O). The amendment requires the court to include a general statement that there may be immigration consequences of conviction in the advice provided to the defendant before the court accepts a plea of guilty or nolo contendere.

For a defendant who is not a citizen of the United States, a criminal conviction may lead to removal, exclusion, and the inability to become a citizen. In Padilla v. Kentucky, 130 S.Ct. 1473 (2010), the Supreme Court held that a defense attorney's failure to advise the defendant concerning the risk of deportation fell below the objective standard of reasonable professional assistance guaranteed by the Sixth Amendment.

The amendment mandates a generic warning, not specific advice concerning the defendant's individual situation. Judges in many districts already include a warning about immigration consequences in the plea colloquy, and the amendment adopts this practice as good policy. The Committee concluded that the most effective and efficient method of conveying this information is to provide it to every defendant, without attempting to determine the defendant's citizenship.

Changes Made After Publication and Comment. The Committee Note was revised to make it clear that the court is to give a general statement that there may be immigration consequences, not specific advice concerning a defendant's individual situation.

REFERENCES IN TEXT

The Federal Rules of Evidence, referred to in subd. (f), are set out in the Appendix to Title 28, Judiciary and Judicial Procedure.

AMENDMENT BY PUBLIC LAW

1988—Subd. (c)(1). Pub. L. 100–690 inserted "or term of supervised release" after "special parole term".

1975—Pub. L. 94–64 amended subds. (c) and (e)(1)–(4), (6) generally.

EFFECTIVE DATE OF 1979 AMENDMENT

Amendment of subd. (e)(6) of this rule by order of the United States Supreme Court of Apr. 30, 1979, effective Dec. 1, 1980, see section 1(1) of Pub. L. 96–42, July 31, 1979, 93 Stat. 326, set out as a note under section 2074 of Title 28, Judiciary and Judicial Procedure.

EFFECTIVE DATE OF AMENDMENTS PROPOSED APRIL 22, 1974; EFFECTIVE DATE OF 1975 AMENDMENTS

Amendments of this rule embraced in the order of the United States Supreme Court on Apr. 22, 1974, and the amendments of this rule made by section 3 of Pub. L. 94–64, effective Dec. 1, 1975, except with respect to the amendment adding subd. (e)(6) of this rule, effective Aug. 1, 1975, see section 2 of Pub. L. 94–64, set out as a note under rule 4 of these rules.

Rule 12. Pleadings and Pretrial Motions

(a) Pleadings. The pleadings in a criminal proceeding are the indictment, the information, and the pleas of not guilty, guilty, and nolo contendere.

(b) Pretrial Motions.

(1) In General. A party may raise by pretrial motion any defense, objection, or request that the court can determine without a trial on the merits. Rule 47 applies to a pretrial motion.

(2) Motions That May Be Made at Any Time. A motion that the court lacks jurisdiction may be made at any time while the case is pending.

(3) Motions That Must Be Made Before Trial. The following defenses, objections, and requests must be raised by pretrial motion if the basis for the motion is then reasonably available and the motion can be determined without a trial on the merits:

(A) a defect in instituting the prosecution, including:

(i) improper venue;

(ii) preindictment delay;

(iii) a violation of the constitutional right to a speedy trial;

(iv) selective or vindictive prosecution; and

(v) an error in the grand-jury proceeding or preliminary hearing;

(B) a defect in the indictment or information, including:

(i) joining two or more offenses in the same count (duplicity);

(ii) charging the same offense in more than one count (multiplicity);

(iii) lack of specificity;

53

(iv) improper joinder; and

(v) failure to state an offense;

(C) suppression of evidence;

(D) severance of charges or defendants under Rule 14; and

(E) discovery under Rule 16.

(4) Notice of the Government's Intent to Use Evidence.

(A) At the Government's Discretion. At the arraignment or as soon afterward as practicable, the government may notify the defendant of its intent to use specified evidence at trial in order to afford the defendant an opportunity to object before trial under Rule 12(b)(3)(C).

(B) At the Defendant's Request. At the arraignment or as soon afterward as practicable, the defendant may, in order to have an opportunity to move to suppress evidence under Rule 12(b)(3)(C), request notice of the government's intent to use (in its evidence-in-chief at trial) any evidence that the defendant may be entitled to discover under Rule 16.

(c) Deadline for a Pretrial Motion; Consequences of Not Making a Timely Motion.

(1) Setting the Deadline. The court may, at the arraignment or as soon afterward as practicable, set a deadline for the parties to make pretrial motions and may also schedule a motion hearing. If the court does not set one, the deadline is the start of trial.

(2) Extending or Resetting the Deadline. At any time before trial, the court may extend or reset the deadline for pretrial motions.

(3) Consequences of Not Making a Timely Motion Under Rule 12(b)(3). If a party does not meet the deadline for making a Rule 12(b)(3) motion, the motion is untimely. But a court may consider the defense, objection, or request if the party shows good cause.

(d) Ruling on a Motion. The court must decide every pretrial motion before trial unless it finds good cause to defer a ruling. The court must not defer ruling on a pretrial motion if the deferral will adversely affect a party's right to appeal. When factual issues are involved in deciding a motion, the court must state its essential findings on the record.

(e) [Reserved]

(f) Recording the Proceedings. All proceedings at a motion hearing, including any findings of fact and conclusions of law made orally by the court, must be recorded by a court reporter or a suitable recording device.

(g) Defendant's Continued Custody or Release Status. If the court grants a motion to dismiss based on a defect in instituting the prosecution, in the indictment, or in the information, it may order the defendant to be released or detained under 18 U.S.C. §3142 for a specified time until a new indictment or information is filed. This rule does not affect any federal statutory period of limitations.

(h) Producing Statements at a Suppression Hearing. Rule 26.2 applies at a suppression hearing under Rule 12(b)(3)(C). At a suppression hearing, a law enforcement officer is considered a government witness.

(As amended Apr. 22, 1974, eff. Dec. 1, 1975; Pub. L. 94–64, §3(11), (12), July 31, 1975, 89 Stat. 372; Apr. 28, 1983, eff. Aug. 1, 1983; Mar. 9, 1987, eff. Aug. 1, 1987; Apr. 22, 1993, eff. Dec. 1, 1993; Apr. 29, 2002, eff. Dec. 1, 2002; Apr. 25, 2014, eff. Dec. 1, 2014.)

NOTES OF ADVISORY COMMITTEE ON RULES—1944

Note to Subdivision (a). 1. This rule abolishes pleas to the jurisdiction, pleas in abatement, demurrers, special pleas in bar, and motions to quash. A motion to dismiss or for other appropriate relief is substituted for the purpose of raising all defenses and objections heretofore interposed in any of the foregoing modes. "This should result in a reduction of opportunities for dilatory tactics and, at the same time, relieve the defense of embarrassment. Many competent practitioners have been baffled and mystified by the distinctions between pleas in abatement, pleas in bar, demurrers, and motions to quash, and have, at times, found difficulty in determining which of these should be invoked." Homer Cummings, 29 A.B.A.Jour. 655. See also, Medalie, 4 Lawyers Guild R. (3)1, 4.

2. A similar change was introduced by the Federal Rules of Civil Procedure (Rule 7(a)) which has proven successful. It is also proposed by the A.L.I. Code of Criminal Procedure (Sec. 209).

Note to Subdivision (b)(1) and (2). These two paragraphs classify into two groups all objections and defenses to be interposed by motion prescribed by Rule 12(a). In one group are defenses and objections which must be raised by motion, failure to do so constituting a waiver. In the other group are defenses and objections which at the defendant's option may be raised by motion, failure to do so, however, not constituting a waiver. (Cf. Rule 12 of Federal Rules of Civil Procedure [28 U.S.C., Appendix].)

In the first of these groups are included all defenses and objections that are based on defects in the institution of the prosecution or in the indictment and information, other than lack of jurisdiction or failure to charge an offense. All such defenses and objections must be included in a single motion. (Cf. Rule 12(g) of Federal Rules of Civil Procedure [28 U.S.C., Appendix].) Among the defenses and objections in this group are the following: Illegal selection or organization of the grand jury, disqualification of individual grand jurors, presence of unauthorized persons in the grand jury room, other irregularities in grand jury proceedings, defects in indictment or information other than lack of jurisdiction or failure to state an offense, etc. The provision that these defenses and objections are waived if not raised by motion substantially continues existing law, as they are waived at present unless raised before trial by plea in abatement, demurrer, motion to quash, etc.

In the other group of objections and defenses, which the defendant at his option may raise by motion before trial, are included all defenses and objections which are capable of determination without a trial of the general issue. They include such matters as former jeopardy, former conviction, former acquittal, statute of limitations, immunity, lack of jurisdiction, failure of indictment or information to state an offense, etc. Such matters have been heretofore raised by demurrers, special pleas in bar and motions to quash.

Note to Subdivision (b)(3). This rule, while requiring the motion to be made before pleading, vests discretionary authority in the court to permit the motion to be made within a reasonable time thereafter. The rule supersedes 18 U.S.C. 556a [now 3288, 3289], fixing a definite limitation of time for pleas in abatement and motions to quash. The rule also eliminates the requirement for technical withdrawal of a plea if it is desired to interpose a preliminary objection or defense after the plea has been entered. Under this rule a plea will be permitted to stand in the meantime.

Note to Subdivision (b)(4). This rule substantially restates existing law. It leaves with the court discretion to determine in advance of trial defenses and objections raised by motion or to defer them for determination at the trial. It preserves the right to jury trial in those cases in which the right is given under the Constitution or by statute. In all other cases it vests in the court authority to determine issues of fact in such manner as the court deems appropriate.

Note to Subdivision (b)(5). 1. The first sentence substantially restates existing law, 18 U.S.C. [former] 561 (Indictments and presentments; judgment on demurrer), which provides that in case a demurrer to an indictment or information is overruled, the judgment shall be respondeat ouster.

2. The last sentence of the rule that "Nothing in this rule shall be deemed to affect the provisions of any act of Congress relating to periods of limitations" is intended to preserve the provisions of statutes which permit a reindictment if the original indictment is found defective or is dismissed for other irregularities and the statute of limitations has run in the meantime, 18 U.S.C. 587 [now 3288] (Defective indictment; defect found after period of limitations; reindictment); Id. sec. 588 [now 3289] (Defective indictment; defect found before period of limitations; reindictment); Id. sec. 589 [now 3288, 3289] (Defective indictment; defense of limitations to new

indictment); Id. sec. 556a [now 3288, 3289] (Indictments and presentments; objections to drawing or qualification of grand jury; time for filing; suspension of statute of limitations).

NOTES OF ADVISORY COMMITTEE ON RULES—1974 AMENDMENT

Subdivision (a) remains as it was in the old rule. It "speaks only of defenses and objections that prior to the rules could have been raised by a plea, demurrer, or motion to quash" (C. Wright, Federal Practice and Procedure: Criminal §191 at p. 397 (1969)), and this might be interpreted as limiting the scope of the rule. However, some courts have assumed that old rule 12 does apply to pretrial motions generally, and the amendments to subsequent subdivisions of the rule should make clear that the rule is applicable to pretrial motion practice generally. (See e.g., rule 12(b)(3), (4), (5) and rule 41(e).)

Subdivision (b) is changed to provide for some additional motions and requests which must be made prior to trial. Subdivisions (b)(1) and (2) are restatements of the old rule.

Subdivision (b)(3) makes clear that objections to evidence on the ground that it was illegally obtained must be raised prior to trial. This is the current rule with regard to evidence obtained as a result of an illegal search. See rule 41(e); C. Wright, Federal Practice and Procedure: Criminal §673 (1969, Supp. 1971). It is also the practice with regard to other forms of illegality such as the use of unconstitutional means to obtain a confession. See C. Wright, Federal Practice and Procedure: Criminal §673 at p. 108 (1969). It seems apparent that the same principle should apply whatever the claimed basis for the application of the exclusionary rule of evidence may be. This is consistent with the court's statement in Jones v. United States, 362 U.S. 257, 264, 80 S.Ct. 725, 4 L.Ed.2d 697 (1960):

This provision of Rule 41(e), requiring the motion to suppress to be made before trial, is a crystallization of decisions of this Court requiring that procedure, and is designed to eliminate from the trial disputes over police conduct not immediately relevant to the question of guilt. (Emphasis added.)

Subdivision (b)(4) provides for a pretrial request for discovery by either the defendant or the government to the extent to which such discovery is authorized by rule 16.

Subdivision (b)(5) provides for a pretrial request for a severance as authorized in rule 14.

Subdivision (c) provides that a time for the making of motions shall be fixed at the time of the arraignment or as soon thereafter as practicable by court rule or direction of a judge. The rule leaves to the individual judge whether the motions may be oral or written. This and other amendments to rule 12 are designed to make possible and to encourage the making of motions prior to trial, whenever possible, and in a single hearing rather than in a series of hearings. This is the recommendation of the American Bar Association's Committee on Standards Relating to Discovery and Procedure Before Trial (Approved Draft, 1970); see especially §§5.2 and 5.3. It also is the procedure followed in those jurisdictions which have used the so-called "omnibus hearing" originated by Judge James Carter in the Southern District of California. See 4 Defender Newsletter 44 (1967); Miller, The Omnibus Hearing—An Experiment in Federal Criminal Discovery, 5 San Diego L.Rev. 293 (1968); American Bar Association, Standards Relating to Discovery and Procedure Before Trial, Appendices B, C, and D (Approved Draft, 1970). The omnibus hearing is also being used, on an experimental basis, in several other district courts. Although the Advisory Committee is of the view that it would be premature to write the omnibus hearing procedure into the rules, it is of the view that the single pretrial hearing should be made possible and its use encouraged by the rules.

There is a similar trend in state practice. See, e.g., State ex rel. Goodchild v. Burke, 27 Wis.2d 244, 133 N.W.2d 753 (1965); State ex rel. Rasmussen v. Tahash, 272 Minn. 539, 141 N.W.2d 3 (1965).

The rule provides that the motion date be set at "the arraignment or as soon thereafter as practicable." This is the practice in some federal courts including those using the omnibus hearing. (In order to obtain the advantage of the omnibus hearing, counsel routinely plead not guilty at the initial arraignment on the information or indictment and then may indicate a desire to change the plea to guilty following the omnibus hearing. This practice builds a more adequate record in guilty plea cases.) The rule further provides that the date may be set before the arraignment if local rules of court so provide.

Subdivision (d) provides a mechanism for insuring that a defendant knows of the government's intention to use evidence to which the defendant may want to object. On some occasions the resolution of the admissibility issue prior to trial may be advantageous to the government. In these situations the attorney for the government can make effective defendant's obligation to make his motion to suppress prior to trial by giving defendant notice of the government's intention to use certain evidence. For example, in United States v. Desist, 384 F.2d 889, 897 (2d Cir. 1967), the court said:

Early in the pre-trial proceedings, the Government commendably informed both the court and defense counsel that an electronic listening device had been used in investigating the case, and suggested a hearing be held as to its legality.

See also the "Omnibus Crime Control and Safe Streets Act of 1968," 18 U.S.C. §2518(9):

The contents of any intercepted wire or oral communication or evidence derived therefrom shall not be received in evidence or otherwise disclosed in any trial, hearing, or other proceeding in a Federal or State court unless each party, not less than ten days before the trial, hearing, or proceeding, has been furnished with a copy of the court order, and accompanying application, under which the interception was authorized or approved.

In cases in which defendant wishes to know what types of evidence the government intends to use so that he can make his motion to suppress prior to trial, he can request the government to give notice of its intention to use specified evidence which the defendant is entitled to discover under rule 16. Although the defendant is already entitled to discovery of such evidence prior to trial under rule 16, rule 12 makes it possible for him to avoid the necessity of moving to suppress evidence which the government does not intend to use. No sanction is provided for the government's failure to comply with the court's order because the committee believes that attorneys for the government will in fact comply and that judges have ways of insuring compliance. An automatic exclusion of such evidence, particularly where the failure to give notice was not deliberate, seems to create too heavy a burden upon the exclusionary rule of evidence, especially when defendant has opportunity for broad discovery under rule 16. Compare ABA Project on Standards for Criminal Justice, Standards Relating to Electronic Surveillance (Approved Draft, 1971) at p. 116:

A failure to comply with the duty of giving notice could lead to the suppression of evidence. Nevertheless, the standards make it explicit that the rule is intended to be a matter of procedure which need not under appropriate circumstances automatically dictate that evidence otherwise admissible be suppressed.

Pretrial notice by the prosecution of its intention to use evidence which may be subject to a motion to suppress is increasingly being encouraged in state practice. See, e.g., State ex rel. Goodchild v. Burke, 27 Wis.2d 244, 264, 133 N.W.2d 753, 763 (1965):

In the interest of better administration of criminal justice we suggest that wherever practicable the prosecutor should within a reasonable time before trial notify the defense as to whether any alleged confession or admission will be offered in evidence at the trial. We also suggest, in cases where such notice is given by the prosecution, that the defense, if it intends to attack the confession or admission as involuntary, notify the prosecutor of a desire by the defense for a special determination on such issue.

See also State ex rel. Rasmussen v. Tahash, 272 Minn. 539, 553–556, 141 N.W.2d 3, 13–15 (1965):

At the time of arraignment when a defendant pleads not guilty, or as soon as possible thereafter, the state will advise the court as to whether its case against the defendant will include evidence obtained as the result of a search and seizure; evidence discovered because of a confession or statements in the nature of a confession obtained from the defendant; or confessions or statements in the nature of confessions.

Upon being so informed, the court will formally advise the attorney for the defendant (or the defendant himself if he refuses legal counsel) that he may, if he chooses, move the court to suppress the evidence so secured or the confession so obtained if his contention is that such evidence was secured or confession obtained in violation of defendant's constitutional rights. * * *

The procedure which we have outlined deals only with evidence obtained as the result of a search and seizure and evidence consisting of or produced by confession on the part of the defendant. However, the steps which have been suggested as a method of dealing with evidence of this type will indicate to counsel and to the trial courts that the pretrial consideration of other evidentiary problems, the resolution of which is needed to assure the integrity of the trial when conducted, will be most useful and that this court encourages the use of such procedures whenever practical.

Subdivision (e) provides that the court shall rule on a pretrial motion before trial unless the court orders that it be decided upon at the trial of the general issue or after verdict. This is the old rule. The reference to issues which must be tried by the jury is dropped as unnecessary, without any intention of changing current law or practice. The old rule begs the question of when a jury decision is required at the trial, providing only that a jury is necessary if "required by the Constitution or an act of Congress." It will be observed that subdivision (e) confers general authority to defer the determination of any pretrial motion until after verdict. However, in the case of a motion to suppress evidence the power should be exercised in the light of the possibility that if the motion is ultimately granted a retrial of the defendant may not be permissible.

Subdivision (f) provides that a failure to raise the objections or make the requests specified in subdivision (b) constitutes a waiver thereof, but the court is allowed to grant relief from the waiver if adequate cause is shown. See C. Wright, Federal Practice and Procedure: Criminal §192 (1969), where it is pointed out that the old rule is unclear as to whether the waiver results only from a failure to raise the issue prior to trial or from the failure to do so at the time fixed by the judge for a hearing. The amendment makes clear that the defendant and, where appropriate, the government have an obligation to raise the issue at the motion date set by the judge pursuant to subdivision (c).

Subdivision (g) requires that a verbatim record be made of pretrial motion proceedings and requires the judge to make a record of his findings of fact and conclusions of law. This is desirable if pretrial rulings are to be subject to post-conviction review on the record. The judge may find and rule orally from the bench, so long as a verbatim record is taken. There is no necessity of a separate written memorandum containing the judge's findings and conclusions.

Subdivision (h) is essentially old rule 12(b)(5) except for the deletion of the provision that defendant may plead if the motion is determined adversely to him or, if he has already entered a plea, that that plea stands. This language seems unnecessary particularly in light of the experience in some district courts where a pro forma plea of not guilty is entered at the arraignment, pretrial motions are later made, and depending upon the outcome the defendant may then change his plea to guilty or persist in his plea of not guilty.

NOTES OF COMMITTEE ON THE JUDICIARY, HOUSE REPORT NO. 94–247; 1975 AMENDMENT

A. Amendments Proposed by the Supreme Court. Rule 12 of the Federal Rules of Criminal Procedure deals with pretrial motions and pleadings. The Supreme Court proposed several amendments to it. The more significant of these are set out below.

Subdivision (b) as proposed to be amended provides that the pretrial motions may be oral or written, at the court's discretion. It also provides that certain types of motions must be made before trial.

Subdivision (d) as proposed to be amended provides that the government, either on its own or in response to a request by the defendant, must notify the defendant of its intention to use certain evidence in order to give the defendant an opportunity before trial to move to suppress that evidence.

Subdivision (e) as proposed to be amended permits the court to defer ruling on a pretrial motion until the trial of the general issue or until after verdict.

Subdivision (f) as proposed to be amended provides that the failure before trial to file motions or requests or to raise defenses which must be filed or raised prior to trial, results in a waiver. However, it also provides that the court, for cause shown, may grant relief from the waiver.

Subdivision (g) as proposed to be amended requires that a verbatim record be made of the pretrial motion proceedings and that the judge make a record of his findings of fact and conclusions of law.

B. Committee Action. The Committee modified subdivision (e) to permit the court to defer its ruling on a pretrial motion until after the trial only for good cause. Moreover, the court cannot defer its ruling if to do so will adversely affect a party's right to appeal. The Committee believes that the rule proposed by the Supreme Court could deprive the government of its appeal rights under statutes like section 3731 of title 18 of the United States Code. Further, the Committee hopes to discourage the tendency to reserve rulings on pretrial motions until after verdict in the hope that the jury's verdict will make a ruling unnecessary.

The Committee also modified subdivision (h), which deals with what happens when the court grants a pretrial motion based upon a defect in the institution of the prosecution or in the indictment or information. The Committee's change provides that when such a motion is granted, the court may order that the defendant be continued in custody or that his bail be continued for a specified time. A defendant should not automatically be continued in custody when such a motion is granted. In order to continue the defendant in custody, the court must not only determine that there is probable cause, but it must also determine, in effect, that there is good cause to have the defendant arrested.

NOTES OF ADVISORY COMMITTEE ON RULES—1983 AMENDMENT

Note to Subdivision (i). As noted in the recent decision of United States v. Raddatz, 447 U.S. 667 (1980), hearings on pretrial suppression motions not infrequently necessitate a determination of the credibility of witnesses. In such a situation, it is particularly important, as also highlighted by Raddatz, that the record include some other evidence which tends to either verify or controvert the assertions of the witness. (This is especially true in light of the Raddatz holding that a district judge, in order to make an independent evaluation of credibility, is not required to rehear testimony on which a magistrate based his findings and recommendations following a suppression hearing before the magistrate.) One kind of evidence which can often fulfill this function is prior statements of the testifying witness, yet courts have consistently held that in light of the Jencks Act, 18 U.S.C. §3500, such production of statements cannot be compelled at a pretrial suppression hearing. United States v. Spagnuolo, 515 F.2d 818 (9th Cir. 1975); United States v. Sebastian, 497 F.2d 1267 (2nd Cir. 1974); United States v. Montos, 421 F.2d 215 (5th Cir. 1970). This result, which finds no express Congressional approval in the legislative history of the Jencks Act, see United States v. Sebastian, supra; United States v. Covello, 410 F.2d 536 (2d Cir. 1969), would be obviated by new subdivision (i) of rule 12.

This change will enhance the accuracy of the factual determinations made in the context of pretrial suppression hearings. As noted in United States v. Sebastian, supra, it can be argued most persuasively that the case for pre-trial disclosure is strongest in the framework of a suppression hearing. Since findings at such a hearing as to admissibility of challenged evidence will often determine the result at trial and, at least in the case of fourth amendment suppression motions, cannot be relitigated later before the trier of fact, pre-trial production of the statements of witnesses would aid defense counsel's impeachment efforts at perhaps the most crucial point in the case. * * * [A] government witness at the suppression hearing may not appear at trial so that defendants could never test his credibility with the benefits of Jencks Act material.

The latter statement is certainly correct, for not infrequently a police officer who must testify on a motion to suppress as to the circumstances of an arrest or search will not be called at trial because he has no information necessary to the determination of defendant's guilt. See, e.g., United States v. Spagnuolo, supra (dissent notes that "under the prosecution's own admission, it did not intend to produce at trial the witnesses called at the pre-trial suppression hearing"). Moreover, even if that person did testify at the trial, if that testimony went to a different subject matter, then under rule 26.2(c) only portions of prior statements covering the same subject matter need be produced, and thus portions which might contradict the suppression hearing testimony would not be revealed. Thus, while it may be true, as declared in United States v. Montos, supra, that "due process does not require premature production at pre-trial hearings on motions to suppress of statements ultimately subject to discovery under the Jencks Act," the fact of the matter is that those statements—or, the essential portions thereof—are not necessarily subject to later discovery.

Moreover, it is not correct to assume that somehow the problem can be solved by leaving the suppression issue "open" in some fashion for resolution once the trial is under way, at which time the prior statements will be produced. In United States v. Spagnuolo, supra, the court responded to the defendant's dilemma of inaccessible prior statements by saying that the suppression motion could simply be deferred until trial. But, under the current version of rule 12 this is not possible; subdivision (b) declares that motions to suppress "must" be made before trial, and subdivision (e) says such motions cannot be deferred for determination at trial "if a party's right to appeal is adversely affected," which surely is the case as to suppression motions. As for the possibility of the trial judge reconsidering the motion to suppress on the basis of prior statements produced at trial and casting doubt on the credibility of a suppression hearing witness, it is not a desirable or adequate solution. For one thing, as already noted, there is no assurance that the prior statements will be forthcoming. Even if they are, it is not efficient to delay the continuation of the trial to undertake a reconsideration of matters which could have been resolved in advance of trial had the critical facts then been available. Furthermore, if such reconsideration is regularly to be expected of the trial judge, then this would give rise on appeal to unnecessary issues of the kind which confronted the court in United States v. Montos, supra—whether the trial judge was obligated either to conduct a new hearing or to make a new determination in light of the new evidence.

The second sentence of subdivision (i) provides that a law enforcement officer is to be deemed a witness called by the government. This means that when such a federal, state or local officer has testified at a suppression hearing, the defendant will be entitled to any statement of the officer in the possession of the government and relating to the subject matter concerning which the witness has testified, without regard to whether the officer was in fact called by the government or the defendant. There is considerable variation in local practice as to whether the arresting or searching officer is considered the witness of the defendant or of the government, but the need for the prior statement exists in either instance.

The second sentence of subdivision (i) also provides that upon a claim of privilege the court is to excise the privileged matter before turning over the statement. The situation most likely to arise is that in which the prior statement of the testifying officer identifies an informant who supplied some or all of the probable cause information to the police. Under McCray v. Illinois, 386 U.S. 300 (1967), it is for the judge who hears the motion to decide whether disclosure of the informant's identity is necessary in the particular case. Of course, the government in any case may prevent disclosure of the informant's identity by terminating reliance upon information from that informant.

NOTES OF ADVISORY COMMITTEE ON RULES——1987 AMENDMENT

The amendments are technical. No substantive change is intended.

NOTES OF ADVISORY COMMITTEE ON RULES——1993 AMENDMENT

The amendment to subdivision (i) is one of a series of contemporaneous amendments to Rules 26.2, 32(f), 32.1, 46, and Rule 8 of the Rules Governing §2255 Hearings, which extended Rule 26.2, Production of Witness Statements, to other proceedings or hearings conducted under the Rules of Criminal Procedure. Rule 26.2(c) now explicitly states that the trial court may excise privileged matter from the requested witness statements. That change rendered similar language in Rule 12(i) redundant.

COMMITTEE NOTES ON RULES——2002 AMENDMENT

The language of Rule 12 has been amended as part of the general restyling of the Criminal Rules to make them more easily understood and to make style and terminology consistent throughout the rules. These changes are intended to be stylistic only, except as noted below.

The last sentence of current Rule 12(a), referring to the elimination of "all other pleas, and demurrers and motions to quash" has been deleted as unnecessary.

Rule 12(b) is modified to more clearly indicate that Rule 47 governs any pretrial motions filed under Rule 12, including form and content. The new provision also more clearly delineates those motions that must be filed pretrial and those that may be filed pretrial. No change in practice is intended.

Rule 12(b)(4) is composed of what is currently Rule 12(d). The Committee believed that that provision, which addresses the government's requirement to disclose discoverable information for the purpose of facilitating timely defense objections and motions, was more appropriately associated with the pretrial motions specified in Rule 12(b)(3).

Rule 12(c) includes a non-stylistic change. The reference to the "local rule" exception has been deleted to make it clear that judges should be encouraged to set deadlines for motions. The Committee believed that doing so promotes more efficient case management, especially when there is a heavy docket of pending cases. Although the rule permits some discretion in setting a date for motion hearings, the Committee believed that doing so at an early point in the proceedings would also promote judicial economy.

Moving the language in current Rule 12(d) caused the relettering of the subdivisions following Rule 12(c).

Although amended Rule 12(e) is a revised version of current Rule 12(f), the Committee intends to make no change in the current law regarding waivers of motions or defenses.

COMMITTEE NOTES ON RULES——2014 AMENDMENT

Rule 12(b)(1). The language formerly in (b)(2), which provided that "any defense, objection, or request that the court can determine without trial of the general issue" may be raised by motion before trial, has been relocated here. The more modern phrase "trial on the merits" is substituted for the more archaic phrase "trial of the general issue." No change in meaning is intended.

Rule 12(b)(2). As revised, subdivision (b)(2) states that lack of jurisdiction may be raised at any time the case is pending. This provision was relocated from its previous placement at the end of subsection (b)(3)(B) and restyled. No change in meaning is intended.

Rule 12(b)(3). The amendment clarifies which motions must be raised before trial.

The introductory language includes two important limitations. The basis for the motion must be one that is "then reasonably available" and the motion must be one that the court can determine "without trial on the merits." The types of claims subject to Rule 12(b)(3) generally will be available before trial and they can—and should—be resolved then. The Committee recognized, however, that in some cases, a party may not have access to the information needed to raise particular claims that fall within the general categories subject to Rule 12(b)(3) prior to trial. The "then reasonably available" language is intended to ensure that a claim a party could not have raised on time is not subject to the limitation on review imposed by Rule 12(c)(3). Additionally, only those issues that can be determined "without a trial on the merits" need be raised by motion before trial. Just as in (b)(1), the more modern phrase "trial on the merits" is substituted for the more archaic phrase "trial of the general issue." No change in meaning is intended.

The rule's command that motions alleging "a defect in instituting the prosecution" and "errors in the indictment or information" must be made before trial is unchanged. The amendment adds a nonexclusive list of commonly raised claims under each category to help ensure that such claims are not overlooked. The Rule is not intended to and does not affect or supersede statutory provisions that establish the time to make specific motions, such as motions under the Jury Selection and Service Act, 18 U.S.C. §1867(a) [28 U.S.C. §1867(a)].

Rule 12(b)(3)(B) has also been amended to remove language that allowed the court at any time while the case is pending to hear a claim that the "indictment or information fails . . . to state an offense." This specific charging error was previously considered fatal whenever raised and was excluded from the general requirement that charging deficiencies be raised prior to trial. The Supreme Court abandoned any jurisdictional justification for the exception in United States v. Cotton, 535 U.S. 625, 629-31 (2002) (overruling Ex parte Bain, 121 U.S. 1 (1887), "[i]nsofar as it held that a defective indictment deprives a court of jurisdiction").

Rule 12(c). As revised, subdivision (c) governs both the deadline for making pretrial motions and the consequences of failing to meet the deadline for motions that must be made before trial under Rule 12(b)(3).

As amended, subdivision (c) contains three paragraphs. Paragraph (c)(1) retains the existing provisions for establishing the time when pretrial motions must be made, and adds a sentence stating that unless the court sets a deadline, the deadline for pretrial motions is the start of trial, so that motions may be ruled upon before jeopardy attaches. Subdivision (e) of the present rule contains the language "or by any extension the court provides," which anticipates that a district court has broad discretion to extend, reset, or decline to extend or reset, the deadline for pretrial motions. New paragraph (c)(2) recognizes this discretion explicitly and relocates the Rule's mention of it to a more logical place—after the provision concerning setting the deadline and before the provision concerning the consequences of not meeting the deadline. No change in meaning is intended.

New paragraph (c)(3) governs the review of untimely claims, previously addressed in Rule 12(e). Rule 12(e) provided that a party "waives" a defense not raised within the time set under Rule 12(c). Although the term waiver in the context of a criminal case ordinarily refers to the intentional relinquishment of a known right, Rule 12(e) has never required any determination that a party who failed to make a timely motion intended to relinquish a defense, objection, or request that was not raised in a timely fashion. Accordingly, to avoid possible confusion the Committee decided not to employ the term "waiver" in new paragraph (c)(3).

New paragraph 12(c)(3) retains the existing standard for untimely claims. The party seeking relief must show "good cause" for failure to raise a claim by the deadline, a flexible standard that requires consideration of all interests in the particular case.

Rule 12(e). The effect of failure to raise issues by a pretrial motion has been relocated from (e) to (c)(3).

Changes Made After Publication and Comment. Language that had been deleted from Rule 12(b)(2) as unnecessary was restored and relocated in (b)(1). The change begins the Rule's treatment of pretrial motions with an appropriate general statement and responds to concerns that the deletion might have been perceived as unintentionally restricting the district courts' authority to rule on pretrial motions. The references to "double jeopardy" and "statute of limitations" were dropped from the nonexclusive list in (b)(3)(A) to permit further debate over the treatment of such claims. New paragraph (c)(2) was added to state explicitly the district court's authority to extend or reset the deadline for pretrial motions; this authority had been recognized implicitly in language being deleted from Rule 12(e). In subdivision (c), the cross reference to Rule 52 was omitted as unnecessarily controversial. In subparagraph (c)(3), the current language "good cause" was retained for all claims and subparagraph (c)(3)(B) was omitted. Finally, the Committee Note was amended to reflect these post-publication changes and to state explicitly that the rule is not intended to change or supersede statutory deadlines under provisions such as the Jury Selection and Service Act.

AMENDMENT BY PUBLIC LAW

1975—Pub. L. 94–64 amended subds. (e) and (h) generally.

EFFECTIVE DATE OF AMENDMENTS PROPOSED APRIL 22, 1974; EFFECTIVE DATE OF 1975 AMENDMENTS

Amendments of this rule embraced in the order of the United States Supreme Court on Apr. 22, 1974, and the amendments of this rule made by section 3 of Pub. L. 94–64, effective Dec. 1, 1975, see section 2 of Pub. L. 94–64, set out as a note under rule 4 of these rules.

Rule 12.1. Notice of an Alibi Defense

(a) Government's Request for Notice and Defendant's Response.
(1) Government's Request. An attorney for the government may request in writing that the defendant notify an attorney for the government of any intended alibi defense. The request must state the time, date, and place of the alleged offense.
(2) Defendant's Response. Within 14 days after the request, or at some other time the court sets, the defendant must serve written notice on an attorney for the government of any intended alibi defense. The defendant's notice must state:
(A) each specific place where the defendant claims to have been at the time of the alleged offense; and
(B) the name, address, and telephone number of each alibi witness on whom the defendant intends to rely.

(b) Disclosing Government Witnesses.
(1) Disclosure.
(A) In General. If the defendant serves a Rule 12.1(a)(2) notice, an attorney for the government must disclose in writing to the defendant or the defendant's attorney:
(i) the name of each witness—and the address and telephone number of each witness other than a victim—that the government intends to rely on to establish that the defendant was present at the scene of the alleged offense; and
(ii) each government rebuttal witness to the defendant's alibi defense.

(B) Victim's Address and Telephone Number. If the government intends to rely on a victim's testimony to establish that the defendant was present at the scene of the alleged offense and the defendant establishes a need for the victim's address and telephone number, the court may:
(i) order the government to provide the information in writing to the defendant or the defendant's attorney; or
(ii) fashion a reasonable procedure that allows preparation of the defense and also protects the victim's interests.

(2) Time to Disclose. Unless the court directs otherwise, an attorney for the government must give its Rule 12.1(b)(1) disclosure within 14 days after the defendant serves notice of an intended alibi defense under Rule 12.1(a)(2), but no later than 14 days before trial.

(c) Continuing Duty to Disclose.

(1) In General. Both an attorney for the government and the defendant must promptly disclose in writing to the other party the name of each additional witness——and the address and telephone number of each additional witness other than a victim——if:

    (A) the disclosing party learns of the witness before or during trial; and

    (B) the witness should have been disclosed under Rule 12.1(a) or (b) if the disclosing party had known of the witness earlier.

(2) Address and Telephone Number of an Additional Victim Witness. The address and telephone number of an additional victim witness must not be disclosed except as provided in Rule 12.1 (b)(1)(B).

(d) Exceptions. For good cause, the court may grant an exception to any requirement of Rule 12.1(a)–(c).

(e) Failure to Comply. If a party fails to comply with this rule, the court may exclude the testimony of any undisclosed witness regarding the defendant's alibi. This rule does not limit the defendant's right to testify.

(f) Inadmissibility of Withdrawn Intention. Evidence of an intention to rely on an alibi defense, later withdrawn, or of a statement made in connection with that intention, is not, in any civil or criminal proceeding, admissible against the person who gave notice of the intention.

(Added Apr. 22, 1974, eff. Dec. 1, 1975; amended Pub. L. 94–64, §3(13), July 31, 1975, 89 Stat. 372; Apr. 29, 1985, eff. Aug. 1, 1985; Mar. 9, 1987, eff. Aug. 1, 1987; Apr. 29, 2002, eff. Dec. 1, 2002; Apr. 23, 2008, eff. Dec. 1, 2008; Mar. 26, 2009, eff. Dec. 1, 2009.)

NOTES OF ADVISORY COMMITTEE ON RULES——1974

Rule 12.1 is new. See rule 87 of the United States District Court Rules for the District of Columbia for a somewhat comparable provision.

The Advisory Committee has dealt with the issue of notice of alibi on several occasions over the course of the past three decades. In the Preliminary Draft of the Federal Rules of Criminal Procedure, 1943, and the Second Preliminary Draft, 1944, an alibi-notice rule was proposed. But the Advisory Committee was closely divided upon whether there should be a rule at all and, if there were to be a rule, what the form of the rule should be. Orfield, The Preliminary Draft of the Federal Rules of Criminal Procedure, 22 Texas L.Rev. 37, 57–58 (1943). The principal disagreement was whether the prosecutor or the defendant should initiate the process. The Second Preliminary Draft published in 1944 required the defendant to initiate the process by a motion to require the government to state with greater particularity the time and place it would rely on. Upon receipt of this information, defendant was required to give his notice of alibi. This formulation was "vehemently objected" to by five members of the committee (out of a total of eighteen) and two alternative rule proposals were submitted to the Supreme Court. Both formulations——one requiring the prosecutor to initiate the process, the other requiring the defendant to initiate the process——were rejected by the Court. See Epstein, Advance Notice of Alibi, 55 J.Crim.L., C. & P.S. 29, 30 (1964), in which the view is expressed that the unresolved split over the rule "probably caused" the court to reject an alibi-notice rule.

Rule 12.1 embodies an intermediate position. The initial burden is upon the defendant to raise the defense of alibi, but he need not specify the details of his alibi defense until the government specifies the time, place, and date of alleged offense. Each party must, at the appropriate time, disclose the names and addresses of witnesses.

In 1962 the Advisory Committee drafted an alibi-notice rule and included it in the Preliminary Draft of December 1962, rule 12A at pp. 5–6. This time the Advisory Committee withdrew the rule without submitting it to the Standing Committee on Rules of Practice and Procedure. Wright, Proposed Changes in Federal Civil, Criminal, and Appellate Procedure, 35 F.R.D. 317, 326 (1964). Criticism of the December 1962 alibi-notice rule centered on constitutional questions and questions of general fairness to the defendant. See Everett, Discovery in Criminal Cases——In Search of a Standard, 1964 Duke L.J. 477, 497–499.

Doubts about the constitutionality of a notice-of-alibi rule were to some extent resolved by Williams v. Florida, 399 U.S. 78, 90 S.Ct. 1893, 26 L.Ed.2d 446 (1970). In that case the court sustained the constitutionality of the Florida notice-of-alibi statute, but left unresolved two important questions.

(1) The court said that it was not holding that a notice-of-alibi requirement was valid under conditions where a defendant does not enjoy "reciprocal discovery against the State." 399 U.S. at 82 n. 11, 90 S.Ct. 1893. Under the revision of rule 16, the defendant is entitled to substantially enlarged discovery in federal cases, and it would seem appropriate to conclude that the rules will comply with the "reciprocal discovery" qualification of the Williams decision. [See, Wardius v. Oregon, 412 U.S. 470, 93 S.Ct. 2208, 37 L.Ed.2d 82 (1973) was decided after the approval of proposed Rule 12.1 by the Judicial Conference of the United States. In that case the Court held the Oregon Notice-of-Alibi statute unconstitutional because of the failure to give the defendant adequate reciprocal discovery rights.]

(2) The court said that it did not consider the question of the "validity of the threatened sanction, had petitioner chosen not to comply with the notice-of-alibi rule." 399 U.S. at 83 n. 14, 90 S.Ct. 1893. This issue remains unresolved. [See Wardius v. Oregon, 412 U.S. at 472, Note 4, 93 S.Ct. 2208.] Rule 12.1(e) provides that the court may exclude the testimony of any witness whose name has not been disclosed pursuant to the requirements of the rule. The defendant may, however, testify himself. Prohibiting from testifying a witness whose name was not disclosed is a common provision in state statutes. See Epstein, supra, at 35. It is generally assumed that the sanction is essential if the notice-of-alibi rule is to have practical significance. See Epstein, supra, at 36. The use of the term "may" is intended to make clear that the judge may allow the alibi witness to testify if, under the particular circumstances, there is cause shown for the failure to conform to the requirements of the rules. This is further emphasized by subdivision (f) which provides for exceptions whenever "good cause" is shown for the exception.

The Supreme Court of Illinois recently upheld an Illinois statute which requires a defendant to give notice of his alibi witnesses although the prosecution is not required to disclose its alibi rebuttal witnesses. People v. Holiday, 47 Ill.2d 300, 265 N.E.2d 634 (1970). Because the defense complied with the requirement, the court did not have to consider the propriety of penalizing noncompliance.

The requirement of notice of alibi seems to be an increasingly common requirement of state criminal procedure. State statutes and court rules are cited in 399 U.S. at 82 n. 11, 90 S.Ct. 1893. See also Epstein, supra.

Rule 12.1 will serve a useful purpose even though rule 16 now requires disclosure of the names and addresses of government and defense witnesses. There are cases in which the identity of defense witnesses may be known, but it may come as a surprise to the government that they intend to testify as to an alibi and there may be no advance notice of the details of the claimed alibi. The result often is an unnecessary interruption and delay in the trial to enable the government to conduct an appropriate investigation. The objective of rule 12.1 is to prevent this by providing a mechanism which will enable the parties to have specific information in advance of trial to prepare to meet the issue of alibi during the trial.

NOTES OF COMMITTEE ON THE JUDICIARY, HOUSE REPORT NO. 94–247; 1975 AMENDMENT

A. Amendments Proposed by the Supreme Court. Rule 12.1 is a new rule that deals with the defense of alibi. It provides that a defendant must notify the government of his intention to rely upon the defense of alibi. Upon receipt of such notice, the government must advise the defendant of the specific time, date, and place at which the offense is alleged to have been committed. The defendant must then inform the government of the specific place at which he claims to have been when the offense is alleged to have been committed, and of the names and addresses of the witnesses on whom he intends to rely to establish his alibi. The government must then inform the defendant of the names and addresses of the witnesses on whom it will rely to establish the defendant's presence at the scene of the crime. If either party fails to comply with the provisions of the rule, the court may exclude the testimony of any witness whose identity is not disclosed. The rule does not attempt to limit the right of the defendant to testify in his own behalf.

B. Committee Action. The Committee disagrees with the defendant-triggered procedures of the rule proposed by the Supreme Court. The major purpose of a notice-of-alibi rule is to prevent unfair surprise to the prosecution. The Committee, therefore, believes that it should be up to the prosecution to trigger the alibi defense discovery procedures. If the prosecution is worried about being surprised by an alibi defense, it can trigger the alibi defense discovery procedures. If the government fails to trigger the procedures and if the defendant raises an alibi defense at trial, then the government cannot claim surprise and get a continuance of the trial.

The Committee has adopted a notice-of-alibi rule similar to the one now used in the District of Columbia. [See Rule 2–5(b) of the Rules of the United States District Court for the District of Columbia. See also Rule 16–1 of the Rules of Criminal Procedure for the Superior Court of the District of Columbia.] The rule is prosecution-triggered. If the prosecutor notifies the defendant of the time, place, and date of the alleged offense, then the defendant has 10 days in which to notify the prosecutor of his intention to rely upon an alibi defense, specify where he claims to have been at the time of the alleged offense, and provide a list of his alibi witnesses. The prosecutor, within 10 days but no later than 10 days before trial, must then provide the defendant with a list of witnesses who will place the defendant at the scene of the alleged crime and those witnesses who will be used to rebut the defendant's alibi witnesses.

The Committee's rule does not operate only to the benefit of the prosecution. In fact, its rule will provide the defendant with more information than the rule proposed by the Supreme Court. The rule proposed by the Supreme Court permits the defendant to obtain a list of only those witnesses who will place him at the scene of the crime. The defendant, however, would get the names of these witnesses anyway as part of his discovery under Rule 16(a)(1)(E). The Committee rule not only requires the prosecution to provide the names of witnesses who place the defendant at the scene of the crime, but it also requires the prosecution to turn over the names of those witnesses who will be called in rebuttal to the defendant's alibi witnesses. This is information that the defendant is not otherwise entitled to discover.

NOTES OF ADVISORY COMMITTEE ON RULES—1985 AMENDMENT

Note to Subdivision (f). This clarifying amendment is intended to serve the same purpose as a comparable change made in 1979 to similar language in Rule 11(e)(6). The change makes it clear that evidence of a withdrawn intent or of statements made in connection therewith is thereafter inadmissible against the person who gave the notice in any civil or criminal proceeding, without regard to whether the proceeding is against that person.

NOTES OF ADVISORY COMMITTEE ON RULES—1987 AMENDMENT

The amendments are technical. No substantive change is intended.

COMMITTEE NOTES ON RULES—2002 AMENDMENT

The language of Rule 12.1 has been amended as part of the general restyling of the Criminal Rules to make them more easily understood and to make style and terminology consistent throughout the rules. These changes are intended to be stylistic only, except as noted below.

Current Rules 12.1(d) and 12.1(e) have been switched in the amended rule to improve the organization of the rule.

Finally, the amended rule includes a new requirement that in providing the names and addresses of alibi and any rebuttal witnesses, the parties must also provide the phone numbers of those witnesses. See Rule 12.1(a)(2), Rule 12.1(b)(1), and Rule 12.1(c). The Committee believed that requiring such information would facilitate locating and interviewing those witnesses.

COMMITTEE NOTES ON RULES—2008 AMENDMENT

Subdivisions (b) and (c). The amendment implements the Crime Victims' Rights Act, which states that victims have the right to be reasonably protected from the accused and to be treated with respect for the victim's dignity and privacy. See 18 U.S.C. §3771(a)(1) & (8). The rule provides that a victim's address and telephone number should not automatically be provided to the defense when an alibi defense is raised. If a defendant establishes a need for this information, the court has discretion to order its disclosure or to fashion an alternative procedure that provides the defendant with the information necessary to prepare a defense, but also protects the victim's interests.

In the case of victims who will testify concerning an alibi claim, the same procedures and standards apply to both the prosecutor's initial disclosure and the prosecutor's continuing duty to disclose under subdivision (c).

Changes Made to Proposed Amendment Released for Public Comment. The Committee made very minor changes in the text at the suggestion of the Style Consultant. The Committee revised the Note in response to public comments, omitting the suggestion that the court might upon occasion have the defendant and victim meet.

COMMITTEE NOTES ON RULES—2009 AMENDMENT

The times set in the former rule at 10 days have been revised to 14 days. See the Committee Note to Rule 45(a).

AMENDMENT BY PUBLIC LAW

1975—Pub. L. 94–64 amended Rule 12.1 generally.

EFFECTIVE DATE OF RULE; EFFECTIVE DATE OF 1975 AMENDMENTS

This rule, and the amendments of this rule made by section 3 of Pub. L. 94–64, effective Dec. 1, 1975, see section 2 of Pub. L. 94–64, set out as a note under rule 4 of these rules.

Rule 12.2. Notice of an Insanity Defense; Mental Examination

(a) Notice of an Insanity Defense. A defendant who intends to assert a defense of insanity at the time of the alleged offense must so notify an attorney for the government in writing within the time provided for filing a pretrial motion, or at any later time the court sets, and file a copy of the notice with the clerk. A defendant who fails to do so cannot rely on an insanity defense. The court may, for good cause, allow the defendant to file the notice late, grant additional trial-preparation time, or make other appropriate orders.

(b) Notice of Expert Evidence of a Mental Condition. If a defendant intends to introduce expert evidence relating to a mental disease or defect or any other mental condition of the defendant bearing on either (1) the issue of guilt or (2) the issue of punishment in a capital case, the defendant must—within the time provided for filing a pretrial motion or at any later time the court sets—notify an attorney for the government in writing of this intention and file a copy of the notice with the clerk. The court may, for good cause, allow the defendant to file the notice late, grant the parties additional trial-preparation time, or make other appropriate orders.

(c) Mental Examination.

(1) Authority to Order an Examination; Procedures.

(A) The court may order the defendant to submit to a competency examination under 18 U.S.C. §4241.

(B) If the defendant provides notice under Rule 12.2(a), the court must, upon the government's motion, order the defendant to be examined under 18 U.S.C. §4242. If the defendant provides notice under Rule 12.2(b) the court may, upon the government's motion, order the defendant to be examined under procedures ordered by the court.

(2) Disclosing Results and Reports of Capital Sentencing Examination. The results and reports of any examination conducted solely under Rule 12.2(c)(1) after notice under Rule 12.2(b)(2) must be sealed and must not be disclosed to any attorney for the government or the defendant unless the defendant is found guilty of one or more capital crimes and the defendant confirms an intent to offer during sentencing proceedings expert evidence on mental condition.

(3) Disclosing Results and Reports of the Defendant's Expert Examination. After disclosure under Rule 12.2(c)(2) of the results and reports of the government's examination, the defendant must disclose to the government the results and reports of any examination on mental condition conducted by the defendant's expert about which the defendant intends to introduce expert evidence.

(4) Inadmissibility of a Defendant's Statements. No statement made by a defendant in the course of any examination conducted under this rule (whether conducted with or without the defendant's consent), no testimony by the expert based on the statement, and no other fruits of the statement may be admitted into evidence against the defendant in any criminal proceeding except on an issue regarding mental condition on which the defendant:

(A) has introduced evidence of incompetency or evidence requiring notice under Rule 12.2(a) or (b)(1), or

(B) has introduced expert evidence in a capital sentencing proceeding requiring notice under Rule 12.2(b)(2).

(d) Failure to Comply.

(1) Failure to Give Notice or to Submit to Examination. The court may exclude any expert evidence from the defendant on the issue of the defendant's mental disease, mental defect, or any other mental condition bearing on the defendant's guilt or the issue of punishment in a capital case if the defendant fails to:

(A) give notice under Rule 12.2(b); or

(B) submit to an examination when ordered under Rule 12.2(c).

(2) Failure to Disclose. The court may exclude any expert evidence for which the defendant has failed to comply with the disclosure requirement of Rule 12.2(c)(3).

(e) Inadmissibility of Withdrawn Intention. Evidence of an intention as to which notice was given under Rule 12.2(a) or (b), later withdrawn, is not, in any civil or criminal proceeding, admissible against the person who gave notice of the intention.

(Added Apr. 22, 1974, eff. Dec. 1, 1975; amended Pub. L. 94–64, §3(14), July 31, 1975, 89 Stat. 373; Apr. 28, 1983, eff. Aug. 1, 1983; Pub. L. 98–473, title II, §404, Oct. 12, 1984, 98 Stat. 2067; Pub. L. 98–596, §11(a), (b), Oct. 30, 1984, 98 Stat. 3138; Apr. 29, 1985, eff. Aug. 1, 1985; Pub. L. 99–646, §24, Nov. 10, 1986, 100 Stat. 3597; Mar. 9, 1987, eff. Aug. 1, 1987; Apr. 29, 2002, eff. Dec. 1, 2002; Apr. 25, 2005, eff. Dec. 1, 2005.)

NOTES OF ADVISORY COMMITTEE ON RULES—1974

Rule 12.2 is designed to require a defendant to give notice prior to trial of his intention (1) to rely upon the defense of insanity or (2) to introduce expert testimony of mental disease or defect on the theory that such mental condition is inconsistent with the mental state required for the offense charged. This rule does not deal with the issue of mental competency to stand trial.

The objective is to give the government time to prepare to meet the issue, which will usually require reliance upon expert testimony. Failure to give advance notice commonly results in the necessity for a continuance in the middle of a trial, thus unnecessarily delaying the administration of justice.

A requirement that the defendant give notice of his intention to rely upon the defense of insanity was proposed by the Advisory Committee in the Second Preliminary Draft of Proposed Amendments (March 1964), rule 12.1, p. 7. The objective of the 1964 proposal was explained in a brief Advisory Committee Note:

Under existing procedure although insanity is a defense, once it is raised the burden to prove sanity beyond a reasonable doubt rests with the government. Davis v. United States, 160 U.S. 469, 16 S.Ct. 353, 40 L.Ed. 499 (1895). This rule requires pretrial notice to the government of an insanity defense, thus permitting it to prepare to meet the issue. Furthermore, in Lynch v. Overholser, 369 U.S. 705, 82 S.Ct. 1063, 8 L.Ed.2d 211 (1962), the Supreme Court held that, at least in the face of a mandatory commitment statute, the defendant had a right to determine whether or not to raise the issue of insanity. The rule gives the defendant a method of raising the issue and precludes any problem of deciding whether or not the defendant relied on insanity.

The Standing Committee on Rules of Practice and Procedure decided not to recommend the proposed Notice of Insanity rule to the Supreme Court. Reasons were not given.

Requiring advance notice of the defense of insanity is commonly recommended as a desirable procedure. The Working Papers of the National Commission on Reform of Federal Criminal Laws, Vol. 1, p. 254 (1970), state in part:

It is recommended that procedural reform provide for advance notice that evidence of mental disease or defect will be relied upon in defense. . . .

Requiring advance notice is proposed also by the American Law Institute's Model Penal Code, §4.03 (P.O.D. 1962). The commentary in Tentative Draft No. 4 at 193–194 (1955) indicates that, as of that time, six states required pretrial notice and an additional eight states required that the defense of insanity be specially pleaded.

For recent state statutes see N.Y. CPL §250.10 (McKinney's Consol. Laws, c. 11–A, 1971) enacted in 1970 which provides that no evidence by a defendant of a mental disease negativing criminal responsibility shall be allowed unless defendant has served notice on the prosecutor of his intention to rely upon such defense. See also New Jersey Penal Code (Final Report of the New Jersey Criminal Law Revision Commission, Oct. 1971) §2c: 4–3; New Jersey Court Rule 3:12; State v. Whitlow, 45 N.J. 3, 22 n. 3, 210 T.2d 763 (1965), holding the requirement of notice to be both appropriate and not in violation of the privilege against self-incrimination.

Subdivision (a) deals with notice of the "defense of insanity." In this context the term insanity has a well-understood meaning. See, e.g., Tydings, A Federal Verdict of Not Guilty by Reason of Insanity and a Subsequent Commitment Procedure, 27 Md.L.Rev. 131 (1967). Precisely how the defense of insanity is phrased does, however, differ somewhat from circuit to circuit. See Study Draft of a New Federal Criminal Code, §503 Comment at 37 (USGPO 1970). For a more extensive discussion of present law, see Working Papers of the National Commission on Reform of Federal Criminal Laws, Vol. 1, pp. 229–247 (USGPO 1970). The National Commission recommends the adoption of a single test patterned after the proposal of the American Law Institute's Model Penal Code. The proposed definition provides in part:

In any prosecution for an offense lack of criminal responsibility by reason of mental disease or defect is a defense. [Study Draft of a New Federal Criminal Code §503 at 36–37.]

Should the proposal of the National Commission be adopted by the Congress, the language of subdivision (a) probably ought to be changed to read "defense of lack of criminal responsibility by reason of mental disease or defect" rather than "defense of insanity."

Subdivision (b) is intended to deal with the issue of expert testimony bearing upon the issue of whether the defendant had the "mental state required for the offense charged."

There is some disagreement as to whether it is proper to introduce evidence of mental disease or defect bearing not upon the defense of insanity, but rather upon the existence of the mental state required by the offense charged. The American Law Institute's Model Penal Code takes the position that such evidence is admissible [§4.02(1) (P.O.D. 1962)]. See also People v. Gorshen, 51 Cal.2d 716, 336 P.2d 492 (1959).

The federal cases reach conflicting conclusions. See Rhodes v. United States, 282 F.2d 59, 62 (4th Cir. 1960):

61

The proper way would have been to ask the witness to describe the defendant's mental condition and symptoms, his pathological beliefs and motivations, if he was thus afflicted, and to explain how these influenced or could have influenced his behavior, particularly his mental capacity knowingly to make the false statement charged, or knowingly to forge the signatures * * *.

Compare Fisher v. United States, 328 U.S. 463, 66 S.Ct. 1318, 90 L.Ed. 1382 (1946).

Subdivision (b) does not attempt to decide when expert testimony is admissible on the issue of the requisite mental state. It provides only that the defendant must give pretrial notice when he intends to introduce such evidence. The purpose is to prevent the need for a continuance when such evidence is offered without prior notice. The problem of unnecessary delay has arisen in jurisdictions which do not require prior notice of an intention to use expert testimony on the issue of mental state. Referring to this, the California Special Commission on Insanity and Criminal Offenders, First Report 30 (1962) said:

The abuses of the present system are great. Under a plea of "not guilty" without any notice to the people that the defense of insanity will be relied upon, defendant has been able to raise the defense upon the trial of the issue as to whether he committed the offense charged.

As an example of the delay occasioned by the failure to heretofore require a pretrial notice by the defendant, see United States v. Albright, 388 F.2d 719 (4th Cir. 1968), where a jury trial was recessed for 23 days to permit a psychiatric examination by the prosecution when the defendant injected a surprise defense of lack of mental competency.

Subdivision (c) gives the court the authority to order the defendant to submit to a psychiatric examination by a psychiatrist designated by the court. A similar provision is found in ALI, Model Penal Code §4.05(1) (P.O.D. 1962). This is a common provision of state law, the constitutionality of which has been sustained. Authorities are collected in ALI, Model Penal Code, pp. 195–196 Tent. Draft No. 4, (1955). For a recent proposal, see the New Jersey Penal Code §2c: 4–5 (Final Report of the New Jersey Criminal Law Revision Commission, Oct. 1971) authorizing appointment of "at least one qualified psychiatrist to examine and report upon the mental condition of the defendant." Any issue of self-incrimination which might arise can be dealt with by the court as, for example, by a bifurcated trial which deals separately with the issues of guilt and of mental responsibility. For statutory authority to appoint a psychiatrist with respect to competency to stand trial, see 18 U.S.C. §4244.

Subdivision (d) confers authority on the court to exclude expert testimony in behalf of a defendant who has failed to give notice under subdivision (b) or who refuses to be examined by a court-appointed psychiatrist under subdivision (c). See State v. Whitlow, 45 N.J. 3, 23, 210 A.2d 763 (1965), which indicates that it is proper to limit or exclude testimony by a defense psychiatrist whenever defendant refuses to be examined.

NOTES OF COMMITTEE ON THE JUDICIARY, HOUSE REPORT NO. 94–247; 1975 AMENDMENT

A. Amendments Proposed by the Supreme Court. Rule 12.2 is a new rule that deals with defense based upon mental condition. It provides that: (1) The defendant must notify the prosecution in writing of his intention to rely upon the defense of insanity. If the defendant fails to comply, "insanity may not be raised as a defense." (2) If the defendant intends to introduce expert testimony relating to mental disease or defect on the issue whether he had the requisite mental state, he must notify the prosecution in writing. (3) The court, on motion of the prosecution, may order the defendant to submit to a psychiatric examination by a court-appointed psychiatrist. (4) If the defendant fails to undergo the court-ordered psychiatric examination, the court may exclude any expert witness the defendant offers on the issue of his mental state.

B. Committee Action. The Committee agrees with the proposed rule but has added language concerning the use of statements made to a psychiatrist during the course of a psychiatric examination provided for by Rule 12.2. The language provides:

No statement made by the accused in the course of any examination provided for by this rule, whether the examination shall be with or without the consent of the accused, shall be admitted in evidence against the accused before the judge who or jury which determines the guilt of the accused, prior to the determination of guilt.

The purpose of this rule is to secure the defendant's fifth amendment right against self-incrimination. See State v. Raskin, 34 Wis.2d 607, 150 N.W.2d 318 (1967). The provision is flexible and does not totally preclude the use of such statements. For example, the defendant's statement can be used at a separate determination of the issue of sanity or for sentencing purposes once guilt has been determined. A limiting instruction to the jury in a single trial to consider statements made to the psychiatrist only on the issue of sanity would not satisfy the requirements of the rule as amended. The prejudicial effect on the determination of guilt would be inescapable.

The Committee notes that the rule does not attempt to resolve the issue whether the court can constitutionally compel a defendant to undergo a psychiatric examination when the defendant is unwilling to undergo one. The provisions of subdivision (c) are qualified by the phrase, "In an appropriate case." If the court cannot constitutionally compel an unwilling defendant to undergo a psychiatric examination, then the provisions of subdivision (c) are inapplicable in every instance where the defendant is unwilling to undergo a court-ordered psychiatric examination. The Committee, by its approval of subdivision (c), intends to take no stand whatever on the constitutional question.

CONFERENCE COMMITTEE NOTES, HOUSE REPORT NO. 94–414; 1975 AMENDMENT

Rule 12.2(c) deals with court-ordered psychiatric examinations. The House version provides that no statement made by a defendant during a court-ordered psychiatric examination could be admitted in evidence against the defendant before the trier of fact that determines the issue of guilt prior to the determination of guilt. The Senate version deletes this provision.

The Conference adopts a modified House provision and restores to the bill the language of H.R. 6799 as it was originally introduced. The Conference adopted language provides that no statement made by the defendant during a psychiatric examination provided for by the rule shall be admitted against him on the issue of guilt in any criminal proceeding.

The Conference believes that the provision in H.R. 6799 as originally introduced in the House adequately protects the defendant's fifth amendment right against self-incrimination. The rule does not preclude use of statements made by a defendant during a court-ordered psychiatric examination. The statements may be relevant to the issue of defendant's sanity and admissible on that issue. However, a limiting instruction would not satisfy the rule if a statement is so prejudicial that a limiting instruction would be ineffective. Cf. practice under 18 U.S.C. 4244.

NOTES OF ADVISORY COMMITTEE ON RULES—1983 AMENDMENT

Note to Subdivision (b). Courts have recently experienced difficulty with the question of what kind of expert testimony offered for what purpose falls within the notice requirement of rule 12.2(b). See, e.g., United States v. Hill, 655 F.2d 512 (3d Cir. 1980) (rule not applicable to tendered testimony of psychologist concerning defendant's susceptibility of inducement, offered to reinforce defendant's entrapment defense); United States v. Webb, 625 F.2d 709 (5th Cir. 1980) (rule not applicable to expert testimony tendered to show that defendant lacked the "propensity to commit a violent act," as this testimony was offered "to prove that Webb did not commit the offense charged," shooting at a helicopter, "not that certain conduct was unaccompanied by criminal intent"); United States v. Perl, 584 F.2d 1316 (4th Cir. 1978) (because entrapment defense properly withheld from jury, it was unnecessary to decide if the district court erred in holding rule applicable to tendered testimony of the doctor that defendant had increased susceptibility to suggestion as a result of medication he was taking); United States v. Olson, 576 F.2d 1267 (8th Cir. 1978) (rule applicable to tendered testimony of an alcoholism and drug therapist that defendant was not responsible for his actions because of a problem with alcohol); United States v. Staggs, 553 F.2d 1073 (7th Cir. 1977) (rule applicable to tendered testimony of psychologist that defendant, charged with assaulting federal officer, was more likely to hurt himself than to direct his aggressions toward others, as this testimony bears upon whether defendant intended to put victim in apprehension when he picked up the gun).

What these cases illustrate is that expert testimony about defendant's mental condition may be tendered in a wide variety of circumstances well beyond the situation clearly within rule 12.2(b), i.e., where a psychiatrist testifies for the defendant regarding his diminished capacity. In all of these situations and others like them, there is good reason to make applicable the notice provisions of rule 12.2(b). This is because in all circumstances in which the defendant plans to offer expert testimony concerning his mental condition at the time of the crime charged, advance disclosure to the government will serve "to permit adequate pretrial preparation, to prevent surprise at trial, and to avoid the necessity of delays during trial." 2 A.B.A. Standards for Criminal Justice 11–55 (2d 1980). Thus, while the district court in United States v. Hill, 481 F.Supp. 558 (E.D.Pa. 1979), incorrectly concluded that present rule 12.2(b) covers testimony by a psychologist bearing on the defense of entrapment, the court quite properly concluded that the government would be seriously disadvantaged by lack of notice. This would have meant that the government would not have been equipped to cross-examine the expert, that any expert called by the government would not have had an opportunity to hear the defense expert testify, and that the government would not have had an opportunity to conduct the kind of investigation needed to acquire rebuttal testimony on defendant's claim that he was especially susceptible to inducement. Consequently, rule 12.2(b) has been expanded to cover all of the aforementioned situations.

Note to Subdivision (c). The amendment of the first sentence of subdivision (c), recognizing that the government may seek to have defendant subjected to a mental examination by an expert other than a psychiatrist, is prompted by the same considerations discussed above. Because it is possible that the defendant will submit to examination by an expert of his own other than a psychiatrist, it is necessary to recognize that it will sometimes be appropriate for defendant to be examined by a government expert other than a psychiatrist.

The last sentence of subdivision (c) has been amended to more accurately reflect the Fifth Amendment considerations at play in this context. See Estelle v. Smith, 451 U.S. 454 (1981), holding that self-incrimination protections are not inevitably limited to the guilt phase of a trial and that the privilege, when applicable, protects against use of defendant's statement and also the fruits thereof, including expert testimony based upon defendant's statements to the expert. Estelle also intimates that "a defendant can be required to submit to a sanity examination," and presumably some other form of mental examination, when "his silence may deprive the State of the only effective means it has of controverting his proof on an issue that he interjected into the case."

Note to Subdivision (d). The broader term "mental condition" is appropriate here in light of the above changes to subdivisions (b) and (c).

Note to Subdivision (e). New subdivision (e), generally consistent with the protection afforded in rule 12.1(f) with respect to notice of alibi, ensures that the notice required under subdivision (b) will not deprive the defendant of an opportunity later to elect not to utilize any expert testimony. This provision is consistent with Williams v. Florida, 399 U.S. 78 (1970), holding the privilege against self-incrimination is not violated by requiring the defendant to give notice of a defense where the defendant retains the "unfettered choice" of abandoning the defense.

DISSENTING STATEMENT OF JUSTICE O'CONNOR TO 1983 AMENDMENT

With one minor reservation, I join the Court in its adoption of the proposed amendments. They represent the product of considerable effort by the Advisory Committee, and they will institute desirable reforms. My sole disagreement with the Court's action today lies in its failure to recommend correction of an apparent error in the drafting of Proposed Rule 12.2(e).

As proposed, Rule 12.2(e) reads:

"Evidence of an intention as to which notice was given under subdivision (a) or (b), later withdrawn, is not admissible in any civil or criminal proceeding against the person who gave notice of the intention."
Identical language formerly appeared in Fed. Rules Crim. Proc. 11(e)(6) and Fed. Rules Evid. 410, each of which stated that
"[Certain material] is not admissible in any civil or criminal proceeding against the defendant."
Those rules were amended, Supreme Court Order April 30, 1979, 441 U.S. 970, 987, 1007, Pub. Law 96–42, approved July 31, 1979, 93 Stat. 326. After the amendments, the relevant language read,
"[Certain material] is not, in any civil or criminal proceeding, admissible against the defendant."
As the Advisory Committee explained, this minor change was necessary to eliminate an ambiguity. Before the amendment, the word "against" could be read as referring either to the kind of proceeding in which the evidence was offered or to the purpose for which it was offered. Thus, for instance, if a person was a witness in a suit but not a party, it was unclear whether the evidence could be used to impeach him. In such a case, the use would be against the person, but the proceeding would not be against him. Similarly, if the person wished to introduce the evidence in a proceeding in which he was the defendant, the use, but not the proceeding, would be against him. To eliminate the ambiguity, the Advisory Committee proposed the amendment clarifying that the evidence was inadmissible against the person, regardless of whether the particular proceeding was against the person. See Adv. Comm. Note to Fed. Rules Crim. Proc. 11(e)(6); Adv. Comm. Note to Fed. Rules Evid. 410.
The same ambiguity inheres in the proposed version of Rule 12.2(e). We should recommend that it be eliminated now. To that extent, I respectfully dissent.

NOTES OF ADVISORY COMMITTEE ON RULES—1985 AMENDMENT

Note to Subdivision (e). This clarifying amendment is intended to serve the same purpose as a comparable change made in 1979 to similar language in Rule 11(e)(6). The change makes it clear that evidence of a withdrawn intent is thereafter inadmissible against the person who gave the notice in any civil or criminal proceeding, without regard to whether the proceeding is against that person.

NOTES OF ADVISORY COMMITTEE ON RULES—1987 AMENDMENT

The amendments are technical. No substantive change is intended.

COMMITTEE NOTES ON RULES—2002 AMENDMENT

The language of Rule 12.2 has been amended as part of the general restyling of the Criminal Rules to make them more easily understood and to make style and terminology consistent throughout the rules. These changes are intended to be stylistic only, except as noted below.

The substantive changes to Rule 12.2 are designed to address five issues. First, the amendment clarifies that a court may order a mental examination for a defendant who has indicated an intention to raise a defense of mental condition bearing on the issue of guilt. Second, the defendant is required to give notice of an intent to present expert evidence of the defendant's mental condition during a capital sentencing proceeding. Third, the amendment addresses the ability of the trial court to order a mental examination for a defendant who has given notice of an intent to present evidence of mental condition during capital sentencing proceedings and when the results of that examination may be disclosed. Fourth, the amendment addresses the timing of disclosure of the results and reports of the defendant's expert examination. Finally, the amendment extends the sanctions for failure to comply with the rule's requirements to the punishment phase of a capital case.

Under current Rule 12.2(b), a defendant who intends to offer expert testimony on the issue of his or her mental condition on the question of guilt must provide a pretrial notice of that intent. The amendment extends that notice requirement to a defendant who intends to offer expert evidence, testimonial or otherwise, on his or her mental condition during a capital sentencing proceeding. As several courts have recognized, the better practice is to require pretrial notice of that intent so that any mental examinations can be conducted without unnecessarily delaying capital sentencing proceedings. See, e.g., United States v. Beckford, 962 F. Supp. 748, 754–64 (E.D. Va. 1997); United States v. Haworth, 942 F. Supp. 1406, 1409 (D.N.M. 1996). The amendment adopts that view.

Revised Rule 12.2(c)(1) addresses and clarifies the authority of the court to order mental examinations for a defendant—to determine competency of a defendant to stand trial under 18 U.S.C. §4241; to determine the defendant's sanity at the time of the alleged offense under 18 U.S.C. §4242; or in those cases where the defendant intends to present expert testimony on his or her mental condition. Rule 12.2(c)(1)(A) reflects the traditional authority of the court to order competency examinations. With regard to examinations to determine insanity at the time of the offense, current Rule 12.2(c) implies that the trial court may grant a government motion for a mental examination of a defendant who has indicated under Rule 12.2(a) an intent to raise the defense of insanity. But the corresponding statute, 18 U.S.C. §4242, requires the court to order an examination if the defendant has provided notice of an intent to raise that defense and the government moves for the examination. Revised Rule 12.2(c)(1)(B) now conforms the rule to §4242. Any examination conducted on the issue of the insanity defense would thus be conducted in accordance with the procedures set out in that statutory provision.

Revised Rule 12.2(c)(1)(B) also addresses those cases where the defendant is not relying on an insanity defense, but intends to offer expert testimony on the issue of mental condition. While the authority of a trial court to order a mental examination of a defendant who has registered an intent to raise the insanity defense seems clear, the authority under the rule to order an examination of a defendant who intends only to present expert testimony on his or her mental condition on the issue of guilt is not as clear. Some courts have concluded that a court may order such an examination. See, e.g., United States v. Stackpole, 811 F.2d 689, 697 (1st Cir. 1987); United States v. Buchbinder, 796 F.2d 910, 915 (1st Cir. 1986); and United States v. Halbert, 712 F.2d 388 (9th Cir. 1983). In United States v. Davis, 93 F.3d 1286 (6th Cir. 1996), however, the court in a detailed analysis of the issue concluded that the district court lacked the authority under the rule to order a mental examination of a defendant who had provided notice of an intent to offer evidence on a defense of diminished capacity. The court noted first that the defendant could not be ordered to undergo commitment and examination under 18 U.S.C. §4242, because that provision relates to situations when the defendant intends to rely on the defense of insanity. The court also rejected the argument that the examination could be ordered under Rule 12.2(c) because this was, in the words of the rule, an "appropriate case." The court concluded, however, that the trial court had the inherent authority to order such an examination.

The amendment clarifies that the authority of a court to order a mental examination under Rule 12.2(c)(1)(B) extends to those cases when the defendant has provided notice, under Rule 12.2(b), of an intent to present expert testimony on the defendant's mental condition, either on the merits or at capital sentencing. See, e.g., United States v. Hall, 152 F.3d 381 (5th Cir. 1998), cert. denied, 119 S. Ct. 1767 (1999).

The amendment to Rule 12.2(c)(1) is not intended to affect any statutory or inherent authority a court may have to order other mental examinations.

The amendment leaves to the court the determination of what procedures should be used for a court-ordered examination on the defendant's mental condition (apart from insanity). As currently provided in the rule, if the examination is being ordered in connection with the defendant's stated intent to present an insanity defense, the procedures are dictated by 18 U.S.C. §4242. On the other hand, if the examination is being ordered in conjunction with a stated intent to present expert testimony on the defendant's mental condition (not amounting to a defense of insanity) either at the guilt or sentencing phases, no specific statutory counterpart is available. Accordingly, the court is given the discretion to specify the procedures to be used. In so doing, the court may certainly be informed by other provisions, which address hearings on a defendant's mental condition. See, e.g., 18 U.S.C. §4241, et seq.

Additional changes address the question when the results of an examination ordered under Rule 12.2(b)(2) may, or must, be disclosed. The Supreme Court has recognized that use of a defendant's statements during a court-ordered examination may compromise the defendant's right against self-incrimination. See Estelle v. Smith, 451 U.S. 454 (1981) (defendant's privilege against self-incrimination violated when he was not advised of right to remain silent during court-ordered examination and prosecution introduced statements during capital sentencing hearing). But subsequent cases have indicated that the defendant waives the privilege if the defendant introduces expert testimony on his or her mental condition. See, e.g., Powell v. Texas, 492 U.S. 680, 683–84 (1989); Buchanan v. Kentucky, 483 U.S. 402, 421–24 (1987); Presnell v. Zant, 959 F.2d 1524, 1533 (11th Cir. 1992); Williams v. Lynaugh, 809 F.2d 1063, 1068 (5th Cir. 1987); United States v. Madrid, 673 F.2d 1114, 1119-21 (10th Cir. 1982). That view is reflected in Rule 12.2(c), which indicates that the statements of the defendant may be used against the defendant only after the defendant has introduced testimony on his or her mental condition. What the current rule does not address is if, and to what extent, the prosecution may see the results of the examination, which may include the defendant's statements, when evidence of the defendant's mental condition is being presented solely at a capital sentencing proceeding.

The proposed change in Rule 12.2(c)(2) adopts the procedure used by some courts to seal or otherwise insulate the results of the examination until it is clear that the defendant will introduce expert evidence about his or her mental condition at a capital sentencing hearing; i.e., after a verdict of guilty on one or more capital crimes, and a reaffirmation by the defendant of an intent to introduce expert mental-condition evidence in the sentencing phase. See, e.g., United States v. Beckford, 962 F. Supp. 748 (E.D. Va. 1997). Most courts that have addressed the issue have recognized that if the government obtains early access to the accused's statements, it will be required to show that it has not made any derivative use of that evidence. Doing so can consume time and resources. See, e.g., United States v. Hall, supra, 152 F.3d at 398 (noting that sealing of record, although not constitutionally required, "likely advances interests of judicial economy by avoiding litigation over [derivative use issue]").

Except as provided in Rule 12.2(c)(3), the rule does not address the time for disclosing results and reports of any expert examination conducted by the defendant. New Rule 12.2(c)(3) provides that upon disclosure under subdivision (c)(2) of the results and reports of the government's examination, disclosure of the results and reports of the defendant's expert examination is mandatory, if the defendant intends to introduce expert evidence relating to the examination.

Rule 12.2(c), as previously written, restricted admissibility of the defendant's statements during the course of an examination conducted under the rule to an issue respecting mental condition on which the defendant "has introduced testimony"—expert or otherwise. As amended, Rule 12.2(c)(4) provides that the admissibility of such evidence in a capital sentencing proceeding is triggered only by the defendant's introduction of expert evidence. The Committee believed that, in this context, it was appropriate to limit the government's ability to use the results of its expert mental examination to instances in which the defendant has first introduced expert evidence on the issue.

Rule 12.2(d) has been amended to extend sanctions for failure to comply with the rule to the penalty phase of a capital case. The selection of an appropriate remedy for the failure of a defendant to provide notice or submit to an examination under subdivisions (b) and (c) is entrusted to the discretion of the court. While subdivision (d) recognizes that the court may exclude the evidence of the defendant's own expert in such a situation, the court should also consider "the effectiveness of less severe sanctions, the impact of preclusion on the evidence at trial and the outcome of the case, the extent of prosecutorial surprise or prejudice, and whether the violation was willful." Taylor v. Illinois, 484 U.S. 400, 414 n.19 (1988) (citing Fendler v. Goldsmith, 728 F.2d 1181 (9th Cir. 1983)).

COMMITTEE NOTES ON RULES—2005 AMENDMENT

The amendment to Rule 12.2(d) fills a gap created in the 2002 amendments to the rule. The substantively amended rule that took effect December 1, 2002, permits a sanction of exclusion of "any expert evidence" for failure to give notice or failure to submit to an examination, but provides no sanction for failure to disclose reports. The proposed amendment is designed to address that specific issue.

Rule 12.2(d)(1) is a slightly restructured version of current Rule 12.2(d). Rule 12.2(d)(2) is new and permits the court to exclude any expert evidence for failure to comply with the disclosure requirement in Rule 12.2(c)(3). The sanction is intended to relate only to the evidence related to the matters addressed in the report, which the defense failed to disclose. Unlike the broader sanction for the two violations listed in Rule 12.2(d)(1)—which can substantially affect the entire hearing—the Committee believed that it would be overbroad to expressly authorize exclusion of "any" expert evidence, even evidence unrelated to the results and reports that were not disclosed, as required in Rule 12.2(c)(3).

The rule assumes that the sanction of exclusion will result only where there has been a complete failure to disclose the report. If the report is disclosed, albeit in an untimely fashion, other relief may be appropriate, for example, granting a continuance to the government to review the report.

Changes Made After Publication and Comment. The Committee made no additional changes to Rule 12.2, following publication.

AMENDMENT BY PUBLIC LAW

1986—Subd. (c). Pub. L. 99—646 inserted "4241 or" before "4242".

1984—Subd. (a). Pub. L. 98—473, §404(a), substituted "offense" for "crime".

Subd. (b). Pub. L. 98—473, §404(b), which directed the amendment of subd. (b) by deleting "other condition bearing upon the issue of whether he had the mental state required for the offense charged" and inserting in lieu thereof "any other mental condition bearing upon the issue of guilt", was repealed by section 11(b) of Pub. L. 98—596.

Subd. (c). Pub. L. 98—596, §11(a)(1), substituted "to an examination pursuant to 18 U.S.C. 4242" for "to a mental examination by a psychiatrist or other expert designated for this purpose in the order of the court".

Pub. L. 98—473, §404(c), which directed the amendment of subd. (c) by deleting "to a psychiatric examination by a psychiatrist designated for this purpose in the order of the court" and inserting in lieu thereof "to an examination pursuant to 18 U.S.C. 4242" could not be executed because the phrase to be deleted did not appear. See amendment note for section 11(a)(1) of Pub. L. 98—596 above.

Subd. (d). Pub. L. 98—596, §11(a)(2), substituted "guilt" for "mental condition".

Pub. L. 98—473, §404(d), which directed the amendment of subd. (d) by deleting "mental state" and inserting in lieu thereof "guilt", was repealed by section 11(b) of Pub. L. 98—596.

1975—Pub. L. 94—64 amended subd. (c) generally.

EFFECTIVE DATE OF 1984 AMENDMENT

Pub. L. 98—596, §11(c), Oct. 30, 1984, 98 Stat. 3138, provided that: "The amendments and repeals made by subsections (a) and (b) of this section [amending this rule] shall apply on and after the enactment of the joint resolution entitled 'Joint resolution making continuing appropriations for the fiscal year 1985, and for other purposes', H.J. Res. 648, Ninety-eighth Congress [Pub. L. 98—473, Oct. 12, 1984]."

EFFECTIVE DATE OF RULE; EFFECTIVE DATE OF 1975 AMENDMENTS

This rule, and the amendments of this rule made by section 3 of Pub. L. 94—64, effective Dec. 1, 1975, see section 2 of Pub. L. 94—64, set out as a note under rule 4 of these rules.

Rule 12.3. Notice of a Public-Authority Defense

(a) Notice of the Defense and Disclosure of Witnesses.
(1) Notice in General. If a defendant intends to assert a defense of actual or believed exercise of public authority on behalf of a law enforcement agency or federal intelligence agency at the time of the alleged offense, the defendant must so notify an attorney for the government in writing and must file a copy of the notice with the clerk within the time provided for filing a pretrial motion, or at any later time the court sets. The notice filed with the clerk must be under seal if the notice identifies a federal intelligence agency as the source of public authority.
(2) Contents of Notice. The notice must contain the following information:
(A) the law enforcement agency or federal intelligence agency involved;
(B) the agency member on whose behalf the defendant claims to have acted; and
(C) the time during which the defendant claims to have acted with public authority.

(3) Response to the Notice. An attorney for the government must serve a written response on the defendant or the defendant's attorney within 14 days after receiving the defendant's notice, but no later than 21 days before trial. The response must admit or deny that the defendant exercised the public authority identified in the defendant's notice.
(4) Disclosing Witnesses.
(A) Government's Request. An attorney for the government may request in writing that the defendant disclose the name, address, and telephone number of each witness the defendant intends to rely on to establish a public-authority defense. An attorney for the government may serve the request when the government serves its response to the defendant's notice under Rule 12.3(a)(3), or later, but must serve the request no later than 21 days before trial.
(B) Defendant's Response. Within 14 days after receiving the government's request, the defendant must serve on an attorney for the government a written statement of the name, address, and telephone number of each witness.
(C) Government's Reply. Within 14 days after receiving the defendant's statement, an attorney for the government must serve on the defendant or the defendant's attorney a written statement of the name of each witness—and the address and telephone number of each witness other than a victim—that the government intends to rely on to oppose the defendant's public-authority defense.
(D) Victim's Address and Telephone Number. If the government intends to rely on a victim's testimony to oppose the defendant's public-authority defense and the defendant establishes a need for the victim's address and telephone number, the court may:
(i) order the government to provide the information in writing to the defendant or the defendant's attorney; or
(ii) fashion a reasonable procedure that allows for preparing the defense and also protects the victim's interests.

(5) Additional Time. The court may, for good cause, allow a party additional time to comply with this rule.

(b) Continuing Duty to Disclose.
(1) In General. Both an attorney for the government and the defendant must promptly disclose in writing to the other party the name of any additional witness—and the address, and telephone number of any additional witness other than a victim—if:
(A) the disclosing party learns of the witness before or during trial; and
(B) the witness should have been disclosed under Rule 12.3(a)(4) if the disclosing party had known of the witness earlier.

(2) Address and Telephone Number of an Additional Victim-Witness. The address and telephone number of an additional victim-witness must not be disclosed except as provided in Rule 12.3(a)(4)(D).

(c) Failure to Comply. If a party fails to comply with this rule, the court may exclude the testimony of any undisclosed witness regarding the public-authority defense. This rule does not limit the defendant's right to testify.
(d) Protective Procedures Unaffected. This rule does not limit the court's authority to issue appropriate protective orders or to order that any filings be under seal.
(e) Inadmissibility of Withdrawn Intention. Evidence of an intention as to which notice was given under Rule 12.3(a), later withdrawn, is not, in any civil or criminal proceeding, admissible against the person who gave notice of the intention.

(Added Pub. L. 100—690, title VI, §6483, Nov. 18, 1988, 102 Stat. 4382; amended Apr. 29, 2002, eff. Dec. 1, 2002; Mar. 26, 2009, eff. Dec. 1, 2009; Apr. 28, 2010, eff. Dec. 1, 2010.)

The language of Rule 12.3 has been amended as part of the general restyling of the Criminal Rules to make them more easily understood and to make style and terminology consistent throughout the rules. These changes are intended to be stylistic only, except as noted below.

Substantive changes have been made in Rule 12.3(a)(4) and 12.3(b). As in Rule 12.1, the Committee decided to include in the restyled rule the requirement that the parties provide the telephone numbers of any witnesses disclosed under the rule.

The times set in the former rule at 7, 10, or 20 days have been revised to 14 or 21 days. See the Committee Note to Rule 45(a).

Subdivisions (a) and (b). The amendment implements the Crime Victims' Rights Act, which states that victims have the right to be reasonably protected from the accused, and to be treated with respect for the victim's dignity and privacy. See 18 U.S.C. §3771(a)(1) & (8). The rule provides that a victim's address and telephone number should not automatically be provided to the defense when a public-authority defense is raised. If a defendant establishes a need for this information, the court has discretion to order its disclosure or to fashion an alternative procedure that provides the defendant with the information necessary to prepare a defense, but also protects the victim's interests.

In the case of victims who will testify concerning a public-authority claim, the same procedures and standards apply to both the prosecutor's initial disclosure and the prosecutor's continuing duty to disclose under subdivision (b).

Changes Made to Proposed Amendment Released for Public Comment. No changes were made after the amendment was released for public comment.

Rule 12.4. Disclosure Statement

(a) Who Must File.
(1) Nongovernmental Corporate Party. Any nongovernmental corporate party to a proceeding in a district court must file a statement that identifies any parent corporation and any publicly held corporation that owns 10% or more of its stock or states that there is no such corporation.
(2) Organizational Victim. Unless the government shows good cause, it must file a statement identifying any organizational victim of the alleged criminal activity. If the organizational victim is a corporation, the statement must also disclose the information required by Rule 12.4(a)(1) to the extent it can be obtained through due diligence.

(b) Time to File; Later Filing. A party must:
(1) file the Rule 12.4(a) statement within 28 days after the defendant's initial appearance; and
(2) promptly file a later statement if any required information changes.

(Added Apr. 29, 2002, eff. Dec. 1, 2002; amended Apr. 26, 2018, eff. Dec. 1, 2018.)

Rule 12.4 is a new rule modeled after Federal Rule of Appellate Procedure 26.1 and parallels similar provisions being proposed in new Federal Rule of Civil Procedure 7.1. The purpose of the rule is to assist judges in determining whether they must recuse themselves because of a "financial interest in the subject matter in controversy." Code of Judicial Conduct, Canon 3C(1)(c)(1972). It does not, however, deal with other circumstances that might lead to disqualification for other reasons.

Under Rule 12.4(a)(1), any nongovernmental corporate party must file a statement that indicates whether it has any parent corporation that owns 10% or more of its stock or indicates that there is no such corporation. Although the term "nongovernmental corporate party" will almost always involve organizational defendants, it might also cover any third party that asserts an interest in property to be forfeited under new Rule 32.2.

Rule 12.4(a)(2) requires an attorney for the government to file a statement that lists any organizational victims of the alleged criminal activity; the purpose of this disclosure is to alert the court to the fact that a possible ground for disqualification might exist. Further, if the organizational victim is a corporation, the statement must include the same information required of any nongovernmental corporate party. The rule requires an attorney for the government to use due diligence in obtaining that information from a corporate organizational victim, recognizing that the timing requirements of Rule 12.4(b) might make it difficult to obtain the necessary information by the time the initial appearance is conducted.

Although the disclosures required by Rule 12.4 may seem limited, they are calculated to reach the majority of circumstances that are likely to call for disqualification on the basis of information that a judge may not know or recollect. Framing a rule that calls for more detailed disclosure is problematic and will inevitably require more information than is necessary for purposes of automatic recusal. Unnecessary disclosure of volumes of information may create the risk that a judge will overlook the one bit of information that might require disqualification, and may also create the risk that courts will experience unnecessary disqualifications rather than attempt to unravel a potentially difficult question.

The same concerns about overbreadth are potentially present in any local rules that might address this topic. Rule 12.4 does not address the promulgation of any local rules that might address the same issue, or supplement the requirements of the rule.

The rule does not cover disclosure of all financial information that could be relevant to a judge's decision whether to recuse himself or herself from a case. The Committee believes that with the various disclosure practices in the federal courts and with the development of technology, more comprehensive disclosure may be desirable and feasible.

Rule 12.4(b)(1) indicates that the time for filing the disclosure statement is at the point when the defendant enters an initial appearance under Rule 5. Although there may be other instances where an earlier appearance of a party in a civil proceeding would raise concerns about whether the presiding judicial officer should be notified of a possible grounds for recusal, the Committee believed that in criminal cases, the most likely time for that to occur is at the initial appearance and that it was important to set a uniform triggering event for disclosures under this rule.

Finally, Rule 12.4(b)(2) requires the parties to file supplemental statements with the court if there are any changes in the information required in the statement.

Subdivision (a). Rule 12.4 requires the government to identify organizational victims to assist judges in complying with their obligations under the Code of Conduct for United States Judges. The 2009 amendments to Canon 3(C)(1)(c) of the Code require recusal only when a judge has an "interest that could be affected substantially by the outcome of the proceeding." In some cases, there are numerous organizational victims, but the impact of the crime on each is relatively small. In such cases, the amendment allows the government to show good cause to be relieved of making the disclosure statements because the organizations' interests could not be "affected substantially by the outcome of the proceeding."

Subdivision (b). The amendment specifies that the time for making the disclosures is within 28 days after the initial appearance.

Because a filing made after the 28-day period may disclose organizational victims in cases in which none were previously known or disclosed, the caption and text have been revised to refer to a later, rather than a supplemental, filing. The text was also revised to be more concise and to parallel Civil Rule 7.1(b)(2).

Rule 13. Joint Trial of Separate Cases

The court may order that separate cases be tried together as though brought in a single indictment or information if all offenses and all defendants could have been joined in a single indictment or information.

(As amended Apr. 29, 2002, eff. Dec. 1, 2002.)

NOTES OF ADVISORY COMMITTEE ON RULES—1944

This rule is substantially a restatement of existing law, 18 U.S.C. [former] 557 (Indictments and presentments; joinder of charges); Logan v. United States, 144 U.S. 263, 296; Showalter v. United States, 260 F. 719 (C.C.A. 4th)—cert. den., 250 U.S. 672; Hostetter v. United States, 16 F.2d 921 (C.C.A. 8th); Capone v. United States, 51 F.2d 609, 619–620 (C.C.A. 7th).

COMMITTEE NOTES ON RULES—2002 AMENDMENT

The language of Rule 13 has been amended as part of the general restyling of the Criminal Rules to make them more easily understood and to make style and terminology consistent throughout the rules. These changes are intended to be stylistic only.

Rule 14. Relief from Prejudicial Joinder

(a) Relief. If the joinder of offenses or defendants in an indictment, an information, or a consolidation for trial appears to prejudice a defendant or the government, the court may order separate trials of counts, sever the defendants' trials, or provide any other relief that justice requires.

(b) Defendant's Statements. Before ruling on a defendant's motion to sever, the court may order an attorney for the government to deliver to the court for in camera inspection any defendant's statement that the government intends to use as evidence.

(As amended Feb. 28, 1966, eff. July 1, 1966; Apr. 29, 2002, eff. Dec. 1, 2002.)

NOTES OF ADVISORY COMMITTEE ON RULES—1944

This rule is a restatement of existing law under which severance and other similar relief is entirely in the discretion of the court, 18 U.S.C. [former] 557 (Indictments and presentments; joinder of charges); Pointer v. United States, 151 U.S. 396; Pierce v. United States, 160 U.S. 355; United States v. Ball, 163 U.S. 662, 673; Stilson v. United States, 250 U.S. 583.

NOTES OF ADVISORY COMMITTEE ON RULES—1966 AMENDMENT

A defendant may be prejudiced by the admission in evidence against a co-defendant of a statement or confession made by that co-defendant. This prejudice cannot be dispelled by cross-examination if the co-defendant does not take the stand. Limiting instructions to the jury may not in fact erase the prejudice. While the question whether to grant a severance is generally left within the discretion of the trial court, recent Fifth Circuit cases have found sufficient prejudice involved to make denial of a motion for severance reversible error. See Schaffer v. United States, 221 F.2d 17 (5th Cir. 1955); Barton v. United States, 263 F.2d 894 (5th Cir. 1959). It has even been suggested that when the confession of the co-defendant comes as a surprise at the trial, it may be error to deny a motion or a mistrial. See Belvin v. United States, 273 F.2d 583 (5th Cir. 1960).

The purpose of the amendment is to provide a procedure whereby the issue of possible prejudice can be resolved on the motion for severance. The judge may direct the disclosure of the confessions or statements of the defendants to him for in camera inspection as an aid to determining whether the possible prejudice justifies ordering separate trials. Cf. note, Joint and Single Trials Under Rules 8 and 14 of the Federal Rules of Criminal Procedure, 74 Yale L.J. 551, 565 (1965).

COMMITTEE NOTES ON RULES—2002 AMENDMENT

The language of Rule 14 has been amended as part of the general restyling of the Criminal Rules to make them more easily understood and to make style and terminology consistent throughout the rules. These changes are intended to be stylistic only.

The reference to a defendant's "confession" in the last sentence of the current rule has been deleted. The Committee believed that the reference to the "defendant's statements" in the amended rule would fairly embrace any confessions or admissions by a defendant.

Rule 15. Depositions

(a) When Taken.

(1) In General. A party may move that a prospective witness be deposed in order to preserve testimony for trial. The court may grant the motion because of exceptional circumstances and in the interest of justice. If the court orders the deposition to be taken, it may also require the deponent to produce at the deposition any designated material that is not privileged, including any book, paper, document, record, recording, or data.

(2) Detained Material Witness. A witness who is detained under 18 U.S.C. §3144 may request to be deposed by filing a written motion and giving notice to the parties. The court may then order that the deposition be taken and may discharge the witness after the witness has signed under oath the deposition transcript.

(b) Notice.

(1) In General. A party seeking to take a deposition must give every other party reasonable written notice of the deposition's date and location. The notice must state the name and address of each deponent. If requested by a party receiving the notice, the court may, for good cause, change the deposition's date or location.

(2) To the Custodial Officer. A party seeking to take the deposition must also notify the officer who has custody of the defendant of the scheduled date and location.

(c) Defendant's Presence.

(1) Defendant in Custody. Except as authorized by Rule 15(c)(3), the officer who has custody of the defendant must produce the defendant at the deposition and keep the defendant in the witness's presence during the examination, unless the defendant:

(A) waives in writing the right to be present; or

(B) persists in disruptive conduct justifying exclusion after being warned by the court that disruptive conduct will result in the defendant's exclusion.

(2) Defendant Not in Custody. Except as authorized by Rule 15(c)(3), a defendant who is not in custody has the right upon request to be present at the deposition, subject to any conditions imposed by the court. If the government tenders the defendant's expenses as provided in Rule 15(d) but the defendant still fails to appear, the defendant—absent good cause—waives both the right to appear and any objection to the taking and use of the deposition based on that right.

(3) Taking Depositions Outside the United States Without the Defendant's Presence. The deposition of a witness who is outside the United States may be taken without the defendant's presence if the court makes case-specific findings of all the following:

(A) the witness's testimony could provide substantial proof of a material fact in a felony prosecution;

(B) there is a substantial likelihood that the witness's attendance at trial cannot be obtained;

(C) the witness's presence for a deposition in the United States cannot be obtained;

(D) the defendant cannot be present because:

(i) the country where the witness is located will not permit the defendant to attend the deposition;

(ii) for an in-custody defendant, secure transportation and continuing custody cannot be assured at the witness's location; or

(iii) for an out-of-custody defendant, no reasonable conditions will assure an appearance at the deposition or at trial or sentencing; and

(E) the defendant can meaningfully participate in the deposition through reasonable means.

(d) Expenses. If the deposition was requested by the government, the court may—or if the defendant is unable to bear the deposition expenses, the court must—order the government to pay:

(1) any reasonable travel and subsistence expenses of the defendant and the defendant's attorney to attend the deposition; and

(2) the costs of the deposition transcript.

(e) Manner of Taking. Unless these rules or a court order provides otherwise, a deposition must be taken and filed in the same manner as a deposition in a civil action, except that:

(1) A defendant may not be deposed without that defendant's consent.

(2) The scope and manner of the deposition examination and cross-examination must be the same as would be allowed during trial.

(3) The government must provide to the defendant or the defendant's attorney, for use at the deposition, any statement of the deponent in the government's possession to which the defendant would be entitled at trial.

(f) Admissibility and Use as Evidence. An order authorizing a deposition to be taken under this rule does not determine its admissibility. A party may use all or part of a deposition as provided by the Federal Rules of Evidence.

(g) Objections. A party objecting to deposition testimony or evidence must state the grounds for the objection during the deposition.

(h) Depositions by Agreement Permitted. The parties may by agreement take and use a deposition with the court's consent.

(As amended Apr. 22, 1974, eff. Dec. 1, 1975; Pub. L. 94–64, §3(15)–(19), July 31, 1975, 89 Stat. 373, 374; Pub. L. 98–473, title II, §209(b), Oct. 12, 1984, 98 Stat. 1986; Mar. 9, 1987, eff. Aug. 1, 1987; Apr. 29, 2002, eff. Dec. 1, 2002; Apr. 23, 2012, eff. Dec. 1, 2012.)

NOTES OF ADVISORY COMMITTEE ON RULES—1944

Note to Subdivision (a). 1. This rule continues the existing law permitting defendants to take depositions in certain limited classes of cases under dedimus potestatem and in perpetuam rei memoriam, 28 U.S.C. [former] 644. This statute has been generally held applicable to criminal cases, Clymer v. United States, 38 F.2d 581 (C.C.A. 10th); Wong Yim v. United States, 118 F.2d 667 (C.C.A. 9th)—cert. den., 313 U.S. 589; United States v. Cameron, 15 F. 794 (C.C.E.D.Mo.); United States v. Hofmann, 24 F.Supp. 847 (S.D.N.Y.). Contra, Luxemberg v. United States, 45 F.2d 497 (C.C.A. 4th)—cert. den., 283 U.S. 820. The rule continues the limitation of the statute that the taking of depositions is to be restricted to cases in which they are necessary "in order to prevent a failure of justice."

2. Unlike the practice in civil cases in which depositions may be taken as a matter of right by notice without permission of the court (Rules 26(a) and 30, Federal Rules of Civil Procedure [28 U.S.C., Appendix]), this rule permits depositions to be taken only by order of the court, made in the exercise of discretion and on notice to all parties. It was contemplated that in criminal cases depositions would be used only in exceptional situations, as has been the practice heretofore.

3. This rule introduces a new feature in authorizing the taking of the deposition of a witness committed for failure to give bail (see Rule 46(b)). This matter is, however, left to the discretion of the court. The purpose of the rule is to afford a method of relief for such a witness, if the court finds it proper to extend it.

Note to Subdivision (b). This subdivision, as well as subdivisions (d) and (f), sets forth the procedure to be followed in the event that the court grants an order for the taking of a deposition. The procedure prescribed is similar to that in civil cases, Rules 28–31, Federal Rules of Civil Procedure [28 U.S.C., Appendix].

Note to Subdivision (c). This rule introduces a new feature for the purpose of protecting the rights of an indigent defendant.

Note to Subdivision (d). See Note to Subdivision (b), supra.

Note to Subdivision (e). In providing when and for what purpose a deposition may be used at the trial, this rule generally follows the corresponding provisions of the Federal Rules of Civil Procedure, Rule 26(d)(3) [28 U.S.C., Appendix]. The only difference is that in civil cases a deposition may be introduced at the trial if the witness is at a greater distance than 100 miles from the place of trial, while this rule requires that the witness be out of the United States. The distinction results from the fact that a subpoena in a civil case runs only within the district where issued or 100 miles from the place of trial (Rule 45(e)(1), Federal Rules of Civil Procedure), while a subpoena in a criminal case runs throughout the United States (see Rule 17(e)(1), infra).

Note to Subdivision (f). See Note to Subdivision (b), supra.

NOTES OF ADVISORY COMMITTEE ON RULES—1974 AMENDMENT

Rule 15 authorizes the taking of depositions by the government. Under former rule 15 only a defendant was authorized to take a deposition.

The revision is similar to Title VI of the Organized Crime Control Act of 1970. The principal difference is that Title VI (18 U.S.C. §3503) limits the authority of the government to take depositions to cases in which the Attorney General certifies that the "proceeding is against a person who is believed to have participated in an organized criminal activity." This limitation is not contained in rule 15.

Dealing with the issue of government depositions so soon after the enactment of 18 U.S.C. §3503 is not inconsistent with the congressional purpose. On the floor of the House, Congressman Poff, a principal spokesman for the proposal, said that the House version was not designed to "limit the Judicial Conference of the United States in the exercise of its rulemaking authority . . . from addressing itself to other problems in this area or from adopting a broader approach." 116 Cong.Rec. 35293 (1970).

The recently enacted Title VI of the Organized Crime Control Act of 1970 (18 U.S.C. §3503) is based upon earlier efforts of the Advisory Committee on Criminal Rules which has over the past twenty-five years submitted several proposals authorizing government depositions.

The earlier drafts of the Federal Rules of Criminal Procedure proposed that the government be allowed to take depositions. Orfield, The Federal Rules of Criminal Procedure, 33 Calif.L.Rev. 543, 559 (1945). The Fifth Draft of what became rule 15 (then rule 20) dated June 1942, was submitted to the Supreme Court for comment. The court had a number of unfavorable comments about allowing government depositions. These comments were not published. The only reference to the fact that the court made comments is in 2 Orfield, Criminal Procedure under the Federal Rules §15:1 (1966); and Orfield, Depositions in Federal Criminal Procedure, 9 S.C.L.Q. 376, 380–381 (1957).

The Advisory Committee, in the 1940's, continued to recommend the adoption of a provision authorizing government depositions. The final draft submitted to the Supreme Court contained a section providing:

The following additional requirements shall apply if the deposition is taken at the instance of the government or of a witness. The officer having custody of a defendant shall be notified of the time and place set for examination, and shall produce him at the examination and keep him in the presence of the witness during the examination. A defendant not in custody shall be given notice and shall have the right to be present at the examination. The government shall pay in advance to the defendant's attorney and a defendant not in custody expenses of travel and subsistence for attendance at the examination.

See 2 Orfield, Criminal Procedure under the Federal Rules §15:3, pp. 447–448 (1966); Orfield, Depositions in Federal Criminal Procedure, 9 S.C.L.Q. 376, 383 (1957).

The Supreme Court rejected this section in this entirety, thus eliminating the provision for depositions by the government. These changes were made without comment.

The proposal to allow government depositions was renewed in the amendments to the Federal Rules of Criminal Procedure in the early 1960's. The Preliminary Draft of Proposed Amendments to Rules of Criminal Procedure for the United States District Courts (December 1962) proposed to amend rule 15 by eliminating the words "of a defendant" from the first sentence of subdivision (a) and adding a subdivision (g) which was practically identical to the subdivision rejected by the Supreme Court in the original draft of the rules.

The Second Preliminary Draft of Proposed Amendments to Rules of Criminal Procedure for the United States District Courts (March 1964) continued to propose allowing governments depositions. Subdivision (g) was substantially modified, however.

The following additional requirements shall apply if the deposition is taken at the instance of the government or a witness. Both the defendant and his attorney shall be given reasonable advance notice of the time and place set for the examination. The officer having custody of a defendant shall be notified of the time and place set for the examination, and shall produce him at the examination and keep him in the presence of the witness during the examination. A defendant not in custody shall have the right to be present at the examination but his failure to appear after notice and tender of expenses shall constitute a waiver of that right. The government shall pay to the defendant's attorney and to a defendant not in custody expenses of travel and subsistence for attendance at the examination. The government shall make available to the defendant for his examination and use at the taking of the deposition any statement of the witness being deposed which is in the possession of the government and which the government would be required to make available to the defendant if the witness were testifying at the trial.

The proposal to authorize government depositions was rejected by the Standing Committee on Rules of Practice and Procedure, C. Wright, Federal Practice and Procedure §241 at 477 (1969). 4 Barron, Federal Practice and Procedure (Supp. 1967). The Report of the Judicial Conference, submitted to the Supreme Court for approval late in 1965, contained no proposal for an amendment to rule 15. See 39 F.R.D. 69, 168–211 (1966).

When the Organized Crime Control Act of 1970 was originally introduced in the Senate (S. 30) it contained a government deposition provision which was similar to the 1964 proposal of the Criminal Rules Advisory Committee, except that the original bill (S. 30) failed to provide standards to control the use of depositions at the trial. For an explanation and defense of the original proposal see McClellan, The Organized Crime Act (S. 30) or Its Critics: Which Threatens Civil Liberties?, 46 Notre Dame Lawyer 55, 100–108 (1970). This omission was remedied, prior to passage, with the addition of what is now 18 U.S.C. §3503(f) which prescribes the circumstances in which a deposition can be used. The standards are the same as those in former rule 15(e) with the addition of language allowing the use of the deposition when "the witness refuses in the trial or hearing to testify concerning the subject of the deposition or the part offered."

Before the Organized Crime Control Act of 1970 was enacted an additional amendment was added providing that the right of the government to take a deposition is limited to cases in which the Attorney General certifies that the defendant is "believed to have participated in an organized criminal activity" [18 U.S.C. §3503(a)]. The argument in favor of the amendment was that the whole purpose of the act was to deal with organized crime and therefore its provisions, including that providing for government depositions, should be limited to organized crime type cases.

There is another aspect of Advisory Committee history which is relevant. In January 1970, the Advisory Committee circulated proposed changes in rule 16, one of which gives the government, when it has disclosed the identity of its witnesses, the right to take a deposition and use it "in the event the witness has become unavailable without the fault of the government or if the witness has changed his testimony." [See Preliminary Draft of Proposed Amendments to the Federal Rules of Criminal Procedure for the United States District Courts, rule 16(a)(1)(vi) (January 1970).] This provision is now incorporated within rule 16(a)(1)(v).

Because neither the court nor the standing committee gave reasons for rejecting the government deposition proposal, it is not possible to know why they were not approved. To the extent that the rejection was based upon doubts as to the constitutionality of such a proposal, those doubts now seem resolved by California v. Green, 399 U.S. 149, 90 S.Ct. 1930, 26 L.Ed.2d 489 (1970).

On the merits, the proposal to allow the government to take depositions is consistent with the revision of rule 16 and with section 804(b)(1) of the Rules of Evidence for the United States Courts and Magistrates (November 1971) which provides that the following is not excluded by the hearsay rule if the declarant is unavailable:

(1) Former Testimony. Testimony given as a witness at another hearing of the same or a different proceeding, or in a deposition taken in compliance with law in the course of another proceeding, at the instance of or against a party with an opportunity to develop the testimony by direct, cross, or redirect examination, with motive and interest similar to those of the party against whom now offered.

Subdivision (a) is revised to provide that the government as well as the defendant is entitled to take a deposition. The phrase "whenever due to special circumstances of the case it is in the interest of justice," is intended to make clear that the decision by the court as to whether to order the taking of a deposition shall be made in the context of the circumstances of the particular case. The principal objective is the preservation of evidence for use at trial. It is not to provide a method of pretrial discovery nor primarily for the purpose of obtaining a basis for later cross-examination of an adverse witness. Discovery is a matter dealt with in rule 16. An obviously important factor is whether a deposition will expedite, rather than delay, the administration of criminal justice. Also important is the presence or absence of factors which determine the use of a deposition at the trial, such as the agreement of the parties to use of the deposition; the possible unavailability of the witness; or the possibility that coercion may be used upon the witness to induce him to change his testimony or not to testify. See rule 16(a)(1)(v).

Subdivision (a) also makes explicit that only the "testimony of a prospective witness of a party" can be taken. This means the party's own witness and does not authorize a discovery deposition of an adverse witness. The language "for use at trial" is intended to give further emphasis to the importance of the criteria for use specified in subdivision (e).

In subdivision (b) reference is made to the defendant in custody. If he is in state custody, a writ of habeas corpus ad testificandum (to produce the prisoner for purposes of testimony) may be required to accomplish his presence.

In subdivision (d) the language "except as otherwise provided in these rules" is meant to make clear that the subpoena provisions of rule 17 control rather than the provisions of the civil rules.

The use of the phrase "and manner" in subdivision (d)(2) is intended to emphasize that the authorization is not to conduct an adverse examination of an opposing witness.

In subdivision (e) the phrase "as substantive evidence" is added to make clear that the deposition can be used as evidence in chief as well as for purposes of impeachment.

Subdivision (e) also makes clear that the deposition can be used as affirmative evidence whenever the witness is available but gives testimony inconsistent with that given in the deposition. A California statute which contained a similar provision was held constitutional in California v. Green, 399 U.S. 149, 90 S.Ct. 1930, 26 L.Ed.2d 489 (1970). This is also consistent with section 801(d)(1) of the Rules of Evidence for United States Courts and Magistrates (Nov. 1971).

Subdivision (f) is intended to insure that a record of objections and the grounds for the objections is made at the time the deposition is taken when the witness is available so that the witness can be examined further, if necessary, on the point of the objection so that there will be an adequate record for the court's later ruling upon the objection.

Subdivision (g) uses the "unavailability" definition of the Rules of Evidence for the United States Courts and Magistrates, 804(a) (Nov. 1971).

Subdivision (h) is intended to make clear that the court always has authority to order the taking of a deposition, or to allow the use of a deposition, where there is an agreement of the parties to the taking or to the use.

NOTES OF COMMITTEE ON THE JUDICIARY, HOUSE REPORT NO. 94—247; 1975 AMENDMENT

A. Amendments Proposed by the Supreme Court. Rule 15 of the Federal Rules of Criminal Procedure provides for the taking of depositions. The present rule permits only the defendant to move that a deposition of a prospective witness be taken. The court may grant the motion if it appears that (a) the prospective witness will be unable to attend or be prevented from attending the trial, (b) the prospective witness' testimony is material, and (c) the prospective witness' testimony is necessary to prevent a failure of justice.

The Supreme Court promulgated several amendments to Rule 15. The more significant amendments are described below.

Subdivision (a) as proposed to be amended permits either party to move the court for the taking of a deposition of a witness. However, a party may only move to take the deposition of one of its own witnesses, not one of the adversary party's witnesses.

Subdivision (c) as proposed to be amended provides that whenever a deposition is taken at the instance of the government or of an indigent defendant, the expenses of the taking of the deposition must be paid by the government.

Subdivision (e) as proposed to be amended provides that part or all of the deposition may be used at trial as substantive evidence if the witness is "unavailable" or if the witness gives testimony inconsistent with his deposition.

Subdivision (b)[(g)] as proposed to be amended defines "unavailable." "Unavailable" as a witness includes situations in which the deponent:

(1) is exempted by ruling of the judge on the ground of privilege from testifying concerning the subject matter of his deposition; or

(2) persists in refusing to testify concerning the subject matter of his deposition despite an order of the judge to do so; or

(3) testifies to a lack of memory of the subject matter of his deposition; or

(4) is unable to be present or to testify at the hearing because of death or then existing physical or mental illness or infirmity; or

(5) is absent from the hearing and the proponent of his deposition has been unable to procure his attendance by process or other reasonable means. A deponent is not unavailable as a witness if his exemption, refusal, claim of lack of memory, inability, or absence is due to the procurement or wrongdoing of the proponent of his deposition for the purpose of preventing the witness from attending or testifying.

B. Committee Action. The Committee narrowed the definition of "unavailability" in subdivision (g). The Committee deleted language from that subdivision that provided that a witness was "unavailable" if the court exempts him from testifying at the trial on the ground of privilege. The Committee does not want to encourage the use of depositions at trial, especially in view of the importance of having live testimony from a witness on the witness stand.

The Committee added a provision to subdivision (b) to parallel the provision of Rule 43(b)(2). This is to make it clear that a disruptive defendant may be removed from the place where a deposition is being taken.

The Committee added language to subdivision (c) to make clear that the government must pay for the cost of the transcript of a deposition when the deposition is taken at the instance of an indigent defendant or of the government. In order to use a deposition at trial, it must be transcribed. The proposed rule did not explicitly provide for payment of the cost of transcribing, and the Committee change rectifies this.

The Committee notes that subdivision (e) permits the use of a deposition when the witness "gives testimony at the trial or hearing inconsistent with his deposition." Since subdivision (e) refers to the rules of evidence, the Committee understands that the Federal Rules of Evidence will govern the admissibility and use of the deposition. The Committee, by adopting subdivision (e) as proposed to be amended by the Supreme Court, intends the Federal Rules of Evidence to govern the admissibility and use of the deposition.

The Committee believes that Rule 15 will not encourage trials by deposition. A deposition may be taken only in "exceptional circumstances" when "it is in the interest of justice that the testimony of a prospective witness of a party be taken and preserved. * * *" A deposition, once it is taken, is not automatically admissible at trial, however. It may only be used at trial if the witness is unavailable, and the rule narrowly defines unavailability. The procedure established in Rule 15 is similar to the procedure established by the Organized Crime Control Act of 1970 for the taking and use of depositions in organized crime cases. See 18 U.S.C. 3503.

CONFERENCE COMMITTEE NOTES, HOUSE REPORT NO. 94—414; 1975 AMENDMENT

Rule 15 deals with the taking of depositions and the use of depositions at trial. Rule 15(e) permits a deposition to be used if the witness is unavailable. Rule 15(g) defines that term.

The Supreme Court's proposal defines five circumstances in which the witness will be considered unavailable. The House version of the bill deletes a provision that said a witness is unavailable if he is exempted at trial, on the ground of privilege, from testifying about the subject matter of his deposition. The Senate version of the bill by cross reference to the Federal Rules of Evidence, restores the Supreme Court proposal.

The Conference adopts the Senate provision.

NOTES OF ADVISORY COMMITTEE ON RULES—1987 AMENDMENT

The amendments are technical. No substantive change is intended.

COMMITTEE NOTES ON RULES—2002 AMENDMENT

The language of Rule 15 has been amended as part of the general restyling of the Criminal Rules to make them more easily understood and to make style and terminology consistent throughout the rules. These changes are intended to be stylistic only, except as noted below.

In Rule 15(a), the list of materials to be produced has been amended to include the expansive term "data" to reflect the fact that in an increasingly technological culture, the information may exist in a format not already covered by the more conventional list, such as a book or document.

The last portion of current Rule 15(b), dealing with the defendant's presence at a deposition, has been moved to amended Rule 15(c).

Revised Rule 15(d) addresses the payment of expenses incurred by the defendant and the defendant's attorney. Under the current rule, if the government requests the deposition, or if the defendant requests the deposition and is unable to pay for it, the court may direct the government to pay for travel and subsistence expenses for both the defendant and the defendant's attorney. In either case, the current rule requires the government to pay for the transcript. Under the amended rule, if the government requested the deposition, the court must require the government to pay reasonable subsistence and travel expenses and the cost of the deposition transcript. If the defendant is unable to pay the deposition expenses, the court must order the government to pay reasonable subsistence and travel expenses and the deposition transcript costs—regardless of who requested the deposition. Although the current rule places no apparent limits on the amount of funds that should be reimbursed, the Committee believed that insertion of the word "reasonable" was consistent with current practice.

Rule 15(f) is intended to more clearly reflect that the admissibility of any deposition taken under the rule is governed not by the rule itself, but instead by the Federal Rules of Evidence.

COMMITTEE NOTES ON RULES—2012 AMENDMENT

Subdivisions (c)(3) and (f). This amendment provides a mechanism for taking depositions in cases in which important witnesses—government and defense witnesses both—live in, or have fled to, countries where they cannot be reached by the court's subpoena power. Although Rule 15 authorizes depositions of witnesses in certain circumstances, the rule to date has not addressed instances where an important witness is not in the United States, there is a substantial likelihood the witness's attendance at trial cannot be obtained, and it would not be possible to securely transport the defendant or a co-defendant to the witness's location for a deposition.

While a party invokes Rule 15 in order to preserve testimony for trial, the rule does not determine whether the resulting deposition will be admissible, in whole or in part. Subdivision (f) provides that in the case of all depositions, questions of admissibility of the evidence obtained are left to the courts to resolve on a case by case basis. Under Rule 15(f), the courts make this determination applying the Federal Rules of Evidence, which state that relevant evidence is admissible except as otherwise provided by the Constitution, statutes, the Rules of Evidence, and other rules prescribed by the Supreme Court. Fed.R.Evid. 402.

Rule 15(c) as amended imposes significant procedural limitations on taking certain depositions in criminal cases. The amended rule authorizes a deposition outside a defendant's physical presence only in very limited circumstances after the trial court makes case-specific findings. Amended Rule 15(c)(3) delineates these circumstances and the specific findings a trial court must make before permitting parties to depose a witness outside the defendant's presence. The party requesting the deposition shoulders the burden of proof—by a preponderance of the evidence—on the elements that must be shown. The amended rule recognizes the important witness confrontation principles and vital law enforcement and other public interests that are involved.

This amendment does not supersede the relevant provisions of 18 U.S.C. §3509, authorizing depositions outside the defendant's physical presence in certain cases involving child victims and witnesses, or any other provision of law.

Changes Made to Proposed Amendment Released for Public Comment. The limiting phrase "in the United States" was deleted from Rule 15(c)(1) and (2) and replaced with the phrase "Except as authorized by Rule 15(c)(3)." The revised language makes clear that foreign depositions under the authority of (c)(3) are exceptions to the provisions requiring the defendant's presence, but other depositions outside the United States remain subject to the general requirements of (c)(1) and (2). For example, a defendant may waive his right to be present at a foreign deposition, and a defendant who attends a foreign deposition may be removed from such a deposition if he is disruptive. In subdivision (c)(3)(D) the introductory phrase was revised to the simpler "because."

In order to restrict foreign depositions outside of the defendant's presence to situations where the deposition serves an important public interest, the limiting phrase "in a felony prosecution" was added to subdivision (c)(3)(A).

The text of subdivision (f) and the Committee Note were revised to state more clearly the limited purpose and effect of the amendment, which is providing assistance in pretrial discovery. Compliance with the procedural requirements for the taking of the foreign testimony does not predetermine admissibility at trial, which is determined on a case-by-case basis, applying the Federal Rules of Evidence and the Constitution.

Other changes were also made in the Committee Note. In conformity with the style conventions governing the rules, citations to cases were deleted, and other changes were made to improve clarity.

REFERENCES IN TEXT

The Federal Rules of Evidence, referred to in subd. (f), are set out in the Appendix to Title 28, Judiciary and Judicial Procedure.

AMENDMENT BY PUBLIC LAW

1984—Subd. (a). Pub. L. 98–473 substituted "detained pursuant to section 3144 of title 18, United States Code" for "committed for failure to give bail to appear to testify at a trial or hearing".

1975—Pub. L. 94–64 amended subds. (a), (b), (c), and (e) generally, struck out subd. (g), and redesignated subd. (h) as (g).

EFFECTIVE DATE OF AMENDMENTS PROPOSED APRIL 22, 1974; EFFECTIVE DATE OF 1975 AMENDMENTS

Amendments of this rule embraced in the order of the United States Supreme Court on Apr. 22, 1974, and the amendments of this rule made by section 3 of Pub. L. 94–64, effective Dec. 1, 1975, see section 2 of Pub. L. 94–64, set out as a note under rule 4 of these rules.

Rule 16. Discovery and Inspection

(a) Government's Disclosure.
    (1) Information Subject to Disclosure.

(A) Defendant's Oral Statement. Upon a defendant's request, the government must disclose to the defendant the substance of any relevant oral statement made by the defendant, before or after arrest, in response to interrogation by a person the defendant knew was a government agent if the government intends to use the statement at trial.

(B) Defendant's Written or Recorded Statement. Upon a defendant's request, the government must disclose to the defendant, and make available for inspection, copying, or photographing, all of the following:

    (i) any relevant written or recorded statement by the defendant if:

      • statement is within the government's possession, custody, or control; and

      • the attorney for the government knows—or through due diligence could know—that the statement exists;

    (ii) the portion of any written record containing the substance of any relevant oral statement made before or after arrest if the defendant made the statement in response to interrogation by a person the defendant knew was a government agent; and

    (iii) the defendant's recorded testimony before a grand jury relating to the charged offense.

(C) Organizational Defendant. Upon a defendant's request, if the defendant is an organization, the government must disclose to the defendant any statement described in Rule 16(a)(1)(A) and (B) if the government contends that the person making the statement:

    (i) was legally able to bind the defendant regarding the subject of the statement because of that person's position as the defendant's director, officer, employee, or agent; or

    (ii) was personally involved in the alleged conduct constituting the offense and was legally able to bind the defendant regarding that conduct because of that person's position as the defendant's director, officer, employee, or agent.

(D) Defendant's Prior Record. Upon a defendant's request, the government must furnish the defendant with a copy of the defendant's prior criminal record that is within the government's possession, custody, or control if the attorney for the government knows—or through due diligence could know—that the record exists.

(E) Documents and Objects. Upon a defendant's request, the government must permit the defendant to inspect and to copy or photograph books, papers, documents, data, photographs, tangible objects, buildings or places, or copies or portions of any of these items, if the item is within the government's possession, custody, or control and:

    (i) the item is material to preparing the defense;

    (ii) the government intends to use the item in its case-in-chief at trial; or

    (iii) the item was obtained from or belongs to the defendant.

(F) Reports of Examinations and Tests. Upon a defendant's request, the government must permit a defendant to inspect and to copy or photograph the results or reports of any physical or mental examination and of any scientific test or experiment if:

    (i) the item is within the government's possession, custody, or control;

    (ii) the attorney for the government knows—or through due diligence could know—that the item exists; and

    (iii) the item is material to preparing the defense or the government intends to use the item in its case-in-chief at trial.

(G) Expert Witnesses. At the defendant's request, the government must give to the defendant a written summary of any testimony that the government intends to use under Rules 702, 703, or 705 of the Federal Rules of Evidence during its case-in-chief at trial. If the government requests discovery under subdivision (b)(1)(C)(ii) and the defendant complies, the government must, at the defendant's request, give to the defendant a written summary of testimony that the government intends to use under Rules 702, 703, or 705 of the Federal Rules of Evidence as evidence at trial on the issue of the defendant's mental condition. The summary provided under this subparagraph must describe the witness's opinions, the bases and reasons for those opinions, and the witness's qualifications.

(2) Information Not Subject to Disclosure. Except as permitted by Rule 16(a)(1)(A)–(D), (F), and (G), this rule does not authorize the discovery or inspection of reports, memoranda, or other internal government documents made by an attorney for the government or other government agent in connection with investigating or prosecuting the case. Nor does this rule authorize the discovery or inspection of statements made by prospective government witnesses except as provided in 18 U.S.C. §3500.

(3) Grand Jury Transcripts. This rule does not apply to the discovery or inspection of a grand jury's recorded proceedings, except as provided in Rules 6, 12(h), 16(a)(1), and 26.2.

(b) Defendant's Disclosure.

(1) Information Subject to Disclosure.

(A) Documents and Objects. If a defendant requests disclosure under Rule 16(a)(1)(E) and the government complies, then the defendant must permit the government, upon request, to inspect and to copy or photograph books, papers, documents, data, photographs, tangible objects, buildings or places, or copies or portions of any of these items if:

    (i) the item is within the defendant's possession, custody, or control; and

    (ii) the defendant intends to use the item in the defendant's case-in-chief at trial.

(B) Reports of Examinations and Tests. If a defendant requests disclosure under Rule 16(a)(1)(F) and the government complies, the defendant must permit the government, upon request, to inspect and to copy or photograph the results or reports of any physical or mental examination and of any scientific test or experiment if:

    (i) the item is within the defendant's possession, custody, or control; and

    (ii) the defendant intends to use the item in the defendant's case-in-chief at trial, or intends to call the witness who prepared the report and the report relates to the witness's testimony.

(C) Expert Witnesses. The defendant must, at the government's request, give to the government a written summary of any testimony that the defendant intends to use under Rules 702, 703, or 705 of the Federal Rules of Evidence as evidence at trial, if—

    (i) the defendant requests disclosure under subdivision (a)(1)(G) and the government complies; or

    (ii) the defendant has given notice under Rule 12.2(b) of an intent to present expert testimony on the defendant's mental condition.

This summary must describe the witness's opinions, the bases and reasons for those opinions, and the witness's qualifications[.]

(2) Information Not Subject to Disclosure. Except for scientific or medical reports, Rule 16(b)(1) does not authorize discovery or inspection of:

    (A) reports, memoranda, or other documents made by the defendant, or the defendant's attorney or agent, during the case's investigation or defense; or

    (B) a statement made to the defendant, or the defendant's attorney or agent, by:

      (i) the defendant;

      (ii) a government or defense witness; or

      (iii) a prospective government or defense witness.

(c) Continuing Duty to Disclose. A party who discovers additional evidence or material before or during trial must promptly disclose its existence to the other party or the court if:

(1) the evidence or material is subject to discovery or inspection under this rule; and

(2) the other party previously requested, or the court ordered, its production.

(d) Regulating Discovery.

(1) Protective and Modifying Orders. At any time the court may, for good cause, deny, restrict, or defer discovery or inspection, or grant other appropriate relief. The court may permit a party to show good cause by a written statement that the court will inspect ex parte. If relief is granted, the court must preserve the entire text of the party's statement under seal.

(2) Failure to Comply. If a party fails to comply with this rule, the court may:

(A) order that party to permit the discovery or inspection; specify its time, place, and manner; and prescribe other just terms and conditions;

(B) grant a continuance;

(C) prohibit that party from introducing the undisclosed evidence; or

(D) enter any other order that is just under the circumstances.

(As amended Feb. 28, 1966, eff. July 1, 1966; Apr. 22, 1974, eff. Dec. 1, 1975; Pub. L. 94–64, §3(20)–(28), July 31, 1975, 89 Stat. 374, 375; Pub. L. 94–149, §5, Dec. 12, 1975, 89 Stat. 806; Apr. 28, 1983, eff. Aug. 1, 1983; Mar. 9, 1987, eff. Aug. 1, 1987; Apr. 30, 1991, eff. Dec. 1, 1991; Apr. 22, 1993, eff. Dec. 1, 1993; Apr. 29, 1994, eff. Dec. 1, 1994; Apr. 11, 1997, eff. Dec. 1, 1997; Apr. 29, 2002, eff. Dec. 1, 2002; Pub. L. 107–273, div. C, title I, §11019(b), Nov. 2, 2002, 117 Stat. 1825; Apr. 16, 2013, eff. Dec. 1, 2013.)

NOTES OF ADVISORY COMMITTEE ON RULES——1944

Whether under existing law discovery may be permitted in criminal cases is doubtful, United States v. Rosenfeld, 57 F.2d 74 (C.C.A. 2d)——cert. den., 286 U.S. 556. The courts have, however, made orders granting to the defendant an opportunity to inspect impounded documents belonging to him, United States v. B. Goedde and Co., 40 F.Supp. 523, 534 (E.D.Ill.). The rule is a restatement of this procedure. In addition, it permits the procedure to be invoked in cases of objects and documents obtained from others by seizure or by process, on the theory that such evidential matter would probably have been accessible to the defendant if it had not previously been seized by the prosecution. The entire matter is left within the discretion of the court.

NOTES OF ADVISORY COMMITTEE ON RULES——1966 AMENDMENT

The extent to which pretrial discovery should be permitted in criminal cases is a complex and controversial issue. The problems have been explored in detail in recent legal literature, most of which has been in favor of increasing the range of permissible discovery. See, e.g. Brennan, The Criminal Prosecution: Sporting Event or Quest for Truth, 1963 Wash.U.L.Q. 279; Everett, Discovery in Criminal Cases——In Search of a Standard, 1964 Duke L.J. 477; Fletcher, Pretrial Discovery in State Criminal Cases, 12 Stan.L.Rev. 293 (1960); Goldstein, The State and the Accused: Balance of Advantage in Criminal Procedure, 69 Yale L.J. 1149, 1172–1198 (1960); Krantz, Pretrial Discovery in Criminal Cases: A Necessity for Fair and Impartial Justice, 42 Neb.L.Rev. 127 (1962); Louisell, Criminal Discovery: Dilemma Real or Apparent, 49 Calif.L.Rev. 56 (1961); Louisell, The Theory of Criminal Discovery and the Practice of Criminal Law, 14 Vand.L.Rev. 921 (1961); Moran, Federal Criminal Rules Changes: Aid or Illusion for the Indigent Defendant? 51 A.B.A.J. 64 (1965); Symposium, Discovery in Federal Criminal Cases, 33 F.R.D. 47–128 (1963); Traynor, Ground Lost and Found in Criminal Discovery, 39 N.Y.U.L.Rev. 228 (1964); Developments in the Law——Discovery, 74 Harv.L.Rev. 940, 1051–1063. Full judicial exploration of the conflicting policy considerations will be found in State v. Tune, 13 N.J. 203, 98 A.2d 881 (1953) and State v. Johnson, 28 N.J. 133, 145 A.2d 313 (1958); cf. State v. Murphy, 36 N.J. 172, 175 A.2d 622 (1961); State v. Moffa, 36 N.J. 219, 176 A.2d 1 (1961). The rule has been revised to expand the scope of pretrial discovery. At the same time provisions are made to guard against possible abuses.

Subdivision (a).——The court is authorized to order the attorney for the government to permit the defendant to inspect and copy or photograph three different types of material:

(1) Relevant written or recorded statements or confessions made by the defendant, or copies thereof. The defendant is not required to designate because he may not always be aware that his statements or confessions are being recorded. The government's obligation is limited to production of such statements as are within the possession, custody or control of the government, the existence of which is known, or by the exercise of due diligence may become known, to the attorney for the government. Discovery of statements and confessions is in line with what the Supreme Court has described as the "better practice" (Cicenia v. LaGay, 357 U.S. 504, 511 (1958)), and with the law in a number of states. See e.g., Del. Rules Crim. Proc., Rule 16; Ill.Stat. Ch. 38, §729; Md. Rules Proc., Rule 728; State v. McGee, 91 Ariz. 101, 370 P.2d 261 (1962); Cash v. Superior Court, 53 Cal.2d 72, 346 P.2d 407 (1959); State v. Bickham, 239 La. 1094, 121 So.2d 207, cert. den. 364 U.S. 874 (1960); People v. Johnson, 356 Mich. 619, 97 N.W.2d 739 (1959); State v. Johnson, supra; People v. Stokes, 24 Miss.2d 755, 204 N.Y.Supp.2d 827 (Ct.Gen.Sess. 1960). The amendment also makes it clear that discovery extends to recorded as well as written statements. For state cases upholding the discovery of recordings, see, e.g., People v. Cartier, 51 Cal.2d 590, 335 P.2d 114 (1959); State v. Minor, 177 A.2d 215 (Del.Super.Ct. 1962).

(2) Relevant results or reports of physical or mental examinations, and of scientific tests or experiments (including fingerprint and handwriting comparisons) made in connection with the particular case, or copies thereof. Again the defendant is not required to designate but the government's obligation is limited to production of items within the possession, custody or control of the government, the existence of which is known, or by the exercise of due diligence may become known, to the attorney for the government. With respect to results or reports of scientific tests or experiments the range of materials which must be produced by the government is further limited to those made in connection with the particular case. Cf. Fla.Stats. §909.18; State v. Superior Court, 90 Ariz. 133, 367 P.2d 6 (1961); People v. Cooper, 53 Cal.2d 755, 770, 3 Cal.Rptr. 148, 157, 349 P.2d 1964, 973 (1960); People v. Stokes, supra, at 762, 204 N.Y.Supp.2d at 835.

(3) Relevant recorded testimony of a defendant before a grand jury. The policy which favors pretrial disclosure to a defendant of his statements to government agents also supports, pretrial disclosure of his testimony before a grand jury. Courts, however, have tended to require a showing of special circumstances before ordering such disclosure. See, e.g., United States v. Johnson, 215 F.Supp. 300 (D.Md. 1963). Disclosure is required only where the statement has been recorded and hence can be transcribed.

Subdivision (b).——This subdivision authorizes the court to order the attorney for the government to permit the defendant to inspect the copy or photograph all other books, papers, documents, tangible objects, buildings or places, or copies or portions thereof, which are within the possession, custody or control of the government. Because of the necessarily broad and general terms in which the items to be discovered are described, several limitations are imposed:

(1) While specific designation is not required of the defendant, the burden is placed on him to make a showing of materiality to the preparation of his defense and that his request is reasonable. The requirement of reasonableness will permit the court to define and limit the scope of the government's obligation to search its files while meeting the legitimate needs of the defendant. The court is also authorized to limit discovery to portions of items sought.

(2) Reports, memoranda, and other internal government documents made by government agents in connection with the investigation or prosecution of the case are exempt from discovery. Cf. Palermo v. United States, 360 U.S. 343 (1959); Ogden v. United States, 303 F.2d 724 (9th Cir. 1962).

(3) Except as provided for reports of examinations and tests in subdivision (a)(2), statements made by government witnesses or prospective government witnesses to agents of the government are also exempt from discovery except as provided by 18 U.S.C. §3500.

73

Subdivision (c).—This subdivision permits the court to condition a discovery order under subdivision (a)(2) and subdivision (b) by requiring the defendant to permit the government to discover similar items which the defendant intends to produce at the trial and which are within his possession, custody or control under restrictions similar to those placed in subdivision (b) upon discovery by the defendant. While the government normally has resources adequate to secure the information necessary for trial, there are some situations in which mutual disclosure would appear necessary to prevent the defendant from obtaining an unfair advantage. For example, in cases where both prosecution and defense have employed experts to make psychiatric examinations, it seems as important for the government to study the opinions of the experts to be called by the defendant in order to prepare for trial as it does for the defendant to study those of the government's witnesses. Or in cases (such as antitrust cases) in which the defendant is well represented and well financed, mutual disclosure so far as consistent with the privilege against self-incrimination would seem as appropriate as in civil cases. State cases have indicated that a requirement that the defendant disclose in advance of trial materials which he intends to use on his own behalf at the trial is not a violation of the privilege against self-incrimination. See Jones v. Superior Court, 58 Cal.2d 56, 22 Cal.Rptr. 879, 372 P.2d 919 (1962); People v. Lopez, 60 Cal.2d 223, 32 Cal.Rptr. 424, 384 P.2d 16 (1963); Traynor, Ground Lost and Found in Criminal Discovery. 39 N.Y.U.L.Rev. 228, 246 (1964); Comment, The Self-Incrimination Privilege: Barrier to Criminal Discovery, 51 Calif.L.Rev. 135 (1963); Note, 76 Harv.L.Rev. 828 (1963).

Subdivision (d).—This subdivision is substantially the same as the last sentence of the existing rule.

Subdivision (e).—This subdivision gives the court authority to deny, restrict or defer discovery upon a sufficient showing. Control of the abuses of discovery is necessary if it is to be expanded in the fashion proposed in subdivisions (a) and (b). Among the considerations to be taken into account by the court will be the safety of witnesses and others, a particular danger of perjury or witness intimidation, the protection of information vital to the national security, and the protection of business enterprises from economic reprisals.

For an example of a use of a protective order in state practice, see People v. Lopez, 60 Cal.2d 223, 32 Cal.Rptr. 424, 384 P.2d 16 (1963). See also Brennan, Remarks on Discovery, 33 F.R.D. 56, 65 (1963); Traynor, Ground Lost and Found in Criminal Discovery, 39 N.Y.U.L.Rev. 228, 244, 250.

In some cases it would defeat the purpose of the protective order if the government were required to make its showing in open court. The problem arises in its most extreme form where matters of national security are involved. Hence a procedure is set out where upon motion by the government the court may permit the government to make its showing, in whole or in part, in a written statement to be inspected by the court in camera. If the court grants relief based on such showing, the government's statement is to be sealed and preserved in the records of the court to be made available to the appellate court in the event of an appeal by the defendant, Cf. 18 U.S.C. §3500.

Subdivision (f).—This subdivision is designed to encourage promptness in making discovery motions and to give the court sufficient control to prevent unnecessary delay and court time consequent upon a multiplication of discovery motions. Normally one motion should encompass all relief sought and a subsequent motion permitted only upon a showing of cause. Where pretrial hearings are used pursuant to Rule 17.1, discovery issues may be resolved at such hearings.

Subdivision (g).—The first sentence establishes a continuing obligation on a party subject to a discovery order with respect to material discovered after initial compliance. The duty provided is to notify the other party, his attorney or the court of the existence of the material. A motion can then be made by the other party for additional discovery and, where the existence of the material is disclosed shortly before or during the trial, for any necessary continuance.

The second sentence gives wide discretion to the court in dealing with the failure of either party to comply with a discovery order. Such discretion will permit the court to consider the reasons why disclosure was not made, the extent of the prejudice, if any, to the opposing party, the feasibility of rectifying that prejudice by a continuance, and any other relevant circumstances.

NOTES OF ADVISORY COMMITTEE ON RULES—1974 AMENDMENT

Rule 16 is revised to give greater discovery to both the prosecution and the defense. Subdivision (a) deals with disclosure of evidence by the government. Subdivision (b) deals with disclosure of evidence by the defendant. The majority of the Advisory Committee is of the view that the two—prosecution and defense discovery—are related and that the giving of a broader right of discovery to the defense is dependent upon giving also a broader right of discovery to the prosecution.

The draft provides for a right of prosecution discovery independent of any prior request for discovery by the defendant. The Advisory Committee is of the view that this is the most desirable approach to prosecution discovery. See American Bar Association, Standards Relating to Discovery and Procedure Before Trial, pp. 7, 43–46 (Approved Draft, 1970).

The language of the rule is recast from "the court may order" or "the court shall order" to "the government shall permit" or "the defendant shall permit." This is to make clear that discovery should be accomplished by the parties themselves, without the necessity of a court order unless there is dispute as to whether the matter is discoverable or a request for a protective order under subdivision (d)(1). The court, however, has the inherent right to enter an order under this rule.

The rule is intended to prescribe the minimum amount of discovery to which the parties are entitled. It is not intended to limit the judge's discretion to order broader discovery in appropriate cases. For example, subdivision (a)(3) is not intended to deny a judge's discretion to order disclosure of grand jury minutes where circumstances make it appropriate to do so.

Subdivision (a)(1)(A) amends the old rule to provide, upon request of the defendant, the government shall permit discovery if the conditions specified in subdivision (a)(1)(A) exist. Some courts have construed the current language as giving the court discretion as to whether to grant discovery of defendant's statements. See United States v. Kaminsky, 275 F.Supp. 365 (S.D.N.Y. 1967), denying discovery because the defendant did not demonstrate that his request for discovery was warranted; United States v. Diliberto, 264 F.Supp. 181 (S.D.N.Y. 1967), holding that there must be a showing of actual need before discovery would be granted; United States v. Louis Carreau, Inc., 42 F.R.D. 408 (S.D.N.Y. 1967), holding that in the absence of a showing of good cause the government cannot be required to disclose defendant's prior statements in advance of trial. In United States v. Louis Carreau, Inc., at p. 412, the court stated that if rule 16 meant that production of the statements was mandatory, the word "shall" would have been used instead of "may." See also United States v. Wallace, 272 F.Supp. 838 (S.D.N.Y. 1967); United States v. Wood, 270 F.Supp. 963 (S.D.N.Y. 1967); United States v. Leighton, 265 F.Supp. 27 (S.D.N.Y. 1967); United States v. Longarzo, 43 F.R.D. 395 (S.D.N.Y. 1967); Loux v. United States, 389 F.2d 911 (9th Cir. 1968); and the discussion of discovery in Discovery in Criminal Cases, 44 F.R.D. 481 (1968). Other courts have held that even though the current rules make discovery discretionary, the defendant need not show cause when he seeks to discover his own statements. See United States v. Aadal, 280 F.Supp. 859 (S.D.N.Y. 1967); United States v. Federmann, 41 F.R.D. 339 (S.D.N.Y. 1967); and United States v. Projansky, 44 F.R.D. 550 (S.D.N.Y. 1968).

The amendment making disclosure mandatory under the circumstances prescribed in subdivision (a)(1)(A) resolves such ambiguity as may currently exist, in the direction of more liberal discovery. See C. Wright, Federal Practice and Procedure: Criminal §253 (1969, Supp. 1971), Rezneck, The New Federal Rules of Criminal Procedure, 54 Geo.L.J. 1276 (1966); Fla.Stat.Ann. §925.05 (Supp. 1971–1972); N.J.Crim.Prac.Rule 35–11(a) (1967). This is done in the view that broad discovery contributes to the fair and efficient administration of criminal justice by providing the defendant with enough information to make an informed decision as to plea; by minimizing the undesirable effect of surprise at the trial; and by otherwise contributing to an accurate determination of the issue of guilt or innocence. This is the ground upon which the American Bar Association Standards Relating to Discovery and Procedure Before Trial (Approved Draft, 1970) has unanimously recommended broader discovery. The United States Supreme Court has said that the pretrial disclosure of a defendant's statements "may be the 'better practice.' " Cicenia v. La Gay, 357 U.S. 504, 511, 78 S.Ct. 1297, 2 L.Ed.2d 1523 (1958). See also Leland v. Oregon, 343 U.S. 790, 72 S.Ct. 1002, 96 L.Ed. 1302 (1952); State v. Johnson, 28 N.J. 133, 145 A.2d 313 (1958).

The requirement that the statement be disclosed prior to trial, rather than waiting until the trial, also contributes to efficiency of administration. It is during the pretrial stage that the defendant usually decides whether to plead guilty. See United States v. Projansky, supra. The pretrial stage is also the time during which many objections to the admissibility of types of evidence ought to be made. Pretrial disclosure ought, therefore, to contribute both to an informed guilty plea practice and to a pretrial resolution of admissibility questions. See ABA, Standards Relating to Discovery and Procedure Before Trial §1.2 and Commentary pp. 40–43 (Approved Draft, 1970).

The American Bar Association Standards mandate the prosecutor to make the required disclosure even though not requested to do so by the defendant. The proposed draft requires the defendant to request discovery, although obviously the attorney for the government may disclose without waiting for a request, and there are situations in which due process will require the prosecution, on its own, to disclose evidence "helpful" to the defense. Brady v. Maryland, 373 U.S. 83, 83 S.Ct. 1194, 10 L.Ed.2d 215 (1963); Giles v. Maryland, 386 U.S. 66, 87 S.Ct. 793, 17 L.Ed.2d 737 (1967).

The requirement in subdivision (a)(1)(A) is that the government produce "statements" without further discussion of what "statement" includes. There has been some recent controversy over what "statements" are subject to discovery under the current rule. See Discovery in Criminal Cases, 44 F.R.D. 481 (1968); C. Wright, Federal Practice and Procedure: Criminal §253, pp. 505–506 (1969, Supp. 1971). The kinds of "statements" which have been held to be within the rule include "substantially verbatim and contemporaneous" statements, United States v. Elife, 43 F.R.D. 23 (S.D.N.Y. 1967); statements which reproduce the defendant's "exact words," United States v. Armantrout, 278 F.Supp. 517 (S.D.N.Y. 1968); a memorandum which was not verbatim but included the substance of the defendant's testimony, United States v. Scharf, 267 F.Supp. 19 (S.D.N.Y. 1967); Summaries of the defendant's statements, United States v. Morrison, 43 F.R.D. 516 (N.D.Ill. 1967); and statements discovered by means of electronic surveillance, United States v. Black, 282 F.Supp. 35 (D.D.C. 1968). The court in United States v. Iovinelli, 276 F.Supp. 629, 631 (N.D.Ill. 1967), declared that "statements" as used in old rule 16 is not restricted to the "substantially verbatim recital of an oral statement" or to statements which are a "recital of past occurrences."

The Jencks Act, 18 U.S.C. §3500, defines "statements" of government witnesses discoverable for purposes of cross-examination as: (1) a "written statement" signed or otherwise approved by a witness, (2) "a stenographic, mechanical, electrical, or other recording, or a transcription thereof, which is a substantially verbatim recital of an oral statement made by said witness to an agent of the government and recorded contemporaneously with the making of such oral statement." 18 U.S.C. §3500(e). The language of the Jencks Act has most often led to a restrictive definition of "statements," confining "statements" to the defendant's "own words." See Hanks v. United States, 388 F.2d 171 (10th Cir. 1968), and Augenblick v. United States, 377 F.2d 586, 180 Ct.Cl. 131 (1967).

The American Bar Association's Standards Relating to Discovery and Procedure Before Trial (Approved Draft, 1970) do not attempt to define "statements" because of a disagreement among members of the committee as to what the definition should be. The majority rejected the restrictive definition of "statements" contained in the Jencks Act, 18 U.S.C. §3500(e), in the view that the defendant ought to be able to see his statement in whatever form it may have been preserved in fairness to the defendant and to discourage the practice, where it exists, of destroying original notes, after transforming them into secondary transcriptions, in order to avoid cross-examination based upon the original notes. See Campbell v. United States, 373 U.S. 487, 83 S.Ct. 1356, 10 L.Ed.2d 501 (1963). The minority favored a restrictive definition of "statements" in the view that the use of other than "verbatim" statements would subject witnesses to unfair cross-examination. See American Bar Association's Standards Relating to Discovery and Procedure Before Trial pp. 61–64 (Approved Draft, 1970). The draft of subdivision (a)(1)(A) leaves the matter of the meaning of the term unresolved and thus left for development on a case-by-case basis.

Subdivision (a)(1)(A) also provides for mandatory disclosure of a summary of any oral statement made by defendant to a government agent which the attorney for the government intends to use in evidence. The reasons for permitting the defendant to discover his own statements seem obviously to apply to the substance of any oral statement which the government intends to use in evidence at the trial. See American Bar Association Standards Relating to Discovery and Procedure Before Trial §2.1(a)(ii) (Approved Draft, 1970). Certainly disclosure will facilitate the raising of objections to admissibility prior to trial. There have been several conflicting decisions under the current rules as to whether the government must disclose the substance of oral statements of the defendant which it has in its possession. Cf. United States v. Baker, 262 F.Supp. 657 (D.C.D.C. 1966); United States v. Curry, 278 F.Supp. 508 (N.D.Ill. 1967); United States v. Morrison, 43 F.R.D. 516 (N.D.Ill. 1967); United States v. Reid, 43 F.R.D. 520 (N.D.Ill. 1967); United States v. Armantrout, 278 F.Supp. 517 (S.D.N.Y. 1968); and United States v. Elife, 43 F.R.D. 23 (S.D.N.Y. 1967). There is, however, considerable support for the policy of disclosing the substance of the defendant's oral statement. Many courts have indicated that this is a "better practice" than denying such disclosure. E.g., United States v. Curry, supra; Loux v. United States, 389 F.2d 911 (9th Cir. 1968); and United States v. Baker, supra.

Subdivision (a)(1)(A) also provides for mandatory disclosure of any "recorded testimony" which defendant gives before a grand jury if the testimony "relates to the offense charged." The present rule is discretionary and is applicable only to those of defendant's statements which are "relevant."

The traditional rationale behind grand jury secrecy—protection of witnesses—does not apply when the accused seeks discovery of his own testimony. Cf. Dennis v. United States, 384 U.S. 855, 86 S.Ct. 1840, 16 L.Ed.2d 973 (1966); and Allen v. United States, 129 U.S.App.D.C. 61, 390 F.2d 476 (1968). In interpreting the rule many judges have granted defendant discovery without a showing of need or relevance. United States v. Gleason, 259 F.Supp. 282 (S.D.N.Y. 1966); United States v. Longarzo, 43 F.R.D. 395 (S.D.N.Y. 1967); and United States v. United Concrete Pipe Corp., 41 F.R.D. 538 (N.D.Tex. 1966). Making disclosure mandatory without a showing of relevance conforms to the recommendation of the American Bar Association Standards Relating to Discovery and Procedure Before Trial §2.1(a)(iii) and Commentary pp. 64–66 (Approved Draft, 1970). Also see Note, Discovery by a Criminal Defendant of His Own Grand-Jury Testimony, 68 Columbia L.Rev. 311 (1968).

In a situation involving a corporate defendant, statements made by present and former officers and employees relating to their employment have been held discoverable as statements of the defendant. United States v. Hughes, 413 F.2d 1244 (5th Cir. 1969). The rule makes clear that such statements are discoverable if the officer or employee was "able legally to bind the defendant in respect to the activities involved in the charges."

Subdivision (a)(1)(B) allows discovery of the defendant's prior criminal record. A defendant may be uncertain of the precise nature of his prior record and it seems therefore in the interest of efficient and fair administration to make it possible to resolve prior to trial any disputes as to the correctness of the relevant criminal record of the defendant.

Subdivision (a)(1)(C) gives a right of discovery of certain tangible objects under the specified circumstances. Courts have construed the old rule as making disclosure discretionary with the judge. Cf. United States v. Kaminsky, 275 F.Supp. 365 (S.D.N.Y. 1967); Gevinson v. United States, 358 F.2d 761 (5th Cir. 1966), cert. denied, 385 U.S. 823, 87 S.Ct. 51, 17 L.Ed.2d 60 (1966); and United States v. Tanner, 279 F.Supp. 457 (N.D.Ill. 1967). The old rule requires a "showing of materiality to the preparation of his defense and that the request is reasonable." The new rule requires disclosure if any one of three situations exists: (a) the defendant shows that disclosure of the document or tangible object is material to the defense, (b) the government intends to use the document or tangible object in its presentation of its case in chief, or (c) the document or tangible object was obtained from or belongs to the defendant.

Disclosure of documents and tangible objects which are "material" to the preparation of the defense may be required under the rule of Brady v. Maryland, 373 U.S. 83, 83 S.Ct. 1194, 10 L.Ed.2d 215 (1963), without an additional showing that the request is "reasonable." In Brady the court held that "due process" requires that the prosecution disclose evidence favorable to the accused. Although the Advisory Committee decided not to codify the Brady Rule, the requirement that the government disclose documents and tangible objects "material to the preparation of his defense" underscores the importance of disclosure of evidence favorable to the defendant.

Limiting the rule to situations in which the defendant can show that the evidence is material seems unwise. It may be difficult for a defendant to make this showing if he does not know what the evidence is. For this reason subdivision (a)(1)(C) also contains language to compel disclosure if the government intends to use the property as evidence at the trial or if the property was obtained from or belongs to the defendant. See ABA Standards Relating to Discovery and Procedure Before Trial §2.1(a)(v) and Commentary pp. 68–69 (Approved Draft, 1970). This is probably the result under old rule 16 since the fact that the government intends to use the physical evidence at the trial is probably sufficient proof of "materiality." C. Wright, Federal Practice and Procedure: Criminal §254 especially n. 70 at p. 513 (1969, Supp. 1971). But it seems desirable to make this explicit in the rule itself.

Requiring disclosure of documents and tangible objects which "were obtained from or belong to the defendant" probably is also making explicit in the rule what would otherwise be the interpretation of "materiality." See C. Wright, Federal Practice and Procedure: Criminal §254 at p. 510 especially n. 58 (1969, Supp. 1971).

Subdivision (a)(1)(C) is also amended to add the word "photographs" to the objects previously listed. See ABA Standards Relating to Discovery and Procedure Before Trial §2.1(a)(v) (Approved Draft, 1970).

Subdivision (a)(1)(D) makes disclosure of the reports of examinations and tests mandatory. This is the recommendation of the ABA Standards Relating to Discovery and Procedure Before Trial §2.1(a)(iv) and Commentary pp. 66–68 (Approved Draft, 1970). The obligation of disclosure applies only to scientific tests or experiments "made in connection with the particular case." So limited, mandatory disclosure seems justified because: (1) it is difficult to test expert testimony at trial without advance notice and preparation; (2) it is not likely that such evidence will be distorted or misused if disclosed prior to trial; and (3) to the extent that a test may be favorable to the defense, its disclosure is mandated under the rule of Brady v. Maryland, supra.

Subdivision (a)(1)(E) is new. It provides for discovery of the names of witnesses to be called by the government and of the prior criminal record of these witnesses. Many states have statutes or rules which require that the accused be notified prior to trial of the witnesses to be called against him. See, e.g., Alaska R.Crim.Proc. 7(c); Ariz.R.Crim.Proc. 153, 17 A.R.S. (1956); Ark.Stat.Ann. §43–1001 (1947); Cal.Pen.Code §995n (West 1957); Colo.Rev.Stat.Ann. §§39–3–6, 39–4–2 (1963); Fla.Stat.Ann. §906.29 (1944); Idaho Code Ann. §19–1404 (1948); Ill.Rev.Stat. ch. 38, §114–9 (1970); Ind.Ann.Stat. §9–903 (1856), IC 1971, 35–1–16–3; Iowa Code Ann. §772.3 (1950); Kan.Stat.Ann. §62–931 (1964); Ky.R.Crim. Proc. 6.08 (1962); Mich.Stat.Ann. §28.980, M.C.L.A. §767.40 (Supp.1971); Minn.Stat.Ann. §628.08 (1947); Mo.Ann.Stat. §545.070 (1953); Mont.Rev. Codes Ann. §95–1503 (Supp. 1969); Neb.Rev.Stat. §29–1602 (1964); Nev.Rev.Stat. §173.045 (1967); Okl.Stat. tet. 22, §384 (1951); Ore.Rev.Stat. §132.580 (1969); Tenn. Code Ann. §40–1708 (1955); Utah Code Ann. §77–20–3 (1953). For examples of the ways in which these requirements are implemented, see State v. Mitchell, 181 Kan. 193, 310 P.2d 1063 (1957); State v. Parr, 129 Mont. 175, 283 P.2d 1086 (1955); Phillips v. State, 157 Neb. 419, 59 N.W. 598 (1953).

Witnesses' prior statements must be made available to defense counsel after the witness testifies on direct examination for possible impeachment purposes during trial: 18 U.S.C. §3500.

The American Bar Association's Standards Relating to Discovery and Procedure Before Trial §2.1(a)(i) (Approved Draft, 1970) require disclosure of both the names and the statements of prosecution witnesses. Subdivision (a)(1)(E) requires only disclosure, prior to trial, of names, addresses, and prior criminal record. It does not require disclosure of the witnesses' statements although the rule does not preclude the parties from agreeing to disclose statements prior to trial. This is done, for example, in courts using the so-called "omnibus hearing."

Disclosure of the prior criminal record of witnesses places the defense in the same position as the government, which normally has knowledge of the defendant's record and the record of anticipated defense witnesses. In addition, the defendant often lacks means of procuring this information on his own. See American Bar Association Standards Relating to Discovery and Procedure Before Trial §2.1(a)(vi) (Approved Draft, 1970).

A principal argument against disclosure of the identity of witnesses prior to trial has been the danger to the witness, his being subjected either to physical harm or to threats designed to make the witness unavailable or to influence him to change his testimony. Discovery in Criminal cases, 44 F.R.D. 481, 499–500 (1968); Ratnoff, The New Criminal Deposition Statute in Ohio—Help or Hindrance to Justice?, 19 Case Western Reserve L.Rev. 279, 284 (1968). See, e.g., United States v. Estep, 151 F.Supp. 668, 672–673 (N.D. Tex. 1957):

Ninety percent of the convictions had in the trial court for sale and dissemination of narcotic drugs are linked to the work and the evidence obtained by an informer. If that informer is not to have his life protected there won't be many informers hereafter.

See also the dissenting opinion of Mr. Justice Clark in Roviaro v. United States, 353 U.S. 53, 66–67, 77 S.Ct. 623, 1 L.Ed.2d 639 (1957). Threats of market retaliation against witnesses in criminal antitrust cases are another illustration. Bergen Drug Co. v. Parke, Davis & Company, 307 F.2d 725 (3d Cir. 1962); and House of Materials, Inc. v. Simplicity Pattern Co., 298 F.2d 867 (2d Cir. 1962). The government has two alternatives when it believes disclosure will create an undue risk of harm to the witness: It can ask for a protective order under subdivision (d)(1). See ABA Standards Relating to Discovery and Procedure Before Trial §2.5(b) (Approved Draft, 1970). It can also move the court to allow the perpetuation of a particular witness's testimony for use at trial if the witness is unavailable or later changes his testimony. The purpose of the latter alternative is to make pretrial disclosure possible and at the same time to minimize any inducement to use improper means to force the witness either to not show up or to change his testimony before a jury. See rule 15.

Subdivision (a)(2) is substantially unchanged. It limits the discovery otherwise allowed by providing that the government need not disclose "reports, memoranda, or other internal government documents made by the attorney for the government or other government agents in connection with the investigation or prosecution of the case" or "statements made by government witnesses or prospective government witnesses." The only proposed change is that the "reports, memoranda, or other internal government documents made by the attorney for the government" are included to make clear that the work product of the government attorney is protected. See C. Wright, Federal Practice and Procedure: Criminal §254 n. 92 (1969, Supp. 1971); United States v. Rothman, 179 F.Supp. 935 (W.D.Pa. 1959); Note, "Work Product" in Criminal Discovery, 1966 Wash.U.L.Q. 321; American Bar Association, Standards Relating to Discovery and Procedure Before Trial §2.6(a) (Approved Draft, 1970); cf. Hickman v. Taylor, 329 U.S. 495, 67 S.Ct. 385, 91 L.Ed. 451 (1947). Brady v. Maryland, 373 U.S. 83, 83 S.Ct. 1194, 10 L.Ed2d 215 (1963), requires the disclosure of evidence favorable to the defendant. This is, of course, not changed by this rule.

Subdivision (a)(3) is included to make clear that recorded proceedings of a grand jury are explicitly dealt with in rule 6 and subdivision (a)(1)(A) of rule 16 and thus are not covered by other provisions such as subdivision (a)(1)(C) which deals generally with discovery of documents in the possession, custody, or control of the government.

Subdivision (a)(4) is designed to insure that the government will not be penalized if it makes a full disclosure of all potential witnesses and then decides not to call one or more of the witnesses listed. This is not, however, intended to abrogate the defendant's right to comment generally upon the government's failure to call witnesses in an appropriate case.

Subdivision (b) deals with the government's right to discovery of defense evidence or, put in other terms, with the extent to which a defendant is required to disclose its evidence to the prosecution prior to trial. Subdivision (b) replaces old subdivision (c).

Subdivision (b) enlarges the right of government discovery in several ways: (1) it gives the government the right to discovery of lists of defense witnesses as well as physical evidence and the results of examinations and tests; (2) it requires disclosure if the defendant has the evidence under his control and intends to use it at trial in his case in chief, without the additional burden, required by the old rule, of having to show, in behalf of the government, that the evidence is material and the request reasonable; and (3) it gives the government the right to discovery without conditioning that right upon the existence of a prior request for discovery by the defendant.

Although the government normally has resources adequate to secure much of the evidence for trial, there are situations in which pretrial disclosure of evidence to the government is in the interest of effective and fair criminal justice administration. For example, the experimental "omnibus hearing" procedure (see discussion in Advisory Committee Note to rule 12) is based upon an assumption that the defendant, as well as the government, will be willing to disclose evidence prior to trial.

Having reached the conclusion that it is desirable to require broader disclosure by the defendant under certain circumstances, the Advisory Committee has taken the view that it is preferable to give the right of discovery to the government independently of a prior request for discovery by the defendant. This is the recommendation of the American Bar Association Standards Relating to Discovery and Procedure Before Trial, Commentary, pp. 43–46 (Approved Draft, 1970). It is sometimes asserted that making the government's right to discovery conditional will minimize the risk that government discovery will be viewed as an infringement of the defendant's constitutional rights. See discussion in C. Wright, Federal Practice and Procedure: Criminal §256 (1969, Supp.1971); Moore, Criminal Discovery, 19 Hastings L.J. 865 (1968); Wilder, Prosecution Discovery and the Privilege Against Self-Incrimination, 6 Am.Cr.L.Q. 3 (1967). There are assertions that prosecution discovery, even if conditioned upon the defendants being granted discovery, is a violation of the privilege. See statements of Mr. Justice Black and Mr. Justice Douglas, 39 F.R.D. 69, 272, 277–278 19 (1966); C. Wright, Federal Practice and Procedure: Criminal §256 (1969, Supp. 1971). Several states require defense disclosure of an intended defense of alibi and, in some cases, a list of witnesses in support of an alibi defense, without making the requirement conditional upon prior discovery being given to the defense. E.g., Ariz.R.Crim.P. 162(B), 17 A.R.S. (1956); Ind.Ann.Stat. §9–1631 to 9–1633 (1956), IC 1971, 35–5–1–1 to 35–5–1–3; Mich.Comp. Laws Ann. §§768.20, 768.21 (1968); N.Y. CPL §250.20 (McKinney's Consol.Laws, c. 11–A, 1971); and Ohio Rev.Code Ann. §2945.58 (1954). State courts have refused to hold these statutes violative of the privilege against self-incrimination. See State v. Thayer, 124 Ohio St. 1, 176 N.E. 656 (1931), and People v. Rakiec, 260 App.Div. 452, 23 N.Y.S.2d 607, aff'd, 289 N.Y. 306, 45 N.E.2d 812 (1942). See also rule 12.1 and Advisory Committee Note thereto.

Some state courts have held that a defendant may be required to disclose, in advance of trial, evidence which he intends to use on his own behalf at trial without violating the privilege against self-incrimination. See Jones v. Superior Court of Nevada County, 58 Cal.2d 56, 22 Cal.Rptr. 879, 372 P.2d 919 (1962); People v. Lopez, 60 Cal.2d 223, 32 Cal.Rptr. 424, 384 P.2d 16 (1963); Comment, The Self-Incrimination Privilege: Barrier to Criminal Discovery?, 51 Calif.L.Rev. 135 (1963); Note, 76 Harv.L.Rev. 838 (1963). The courts in Jones v. Superior Court of Nevada County, supra, suggests that if mandatory disclosure applies only to those items which the accused intends to introduce in evidence at trial, neither the incriminatory nor the involuntary aspects of the privilege against self-incrimination are present.

On balance the Advisory Committee is of the view that an independent right of discovery for both the defendant and the government is likely to contribute to both effective and fair administration. See Louisell, Criminal Discovery and Self-Incrimination: Roger Traynor Confronts the Dilemma, 53 Calif.L.Rev. 89 (1965), for an analysis of the difficulty of weighing the value of broad discovery against the value which inheres in not requiring the defendant to disclose anything which might work to his disadvantage.

Subdivision (b)(1)(A) provides that the defendant shall disclose any documents and tangible objects which he has in his possession, custody, or control and which he intends to introduce in evidence in his case in chief.

Subdivision (b)(1)(B) provides that the defendant shall disclose the results of physical or mental examinations and scientific tests or experiments if (a) they were made in connection with a particular case; (b) the defendant has them under his control; and (c) he intends to offer them in evidence in his case in chief or which were prepared by a defense witness and the results or reports relate to the witness's testimony. In cases where both prosecution and defense have employed experts to conduct tests such as psychiatric examinations, it seems as important for the government to be able to study the results reached by defense experts which are to be called by the defendant as it does for the defendant to study those of government experts. See Schultz, Criminal Discovery by the Prosecution: Frontier Developments and Some Proposals for the Future, 22 N.Y.U.Intra.L.Rev. 268 (1967); American Bar Association, Standards Relating to Discovery and Procedure Before Trial §3.2 (Supp., Approved Draft, 1970).

Subdivision (b)(1)(C) provides for discovery of a list of witnesses the defendant intends to call in his case in chief. State cases have indicated that disclosure of a list of defense witnesses does not violate the defendant's privilege against self-incrimination. See Jones v. Superior Court of Nevada County, supra, and People v. Lopez, supra. The defendant has the same option as does the government if it is believed that disclosure of the identity of a witness may subject that witness to harm or a threat of harm. The defendant can ask for a protective order under subdivision (d)(1) or can take a deposition in accordance with the terms of rule 15.

Subdivision (b)(2) is unchanged, appearing as the last sentence of subdivision (c) of old rule 16.

Subdivision (b)(3) provides that the defendant's failure to introduce evidence or call witnesses shall not be admissible in evidence against him. In states which require pretrial disclosure of witnesses' identity, the prosecution is not allowed to comment upon the defendant's failure to call a listed witness. See O'Connor v. State, 31 Wis.2d 684, 143 N.W.2d 489 (1966); People v. Mancini, 6 N.Y.2d 853, 188 N.Y.S.2d 559, 160 N.E.2d 91 (1959); and State v. Cocco, 73 Ohio App. 182, 55 N.E.2d 430 (1943). This is not, however, intended to abrogate the government's right to comment generally upon the defendant's failure to call witnesses in an appropriate case, other than the defendant's failure to testify.

Subdivision (c) is a restatement of part of old rule 16(g).

Subdivision (d)(1) deals with the protective order. Although the rule does not attempt to indicate when a protective order should be entered, it is obvious that one would be appropriate where there is reason to believe that a witness would be subject to physical or economic harm if his identity is revealed. See Will v. United States, 389 U.S. 90, 88 S.Ct. 269, 19 L.Ed.2d 305 (1967). The language "by the judge alone" is not meant to be inconsistent with Alderman v. United States, 394 U.S. 165, 89 S.Ct. 961, 22 L.Ed.2d 176 (1969). In Alderman the court points out that there may be appropriate occasions for the trial judge to decide questions relating to pretrial disclosure. See Alderman v. United States, 394 U.S. at 182 n. 14, 89 S.Ct. 961.

Subdivision (d)(2) is a restatement of part of old rule 16(g) and (d).

Old subdivision (f) of rule 16 dealing with time of motions is dropped because rule 12(c) provides the judge with authority to set the time for the making of pretrial motions including requests for discovery. Rule 12 also prescribes the consequences which follow from a failure to make a pretrial motion at the time fixed by the court. See rule 12(f).

NOTES OF COMMITTEE ON THE JUDICIARY, HOUSE REPORT NO. 94–247; 1975 AMENDMENT

A. Amendments Proposed by the Supreme Court. Rule 16 of the Federal Rules of Criminal Procedure regulates discovery by the defendant of evidence in possession of the prosecution, and discovery by the prosecution of evidence in possession of the defendant. The present rule permits the defendant to move the court to discover certain material. The prosecutor's discovery is limited and is reciprocal—that is, if the defendant is granted discovery of certain items, then the prosecution may move for discovery of similar items under the defendant's control.

As proposed to be amended, the rule provides that the parties themselves will accomplish discovery—no motion need be filed and no court order is necessary. The court will intervene only to resolve a dispute as to whether something is discoverable or to issue a protective order.

The proposed rule enlarges the scope of the defendant's discovery to include a copy of his prior criminal record and a list of the names and addresses, plus record of prior felony convictions, of all witnesses the prosecution intends to call during its case-in-chief. It also permits the defendant to discover the substance of any oral statement of his which the prosecution intends to offer at trial, if the statement was given in response to interrogation by any person known by defendant to be a government agent.

77

Proposed subdivision (a)(2) provides that Rule 16 does not authorize the defendant to discover "reports, memoranda, or other internal government documents made by the attorney for the government or other government agents in connection with the investigation or prosecution of the case. . . ."

The proposed rule also enlarges the scope of the government's discovery of materials in the custody of the defendant. The government is entitled to a list of the names and addresses of the witnesses the defendant intends to call during his case-in-chief. Proposed subdivision (b)(2) protects the defendant from having to disclose "reports, memoranda, or other internal defense documents . . . made in connection with the investigation or defense of the case. . . ."

Subdivision (d)(1) of the proposed rule permits the court to deny, restrict, or defer discovery by either party, or to make such other order as is appropriate. Upon request, a party may make a showing that such an order is necessary. This showing shall be made to the judge alone if the party so requests. If the court enters an order after such a showing, it must seal the record of the showing and preserve it in the event there is an appeal.

B. Committee Action. The Committee agrees that the parties should, to the maximum possible extent, accomplish discovery themselves. The court should become involved only when it is necessary to resolve a dispute or to issue an order pursuant to subdivision (d).

Perhaps the most controversial amendments to this rule were those dealing with witness lists. Under present law, the government must turn over a witness list only in capital cases. [Section 3432 of title 18 of the United States Code provides: A person charged with treason or other capital offense shall at least three entire days before commencement of trial be furnished with a copy of the indictment and a list of the veniremen, and of the witnesses to be produced on the trial for proving the indictment, stating the place of abode of each veniremen and witness.] The defendant never needs to turn over a list of his witnesses. The proposed rule requires both the government and the defendant to turn over witness lists in every case, capital or noncapital. Moreover, the lists must be furnished to the adversary party upon that party's request.

The proposed rule was sharply criticized by both prosecutors and defenders. The prosecutors feared that pretrial disclosure of prosecution witnesses would result in harm to witnesses. The defenders argued that a defendant cannot constitutionally be compelled to disclose his witnesses.

The Committee believes that it is desirable to promote greater pretrial discovery. As stated in the Advisory Committee Note,

broader discovery by both the defense and the prosecution will contribute to the fair and efficient administration of criminal justice by aiding in informed plea negotiations, by minimizing the undesirable effect of surprise at trial, and by otherwise contributing to an accurate determination of the issue of guilt or innocence. . . .

The Committee, therefore, endorses the principle that witness lists are discoverable. However, the Committee has attempted to strike a balance between the narrow provisions of existing law and the broad provisions of the proposed rule.

The Committee rule makes the procedures defendant-triggered. If the defendant asks for and receives a list of prosecution witnesses, then the prosecution may request a list of defense witnesses. The witness lists need not be turned over until 3 days before trial. The court can modify the terms of discovery upon a sufficient showing. Thus, the court can require disclosure of the witness lists earlier than 3 days before trial, or can permit a party not to disclose the identity of a witness before trial.

The Committee provision promotes broader discovery and its attendant values—informed disposition of cases without trial, minimizing the undesirable effect of surprise, and helping insure that the issue of guilt or innocence is accurately determined. At the same time, it avoids the problems suggested by both the prosecutors and the defenders.

The major argument advanced by prosecutors is the risk of danger to their witnesses if their identities are disclosed prior to trial. The Committee recognizes that there may be a risk but believes that the risk is not as great as some fear that it is. Numerous states require the prosecutor to provide the defendant with a list of prosecution witnesses prior to trial. [These States include Alaska, Arizona, Arkansas, California, Colorado, Florida, Idaho, Illinois, Indiana, Iowa, Kansas, Kentucky, Michigan, Minnesota, Missouri, Montana, Nebraska, Nevada, Oklahoma, Oregon, Tennessee, and Utah. See Advisory Committee Note, House Document 93–292, at 60.] The evidence before the Committee indicates that these states have not experienced unusual problems of witness intimidation. [See the comments of the Standing Committee on Criminal Law and Procedure of the State Bar of California in Hearings II, at 302.]

Some federal jurisdictions have adopted an omnibus pretrial discovery procedure that calls upon the prosecutor to give the defendant its witness lists. One such jurisdiction is the Southern District of California. The evidence before the Committee indicates that there has been no unusual problems with witness intimidation in that district. Charles Sevilla, Chief Trial Attorney for the Federal Defenders of San Diego, Inc., which operates in the Southern District of California, testified as follows:

The Government in one of its statements to this committee indicated that providing the defense with witness lists will cause coerced witness perjury. This does not happen. We receive Government witness lists as a matter of course in the Southern District, and it's a rare occasion when there is any overture by a defense witness or by a defendant to a Government witness. It simply doesn't happen except on the rarest of occasion. When the Government has that fear it can resort to the protective order. [Hearings II, at 42.]

Mr. Sevilla's observations are corroborated by the views of the U.S. Attorney for the Southern District of California:

Concerning the modifications to Rule 16, we have followed these procedures informally in this district for a number of years. We were one of the districts selected for the pilot projects of the Omnibus Hearing in 1967 or 1968. We have found that the courts in our district will not require us to disclose names of proposed witnesses when in our judgment to do so would not be advisable. Otherwise we routinely provide defense counsel with full discovery, including names and addresses of witnesses. We have not had any untoward results by following this program, having in mind that the courts will, and have, excused us from discovery where the circumstances warrant. [Hearings I, at 109.]

Much of the prosecutorial criticism of requiring the prosecution to give a list of its witnesses to the defendant reflects an unwillingness to trust judges to exercise sound judgment in the public interest. Prosecutors have stated that they frequently will open their files to defendants in order to induce pleas. [See testimony of Richard L. Thornburgh, United States Attorney for the Western District of Pennsylvania, in Hearings I, at 150.]

Prosecutors are willing to determine on their own when they can do this without jeopardizing the safety of witnesses. There is no reason why a judicial officer cannot exercise the same discretion in the public interest.

The Committee is convinced that in the usual case there is no serious risk of danger to prosecution witnesses from pretrial disclosure of their identities. In exceptional instances, there may be a risk of danger. The Committee rule, however, is capable of dealing with those exceptional instances while still providing for disclosure of witnesses in the usual case.

The Committee recognizes the force of the constitutional arguments advanced by defenders. Requiring a defendant, upon request, to give to the prosecution material which may be incriminating, certainly raises very serious constitutional problems. The Committee deals with these problems by having the defendant trigger the discovery procedures. Since the defendant has no constitutional right to discover any of the prosecution's evidence (unless it is exculpatory within the meaning of Brady v. Maryland, 373 U.S. 83 (1963)), it is permissible to condition his access to nonexculpatory evidence upon his turning over a list of defense witnesses. Rule 16 currently operates in this manner.

The Committee also changed subdivisions (a)(2) and (b)(2), which set forth "work product" exceptions to the general discovery requirements. The subsections proposed by the Supreme Court are cast in terms of the type of document involved (e. g., report), rather than in terms of the content (e. g., legal theory). The Committee recast these provisions by adopting language from Rule 26(b)(3) of the Federal Rules of Civil Procedure.

The Committee notes that subdivision (a)(1)(C) permits the defendant to discover certain items that "were obtained from or belong to the defendant." The Committee believes that, as indicated in the Advisory Committee Note [House Document 93–292, at 59], items that "were obtained from or belong to the defendant" are items that are material to the preparation of his defense.

The Committee added language to subdivision (a)(1)(B) to conform it to provisions in subdivision (a)(1)(A). The rule as changed by the Committee requires the prosecutor to give the defendant such copy of the defendant's prior criminal record as is within the prosecutor's "possession, custody, or control, the existence of which is known, or by the exercise of due diligence may become known" to the prosecutor. The Committee also made a similar conforming change in subdivision (a)(1)(E), dealing with the criminal records of government witnesses. The prosecutor can ordinarily discharge his obligation under these two subdivisions, (a)(1)(B) and (E), by obtaining a copy of the F.B.I. "rap sheet."

The Committee made an additional change in subdivision (a)(1)(E). The proposed rule required the prosecutor to provide the defendant with a record of the felony convictions of government witnesses. The major purpose for letting the defendant discover information about the record of government witnesses, is to provide him with information concerning the credibility of those witnesses. Rule 609(a) of the Federal Rules of Evidence permits a party to attack the credibility of a witness with convictions other than just felony convictions. The Committee, therefore, changed subdivision (a)(1)(E) to require the prosecutor to turn over a record of all criminal convictions, not just felony convictions.

The Committee changed subdivision (d)(1), which deals with protective orders. Proposed (d)(1) required the court to conduct an ex parte proceeding whenever a party so requested. The Committee changed the mandatory language to permissive language. A Court may, not must, conduct an ex parte proceeding if a party so requests. Thus, if a party requests a protective or modifying order and asks to make its showing ex parte, the court has two separate determinations to make. First, it must determine whether an ex parte proceeding is appropriate, bearing in mind that ex parte proceedings are disfavored and not to be encouraged. [An ex parte proceeding would seem to be appropriate if any adversary proceeding would defeat the purpose of the protective or modifying order. For example, the identity of a witness would be disclosed and the purpose of the protective order is to conceal that witness' identity.] Second, it must determine whether a protective or modifying order shall issue.

CONFERENCE COMMITTEE NOTES, HOUSE REPORT NO. 94–414; 1975 AMENDMENT

Rule 16 deals with pretrial discovery by the defendant and the government. The House and Senate versions of the bill differ on Rule 16 in several respects.

A. Reciprocal vs. Independent Discovery for the Government.——The House version of the bill provides that the government's discovery is reciprocal. If the defendant requires and receives certain items from the government, then the government is entitled to get similar items from the defendant. The Senate version of the bill gives the government an independent right to discover material in the possession of the defendant.

The Conference adopts the House provisions.

B. Rule 16(a)(1)(A).——The House version permits an organization to discover relevant recorded grand jury testimony of any witness who was, at the time of the acts charged or of the grand jury proceedings, so situated as an officer or employee as to have been able legally to bind it in respect to the activities involved in the charges. The Senate version limits discovery of this material to testimony of a witness who was, at the time of the grand jury proceeding, so situated as an officer or employee as to have been legally to bind the defendant in respect to the activities involved in the charges.

The Conferees share a concern that during investigations, ex-employees and ex-officers of potential corporate defendants are a critical source of information regarding activities of their former corporate employers. It is not unusual that, at the time of their testimony or interview, these persons may have interests which are substantially adverse to or divergent from the putative corporate defendant. It is also not unusual that such individuals, though no longer sharing a community of interest with the corporation, may nevertheless be subject to pressure from their former employers. Such pressure may derive from the fact that the ex-employees or ex-officers have remained in the same industry or related industry, are employed by competitors, suppliers, or customers of their former employers, or have pension or other deferred compensation arrangements with former employers.

The Conferees also recognize that considerations of fairness require that a defendant corporation or other legal entity be entitled to the grand jury testimony of a former officer or employee if that person was personally involved in the conduct constituting the offense and was able legally to bind the defendant in respect to the conduct in which he was involved.

The Conferees decided that, on balance, a defendant organization should not be entitled to the relevant grand jury testimony of a former officer or employee in every instance. However, a defendant organization should be entitled to it if the former officer or employee was personally involved in the alleged conduct constituting the offense and was so situated as to have been able legally to bind the defendant in respect to the alleged conduct. The Conferees note that, even in those situations where the rule provides for disclosure of the testimony, the Government may, upon a sufficient showing, obtain a protective or modifying order pursuant to Rule 16(d)(1).

The Conference adopts a provision that permits a defendant organization to discover relevant grant jury testimony of a witness who (1) was, at the time of his testimony, so situated as an officer or employee as to have been able legally to bind the defendant in respect to conduct constituting the offense, or (2) was, at the time of the offense, personally involved in the alleged conduct constituting the offense and so situated as an officer or employee as to have been able legally to bind the defendant in respect to that alleged conduct in which he was involved.

C. Rules 16(a)(1)(E) and (b)(1)(C) (witness lists).——The House version of the bill provides that each party, the government and the defendant, may discover the names and addresses of the other party's witnesses 3 days before trial. The Senate version of the bill eliminates these provisions, thereby making the names and addresses of a party's witnesses nondiscoverable. The Senate version also makes a conforming change in Rule 16(d)(1). The Conference adopts the Senate version.

A majority of the Conferees believe it is not in the interest of the effective administration of criminal justice to require that the government or the defendant be forced to reveal the names and addresses of its witnesses before trial. Discouragement of witnesses and improper contact directed at influencing their testimony, were deemed paramount concerns in the formulation of this policy.

D. Rules 16(a)(2) and (b)(2).——Rules 16(a)(2) and (b)(2) define certain types of materials ("work product") not to be discoverable. The House version defines work product to be "the mental impressions, conclusions, opinions, or legal theories of the attorney for the government or other government agents." This is parallel to the definition in the Federal Rules of Civil Procedure. The Senate version returns to the Supreme Court's language and defines work product to be "reports, memoranda, or other internal government documents." This is the language of the present rule.

The Conference adopts the Senate provision.

The Conferees note that a party may not avoid a legitimate discovery request merely because something is labelled "report", "memorandum", or "internal document". For example if a document qualifies as a statement of the defendant within the meaning of the Rule 16(a)(1)(A), then the labelling of that document as "report", "memorandum", or "internal government document" will not shield that statement from discovery. Likewise, if the results of an experiment qualify as the results of a scientific test within the meaning of Rule 16(b)(1)(B), then the results of that experiment are not shielded from discovery even if they are labelled "report", "memorandum", or "internal defense document".

NOTES OF ADVISORY COMMITTEE ON RULES—1983 AMENDMENT

Note to Subdivision (a)(3). The added language is made necessary by the addition of Rule 26.2 and new subdivision (i) of Rule 12, which contemplate the production of statements, including those made to a grand jury, under specified circumstances.

NOTES OF ADVISORY COMMITTEE ON RULES—1987 AMENDMENT

The amendments are technical. No substantive change is intended.

NOTES OF ADVISORY COMMITTEE ON RULES—1991 AMENDMENT

The amendment to Rule 16(a)(1)(A) expands slightly government disclosure to the defense of statements made by the defendant. The rule now requires the prosecution, upon request, to disclose any written record which contains reference to a relevant oral statement by the defendant which was in response to interrogation, without regard to whether the prosecution intends to use the statement at trial. The change recognizes that the defendant has some proprietary interest in statements made during interrogation regardless of the prosecution's intent to make any use of the statements.

The written record need not be a transcription or summary of the defendant's statement but must only be some written reference which would provide some means for the prosecution and defense to identify the statement. Otherwise, the prosecution would have the difficult task of locating and disclosing the myriad oral statements made by a defendant, even if it had no intention of using the statements at trial. In a lengthy and complicated investigation with multiple interrogations by different government agents, that task could become unduly burdensome.

The existing requirement to disclose oral statements which the prosecution intends to introduce at trial has also been changed slightly. Under the amendment, the prosecution must also disclose any relevant oral statement which it intends to use at trial, without regard to whether it intends to introduce the statement. Thus, an oral statement by the defendant which would only be used for impeachment purposes would be covered by the rule.

The introductory language to the rule has been modified to clarify that without regard to whether the defendant's statement is oral or written, it must at a minimum be disclosed. Although the rule does not specify the means for disclosing the defendant's statements, if they are in written or recorded form, the defendant is entitled to inspect, copy, or photograph them.

NOTES OF ADVISORY COMMITTEE ON RULES—1993 AMENDMENT

New subdivisions (a)(1)(E) and (b)(1)(C) expand federal criminal discovery by requiring disclosure of the intent to rely on expert opinion testimony, what the testimony will consist of, and the bases of the testimony. The amendment is intended to minimize surprise that often results from unexpected expert testimony, reduce the need for continuances, and to provide the opponent with a fair opportunity to test the merit of the expert's testimony through focused cross-examination. See Eads, Adjudication by Ambush: Federal Prosecutors' Use of Nonscientific Experts in a System of Limited Criminal Discovery, 67 N. C. L. Rev. 577, 622 (1989).

Like other provisions in Rule 16, subdivision (a)(1)(E) requires the government to disclose information regarding its expert witnesses if the defendant first requests the information. Once the requested information is provided, the government is entitled, under (b)(1)(C) to reciprocal discovery of the same information from the defendant. The disclosure is in the form of a written summary and only applies to expert witnesses that each side intends to call. Although no specific timing requirements are included, it is expected that the parties will make their requests and disclosures in a timely fashion.

With increased use of both scientific and nonscientific expert testimony, one of counsel's most basic discovery needs is to learn that an expert is expected to testify. See Gianelli, Criminal Discovery, Scientific Evidence, and DNA, 44 Vand. L. Rev. 793 (1991); Symposium on Science and the Rules of Legal Procedure, 101 F.R.D. 599 (1983). This is particularly important if the expert is expected to testify on matters which touch on new or controversial techniques or opinions. The amendment is intended to meet this need by first, requiring notice of the expert's qualifications which in turn will permit the requesting party to determine whether in fact the witness is an expert within the definition of Federal Rule of Evidence 702. Like Rule 702, which generally provides a broad definition of who qualifies as an "expert," the amendment is broad in that it includes both scientific and nonscientific experts. It does not distinguish between those cases where the expert will be presenting testimony on novel scientific evidence. The rule does not extend, however, to witnesses who may offer only lay opinion testimony under Federal Rule of Evidence 701. Nor does the amendment extend to summary witnesses who may testify under Federal Rule of Evidence 1006 unless the witness is called to offer expert opinions apart from, or in addition to, the summary evidence.

Second, the requesting party is entitled to a summary of the expected testimony. This provision is intended to permit more complete pretrial preparation by the requesting party. For example, this should inform the requesting party whether the expert will be providing only background information on a particular issue or whether the witness will actually offer an opinion. In some instances, a generic description of the likely witness and that witness's qualifications may be sufficient, e.g., where a DEA laboratory chemist will testify, but it is not clear which particular chemist will be available.

Third, and perhaps most important, the requesting party is to be provided with a summary of the bases of the expert's opinion. Rule 16(a)(1)(D) covers disclosure and access to any results or reports of mental or physical examinations and scientific testing. But the fact that no formal written reports have been made does not necessarily mean that an expert will not testify at trial. At least one federal court has concluded that that provision did not otherwise require the government to disclose the identify of its expert witnesses where no reports had been prepared. See, e.g., United States v. Johnson, 713 F.2d 654 (11th Cir. 1983, cert. denied, 484 U.S. 956 (1984) (there is no right to witness list and Rule 16 was not implicated because no reports were made in the case). The amendment should remedy that problem. Without regard to whether a party would be entitled to the underlying bases for expert testimony under other provisions of Rule 16, the amendment requires a summary of the bases relied upon by the expert. That should cover not only written and oral reports, tests, reports, and investigations, but any information that might be recognized as a legitimate basis for an opinion under Federal Rule of Evidence 703, including opinions of other experts.

The amendments are not intended to create unreasonable procedural hurdles. As with other discovery requests under Rule 16, subdivision (d) is available to either side to seek ex parte a protective or modifying order concerning requests for information under (a)(1)(E) or (b)(1)(C).

NOTES OF ADVISORY COMMITTEE ON RULES—1994 AMENDMENT

The amendment is intended to clarify that the discovery and disclosure requirements of the rule apply equally to individual and organizational defendants. See In re United States, 918 F.2d 138 (11th Cir. 1990) (rejecting distinction between individual and organizational defendants). Because an organizational defendant may not know what its officers or agents have said or done in regard to a charged offense, it is important that it have access to statements made by persons whose statements or actions could be binding on the defendant. See also United States v. Hughes, 413 F.2d 1244, 1251–52 (5th Cir. 1969), vacated as moot, 397 U.S. 93 (1970) (prosecution of corporations "often resembles the most complex civil cases, necessitating a vigorous probing of the mass of detailed facts to seek out the truth").

The amendment defines defendant in a broad, nonexclusive fashion. See also 18 U.S.C. §18 (the term "organization" includes a person other than an individual). And the amendment recognizes that an organizational defendant could be bound by an agent's statement, see, e.g., Federal Rule of Evidence 801(d)(2), or be vicariously liable for an agent's actions. The amendment contemplates that, upon request of the defendant, the Government will disclose any statements within the purview of the rule and made by persons whom the government contends to be among the classes of persons described in the rule. There is no requirement that the defense stipulate or admit that such persons were in a position to bind the defendant.

Notes of Advisory Committee on Rules—1997 Amendment

Subdivision (a)(1)(E). Under Rule 16(a)(1)(E), as amended in 1993, the defense is entitled to disclosure of certain information about expert witnesses which the government intends to call during the trial. And if the government provides that information, it is entitled to reciprocal discovery under (b)(1)(C). This amendment is a parallel reciprocal disclosure provision which is triggered by a government request for information concerning defense expert witnesses as to the defendant's mental condition, which is provided for in an amendment to (b)(1)(C), infra.

Subdivision (b)(1)(C). Amendments in 1993 to Rule 16 included provisions for pretrial disclosure of information, including names and expected testimony of both defense and government expert witnesses. Those disclosures are triggered by defense requests for the information. If the defense makes such requests and the government complies, the government is entitled to similar, reciprocal discovery. The amendment to Rule 16(b)(1)(C) provides that if the defendant has notified the government under Rule 12.2 of an intent to rely on expert testimony to show the defendant's mental condition, the government may request the defense to disclose information about its expert witnesses. Although Rule 12.2 insures that the government will not be surprised by the nature of the defense or that the defense intends to call an expert witness, that rule makes no provision for discovery of the identity, the expected testimony, or the qualifications of the expert witness. The amendment provides the government with the limited right to respond to the notice provided under Rule 12.2 by requesting more specific information about the expert. If the government requests the specified information, and the defense complies, the defense is entitled to reciprocal discovery under an amendment to subdivision (a)(1)(E), supra.

Committee Notes on Rules—2002 Amendment

The language of Rule 16 has been amended as part of the general restyling of the Criminal Rules to make them more easily understood and to make style and terminology consistent throughout the rules. These changes are intended to be stylistic only, except as noted below.

Current Rule 16(a)(1)(A) is now located in Rule 16(a)(1)(A), (B), and (C). Current Rule 16(a)(1)(B), (C), (D), and (E) have been relettered.

Amended Rule 16(b)(1)(B) includes a change that may be substantive in nature. Rule 16(a)(1)(E) and 16(a)(1)(F) require production of specified information if the government intends to "use" the information "in its case-in-chief at trial." The Committee believed that the language in revised Rule 16(b)(1)(B), which deals with a defendant's disclosure of information to the government, should track the similar language in revised Rule 16(a)(1). In Rule 16(b)(1)(B)(ii), the Committee changed the current provision which reads: "the defendant intends to introduce as evidence" to the "defendant intends to use the item . . ." The Committee recognized that this might constitute a substantive change in the rule but believed that it was a necessary conforming change with the provisions in Rule 16(a)(1)(E) and (F), noted supra, regarding use of evidence by the government.

In amended Rule 16(d)(1), the last phrase in the current subdivision—which refers to a possible appeal of the court's discovery order—has been deleted. In the Committee's view, no substantive change results from that deletion. The language is unnecessary because the court, regardless of whether there is an appeal, will have maintained the record.

Finally, current Rule 16(e), which addresses the topic of notice of alibi witnesses, has been deleted as being unnecessarily duplicative of Rule 12.1.

Committee Notes on Rules—2013 Amendment

Subdivision (a). Paragraph (a)(2) is amended to clarify that the 2002 restyling of Rule 16 did not change the protection afforded to government work product.

Prior to restyling in 2002, Rule 16(a)(1)(C) required the government to allow the defendant to inspect and copy "books, papers, [and] documents" material to his defense. Rule 16(a)(2), however, stated that except as provided by certain enumerated subparagraphs—not including Rule 16(a)(1)(C)—Rule 16(a) did not authorize the discovery or inspection of reports, memoranda, or other internal government documents made by the attorney for the government. Reading these two provisions together, the Supreme Court concluded that "a defendant may examine documents material to his defense, but, under Rule 16(a)(2), he may not examine Government work product." United States v. Armstrong, 517 U.S. 456, 463 (1996).

With one exception not relevant here, the 2002 restyling of Rule 16 was intended to work no substantive change. Nevertheless, because restyled Rule 16(a)(2) eliminated the enumerated subparagraphs of its successor and contained no express exception for the materials previously covered by Rule 16(a)(1)(C) (redesignated as subparagraph (a)(1)(E)), some courts have been urged to construe the restyled rule as eliminating protection for government work product.

Courts have uniformly declined to construe the restyling changes to Rule 16(a)(2) to effect a substantive alteration in the scope of protection previously afforded to government work product by that rule. Correctly recognizing that restyling was intended to effect no substantive change, courts have invoked the doctrine of the scrivener's error to excuse confusion caused by the elimination of the enumerated subparagraphs from the restyled rules. See, e.g., United States v. Rudolph, 224 F.R.D. 503, 504–11 (N.D. Ala. 2004), and United States v. Fort, 472 F.3d 1106, 1110 n.2 (9th Cir. 2007) (adopting the Rudolph court's analysis).

By restoring the enumerated subparagraphs, the amendment makes it clear that a defendant's pretrial access to books, papers, and documents under Rule 16(a)(1)(E) remains subject to the limitations imposed by Rule 16(a)(2).

Changes Made After Publication and Comment. No changes were made after publication and comment.

References in Text

The Federal Rules of Evidence, referred to in subds. (a)(1)(G) and (b)(1)(C), are set out in the Appendix to Title 28, Judiciary and Judicial Procedure.

Amendment by Public Law

2002—Subd. (a)(1)(G). Pub. L. 107–273, §11019(b)(1), amended subpar. (G) generally.

Subd. (b)(1)(C). Pub. L. 107–273, §11019(b)(2), amended subpar. (C) generally.

1975—Subd. (a)(1). Pub. L. 94–64 amended subpars. (A), (B), and (D) generally, and struck out subpar. (E).

Subd. (a)(4). Pub. L. 94–149 struck out par. (4) "Failure to Call Witness. The fact that a witness' name is on a list furnished under this rule shall not be grounds for comment upon a failure to call the witness."

Subd. (b)(1). Pub. L. 94–64 amended subpars. (A) and (B) generally, and struck out subpar. (C).

Subd. (b)(3). Pub. L. 94–149 struck out par. (3) "Failure to Call Witness. The fact that a witness' name is on a list furnished under this rule shall not be grounds for a comment upon a failure to call a witness."

Subd. (c). Pub. L. 94–64 amended subd. (c) generally.

Subd. (d)(1). Pub. L. 94–64 amended par. (1) generally.

EFFECTIVE DATE OF 2002 AMENDMENT

Pub. L. 107–273, div. C, title I, §11019(c), Nov. 2, 2002, 116 Stat. 1826, provided that: "The amendments made by subsection (b) [amending this rule] shall take effect on December 1, 2002."

EFFECTIVE DATE OF AMENDMENTS PROPOSED APRIL 22, 1974; EFFECTIVE DATE OF 1975 AMENDMENTS

Amendments of this rule embraced in the order of the United States Supreme Court on Apr. 22, 1974, and the amendments of this rule made by section 3 of Pub. L. 94–64, effective Dec. 1, 1975, see section 2 of Pub. L. 94–64, set out as a note under rule 4 of these rules.

Rule 16.1. Pretrial Discovery Conference; Request for Court Action

(a) Discovery Conference. No later than 14 days after the arraignment, the attorney for the government and the defendant's attorney must confer and try to agree on a timetable and procedures for pretrial disclosure under Rule 16.

(b) Request for Court Action. After the discovery conference, one or both parties may ask the court to determine or modify the time, place, manner, or other aspects of disclosure to facilitate preparation for trial.

(Added Apr. 25, 2019, eff. Dec. 1, 2019.)

COMMITTEE NOTES ON RULES—2019

This new rule requires the attorney for the government and counsel for the defendant to confer early in the process, no later than 14 days after arraignment, about the timetable and procedures for pretrial disclosure. The new requirement is particularly important in cases involving electronically stored information (ESI) or other voluminous or complex discovery.

For practical reasons, the rule does not require attorneys for the government to confer with defendants who are not represented by counsel. However, neither does the rule limit existing judicial discretion to manage discovery in cases involving pro se defendants, and courts must ensure such defendants have full access to discovery.

The rule states a general procedure that the parties can adapt to the circumstances. Simple cases may require only a brief informal conversation to settle the timing and procedures for discovery. Agreement may take more effort as case complexity and technological challenges increase.

Moreover, the rule does not (1) modify statutory safeguards provided in security and privacy laws such as the Jencks Act or the Classified Information Procedures Act, (2) displace local rules or standing orders that supplement and are consistent with its requirements, or (3) limit the authority of the district court to determine the timetable and procedures for disclosure.

Because technology changes rapidly, the rule does not attempt to state specific requirements for the manner or timing of disclosure in cases involving ESI. However, counsel should be familiar with best practices. For example, the Department of Justice, the Administrative Office of the U.S. Courts, and the Joint Working Group on Electronic Technology in the Criminal Justice System (JETWG) have published "Recommendations for Electronically Stored Information (ESI) Discovery Production in Federal Criminal Cases" (2012).

Subsection (b) allows one or more parties to request that the court determine or modify the timing, manner, or other aspects of the disclosure to facilitate trial preparation.

This rule focuses exclusively on the process, manner and timing of pretrial disclosures, and does not address modification of the trial date. The Speedy Trial Act, 18 U.S.C. §§3161–3174, governs whether extended time for discovery may be excluded from the time within which trial must commence.

Rule 17. Subpoena

(a) Content. A subpoena must state the court's name and the title of the proceeding, include the seal of the court, and command the witness to attend and testify at the time and place the subpoena specifies. The clerk must issue a blank subpoena—signed and sealed—to the party requesting it, and that party must fill in the blanks before the subpoena is served.

(b) Defendant Unable to Pay. Upon a defendant's ex parte application, the court must order that a subpoena be issued for a named witness if the defendant shows an inability to pay the witness's fees and the necessity of the witness's presence for an adequate defense. If the court orders a subpoena to be issued, the process costs and witness fees will be paid in the same manner as those paid for witnesses the government subpoenas.

(c) Producing Documents and Objects.

(1) In General. A subpoena may order the witness to produce any books, papers, documents, data, or other objects the subpoena designates. The court may direct the witness to produce the designated items in court before trial or before they are to be offered in evidence. When the items arrive, the court may permit the parties and their attorneys to inspect all or part of them.

(2) Quashing or Modifying the Subpoena. On motion made promptly, the court may quash or modify the subpoena if compliance would be unreasonable or oppressive.

(3) Subpoena for Personal or Confidential Information About a Victim. After a complaint, indictment, or information is filed, a subpoena requiring the production of personal or confidential information about a victim may be served on a third party only by court order. Before entering the order and unless there are exceptional circumstances, the court must require giving notice to the victim so that the victim can move to quash or modify the subpoena or otherwise object.

(d) Service. A marshal, a deputy marshal, or any nonparty who is at least 18 years old may serve a subpoena. The server must deliver a copy of the subpoena to the witness and must tender to the witness one day's witness-attendance fee and the legal mileage allowance. The server need not tender the attendance fee or mileage allowance when the United States, a federal officer, or a federal agency has requested the subpoena.

(e) Place of Service.

(1) In the United States. A subpoena requiring a witness to attend a hearing or trial may be served at any place within the United States.

(2) In a Foreign Country. If the witness is in a foreign country, 28 U.S.C. §1783 governs the subpoena's service.

(f) Issuing a Deposition Subpoena.

(1) Issuance. A court order to take a deposition authorizes the clerk in the district where the deposition is to be taken to issue a subpoena for any witness named or described in the order.

(2) Place. After considering the convenience of the witness and the parties, the court may order—and the subpoena may require—the witness to appear anywhere the court designates.

(g) Contempt. The court (other than a magistrate judge) may hold in contempt a witness who, without adequate excuse, disobeys a subpoena issued by a federal court in that district. A magistrate judge may hold in contempt a witness who, without adequate excuse, disobeys a subpoena issued by that magistrate judge as provided in 28 U.S.C. §636(e).

(h) Information Not Subject to a Subpoena. No party may subpoena a statement of a witness or of a prospective witness under this rule. Rule 26.2 governs the production of the statement.

(As amended Dec. 27, 1948, eff. Oct. 20, 1949; Feb. 28, 1966, eff. July 1, 1966; Apr. 24, 1972, eff. Oct. 1, 1972; Apr. 22, 1974, eff. Dec. 1, 1975; Pub. L. 94–64, §3(29), July 31, 1975, 89 Stat. 375; Apr. 30, 1979, eff. Dec. 1, 1980; Mar. 9, 1987, eff. Aug. 1, 1987; Apr. 22, 1993, eff. Dec. 1, 1993; Apr. 29, 2002, eff. Dec. 1, 2002; Apr. 23, 2008, eff. Dec. 1, 2008.)

NOTES OF ADVISORY COMMITTEE ON RULES——1944

Note to Subdivision (a). This rule is substantially the same as Rule 45(a) of the Federal Rules of Civil Procedure [28 U.S.C., Appendix].

Note to Subdivision (b). This rule preserves the existing right of an indigent defendant to secure attendance of witnesses at the expense of the Government, 28 U.S.C. [former] 656 (Witnesses for indigent defendants). Under existing law, however, the right is limited to witnesses who are within the district in which the court is held or within one hundred miles of the place of trial. No procedure now exists whereby an indigent defendant can procure at Government expense the attendance of witnesses found in another district and more than 100 miles of the place of trial. This limitation is abrogated by the rule so that an indigent defendant will be able to secure the attendance of witnesses at the expense of the Government no matter where they are located. The showing required by the rule to justify such relief is the same as that now exacted by 28 U.S.C. [former] 656.

Note to Subdivision (c). This rule is substantially the same as Rule 45(b) of the Federal Rules of Civil Procedure [28 U.S.C., Appendix].

Note to Subdivision (d). This rule is substantially the same as Rule 45(c) of the Federal Rules of Civil Procedure [28 U.S.C., Appendix]. The provision permitting persons other than the marshal to serve the subpoena, and requiring the payment of witness fees in Government cases is new matter.

Note to Subdivision (e)(1). This rule continues existing law, 28 U.S.C. [former] 654 (Witnesses; subpoenas; may run into another district). The rule is different in civil cases in that in such cases, unless a statute otherwise provides, a subpoena may be served only within the district or within 100 miles of the place of trial, 28 U.S.C. [former] 654; Rule 45(e)(1) of the Federal Rules of Civil Procedure [28 U.S.C., Appendix].

Note to Subdivision (e)(2). This rule is substantially the same as Rule 45(e)(2) of the Federal Rules of Civil Procedure [28 U.S.C., Appendix]. See Blackmer v. United States, 284 U.S. 421, upholding the validity of the statute referred to in the rule.

Note to Subdivision (f). This rule is substantially the same as Rule 45(d) of the Federal Rules of Civil Procedure [28 U.S.C, Appendix].

Note to Subdivision (g). This rule is substantially the same as Rule 45(f) of the Federal Rules of Civil Procedure [28 U.S.C, Appendix].

NOTES OF ADVISORY COMMITTEE ON RULES——1948 AMENDMENT

The amendment is to substitute proper reference to Title 28 in place of the repealed act.

NOTES OF ADVISORY COMMITTEE ON RULES——1966 AMENDMENT

Subdivision (b).——Criticism has been directed at the requirement that an indigent defendant disclose in advance the theory of his defense in order to obtain the issuance of a subpoena at government expense while the government and defendants able to pay may have subpoenas issued in blank without any disclosure. See Report of the Attorney General's Committee on Poverty and the Administration of Criminal Justice (1963) p. 27. The Attorney General's Committee also urged that the standard of financial inability to pay be substituted for that of indigency. Id. at 40–41. In one case it was held that the affidavit filed by an indigent defendant under this subdivision could be used by the government at his trial for purposes of impeachment. Smith v. United States, 312 F.2d 867 (D.C.Cir. 1962). There has also been doubt as to whether the defendant need make a showing beyond the face of his affidavit in order to secure issuance of a subpoena. Greenwell v. United States, 317 F.2d 108 (D.C.Cir. 1963).

The amendment makes several changes. The references to a judge are deleted since applications should be made to the court. An ex parte application followed by a satisfactory showing is substituted for the requirement of a request or motion supported by affidavit. The court is required to order the issuance of a subpoena upon finding that the defendant is unable to pay the witness fees and that the presence of the witness is necessary to an adequate defense.

Subdivision (d).——The subdivision is revised to bring it into conformity with 28 U.S.C. §1825.

NOTES OF ADVISORY COMMITTEE ON RULES——1972 AMENDMENT

Subdivisions (a) and (g) are amended to reflect the existence of the "United States magistrate," a phrase defined in rule 54.

NOTES OF ADVISORY COMMITTEE ON RULES——1974 AMENDMENT

Subdivision (f)(2) is amended to provide that the court has discretion over the place at which the deposition is to be taken. Similar authority is conferred by Civil Rule 45(d)(2). See C. Wright, Federal Practice and Procedure: Criminal §278 (1969).

Ordinarily the deposition should be taken at the place most convenient for the witness but, under certain circumstances, the parties may prefer to arrange for the presence of the witness at a place more convenient to counsel.

NOTES OF COMMITTEE ON THE JUDICIARY, HOUSE REPORT NO. 94–247; 1975 AMENDMENT

A. Amendments Proposed by the Supreme Court. Rule 17 of the Federal Rules of Criminal Procedure deals with subpoenas. Subdivision (f)(2) as proposed by the Supreme Court provides:

> The witness whose deposition is to be taken may be required by subpoena to attend at any place designated by the trial court.

B. Committee Action. The Committee added language to the proposed amendment that directs the court to consider the convenience of the witness and the parties when compelling a witness to attend where a deposition will be taken.

NOTES OF ADVISORY COMMITTEE ON RULES——1979 AMENDMENT

Note to Subdivision (h). This addition to rule 17 is necessary in light of proposed rule 26.2, which deals with the obtaining of statements of government and defense witnesses.

NOTES OF ADVISORY COMMITTEE ON RULES——1987 AMENDMENT

The amendments are technical. No substantive change is intended.

The Rule is amended to conform to the Judicial Improvements Act of 1990 [P.L. 101–650, Title III, Section 321] which provides that each United States magistrate appointed under section 631 of title 28, United States Code, shall be known as a United States magistrate judge.

Committee Notes on Rules——2002 Amendment

The language of Rule 17 has been amended as part of the general restyling of the Criminal Rules to make them more easily understood and to make style and terminology consistent throughout the rules. These changes are intended to be stylistic only, except as noted below.

A potential substantive change has been made in Rule 17(c)(1); the word "data" has been added to the list of matters that may be subpoenaed. The Committee believed that inserting that term will reflect the fact that in an increasingly technological culture, the information may exist in a format not already covered by the more conventional list, such as a book or document.

Rule 17(g) has been amended to recognize the contempt powers of a court (other than a magistrate judge) and a magistrate judge.

Committee Notes on Rules——2008 Amendment

Subdivision (c)(3). This amendment implements the Crime Victims' Rights Act, codified at 18 U.S.C. §3771(a)(8), which states that victims have a right to respect for their "dignity and privacy." The rule provides a protective mechanism when the defense subpoenas a third party to provide personal or confidential information about a victim. Third party subpoenas raise special concerns because a third party may not assert the victim's interests, and the victim may be unaware of the subpoena. Accordingly, the amendment requires judicial approval before service of a subpoena seeking personal or confidential information about a victim from a third party. The phrase "personal or confidential information," which may include such things as medical or school records, is left to case development.

The amendment provides a mechanism for notifying the victim, and makes it clear that a victim may move to quash or modify the subpoena under Rule 17(c)(2)——or object by other means such as a letter——on the grounds that it is unreasonable or oppressive. The rule recognizes, however, that there may be exceptional circumstances in which this procedure may not be appropriate. Such exceptional circumstances would include, evidence that might be lost or destroyed if the subpoena were delayed or a situation where the defense would be unfairly prejudiced by premature disclosure of a sensitive defense strategy. The Committee leaves to the judgment of the court a determination as to whether the judge will permit the question whether such exceptional circumstances exist to be decided ex parte and authorize service of the third-party subpoena without notice to anyone.

The amendment applies only to subpoenas served after a complaint, indictment, or information has been filed. It has no application to grand jury subpoenas. When the grand jury seeks the production of personal or confidential information, grand jury secrecy affords substantial protection for the victim's privacy and dignity interests.

Changes Made to Proposed Amendment Released for Public Comment. The proposed amendment omits the language providing for ex parte issuance of a court order authorizing a subpoena to a third party for private or confidential information about a victim. The last sentence of the amendment was revised to provide that unless there are exceptional circumstances the court must give the victim notice before a subpoena seeking the victim's personal or confidential information can be served upon a third party. It was also revised to add the language "or otherwise object" to make it clear that the victim's objection might be lodged by means other than a motion, such as a letter to the court.

Amendment by Public Law

1975——Subd. (f)(2). Pub. L. 94–64 amended par. (2) generally.

Effective Date of 1979 Amendment

Amendment of this rule by addition of subd. (h) by order of the United States Supreme Court of Apr. 30, 1979, effective Dec. 1, 1980, see section 1(1) of Pub. L. 96–42, July 31, 1979, 93 Stat. 326, set out as a note under section 2074 of Title 28, Judiciary and Judicial Procedure.

Effective Date of Amendments Proposed April 22, 1974; Effective Date of 1975 Amendments

Amendments of this rule embraced in the order of the United States Supreme Court on Apr. 22, 1974, and the amendments of this rule made by section 3 of Pub. L. 94–64, effective Dec. 1, 1975, see section 2 of Pub. L. 94–64, set out as a note under rule 4 of these rules.

Supersedure

Provision of subd. (d) of this rule that witness shall be tendered the fee for 1 day's attendance and mileage allowed by law as superseded by section 1825 of Title 28, Judiciary and Judicial Procedure, see such section and Reviser's Note thereunder.

Rule 17.1. Pretrial Conference

On its own, or on a party's motion, the court may hold one or more pretrial conferences to promote a fair and expeditious trial. When a conference ends, the court must prepare and file a memorandum of any matters agreed to during the conference. The government may not use any statement made during the conference by the defendant or the defendant's attorney unless it is in writing and is signed by the defendant and the defendant's attorney.

(Added Feb. 28, 1966, eff. July 1, 1966; amended Mar. 9, 1987, eff. Aug. 1, 1987; Apr. 29, 2002, eff. Dec. 1, 2002.)

Notes of Advisory Committee on Rules——1966

This new rule establishes a basis for pretrial conferences with counsel for the parties in criminal cases within the discretion of the court. Pretrial conferences are now being utilized to some extent even in the absence of a rule. See, generally, Brewster, Criminal Pre-Trials——Useful Techniques, 29 F.R.D. 442 (1962); Estes, Pre-Trial Conferences in Criminal Cases, 23 F.R.D. 560 (1959); Kaufman, Pre-Trial in Criminal Cases, 23 F.R.D. 551 (1959); Kaufman, Pre-Trial in Criminal Cases, 42 J.Am.Jud.Soc. 150 (1959); Kaufman, The Appalachian Trial: Further Observations on Pre-Trial in Criminal Cases, 44 J.Am.Jud.Soc. 53 (1960); West, Criminal Pre-Trials——Useful Techniques, 29 F.R.D. 436 (1962); Handbook of Recommended Procedures for the Trial of Protracted Cases, 25 F.R.D. 399–403, 468–470 (1960). Cf. Mo.Sup.Ct. Rule 25.09; Rules Governing the N.J. Courts, §3:5–3.

The rule is cast in broad language so as to accommodate all types of pretrial conferences. As the third sentence suggests, in some cases it may be desirable or necessary to have the defendant present. See Committee on Pretrial Procedure of the Judicial Conference of the United States, Recommended Procedures in Criminal Pretrials, 37 F.R.D. 95 (1965).

Notes of Advisory Committee on Rules——1987 Amendment

The amendments are technical. No substantive change is intended.

Committee Notes——2002 Amendment

The language of Rule 17.1 has been amended as part of the general restyling of the Criminal Rules to make them more easily understood and to make style and terminology consistent throughout the rules. These changes are intended to be stylistic only, except as noted below.

Current Rule 17.1 prohibits the court from holding a pretrial conference where the defendant is not represented by counsel. It is unclear whether this would bar such a conference when the defendant invokes the constitutional right to self-representation. See Faretta v. California, 422 U.S. 806 (1975). The amended version makes clear that a pretrial conference may be held in these circumstances. Moreover, the Committee believed that pretrial conferences might be particularly useful in those cases where the defendant is proceeding pro se.

TITLE V. VENUE

Rule 18. Place of Prosecution and Trial

Unless a statute or these rules permit otherwise, the government must prosecute an offense in a district where the offense was committed. The court must set the place of trial within the district with due regard for the convenience of the defendant, any victim, and the witnesses, and the prompt administration of justice.

(As amended Feb. 28, 1966, eff. July 1, 1966; Apr. 30, 1979, eff. Aug. 1, 1979; Apr. 29, 2002, eff. Dec. 1, 2002; Apr. 23, 2008, eff. Dec. 1, 2008.)

NOTES OF ADVISORY COMMITTEE ON RULES——1944

1. The Constitution of the United States, Article III. Section 2, Paragraph 3, provides:

The Trial of all Crimes, except in Cases of Impeachment, shall be by Jury; and such Trial shall be held in the State where the said Crimes shall have been committed; but when not committed within any State, the Trial shall be at such Place or Places as the Congress may by Law have directed.

Amendment VI provides:

In all criminal prosecutions, the accused shall enjoy the right to a speedy and public trial, by an impartial jury of the State and district wherein the crime shall have been committed, which district shall have been previously ascertained by law * * *

28 U.S.C. former §114 (now §§1393, 1441) provides:

All prosecutions for crimes or offenses shall be had within the division of such districts where the same were committed, unless the court, or the judge thereof, upon the application of the defendant, shall order the cause to be transferred for prosecution to another division of the district.

The word "prosecutions," as used in this statute, does not include the finding and return of an indictment. The prevailing practice of impaneling a grand jury for the entire district at a session in some division and of distributing the indictments among the divisions in which the offenses were committed is deemed proper and legal, Salinger v. Loisel, 265 U.S. 224, 237. The court stated that this practice is "attended with real advantages." The rule is a restatement of existing law and is intended to sanction the continuance of this practice. For this reason, the rule requires that only the trial be held in the division in which the offense was committed and permits other proceedings to be had elsewhere in the same district.

2. Within the framework of the foregoing constitutional provisions and the provisions of the general statute, 28 U.S.C. 114 [now 1393, 1441], supra, numerous statutes have been enacted to regulate the venue of criminal proceedings, particularly in respect to continuing offenses and offenses consisting of several transactions occurring in different districts. Armour Packing Co. v. United States, 209 U.S. 56, 73–77; United States v. Johnson, 323 U.S. 273. These special venue provisions are not affected by the rule. Among these statutes are the following:

U.S.C., Title 8:

Section 138 [see 1326, 1328, 1329] (Importation of aliens for immoral purposes; attempt to reenter after deportation; penalty)

U.S.C., Title 15:

Section 78aa (Regulation of Securities Exchanges; jurisdiction of offenses and suits)
Section 79y (Control of Public Utility Holding Companies; jurisdiction of offenses and suits)
Section 80a–43 (Investment Companies; jurisdiction of offenses and suits)
Section 80b–14 (Investment Advisers; jurisdiction of offenses and suits)
Section 298 (Falsely Stamped Gold or Silver, etc., violations of law; penalty; jurisdiction of prosecutions)
Section 715i (Interstate Transportation of Petroleum Products; restraining violations; civil and criminal proceedings; jurisdiction of District Courts; review)
Section 717u (Natural Gas Act; jurisdiction of offenses; enforcement of liabilities and duties)

U.S.C., Title 18:

Section 39 [now 5, 3241] (Enforcement of neutrality; United States defined; jurisdiction of offenses; prior offenses; partial invalidity of provisions)
Section 336 [now 1302] (Lottery, or gift enterprise circulars not mailable; place of trial)
Section 338a [now 876, 3239] (Mailing threatening communications)
Section 338b [now 877, 3239] (Same; mailing in foreign country for delivery in the United States)
Section 345 [now 1717] (Using or attempting to use mails for transmission of matter declared nonmailable by title; jurisdiction of offense)
Section 396e [now 1762] (Transportation or importation of convict-made goods with intent to use in violation of local law; jurisdiction of violations)
Section 401 [now 2421] (White slave traffic; jurisdiction of prosecutions)
Section 408 [now 10, 2311 to 2313] (Motor vehicles; transportation, etc., of stolen vehicles)
Section 408d [now 875, 3239] (Threatening communications in interstate commerce)
Section 408e [now 1073] (Moving in interstate or foreign commerce to avoid prosecution for felony or giving testimony)
Section 409 [now 659, 660, 2117] (Larceny, etc., of goods in interstate or foreign commerce; penalty)
Section 412 [now 660] (Embezzlement, etc., by officers of carrier; jurisdiction; double jeopardy)
Section 418 [now 3237] (National Stolen Property Act; jurisdiction)
Section 419d [now 3237] (Transportation of stolen cattle in interstate or foreign commerce; jurisdiction of offense)
Section 420d [now 1951] (Interference with trade and commerce by violence, threats, etc., jurisdiction of offenses)
Section 494 [now 1654] (Arming vessel to cruise against citizen; trials)
Section 553 [now 3236] (Place of committal of murder or manslaughter determined)

U.S.C., Title 21:

Section 17 (Introduction into, or sale in, State or Territory or District of Columbia of dairy or food products falsely labeled or branded; penalty; jurisdiction of prosecutions)
Section 118 (Prevention of introduction and spread of contagion; duty of district attorneys)

U.S.C., Title 28:

Section 101 [now 18 U.S.C. 3235] (Capital cases)

Section 102 [now 18 U.S.C. 3238] (Offenses on the high seas)
Section 103 [now 18 U.S.C. 3237] (Offenses begun in one district and completed in another)
Section 121 [now 18 U.S.C. 3240] (Creation of new district or division)

U.S.C., Title 47:
Section 33 (Submarine Cables; jurisdiction and venue of actions and offenses)
Section 505 (Special Provisions Relating to Radio; venue of trials)

U.S.C., Title 49:
Section 41 [now 11902, 11903, 11915, 11916] (Legislation Supplementary to Interstate Commerce Act; liability of corporation carriers and agents; offenses and penalties—(1) Liability of corporation common carriers; offenses; penalties; Jurisdiction)
Section 623 [repealed] (Civil Aeronautics Act; venue and prosecution of offenses)

NOTES OF ADVISORY COMMITTEE ON RULES—1966 AMENDMENT

The amendment eliminates the requirement that the prosecution shall be in a division in which the offense was committed and vests discretion in the court to fix the place of trial at any place within the district with due regard to the convenience of the defendant and his witnesses.

The Sixth Amendment provides that the defendant shall have the right to a trial "by an impartial jury of the State and district wherein the crime shall have been committed, which district shall have been previously ascertained by law. * * *" There is no constitutional right to trial within a division. See United States v. Anderson, 328 U.S. 699, 704, 705 (1946); Barrett v. United States, 169 U.S. 218 (1898); Lafoon v. United States, 250 F.2d 958 (5th Cir. 1958); Carrillo v. Squier, 137 F.2d 648 (9th Cir. 1943); McNealey v. Johnston, 100 F.2d 280, 282 (9th Cir. 1938). Cf. Platt v. Minnesota Mining and Manufacturing Co., 376 U.S. 240 (1964).

The former requirement for venue within the division operated in an irrational fashion. Divisions have been created in only half of the districts, and the differentiation between those districts with and those without divisions often bears no relationship to comparative size or population. In many districts a single judge is required to sit in several divisions and only brief and infrequent terms may be held in particular divisions. As a consequence under the original rule there was often undue delay in the disposition of criminal cases—delay which was particularly serious with respect to defendants who had been unable to secure release on bail pending the holding of the next term of court.

If the court is satisfied that there exists in the place fixed for trial prejudice against the defendant so great as to render the trial unfair, the court may, of course, fix another place of trial within the district (if there be such) where such prejudice does not exist. Cf. Rule 21 dealing with transfers between districts.

NOTES OF ADVISORY COMMITTEE ON RULES—1979 AMENDMENT

This amendment is intended to eliminate an inconsistency between rule 18, which in its present form has been interpreted not to allow trial in a division other than that in which the offense was committed except as dictated by the convenience of the defendant and witnesses, Dupoint v. United States, 388 F.2d 39 (5th Cir. 1968), and the Speedy Trial Act of 1974. This Act provides:

In any case involving a defendant charged with an offense, the appropriate judicial officer, at the earliest practicable time, shall, after consultation with the counsel for the defendant and the attorney for the Government, set the case for trial on a day certain, or list it for trial on a weekly or other short-term trial calendar at a place within the judicial district so as to assure a speedy trial.

18 U.S.C. §3161(a). This provision is intended to "permit the trial of a case at any place within the judicial district. This language was included in anticipation of problems which might occur in districts with statutory divisions, where it could be difficult to set trial outside the division." H.R.Rep. No. 93–1508, 93d Cong., 2d Sess. 29 (1974).

The change does not offend the venue or vicinage provisions of the Constitution. Article III, §2, clause 3 places venue (the geographical location of the trial) "in the State where the said Crimes shall have been committed," while the Sixth Amendment defines the vicinage (the geographical location of the jurors) as "the State and district wherein the crime shall have been committed, which district shall have been previously ascertained by law." The latter provision makes "no reference to a division within a judicial district." United States v. James, 528 F.2d 999 (5th Cir. 1976). "It follows a fortiori that when a district is not separated into divisions, * * * trial at any place within the district is allowable under the Sixth Amendment * * *." United States v. Fernandez, 480 F.2d 726 (2d Cir. 1973). See also Zicarelli v. Gray, 543 F.2d 466 (3d Cir. 1976) and cases cited therein.

Nor is the change inconsistent with the Declaration of Policy in the Jury Selection and Service Act of 1968, which reads:

It is the policy of the United States that all litigants in Federal courts entitled to trial by jury shall have the right to grand and petit juries selected at random from a fair cross section of the community in the district or division wherein the court convenes.

28 U.S.C. §1861. This language does not mean that the Act requires "the trial court to convene not only in the district but also in the division wherein the offense occurred," as:

There is no hint in the statutory history that the Jury Selection Act was intended to do more than provide improved judicial machinery so that grand and petit jurors would be selected at random by the use of objective qualification criteria to ensure a representative cross section of the district or division in which the grand or petit jury sits. United States v. Cates, 485 F.2d 26 (1st Cir. 1974).

The amendment to rule 18 does not eliminate either of the existing considerations which bear upon fixing the place of trial within a district, but simply adds yet another consideration in the interest of ensuring compliance with the requirements of the Speedy Trial Act of 1974. The amendment does not authorize the fixing of the place of trial for yet other reasons. Cf. United States v. Fernandez, 480 F.2d 726 (2d Cir. 1973) (court in the exercise of its supervisory power held improper the fixing of the place of trial "for no apparent reason other than the convenience of the judge").

COMMITTEE NOTES ON RULES—2002 AMENDMENT

The language of Rule 18 has been amended as part of the general restyling of the Criminal Rules to make them more easily understood and to make style and terminology consistent throughout the rules. These changes are intended to be stylistic only.

COMMITTEE NOTES ON RULES—2008 AMENDMENT

The rule requires the court to consider the convenience of victims—as well as the defendant and witnesses—in setting the place for trial within the district. The Committee recognizes that the court has substantial discretion to balance any competing interests.

Changes Made to Proposed Amendment Released for Public Comment. There were no changes in the text of the rule. The Committee Note was amended to delete a statutory reference that commentators found misleading, and to draw attention to the court's discretion to balance the competing interests, which may be more important as the court must consider a new set of interests.

Rule 19. [Reserved]

(a) Consent to Transfer. A prosecution may be transferred from the district where the indictment or information is pending, or from which a warrant on a complaint has been issued, to the district where the defendant is arrested, held, or present if:

(1) the defendant states in writing a wish to plead guilty or nolo contendere and to waive trial in the district where the indictment, information, or complaint is pending, consents in writing to the court's disposing of the case in the transferee district, and files the statement in the transferee district; and

(2) the United States attorneys in both districts approve the transfer in writing.

(b) Clerk's Duties. After receiving the defendant's statement and the required approvals, the clerk where the indictment, information, or complaint is pending must send the file, or a certified copy, to the clerk in the transferee district.

(c) Effect of a Not Guilty Plea. If the defendant pleads not guilty after the case has been transferred under Rule 20(a), the clerk must return the papers to the court where the prosecution began, and that court must restore the proceeding to its docket. The defendant's statement that the defendant wished to plead guilty or nolo contendere is not, in any civil or criminal proceeding, admissible against the defendant.

(d) Juveniles.

(1) Consent to Transfer. A juvenile, as defined in 18 U.S.C. §5031, may be proceeded against as a juvenile delinquent in the district where the juvenile is arrested, held, or present if:

(A) the alleged offense that occurred in the other district is not punishable by death or life imprisonment;

(B) an attorney has advised the juvenile;

(C) the court has informed the juvenile of the juvenile's rights——including the right to be returned to the district where the offense allegedly occurred——and the consequences of waiving those rights;

(D) the juvenile, after receiving the court's information about rights, consents in writing to be proceeded against in the transferee district, and files the consent in the transferee district;

(E) the United States attorneys for both districts approve the transfer in writing; and

(F) the transferee court approves the transfer.

(2) Clerk's Duties. After receiving the juvenile's written consent and the required approvals, the clerk where the indictment, information, or complaint is pending or where the alleged offense occurred must send the file, or a certified copy, to the clerk in the transferee district.

(As amended Feb. 28, 1966, eff. July 1, 1966; Apr. 22, 1974, eff. Dec. 1, 1975; Pub. L. 94–64, §3(30), July 31, 1975, 89 Stat. 375; Apr. 28, 1982, eff. Aug. 1, 1982; Mar. 9, 1987, eff. Aug. 1, 1987; Apr. 29, 2002, eff. Dec. 1, 2002.)

NOTES OF ADVISORY COMMITTEE ON RULES——1944

This rule introduces a new procedure in the interest of defendants who intend to plead guilty and are arrested in a district other than that in which the prosecution has been instituted. This rule would accord to a defendant in such a situation an opportunity to secure a disposition of the case in the district where the arrest takes place, thereby relieving him of whatever hardship may be involved in a removal to the place where the prosecution is pending. In order to prevent possible interference with the administration of justice, however, the consent of the United States attorneys involved is required.

NOTES OF ADVISORY COMMITTEE ON RULES——1966 AMENDMENT

Rule 20 has proved to be most useful. In some districts, however, literal compliance with the procedures spelled out by the rule has resulted in unnecessary delay in the disposition of cases. This delay has been particularly troublesome where the defendant has been arrested prior to the filing of an indictment or information against him. See e.g., the procedure described in Donovan v. United States, 205 F.2d 557 (10th Cir. 1953). Furthermore, the benefit of the rule has not been available to juveniles electing to be proceeded against under 18 U.S.C. §§5031—5037. In an attempt to clarify and simplify the procedure the rule has been recast into four subdivisions.

Subdivision (a).——This subdivision is intended to apply to the situation in which an indictment or information is pending at the time at which the defendant indicates his desire to have the transfer made. Two amendments are made to the present language of the rule. In the first sentence the words "or held" and "or is held" are added to make it clear that a person already in state or federal custody within a district may request a transfer of federal charges pending against him in another district. See 4 Barron, Federal Practice and Procedure 146 (1951). The words "after receiving a copy of the indictment or information" are deleted.

The defendant should be permitted, if he wishes, to initiate transfer proceedings under the Rule without waiting for a copy of the indictment or information to be obtained. The defendant is protected against prejudice by the fact that under subdivision (c) he can, in effect, rescind his action by pleading not guilty after the transfer has been completed.

Subdivision (b).——This subdivision is intended to apply to the situation in which no indictment or information is pending but the defendant has been arrested on a warrant issued upon a complaint in another district. Under the procedure set out he may initiate the transfer proceedings without waiting for the filing of an indictment or information in the district where the complaint is pending. Also it is made clear that the defendant may validate an information previously filed by waiving indictment in open court when he is brought before the court to plead. See United States v. East, 5 F.R.D. 389. (N.D. Ind. 1946); Potter v. United States, 36 F.R.D. 394 (W.D. Mo. 1965). Here again the defendant is fully protected by the fact that at the time of pleading in the transferee court he may then refuse to waive indictment and rescind the transfer by pleading not guilty.

Subdivision (c).——The last two sentences of the original rule are included here. The last sentence is amended to forbid use against the defendant of his statement that he wishes to plead guilty or nolo contendere whether or not he was represented by counsel when it was made. Since under the amended rule the defendant may make his statement prior to receiving a copy of the indictment or information, it would be unfair to permit use of that statement against him.

Subdivision (d).——Under 18 U.S.C. §5033 a juvenile who has committed an act in violation of the law of the United States in one district and is apprehended in another must be returned to the district "having cognizance of the alleged violation" before he can consent being proceeded against as a juvenile delinquent. This subdivision will permit a juvenile after he has been advised by counsel and with the approval of the court and the United States attorney to consent to be proceeded against in the district in which he is arrested or held. Consent is required only of the United States attorney in the district of the arrest in order to permit expeditious handling of juvenile cases. If it is necessary to recognize special interests of particular districts where offenses are committed——e.g., the District of Columbia with its separate Juvenile Court (District of Columbia Code §11–1551(a))——the Attorney General may do so through his Administrative control over United States Attorneys.

Subdivision (e).——This subdivision is added to make it clear that a defendant who appears in one district in response to a summons issued in the district where the offense was committed may initiate transfer proceedings under the rule.

NOTES OF ADVISORY COMMITTEE ON RULES——1974 AMENDMENT

Rule 20 is amended to provide that a person "present" in a district other than the district in which he is charged with a criminal offense may, subject to the other provisions of rule 20, plead guilty in the district in which he is "present." See rule 6(b), Rules of Procedure for the Trial of Minor Offenses Before Magistrates.

Under the former rule, practice was to have the district in which the offense occurred issue a bench warrant authorizing the arrest of the defendant in the district in which he was located. This is a procedural complication which serves no interest of either the government or the defense and therefore can properly be dispensed with.

Making the fact that a defendant is "present" in the district an adequate basis for allowing him to plead guilty there makes it unnecessary to retain subdivision (e) which makes appearance in response to a summons equivalent to an arrest. Dropping (e) will eliminate some minor ambiguity created by that subdivision. See C. Wright, Federal Practice and Procedure: Criminal §322 n. 26, p. 612 (1969, Supp. 1971).

There are practical advantages which will follow from the change. In practice a person may turn himself in in a district other than that in which the prosecution is pending. It may be more convenient to have him plead in the district in which he is present rather than having him or the government incur the expense of his return to the district in which the charge is pending.

The danger of "forum shopping" can be controlled by the requirement that both United States Attorneys agree to the handling of the case under provisions of this rule.

NOTES OF COMMITTEE ON THE JUDICIARY, HOUSE REPORT NO. 94–247; 1975 AMENDMENT

A. Amendments Proposed by the Supreme Court. Rule 20 of the Federal Rules of Criminal Procedure deals with transferring a defendant from one district to another for the purpose of pleading and being sentenced. It deals with the situation where a defendant is located in one district (A) and is charged with a crime in another district (B). Under the present rule, if such a defendant desires to waive trial and plead guilty or nolo contendere, a judge in district B would issue a bench warrant for the defendant, authorizing his arrest in district A and his transport to district B for the purpose of pleading and being sentenced.

The Supreme Court amendments permit the defendant in the above example to plead guilty or nolo contendere in district A, if the United States Attorneys for districts A and B consent.

B. Committee Action. The Committee has added a conforming amendment to subdivision (d), which establishes procedures for dealing with defendants who are juveniles.

NOTES OF ADVISORY COMMITTEE ON RULES—1982 AMENDMENT

This amendment to subdivision (b) is intended to expedite transfer proceedings under Rule 20. At present, considerable delay—sometimes as long as three or four weeks—occurs in subdivision (b) cases, that is, where no indictment or information is pending. This time is spent on the transmittal of defendant's statement to the district where the complaint is pending, the filing of an information or return of an indictment there, and the transmittal of papers in the case from that district to the district where the defendant is present. Under the amendment, the defendant, by also waiving venue, would make it possible for charges to be filed in the district of his arrest or presence. This would advance the interests of both the prosecution and defendant in a timely entry of a plea of guilty. No change has been made in the requirement that the transfer occur with the consent of both United States attorneys.

NOTES OF ADVISORY COMMITTEE ON RULES—1987 AMENDMENT

The amendments are technical. No substantive change is intended.

COMMITTEE NOTES ON RULES—2002 AMENDMENT

The language of Rule 20 has been amended as part of the general restyling of the Criminal Rules to make them more easily understood and to make style and terminology consistent throughout the rules. These changes are intended to be stylistic only, except as noted below.

New Rule 20(d)(2) applies to juvenile cases and has been added to parallel a similar provision in new Rule 20(b). The new provision provides that after the court has determined that the provisions in Rule 20(d)(1) have been completed and the transfer is approved, the file (or certified copy) must be transmitted from the original court to the transferee court.

AMENDMENT BY PUBLIC LAW

1975—Subd. (d). Pub. L. 94–64 amended subd. (d) generally.

EFFECTIVE DATE OF AMENDMENTS PROPOSED APRIL 22, 1974; EFFECTIVE DATE OF 1975 AMENDMENTS

Amendments of this rule embraced in the order of the United States Supreme Court on Apr. 22, 1974, and the amendments of this rule made by section 3 of Pub. L. 94–64, effective Dec. 1, 1975, see section 2 of Pub. L. 94–64, set out as a note under rule 4 of these rules.

Rule 21. Transfer for Trial

(a) For Prejudice. Upon the defendant's motion, the court must transfer the proceeding against that defendant to another district if the court is satisfied that so great a prejudice against the defendant exists in the transferring district that the defendant cannot obtain a fair and impartial trial there.

(b) For Convenience. Upon the defendant's motion, the court may transfer the proceeding, or one or more counts, against that defendant to another district for the convenience of the parties, any victim, and the witnesses, and in the interest of justice.

(c) Proceedings on Transfer. When the court orders a transfer, the clerk must send to the transferee district the file, or a certified copy, and any bail taken. The prosecution will then continue in the transferee district.

(d) Time to File a Motion to Transfer. A motion to transfer may be made at or before arraignment or at any other time the court or these rules prescribe.

(As amended Feb. 28, 1966, eff. July 1, 1966; Mar. 9, 1987, eff. Aug. 1, 1987; Apr. 29, 2002, eff. Dec. 1, 2002; Apr. 28, 2010, eff. Dec. 1, 2010.)

NOTES OF ADVISORY COMMITTEE ON RULES—1944

Note to Subdivisions (a) and (b). 1. This rule introduces an addition to existing law. "Lawyers not thoroughly familiar with Federal practice are somewhat astounded to learn that they may not move for a change of venue, even if they are able to demonstrate that public feeling in the vicinity of the crime may render impossible a fair and impartial trial. This seems to be a defect in the federal law, which the proposed rules would cure." Homer Cummings, 29 A.B.A.Jour. 655; Medalie, 4 Lawyers Guild R. (3)1, 5.

2. The rule provides for two kinds of motions that may be made by the defendant for a change of venue. The first is a motion on the ground that so great a prejudice exists against the defendant that he cannot obtain a fair and impartial trial in the district or division where the case is pending. Express provisions to a similar effect are found in many State statutes. See, e.g., Ala. Code (1940), Title 15, sec. 267; Cal.Pen.Code (Deering, 1941), sec. 1033; Conn.Gen.Stat. (1930), sec. 6445; Mass.Gen.Laws (1932) c. 277, sec. 51 (in capital cases); N.Y. Code of Criminal Procedure, sec. 344. The second is a motion for a change of venue in cases involving an offense alleged to have been committed in more than one district or division. In such cases the court, on defendant's motion, will be authorized to transfer the case to another district or division in which the commission of the offense is charged, if the court is satisfied that it is in the interest of justice to do so. The effect of this provision would be to modify the existing practice under which in such cases the Government has the final choice of the jurisdiction where the prosecution should be conducted. The matter will now be left in the discretion of the court.

3. The rule provides for a change of venue only on defendant's motion and does not extend the same right to the prosecution, since the defendant has a constitutional right to a trial in the district where the offense was committed. Constitution of the United States, Article III, Sec. 2, Par. 3; Amendment VI. By making a motion for a change of venue, however, the defendant waives this constitutional right.

4. This rule is in addition to and does not supersede existing statutes enabling a party to secure a change of judge on the ground of personal bias or prejudice, 28 U.S.C. 25 [now 144]; or enabling the defendant to secure a change of venue as of right in certain cases involving offenses committed in more than one district, 18 U.S.C. 338a(d) [now 876, 3239] (Mailing threatening communications); Id. sec. 403d(d) [now 875, 3239] (Threatening communications in interstate commerce).

Note to Subdivision (c). Cf. 28 U.S.C. 114 [now 1393, 1441] and Rule 20, supra.

NOTES OF ADVISORY COMMITTEE ON RULES——1966 AMENDMENT

Subdivision (a).——All references to divisions are eliminated in accordance with the amendment to Rule 18 eliminating division venue. The defendant is given the right to a transfer only when he can show that he cannot obtain a fair and impartial trial at any place fixed by law for holding court in the district. Transfers within the district to avoid prejudice will be within the power of the judge to fix the place of trial as provided in the amendments to Rule 18. It is also made clear that on a motion to transfer under this subdivision the court may select the district to which the transfer may be made. Cf. United States v. Parr, 17 F.R.D. 512, 519 (S.D.Tex. (1955); Parr v. United States, 351 U.S. 513 (1956).

Subdivision (b).——The original rule limited change of venue for reasons other than prejudice in the district to those cases where venue existed in more than one district. Upon occasion, however, convenience of the parties and witnesses and the interest of justice would best be served by trial in a district in which no part of the offense was committed. See, e.g., Travis v. United States, 364 U.S. 631 (1961), holding that the only venue of a charge of making or filing a false non-Communist affidavit required by §9(h) of the National Labor Relations Act is in Washington, D.C. even though all the relevant witnesses may be located at the place where the affidavit was executed and mailed. See also Barber, Venue in Federal Criminal Cases: A Plea for Return to Principle, 42 Tex.L.Rev. 39 (1963); Wright, Proposed Changes in Federal Civil, Criminal and Appellate Procedure, 35 F.R.D. 317, 329 (1964). The amendment permits a transfer in any case on motion of the defendant on a showing that it would be for the convenience of parties and witnesses, and in the interest of justice. Cf. 28 U.S.C. §1404(a), stating a similar standard for civil cases. See also Platt v. Minnesota Min. & Mfg. Co., 376 U.S.C. 240 (1964). Here, as in subdivision (a), the court may select the district to which the transfer is to be made. The amendment also makes it clear that the court may transfer all or part of the offenses charged in a multi-count indictment or information. Cf. United States v. Choate, 276 F.2d 724 (5th Cir. 1960). References to divisions are eliminated in accordance with the amendment to Rule 18.

Subdivision (c).——The reference to division is eliminated in accordance with the amendment to Rule 18.

NOTES OF ADVISORY COMMITTEE ON RULES——1987 AMENDMENT

The amendments are technical. No substantive change is intended.

COMMITTEE NOTES ON RULES——2002 AMENDMENT

The language of Rule 21 has been amended as part of the general restyling of the Criminal Rules to make them more easily understood and to make style and terminology consistent throughout the rules. These changes are intended to be stylistic only.

Amended Rule 21(d) consists of what was formerly Rule 22. The Committee believed that the substance of Rule 22, which addressed the issue of the timing of motions to transfer, was more appropriate for inclusion in Rule 21.

COMMITTEE NOTES ON RULES——2010 AMENDMENT

Subdivision (b). This amendment requires the court to consider the convenience of victims——as well as the convenience of the parties and witnesses and the interests of justice——in determining whether to transfer all or part of the proceeding to another district for trial. The Committee recognizes that the court has substantial discretion to balance any competing interests.

Changes Made to Proposed Amendment Released for Public Comment. No changes were made after the amendment was released for public comment.

Rule 22. [Transferred]

COMMITTEE NOTES ON RULES——2002 AMENDMENT

Rule 22 has been abrogated. The substance of the rule is now located in Rule 21(d).

TITLE VI. TRIAL

Rule 23. Jury or Nonjury Trial

(a) Jury Trial. If the defendant is entitled to a jury trial, the trial must be by jury unless:
    (1) the defendant waives a jury trial in writing;
    (2) the government consents; and
    (3) the court approves.

(b) Jury Size.
    (1) In General. A jury consists of 12 persons unless this rule provides otherwise.
    (2) Stipulation for a Smaller Jury. At any time before the verdict, the parties may, with the court's approval, stipulate in writing that:
        (A) the jury may consist of fewer than 12 persons; or
        (B) a jury of fewer than 12 persons may return a verdict if the court finds it necessary to excuse a juror for good cause after the trial begins.

    (3) Court Order for a Jury of 11. After the jury has retired to deliberate, the court may permit a jury of 11 persons to return a verdict, even without a stipulation by the parties, if the court finds good cause to excuse a juror.

(c) Nonjury Trial. In a case tried without a jury, the court must find the defendant guilty or not guilty. If a party requests before the finding of guilty or not guilty, the court must state its specific findings of fact in open court or in a written decision or opinion.

(As amended Feb. 28, 1966, eff. July 1, 1966; Pub. L. 95–78, §2(b), July 30, 1977, 91 Stat. 320; Apr. 28, 1983, eff. Aug. 1, 1983; Apr. 29, 2002, eff. Dec. 1, 2002.)

NOTES OF ADVISORY COMMITTEE ON RULES——1944

Note to Subdivision (a). 1. This rule is a formulation of the constitutional guaranty of trial by jury, Constitution of the United States, Article III, Sec. 2, Par. 3: "The Trial of all Crimes, except in Cases of Impeachment, shall be by Jury * * *"; Amendment VI: "In all criminal prosecutions, the accused shall enjoy the right to a speedy and public trial, by an impartial jury * * *." The right to a jury trial, however, does not apply to petty offenses, District of Columbia v. Clawans, 300 U.S. 617; Schick v. United States, 195 U.S. 65; Frankfurter and Corcoran, 39 Harv.L.R. 917. Cf. Rule 38(a) of the Federal Rules of Civil Procedure [28 U.S.C., Appendix].

2. The provision for a waiver of jury trial by the defendant embodies existing practice, the constitutionality of which has been upheld, Patton v. United States, 281 U.S. 276; Adams v. United States ex rel. McCann, 317 U.S. 269; Cf. Rules 38 and 39 of Federal Rules of Civil Procedure [28 U.S.C., Appendix]. Many States by express statutory provision permit waiver of jury trial in criminal cases. See A.L.I. Code of Criminal Procedure Commentaries, pp. 807–811.

Note to Subdivision (b). This rule would permit either a stipulation before the trial that the case be tried by a jury composed of less than 12 or a stipulation during the trial consenting that the case be submitted to less than 12 jurors. The second alternative is useful in case it becomes necessary during the trial to excuse a juror owing to illness or for some other cause and no alternate juror is available. The rule is a restatement of existing practice, the constitutionality of which was approved in Patton v. United States, 281 U.S. 276.

Note to Subdivision (c). This rule changes existing law in so far as it requires the court in a case tried without a jury to make special findings of fact if requested. Cf. Connecticut practice, under which a judge in a criminal case tried by the court without a jury makes findings of fact, State v. Frost, 105 Conn. 326.

NOTES OF ADVISORY COMMITTEE ON RULES—1966 AMENDMENT
This amendment adds to the rule a provision added to Civil Rule 52(a) in 1946.

NOTES OF ADVISORY COMMITTEE ON RULES—1977 AMENDMENT
The amendment to subdivision (b) makes it clear that the parties, with the approval of the court, may enter into an agreement to have the case decided by less than twelve jurors if one or more jurors are unable or disqualified to continue. For many years the Eastern District of Virginia has used a form entitled, "Waiver of Alternate Jurors." In a substantial percentage of cases the form is signed by the defendant, his attorney, and the Assistant United States Attorney in advance of trial, generally on the morning of trial. It is handled automatically by the courtroom deputy clerk who, after completion, exhibits it to the judge.

This practice would seem to be authorized by existing rule 23(b), but there has been some doubt as to whether the pretrial stipulation is effective unless again agreed to by a defendant at the time a juror or jurors have to be excused. See 8 J. Moore, Federal Practice 23.04 (2d. ed. Cipes, 1969); C. Wright, Federal Practice and Procedure: Criminal §373 (1969). The proposed amendment is intended to make clear that the pretrial stipulation is an effective waiver, which need not be renewed at the time the incapacity or disqualification of the juror becomes known.

In view of the fact that a defendant can make an effective pretrial waiver of trial by jury or by a jury of twelve, it would seem to follow that he can also effectively waive trial by a jury of twelve in situations where a juror or jurors cannot continue to serve.

As has been the practice under rule 23(b), a stipulation addressed to the possibility that some jurors may later be excused need not be open-ended. That is, the stipulation may be conditioned upon the jury not being reduced below a certain size. See, e.g., Williams v. United States, 332 F.2d 36 (7th Cir. 1964) (agreement to proceed if no more than 2 jurors excused for illness); Rogers v. United States, 319 F.2d 5 (7th Cir. 1963) (same).

Subdivision (c) is changed to make clear the deadline for making a request for findings of fact and to provide that findings may be oral. The oral findings, of course, become a part of the record, as findings of fact are essential to proper appellate review on a conviction resulting from a nonjury trial. United States v. Livingston, 459 F.2d 797 (3d Cir. 1972).

The meaning of current subdivision (c) has been in some doubt because there is no time specified within which a defendant must make a "request" that the court "find the facts specially." See, e.g., United States v. Rivera, 444 F.2d 136 (2d Cir. 1971), where the request was not made until the sentence had been imposed. In the opinion the court said:

This situation might have raised the interesting and apparently undecided question of when a request for findings under Fed. R. Crim. P. 23(c) is too late, since Rivera's request was not made until the day after sentence was imposed. See generally Benchwick v. United States, 297 F.2d 330, 335 (9th Cir. 1961); United States v. Morris, 263 F.2d 594 (7th Cir. 1959).

NOTES OF COMMITTEE ON THE JUDICIARY, SENATE REPORT NO. 95–354; 1977 AMENDMENTS PROPOSED BY THE SUPREME COURT
Subsection (b) of section 2 of the bill simply approves the Supreme Court proposed changes in subdivisions (b) and (c) of rule 23 for the reasons given by the Advisory Committee on Rules of Practice and Procedure to the Judicial Conference.

CONGRESSIONAL APPROVAL OF PROPOSED 1977 AMENDMENTS
Pub. L. 95–78, §2(b), July 30, 1977, 91 Stat. 320, provided that: "The amendments proposed by the Supreme Court [in its order of Apr. 26, 1977] to subdivisions (b) and (c) of rule 23 of such Rules of Criminal Procedure [subd. (b) and (c) of this rule] are approved."

NOTES OF ADVISORY COMMITTEE ON RULES—1983 AMENDMENT
Note to Subdivision (b). The amendment to subdivision (b) addresses a situation which does not occur with great frequency but which, when it does occur, may present a most difficult issue concerning the fair and efficient administration of justice. This situation is that in which, after the jury has retired to consider its verdict and any alternate jurors have been discharged, one of the jurors is seriously incapacitated or otherwise found to be unable to continue service upon the jury. The problem is acute when the trial has been a lengthy one and consequently the remedy of mistrial would necessitate a second expenditure of substantial prosecution, defense and court resources. See, e.g., United States v. Meinster, 484 F.Supp. 442 (S.D.Fla. 1980), aff'd sub nom. United States v. Phillips, 664 F.2d 971 (5th Cir. 1981) (juror had heart attack during deliberations after "well over four months of trial"); United States v. Barone, 83 F.R.D. 565 (S.D. Fla. 1979) (juror removed upon recommendation of psychiatrist during deliberations after "approximately six months of trial").

It is the judgment of the Committee that when a juror is lost during deliberations, especially in circumstances like those in Barone and Meinster, it is essential that there be available a course of action other than mistrial. Proceeding with the remaining 11 jurors, though heretofore impermissible under rule 23(b) absent stipulation by the parties and approval of the court, United States v. Taylor, 507 F.2d 166 (5th Cir. 1975), is constitutionally permissible. In Williams v. Florida, 399 U.S. 78 (1970), the Court concluded

the fact that the jury at common law was composed of precisely 12 is an historical accident, unnecessary to effect the purposes of the jury system and wholly without significance "except to mystics." * * * To read the Sixth Amendment as forever codifying a feature so incidental to the real purpose of the Amendment is to ascribe a blind formalism to the Framers which would require considerably more evidence than we have been able to discover in the history and language of the Constitution or in the reasoning of our past decisions. * * * Our holding does no more than leave these considerations to Congress and the States, unrestrained by an interpretation of the Sixth Amendment which would forever dictate the precise number which can constitute a jury.

Williams held that a six-person jury was constitutional because such a jury had the "essential feature of a jury," i.e., "the interposition between the accused and his accuser of the common-sense judgment of a group of laymen, and in the community participation and shared responsibility which results from that group's determination of guilt or innocence," necessitating only a group "large enough to promote group deliberation, free from outside attempts at intimidation, and to provide a fair possibility for obtaining a representative cross section of the community." This being the case, quite clearly the occasional use of a jury of slightly less than 12, as contemplated by the amendment to rule 23(b), is constitutional. Though the alignment of the Court and especially the separate opinion by Justice Powell in Apodoca v. Oregon, 406 U.S. 404 (1972), makes it at best uncertain whether less-than-unanimous verdicts would be constitutionally permissible in federal trials, it hardly follows that a requirement of unanimity of a group slightly less than 12 is similarly suspect.

The Meinster case clearly reflects the need for a solution other than mistrial. There twelve defendants were named in a 36-count, 100-page indictment for RICO offenses and related violations, and the trial lasted more than four months. Before the jury retired for deliberations, the trial judge inquired of defense counsel whether they would now agree to a jury of less than 12 should a juror later be unable to continue during the deliberations which were anticipated to be lengthy. All defense counsel rejected that proposal. When one juror was excused a day later after suffering a heart attack, all defense counsel again rejected the proposal that deliberations continue with the remaining 11 jurors. Thus, the solution now provided in rule 23(b), stipulation to a jury of less than 12, was not possible in that case, just as it will not be possible in any case in which defense counsel believe some tactical advantage will be gained by retrial. Yet, to declare a mistrial at that point would have meant that over four months of trial time would have gone for naught and that a comparable period of time would have to be expended on retrial. For a variety of reasons, not the least of which is the impact such a retrial would have upon that court's ability to comply with speedy trial limits in other cases, such a result is most undesirable.

That being the case, it is certainly understandable that the trial judge in Meinster (as in Barone) elected to substitute an alternate juror at that point. Given the rule 23(b) bar on a verdict of less than 12 absent stipulation, United States v. Taylor, supra, such substitution seemed the least objectionable course of action. But in terms of what change in the Federal Rules of Criminal Procedure is to be preferred in order to facilitate response to such situations in the future, the judgment of the Advisory Committee is that it is far better to permit the deliberations to continue with a jury of 11 than to make a substitution at that point.

In rejecting the substitution-of-juror alternative, the Committee's judgment is in accord with that of most commentators and many courts.

> There have been proposals that the rule should be amended to permit an alternate to be substituted if a regular juror becomes unable to perform his duties after the case has been submitted to the jury. An early draft of the original Criminal Rules had contained such a provision, but it was withdrawn when the Supreme Court itself indicated to the Advisory Committee on Criminal Rules doubts as to the desirability and constitutionality of such a procedure. These doubts are as forceful now as they were a quarter century ago. To permit substitution of an alternate after deliberations have begun would require either that the alternate participate though he has missed part of the jury discussion, or that he sit in with the jury in every case on the chance he might be needed. Either course is subject to practical difficulty and to strong constitutional objection.

Wright, Federal Practice and Procedure, §388 (1969). See also Moore, Federal Practice par. 24.05 (2d ed. Cipes 1980) ("The inherent coercive effect upon an alternate who joins a jury leaning heavily toward a guilty verdict may result in the alternate reaching a premature guilty verdict"); 3 ABA Standards for Criminal Justice §15—2.7, commentary (2d ed. 1980) ("It is not desirable to allow a juror who is unfamiliar with the prior deliberations to suddenly join the group and participate in the voting without the benefit of earlier group discussion"); United States v. Lamb, 529 F.2d 1153 (9th Cir. 1975); People v. Ryan, 19 N.Y.2d 100, 224 N.E.2d 710 (1966). Compare People v. Collins, 17 Cal.3d 687, 131 Cal.Rptr. 782, 522 P.2d 742 (1976); Johnson v. State, 267 Ind. 256, 396 N.E.2d 623 (1977).

The central difficulty with substitution, whether viewed only as a practical problem or a question of constitutional dimensions (procedural due process under the Fifth Amendment or jury trial under the Sixth Amendment), is that there does not appear to be any way to nullify the impact of what has occurred without the participation of the new juror. Even were it required that the jury "review" with the new juror their prior deliberations or that the jury upon substitution start deliberations anew, it still seems likely that the continuing jurors would be influenced by the earlier deliberations and that the new juror would be somewhat intimidated by the others by virtue of being a newcomer to the deliberations. As for the possibility of sending in the alternates at the very beginning with instructions to listen but not to participate until substituted, this scheme is likewise attended by practical difficulties and offends "the cardinal principle that the deliberations of the jury shall remain private and secret in every case." United States v. Virginia Erection Corp., 335 F.2d 868 (4th Cir. 1964).

The amendment provides that if a juror is excused after the jury has retired to consider its verdict, it is within the discretion of the court whether to declare a mistrial or to permit deliberations to continue with 11 jurors. If the trial has been brief and not much would be lost by retrial, the court might well conclude that the unusual step of allowing a jury verdict by less than 12 jurors absent stipulation should not be taken. On the other hand, if the trial has been protracted the court is much more likely to opt for continuing with the remaining 11 jurors.

Committee Notes on Rules—2002 Amendment

The language of Rule 23 has been amended as part of the general restyling of the Criminal Rules to make them more easily understood and to make style and terminology consistent throughout the rules. These changes are intended to be stylistic only.

In current Rule 23(b), the term "just cause" has been replaced with the more familiar term "good cause," that appears in other rules. No change in substance is intended.

Effective Date of 1977 Amendment

Amendment of this rule by order of the United States Supreme Court on Apr. 26, 1976, approved by Pub. L. 95—78, effective Oct. 1, 1977, see section 4 of Pub. L. 95—78, set out as an Effective Date of Pub. L. 95—78 note under section 2074 of Title 28, Judiciary and Judicial Procedure.

Rule 24. Trial Jurors

(a) Examination.

(1) In General. The court may examine prospective jurors or may permit the attorneys for the parties to do so.

(2) Court Examination. If the court examines the jurors, it must permit the attorneys for the parties to:

(A) ask further questions that the court considers proper; or

(B) submit further questions that the court may ask if it considers them proper.

(b) Peremptory Challenges. Each side is entitled to the number of peremptory challenges to prospective jurors specified below. The court may allow additional peremptory challenges to multiple defendants, and may allow the defendants to exercise those challenges separately or jointly.

(1) Capital Case. Each side has 20 peremptory challenges when the government seeks the death penalty.

(2) Other Felony Case. The government has 6 peremptory challenges and the defendant or defendants jointly have 10 peremptory challenges when the defendant is charged with a crime punishable by imprisonment of more than one year.

(3) Misdemeanor Case. Each side has 3 peremptory challenges when the defendant is charged with a crime punishable by fine, imprisonment of one year or less, or both.

(c) Alternate Jurors.

(1) In General. The court may impanel up to 6 alternate jurors to replace any jurors who are unable to perform or who are disqualified from performing their duties.

(2) Procedure.

(A) Alternate jurors must have the same qualifications and be selected and sworn in the same manner as any other juror.

(B) Alternate jurors replace jurors in the same sequence in which the alternates were selected. An alternate juror who replaces a juror has the same authority as the other jurors.

91

(3) Retaining Alternate Jurors. The court may retain alternate jurors after the jury retires to deliberate. The court must ensure that a retained alternate does not discuss the case with anyone until that alternate replaces a juror or is discharged. If an alternate replaces a juror after deliberations have begun, the court must instruct the jury to begin its deliberations anew.

(4) Peremptory Challenges. Each side is entitled to the number of additional peremptory challenges to prospective alternate jurors specified below. These additional challenges may be used only to remove alternate jurors.

(A) One or Two Alternates. One additional peremptory challenge is permitted when one or two alternates are impaneled.

(B) Three or Four Alternates. Two additional peremptory challenges are permitted when three or four alternates are impaneled.

(C) Five or Six Alternates. Three additional peremptory challenges are permitted when five or six alternates are impaneled.

(As amended Feb. 28, 1966, eff. July 1, 1966; Mar. 9, 1987, eff. Aug. 1, 1987; Apr. 26, 1999, eff. Dec. 1, 1999; Apr. 29, 2002, eff. Dec. 1, 2002.)

NOTES OF ADVISORY COMMITTEE ON RULES——1944

Note to Subdivision (a). This rule is similar to Rule 47(a) of the Federal Rules of Civil Procedure [28 U.S.C., Appendix] and also embodies the practice now followed by many Federal courts in criminal cases. Uniform procedure in civil and criminal cases on this point seems desirable.

Note to Subdivision (b). This rule embodies existing law, 28 U.S.C. 424 [now 1870] (Challenges), with the following modifications. In capital cases the number of challenges is equalized as between the defendant and the United States so that both sides have 20 challenges, which only the defendant has at present. While continuing the existing rule that multiple defendants are deemed a single party for purposes of challenges, the rule vests in the court discretion to allow additional peremptory challenges to multiple defendants and to permit such challenges to be exercised separately or jointly. Experience with cases involving numerous defendants indicates the desirability of this modification.

Note to Subdivision (c). This rule embodies existing law, 28 U.S.C. [former] 417a (Alternate jurors), as well as the practice prescribed for civil cases by Rule 47(b) of the Federal Rules of Civil Procedure [28 U.S.C., Appendix], except that the number of possible alternate jurors that may be impaneled is increased from two to four, with a corresponding adjustment of challenges.

NOTES OF ADVISORY COMMITTEE ON RULES——1966 AMENDMENT

Experience has demonstrated that four alternate jurors may not be enough for some lengthy criminal trials. See e.g., United States v. Bentvena, 288 F.2d 442 (2d Cir. 1961); Reports of the Proceedings of the Judicial Conference of the United States, 1961, p. 104. The amendment to the first sentence increases the number authorized from four to six. The fourth sentence is amended to provide an additional peremptory challenge where a fifth or sixth alternate juror is used.

The words "or are found to be" are added to the second sentence to make clear that an alternate juror may be called in the situation where it is first discovered during the trial that a juror was unable or disqualified to perform his duties at the time he was sworn. See United States v. Goldberg, 330 F.2d 30 (3rd Cir. 1964), cert. den. 377 U.S. 953 (1964).

CONGRESSIONAL DISAPPROVAL OF PROPOSED 1977 AMENDMENT

Pub. L. 95–78, §2(c), July 30, 1977, 91 Stat. 320, effective Oct. 1, 1977, provided that: "The amendment proposed by the Supreme Court [in its order of Apr. 26, 1977] to rule 24 of such Rules of Criminal Procedure is disapproved and shall not take effect."

NOTES OF ADVISORY COMMITTEE ON RULES——1987 AMENDMENT

The amendments are technical. No substantive change is intended.

COMMITTEE NOTES ON RULES——1999 AMENDMENT

As currently written, Rule 24(c) explicitly requires the court to discharge all of the alternate jurors—who have not been selected to replace other jurors—when the jury retires to deliberate. That requirement is grounded on the concern that after the case has been submitted to the jury, its deliberations must be private and inviolate. United States v. Houlihan, 92 F.3d 1271, 1285 (1st Cir. 1996), citing United States v. Virginia Election Corp., 335 F.2d 868, 872 (4th Cir. 1964).

Rule 23(b) provides that in some circumstances a verdict may be returned by eleven jurors. In addition, there may be cases where it is better to retain the alternates when the jury retires, insulate them from the deliberation process, and have them available should one or more vacancies occur in the jury. That might be especially appropriate in a long, costly, and complicated case. To that end the Committee believed that the court should have the discretion to decide whether to retain or discharge the alternates at the time the jury retires to deliberate and to use Rule 23(b) to proceed with eleven jurors or to substitute a juror or jurors with alternate jurors who have not been discharged.

In order to protect the sanctity of the deliberative process, the rule requires the court to take appropriate steps to insulate the alternate jurors. That may be done, for example, by separating the alternates from the deliberating jurors and instructing the alternate jurors not to discuss the case with any other person until they replace a regular juror. See, e.g., United States v. Olano, 507 U.S. 725 (1993) (not plain error to permit alternate jurors to sit in during deliberations); United States v. Houlihan, 92 F.3d 1271, 1286–88 (1st Cir. 1996) (harmless error to retain alternate jurors in violation of Rule 24(c); in finding harmless error the court cited the steps taken by the trial judge to insulate the alternates). If alternates are used, the jurors must be instructed that they must begin their deliberations anew.

Finally, subsection (c) has been reorganized and restyled.

GAP Report——Rule 24(c). The final sentence of Rule 24(c) was moved from the committee note to the rule to emphasize that if an alternate replaces a juror during deliberations, the court shall instruct the jury to begin its deliberations anew.

COMMITTEE NOTES ON RULES——2002 AMENDMENT

The language of Rule 24 has been amended as part of the general restyling of the Criminal Rules to make them more easily understood and to make style and terminology consistent throughout the rules. These changes are intended to be stylistic only, except as noted below.

In restyling Rule 24(a), the Committee deleted the language that authorized the defendant to conduct voir dire of prospective jurors. The Committee believed that the current language was potentially ambiguous and could lead one incorrectly to conclude that a defendant, represented by counsel, could personally conduct voir dire or additional voir dire. The Committee believed that the intent of the current provision was to permit a defendant to participate personally in voir dire only if the defendant was acting pro se. Amended Rule 24(a) refers only to attorneys for the parties, i.e., the defense counsel and the attorney for the government, with the understanding that if the defendant is not represented by counsel, the court may still, in its discretion, permit the defendant to participate in voir dire. In summary, the Committee intends no change in practice.

Finally, the rule authorizes the court in multi-defendant cases to grant additional peremptory challenges to the defendants. If the court does so, the prosecution may request additional challenges in a multi-defendant case, not to exceed the total number available to the defendants jointly. The court, however, is not required to equalize the number of challenges where additional challenges are granted to the defendant.

Rule 25. Judge's Disability

(a) During Trial. Any judge regularly sitting in or assigned to the court may complete a jury trial if:

    (1) the judge before whom the trial began cannot proceed because of death, sickness, or other disability; and

    (2) the judge completing the trial certifies familiarity with the trial record.

(b) After a Verdict or Finding of Guilty.

    (1) In General. After a verdict or finding of guilty, any judge regularly sitting in or assigned to a court may complete the court's duties if the judge who presided at trial cannot perform those duties because of absence, death, sickness, or other disability.

    (2) Granting a New Trial. The successor judge may grant a new trial if satisfied that:

        (A) a judge other than the one who presided at the trial cannot perform the post-trial duties; or

        (B) a new trial is necessary for some other reason.

(As amended Feb. 28, 1966, eff. July 1, 1966; Mar. 9, 1987, eff. Aug. 1, 1987; Apr. 29, 2002, eff. Dec. 1, 2002.)

NOTES OF ADVISORY COMMITTEE ON RULES—1944

This rule is similar to Rule 63 of the Federal Rules of Civil Procedure [28 U.S.C., Appendix]. See also, 28 U.S.C. [former] 776 (Bill of exceptions; authentication; signing of by judge).

NOTES OF ADVISORY COMMITTEE ON RULES—1966 AMENDMENT

In September, 1963, the Judicial Conference of the United States approved a recommendation of its Committee on Court Administration that provision be made for substitution of a judge who becomes disabled during trial. The problem has become serious because of the increase in the number of long criminal trials. See 1963 Annual Report of the Director of the Administrative Office of the United States Courts, p. 114, reporting a 25% increase in criminal trials lasting more than one week in fiscal year 1963 over 1962.

Subdivision (a).—The amendment casts the rule into two subdivisions and in subdivision (a) provides for substitution of a judge during a jury trial upon his certification that he has familiarized himself with the record of the trial. For similar provisions see Alaska Rules of Crim. Proc., Rule 25; California Penal Code, §1053.

Subdivision (b).—The words "from the district" are deleted to permit the local judge to act in those situations where a judge who has been assigned from within the district to try the case is, at the time for sentence, etc., back at his regular place of holding court which may be several hundred miles from the place of trial. It is not intended, of course, that substitutions shall be made where the judge who tried the case is available within a reasonable distance from the place of trial.

NOTES OF ADVISORY COMMITTEE ON RULES—1987 AMENDMENT

The amendments are technical. No substantive change is intended.

COMMITTEE NOTES ON RULES—2002 AMENDMENT

The language of Rule 25 has been amended as part of the general restyling of the Criminal Rules to make them more easily understood and to make style and terminology consistent throughout the rules. These changes are intended to be stylistic only.

Rule 25(b)(2) addresses the possibility of a new trial when a judge determines that no other judge could perform post-trial duties or when the judge determines that there is some other reason for doing so. The current rule indicates that those reasons must be "appropriate." The Committee, however, believed that a better term would be "necessary," because that term includes notions of manifest necessity. No change in meaning or practice is intended.

Rule 26. Taking Testimony

In every trial the testimony of witnesses must be taken in open court, unless otherwise provided by a statute or by rules adopted under 28 U.S.C. §§2072–2077.

(As amended Nov. 20, 1972, eff. July 1, 1975; Apr. 29, 2002, eff. Dec. 1, 2002.)

NOTES OF ADVISORY COMMITTEE ON RULES—1944

1. This rule contemplates the development of a uniform body of rules of evidence to be applicable in trials of criminal cases in the Federal courts. It is based on Funk v. United States, 290 U.S. 371, and Wolfle v. United States, 291 U.S. 7, which indicated that in the absence of statute the Federal courts in criminal cases are not bound by the State law of evidence, but are guided by common law principles as interpreted by the Federal courts "in the light of reason and experience." The rule does not fetter the applicable law of evidence to that originally existing at common law. It is contemplated that the law may be modified and adjusted from time to time by judicial decisions. See Homer Cummings, 29 A.B.A.Jour. 655; Vanderbilt, 29 A.B.A.Jour. 377; Holtzoff, 12 George Washington L.R. 119, 131–132; Holtzoff, 3 F.R.D. 445, 453; Howard, 51 Yale L.Jour. 763; Medalie, 4 Lawyers Guild R. (3)1, 5–6.

2. This rule differs from the corresponding rule for civil cases (Federal Rules of Civil Procedure, Rule 43(a) [28 U.S.C., Appendix]), in that this rule contemplates a uniform body of rules of evidence to govern in criminal trials in the Federal courts, while the rule for civil cases prescribes partial conformity to State law and, therefore, results in a divergence as between various districts. Since in civil actions in which Federal jurisdiction is based on diversity of citizenship, the State substantive law governs the rights of the parties, uniformity of rules of evidence among different districts does not appear necessary. On the other hand, since all Federal crimes are statutory and all criminal prosecutions in the Federal courts are based on acts of Congress, uniform rules of evidence appear desirable if not essential in criminal cases, as otherwise the same facts under differing rules of evidence may lead to a conviction in one district and to an acquittal in another.

3. This rule expressly continues existing statutes governing the admissibility of evidence and the competency and privileges of witnesses. Among such statutes are the following:

U.S.C., Title 8:

Section 138 [see 1326, 1328, 1329] (Importation of aliens for immoral purposes; attempt to re-enter after deportation; penalty)

U.S.C., Title 28:

Section 632 [now 18 U.S.C. 3481] (Competency of witnesses governed by State laws; defendants in criminal cases)
Section 633 [former] (Competency of witnesses governed by State laws; husband or wife of defendant in prosecution for bigamy)
Section 634 [former] (Testimony of witnesses before Congress)
Section 638 [now 1731] (Comparison of handwriting to determine genuineness)
Section 695 [now 1732] (Admissibility)
Section 695a [now 18 U.S.C. 3491] (Foreign documents)

U.S.C., Title 46:

NOTES OF ADVISORY COMMITTEE ON RULES—1972 AMENDMENT

The first sentence is retained, with appropriate narrowing of the title, since its subject is not covered in the Rules of Evidence. The second sentence is deleted because the Rules of Evidence govern admissibility of evidence, competency of witnesses, and privilege. The language is broadened, however, to take account of the Rules of Evidence and any other rules adopted by the Supreme Court.

COMMITTEE NOTES ON RULES—2002 AMENDMENT

The language of Rule 26 has been amended as part of the general restyling of the Criminal Rules to make them more easily understood and to make style and terminology consistent throughout the rules. These changes are intended to be stylistic only, except as noted below.

Rule 26 is amended, by deleting the word "orally," to accommodate witnesses who are not able to present oral testimony in open court and may need, for example, a sign language interpreter. The change conforms the rule, in that respect, to Federal Rule of Civil Procedure 43.

EFFECTIVE DATE OF AMENDMENT PROPOSED NOVEMBER 20, 1972

Amendment of this rule embraced by the order entered by the Supreme Court of the United States on November 20, 1972, effective on the 180th day beginning after January 2, 1975, see section 3 of Pub. L. 93–595, Jan. 2, 1975, 88 Stat. 1959, set out as a note under section 2074 of Title 28, Judiciary and Judicial Procedure.

Rule 26.1. Foreign Law Determination

A party intending to raise an issue of foreign law must provide the court and all parties with reasonable written notice. Issues of foreign law are questions of law, but in deciding such issues a court may consider any relevant material or source—including testimony—without regard to the Federal Rules of Evidence.

(Added Feb. 28, 1966, eff. July 1, 1966; amended Nov. 20, 1972, eff. July 1, 1975; Apr. 29, 2002, eff. Dec. 1, 2002.)

NOTES OF ADVISORY COMMITTEE ON RULES—1966

The original Federal Rules of Criminal Procedure did not contain a provision explicitly regulating the determination of foreign law. The resolution of issues of foreign law, when relevant in federal criminal proceedings, falls within the general compass of Rule 26 which provides for application of "the [evidentiary] principles of the common law as they may be interpreted by the courts of the United States in the light of reason and experience." See Green, Preliminary Report on the Advisability and Feasibility of Developing Uniform Rules of Evidence for the United States District Courts 6–7, 17–18 (1962). Although traditional "commonlaw" methods for determining foreign-country law have proved inadequate, the courts have not developed more appropriate practices on the basis of this flexible rule. Cf. Green, op. cit. supra at 26–28. On the inadequacy of common-law procedures for determining foreign law, see, e.g., Nussbaum, Proving the Law of Foreign Countries, 3 Am.J.Comp.L. 60 (1954).

Problems of foreign law that must be resolved in accordance with the Federal Rules of Criminal Procedure are most likely to arise in places such as Washington, D.C., the Canal Zone, Guam, and the Virgin Islands, where the federal courts have general criminal jurisdiction. However, issues of foreign law may also arise in criminal proceedings commenced in other federal districts. For example, in an extradition proceeding, reasonable ground to believe that the person sought to be extradited is charged with, or was convicted of, a crime under the laws of the demanding state must generally be shown. See Factor v. Laubenheimer, 290 U.S. 276 (1933); Fernandez v. Phillips, 268 U.S. 311 (1925); Bishop International Law: Cases and Materials (2d ed. 1962). Further, foreign law may be invoked to justify non-compliance with a subpoena duces tecum, Application of Chase Manhattan Bank, 297 F.2d 611 (2d Cir. 1962), and under certain circumstances, as a defense to prosecution. Cf. American Banana Co. v. United Fruit Co., 213 U.S. 347 (1909). The content of foreign law may also be relevant in proceedings arising under 18 U.S.C. §§1201, 2312–2317.

Rule 26.1 is substantially the same as Civil Rule 44.1. A full explanation of the merits and practicability of the rule appear in the Advisory Committee's Note to Civil Rule 44.1. It is necessary here to add only one comment to the explanations there made. The second sentence of the rule frees the court from the restraints of the ordinary rules of evidence in determining foreign law. This freedom, made necessary by the peculiar nature of the issue of foreign law, should not constitute an unconstitutional deprivation of the defendant's rights to confrontation of witnesses. The issue is essentially one of law rather than of fact. Furthermore, the cases have held that the Sixth Amendment does not serve as a rigid barrier against the development of reasonable and necessary exceptions to the hearsay rule. See Kay v. United States, 255 F.2d 476, 480 (4th Cir. 1958), cert. den., 358 U.S. 825 (1958); Matthews v. United States, 217 F.2d 409, 418 (5th Cir. 1954); United States v. Leathers, 135 F.2d 507 (2d Cir. 1943); and cf., Painter v. Texas, 85 S.Ct. 1065 (1965); Douglas v. Alabama, 85 S.Ct. 1074 (1965).

NOTES OF ADVISORY COMMITTEE ON RULES—1972 AMENDMENT

Since the purpose is to free the judge, in determining foreign law, from restrictive evidentiary rules, the reference is made to the Rules of Evidence generally.

COMMITTEE NOTES ON RULES—2002 AMENDMENT

The language of Rule 26.1 has been amended as part of the general restyling of the Criminal Rules to make them more easily understood and to make style and terminology consistent throughout the rules. These changes are intended to be stylistic only.

REFERENCES IN TEXT

The Federal Rules of Evidence, referred to in text, are set out in the Appendix to Title 28, Judiciary and Judicial Procedure.

EFFECTIVE DATE OF AMENDMENT PROPOSED NOVEMBER 20, 1972

Amendment of this rule embraced by the order entered by the Supreme Court of the United States on November 20, 1972, effective on the 180th day beginning after January 2, 1975, see section 3 of Pub. L. 93–595, Jan. 2, 1975, 88 Stat. 1959, set out as a note under section 2074 of Title 28, Judiciary and Judicial Procedure.

Rule 26.2. Producing a Witness's Statement

(a) Motion to Produce. After a witness other than the defendant has testified on direct examination, the court, on motion of a party who did not call the witness, must order an attorney for the government or the defendant and the defendant's attorney to produce, for the examination and use of the moving party, any statement of the witness that is in their possession and that relates to the subject matter of the witness's testimony.

(b) Producing the Entire Statement. If the entire statement relates to the subject matter of the witness's testimony, the court must order that the statement be delivered to the moving party.

(c) Producing a Redacted Statement. If the party who called the witness claims that the statement contains information that is privileged or does not relate to the subject matter of the witness's testimony, the court must inspect the statement in camera. After excising any privileged or unrelated portions, the court must order delivery of the redacted statement to the moving party. If the defendant objects to an excision, the court must preserve the entire statement with the excised portion indicated, under seal, as part of the record.

(d) Recess to Examine a Statement. The court may recess the proceedings to allow time for a party to examine the statement and prepare for its use.

(e) Sanction for Failure to Produce or Deliver a Statement. If the party who called the witness disobeys an order to produce or deliver a statement, the court must strike the witness's testimony from the record. If an attorney for the government disobeys the order, the court must declare a mistrial if justice so requires.

(f) "Statement" Defined. As used in this rule, a witness's "statement" means:

(1) a written statement that the witness makes and signs, or otherwise adopts or approves;

(2) a substantially verbatim, contemporaneously recorded recital of the witness's oral statement that is contained in any recording or any transcription of a recording; or

(3) the witness's statement to a grand jury, however taken or recorded, or a transcription of such a statement.

(g) Scope. This rule applies at trial, at a suppression hearing under Rule 12, and to the extent specified in the following rules:

(1) Rule 5.1(h) (preliminary hearing);

(2) Rule 32(i)(2) (sentencing);

(3) Rule 32.1(e) (hearing to revoke or modify probation or supervised release);

(4) Rule 46(j) (detention hearing); and

(5) Rule 8 of the Rules Governing Proceedings under 28 U.S.C. §2255.

(Added Apr. 30, 1979, eff. Dec. 1, 1980; amended Mar. 9, 1987, eff. Aug. 1, 1987; Apr. 22, 1993, eff. Dec. 1, 1993; Apr. 24, 1998, eff. Dec. 1, 1998; Apr. 29, 2002, eff. Dec. 1, 2002.)

NOTES OF ADVISORY COMMITTEE ON RULES——1979

S. 1437, 95th Cong., 1st Sess. (1977), would place in the criminal rules the substance of what is now 18 U.S.C. §3500 (the Jencks Act). Underlying this and certain other additions to the rules contemplated by S. 1437 is the notion that provisions which are purely procedural in nature should appear in the Federal Rules of Criminal Procedure rather than in Title 18. See Reform of the Federal Criminal Laws, Part VI: Hearings on S. 1, S. 716, and S. 1400, Subcomm. on Criminal Laws and Procedures, Senate Judiciary Comm., 93rd Cong., 1st Sess. (statement of Judge Albert B. Maris, at page 5503). Rule 26.2 is identical to the S.1437 rule except as indicated by the marked additions and deletions. As those changes show, rule 26.2 provides for production of the statements of defense witnesses at trial in essentially the same manner as is now provided for with respect to the statements of government witnesses. Thus, the proposed rule reflects these two judgments: (i) that the subject matter——production of the statements of witnesses——is more appropriately dealt with in the criminal rules; and (ii) that in light of United States v. Nobles, 422 U.S. 225 (1975), it is important to establish procedures for the production of defense witnesses' statements as well. The rule is not intended to discourage the practice of voluntary disclosure at an earlier time so as to avoid delays at trial.

In Nobles, defense counsel sought to introduce the testimony of a defense investigator who prior to trial had interviewed prospective prosecution witnesses and had prepared a report embodying the essence of their conversation. When the defendant called the investigator to impeach eyewitness testimony identifying the defendant as the robber, the trial judge granted the prosecutor the right to inspect those portions of the investigator's report relating to the witnesses' statements, as a potential basis for cross-examination of the investigator. When the defense declined to produce the report, the trail judge refused to permit the investigator to testify. The Supreme Court unanimously upheld the trail court's actions, finding that neither the Fifth nor Sixth Amendments nor the attorney work product doctrine prevented disclosure of such a document at trial. Noting "the federal judiciary's inherent power to require the prosecution to produce the previously recorded statements of its witnesses so that the defense may get the full benefit of cross-examinations and the truth-finding process may be enhanced," the Court rejected the notion "that the Fifth amendment renders criminal discovery 'basically a one-way street,' " and thus concluded that "in a proper case, the prosecution can call upon that same power for production of witness statements that facilitate 'full disclosure of all the [relevant] facts.' "

The rule, consistent with the reasoning in Nobles, is designed to place the disclosure of prior relevant statements of a defense witness in the possession of the defense on the same legal footing as is the disclosure of prior statements of prosecution witnesses in the hands of the government under the Jencks Act, 18 U.S.C. §3500 (which S. 1437 would replace with the rule set out therein). See United States v. Pulvirenti, 408 F.Supp. 12 (E.D.Mich. 1976), holding that under Nobles "[t]he obligation [of disclosure] placed on the defendant should be the reciprocal of that placed upon the government * * * [as] defined by the Jencks Act." Several state courts have likewise concluded that witness statements in the hands of the defense at trial should be disclosed on the same basis that prosecution witness statements are disclosed, in order to promote the concept of the trail as a search for truth. See, e.g., People v. Sanders, 110 Ill.App.2d 85, 249 N.E.2d 124 (1969); State v. Montague, 55 N.J. 371, 262 A.2d 398 (1970); People v. Damon, 24 N.Y.2d 256, 299 N.Y.S.2d 830, 247 N.E.2d 651 (1959).

The rule, with minor exceptions, makes the procedure identical for both prosecution and defense witnesses, including the provision directing the court, whenever a claim is made that disclosure would be improper because the statement contains irrelevant matter, to examine the statements in camera and excise such matter as should not be disclosed. This provision acts as a safeguard against abuse and will enable a defendant who believes that a demand is being improperly made to secure a swift and just resolution of the issue.

The treatment as to defense witnesses of necessity differs slightly from the treatment as to prosecution witnesses in terms of the sanction for a refusal to comply with the court's disclosure order. Under the Jencks Act and the rule proposed in S. 1437, if the prosecution refuses to abide by the court's order, the court is required to strike the witness's testimony unless in its discretion it determines that the more serious sanction of a mistrial in favor of the accused is warranted. Under this rule, if a defendant refuses to comply with the court's disclosure order, the court's only alternative is to enter an order striking or precluding the testimony of the witness, as was done in Nobles.

Under subdivision (a) of the rule, the motion for production may be made by "a party who did not call the witness." Thus, it also requires disclosure of statements in the possession of either party when the witness is called neither by the prosecution nor the defense but by the court pursuant to the Federal Rules of Evidence. Present law does not deal with this situation, which consistency requires be treated in an identical manner as the disclosure of statements of witnesses called by a party to the case.

NOTES OF ADVISORY COMMITTEE ON RULES——1987 AMENDMENT

The amendments are technical. No substantive change is intended.

NOTES OF ADVISORY COMMITTEE ON RULES——1993 AMENDMENT

New subdivision (g) recognizes other contemporaneous amendments in the Rules of Criminal Procedure which extend the application of Rule 26.2 to other proceedings. Those changes are thus consistent with the extension of Rule 26.2 in 1983 to suppression hearings conducted under Rule 12. See Rule 12(i).

In extending Rule 26.2 to suppression hearings in 1983, the Committee offered several reasons. First, production of witness statements enhances the ability of the court to assess the witnesses' credibility and thus assists the court in making accurate factual determinations at suppression hearings. Second, because witnesses testifying at a suppression hearing may not necessarily testify at the trial itself, waiting until after a witness testifies at trial before requiring production of that witness's statement would be futile. Third, the Committee believed that it would be feasible to leave the suppression issue open until trial, where Rule 26.2 would then be applicable. Finally, one of the central reasons for requiring production of statements at suppression hearings was the recognition that by its nature, the results of a suppression hearing have a profound and ultimate impact on the issues presented at trial.

The reasons given in 1983 for extending Rule 26.2 to a suppression hearing are equally compelling with regard to other adversary type hearings which ultimately depend on accurate and reliable information. That is, there is a continuing need for information affecting the credibility of witnesses who present testimony. And that need exists without regard to whether the witness is presenting testimony at a pretrial hearing, at a trial, or at a post-trial proceeding.

As noted in the 1983 Advisory Committee Note to Rule 12(i), the courts have generally declined to extend the Jencks Act, 18 U.S.C. §3500, beyond the confines of actual trial testimony. That result will be obviated by the addition of Rule 26.2(g) and amendments to the Rules noted in that new subdivision.

95

Although amendments to Rules 32, 32.1, 46, and Rule 8 of the Rules Governing Proceedings under 28 U.S.C. §2255 specifically address the requirement of producing a witness's statement, Rule 26.2 has become known as the central "rule" requiring production of statements. Thus, the references in the Rule itself will assist the bench and bar in locating other Rules which include similar provisions.

The amendment to Rule 26.2 and the other designated Rules is not intended to require production of a witness's statement before the witness actually testifies.

Minor conforming amendments have been made to subsection (d) to reflect that Rule 26.2 will be applicable to proceedings other than the trial itself. And language has been added to subsection (c) to recognize explicitly that privileged matter may be excised from the witness's prior statement.

COMMITTEE NOTES ON RULES—1998 AMENDMENT

The amendment to subdivision (g) mirrors similar amendments made in 1993 to this rule and to other Rules of Criminal Procedure which extended the application of Rule 26.2 to other proceedings, both pretrial and post-trial. This amendment extends the requirement of producing a witness' statement to preliminary examinations conducted under Rule 5.1.

Subdivision (g)(1) has been amended to reflect changes to Rule 32.

Changes Made to Rule 26.2 After Publication ("GAP Report"). The Committee made no changes to the published draft.

COMMITTEE NOTES ON RULES—2002 AMENDMENT

The language of Rule 26.2 has been amended as part of the general restyling of the Criminal Rules to make them more easily understood and to make style and terminology consistent throughout the rules. These changes are intended to be stylistic only, except as noted below.

Current Rule 26.2(c) states that if the court withholds a portion of a statement, over the defendant's objection, "the attorney for the government" must preserve the statement. The Committee believed that the better rule would be for the court to simply seal the entire statement as a part of the record, in the event that there is an appeal.

Also, the terminology in Rule 26.2(c) has been changed. The rule now speaks in terms of a "redacted" statement instead of an "excised" statement. No change in practice is intended.

Finally, the list of proceedings in Rule 26.2(g) has been placed in rule-number order.

REFERENCES IN TEXT

The Rules Governing Proceedings under 28 U.S.C. §2255, referred to in subd. (g)(5), are set out under section 2255 of Title 28, Judiciary and Judicial Procedure.

EFFECTIVE DATE OF RULE

This rule added by order of the United States Supreme Court of Apr. 30, 1979, effective Dec. 1, 1980, see section 1(1) of Pub. L. 96–42, July 31, 1979, 93 Stat. 326, set out as a note under section 2074 of Title 28, Judiciary and Judicial Procedure.

Rule 26.3. Mistrial

Before ordering a mistrial, the court must give each defendant and the government an opportunity to comment on the propriety of the order, to state whether that party consents or objects, and to suggest alternatives.

(Added Apr. 22, 1993, eff. Dec. 1, 1993; amended Apr. 29, 2002, eff. Dec. 1, 2002.)

NOTES OF ADVISORY COMMITTEE ON RULES—1993

Rule 26.3 is a new rule designed to reduce the possibility of an erroneously ordered mistrial which could produce adverse and irretrievable consequences. The Rule is not designed to change the substantive law governing mistrials. Instead it is directed at providing both sides an opportunity to place on the record their views about the proposed mistrial order. In particular, the court must give each side an opportunity to state whether it objects or consents to the order.

Several cases have held that retrial of a defendant was barred by the Double Jeopardy Clause of the Constitution because the trial court had abused its discretion in declaring a mistrial. See United States v. Dixon, 913 F.2d 1305 (8th Cir. 1990); United States v. Bates, 917 F.2d 388 (9th Cir. 1990). In both cases the appellate courts concluded that the trial court had acted precipitately and had failed to solicit the parties' views on the necessity of a mistrial and the feasibility of any alternative action. The new Rule is designed to remedy that situation.

The Committee regards the Rule as a balanced and modest procedural device that could benefit both the prosecution and the defense. While the Dixon and Bates decisions adversely affected the government's interest in prosecuting serious crimes, the new Rule could also benefit defendants. The Rule ensures that a defendant has the opportunity to dissuade a judge from declaring a mistrial in a case where granting one would not be an abuse of discretion, but the defendant believes that the prospects for a favorable outcome before that particular court, or jury, are greater than they might be upon retrial.

COMMITTEE NOTES ON RULES—2002 AMENDMENT

The language of Rule 26.3 has been amended as part of the general restyling of the Criminal Rules to make them more easily understood and to make style and terminology consistent throughout the rules. These changes are intended to be stylistic only.

Rule 27. Proving an Official Record

A party may prove an official record, an entry in such a record, or the lack of a record or entry in the same manner as in a civil action.

(As amended Apr. 29, 2002, eff. Dec. 1, 2002.)

NOTES OF ADVISORY COMMITTEE ON RULES—1944

This rule incorporates by reference Rule 44 of the Federal Rules of Civil Procedure, 28 U.S.C., Appendix, which provided a simple and uniform method of proving public records and entry or lack of entry therein. The rule does not supersede statutes regulating modes of proof in respect to specific official records. In such cases parties have the option of following the general rule or the pertinent statute. Among the many statutes are:

U.S.C., Title 28:

Section 661 [now 1733] (Copies of department or corporation records and papers; admissibility; seal)
Section 662 [now 1733] (Same; in office of General Counsel of the Treasury)
Section 663 [now 1733] (Instruments and papers of Comptroller of Currency; admissibility)

96

Section 664 [now 1733] (Organization certificates of national banks; admissibility)
Section 665 [now 1733] (Transcripts from books of Treasury in suits against delinquents; admissibility)
Section 666 [now 1733] (Same; certificate by Secretary or Assistant Secretary)
Section 668 [now 18 U.S.C. 3497] (Same; indictments for embezzlement of public moneys)
Section 669 [former] (Copies of returns in returns office admissible)
Section 670 [now 1743] (Admissibility of copies of statements of demands by Post Office Department)
Section 671 [now 1733] (Admissibility of copies of post office records and statement of accounts)
Section 672 [see 1733] (Admissibility of copies of records in General Land Office)
Section 673 [now 1744] (Admissibility of copies of records, and so forth, of Patent Office)
Section 674 [now 1745] (Copies of foreign letters patent as prima facie evidence)
Section 675 [former] (Copies of specifications and drawings of patents admissible)
Section 676 [now 1736] (Extracts from Journals of Congress admissible when injunction of secrecy removed)
Section 677 [now 1740] (Copies of records in offices of United States consuls admissible)
Section 678 [former] (Books and papers in certain district courts)
Section 679 [former] (Records in clerks' offices, western district of North Carolina)
Section 680 [former] (Records in clerks' offices of former district of California)
Section 681 [now 1734] (Original records lost or destroyed; certified copy admissible)
Section 682 [now 1734] (Same; when certified copy not obtainable)
Section 685 [now 1735] (Same; certified copy of official papers)
Section 687 [now 1738] (Authentication of legislative acts; proof of judicial proceedings of State)
Section 688 [now 1739] (Proofs of records in offices not pertaining to courts)
Section 689 [now 1742] (Copies of foreign records relating to land titles)
Section 695a–695h [now 18 U.S.C. 3491–3496; 22 U.S.C. 1204; 1741] (Foreign documents)

U.S.C., Title 1:
Section 30 [now 112] (Statutes at Large; contents; admissibility in evidence)
Section 30a [now 113] ("Little and Brown's" edition of laws and treaties competent evidence of Acts of Congress)
Section 54 [now 204] (Codes and Supplements as establishing prima facie the Laws of United States and District of Columbia, citation of Codes and Supplements)
Section 55 [now 209] (Copies of Supplements to Code of Laws of United States and of District of Columbia Code and Supplements; conclusive evidence of original)

U.S.C., Title 5:
Section 490 [see 28 U.S.C. 1733] (Records of Department of Interior; authenticated copies as evidence)

U.S.C., Title 8:
Section 717(b) [see 1435, 1482] (Former citizens of United States excepted from certain requirements; citizenship lost by spouse's alienage or loss of United States citizenship, or by entering armed forces of foreign state or acquiring its nationality)
Section 727(g) [see 1443] (Administration of naturalization laws; rules and regulations; instruction in citizenship; forms; oaths; depositions; documents in evidence; photographic studio)

U.S.C., Title 15:
Section 127 [see 1057(e)] (Trade-marks; copies of records as evidence)

U.S.C., Title 20:
Section 52 (Smithsonian Institution; evidence of title to site and buildings)

U.S.C., Title 25:
Section 6 (Bureau of Indian Affairs; seal; authenticated and certified documents; evidence)

U.S.C., Title 31:
Section 46 [see 704] (Laws governing General Accounting Office; copies of books, records, etc., thereof as evidence)

U.S.C., Title 38:
Section 11g [see 302] (Seal of Veterans' Administration; authentication of copies of records)

U.S.C., Title 43:
Section 57 (Authenticated copies or extracts from records as evidence)
Section 58 (Transcripts from records of Louisiana)
Section 59 (Official papers in office of surveyor general in California; papers; copies)
Section 83 (Transcripts of records as evidence)

U.S.C., Title 44:
Section 300h [now 2112] (National Archives; seal; reproduction of archives; fee; admissibility in evidence of reproductions)
Section 307 [now 1507] (Filing document as constructive notice; publication in Register as presumption of validity; judicial notice; citation)

U.S.C., Title 47:
Section 412 (Documents filed with Federal Communications Commission as public records; prima facie evidence; confidential records)

U.S.C., Title 49:
Section 16 [now 10303] (Orders of Commission and enforcement thereof; forfeitures—(13) copies of schedules, tariffs, contracts, etc., kept as public records; evidence)

COMMITTEE NOTES ON RULES—2002 AMENDMENT

The language of Rule 27 has been amended as part of the general restyling of the Criminal Rules to make them more easily understood and to make style and terminology consistent throughout the rules. These changes are intended to be stylistic only.

Rule 28. Interpreters

The court may select, appoint, and set the reasonable compensation for an interpreter, including an interpreter for the victim. The compensation must be paid from funds provided by law or by the government, as the court may direct.

(As amended Feb. 28, 1966, eff. July 1, 1966; Nov. 20, 1972, eff. July 1, 1975; Apr. 29, 2002, eff. Dec. 1, 2002; Pub. L. 114–324, §2(c), Dec. 16, 2016, 130 Stat. 1948.)

NOTES OF ADVISORY COMMITTEE ON RULES——1944

The power of the court to call its own witnesses, though rarely invoked, is recognized in the Federal courts, Young v. United States, 107 F.2d 490 (C.C.A. 5th); Litsinger v. United States, 44 F.2d 45 (C.C.A. 7th). This rule provides a procedure whereby the court may, if it chooses, exercise this power in connection with expert witnesses. The rule is based, in part, on the Uniform Expert Testimony Act, drafted by the Commissioners on Uniform State Laws, Hand Book of the National Conference of Commissioners on Uniform State Laws (1937), 337; see, also, Wigmore——Evidence, 3d Ed., sec. 563; A.L.I. Code of Criminal Procedure, secs. 307–309; National Commission on Law of Observance and Enforcement——Report on Criminal Procedure, 37. Similar provisions are found in the statutes of a number of States: Wisconsin——Wis.Stat. (1941), sec. 357.12; Indiana——Ind.Stat.Ann. (Burns, 1933), sec. 9–1702; California——Cal.Pen.Code (Deering, 1941), sec. 1027.

NOTES OF ADVISORY COMMITTEE ON RULES——1966 AMENDMENT

Subdivision (a).——The original rule is made a separate subdivision. The amendment permits the court to inform the witness of his duties in writing since it often constitutes an unnecessary inconvenience and expense to require the witness to appear in court for such purpose.

Subdivision (b).——This new subdivision authorizes the court to appoint and provide for the compensation of interpreters. General language is used to give discretion to the court to appoint interpreters in all appropriate situations. Interpreters may be needed to interpret the testimony of non-English speaking witnesses or to assist non-English speaking defendants in understanding the proceedings or in communicating with assigned counsel. Interpreters may also be needed where a witness or a defendant is deaf.

NOTES OF ADVISORY COMMITTEE ON RULES——1972 AMENDMENT

Subdivision (a). This subdivision is stricken, since the subject of court-appointed expert witnesses is covered in Evidence Rule 706 in detail.

Subdivision (b). The provisions of subdivision (b) are retained. Although Evidence Rule 703 specifies the qualifications of interpreters and the form of oath to be administered to them, it does not cover their appointment or compensation.

COMMITTEE NOTES ON RULES——2002 AMENDMENT

The language of Rule 28 has been amended as part of the general restyling of the Criminal Rules to make them more easily understood and to make style and terminology consistent throughout the rules. These changes are intended to be stylistic only.

AMENDMENT BY PUBLIC LAW

2016——Pub. L. 114–324 inserted ", including an interpreter for the victim" after "compensation for an interpreter".

EFFECTIVE DATE OF AMENDMENT PROPOSED NOVEMBER 20, 1972

Amendment of this rule embraced by the order entered by the Supreme Court of the United States on November 20, 1972, effective on the 180th day beginning after January 2, 1975, see section 3 of Pub. L. 93–595, Jan. 2, 1975, 88 Stat. 1959, set out as a note under section 2074 of Title 28, Judiciary and Judicial Procedure.

Rule 29. Motion for a Judgment of Acquittal

(a) Before Submission to the Jury. After the government closes its evidence or after the close of all the evidence, the court on the defendant's motion must enter a judgment of acquittal of any offense for which the evidence is insufficient to sustain a conviction. The court may on its own consider whether the evidence is insufficient to sustain a conviction. If the court denies a motion for a judgment of acquittal at the close of the government's evidence, the defendant may offer evidence without having reserved the right to do so.

(b) Reserving Decision. The court may reserve decision on the motion, proceed with the trial (where the motion is made before the close of all the evidence), submit the case to the jury, and decide the motion either before the jury returns a verdict or after it returns a verdict of guilty or is discharged without having returned a verdict. If the court reserves decision, it must decide the motion on the basis of the evidence at the time the ruling was reserved.

(c) After Jury Verdict or Discharge.

(1) Time for a Motion. A defendant may move for a judgment of acquittal, or renew such a motion, within 14 days after a guilty verdict or after the court discharges the jury, whichever is later.

(2) Ruling on the Motion. If the jury has returned a guilty verdict, the court may set aside the verdict and enter an acquittal. If the jury has failed to return a verdict, the court may enter a judgment of acquittal.

(3) No Prior Motion Required. A defendant is not required to move for a judgment of acquittal before the court submits the case to the jury as a prerequisite for making such a motion after jury discharge.

(d) Conditional Ruling on a Motion for a New Trial.

(1) Motion for a New Trial. If the court enters a judgment of acquittal after a guilty verdict, the court must also conditionally determine whether any motion for a new trial should be granted if the judgment of acquittal is later vacated or reversed. The court must specify the reasons for that determination.

(2) Finality. The court's order conditionally granting a motion for a new trial does not affect the finality of the judgment of acquittal.

(3) Appeal.

(A) Grant of a Motion for a New Trial. If the court conditionally grants a motion for a new trial and an appellate court later reverses the judgment of acquittal, the trial court must proceed with the new trial unless the appellate court orders otherwise.

(B) Denial of a Motion for a New Trial. If the court conditionally denies a motion for a new trial, an appellee may assert that the denial was erroneous. If the appellate court later reverses the judgment of acquittal, the trial court must proceed as the appellate court directs.

(As amended Feb. 28, 1966, eff. July 1, 1966; Pub. L. 99–646, §54(a), Nov. 10, 1986, 100 Stat. 3607; Apr. 29, 1994, eff. Dec. 1, 1994; Apr. 29, 2002, eff. Dec. 1, 2002; Apr. 25, 2005, eff. Dec. 1, 2005; Mar. 26, 2009, eff. Dec. 1, 2009.)

NOTES OF ADVISORY COMMITTEE ON RULES——1944

Note to Subdivision (a). 1. The purpose of changing the name of a motion for a directed verdict to a motion for judgment of acquittal is to make the nomenclature accord with the realities. The change of nomenclature, however, does not modify the nature of the motion or enlarge the scope of matters that may be considered.

2. The second sentence is patterned on New York Code of Criminal Procedure, sec. 410.

3. The purpose of the third sentence is to remove the doubt existing in a few jurisdictions on the question whether the defendant is deemed to have rested his case if he moves for a directed verdict at the close of the prosecution's case. The purpose of the rule is expressly to preserve the right of the defendant to offer evidence in his own behalf, if such motion is denied. This is a restatement of the prevailing practice, and is also in accord with the practice prescribed for civil cases by Rule 50(a) of the Federal Rules of Civil Procedure [28 U.S.C., Appendix].

Note to Subdivision (b). This rule is in substance similar to Rule 50(b) of the Federal Rules of Civil Procedure, 28 U.S.C., Appendix, and permits the court to render judgment for the defendant notwithstanding a verdict of guilty. Some Federal courts have recognized and approved the use of a judgment non obstante veredicto for the defendant in a criminal case, Ex parte United States, 101 F.2d 870 (C.C.A. 7th), affirmed by an equally divided court, United States v. Stone, 308 U.S. 519. The rule sanctions this practice.

NOTES OF ADVISORY COMMITTEE ON RULES—1966 AMENDMENT

Subdivision (a).—A minor change has been made in the caption.

Subdivision (b).—The last three sentences are deleted with the matters formerly covered by them transferred to the new subdivision (c).

Subdivision (c).—The new subdivision makes several changes in the former procedure. A motion for judgment of acquittal may be made after discharge of the jury whether or not a motion was made before submission to the jury. No legitimate interest of the government is intended to be prejudiced by permitting the court to direct an acquittal on a post-verdict motion. The constitutional requirement of a jury trial in criminal cases is primarily a right accorded to the defendant. Cf. Adams v. United States, ex rel. McCann, 317 U.S. 269 (1942); Singer v. United States, 380 U.S. 24 (1965); Note, 65 Yale L.J. 1032 (1956).

The time in which the motion may be made has been changed to 7 days in accordance with the amendment to Rule 45(a) which by excluding Saturday from the days to be counted when the period of time is less than 7 days would make 7 days the normal time for a motion required to be made in 5 days. Also the court is authorized to extend the time as is provided for motions for new trial (Rule 33) and in arrest of judgment (Rule 34).

References in the original rule to the motion for a new trial as an alternate to the motion for judgment of acquittal and to the power of the court to order a new trial have been eliminated. Motions for new trial are adequately covered in Rule 33. Also the original wording is subject to the interpretation that a motion for judgment of acquittal gives the court power to order a new trial even though the defendant does not wish a new trial and has not asked for one.

NOTES OF ADVISORY COMMITTEE ON RULES—1994 AMENDMENT

The amendment permits the reservation of a motion for a judgment of acquittal made at the close of the government's case in the the same manner as the rule now permits for motions made at the close of all of the evidence. Although the rule as written did not permit the court to reserve such motions made at the end of the government's case, trial courts on occasion have nonetheless reserved ruling. See, e.g., United States v. Bruno, 873 F.2d 555 (2d Cir.), cert. denied, 110 S.Ct. 125 (1989); United States v. Reifsteck, 841 F.2d 701 (6th Cir. 1988). While the amendment will not affect a large number of cases, it should remove the dilemma in those close cases in which the court would feel pressured into making an immediate, and possibly erroneous, decision or violating the rule as presently written by reserving its ruling on the motion.

The amendment also permits the trial court to balance the defendant's interest in an immediate resolution of the motion against the interest of the government in proceeding to a verdict thereby preserving its right to appeal in the event a verdict of guilty is returned but is then set aside by the granting of a judgment of acquittal. Under the double jeopardy clause the government may appeal the granting of a motion for judgment of acquittal only if there would be no necessity for another trial, i.e., only where the jury has returned a verdict of guilty. United States v. Martin Linen Supply Co., 430 U.S. 564 (1977). Thus, the government's right to appeal a Rule 29 motion is only preserved where the ruling is reserved until after the verdict.

In addressing the issue of preserving the government's right to appeal and at the same time recognizing double jeopardy concerns, the Supreme Court observed:

We should point out that it is entirely possible for a trial court to reconcile the public interest in the Government's right to appeal from an erroneous conclusion of law with the defendant's interest in avoiding a second prosecution. In United States v. Wilson, 420 U.S. 332 (1975), the court permitted the case to go to the jury, which returned a verdict of guilty, but it subsequently dismissed the indictment for preindictment delay on the basis of evidence adduced at trial. Most recently in United States v. Ceccolini, 435 U.S. 268 (1978), we described similar action with approval: 'The District Court had sensibly made its finding on the factual question of guilt or innocence, and then ruled on the motion to suppress; a reversal of these rulings would require no further proceeding in the District Court, but merely a reinstatement of the finding of guilt.' Id. at 271.

United States v. Scott, 437 U.S. 82, 100 n. 13 (1978). By analogy, reserving a ruling on a motion for judgment of acquittal strikes the same balance as that reflected by the Supreme Court in Scott.

Reserving a ruling on a motion made at the end of the government's case does pose problems, however, where the defense decides to present evidence and run the risk that such evidence will support the government's case. To address that problem, the amendment provides that the trial court is to consider only the evidence submitted at the time of the motion in making its ruling, whenever made. And in reviewing a trial court's ruling, the appellate court would be similarly limited.

COMMITTEE NOTES ON RULES—2002 AMENDMENT

The language of Rule 29 has been amended as part of the general restyling of the Criminal Rules to make them more easily understood and to make style and terminology consistent throughout the rules. These changes are intended to be stylistic only, except as noted below.

In Rule 29(a), the first sentence abolishing "directed verdicts" has been deleted because it is unnecessary. The rule continues to recognize that a judge may sua sponte enter a judgment of acquittal.

Rule 29(c)(1) addresses the issue of the timing of a motion for judgment of acquittal. The amended rule now includes language that the motion must be made within 7 days after a guilty verdict or after the judge discharges the jury, whichever occurs later. That change reflects the fact that in a capital case or in a case involving criminal forfeiture, for example, the jury may not be discharged until it has completed its sentencing duties. The court may still set another time for the defendant to make or renew the motion, if it does so within the 7-day period.

COMMITTEE NOTES ON RULES—2005 AMENDMENT

Rule 29(c) has been amended to remove the requirement that the court must act within seven days after a guilty verdict or after the court discharges the jury, if it sets another time for filing a motion for a judgment of acquittal. This amendment parallels similar changes to Rules 33 and 34. Further, a conforming amendment has been made to Rule 45(b)(2).

Currently, Rule 29(c) requires the defendant to move for a judgment of acquittal within seven days of the guilty verdict, or after the court discharges the jury, whichever occurs later, or some other time set by the court in an order issued within that same seven-day period. Similar provisions exist in Rules 33 and 34. Courts have held that the seven-day rule is jurisdictional. Thus, if a defendant files a request for an extension of time to file a motion for a judgment of acquittal within the seven-day period, the court must rule on that motion or request within the same seven-day period. If for some reason the court does not rule on the request within the seven days, it loses jurisdiction to act on the underlying substantive motion. See, e.g., United States v. Smith, 331 U.S. 469, 473–474 (1947) (rejecting argument that trial court had power to grant new trial on its own motion after expiration of time in Rule 33); United States v. Marquez, 291 F.3d 23, 27–28 (D.C. Cir. 2002) (citing language of Rule 33, and holding that "district court forfeited the power to act when it failed to . . . fix a new time for filing a motion for a new trial within seven days of the verdict").

Assuming that the current rule was intended to promote finality, there is nothing to prevent the court from granting a significant extension of time, so long as it does so within the seven-day period. Thus, the Committee believed that the rule should be amended to be consistent with all of the other timing requirements in the rules, which do not force the court to act on a motion to extend the time for filing within a particular period of time or lose jurisdiction to do so.

Accordingly, the amendment deletes the language regarding the court's acting within seven days to set the time for filing. Read in conjunction with the conforming amendment to Rule 45(b), the defendant is still required to file a timely motion for a judgment of acquittal under Rule 29 within the seven-day period specified. The defendant may, under Rule 45, seek an extension of time to file the underlying motion as long as the defendant does so within the seven-day period. But the court itself is not required to act on that motion within any particular time. Further, under Rule 45(b)(1)(B), if for some reason the defendant fails to file the underlying motion within the specified time, the court may nonetheless consider that untimely motion if the court determines that the failure to file it on time was the result of excusable neglect.

Changes Made After Publication and Comment. The Committee made no substantive changes to Rule 29 following publication.

COMMITTEE NOTES ON RULES—2009 AMENDMENT

Former Rules 29, 33, and 34 adopted 7-day periods for their respective motions. This period has been expanded to 14 days. Experience has proved that in many cases it is not possible to prepare a satisfactory motion in 7 days, even under the former rule that excluded intermediate Saturdays, Sundays, and legal holidays. This led to frequent requests for continuances, and the filing of bare bones motions that required later supplementation. The 14-day period—including intermediate Saturdays, Sundays, and legal holidays as provided by Rule 45(a)—sets a more realistic time for the filing of these motions.

AMENDMENT BY PUBLIC LAW

1986—Subd. (d). Pub. L. 99–646 added subd. (d).

EFFECTIVE DATE OF 1986 AMENDMENT

Pub. L. 99–646, §54(b), Nov. 10, 1986, 100 Stat. 3607, provided that: "The amendments made by this section [amending this rule] shall take effect 30 days after the date of the enactment of this Act [Nov. 10, 1986]."

Rule 29.1. Closing Argument

Closing arguments proceed in the following order:
(a) the government argues;
(b) the defense argues; and
(c) the government rebuts.

(Added Apr. 22, 1974, eff. Dec. 1, 1975; amended Apr. 29, 2002, eff. Dec. 1, 2002.)

NOTES OF ADVISORY COMMITTEE ON RULES—1974

This rule is designed to control the order of closing argument. It reflects the Advisory Committee's view that it is desirable to have a uniform federal practice. The rule is drafted in the view that fair and effective administration of justice is best served if the defendant knows the arguments actually made by the prosecution in behalf of conviction before the defendant is faced with the decision whether to reply and what to reply.

NOTES OF COMMITTEE ON THE JUDICIARY, HOUSE REPORT NO. 94–247; 1975 AMENDMENT

A. Amendments Proposed by the Supreme Court. Rule 29.1 is a new rule that was added to regulate closing arguments. It prescribes that the government shall make its closing argument and then the defendant shall make his. After the defendant has argued, the government is entitled to reply in rebuttal.

B. Committee Action. The Committee endorses and adopts this proposed rule in its entirety. The Committee believes that as the Advisory Committee Note has stated, fair and effective administration of justice is best served if the defendant knows the arguments actually made by the prosecution in behalf of conviction before the defendant is faced with the decision whether to reply and what to reply. Rule 29.1 does not specifically address itself to what happens if the prosecution waives its initial closing argument. The Committee is of the view that the prosecutor, when he waives his initial closing argument, also waives his rebuttal. [See the remarks of Senior United States Circuit Judge J. Edward Lumbard in Hearings II, at 207.]

COMMITTEE NOTES ON RULES—2002 AMENDMENT

The language of Rule 29.1 has been amended as part of the general restyling of the Criminal Rules to make them more easily understood and to make style and terminology consistent throughout the rules. These changes are intended to be stylistic only.

EFFECTIVE DATE

This rule effective Dec. 1, 1975, see section 2 of Pub. L. 94–64, set out as a note under rule 4 of these rules.

Rule 30. Jury Instructions

(a) In General. Any party may request in writing that the court instruct the jury on the law as specified in the request. The request must be made at the close of the evidence or at any earlier time that the court reasonably sets. When the request is made, the requesting party must furnish a copy to every other party.
(b) Ruling on a Request. The court must inform the parties before closing arguments how it intends to rule on the requested instructions.
(c) Time for Giving Instructions. The court may instruct the jury before or after the arguments are completed, or at both times.
(d) Objections to Instructions. A party who objects to any portion of the instructions or to a failure to give a requested instruction must inform the court of the specific objection and the grounds for the objection before the jury retires to deliberate. An opportunity must be given to object out of the jury's hearing and, on request, out of the jury's presence. Failure to object in accordance with this rule precludes appellate review, except as permitted under Rule 52(b).

(As amended Feb. 28, 1966, eff. July 1, 1966; Mar. 9, 1987, eff. Aug. 1, 1987; Apr. 25, 1988, eff. Aug. 1, 1988; Apr. 29, 2002, eff. Dec. 1, 2002.)

NOTES OF ADVISORY COMMITTEE ON RULES—1944

This rule corresponds to Rule 51 of the Federal Rules of Civil Procedure [28 U.S.C., Appendix], the second sentence alone being new. It seemed appropriate that on a point such as instructions to juries there should be no difference in procedure between civil and criminal cases.

NOTES OF ADVISORY COMMITTEE ON RULES—1966 AMENDMENT

The amendment requires the court, on request of any party, to require the jury to withdraw in order to permit full argument of objections to instructions.

NOTES OF ADVISORY COMMITTEE ON RULES—1987 AMENDMENT

In its current form, Rule 30 requires that the court instruct the jury after the arguments of counsel. In some districts, usually where the state practice is otherwise, the parties prefer to stipulate to instruction before closing arguments. The purpose of the amendment is to give the court discretion to instruct the jury before or after closing arguments, or at both times. The amendment will permit courts to continue instructing the jury after arguments as Rule 30 had previously required. It will also permit courts to instruct before arguments in order to give the parties an opportunity to argue to the jury in light of the exact language used by the court. See generally Raymond, Merits and Demerits of the Missouri System in Instructing Juries, 5 St. Louis U.L.J. 317 (1959). Finally, the amendment plainly indicates that the court may instruct both before and after arguments, which assures that the court retains power to remedy omissions in pre-argument instructions or to add instructions necessitated by the arguments.

The amendment is technical. No substantive change is intended.

The language of Rule 30 has been amended as part of the general restyling of the Criminal Rules to make them more easily understood and to make style and terminology consistent throughout the rules. These changes are intended to be stylistic only, except as noted below.

Rule 30(a) reflects a change in the timing of requests for instructions. As currently written, the trial court may not direct the parties to file such requests before trial without violating Rules 30 and 57. While the amendment falls short of requiring all requests to be made before trial in all cases, the amendment permits a court to do so in a particular case or as a matter of local practice under local rules promulgated under Rule 57. The rule does not preclude the practice of permitting the parties to supplement their requested instructions during the trial.

Rule 30(d) clarifies what, if anything, counsel must do to preserve a claim of error regarding an instruction or failure to instruct. The rule retains the requirement of a contemporaneous and specific objection (before the jury retires to deliberate). As the Supreme Court recognized in Jones v. United States, 527 U.S. 373 (1999), read literally, current Rule 30 could be construed to bar any appellate review absent a timely objection when in fact a court may conduct a limited review under a plain error standard. The amendment does not address the issue of whether objections to the instructions must be renewed after the instructions are given, in order to preserve a claim of error. No change in practice is intended by the amendment.

Rule 31. Jury Verdict

(a) Return. The jury must return its verdict to a judge in open court. The verdict must be unanimous.

(b) Partial Verdicts, Mistrial, and Retrial.

(1) Multiple Defendants. If there are multiple defendants, the jury may return a verdict at any time during its deliberations as to any defendant about whom it has agreed.

(2) Multiple Counts. If the jury cannot agree on all counts as to any defendant, the jury may return a verdict on those counts on which it has agreed.

(3) Mistrial and Retrial. If the jury cannot agree on a verdict on one or more counts, the court may declare a mistrial on those counts. The government may retry any defendant on any count on which the jury could not agree.

(c) Lesser Offense or Attempt. A defendant may be found guilty of any of the following:

(1) an offense necessarily included in the offense charged;

(2) an attempt to commit the offense charged; or

(3) an attempt to commit an offense necessarily included in the offense charged, if the attempt is an offense in its own right.

(d) Jury Poll. After a verdict is returned but before the jury is discharged, the court must on a party's request, or may on its own, poll the jurors individually. If the poll reveals a lack of unanimity, the court may direct the jury to deliberate further or may declare a mistrial and discharge the jury.

(As amended Apr. 24, 1972, eff. Oct. 1, 1972; Apr. 24, 1998, eff. Dec. 1, 1998; Apr. 17, 2000, eff. Dec. 1, 2000; Apr. 29, 2002, eff. Dec. 1, 2002.)

Note to Subdivision (a). This rule is a restatement of existing law and practice. It does not embody any regulation of sealed verdicts, it being contemplated that this matter would be governed by local practice in the various district courts. The rule does not affect the existing statutes relating to qualified verdicts in cases in which capital punishment may be imposed, 18 U.S.C. 408a [now 1201] (Kidnapped persons); sec. 412a [now 1992] (Wrecking trains); sec. 567 [now 1111] (Verdicts; qualified verdicts).

Note to Subdivision (b). This rule is a restatement of existing law, 18 U.S.C. [former] 566 (Verdicts; several joint defendants).

Note to Subdivision (c). This rule is a restatement of existing law, 18 U.S.C. [former] 565 (Verdicts; less offense than charged).

Note to Subdivision (d). This rule is a restatement of existing law and practice, Mackett v. United States, 90 F.2d 462, 465 (C.C.A. 7th); Bruce v. Chestnut Farms Chevy Chase Dairy, 126 F.2d 224, App.D.C.

Subdivision (e) is new. It is intended to provide procedural implementation of the recently enacted criminal forfeiture provision of the Organized Crime Control Act of 1970, Title IX, §1963, and the Comprehensive Drug Abuse Prevention and Control Act of 1970, Title II, §408(a)(2).

The assumption of the draft is that the amount of the interest or property subject to criminal forfeiture is an element of the offense to be alleged and proved. See Advisory Committee Note to rule 7(c)(2).

Although special verdict provisions are rare in criminal cases, they are not unknown. See United States v. Spock, 416 F. 2d 165 (1st Cir. 1969), especially footnote 41 where authorities are listed.

The right of a party to have the jury polled is an "undoubted right." Humphries v. District of Columbia, 174 U.S. 190, 194 (1899). Its purpose is to determine with certainty that "each of the jurors approves of the verdict as returned; that no one has been coerced or induced to sign a verdict to which he does not fully assent." Id.

Currently, Rule 31(d) is silent on the precise method of polling the jury. Thus, a court in its discretion may conduct the poll collectively or individually. As one court has noted, although the prevailing view is that the method used is a matter within the discretion of the trial court, United States v. Miller, 59 F.3d 417, 420 (3d Cir. 1995) (citing cases), the preference, nonetheless of the appellate and trial courts, seems to favor individual polling. Id. (citing cases). That is the position taken in the American Bar Association Standards for Criminal Justice §15—4.5. Those sources favoring individual polling observe that conducting a poll of the jurors collectively saves little time and does not always adequately insure that an individual juror who has been forced to join the majority during deliberations will voice dissent from a collective response. On the other hand, an advantage to individual polling is the "likelihood that it will discourage post-trial efforts to challenge the verdict on allegations of coercion on the part of some of the jurors." Miller, Id. at 420 (citing Audette v. Isaksen Fishing Corp., 789 F.2d 956, 961, n. 6 (1st Cir. 1986)).

The Committee is persuaded by the authorities and practice that there are advantages of conducting an individual poll of the jurors. Thus, the rule requires that the jurors be polled individually when a polling is requested, or when polling is directed sua sponte by the court. The amendment, however, leaves to the court the discretion as to whether to conduct a separate poll for each defendant, each count of the indictment or complaint, or on other issues.

Changes Made to Rule 31 After Publication ("GAP Report"). The Committee changed the rule to require that any polling of the jury must be done before the jury is discharged and it incorporated suggested style changes submitted by the Style Subcommittee.

The rule is amended to reflect the creation of new Rule 32.2, which now governs criminal forfeiture procedures.

GAP Report—Rule 31. The Committee made no changes to the published draft amendment to Rule 31.

The language of Rule 31 has been amended as part of the general restyling of the Criminal Rules to make them more easily understood and to make style and terminology consistent throughout the rules. These changes are intended to be stylistic only.

Rule 31(b) has been amended to clarify that a jury may return partial verdicts, either as to multiple defendants or multiple counts, or both. See, e.g., United States v. Cunningham, 145 F.3d 1385, 1388–90 (D.C. Cir. 1998) (partial verdicts on multiple defendants and counts). No change in practice is intended.

TITLE VII. POST-CONVICTION PROCEDURES

Rule 32. Sentencing and Judgment

(a) [Reserved.]

(b) Time of Sentencing.

(1) In General. The court must impose sentence without unnecessary delay.

(2) Changing Time Limits. The court may, for good cause, change any time limits prescribed in this rule.

(c) Presentence Investigation.

(1) Required Investigation.

(A) In General. The probation officer must conduct a presentence investigation and submit a report to the court before it imposes sentence unless:

(i) 18 U.S.C. §3593(c) or another statute requires otherwise; or

(ii) the court finds that the information in the record enables it to meaningfully exercise its sentencing authority under 18 U.S.C. §3553, and the court explains its finding on the record.

(B) Restitution. If the law permits restitution, the probation officer must conduct an investigation and submit a report that contains sufficient information for the court to order restitution.

(2) Interviewing the Defendant. The probation officer who interviews a defendant as part of a presentence investigation must, on request, give the defendant's attorney notice and a reasonable opportunity to attend the interview.

(d) Presentence Report.

(1) Applying the Advisory Sentencing Guidelines. The presentence report must:

(A) identify all applicable guidelines and policy statements of the Sentencing Commission;

(B) calculate the defendant's offense level and criminal history category;

(C) state the resulting sentencing range and kinds of sentences available;

(D) identify any factor relevant to:

(i) the appropriate kind of sentence, or

(ii) the appropriate sentence within the applicable sentencing range; and

(E) identify any basis for departing from the applicable sentencing range.

(2) Additional Information. The presentence report must also contain the following:

(A) the defendant's history and characteristics, including:

(i) any prior criminal record;

(ii) the defendant's financial condition; and

(iii) any circumstances affecting the defendant's behavior that may be helpful in imposing sentence or in correctional treatment;

(B) information that assesses any financial, social, psychological, and medical impact on any victim;

(C) when appropriate, the nature and extent of nonprison programs and resources available to the defendant;

(D) when the law provides for restitution, information sufficient for a restitution order;

(E) if the court orders a study under 18 U.S.C. §3552(b), any resulting report and recommendation;

(F) a statement of whether the government seeks forfeiture under Rule 32.2 and any other law; and

(G) any other information that the court requires, including information relevant to the factors under 18 U.S.C. §3553(a).

(3) Exclusions. The presentence report must exclude the following:

(A) any diagnoses that, if disclosed, might seriously disrupt a rehabilitation program;

(B) any sources of information obtained upon a promise of confidentiality; and

(C) any other information that, if disclosed, might result in physical or other harm to the defendant or others.

(e) Disclosing the Report and Recommendation.

(1) Time to Disclose. Unless the defendant has consented in writing, the probation officer must not submit a presentence report to the court or disclose its contents to anyone until the defendant has pleaded guilty or nolo contendere, or has been found guilty.

(2) Minimum Required Notice. The probation officer must give the presentence report to the defendant, the defendant's attorney, and an attorney for the government at least 35 days before sentencing unless the defendant waives this minimum period.

(3) Sentence Recommendation. By local rule or by order in a case, the court may direct the probation officer not to disclose to anyone other than the court the officer's recommendation on the sentence.

(f) Objecting to the Report.

(1) Time to Object. Within 14 days after receiving the presentence report, the parties must state in writing any objections, including objections to material information, sentencing guideline ranges, and policy statements contained in or omitted from the report.

(2) Serving Objections. An objecting party must provide a copy of its objections to the opposing party and to the probation officer.

(3) Action on Objections. After receiving objections, the probation officer may meet with the parties to discuss the objections. The probation officer may then investigate further and revise the presentence report as appropriate.

(g) Submitting the Report. At least 7 days before sentencing, the probation officer must submit to the court and to the parties the presentence report and an addendum containing any unresolved objections, the grounds for those objections, and the probation officer's comments on them.

(h) Notice of Possible Departure from Sentencing Guidelines. Before the court may depart from the applicable sentencing range on a ground not identified for departure either in the presentence report or in a party's prehearing submission, the court must give the parties reasonable notice that it is contemplating such a departure. The notice must specify any ground on which the court is contemplating a departure.

(i) Sentencing.

(1) In General. At sentencing, the court:

(A) must verify that the defendant and the defendant's attorney have read and discussed the presentence report and any addendum to the report;

(B) must give to the defendant and an attorney for the government a written summary of—or summarize in camera—any information excluded from the presentence report under Rule 32(d)(3) on which the court will rely in sentencing, and give them a reasonable opportunity to comment on that information;

(C) must allow the parties' attorneys to comment on the probation officer's determinations and other matters relating to an appropriate sentence; and

(D) may, for good cause, allow a party to make a new objection at any time before sentence is imposed.

(2) Introducing Evidence; Producing a Statement. The court may permit the parties to introduce evidence on the objections. If a witness testifies at sentencing, Rule 26.2(a)–(d) and (f) applies. If a party fails to comply with a Rule 26.2 order to produce a witness's statement, the court must not consider that witness's testimony.

(3) Court Determinations. At sentencing, the court:

(A) may accept any undisputed portion of the presentence report as a finding of fact;

(B) must—for any disputed portion of the presentence report or other controverted matter—rule on the dispute or determine that a ruling is unnecessary either because the matter will not affect sentencing, or because the court will not consider the matter in sentencing; and

(C) must append a copy of the court's determinations under this rule to any copy of the presentence report made available to the Bureau of Prisons.

(4) Opportunity to Speak.

(A) By a Party. Before imposing sentence, the court must:

(i) provide the defendant's attorney an opportunity to speak on the defendant's behalf;

(ii) address the defendant personally in order to permit the defendant to speak or present any information to mitigate the sentence; and

(iii) provide an attorney for the government an opportunity to speak equivalent to that of the defendant's attorney.

(B) By a Victim. Before imposing sentence, the court must address any victim of the crime who is present at sentencing and must permit the victim to be reasonably heard.

(C) In Camera Proceedings. Upon a party's motion and for good cause, the court may hear in camera any statement made under Rule 32(i)(4).

(j) Defendant's Right to Appeal.

(1) Advice of a Right to Appeal.

(A) Appealing a Conviction. If the defendant pleaded not guilty and was convicted, after sentencing the court must advise the defendant of the right to appeal the conviction.

(B) Appealing a Sentence. After sentencing—regardless of the defendant's plea—the court must advise the defendant of any right to appeal the sentence.

(C) Appeal Costs. The court must advise a defendant who is unable to pay appeal costs of the right to ask for permission to appeal in forma pauperis.

(2) Clerk's Filing of Notice. If the defendant so requests, the clerk must immediately prepare and file a notice of appeal on the defendant's behalf.

(k) Judgment.

(1) In General. In the judgment of conviction, the court must set forth the plea, the jury verdict or the court's findings, the adjudication, and the sentence. If the defendant is found not guilty or is otherwise entitled to be discharged, the court must so order. The judge must sign the judgment, and the clerk must enter it.

(2) Criminal Forfeiture. Forfeiture procedures are governed by Rule 32.2.

(As amended Feb. 28, 1966, eff. July 1, 1966; Apr. 24, 1972, eff. Oct. 1, 1972; Apr. 22, 1974, eff. Dec. 1, 1975; Pub. L. 94–64, §3(31)–(34), July 31, 1975, 89 Stat. 376; Apr. 30, 1979, eff. Aug. 1, 1979, and Dec. 1, 1980; Pub. L. 97–291, §3, Oct. 12, 1982, 96 Stat. 1249; Apr. 28, 1983, eff. Aug. 1, 1983; Pub. L. 98–473, title II, §215(a), Oct. 12, 1984, 98 Stat. 2014; Pub. L. 99–646, §25(a), Nov. 10, 1986, 100 Stat. 3597; Mar. 9, 1987, eff. Aug. 1, 1987; Apr. 25, 1989, eff. Dec. 1, 1989; Apr. 30, 1991, eff. Dec. 1, 1991; Apr. 22, 1993, eff. Dec. 1, 1993; Apr. 29, 1994, eff. Dec. 1, 1994; Pub. L. 103–322, title XXIII, §230101(b), Sept. 13, 1994, 108 Stat. 2078; Apr. 23, 1996, eff. Dec. 1, 1996; Pub. L. 104–132, title II, §207(a), Apr. 24, 1996, 110 Stat. 1236; Apr. 17, 2000, eff. Dec. 1, 2000; Apr. 29, 2002, eff. Dec. 1, 2002; Apr. 30, 2007, eff. Dec. 1, 2007; Apr. 23, 2008, eff. Dec. 1, 2008; Mar. 26, 2009, eff. Dec. 1, 2009; Apr. 26, 2011, eff. Dec. 1, 2011.)

NOTES OF ADVISORY COMMITTEE ON RULES——1944

Note to Subdivision (a). This rule is substantially a restatement of existing procedure. Rule I of the Criminal Appeals Rules of 1933, 292 U.S. 661. See Rule 43 relating to the presence of the defendant.

Note to Subdivision (b). This rule is substantially a restatement of existing procedure. Rule I of the Criminal Appeals Rules of 1933, 292 U.S. 661.

Note to Subdivision (c). The purpose of this provision is to encourage and broaden the use of presentence investigations, which are now being utilized to good advantage in many cases. See, "The Presentence Investigation" published by Administrative Office of the United States Courts, Division of Probation.

Note to Subdivision (d). This rule modifies existing practice by abrogating the ten-day limitation on a motion for leave to withdraw a plea of guilty. See Rule II (4) of the Criminal Appeals Rules of 1933, 292 U.S. 661.

Note to Subdivision (e). See 18 U.S.C. 724 et seq. [now 3651 et seq.].

NOTES OF ADVISORY COMMITTEE ON RULES——1966 AMENDMENT

Subdivision (a)(1).——The amendment writes into the rule the holding of the Supreme Court that the court before imposing sentence must afford an opportunity to the defendant personally to speak in his own behalf. See Green v. United States, 365 U.S. 301 (1961); Hill v. United States, 368 U.S. 424 (1962). The amendment also provides an opportunity for counsel to speak on behalf of the defendant.

Subdivision (a)(2).——This amendment is a substantial revision and a relocation of the provision originally found in Rule 37(a)(2): "When a court after trial imposes sentence upon a defendant not represented by counsel, the defendant shall be advised of his right to appeal and if he so requests, the clerk shall prepare and file forthwith a notice of appeal on behalf of the defendant." The court is required to advise the defendant of his right to appeal in all cases which have gone to trial after plea of not guilty because situations arise in which a defendant represented by counsel at the trial is not adequately advised by such counsel of his right to appeal. Trial counsel may not regard his responsibility as extending beyond the time of imposition of sentence. The defendant may be removed from the courtroom immediately upon sentence and held in custody under circumstances which make it difficult for counsel to advise him. See, e.g., Hodges v. United States, 368 U.S. 139 (1961). Because indigent defendants are most likely to be without effective assistance of counsel at this point in the proceedings, it is also provided that defendants be notified of the right of a person without funds to apply for leave to appeal in forma pauperis. The provision is added here because this rule seems the most appropriate place to set forth a procedure to be followed by the court at the time of sentencing.

Subdivision (c)(2).—It is not a denial of due process of law for a court in sentencing to rely on a report of a presentence investigation without disclosing such report to the defendant or giving him an opportunity to rebut it. Williams v. New York, 337 U.S. 241 (1949); Williams v. Oklahoma, 358 U.S. 576 (1959). However, the question whether as a matter of policy the defendant should be accorded some opportunity to see and refute allegations made in such reports has been the subject of heated controversy. For arguments favoring disclosure, see Tappan, Crime, Justice, and Correction, 558 (1960); Model Penal Code, 54–55 (Tent. Draft No. 2, 1954); Thomsen, Confidentiality of the Presentence Report: A Middle Position, 28 Fed.Prob., March 1964, p. 8; Wyzanski, A Trial Judge's Freedom and Responsibility, 65 Harv.L.Rev. 1281, 1291–2 (1952); Note, Employment of Social Investigation Reports in Criminal and Juvenile Proceedings, 58 Colum.L.Rev. 702 (1958); cf. Kadish, The Advocate and the Expert: Counsel in the Peno-Correctional Process, 45 Minn.L.Rev. 803, 806, (1961). For arguments opposing disclosure, see Barnett and Gronewold, Confidentiality of the Presentence Report, 26 Fed.Prob. March 1962, p. 26; Judicial Conference Committee on Administration of the Probation System, Judicial Opinion on Proposed Change in Rule 32(c) of the Federal Rules of Criminal Procedure—a Survey (1964); Keve, The Probation Officer Investigates, 6–15 (1960); Parsons, The Presentence Investigation Report Must be Preserved as a Confidential Document, 28 Fed.Prob. March 1964, p. 3; Sharp, The Confidential Nature of Presentence Reports, 5 Cath.U.L.Rev. 127 (1955); Wilson, A New Arena is Emerging to Test the Confidentiality of Presentence Reports, 25 Fed.Prob. Dec. 1961, p. 6; Federal Judge's Views on Probation Practices, 24 Fed.Prob. March 1960, p. 10.

In a few jurisdictions the defendant is given a right of access to the presentence report. In England and California a copy of the report is given to the defendant in every case. English Criminal Justice Act of 1948, 11 & 12 Geo. 6, c. 58, §43; Cal.Pen.C. §1203. In Alabama the defendant has a right to inspect the report. Ala. Code, Title 42, §23. In Ohio and Virginia the probation officer reports in open court and the defendant is given the right to examine him on his report. Ohio Rev. Code, §2947.06; Va. Code, §53–278.1. The Minnesota Criminal Code of 1963, §609.115(4), provides that any presentence report "shall be open for inspection by the prosecuting attorney and the defendant's attorney prior to sentence and on the request of either of them a summary hearing in chambers shall be held on any matter brought in issue, but confidential sources of information shall not be disclosed unless the court otherwise directs." Cf. Model Penal Code §7.07(5) (P.O.D. 1962): "Before imposing sentence, the Court shall advise the defendant or his counsel of the factual contents and the conclusions of any presentence investigation or psychiatric examination and afford fair opportunity, if the defendant so requests, to controvert them. The sources of confidential information need not, however, be disclosed."

Practice in the federal courts is mixed, with a substantial minority of judges permitting disclosure while most deny it. See the recent survey prepared for the Judicial Conference of the District of Columbia by the Junior Bar Section of the Bar Association of the District of Columbia, reported in Conference Papers on Discovery in Federal Criminal Cases, 33 F.R.D. 101, 125–127 (1963). See also Gronewold, Presentence Investigation Practices in the Federal Probation System, Fed.Prob. Sept. 1958, pp. 27, 31. For divergent judicial opinions see Smith v. United States, 223 F.2d 750, 754 (5th Cir. 1955) (supporting disclosure); United States v. Durham, 181 F.Supp. 503 (D.D.C. 1960) (supporting secrecy).

Substantial objections to compelling disclosure in every case have been advanced by federal judges, including many who in practice often disclose all or parts of presentence reports. See Judicial Conference Committee on the Administration of the Probation System, Judicial Opinion on Proposed Change in Rule 32(c) of the Federal Rules of Criminal Procedure—A Survey (1964). Hence, the amendment goes no further than to make it clear that courts may disclose all or part of the presentence report to the defendant or to his counsel. It is hoped that courts will make increasing use of their discretion to disclose so that defendants generally may be given full opportunity to rebut or explain facts in presentence reports which will be material factors in determining sentences. For a description of such a practice in one district, see Thomsen, Confidentiality of the Presentence Report: A Middle Position, 28 Fed.Prob., March 1964, p. 8.

It is also provided that any material disclosed to the defendant or his counsel shall be disclosed to the attorney for the government. Such disclosure will permit the government to participate in the resolution of any factual questions raised by the defendant.

Subdivision (f).—This new subdivision writes into the rule the procedure which the cases have derived from the provision in 18 U.S.C. §3653 that a person arrested for violation of probation "shall be taken before the court" and that thereupon the court may revoke the probation. See Escoe v. Zerbst, 295 U.S. 490 (1935); Brown v. United States, 236 F.2d 253 (9th Cir. 1956) certiorari denied 356 U.S. 922 (1958). Compare Model Penal Code §301.4 (P.O.D. 1962); Hink, The Application of Constitutional Standards of Protection to Probation, 29 U.Chi.L.Rev. 483 (1962).

NOTES OF ADVISORY COMMITTEE ON RULES—1972 AMENDMENT

Subdivision (b)(2) is new. It is intended to provide procedural implementation of the recently enacted criminal forfeiture provisions of the Organized Crime Control Act of 1970, Title IX, §1963, and the Comprehensive Drug Abuse Prevention and Control Act of 1970, Title II, §408(a)(2).

18 U.S.C. §1963(c) provides for property seizure and disposition. In part it states:

(c) Upon conviction of a person under this section, the court shall authorize the Attorney General to seize all property or other interest declared forfeited under this section upon such terms and conditions as the court shall deem proper.

Although not specifically provided for in the Comprehensive Drug Abuse Prevention and Control Act of 1970, the provision of Title II, §408(a)(2) forfeiting "profits" or "interest" will need to be implemented procedurally, and therefore new rule 32(b)(2) will be applicable also to that legislation.

For a brief discussion of the procedural implications of a criminal forfeiture, see Advisory Committee Note to rule 7(c)(2).

NOTES OF ADVISORY COMMITTEE ON RULES—1974 AMENDMENT

Subdivision (a)(1) is amended by deleting the reference to commitment or release pending sentencing. This issue is dealt with explicitly in the proposed revision of rule 46(c).

Subdivision (a)(2) is amended to make clear that there is no duty on the court to advise the defendant of the right to appeal after sentence is imposed following a plea of guilty or nolo contendere.

To require the court to advise the defendant of a right to appeal after a plea of guilty, accepted pursuant to the increasingly stringent requirements of rule 11, is likely to be confusing to the defendant. See American Bar Association Standards Relating to Criminal Appeals §2.1(b) (Approved Draft, 1970), limiting the court's duty to advice to "contested cases."

The Advisory Committee is of the opinion that such advice, following a sentence imposed after a plea of guilty, will merely tend to build false hopes and encourage frivolous appeals, with the attendant expense to the defendant or the taxpayers.

Former rule 32(a)(2) imposes a duty only upon conviction after "trial on a plea of not guilty." The few federal cases dealing with the question have interpreted rule 32(a)(2) to say that the court has no duty to advise defendant of his right to appeal after conviction following a guilty plea. Burton v. United States, 307 F.Supp. 448, 450 (D.Ariz. 1970); Alaway v. United States, 280 F.Supp. 326, 336 (C.D.Calif. 1968); Crow v. United States, 397 F.2d 284, 285 (10th Cir. 1968).

Prior to the 1966 amendment of rule 32, the court's duty was even more limited. At that time [rule 37(a)(2)] the court's duty to advise was limited to those situations in which sentence was imposed after trial upon a not guilty plea of a defendant not represented by counsel. 8A J. Moore, Federal Practice 32.01[3] (2d ed. Cipes 1969); C. Wright, Federal Practice and Procedure: Criminal §528 (1969); 5 L. Orfield, Criminal Procedure Under the Federal Rules §32:11 (1967).

With respect to appeals in forma pauperis, see appellate rule 24.

Subdivision (c)(1) makes clear that a presentence report is required except when the court otherwise directs for reasons stated of record. The requirement of reasons on the record for not having a presentence report is intended to make clear that such a report ought to be routinely required except in cases where there is a reason for not doing so. The presentence report is of great value for correctional purposes and will serve as a valuable aid in reviewing sentences to the extent that sentence review may be authorized by future rule change. For an analysis of the current rule as it relates to the situation in which a presentence investigation is required, see C. Wright, Federal Practice and Procedure: Criminal §522 (1969); 8A J. Moore, Federal Practice 32.03[1] (2d ed. Cipes 1969).

Subdivision (c)(1) is also changed to permit the judge, after obtaining defendant's consent, to see the presentence report in order to decide whether to accept a plea agreement, and also to expedite the imposition of sentence in a case in which the defendant has indicated that he may plead guilty or nolo contendere.

Former subdivision (c)(1) provides that "The report shall not be submitted to the court * * * unless the defendant has pleaded guilty * * *." This precludes a judge from seeing a presentence report prior to the acceptance of the plea of guilty. L. Orfield, Criminal Procedure Under the Federal Rules §32:35 (1967); 8A J. Moore, Federal Practice 32.03[2], p. 32–22 (2d ed. Cipes 1969); C. Wright, Federal Practice and Procedure: Criminal §523, p. 392 (1969); Gregg v. United States, 394 U.S. 489, 89 S.Ct. 1134, 22 L.Ed.2d 442 (1969).

Because many plea agreements will deal with the sentence to be imposed, it will be important, under rule 11, for the judge to have access to sentencing information as a basis for deciding whether the plea agreement is an appropriate one.

It has been suggested that the problem be dealt with by allowing the judge to indicate approval of the plea agreement subject to the condition that the information in the presentence report is consistent with what he has been told about the case by counsel. See American Bar Association, Standards Relating to Pleas of Guilty §3.3 (Approved Draft, 1963); President's Commission on Law Enforcement and Administration of Justice. The Challenge of Crime in a Free Society 136 (1967).

Allowing the judge to see the presentence report prior to his decision as to whether to accept the plea agreement is, in the view of the Advisory Committee, preferable to a conditional acceptance of the plea. See Enker, Perspectives on Plea Bargaining, Appendix A of President's Commission on Law Enforcement and Administration of Justice, Task Force Report: The Courts at 117 (1967). It enables the judge to have all of the information available to him at the time he is called upon to decide whether or not to accept the plea of guilty and thus avoids the necessity of a subsequent appearance whenever the information is such that the judge decides to reject the plea agreement.

There is presently authority to have a presentence report prepared prior to the acceptance of the plea of guilty. In Gregg v. United States, 394 U.S. 489, 491, 89 S.Ct. 1134 22 L.Ed.2d 442 (1969), the court said that the "language [of rule 32] clearly permits the preparation of a presentence report before guilty plea or conviction * * *." In footnote 3 the court said:

The history of the rule confirms this interpretation. The first Preliminary Draft of the rule would have required the consent of the defendant or his attorney to commence the investigation before the determination of guilt. Advisory Committee on Rules of Criminal Procedure, Fed.Rules Crim.Proc., Preliminary Draft 130, 133 (1943). The Second Preliminary Draft omitted this requirement and imposed no limitation on the time when the report could be made and submitted to the court. Advisory Committee on Rules of Criminal Procedure, Fed.Rules Crim.Proc. Second Preliminary Draft 126–128 (1944). The third and final draft, which was adopted as Rule 32, was evidently a compromise between those who opposed any time limitation, and those who preferred that the entire investigation be conducted after determination of guilt. See 5 L. Orfield, Criminal Procedure Under the Federal Rules §32.2 (1967).

Where the judge rejects the plea agreement after seeing the presentence report, he should be free to recuse himself from later presiding over the trial of the case. This is left to the discretion of the judge. There are instances involving prior convictions where a judge may have seen a presentence report, yet can properly try a case on a plea of not guilty. Webster v. United States, 330 F.Supp. 1080 (D.C., 1971). Unlike the situation in Gregg v. United States, subdivision (e)(3) provides for disclosure of the presentence report to the defendant, and this will enable counsel to know whether the information thus made available to the judge is likely to be prejudicial. Presently trial judges who decide pretrial motions to suppress illegally obtained evidence are not, for that reason alone, precluded from presiding at a later trial.

Subdivision (c)(3)(A) requires disclosure of presentence information to the defense, exclusive of any recommendation of sentence. The court is required to disclose the report to defendant or his counsel unless the court is of the opinion that disclosure would seriously interfere with rehabilitation, compromise confidentiality, or create risk of harm to the defendant or others.

Any recommendation as to sentence should not be disclosed as it may impair the effectiveness of the probation officer if the defendant is under supervision on probation or parole.

The issue of disclosure of presentence information to the defense has been the subject of recommendations from the Advisory Committee in 1944, 1962, 1964, and 1966. The history is dealt with in considerable detail in C. Wright, Federal Practice and Procedure: Criminal §524 (1969), and 8A J. Moore, Federal Practice 32.03[4] (2d ed. Cipes 1969).

In recent years, three prestigious organizations have recommended that the report be disclosed to the defense. See American Bar Association, Standards Relating to Sentencing Alternatives and Procedures §4.4 (Approved Draft, 1968); American Law Institute Model Penal Code §7.07(5) (P.O.D. 1962); National Council on Crime and Delinquency, Model Sentencing Act §4 (1963). This is also the recommendation of the President's Commission on Law Enforcement and Administration of Justice. The Challenge of Crime in a Free Society (1967) at p. 145.

In the absence of compelling reasons for nondisclosure of special information, the defendant and his counsel should be permitted to examine the entire presentence report.

The arguments for and against disclosure are well known and are effectively set forth in American Bar Association Standards Relating to Sentencing Alternatives and Procedures, §4.4 Commentary at pp. 214–225 (Approved Draft, 1968). See also Lehrich, The Use and Disclosure of Presentence Reports in the United States, 47 F.R.D. 225 (1969).

A careful account of existing practices in Detroit, Michigan and Milwaukee, Wisconsin is found in R. Dawson, Sentencing (1969).

Most members of the federal judiciary have, in the past, opposed compulsory disclosure. See the view of District Judge Edwin M. Stanley, American Bar Association Standards Relating to Sentencing Alternatives and Procedures. Appendix A. (Appendix A also contains the results of a survey of all federal judges showing that the clear majority opposed disclosure.)

The Advisory Committee is of the view that accuracy of sentencing information is important not only to the defendant but also to effective correctional treatment of a convicted offender. The best way of insuring accuracy is disclosure with an opportunity for the defendant and counsel to point out to the court information thought by the defense to be inaccurate, incomplete, or otherwise misleading. Experience in jurisdictions which require disclosure does not lend support to the argument that disclosure will result in less complete presentence reports or the argument that sentencing procedures will become unnecessarily protracted. It is not intended that the probation officer would be subjected to any rigorous examination by defense counsel, or that he will even be sworn to testify. The proceedings may be very informal in nature unless the court orders a full hearing.

Subdivision (c)(3)(B) provides for situations in which the sentencing judge believes that disclosure should not be made under the criteria set forth in subdivision (c)(3)(A). He may disclose only a summary of that factual information "to be relied on in determining sentence." This is similar to the proposal of the American Bar Association Standards Relating to Sentencing Alternatives and Procedures §4.4(b) and Commentary at pp. 216–224.

Subdivision (c)(3)(D) provides for the return of disclosed presentence reports to insure that they do not become available to unauthorized persons. See National Council on Crime and Delinquency, Model Sentencing Act §4 (1963): "Such reports shall be part of the record but shall be sealed and opened only on order of the court."

Subdivision (c)(3)(E) makes clear that diagnostic studies under 18 U.S.C. §§4208(b), 5010(c), or 5034 are covered by this rule and also that 18 U.S.C. §4252 is included within the disclosure provisions of subdivision (c). Section 4252 provides for the presentence examination of an "eligible offender" who is believed to be an addict to determine whether "he is an addict and is likely to be rehabilitated through treatment."

Both the Organized Crime Control Act of 1970 [§3775(b)] and the Comprehensive Drug Abuse Prevention and Control Act of 1970 [§409(b)] have special provisions for presentence investigation in the implementation of the dangerous special offender provision. It is however, unnecessary to incorporate them by reference in rule 32 because each contains a specific provision requiring disclosure of the presentence report. The judge does have authority to withhold some information "in extraordinary cases" provided notice is given the parties and the court's reasons for withholding information are made part of the record.

Subdivision (e) is amended to clarify the meaning.

NOTES OF COMMITTEE ON THE JUDICIARY, HOUSE REPORT NO. 94–247; 1975 AMENDMENT
A. Amendments Proposed by the Supreme Court Rule 32 of the Federal Rules of Criminal Procedure deals with sentencing matters.

Proposed subdivision (a)(2) provides that the court is not dutybound to advise the defendant of a right to appeal when the sentence is imposed following a plea of guilty or nolo contendere.

Proposed subdivision (e) provides that the probation service must make a presentence investigation and report unless the court orders otherwise "for reasons stated on the record." The presentence report will not be submitted to the court until after the defendant pleads nolo contendere or guilty, or is found guilty, unless the defendant consents in writing. Upon the defendant's request, the court must permit the defendant to read the presentence report, except for the recommendation as to sentence. However, the court may decline to let the defendant read the report if it contains (a) diagnostic opinion that might seriously disrupt a rehabilitation program, (b) sources of information obtained upon a promise of confidentiality, or (c) any other information that, if disclosed, might result in harm to the defendant or other persons. The court must give the defendant an opportunity to comment upon the presentence report. If the court decides that the defendant should not see the report, then it must provide the defendant, orally or in writing, a summary of the factual information in the report upon which it is relying in determining sentence. No party may keep the report or make copies of it.

B. Committee Action. The Committee added language to subdivision (a)(1) to provide that the attorney for the government may speak to the court at the time of sentencing. The language does not require that the attorney for the government speak but permits him to do so if he wishes.

The Committee recast the language of subdivision (c)(1), which defines when presentence reports must be obtained. The Committee's provision makes it more difficult to dispense with a presentence report. It requires that a presentence report be made unless (a) the defendant waives it, or (b) the court finds that the record contains sufficient information to enable the meaningful exercise of sentencing discretion and explains this finding on the record. The Committee believes that presentence reports are important aids to sentencing and should not be dispensed with easily.

The Committee added language to subdivision (c)(3)(A) that permits a defendant to offer testimony or information to rebut alleged factual inaccuracies in the presentence report. Since the presentence report is to be used by the court in imposing sentence and since the consequence of any significant inaccuracy can be very serious to the defendant, the Committee believes that it is essential that the presentence report be completely accurate in every material respect. The Committee's addition to subdivision (c)(3)(A) will help insure the accuracy of the presentence report.

The Committee added language to subdivision (c)(3)(D) that gives the court the discretion to permit either the prosecutor or the defense counsel to retain a copy of the presentence report. There may be situations when it would be appropriate for either or both of the parties to retain the presentence report. The Committee believes that the rule should give the court the discretion in such situations to permit the parties to retain their copies.

NOTES OF ADVISORY COMMITTEE ON RULES——1979 AMENDMENT
Note to Subdivision (c)(3)(E). The amendment to rule 32(c)(3)(E) is necessary in light of recent changes in the applicable statutes.

Note to Subdivision (f). This subdivision is abrogated. The subject matter is now dealt with in greater detail in proposed new rule 32.1.

NOTES OF ADVISORY COMMITTEE ON RULES——1983 AMENDMENT
Note to Subdivision (a)(1). Subdivision (a)(1) has been amended so as to impose upon the sentencing court the additional obligation of determining that the defendant and his counsel have had an opportunity to read the presentence investigation report or summary thereof. This change is consistent with the amendment of subdivision (c)(3), discussed below, providing for disclosure of the report (or, in the circumstances indicated, a summary thereof) to both defendant and his counsel without request. This amendment is also consistent with the findings of a recent empirical study that under present rule 32 meaningful disclosure is often lacking and "that some form of judicial prodding is necessary to achieve full disclosure." Fennell & Hall, Due Process at Sentencing: An Empirical and Legal Analysis of the Disclosure of Presentence Reports in Federal Courts, 93 Harv.L.Rev. 1613, 1651 (1980):

> The defendant's interest in an accurate and reliable presentence report does not cease with the imposition of sentence. Rather, these interests are implicated at later stages in the correctional process by the continued use of the presentence report as a basic source of information in the handling of the defendant. If the defendant is incarcerated, the presentence report accompanies him to the correctional institution and provides background information for the Bureau of Prisons' classification summary, which, in turn, determines the defendant's classification within the facility, his ability to obtain furloughs, and the choice

of treatment programs. The presentence report also plays a crucial role during parole determination. Section 4207 of the Parole Commission and Reorganization Act directs the parole hearing examiner to consider, if available, the presentence report as well as other records concerning the prisoner. In addition to its general use as background at the parole hearing, the presentence report serves as the primary source of information for calculating the inmate's parole guideline score. Though it is thus important that the defendant be aware now of all these potential uses, the Advisory Committee has considered but not adopted a requirement that the trial judge specifically advise the defendant of these matters. The Committee believes that this additional burden should not be placed upon the trial judge, and that the problem is best dealt with by a form attached to the presentence report, to be signed by the defendant, advising of these potential uses of the report. This suggestion has been forwarded to the Probation Committee of the Judicial Conference.

Note to Subdivision (c)(3)(A), (B) & (C). Three important changes are made in subdivision (c)(3): disclosure of the presentence report is no longer limited to those situations in which a request is made; disclosure is now provided to both defendant and his counsel; and disclosure is now required a reasonable time before sentencing. These changes have been prompted by findings in a recent empirical study that the extent and nature of disclosure of the presentence investigation report in federal courts under current rule 32 is insufficient to ensure accuracy of sentencing information. In 14 districts, disclosure is made only on request, and such requests are received in fewer than 50% of the cases. Forty-two of 92 probation offices do not provide automatic notice to defendant or counsel of the availability of the report; in 18 districts, a majority of the judges do not provide any notice of the availability of the report, and in 20 districts such notice is given only on the day of sentencing. In 28 districts, the report itself is not disclosed until the day of sentencing in a majority of cases. Thirty-one courts generally disclose the report only to counsel and not to the defendant, unless the defendant makes a specific request. Only 13 districts disclose the presentence report to both defendant and counsel prior to the day of sentencing in 90% or more of the cases. Fennell & Hall, supra, at 1640–49.

These findings make it clear that rule 32 in its present form is failing to fulfill its purpose. Unless disclosure is made sufficiently in advance of sentencing to permit the assertion and resolution of claims of inaccuracy prior to the sentencing hearing, the submission of additional information by the defendant when appropriate, and informed comment on the presentence report, the purpose of promoting accuracy by permitting the defendant to contest erroneous information is defeated. Similarly, if the report is not made available to the defendant and his counsel in a timely fashion, and if disclosure is only made on request, their opportunity to review the report may be inadequate. Finally, the failure to disclose the report to the defendant, or to require counsel to review the report with the defendant, significantly reduces the likelihood that false statements will be discovered, as much of the content of the presentence report will ordinarily be outside the knowledge of counsel.

The additional change to subdivision (c)(3)(C) is intended to make it clear that the government's right to disclosure does not depend upon whether the defendant elects to exercise his right to disclosure.

Note to Subdivision (c)(3)(D). Subdivision (c)(3)(D) is entirely new. It requires the sentencing court, as to each matter controverted, either to make a finding as to the accuracy of the challenged factual proposition or to determine that no reliance will be placed on that proposition at the time of sentencing. This new provision also requires that a record of this action accompany any copy of the report later made available to the Bureau of Prisons or Parole Commission.

As noted above, the Bureau of Prisons and the Parole Commission make substantial use of the presentence investigation report. Under current practice, this can result in reliance upon assertions of fact in the report in the making of critical determinations relating to custody or parole. For example, it is possible that the Bureau or Commission, in the course of reaching a decision on such matters as institution assignment, eligibility for programs, or computation of salient factors, will place great reliance upon factual assertions in the report which are in fact untrue and which remained unchallenged at the time of the sentencing because defendant or his counsel deemed the error unimportant in the sentencing context (e.g., where the sentence was expected to conform to an earlier plea agreement, or where the judge said he would disregard certain controverted matter in setting the sentence).

The first sentence of new subdivision (c)(3)(D) is intended to ensure that a record is made as to exactly what resolution occurred as to controverted matter. The second sentence is intended to ensure that this record comes to the attention of the Bureau or Commission when these agencies utilize the presentence investigation report. In current practice, "less than one-fourth of the district courts (twenty of ninety-two) communicate to the correctional agencies the defendant's challenges to information in the presentence report and the resolution of these challenges." Fennell & Hall, supra, at 1680.

New subdivision (c)(3)(D) does not impose an onerous burden. It does not even require the preparation of a transcript. As is now the practice in some courts, these findings and determinations can be simply entered onto a form which is then appended to the report.

Note to Subdivision (c)(3)(E) & (F). Former subdivisions (c)(3)(D) and (E) have been renumbered as (c)(3)(E) and (F). The only change is in the former, necessitated because disclosure is now to defendant and his counsel.

The issue of access to the presentence report at the institution was discussed by the Advisory Committee, but no action was taken on that matter because it was believed to be beyond the scope of the rule-making power. Rule 32 in its present form does not speak to this issue, and thus the Bureau of Prisons and the Parole Commission are free to make provision for disclosure to inmates and their counsel.

Note to Subdivision (d). The amendment to Rule 32(d) is intended to clarify (i) the standard applicable to plea withdrawal under this rule, and (ii) the circumstances under which the appropriate avenue of relief is other than a withdrawal motion under this rule. Both of these matters have been the source of considerable confusion under the present rule. In its present form, the rule declares that a motion to withdraw a plea of guilty or nolo contendere may be made only before sentence is imposed, but then states the standard for permitting withdrawal after sentence. In fact, "there is no limitation upon the time within which relief thereunder may, after sentencing, be sought." United States v. Watson, 548 F.2d 1058 (D.C.Cir. 1977). It has been critically stated that "the Rule offers little guidance as to the applicable standard for a pre-sentence withdrawal of plea," United States v. Michaelson, 552 F.2d 472 (2d Cir. 1977), and that as a result "the contours of [the presentence] standard are not easily defined." Bruce v. United States, 379 F.2d 113 (D.C.Cir. 1967).

By replacing the "manifest injustice" standard with a requirement that, in cases to which it applied, the defendant must (unless taking a direct appeal) proceed under 28 U.S.C. §2255, the amendment avoids language which has been a cause of unnecessary confusion. Under the amendment, a defendant who proceeds too late to come under the more generous "fair and just reason" standard must seek relief under §2255, meaning the applicable standard is that stated in Hill v. United States, 368 U.S. 424 (1962): "a fundamental defect which inherently results in a complete miscarriage of justice" or "an omission inconsistent with the rudimentary demands of fair procedure."

Some authority is to be found to the effect that the rule 32(d) "manifest injustice" standard is indistinguishable from the §2255 standard. In United States v. Hamilton, 553 F.2d 63 (10th Cir. 1977), for example, the court, after first concluding defendant was not entitled to relief under the §2255 "miscarriage of justice" test, then held that "[n]othing is to be gained by the invocation of Rule 32(d)" and its manifest injustice" standard. Some courts, however, have indicated that the rule 32(d) standard provides a somewhat broader basis for relief than §2255. United States v. Dabdoub-Diaz, 599 F.2d 96 (5th Cir. 1979); United States v. Watson, 548 F.2d 1058 (D.C.Cir. 1977); Meyer v. United States, 424 F.2d 1181 (8th Cir.1970); United States v. Kent, 397 F.2d 446 (7th Cir. 1968). It is noteworthy, however, that in Dabdoub-Diaz, Meyer and Kent the defendant did not prevail under either §2255 or Rule 32(d), and that in Watson, though the §2255 case was remanded for consideration as a 32(d) motion, defendant's complaint (that he was not advised of the special parole term, though the sentence he received did not exceed that he was warned about by the court) was one as to which relief had been denied even upon direct appeal from the conviction. United States v. Peters, No. 77–1700 (4th Cir. Dec. 22, 1978).

Indeed, it may more generally be said that the results in §2255 and 32(d) guilty plea cases have been for the most part the same. Relief has often been granted or recognized as available via either of these routes for essentially the same reasons: that there exists a complete constitutional bar to conviction on the offense charged, Brooks v. United States, 424 F.2d 425 (5th Cir. 1970) (§2255), United States v. Bluso, 519 F.2d 473 (4th Cir. 1975) (Rule 32); that the defendant was incompetent at the time of his plea, United States v. Masthers, 539 F.2d 721 (D.C.Cir. 1976) (§2255), Kienlen v. United States, 379 F.2d 20 (10th Cir. 1967) (Rule 32);

and that the bargain the prosecutor made with defendant was not kept, Walters v. Harris, 460 F.2d 988 (4th Cir. 1972) (§2255), United States v. Hawthorne, 502 F.2d 1183 (3rd Cir. 1974) (Rule 32). Perhaps even more significant is the fact that relief has often been denied under like circumstances whichever of the two procedures was used: a mere technical violation of Rule 11, United States v. Timmreck, 441 U.S. 780 (1979) (§2255), United States v. Saft, 558 F.2d 1073 (2d Cir. 1977) (Rule 32); the mere fact defendants expected a lower sentence, United States v. White, 572 F.2d 1007 (4th Cir. 1978) (§2255), Masciola v. United States, 469 F.2d 1057 (3rd Cir. 1972) (Rule 32); or mere familial coercion, Wojtowicz v. United States, 550 F.2d 786 (2d Cir. 1977) (§2255), United States v. Bartoli, 572 F.2d 188 (8th Cir. 1978) (Rule 32).

The one clear instance in which a Rule 32(d) attack might prevail when a §2255 challenge would not is present in those circuits which have reached the questionable result that post-sentence relief under 32(d) is available not merely upon a showing of a "manifest injustice" but also for any deviation from literal compliance with Rule 11. United States v. Cantor, 469 F.2d 435 (3d Cir. 1972). See Advisory Committee Note to Rule 11(h), noting the unsoundness of that position.

The change in Rule 32(d), therefore, is at best a minor one in terms of how post-sentence motions to withdraw pleas will be decided. It avoids the confusion which now obtains as to whether a §2255 petition must be assumed to also be a 32(d) motion and, if so, whether this bears significantly upon how the matter should be decided. See, e.g., United States v. Watson, supra. It also avoids the present undesirable situation in which the mere selection of one of two highly similar avenues of relief, rule 32(d) or §2255, may have significant procedural consequences, such as whether the government can take an appeal from the district court's adverse ruling (possible under §2255 only). Moreover, because §2255 and Rule 32(d) are properly characterized as the "two principal procedures for collateral attack of a federal plea conviction," Borman, The Hidden Right to Direct Appeal From a Federal Conviction, 64 Cornell L.Rev. 319, 327 (1979), this amendment is also in keeping with the proposition underlying the Supreme Court's decision in United States v. Timmreck, supra, namely, that "the concern with finality served by the limitation on collateral attack has special force with respect to convictions based on guilty pleas." The amendment is likewise consistent with ALI Code of Pre-Arraignment Procedure §350.9 (1975) ("Allegations of noncompliance with the procedures provided in Article 350 shall not be a basis for review of a conviction after the appeal period for such conviction has expired, unless such review is required by the Constitution of the United States or of this State or otherwise by the law of this State other than Article 350"); ABA Standards Relating to the Administration of Criminal Justice §14–2.1 (2d ed. 1978) (using "manifest injustice" standard, but listing six specific illustrations each of which would be basis for relief under §2255); Unif.R.Crim.P. 444(e) (Approved Draft, 1974) (using "interest of justice" test, but listing five specific illustrations each of which would be basis for relief under §2255).

The first sentence of the amended rule incorporates the "fair and just" standard which the federal courts, relying upon dictum in Kercheval v. United States, 274 U.S. 220 (1927), have consistently applied to presentence motions. See, e.g., United States v. Strauss, 563 F.2d 127 (4th Cir. 1977); United States v. Bradin, 535 F.2d 1039 (8th Cir. 1976); United States v. Barker, 514 F.2d 208 (D.C.Cir. 1975). Under the rule as amended, it is made clear that the defendant has the burden of showing a "fair and just" reason for withdrawal of the plea. This is consistent with the prevailing view, which is that "the defendant has the burden of satisfying the trial judge that there are valid grounds for withdrawal," see United States v. Michaelson, supra, and cases cited therein. (Illustrative of a reason which would meet this test but would likely fall short of the §2255 test is where the defendant now wants to pursue a certain defense which he for good reason did not put forward earlier, United States v. Barker, supra.)

Although "the terms 'fair and just' lack any pretense of scientific exactness," United States v. Barker, supra, guidelines have emerged in the appellate cases for applying this standard. Whether the movant has asserted his legal innocence is an important factor to be weighed, United States v. Joslin, 434 F.2d 526 (D.C.Cir. 1970), as is the reason why the defenses were not put forward at the time of original pleading. United States v. Needles, 472 F.2d 652 (2d Cir. 1973). The amount of time which has passed between the plea and the motion must also be taken into account.

A swift change of heart is itself strong indication that the plea was entered in haste and confusion * * *. By contrast, if the defendant has long delayed his withdrawal motion, and has had the full benefit of competent counsel at all times, the reasons given to support withdrawal must have considerably more force. United States v. Barker, supra.

If the defendant establishes such a reason, it is then appropriate to consider whether the government would be prejudiced by withdrawal of the plea. Substantial prejudice may be present for a variety of reasons. See United States v. Jerry, 487 F.2d 600 (3d Cir. 1973) (physical evidence had been discarded); United States v. Vasquez-Velasco, 471 F.2d 294 (9th Cir. 1973) (death of chief government witness); United States v. Lombardozzi, 436 F.2d 878 (2d Cir. 1971) (other defendants with whom defendant had been joined for trial had already been tried in a lengthy trial); Farnsworth v. Sanford, 115 F.2d 375 (5th Cir. 1940) (prosecution had dismissed 52 witnesses who had come from all over the country and from overseas bases).

There is currently some disparity in the manner in which presentence motions to withdraw a guilty plea are dealt with. Some courts proceed as if any desire to withdraw the plea before sentence is "fair and just" so long as the government fails to establish that it would be prejudiced by the withdrawal. Illustrative is United States v. Savage, 561 F.2d 554 (4th Cir. 1977), where the defendant pleaded guilty pursuant to a plea agreement that the government would recommend a sentence of 5 years. At the sentencing hearing, the trial judge indicated his unwillingness to follow the government's recommendation, so the defendant moved to withdraw his plea. That motion was denied. On appeal, the court held that there had been no violation of Rule 11, in that refusal to accept the government's recommendation does not constitute a rejection of the plea agreement. But the court then proceeded to hold that absent any showing of prejudice by the government, "the defendant should be allowed to withdraw his plea"; only upon such a showing by the government must the court "weigh the defendant's reasons for seeking to withdraw his plea against the prejudice which the government will suffer." The other view is that there is no occasion to inquire into the matter of prejudice unless the defendant first shows a good reason for being allowed to withdraw his plea. As stated in United States v. Saft, 558 F.2d 1073 (2d Cir. 1977): "The Government is not required to show prejudice when a defendant has shown no sufficient grounds for permitting withdrawal of a guilty plea, although such prejudice may be considered by the district court in exercising its discretion." The second sentence of the amended rule, by requiring that the defendant show a "fair and just" reason, adopts the Saft position and rejects that taken in Savage.

The Savage position, as later articulated in United States v. Strauss, supra, is that the "sounder view, supported by both the language of the rule and by the reasons for it, would be to allow withdrawal of the plea prior to sentencing unless the prosecution has been substantially prejudiced by reliance upon the defendant's plea." (Quoting 2 C. Wright, Federal Practice and Procedure §538, at 474–75 (1969). Although that position may once have been sound, this is no longer the case in light of the recent revisions of Rule 11. Rule 11 now provides for the placing of plea agreements on the record, for full inquiry into the voluntariness of the plea, for detailed advice to the defendant concerning his rights and the consequences of his plea and a determination that the defendant understands these matters, and for a determination of the accuracy of the plea. Given the great care with which pleas are taken under this revised Rule 11, there is no reason to view pleas so taken as merely "tentative," subject to withdrawal before sentence whenever the government cannot establish prejudice.

Were withdrawal automatic in every case where the defendant decided to alter his tactics and present his theory of the case to the jury, the guilty plea would become a mere gesture, a temporary and meaningless formality reversible at the defendant's whim. In fact, however, a guilty plea is no such trifle, but "a grave and solemn act," which is "accepted only with care and discernment."
United States v. Barker, supra, quoting from Brady v. United States, 397 U.S. 742 (1970).

The facts of the Savage case reflect the wisdom of this position. In Savage, the defendant had entered into a plea agreement whereby he agreed to plead guilty in exchange for the government's promise to recommend a sentence of 5 years, which the defendant knew was not binding on the court. Yet, under the approach taken in Savage, the defendant remains free to renege on his plea bargain, notwithstanding full compliance therewith by the attorney for the government, if it later appears to him from the presentence report or the comments of the trial judge or any other source that the court will not follow the government's recommendation. Having bargained for a recommendation pursuant to Rule 11(e)(1)(B), the defendant should not be entitled, in effect, to unilaterally convert the plea agreement into a Rule 11(e)(1)(C) type of agreement (i.e., one with a guarantee of a specific sentence which, if not given, permits withdrawal of the plea).

The first sentence of subdivision (d) provides that the motion, to be judged under the more liberal "fair and just reason" test, must have been made before sentence is imposed, imposition of sentence is suspended, or disposition is had under 18 U.S.C. §4205(c). The latter of these has been added to the rule to make it clear that the lesser standard also governs prior to the second stage of sentencing when the judge, pursuant to that statute, has committed the defendant to the custody of the Attorney General for study pending final disposition. Several circuits have left this issue open, e.g., United States v. McCoy, 477 F.2d 550 (5th Cir. 1973); Callaway v. United States, 367 F.2d 140 (10th Cir. 1966); while some have held that a withdrawal motion filed between tentative and final sentencing should be judged against the presentence standard, United States v. Barker, 514 F.2d 208 (D.C.Cir. 1975); United States v. Thomas, 415 F.2d 1216 (9th Cir. 1969).

Inclusion of the §4205(c) situation under the presentence standard is appropriate. As explained in Barker:

Two reasons of policy have been advanced to explain the near-presumption which Rule 32(d) erects against post-sentence withdrawal motions. The first is that post-sentence withdrawal subverts the "stability" of "final judgments." * * * The second reason is that the post-sentence withdrawal motion often constitutes a veiled attack on the judge's sentencing decision; to grant such motions in lenient fashion might

undermine respect for the courts and fritter away the time and painstaking effort devoted to the sentence process.

* * * Concern for the "stability of final judgments" has little application to withdrawal motions filed between tentative and final sentencing under Section 4208(b) [now 4205(c)]. The point at which a defendant's judgment of conviction becomes "final" for purposes of appeal—whether at tentative or at final sentencing—is wholly within the defendant's discretion. * * * Concern for the integrity of the sentencing process is, however, another matter. The major point, in our view, is that tentative sentencing under Section 4208(b) [now 4205(c)] leaves the defendant ignorant of his final sentence. He will therefore be unlikely to use a withdrawal motion as an oblique attack on the judge's sentencing policy. The relative leniency of the "fair and just" standard is consequently not out of place.

NOTES OF ADVISORY COMMITTEE ON RULES——1987 AMENDMENT

The amendments are technical. No substantive change is intended.

NOTES OF ADVISORY COMMITTEE ON RULES——1989 AMENDMENT

The amendment to subdivision (a)(1) is intended to clarify that the court is expected to proceed without unnecessary delay, and that it may be necessary to delay sentencing when an applicable sentencing factor cannot be resolved at the time set for sentencing. Often, the factor will relate to a defendant's agreement to cooperate with the government. But, other factors may be capable of resolution if the court delays sentencing while additional information is generated. As currently written, the rule might imply that a delay requested by one party or suggested by the court sua sponte might be unreasonable. The amendment rids the rule of any such implication and provides the sentencing court with desirable discretion to assure that relevant factors are considered and accurately resolved. In exercising this discretion, the court retains under the amendment the authority to refuse to delay sentencing when a delay is inappropriate under the circumstances.

In amending subdivision (c)(1), the Committee conformed the rule to the current practice in some courts: i.e., to permit the defendant and the prosecutor to see a presentence report prior to a plea of guilty if the court, with the written consent of the defendant, receives the report at that time. The amendment permits, but does not require, disclosure of the report with the written consent of the defendant.

The amendment to change the "reasonable time" language in subdivision (c)(3)(A) to at least 10 days prior to sentencing, unless the defendant waives the minimum period, conforms the rule to 18 U.S.C. 3552(d). Nothing in the statue [sic] or the rule prohibits a court from requiring disclosure at an earlier time before sentencing. The inclusion of a specific waiver provision is intended to conform the rule to the statute and is not intended to suggest that waiver of other rights is precluded when no specific waiver provision is set forth in a rule or portion thereof.

The language requiring the court to provide the defendant and defense counsel with a copy of the presentence report complements the abrogation of subdivision (E), which had required the defense to return the probation report. Because a defendant or the government may seek to appeal a sentence, an option that is permitted under some circumstances, there will be cases in which the defendant has a need for the presentence report during the preparation of, or the response to, an appeal. This is one reason why the Committee decided that the defendant should not be required to return the nonconfidential portions of the presentence report that have been disclosed. Another reason is that district courts may find it desirable to adopt portions of the presentence report when making findings of fact under the guidelines. They would be inhibited unnecessarily from relying on careful, accurate presentence reports if such reports could not be retained by defendants. A third reason why defendant should be able to retain the reports disclosed to them is that the Supreme Court's decision in United States Department of Justice v. Julian, 486 U.S. 1 (1988), 108 S.Ct. 1606 (1988), suggests that defendants will routinely be able to secure their reports through Freedom of Information Act suits. No public interest is served by continuing to require the return of reports, and unnecessary FOIA litigation should be avoided as a result of the amendment to Rule 32.

The amended rule does not direct whether the defendant or the defendant's lawyer should retain the presentence report. In exceptional cases where retention of a report in a local detention facility might pose a danger to persons housed there, the district judge may direct that the defendant not personally retain a copy of the report until the defendant has been transferred to the facility where the sentence will be served.

Because the parties need not return the presentence report to the probation officer, the Solicitor General should be able to review the report in deciding whether to permit the United States to appeal a sentence under the Sentencing Reform Act of 1984, 18 U.S.C. §3551 et seq.

Although the Committee was concerned about the potential unfairness of having confidential or diagnostic material included in presentence reports but not disclosed to a defendant who might be adversely affected by such material, it decided not to recommend at this time a change in the rule which would require complete disclosure. Some diagnostic material might be particularly useful when a court imposes probation, and might well be harmful to the defendant if disclosed. Moreover, some of this material might assist correctional officials in prescribing treatment programs for an incarcerated defendant. Information provided by confidential sources and information posing a possible threat of harm to third parties was particularly troubling to the Committee, since this information is often extremely negative and thus potentially harmful to a defendant. The Committee concluded, however, that it was preferable to permit the probation officer to include this information in a report so that the sentencing court may determine whether is [it] ought to be disclosed to the defendant. If the court determines that it should not be disclosed, it will have to decide whether to summarize the contents of the information or to hold that no finding as to the undisclosed information will be made because such information will not be taken into account in sentencing. Substantial due process problems may arise if a court attempts to summarize information in a presentence report, the defendant challenges the information, and the court attempts to make a finding as to the accuracy of the information without disclosing to the defendant the source of the information or the details placed before the court. In deciding not to require disclosure of everything in a presentence report, the Committee made no judgment that findings could validly be made based upon nondisclosed information.

Finally, portions of the rule were gender-neutralized.

NOTES OF ADVISORY COMMITTEE ON RULES——1991 AMENDMENT

The amendments are technical. No substantive changes are intended.

NOTES OF ADVISORY COMMITTEE ON RULES——1993 AMENDMENT

The original subdivision (e) has been deleted due to statutory changes affecting the authority of a court to grant probation. See 18 U.S.C. 3561(a). Its replacement is one of a number of contemporaneous amendments extending Rule 26.2 to hearings and proceedings other than the trial itself. The amendment to Rule 32 specifically codifies the result in cases such as United States v. Rosa, 891 F.2d 1074 (3d. Cir. 1989). In that case the defendant pleaded guilty to a drug offense. During sentencing the defendant unsuccessfully attempted to obtain Jencks Act materials relating to a co-accused who testified as a government witness at sentencing. In concluding that the trial court erred in not ordering the government to produce its witness's statement, the court stated:

109

We believe the sentence imposed on a defendant is the most critical stage of criminal proceedings, and is, in effect, the "bottom-line" for the defendant, particularly where the defendant has pled guilty. This being so, we can perceive no purpose in denying the defendant the ability to effectively cross-examine a government witness where such testimony may, if accepted, and substantially to the defendant's sentence. In such a setting, we believe that the rationale of Jencks v. United States . . . and the purpose of the Jencks Act would be disserved if the government at such a grave stage of a criminal proceeding could deprive the accused of material valuable not only to the defense but to his very liberty. Id. at 1079.

The court added that the defendant had not been sentenced under the new Sentencing Guidelines and that its decision could take on greater importance under those rules. Under Guideline sentencing, said the court, the trial judge has less discretion to moderate a sentence and is required to impose a sentence based upon specific factual findings which need not be established beyond a reasonable doubt. Id at n. 3.

Although the Rosa decision decided only the issue of access by the defendant to Jencks material, the amendment parallels Rules 26.2 (applying Jencks Act to trial) and 12(i) (applying Jencks Act to suppression hearing) in that both the defense and the prosecution are entitled to Jencks material.

Production of a statement is triggered by the witness's oral testimony. The sanction provision rests on the assumption that the proponent of the witness's testimony has deliberately elected to withhold relevant material.

NOTES OF ADVISORY COMMITTEE ON RULES——1994 AMENDMENT

The amendments to Rule 32 are intended to accomplish two primary objectives. First, the amendments incorporate elements of a "Model Local Rule for Guideline Sentencing" which was proposed by the Judicial Conference Committee on Probation Administration in 1987. That model rule and the accompanying report were prepared to assist trial judges in implementing guideline sentencing mandated by the Sentencing Reform Act of 1984. See Committee on the Admin. of the Probation Sys., Judicial Conference of the U.S., Recommended Procedures for Guideline Sentencing and Commentary: Model Local Rule for Guideline Sentencing, Reprinted in T. Hutchinson & D. Yellen, Federal Sentencing Law and Practice, app. 8, at 431 (1989). It was anticipated that sentencing hearings would become more complex due to the new fact finding requirements imposed by guideline sentencing methodology. See U.S.S.G. §6A1.2. Accordingly, the model rule focused on preparation of the presentence report as a means of identifying and narrowing the issues to be decided at the sentencing hearing.

Second, in the process of effecting those amendments, the rule was reorganized. Over time, numerous amendments to the rule had created a sort of hodge podge; the reorganization represents an attempt to reflect an appropriate sequential order in the sentencing procedures.

Subdivision (a). Subdivision (a) retains the general mandate that sentence be imposed without unnecessary delay thereby permitting the court to regulate the time to be allowed for the probation officer to complete the presentence investigation and submit the report. The only requirement is that sufficient time be allowed for completion of the process prescribed by subdivision (b)(6) unless the time periods established in the subdivision are shortened or lengthened by the court for good cause. Such limits are not intended to create any new substantive right for the defendant or the Government which would entitle either to relief if a time limit prescribed in the rule is not kept.

The remainder of subdivision (a), which addressed the sentencing hearing, is now located in subdivision (c).

Subdivision (b). Subdivision (b) (formerly subdivision (c)), which addresses the presentence investigation, has been modified in several respects.

First, subdivision (b)(2) is a new provision which provides that, on request, defense counsel is entitled to notice and a reasonable opportunity to be present at any interview of the defendant conducted by the probation officer. Although the courts have not held that presentence interviews are a critical stage of the trial for purposes of the Sixth Amendment right to counsel, the amendment reflects case law which has indicated that requests for counsel to be present should be honored. See, e.g., United States v. Herrera-Figueroa, 918 F.2d 1430, 1437 (9th Cir. 1990) (court relied on its supervisory power to hold that probation officers must honor request for counsel's presence); United States v. Tisdale, 952 F.2d 934, 940 (6th Cir. 1992) (court agreed with rule requiring probation officers to honor defendant's request for attorney or request from attorney not to interview defendant in absence of counsel). The Committee believes that permitting counsel to be present during such interviews may avoid unnecessary misunderstandings between the probation officer and the defendant. The rule does not further define the term "interview." The Committee intended for the provision to apply to any communication initiated by the probation officer where he or she is asking the defendant to provide information which will be used in preparation of the presentence investigation. Spontaneous or unplanned encounters between the defendant and the probation officer would normally not fall within the purview of the rule. The Committee also believed that the burden should rest on defense counsel, having received notice, to respond as promptly as possible to enable timely completion of the presentence report.

Subdivision (b)(6), formerly (c)(3), includes several changes which recognize the key role the presentence report is playing under guideline sentencing. The major thrust of these changes is to address the problem of resolving objections by the parties to the probation officer's presentence report. Subdivision (b)(6)(A) now provides that the probation officer must present the presentence report to the parties not later than 35 days before the sentencing hearing (rather than 10 days before imposition of the sentence) in order to provide some additional time to the parties and the probation officer to attempt to resolve objections to the report. There has been a slight change in the practice of deleting from the copy of the report given to the parties certain information specified in (b)(6)(A). Under that new provision (changing former subdivision (c)(3)(A)), the court has the discretion (in an individual case or in accordance with a local rule) to direct the probation officer to withhold any final recommendation concerning the sentence. Otherwise, the recommendation, if any, is subject to disclosure. The prior practice of not disclosing confidential information, or other information which might result in harm to the defendant or other persons, is retained in (b)(5).

New subdivisions (b)(6)(B), (C), and (D) now provide explicit deadlines and guidance on resolving disputes about the contents of the presentence report. The amendments are intended to provide early resolution of such disputes by (1) requiring the parties to provide the probation officer with a written list of objections to the report within 14 days of receiving the report; (2) permitting the probation officer to meet with the defendant, the defendant's counsel, and the attorney for the Government to discuss objections to the report, conduct an additional investigation, and to make revisions to the report as deemed appropriate; (3) requiring the probation officer to submit the report to the court and the parties not later than 7 days before the sentencing hearing, noting any unresolved disputes; and (4) permitting the court to treat the report as its findings of fact, except for the parties' unresolved objections. Although the rule does not explicitly address the question of whether counsel's objections to the report are to be filed with the court, there is nothing in the rule which would prohibit a court from requiring the parties to file their original objections or have them included as an addendum to the presentence report.

This procedure, which generally mirrors the approach in the Model Local Rule for Guideline Sentencing, supra, is intended to maximize judicial economy by providing for more orderly sentencing hearings while also providing fair opportunity for both parties to review, object to, and comment upon, the probation officer's report in advance of the sentencing hearing. Under the amendment, the parties would still be free at the sentencing hearing to comment on the presentence report, and in the discretion of the court, to introduce evidence concerning their objections to the report.

Subdivision (c). Subdivision (c) addresses the imposition of sentence and makes no major changes in current practice. The provision consists largely of material formerly located in subdivision (a). Language formerly in (a)(1) referring to the court's disclosure to the parties of the probation officer's determination of the sentencing classifications and sentencing guideline range is now located in subdivisions (b)(4)(B) and (c)(1). Likewise, the brief reference in former (a)(1) to the ability of the parties to comment on the probation officer's determination of sentencing classifications and sentencing guideline range is now located in (c)(1) and (c)(3).

Subdivision (c)(1) is not intended to require that resolution of objections and imposition of the sentence occur at the same time or during the same hearing. It requires only that the court rule on any objections before sentence is imposed. In considering objections during the sentencing hearing, the court may in its discretion, permit the parties to introduce evidence. The rule speaks in terms of the court's discretion, but the Sentencing Guidelines specifically provide that the court must provide the parties with a reasonable opportunity to offer information concerning a sentencing factor reasonably in dispute. See U.S.S.G. §6A1.3(a). Thus, it may be an abuse of discretion not to permit the introduction of additional evidence. Although the rules of evidence do not apply to sentencing proceedings, see Fed. R. Evid. 1101(d)(3), the court clearly has discretion in determining the mode, timing, and extent of the evidence offered. See, e.g., United States v. Zuleta-Alvarez, 922 F.2d 33, 36 (1st Cir. 1990) (trial court did not err in denying defendant's late request to introduce rebuttal evidence by way of cross-examination).

Subdivision (c)(1) (formerly subdivision (c)(3)(D)) indicates that the court need not resolve controverted matters which will "not be taken into account in, or will not affect, sentencing." The words "will not affect" did not exist in the former provision but were added in the revision in recognition that there might be situations, due to overlaps in the sentencing ranges, where a controverted matter would not alter the sentence even if the sentencing range were changed.

The provision for disclosure of a witness' statements, which was recently proposed as an amendment to Rule 32 as new subdivision (e), is now located in subdivision (c)(2).

Subdivision (c)(3) includes minor changes. First, if the court intends to rely on information otherwise excluded from the presentence report under subdivision (b)(5), that information is to be summarized in writing and submitted to the defendant and the defendant's counsel. Under the former provision in (c)(3)(A), such information could be summarized orally. Once the information is presented, the defendant and the defendant's counsel are to be given a reasonable opportunity to comment; in appropriate cases, that may require a continuance of the sentencing proceedings.

Subdivision (c)(5), concerning notification of the right to appeal, was formerly included in subdivision (a)(2). Although the provision has been rewritten, the Committee intends no substantive change in practice. That is, the court may, but is not required to, advise a defendant who has entered a guilty plea, nolo contendere plea or a conditional guilty plea of any right to appeal (such as an appeal challenging jurisdiction). However, the duty to advise the defendant in such cases extends only to advice on the right to appeal any sentence imposed.

Subdivision (d). Subdivision (d), dealing with entry of the court's judgment, is former subdivision (b).

Subdivision (e). Subdivision (e), which addresses the topic of withdrawing pleas, was formerly subdivision (d). Both provisions remain the same except for minor stylistic changes.

Under present practice, the court may permit, but is not required to hear, victim allocution before imposing sentence. The Committee considered, but rejected, a provision which would have required the court to hear victim allocution at sentencing.

NOTES OF ADVISORY COMMITTEE ON RULES—1996 AMENDMENT

Subdivision (d)(2). A provision for including a verdict of criminal forfeiture as a part of the sentence was added in 1972 to Rule 32. Since then, the rule has been interpreted to mean that any forfeiture order is a part of the judgment of conviction and cannot be entered before sentencing. See, e.g., United States v. Alexander, 772 F.Supp. 440 (D. Minn. 1990).

Delaying forfeiture proceedings, however, can pose real problems, especially in light of the implementation of the Sentencing Reform Act in 1987 and the resulting delays between verdict and sentencing in complex cases. First, the government's statutory right to discover the location of property subject to forfeiture is triggered by entry of an order of forfeiture. See 18 U.S.C. §1963(k) and 21 U.S.C. §853(m). If that order is delayed until sentencing, valuable time may be lost in locating assets which may have become unavailable or unusable. Second, third persons with an interest in the property subject to forfeiture must also wait to petition the court to begin ancillary proceedings until the forfeiture order has been entered. See 18 U.S.C. §1963(l) and 21 U.S.C. §853(m). And third, because the government cannot actually seize the property until an order of forfeiture is entered, it may be necessary for the court to enter restraining orders to maintain the status quo.

The amendment to Rule 32 is intended to address these concerns by specifically recognizing the authority of the court to enter a preliminary forfeiture order before sentencing. Entry of an order of forfeiture before sentencing rests within the discretion of the court, which may take into account anticipated delays in sentencing, the nature of the property, and the interests of the defendant, the government, and third persons.

The amendment permits the court to enter its order of forfeiture at any time before sentencing. Before entering the order of forfeiture, however, the court must provide notice to the defendant and a reasonable opportunity to be heard on the question of timing and form of any order of forfeiture.

The rule specifies that the order, which must ultimately be made a part of the sentence and included in the judgment, must contain authorization for the Attorney General to seize the property in question and to conduct appropriate discovery and to begin any necessary ancillary proceedings to protect third parties who have an interest in the property.

CONGRESSIONAL MODIFICATION OF PROPOSED 1994 AMENDMENT

Section 230101(a) of Pub. L. 103–322 [set out as a note under section 2074 of Title 28, Judiciary and Judicial Procedure] provided that the amendment proposed by the Supreme Court [in its order of Apr. 29, 1994] affecting rule 32 of the Federal Rules of Criminal Procedure [this rule] would take effect on Dec. 1, 1994, as otherwise provided by law, and as amended by section 230101(b) of Pub. L. 103–322. See 1994 Amendment note below.

COMMITTEE NOTES ON RULES—2000 AMENDMENT

The rule is amended to reflect the creation of new Rule 32.2, which now governs criminal forfeiture procedures.

COMMITTEE NOTES ON RULES—2002 AMENDMENT

The language of Rule 32 has been amended as part of the general restyling of the Criminal Rules to make them more easily understood and to make style and terminology consistent throughout the rules. These changes are intended to be stylistic only, except as noted below.

The rule has been completely reorganized to make it easier to follow and apply. For example, the definitions in the rule have been moved to the first section and the sequencing of the sections generally follows the procedure for presentencing and sentencing procedures.

Revised Rule 32(a) contains definitions that currently appear in Rule 32(f). One substantive change was made in Rule 32(a)(2). The Committee expanded the definition of victims of crimes of violence or sexual abuse to include victims of child pornography under 18 U.S.C. §§2251–2257 (child pornography and related offenses). The Committee considered those victims to be similar to victims of sexual offenses under 18 U.S.C. §§2241–2248, who already possess that right.

Revised Rule 32(d) has been amended to more clearly set out the contents of the presentence report concerning the application of the Sentencing Guidelines.

Current Rule 32(e), which addresses the ability of a defendant to withdraw a guilty plea, has been moved to Rule 11(e).

Rule 32(h) is a new provision that reflects Burns v. United States, 501 U.S. 129, 138–39 (1991). In Burns, the Court held that, before a sentencing court could depart upward on a ground not previously identified in the presentence report as a ground for departure, Rule 32 requires the court to give the parties reasonable notice that it is

111

contemplating such a ruling and to identify the specific ground for the departure. The Court also indicated that because the procedural entitlements in Rule 32 apply equally to both parties, it was equally appropriate to frame the issue as whether notice is required before the sentencing court departs either upward or downward. Id. at 135, n.4.

Revised Rule 32(i)(3) addresses changes to current Rule 32(c)(1). Under the current rule, the court is required to "rule on any unresolved objections to the presentence report." The rule does not specify, however, whether that provision should be read literally to mean every objection that might have been made to the report or only on those objections that might in some way actually affect the sentence. The Committee believed that a broad reading of the current rule might place an unreasonable burden on the court without providing any real benefit to the sentencing process. Revised Rule 32(i)(3) narrows the requirement for court findings to those instances when the objection addresses a "controverted matter." If the objection satisfies that criterion, the court must either make a finding on the objection or decide that a finding is not required because the matter will not affect sentencing or that the matter will not be considered at all in sentencing.

Revised Rule 32(i)(4)(B) provides for the right of certain victims to address the court during sentencing. As noted, supra, revised Rule 32(a)(2) expands the definition of victims to include victims of crimes under 18 U.S.C. §§2251—57 (child pornography and related offenses). Thus, they too will now be permitted to address the court.

Revised Rule 32(i)(1)(B) is intended to clarify language that currently exists in Rule 32(h)(3), that the court must inform both parties that the court will rely on information not in the presentence report and provide them with an opportunity to comment on the information.

Rule 32(i)(4)(C) includes a change concerning who may request an in camera proceeding. Under current Rule 32(c)(4), the parties must file a joint motion for an in camera proceeding to hear the statements by defense counsel, the defendant, the attorney for the government, or any victim. Under the revised rule, any party may move (for good cause) that the court hear in camera any statement—by a party or a victim—made under revised Rule 32(i)(4).

Finally, the Committee considered, but did not adopt, an amendment that would have required the court to rule on any "unresolved objection to a material matter" in the presentence report, whether or not the court will consider it in imposing an appropriate sentence. The amendment was considered because an unresolved objection that has no impact on determining a sentence under the Sentencing Guidelines may affect other important post-sentencing decisions. For example, the Bureau of Prisons consults the presentence report in deciding where a defendant will actually serve his or her sentence of confinement. See A Judicial Guide to the Federal Bureau of Prisons, 11 (United States Department of Justice, Federal Bureau of Prisons 1995) (noting that the "Bureau relies primarily on the Presentence Investigator Report . . ."). And as some courts have recognized, Rule 32 was intended to guard against adverse consequences of a statement in the presentence report that the court may have been found to be false. United States v. Velasquez, 748 F.2d 972, 974 (8th Cir. 1984) (rule designed to protect against evil that false allegation that defendant was notorious alien smuggler would affect defendant for years to come); see also United States v. Brown, 715 F.2d 387, 389 n.2 (5th Cir. 1983) (sentencing report affects "place of incarceration, chances for parole, and relationships with social service and correctional agencies after release from prison").

To avoid unduly burdening the court, the Committee elected not to require resolution of objections that go only to service of sentence. However, because of the presentence report's critical role in post-sentence administration, counsel may wish to point out to the court those matters that are typically considered by the Bureau of Prisons in designating the place of confinement. For example, the Bureau considers:

the type of offense, the length of sentence, the defendant's age, the defendant's release residence, the need for medical or other special treatment, and any placement recommendation made by the court.
A Judicial Guide to the Federal Bureau of Prisons, supra, at 11. Further, a question as to whether or not the defendant has a "drug problem" could have an impact on whether the defendant would be eligible for prison drug abuse treatment programs. 18 U.S.C. §3621(e) (Substance abuse treatment).
If counsel objects to material in the presentence report that could affect the defendant's service of sentence, the court may resolve the objection, but is not required to do so.

COMMITTEE NOTES ON RULES—2007 AMENDMENT

Subdivision (d). The amendment conforms Rule 32(d) to the Supreme Court's decision in United States v. Booker, 543 U.S. 220 (2005). Booker held that the provision of the federal sentencing statute that makes the Guidelines mandatory, 18 U.S.C. §3553(b)(1), violates the Sixth Amendment right to jury trial. With this provision severed and excised, the Court held, the Sentencing Reform Act "makes the Guidelines effectively advisory," and "requires a sentencing court to consider Guidelines ranges, see 18 U.S.C.A. §3553(a)(4) (Supp. 2004), but it permits the court to tailor the sentence in light of other statutory concerns as well, see §3553(a) (Supp. 2004)." Id. at 245—46. Amended subdivision (d)(2)(F) makes clear that the court can instruct the probation office to gather and include in the presentence report any information relevant to the factors articulated in §3553(a). The rule contemplates that a request can be made either by the court as a whole requiring information affecting all cases or a class of cases, or by an individual judge in a particular case.

Changes Made to Proposed Amendment Released for Public Comment. The Committee revised the text of subdivision (d) in response to public comments. In subdivision (d), the Committee revised the title to include the word "Advisory" in order better to reflect the guidelines' role under the Booker decision. It withdrew proposed subdivisions (k) and (h).

Proposed subdivision (h) would have expanded the sentencing court's obligation to give notice to the parties when it intends to rely on grounds not identified in either the presentence report or the parties' submissions. The amendment was intended to respond to the courts' expanded discretion under Booker. In light of a number of recent decisions in the lower courts considering the proper scope of this obligation in light of Booker, the proposed amendment was withdrawn for further study.

Subdivision (k), which would have required that courts use a specified judgment and statement of reasons form, was withdrawn because of the passage of §735 of the USA Patriot Improvement and Reauthorization Act. This legislation amended 28 U.S.C. §994(w) to impose a statutory requirement that sentencing information for each case be provided on "the written statement of reasons form issued by the Judicial Conference and approved by the United States Sentencing Commission." The Criminal Law Committee, which had previously requested that the uniform collection of sentencing information be addressed by an amendment to the rules, withdrew that request in light of the enactment of the statutory requirement.

Finally, here—as in the other Booker rules—the Committee deleted the reference in the Committee Note to the Fifth Amendment from the description of the Supreme Court's decision in Booker.

COMMITTEE NOTES ON RULES—2008 AMENDMENT

Subdivision (a). The Crime Victims' Rights Act, codified as 18 U.S.C. §3771(e), adopted a new definition of the term "crime victim." The new statutory definition has been incorporated in an amendment to Rule 1, which supersedes the provisions that have been deleted here.

Subdivision (c)(1). This amendment implements the victim's statutory right under the Crime Victims' Rights Act to "full and timely restitution as provided in law." See 18 U.S.C. §3771(a)(6). Whenever the law permits restitution, the presentence investigation report should contain information permitting the court to determine whether restitution is appropriate.

Subdivision (d)(2)(B). This amendment implements the Crime Victims' Rights Act, codified at 18 U.S.C. §3771. The amendment makes it clear that victim impact information should be treated in the same way as other information contained in the presentence report. It deletes language requiring victim impact information to be "verified" and "stated in a nonargumentative style" because that language does not appear in the other subparagraphs of Rule 32(d)(2).

Subdivision (i)(4). The deleted language, referring only to victims of crimes of violence or sexual abuse, has been superseded by the Crime Victims' Rights Act, 18 U.S.C. §3771(e). The act defines the term "crime victim" without limiting it to certain crimes, and provides that crime victims, so defined, have a right to be reasonably heard at all public court proceedings regarding sentencing. A companion amendment to Rule 1(b) adopts the statutory definition as the definition of the term "victim" for purposes of the Federal Rules of Criminal Procedure, and explains who may raise the rights of a victim, so the language in this subdivision is no longer needed.

Subdivision (i)(4) has also been amended to incorporate the statutory language of the Crime Victims' Rights Act, which provides that victims have the right "to be reasonably heard" in judicial proceedings regarding sentencing. See 18 U.S.C. §3771(a)(4). The amended rule provides that the judge must speak to any victim present in the courtroom at sentencing. Absent unusual circumstances, any victim who is present should be allowed a reasonable opportunity to speak directly to the judge.

Changes Made to Proposed Amendment Released for Public Comment. No changes were made in the text of the rule. In response to public comments, the Committee Note was amended to make it clear that absent unusual circumstances any victim who is in the courtroom should have a reasonable opportunity to speak directly to the judge.

COMMITTEE NOTES ON RULES——2009 AMENDMENT

Subdivision (d)(2)(G). Rule 32.2(a) requires that the indictment or information provide notice to the defendant of the government's intent to seek forfeiture as part of the sentence. The amendment provides that the same notice be provided as part of the presentence report to the court. This will ensure timely consideration of the issues concerning forfeiture as part of the sentencing process.

Changes Made to Proposed Amendment Released for Public Comment. No changes were made to the proposed amendment to Rule 32.

COMMITTEE NOTES ON RULES——2011 AMENDMENT

Subdivision (d)(2). This technical and conforming amendment reorders two subparagraphs describing the information that may be included in the presentence report so that the provision authorizing the inclusion of any other information the court requires appears at the end of the paragraph. It also rephrases renumbered subdivision (d)(2)(F) for stylistic purposes.

AMENDMENT BY PUBLIC LAW

1996—Subd. (b)(1). Pub. L. 104–132, §207(a)(1), inserted at end "Notwithstanding the preceding sentence, a presentence investigation and report, or other report containing information sufficient for the court to enter an order of restitution, as the court may direct, shall be required in any case in which restitution is required to be ordered."

Subd. (b)(4)(F) to (H). Pub. L. 104–132, §207(a)(2), added subd. (b)(4)(F), and redesignated former subds. (b)(4)(F) and (b)(4)(G) as (b)(4)(G) and (b)(4)(H), respectively.

1994—Subd. (c)(3)(D). Pub. L. 103–322, §230101(b)(4), substituted "opportunity equivalent to that of the defendant's counsel" for "equivalent opportunity".

Subd. (c)(3)(E). Pub. L. 103–322, §230101(b)(1)–(3), added subd. (c)(3)(E).

Subd. (c)(4). Pub. L. 103–322, §230101(b)(5), (6), substituted "(D), and (E)" for "and (D)" and inserted "the victim," before "or the attorney for the Government.".

Subd. (f). Pub. L. 103–322, §230101(b)(7), added subd. (f).

1986—Subd. (c)(2)(B). Pub. L. 99–646 substituted "from" for "than".

1984—Subd. (a)(1). Pub. L. 98–473, §215(a)(1), substituted new subd. (a)(1) for former subd. (a)(1) which read as follows:

"(a) Sentence.

"(1) Imposition of Sentence. Sentence shall be imposed without unreasonable delay. Before imposing sentence the court shall

"(A) determine that the defendant and the defendant's counsel have had the opportunity to read and discuss the presentence investigation report made available pursuant to subdivision (c)(3)(A) or summary thereof made available pursuant to subdivision (c)(3)(B);

"(B) afford counsel an opportunity to speak on behalf of the defendant; and

"(C) address the defendant personally and ask the defendant if the defendant wishes to make a statement in the defendant's own behalf and to present any information in mitigation of punishment.

The attorney for the government shall have an equivalent opportunity to speak to the court."

Subd. (a)(2). Pub. L. 98–473, §215(a)(2), inserted ", including any right to appeal the sentence," after "right to appeal" in first sentence.

Pub. L. 98–473, §215(a)(3), inserted ", except that the court shall advise the defendant of any right to appeal his sentence" after "nolo contendere" in second sentence.

Subd. (c)(1). Pub. L. 98–473, §215(a)(4), amended first sentence generally. Prior to amendment, first sentence read as follows: "The probation service of the court shall make a presentence investigation and report to the court before the imposition of sentence or the granting of probation unless, with the permission of the court, the defendant waives a presentence investigation and report, or the court finds that there is in the record information sufficient to enable the meaningful exercise of sentencing discretion, and the court explains this finding on the record."

Subd. (c)(2). Pub. L. 98–473, §215(a)(5), amended subd. (c)(2) generally. Prior to amendment, subd. (c)(2) read as follows:

"(2) Report. The presentence report shall contain—

"(A) any prior criminal record of the defendant;

"(B) a statement of the circumstances of the commission of the offense and circumstances affecting the defendant's behavior;

"(C) information concerning any harm, including financial, social, psychological, and physical harm, done to or loss suffered by any victim of the offense; and

"(D) any other information that may aid the court in sentencing, including the restitution needs of any victim of the offense."

Subd. (c)(3)(A). Pub. L. 98–473, §215(a)(6), which directed the substitution of ", including the information required by subdivision (c)(2) but not including any final recommendation as to sentence," for "exclusive of any recommendations as to sentence", was executed by substituting the quotation for "exclusive of any recommendation as to sentence" to reflect the probable intent of Congress.

113

Subd. (c)(3)(D). Pub. L. 98–473, §215(a)(7), struck out "or the Parole Commission" before period at end.

Subd. (c)(3)(F). Pub. L. 98–473, §215(a)(8), substituted "pursuant to 18 U.S.C. §3552(b)" for "or the Parole Commission pursuant to 18 U.S.C. §§4205(c), 4252, 5010(e), or 5037(c)".

Subd. (d). Pub. L. 98–473, §215(a)(9), struck out "imposition of sentence is suspended, or disposition is had under 18 U.S.C. §4205(c)," after "is imposed,".

1982—Subdiv. (c)(2). Pub. L. 97–291 substituted provision directing that the presentence report contain any prior criminal record of the defendant, a statement of the circumstances of the commission of the offense and circumstances affecting the defendant's behavior, information concerning any harm, including financial, social, psychological, and physical harm, done to or loss suffered by any victim of the offense, and any other information that may aid the court in sentencing, including the restitution need of any victim of the offense, for provision requiring that the report of the presentence investigation shall contain any prior criminal record of the defendant and such information about his characteristics, his financial condition and the circumstances affecting his behavior as might be helpful in imposing sentence or in granting probation or in the correctional treatment of the defendant, and such other information as might be required by the court.

1975—Pub. L. 94–64 amended subds. (a)(1) and (c)(1), (3)(A), (D) generally.

EFFECTIVE DATE OF 1996 AMENDMENT

Amendment by Pub. L. 104–132 to be effective, to extent constitutionally permissible, for sentencing proceedings in cases in which defendant is convicted on or after Apr. 24, 1996, see section 211 of Pub. L. 104–132, set out as a note under section 2248 of this title.

EFFECTIVE DATE OF 1994 AMENDMENT

Amendment by Pub. L. 103–322 effective Dec. 1, 1994, see section 230101(c) of Pub. L. 103–322, set out as a Victim's Right of Allocution in Sentencing note under section 2074 of Title 28, Judiciary and Judicial Procedure.

EFFECTIVE DATE OF 1986 AMENDMENT

Pub. L. 99–646, §25(b), Nov. 10, 1986, 100 Stat. 3597, provided that: "The amendment made by subsection (a) shall take effect on the taking effect of the amendment made by section 215(a)(5) of the Comprehensive Crime Control Act of 1984 [§215(a)(5) of Pub. L. 98–473, effective Nov. 1, 1987]."

EFFECTIVE DATE OF 1984 AMENDMENT

Amendment by Pub. L. 98–473 effective Nov. 1, 1987, and applicable only to offenses committed after the taking effect of such amendment, see section 235(a)(1) of Pub. L. 98–473, set out as an Effective Date note under section 3551 of this title.

EFFECTIVE DATE OF 1982 AMENDMENT

Amendment by Pub. L. 97–291 effective Oct. 14, 1982, see section 9(a) of Pub. L. 97–291 set out as an Effective Date note under section 1512 of this title.

EFFECTIVE DATE OF 1979 AMENDMENT

Amendment of this rule by abrogation of subd. (f) by order of the United States Supreme Court of Apr. 30, 1979, effective Dec. 1, 1980, see section 1(1) of Pub. L. 96–42, July 31, 1979, 93 Stat. 326, set out as a note under section 2074 of Title 28, Judiciary and Judicial Procedure.

EFFECTIVE DATE OF AMENDMENTS PROPOSED APRIL 22, 1974; EFFECTIVE DATE OF 1975 AMENDMENTS

Amendments of this rule embraced in the order of the United States Supreme Court on Apr. 22, 1974, and the amendments of this rule made by section 3 of Pub. L. 94–64, effective Dec. 1, 1975, see section 2 of Pub. L. 94–64, set out as a note under rule 4 of these rules.

Rule 32.1. Revoking or Modifying Probation or Supervised Release

(a) Initial Appearance.
  (1) Person In Custody. A person held in custody for violating probation or supervised release must be taken without unnecessary delay before a magistrate judge.
    (A) If the person is held in custody in the district where an alleged violation occurred, the initial appearance must be in that district.
    (B) If the person is held in custody in a district other than where an alleged violation occurred, the initial appearance must be in that district, or in an adjacent district if the appearance can occur more promptly there.

  (2) Upon a Summons. When a person appears in response to a summons for violating probation or supervised release, a magistrate judge must proceed under this rule.
  (3) Advice. The judge must inform the person of the following:
    (A) the alleged violation of probation or supervised release;
    (B) the person's right to retain counsel or to request that counsel be appointed if the person cannot obtain counsel; and
    (C) the person's right, if held in custody, to a preliminary hearing under Rule 32.1(b)(1).

  (4) Appearance in the District With Jurisdiction. If the person is arrested or appears in the district that has jurisdiction to conduct a revocation hearing—either originally or by transfer of jurisdiction—the court must proceed under Rule 32.1(b)–(e).
  (5) Appearance in a District Lacking Jurisdiction. If the person is arrested or appears in a district that does not have jurisdiction to conduct a revocation hearing, the magistrate judge must:
    (A) if the alleged violation occurred in the district of arrest, conduct a preliminary hearing under Rule 32.1(b) and either:
      (i) transfer the person to the district that has jurisdiction, if the judge finds probable cause to believe that a violation occurred; or
      (ii) dismiss the proceedings and so notify the court that has jurisdiction, if the judge finds no probable cause to believe that a violation occurred; or

    (B) if the alleged violation did not occur in the district of arrest, transfer the person to the district that has jurisdiction if:
      (i) the government produces certified copies of the judgment, warrant, and warrant application, or produces copies of those certified documents by reliable electronic means; and
      (ii) the judge finds that the person is the same person named in the warrant.

  (6) Release or Detention. The magistrate judge may release or detain the person under 18 U.S.C. §3143(a)(1) pending further proceedings. The burden of establishing by clear and convincing evidence that the person will not flee or pose a danger to any other person or to the community rests with the person.

(b) Revocation.
  (1) Preliminary Hearing.
    (A) In General. If a person is in custody for violating a condition of probation or supervised release, a magistrate judge must promptly conduct a hearing to determine whether there is probable cause to believe that a violation occurred. The person may waive the hearing.

(B) Requirements. The hearing must be recorded by a court reporter or by a suitable recording device. The judge must give the person:

(i) notice of the hearing and its purpose, the alleged violation, and the person's right to retain counsel or to request that counsel be appointed if the person cannot obtain counsel;

(ii) an opportunity to appear at the hearing and present evidence; and

(iii) upon request, an opportunity to question any adverse witness, unless the judge determines that the interest of justice does not require the witness to appear.

(C) Referral. If the judge finds probable cause, the judge must conduct a revocation hearing. If the judge does not find probable cause, the judge must dismiss the proceeding.

(2) Revocation Hearing. Unless waived by the person, the court must hold the revocation hearing within a reasonable time in the district having jurisdiction. The person is entitled to:

(A) written notice of the alleged violation;

(B) disclosure of the evidence against the person;

(C) an opportunity to appear, present evidence, and question any adverse witness unless the court determines that the interest of justice does not require the witness to appear;

(D) notice of the person's right to retain counsel or to request that counsel be appointed if the person cannot obtain counsel; and

(E) an opportunity to make a statement and present any information in mitigation.

(c) Modification.

(1) In General. Before modifying the conditions of probation or supervised release, the court must hold a hearing, at which the person has the right to counsel and an opportunity to make a statement and present any information in mitigation.

(2) Exceptions. A hearing is not required if:

(A) the person waives the hearing; or

(B) the relief sought is favorable to the person and does not extend the term of probation or of supervised release; and

(C) an attorney for the government has received notice of the relief sought, has had a reasonable opportunity to object, and has not done so.

(d) Disposition of the Case. The court's disposition of the case is governed by 18 U.S.C. §3563 and §3565 (probation) and §3583 (supervised release).

(e) Producing a Statement. Rule 26.2(a)—(d) and (f) applies at a hearing under this rule. If a party fails to comply with a Rule 26.2 order to produce a witness's statement, the court must not consider that witness's testimony.

(Added Apr. 30, 1979, eff. Dec. 1, 1980; amended Pub. L. 99–646, §12(b), Nov. 10, 1986, 100 Stat. 3594; Mar. 9, 1987, eff. Aug. 1, 1987; Apr. 25, 1989, eff. Dec. 1, 1989; Apr. 30, 1991, eff. Dec. 1, 1991; Apr. 22, 1993, eff. Dec. 1, 1993; Apr. 29, 2002, eff. Dec. 1, 2002; Apr. 25, 2005, eff. Dec. 1, 2005; Apr. 12, 2006, eff. Dec. 1, 2006; Apr. 28, 2010, eff. Dec. 1, 2010.)

NOTES OF ADVISORY COMMITTEE ON RULES—1979

Note to Subdivision (a)(1). Since Morrissey v. Brewer, 408 U.S. 471 (1972), and Gagnon v. Scarpelli, 411 U.S. 778 (1973), it is clear that a probationer can no longer be denied due process in reliance on the dictum in Escoe v. Zerbst, 295 U.S. 490, 492 (1935), that probation is an "act of grace." See Van Alstyne, The Demise of the Right-Privilege Distinction in Constitutional Law, 81 Harv.L.Rev. 1439 (1968); President's Commission on Law Enforcement and Administration of Justice. Task Force Report: Corrections 86 (1967).

Subdivision (a)(1) requires, consistent with the holding in Scarpelli, that a prompt preliminary hearing must be held whenever "a probationer is held in custody on the ground that he has violated a condition of his probation." See 18 U.S.C. §3653 regarding arrest of the probationer with or without a warrant. If there is to be a revocation hearing but there has not been a holding in custody for a probation violation, there need not be a preliminary hearing. It was the fact of such a holding in custody "which prompted the Court to determine that a preliminary as well as a final revocation hearing was required to afford the petitioner due process of law." United States v. Tucker, 524 F.2d 77 (5th Cir. 1975). Consequently, a preliminary hearing need not be held if the probationer was at large and was not arrested but was allowed to appear voluntarily, United States v. Strada, 503 F.2d 1081 (8th Cir. 1974), or in response to a show cause order which "merely requires his appearance in court," United States v. Langford, 369 F.Supp. 1107 (N.D.Ill. 1973); if the probationer was in custody pursuant to a new charge, Thomas v. United States, 391 F.Supp. 202 (W.D.Pa. 1975), or pursuant to a final conviction of a subsequent offense, United States v. Tucker, supra; or if he was arrested but obtained his release.

Subdivision (a)(1)(A), (B) and (C) list the requirements for the preliminary hearing, as developed in Morrissey and made applicable to probation revocation cases in Scarpelli. Under (A), the probationer is to be given notice of the hearing and its purpose and of the alleged violation of probation. "Although the allegations in a motion to revoke probation need not be as specific as an indictment, they must be sufficient to apprise the probationer of the conditions of his probation which he is alleged to have violated, as well as the dates and events which support the charge." Kartman v. Parratt, 397 F.Supp. 531 (D.Nebr. 1975). Under (B), the probationer is permitted to appear and present evidence in his own behalf. And under (C), upon request by the probationer, adverse witnesses shall be made available for questioning unless the magistrate determines that the informant would be subjected to risk or harm if his identity were disclosed.

Subdivision (a)(1)(D) provides for notice to the probationer of his right to be represented by counsel at the preliminary hearing. Although Scarpelli did not impose as a constitutional requirement a right to counsel in all instances, under 18 U.S.C. §3006A(b) a defendant is entitled to be represented by counsel whenever charged "with a violation of probation."

The federal magistrate (see definition in rule 54(c)) is to keep a record of what transpires at the hearing and, if he finds probable cause of a violation, hold the probationer for a revocation hearing. The probationer may be released pursuant to rule 46(c) pending the revocation hearing.

Note to Subdivision (a)(2). Subdivision (a)(2) mandates a final revocation hearing within a reasonable time to determine whether the probationer has, in fact, violated the conditions of his probation and whether his probation should be revoked. Ordinarily this time will be measured from the time of the probable cause finding (if a preliminary hearing was held) or of the issuance of an order to show cause. However, what constitutes a reasonable time must be determined on the facts of the particular case, such as whether the probationer is available or could readily be made available. If the probationer has been convicted of and is incarcerated for a new crime, and that conviction is the basis of the pending revocation proceedings, it would be relevant whether the probationer waived appearance at the revocation hearing.

The hearing required by rule 32.1(a)(2) is not a formal trial; the usual rules of evidence need not be applied. See Morrissey v. Brewer, supra ("the process should be flexible enough to consider evidence including letters, affidavits, and other material that would not be admissible in an adversary criminal trial"); Rule 1101(d)(e) of the Federal Rules of Evidence (rules not applicable to proceedings "granting or revoking probation"). Evidence that would establish guilt beyond a reasonable doubt is not required to support an order revoking probation. United States v. Francischine, 512 F.2d 827 (5th Cir. 1975). This hearing may be waived by the probationer.

Subdivisions (a)(2)(A)—(E) list the rights to which a probationer is entitled at the final revocation hearing. The final hearing is less a summary one because the decision under consideration is the ultimate decision to revoke rather than a mere determination of probable cause. Thus, the probationer has certain rights not granted at the preliminary hearing: (i) the notice under (A) must by written; (ii) under (B) disclosure of all the evidence against the probationer is required; and (iii) under (D) the probationer does not have to specifically request the right to confront adverse witnesses, and the court may not limit the opportunity to question the witnesses against him.

115

Under subdivision (a)(2)(E) the probationer must be given notice of his right to be represented by counsel. Although Scarpelli holds that the Constitution does not compel counsel in all probation revocation hearings, under 18 U.S.C. §3006A(b) a defendant is entitled to be represented by counsel whenever charged "with a violation of probation."

Revocation of probation is proper if the court finds a violation of the conditions of probation and that such violation warrants revocation. Revocation followed by imprisonment is an appropriate disposition if the court finds on the basis of the original offense and the intervening conduct of the probationer that:

(i) confinement is necessary to protect the public from further criminal activity by the offender; or

(ii) the offender is in need of correctional treatment which can most effectively be provided if he is confined; or

(iii) it would unduly depreciate the seriousness of the violation if probation were not revoked.

See American Bar Association, Standards Relating to Probation §5.1 (Approved Draft, 1970).

If probation is revoked, the probationer may be required to serve the sentence originally imposed, or any lesser sentence, and if imposition of sentence was suspended he may receive any sentence which might have been imposed. 18 U.S.C. §3653. When a split sentence is imposed under 18 U.S.C. §3651 and probation is subsequently revoked, the probationer is entitled to credit for the time served in jail but not for the time he was on probation. Thomas v. United States, 327 F.2d 795 (10th Cir.), cert, denied 377 U.S. 1000 (1964); Schley v. Peyton, 280 F.Supp. 307 (W.D.Va. 1968).

Note to Subdivision (b). Subdivision (b) concerns proceedings on modification of probation (as provided for in 18 U.S.C. §3651). The probationer should have the right to apply to the sentencing court for a clarification or change of conditions. American Bar Association, Standards Relating to Probation §3.1(c) (Approved Draft, 1970). This avenue is important for two reasons: (1) the probationer should be able to obtain resolution of a dispute over an ambiguous term or the meaning of a condition without first having to violate it; and (2) in cases of neglect, overwork, or simply unreasonableness on the part of the probation officer, the probationer should have recourse to the sentencing court when a condition needs clarification or modification.

Probation conditions should be subject to modification, for the sentencing court must be able to respond to changes in the probationer's circumstances as well as new ideas and methods of rehabilitation. See generally ABA Standards, supra, §3.3. The Sentencing court is given the authority to shorten the term or end probation early upon its own motion without a hearing. And while the modification of probation is a part of the sentencing procedure, so that the probationer is ordinarily entitled to a hearing and presence of counsel, a modification favorable to the probationer may be accomplished without a hearing in the presence of defendant and counsel. United States v. Bailey, 343 F.Supp. 76 (W.D.Mo. 1971).

NOTES OF ADVISORY COMMITTEE ON RULES—1987 AMENDMENT

The amendments are technical. No substantive change is intended.

NOTES OF ADVISORY COMMITTEE ON RULES—1989 AMENDMENT

The amendments recognize that convicted defendants may be on supervised release as well as on probation. See 18 U.S.C. §§3583, and 3624(e).

NOTES OF ADVISORY COMMITTEE ON RULES—1991 AMENDMENT

The amendment is technical. No substantive change is intended.

NOTES OF ADVISORY COMMITTEE ON RULES—1993 AMENDMENT

The addition of subdivision (c) is one of several amendments that extend Rule 26.2 to Rules 32(f), 32.1, 46, and Rule 8 of the Rules Governing Proceedings under 28 U.S.C. §2255. As noted in the Committee Note to Rule 26.2, the primary reason for extending that Rule to other hearings and proceedings rests heavily upon the compelling need for accurate information affecting the witnesses' credibility. While that need is certainly clear in a trial on the merits, it is equally compelling, if not more so, in other pretrial and post-trial proceedings in which both the prosecution and defense have high interests at stake. In the case of revocation or modification of probation or supervised release proceedings, not only is the defendant's liberty interest at stake, the government has a stake in protecting the interests of the community.

Requiring production of witness statements at hearings conducted under Rule 32.1 will enhance the procedural due process which the rule now provides and which the Supreme Court required in Morrissey v. Brewer, 408 U.S. 471 (1972) and Gagnon v. Scarpelli, 411 U.S. 778 (1973). Access to prior statements of a witness will enhance the ability of both the defense and prosecution to test the credibility of the other side's witnesses under Rule 32.1(a)(1), (a)(2), and (b) and thus will assist the court in assessing credibility.

A witness's statement must be produced only if the witness testifies.

COMMITTEE NOTES ON RULES—2002 AMENDMENT

The language of Rule 32.1 has been amended as part of the general restyling of the Criminal Rules to make them more easily understood and to make style and terminology consistent throughout the rules. These changes are intended to be stylistic only, except as noted below.

Rule 32.1 has been completely revised and expanded. The Committee believed that it was important to spell out more completely in this rule the various procedural steps that must be met when dealing with a revocation or modification of probation or supervised release. To that end, some language formerly located in Rule 40 has been moved to revised Rule 32.1. Throughout the rule, the terms "magistrate judge," and "court" (see revised Rule 1(b) (Definitions)) are used to reflect that in revocation cases, initial proceedings in both felony and misdemeanor cases will normally be conducted before a magistrate judge, although a district judge may also conduct them. But a district judge must make the revocation decision if the offense of conviction was a felony. See 18 U.S.C. §3401(i) (recognizing that district judge may designate a magistrate judge to conduct a hearing and submit proposed findings of fact and recommendations).

Revised Rule 32.1(a)(1)–(4) is new material. Presently, there is no provision in the rules for conducting initial appearances for defendants charged with violating probation or supervised release—although some districts apply such procedures. Although the rule labels these proceedings as initial appearances, the Committee believed that it was best to separate those proceedings from Rule 5 proceedings, because the procedures differ for persons who are charged with violating conditions of probation or supervised release.

The Committee is also aware that, in some districts, it is not the practice to have an initial appearance for a revocation of probation or supervised release proceeding. Although Rule 32.1(a) will require such an appearance, nothing in the rule prohibits a court from combining the initial appearance proceeding, if convened consistent with the "without unnecessary delay" time requirement of the rule, with the preliminary hearing under Rule 32.1(b).

Revised Rule 32.1(a)(5) is derived from current Rule 40(d).

116

Revised Rule 32.1(a)(6), which is derived from current Rule 46(c), provides that the defendant bears the burden of showing that he or she will not flee or pose a danger pending a hearing on the revocation of probation or supervised release. The Committee believes that the new language is not a substantive change because it makes no change in practice.

Rule 32.1(b)(1)(B)(iii) and Rule 32.1(b)(2)(C) address the ability of a releasee to question adverse witnesses at the preliminary and revocation hearings. Those provisions recognize that the court should apply a balancing test at the hearing itself when considering the releasee's asserted right to cross-examine adverse witnesses. The court is to balance the person's interest in the constitutionally guaranteed right to confrontation against the government's good cause for denying it. See, e.g., Morrissey v. Brewer, 408 U.S. 471, 489 (1972); United States v. Comito, 177 F.3d 1166 (9th Cir. 1999); United States v. Walker, 117 F.3d 417 (9th Cir. 1997); United States v. Zentgraf, 20 F.3d 906 (8th Cir. 1994).

Rule 32.1(c)(2)(A) permits the person to waive a hearing to modify the conditions of probation or supervised release. Although that language is new to the rule, the Committee believes that it reflects current practice.

The remainder of revised Rule 32.1 is derived from the current Rule 32.1.

COMMITTEE NOTES ON RULES—2005 AMENDMENT

The amendments to Rule 32.1(b) and (c) are intended to address a gap in the rule. As noted by the court in United States v. Frazier, 283 F.3d 1242 (11th Cir. 2002) (per curiam), there is no explicit provision in current Rule 32.1 for allocution rights for a person upon revocation of supervised release. In that case the court noted that several circuits had concluded that the right to allocution in Rule 32 extended to supervised release revocation hearings. See United States v. Patterson, 128 F.3d 1259, 1261 (8th Cir. 1997) (Rule 32 right to allocution applies); United States v. Rodriguez, 23 F.3d 919, 921 (5th Cir. 1997) (right of allocution, in Rule 32, applies at revocation proceeding). But the court agreed with the Sixth Circuit that the allocution right in Rule 32 was not incorporated into Rule 32.1. See United States v. Waters, 158 F.3d 933 (6th Cir. 1998) (allocution right in Rule 32 does not apply to revocation proceedings). The Frazier court observed that the problem with the incorporation approach is that it would require application of other provisions specifically applicable to sentencing proceedings under Rule 32, but not expressly addressed in Rule 32.1. 283 F.3d at 1245. The court, however, believed that it would be "better practice" for courts to provide for allocution at revocation proceedings and stated that "[t]he right of allocution seems both important and firmly embedded in our jurisprudence." Id.

The amended rule recognizes the importance of allocution and now explicitly recognizes that right at Rule 32.1(b)(2) revocation hearings, and extends it as well to Rule 32.1(c)(1) modification hearings where the court may decide to modify the terms or conditions of the defendant's probation. In each instance the court is required to give the defendant the opportunity to make a statement and present any mitigating information.

Changes Made After Publication and Comment. The Committee made no changes to Rule 32.1 following publication.

COMMITTEE NOTES ON RULES—2006 AMENDMENT

Subdivision (a)(5)(B)(i). Rule 32.1(a)(5)(B)(i) has been amended to permit the magistrate judge to accept a judgment, warrant, and warrant application by reliable electronic means. Currently, the rule requires the government to produce certified copies of those documents. This amendment parallels similar changes to Rules 5 and 41.

The amendment reflects a number of significant improvements in technology. First, receiving documents by facsimile has become very commonplace and many courts are now equipped to receive filings by electronic means, and indeed, some courts encourage or require that certain documents be filed by electronic means. Second, the technology has advanced to the state where such filings could be sent from, and received at, locations outside the courthouse. Third, electronic media can now provide improved quality of transmission and security measures. In short, in a particular case, using electronic media to transmit a document might be just as reliable and efficient as using a facsimile.

The term "electronic" is used to provide some flexibility to the rule and make allowance for further technological advances in transmitting data. The Committee envisions that the term "electronic" would include use of facsimile transmissions.

The rule requires that if electronic means are to be used to transmit a warrant to the magistrate judge, the means used be "reliable." While the rule does not further define that term, the Committee envisions that a court or magistrate judge would make that determination as a local matter. In deciding whether a particular electronic means, or media, would be reliable, the court might consider first, the expected quality and clarity of the transmission. For example, is it possible to read the contents of the warrant in its entirety, as though it were the original or a clean photocopy? Second, the court may wish to consider whether security measures are available to insure that the transmission is not compromised. In this regard, most courts are now equipped to require that certain documents contain a digital signature, or some other similar system for restricting access. Third, the court may consider whether there are reliable means of preserving the document for later use.

Changes Made After Publication and Comment. The Committee made minor clarifying changes in the published rule at the suggestion of the Style Committee.

COMMITTEE NOTES ON RULES—2010 AMENDMENT

Subdivision (a)(6). This amendment is designed to end confusion regarding the applicability of 18 U.S.C. §3143(a) to release or detention decisions involving persons on probation or supervised release, and to clarify the burden of proof in such proceedings. Confusion regarding the applicability of §3143(a) arose because several subsections of the statute are ill suited to proceedings involving the revocation of probation or supervised release. See United States v. Mincey, 482 F. Supp. 2d 161 (D. Mass. 2007). The amendment makes clear that only subsection 3143(a)(1) is applicable in this context.

The current rule provides that the person seeking release must bear the burden of establishing that he or she will not flee or pose a danger but does not specify the standard of proof that must be met. The amendment incorporates into the rule the standard of clear and convincing evidence.

Changes Made to Proposed Amendment Released for Public Comment. No changes were made after the amendment was released for public comment.

AMENDMENT BY PUBLIC LAW

1986—Subd. (b). Pub. L. 99–646 inserted "to be" after "relief" and inserted provision relating to objection from the attorney for the government after notice of the proposed relief and extension of the term of probation as not favorable to the probationer for the purposes of this rule.

EFFECTIVE DATE OF 1986 AMENDMENT

Pub. L. 99–646, §12(c)(2), Nov. 10, 1986, 100 Stat. 3594, provided that: "The amendments made by subsection (b) [amending this rule] shall take effect 30 days after the date of enactment of this Act [Nov. 10, 1986]."

EFFECTIVE DATE OF RULE

This rule added by order of the United States Supreme Court of Apr. 30, 1979, effective Dec. 1, 1980, see section 1(1) of Pub. L. 96–42, July 31, 1979, 93 Stat. 326, set out as a note under section 2074 of Title 28, Judiciary and Judicial Procedure.

(a) Notice to the Defendant. A court must not enter a judgment of forfeiture in a criminal proceeding unless the indictment or information contains notice to the defendant that the government will seek the forfeiture of property as part of any sentence in accordance with the applicable statute. The notice should not be designated as a count of the indictment or information. The indictment or information need not identify the property subject to forfeiture or specify the amount of any forfeiture money judgment that the government seeks.

(b) Entering a Preliminary Order of Forfeiture.

(1) Forfeiture Phase of the Trial.

(A) Forfeiture Determinations. As soon as practical after a verdict or finding of guilty, or after a plea of guilty or nolo contendere is accepted, on any count in an indictment or information regarding which criminal forfeiture is sought, the court must determine what property is subject to forfeiture under the applicable statute. If the government seeks forfeiture of specific property, the court must determine whether the government has established the requisite nexus between the property and the offense. If the government seeks a personal money judgment, the court must determine the amount of money that the defendant will be ordered to pay.

(B) Evidence and Hearing. The court's determination may be based on evidence already in the record, including any written plea agreement, and on any additional evidence or information submitted by the parties and accepted by the court as relevant and reliable. If the forfeiture is contested, on either party's request the court must conduct a hearing after the verdict or finding of guilty.

(2) Preliminary Order.

(A) Contents of a Specific Order. If the court finds that property is subject to forfeiture, it must promptly enter a preliminary order of forfeiture setting forth the amount of any money judgment, directing the forfeiture of specific property, and directing the forfeiture of any substitute property if the government has met the statutory criteria. The court must enter the order without regard to any third party's interest in the property. Determining whether a third party has such an interest must be deferred until any third party files a claim in an ancillary proceeding under Rule 32.2(c).

(B) Timing. Unless doing so is impractical, the court must enter the preliminary order sufficiently in advance of sentencing to allow the parties to suggest revisions or modifications before the order becomes final as to the defendant under Rule 32.2(b)(4).

(C) General Order. If, before sentencing, the court cannot identify all the specific property subject to forfeiture or calculate the total amount of the money judgment, the court may enter a forfeiture order that:

(i) lists any identified property;

(ii) describes other property in general terms; and

(iii) states that the order will be amended under Rule 32.2(e)(1) when additional specific property is identified or the amount of the money judgment has been calculated.

(3) Seizing Property. The entry of a preliminary order of forfeiture authorizes the Attorney General (or a designee) to seize the specific property subject to forfeiture; to conduct any discovery the court considers proper in identifying, locating, or disposing of the property; and to commence proceedings that comply with any statutes governing third-party rights. The court may include in the order of forfeiture conditions reasonably necessary to preserve the property's value pending any appeal.

(4) Sentence and Judgment.

(A) When Final. At sentencing—or at any time before sentencing if the defendant consents—the preliminary forfeiture order becomes final as to the defendant. If the order directs the defendant to forfeit specific property, it remains preliminary as to third parties until the ancillary proceeding is concluded under Rule 32.2(c).

(B) Notice and Inclusion in the Judgment. The court must include the forfeiture when orally announcing the sentence or must otherwise ensure that the defendant knows of the forfeiture at sentencing. The court must also include the forfeiture order, directly or by reference, in the judgment, but the court's failure to do so may be corrected at any time under Rule 36.

(C) Time to Appeal. The time for the defendant or the government to file an appeal from the forfeiture order, or from the court's failure to enter an order, begins to run when judgment is entered. If the court later amends or declines to amend a forfeiture order to include additional property under Rule 32.2(e), the defendant or the government may file an appeal regarding that property under Federal Rule of Appellate Procedure 4(b). The time for that appeal runs from the date when the order granting or denying the amendment becomes final.

(5) Jury Determination.

(A) Retaining the Jury. In any case tried before a jury, if the indictment or information states that the government is seeking forfeiture, the court must determine before the jury begins deliberating whether either party requests that the jury be retained to determine the forfeitability of specific property if it returns a guilty verdict.

(B) Special Verdict Form. If a party timely requests to have the jury determine forfeiture, the government must submit a proposed Special Verdict Form listing each property subject to forfeiture and asking the jury to determine whether the government has established the requisite nexus between the property and the offense committed by the defendant.

(6) Notice of the Forfeiture Order.

(A) Publishing and Sending Notice. If the court orders the forfeiture of specific property, the government must publish notice of the order and send notice to any person who reasonably appears to be a potential claimant with standing to contest the forfeiture in the ancillary proceeding.

(B) Content of the Notice. The notice must describe the forfeited property, state the times under the applicable statute when a petition contesting the forfeiture must be filed, and state the name and contact information for the government attorney to be served with the petition.

(C) Means of Publication; Exceptions to Publication Requirement. Publication must take place as described in Supplemental Rule G(4)(a)(iii) of the Federal Rules of Civil Procedure, and may be by any means described in Supplemental Rule G(4)(a)(iv). Publication is unnecessary if any exception in Supplemental Rule G(4)(a)(i) applies.

(D) Means of Sending the Notice. The notice may be sent in accordance with Supplemental Rules G(4)(b)(iii)–(v) of the Federal Rules of Civil Procedure.

(7) Interlocutory Sale. At any time before entry of a final forfeiture order, the court, in accordance with Supplemental Rule G(7) of the Federal Rules of Civil Procedure, may order the interlocutory sale of property alleged to be forfeitable.

(c) Ancillary Proceeding; Entering a Final Order of Forfeiture.

(1) In General. If, as prescribed by statute, a third party files a petition asserting an interest in the property to be forfeited, the court must conduct an ancillary proceeding, but no ancillary proceeding is required to the extent that the forfeiture consists of a money judgment.

(A) In the ancillary proceeding, the court may, on motion, dismiss the petition for lack of standing, for failure to state a claim, or for any other lawful reason. For purposes of the motion, the facts set forth in the petition are assumed to be true.

(B) After disposing of any motion filed under Rule 32.2(c)(1)(A) and before conducting a hearing on the petition, the court may permit the parties to conduct discovery in accordance with the Federal Rules of Civil Procedure if the court determines that discovery is necessary or desirable to resolve factual issues. When discovery ends, a party may move for summary judgment under Federal Rule of Civil Procedure 56.

(2) Entering a Final Order. When the ancillary proceeding ends, the court must enter a final order of forfeiture by amending the preliminary order as necessary to account for any third-party rights. If no third party files a timely petition, the preliminary order becomes the final order of forfeiture if the court finds that the defendant

(or any combination of defendants convicted in the case) had an interest in the property that is forfeitable under the applicable statute. The defendant may not object to the entry of the final order on the ground that the property belongs, in whole or in part, to a codefendant or third party; nor may a third party object to the final order on the ground that the third party had an interest in the property.

(3) Multiple Petitions. If multiple third-party petitions are filed in the same case, an order dismissing or granting one petition is not appealable until rulings are made on all the petitions, unless the court determines that there is no just reason for delay.

(4) Ancillary Proceeding Not Part of Sentencing. An ancillary proceeding is not part of sentencing.

(d) Stay Pending Appeal. If a defendant appeals from a conviction or an order of forfeiture, the court may stay the order of forfeiture on terms appropriate to ensure that the property remains available pending appellate review. A stay does not delay the ancillary proceeding or the determination of a third party's rights or interests. If the court rules in favor of any third party while an appeal is pending, the court may amend the order of forfeiture but must not transfer any property interest to a third party until the decision on appeal becomes final, unless the defendant consents in writing or on the record.

(e) Subsequently Located Property; Substitute Property.

(1) In General. On the government's motion, the court may at any time enter an order of forfeiture or amend an existing order of forfeiture to include property that:

(A) is subject to forfeiture under an existing order of forfeiture but was located and identified after that order was entered; or

(B) is substitute property that qualifies for forfeiture under an applicable statute.

(2) Procedure. If the government shows that the property is subject to forfeiture under Rule 32.2(e)(1), the court must:

(A) enter an order forfeiting that property, or amend an existing preliminary or final order to include it; and

(B) if a third party files a petition claiming an interest in the property, conduct an ancillary proceeding under Rule 32.2(c).

(3) Jury Trial Limited. There is no right to a jury trial under Rule 32.2(e).

(Added Apr. 17, 2000, eff. Dec. 1, 2000; amended Apr. 29, 2002, eff. Dec. 1, 2002; Mar. 26, 2009, eff. Dec. 1, 2009.)

COMMITTEE NOTES ON RULES—2000

Rule 32.2 consolidates a number of procedural rules governing the forfeiture of assets in a criminal case. Existing Rules 7(c)(2), 31(e) and 32(d)(2) are also amended to conform to the new rule. In addition, the forfeiture-related provisions of Rule 38(e) are stricken.

Subdivision (a). Subdivision (a) is derived from Rule 7(c)(2) which provides that notwithstanding statutory authority for the forfeiture of property following a criminal conviction, no forfeiture order may be entered unless the defendant was given notice of the forfeiture in the indictment or information. As courts have held, subdivision (a) is not intended to require that an itemized list of the property to be forfeited appear in the indictment or information itself. The subdivision reflects the trend in caselaw interpreting present Rule 7(c). Under the most recent cases, Rule 7(c) sets forth a requirement that the government give the defendant notice that it will be seeking forfeiture in accordance with the applicable statute. It does not require a substantive allegation in which the property subject to forfeiture, or the defendant's interest in the property, must be described in detail. See United States v. DeFries, 129 F.3d 1293 (D.C.Cir. 1997) (it is not necessary to specify in either the indictment or a bill of particulars that the government is seeking forfeiture of a particular asset, such as the defendant's salary; to comply with Rule 7(c), the government need only put the defendant on notice that it will seek to forfeit everything subject to forfeiture under the applicable statute, such as all property "acquired or maintained" as a result of a RICO violation). See also United States v. Moffitt, Zwerling & Kemler, P.C., 83 F.3d 660, 665 (4th Cir. 1996), aff'g 846 F. Supp. 463 (E.D. Va. 1994) (Moffitt I) (indictment need not list each asset subject to forfeiture; under Rule 7(c), this can be done with bill of particulars); United States v. Voigt, 89 F.3d 1050 (3rd Cir. 1996) (court may amend order of forfeiture at any time to include substitute assets).

Subdivision (b). Subdivision (b) replaces Rule 31(e) which provides that the jury in a criminal case must return a special verdict "as to the extent of the interest or property subject to forfeiture." See United States v. Saccoccia, 58 F.3d 754 (1st Cir. 1995) (Rule 31(e) only applies to jury trials; no special verdict required when defendant waives right to jury on forfeiture issues).

One problem under Rule 31(e) concerns the scope of the determination that must be made prior to entering an order of forfeiture. This issue is the same whether the determination is made by the court or by the jury.

As mentioned, the current rule requires the jury to return a special verdict "as to the extent of the interest or property subject to forfeiture." Some courts interpret this to mean only that the jury must answer "yes" or "no" when asked if the property named in the indictment is subject to forfeiture under the terms of the forfeiture statute— e.g. was the property used to facilitate a drug offense? Other courts also ask the jury if the defendant has a legal interest in the forfeited property. Still other courts, including the Fourth Circuit, require the jury to determine the extent of the defendant's interest in the property vis a vis third parties. See United States v. Ham, 58 F.3d 78 (4th Cir. 1995) (case remanded to the district court to impanel a jury to determine, in the first instance, the extent of the defendant's forfeitable interest in the subject property).

The notion that the "extent" of the defendant's interest must be established as part of the criminal trial is related to the fact that criminal forfeiture is an in personam action in which only the defendant's interest in the property may be forfeited. United States v. Riley, 78 F.3d 367 (8th Cir. 1996). When the criminal forfeiture statutes were first enacted in the 1970's, it was clear that a forfeiture of property other than the defendant's could not occur in a criminal case, but there was no mechanism designed to limit the forfeiture to the defendant's interest. Accordingly, Rule 31(e) was drafted to make a determination of the "extent" of the defendant's interest part of the verdict.

The problem is that third parties who might have an interest in the forfeited property are not parties to the criminal case. At the same time, a defendant who has no interest in property has no incentive, at trial, to dispute the government's forfeiture allegations. Thus, it was apparent by the 1980's that Rule 31(e) was an inadequate safeguard against the inadvertent forfeiture of property in which the defendant held no interest.

In 1984, Congress addressed this problem when it enacted a statutory scheme whereby third party interests in criminally forfeited property are litigated by the court in an ancillary proceeding following the conclusion of the criminal case and the entry of a preliminary order of forfeiture. See 21 U.S.C. §853(n); 18 U.S.C. §1963(l). Under this scheme, the court orders the forfeiture of the defendant's interest in the property—whatever that interest may be—in the criminal case. At that point, the court conducts a separate proceeding in which all potential third party claimants are given an opportunity to challenge the forfeiture by asserting a superior interest in the property. This proceeding does not involve relitigation of the forfeitability of the property; its only purpose is to determine whether any third party has a legal interest in the forfeited property.

The notice provisions regarding the ancillary proceeding are equivalent to the notice provisions that govern civil forfeitures. Compare 21 U.S.C. §853(n)(1) with 19 U.S.C. §1607(a); see United States v. Bouler, 927 F. Supp. 911 (W.D.N.C. 1996) (civil notice rules apply to ancillary criminal proceedings). Notice is published and sent to third parties that have a potential interest. See United States v. BCCI Holdings (Luxembourg) S.A. (In re Petition of Indosuez Bank), 916 F. Supp. 1276 (D.D.C. 1996) (discussing steps taken by government to provide notice of criminal forfeiture to third parties). If no one files a claim, or if all claims are denied following a hearing, the forfeiture becomes final and the United States is deemed to have clear title to the property. 21 U.S.C. §853(n)(7); United States v. Hentz, 1996 WL 355327 (E.D. Pa. June 20, 1996) (once third party fails to file a claim in the ancillary proceeding, government has clear title under §853(n)(7) and can market the property notwithstanding third party's name on the deed).

Thus, the ancillary proceeding has become the forum for determining the extent of the defendant's forfeitable interest in the property. This allows the court to conduct a proceeding in which all third party claimants can participate and which ensures that the property forfeited actually belongs to the defendant.

Since the enactment of the ancillary proceeding statutes, the requirement in Rule 31(e) that the court (or jury) determine the extent of the defendant's interest in the property as part of the criminal trial has become an unnecessary anachronism that leads more often than not to duplication and a waste of judicial resources. There is no longer any reason to delay the conclusion of the criminal trial with a lengthy hearing over the extent of the defendant's interest in property when the same issues will have to be litigated a second time in the ancillary proceeding if someone files a claim challenging the forfeiture. For example, in United States v. Messino, 917 F. Supp. 1307 (N.D. Ill. 1996), the court allowed the defendant to call witnesses to attempt to establish that they, not he, were the true owners of the property. After the jury rejected this evidence and the property was forfeited, the court conducted an ancillary proceeding in which the same witnesses litigated their claims to the same property.

A more sensible procedure would be for the court, once it (or a jury) determines that property was involved in the criminal offense for which the defendant has been convicted, to order the forfeiture of whatever interest a defendant may have in the property without having to determine exactly what that interest is. If third parties assert that they have an interest in all or part of the property, those interests can be adjudicated at one time in the ancillary proceeding.

This approach would also address confusion that occurs in multi-defendant cases where it is clear that each defendant should forfeit whatever interest he may have in the property used to commit the offense, but it is not at all clear which defendant is the actual owner of the property. For example, suppose A and B are co-defendants in a drug and money laundering case in which the government seeks to forfeit property involved in the scheme that is held in B's name but of which A may be the true owner. It makes no sense to invest the court's time in determining which of the two defendants holds the interest that should be forfeited. Both defendants should forfeit whatever interest they may have. Moreover, if under the current rule the court were to find that A is the true owner of the property, then B would have the right to file a claim in the ancillary proceeding where he may attempt to recover the property despite his criminal conviction. United States v. Real Property in Waterboro, 64 F.3d 752 (1st Cir. 1995) (co-defendant in drug/money laundering case who is not alleged to be the owner of the property is considered a third party for the purpose of challenging the forfeiture of the other co-defendant's interest).

The new rule resolves these difficulties by postponing the determination of the extent of the defendant's interest until the ancillary proceeding. As provided in (b)(1), the court, as soon as practicable after the verdict or finding of guilty in the criminal case, would determine if the property was subject to forfeiture in accordance with the applicable statute, e.g., whether the property represented the proceeds of the offense, was used to facilitate the offense, or was involved in the offense in some other way. The determination could be made based on the evidence in the record from the criminal trial or the facts set forth in a written plea agreement submitted to the court at the time of the defendant's guilty plea, or the court could hold a hearing to determine if the requisite relationship existed between the property and the offense. Subdivision (b)(2) provides that it is not necessary to determine at this stage what interest any defendant might have in the property. Instead, the court would order the forfeiture of whatever interest each defendant might have in the property and conduct the ancillary proceeding.

Subdivision (b)(1) recognizes that there are different kinds of forfeiture judgments in criminal cases. One type is a personal judgment for a sum of money; another is a judgment forfeiting a specific asset. See, e.g., United States v. Voigt, 89 F.3d 1050 (3d Cir. 1996) (government is entitled to a personal money judgment equal to the amount involved in the money laundering offense, as well as order forfeiting specific assets involved in, or traceable to, the offense; in addition, if the statutory requirements are met, the government may be entitled to forfeit substitute assets); United States v. Cleveland, 1997 WL 537707 (E.D. La. Aug. 26, 1997), modified, 1997 WL 602186 (E.D. La. Sept. 29, 1997) (government entitled to a money judgment equal to the amount of money defendant laundered in money laundering case). The finding the court is required to make will depend on the nature of the forfeiture judgment. A number of cases have approved use of money judgment forfeitures. The Committee takes no position on the correctness of those rulings.

To the extent that the government is seeking forfeiture of a particular asset, such as the money on deposit in a particular bank account that is alleged to be the proceeds of a criminal offense, or a parcel of land that is traceable to that offense, the court must find that the government has established the requisite nexus between the property and the offense. To the extent that the government is seeking a money judgment, such as a judgment for the amount of money derived from a drug trafficking offense or the amount involved in a money laundering offense where the actual property subject to forfeiture has not been found or is unavailable, the court must determine the amount of money that the defendant should be ordered to forfeit.

The court may make the determination based on evidence in the record, or on additional evidence submitted by the defendant or evidence submitted by the government in support of the motion for the entry of a judgment of forfeiture. The defendant would have no standing to object to the forfeiture on the ground that the property belonged to someone else.

Under subdivision (b)(2), if the court finds that property is forfeitable, it must enter a preliminary order of forfeiture. It also recognizes that any determination of a third person's interest in the property is deferred until an ancillary proceeding, if any, is held under subdivision (c).

Subdivision (b)(3) replaces Rule 32(d)(2) (effective December 1996). It provides that once the court enters a preliminary order of forfeiture directing the forfeiture of whatever interest each defendant may have in the forfeited property, the government may seize the property and commence an ancillary proceeding to determine the interests of any third party. The subdivision also provides that the Attorney General may designate someone outside of the Department of Justice to seize forfeited property. This is necessary because in cases in which the lead investigative agency is in the Treasury Department, for example, the seizure of the forfeited property is typically handled by agencies other than the Department of Justice.

If no third party files a claim, the court, at the time of sentencing, will enter a final order forfeiting the property in accordance with subdivision (c)(2), discussed infra. If a third party files a claim, the order of forfeiture will become final as to the defendant at the time of sentencing but will be subject to amendment in favor of a third party pending the conclusion of the ancillary proceeding.

Because the order of forfeiture becomes final as to the defendant at the time of sentencing, his right to appeal from that order begins to run at that time. As courts have held, because the ancillary hearing has no bearing on the defendant's right to the property, the defendant has no right to appeal when a final order is, or is not, amended to recognize third party rights. See, e.g., United States v. Christunas, 126 F.3d 765 (6th Cir. 1997) (preliminary order of forfeiture is final as to the defendant and is immediately appealable).

Because it is not uncommon for sentencing to be postponed for an extended period to allow a defendant to cooperate with the government in an ongoing investigation, the rule would allow the order of forfeiture to become final as to the defendant before sentencing, if the defendant agrees to that procedure. Otherwise, the government would be unable to dispose of the property until the sentencing took place.

Subdivision (b)(4) addresses the right of either party to request that a jury make the determination of whether any property is subject to forfeiture. The provision gives the defendant, in all cases where a jury has returned a guilty verdict, the option of asking that the jury be retained to hear additional evidence regarding the forfeitability of the property. The only issue for the jury in such cases would be whether the government has established the requisite nexus between the property and the offense. For example, if the defendant disputes the government's allegation that a parcel of real property is traceable to the offense, the defendant would have the right to request that the jury hear evidence on that issue, and return a special verdict, in a bifurcated proceeding that would occur after the jury returns the guilty verdict. The government would have the same option of requesting a special jury verdict on this issue, as is the case under current law. See Rule 23(a) (trial by jury may be waived only with the consent of the government).

When Rule 31(e) was promulgated, it was assumed that criminal forfeiture was akin to a separate criminal offense on which evidence would be presented and the jury would have to return a verdict. In Libretti v. United States, 516 U.S. 29 (1995), however, the Supreme Court held that criminal forfeiture constitutes an aspect of the sentence imposed in a criminal case and that the defendant has no constitutional right to have the jury determine any part of the forfeiture. The special verdict requirement in Rule 31(e), the Court said, is in the nature of a statutory right that can be modified or repealed at any time.

Even before Libretti, lower courts had determined that criminal forfeiture is a sentencing matter and concluded that criminal trials therefore should be bifurcated so that the jury first returns a verdict on guilt or innocence and then returns to hear evidence regarding the forfeiture. In the second part of the bifurcated proceeding, the jury is instructed that the government must establish the forfeitability of the property by a preponderance of the evidence. See United States v. Myers, 21 F.3d 826 (8th Cir. 1994) (preponderance standard applies because criminal forfeiture is part of the sentence in money laundering cases); United States v. Voigt, 89 F.3d 1050 (3rd Cir. 1996) (following Myers); United States v. Smith, 966 F.2d 1045, 1050–53 (6th Cir. 1992) (same for drug cases); United States v. Bieri, 21 F.3d 819 (8th Cir. 1994) (same).

Although an argument could be made under Libretti, that a jury trial is no longer appropriate on any aspect of the forfeiture issue, which is a part of sentencing, the Committee decided to retain the right for the parties, in a trial held before a jury, to have the jury determine whether the government has established the requisite statutory nexus between the offense and the property to be forfeited. The jury, however, would not have any role in determining whether a defendant had an interest in the property to be forfeited. This is a matter for the ancillary proceeding which, by statute, is conducted "before the court alone, without a jury." See 21 U.S.C. §853(n)(2).

Subdivision (c). Subdivision (c) sets forth a set of rules governing the conduct of the ancillary proceeding. When the ancillary hearing provisions were added to 18 U.S.C. §1963 and 21 U.S.C. §853 in 1984, Congress apparently assumed that the proceedings under the new provisions would involve simple questions of ownership that could, in the ordinary case, be resolved in 30 days. See 18 U.S.C. §1963(l)(4). Presumably for that reason, the statute contains no procedures governing motions practice or discovery such as would be available in an ordinary civil case. Subdivision (c)(1) makes clear that no ancillary proceeding is required to the extent that the order of forfeiture consists of a money judgment. A money judgment is an in personam judgment against the defendant and not an order directed at specific assets in which any third party could have any interest.

Experience has shown that ancillary hearings can involve issues of enormous complexity that require years to resolve. See United States v. BCCI Holdings (Luxembourg) S.A., 833 F. Supp. 9 (D.D.C. 1993) (ancillary proceeding involving over 100 claimants and $451 million); United States v. Porcelli, CR–85–00756 (CPS), 1992 U.S. Dist. LEXIS 17928 (E.D.N.Y. Nov. 5, 1992) (litigation over third party claim continuing 6 years after RICO conviction). In such cases, procedures akin to those available under the Federal Rules of Civil Procedure should be available to the court and the parties to aid in the efficient resolution of the claims.

Because an ancillary hearing is connected to a criminal case, it would not be appropriate to make the Civil Rules applicable in all respects. The amendment, however, describes several fundamental areas in which procedures analogous to those in the Civil Rules may be followed. These include the filing of a motion to dismiss a claim, conducting discovery, disposing of a claim on a motion for summary judgment, and appealing a final disposition of a claim. Where applicable, the amendment follows the prevailing case law on the issue. See, e.g., United States v. Lavin, 942 F.2d 177 (3rd Cir. 1991) (ancillary proceeding treated as civil case for purposes of applying Rules of Appellate Procedure); United States v. BCCI Holdings (Luxembourg) S.A. (In re Petitions of General Creditors), 919 F. Supp. 31 (D.D.C. 1996) ("If a third party fails to allege in its petition all elements necessary for recovery, including those relating to standing, the court may dismiss the petition without providing a hearing"); United States v. BCCI (Holdings) Luxembourg S.A. (In re Petition of Department of Private Affairs), 1993 WL 760232 (D.D.C. Dec. 8, 1993) (applying court's inherent powers to permit third party to obtain discovery from defendant in accordance with civil rules). The provision governing appeals in cases where there are multiple claims is derived from Fed. R. Civ. P. 54(b). See also United States v. BCCI Holdings (Luxembourg) S.A. (Petition of Banque Indosuez), 961 F. Supp. 282 (D.D.C. 1997) (in resolving motion to dismiss court assumes all facts pled by third party petitioner to be true, applying Rule 12(b)(6) and denying government's motion because whether claimant had superior title turned on factual dispute; government acted reasonably in not making any discovery requests in ancillary proceeding until court ruled on its motion to dismiss).

Subdivision (c)(2) provides for the entry of a final order of forfeiture at the conclusion of the ancillary proceeding. Under this provision, if no one files a claim in the ancillary proceeding, the preliminary order would become the final order of forfeiture, but the court would first have to make an independent finding that at least one of the defendants had an interest in the property such that it was proper to order the forfeiture of the property in a criminal case. In making that determination, the court may rely upon reasonable inferences. For example, the fact that the defendant used the property in committing the crime and no third party claimed an interest in the property may give rise to the inference that the defendant had a forfeitable interest in the property.

This subdivision combines and preserves two established tenets of current law. One is that criminal forfeitures are in personam actions that are limited to the property interests of the defendant. (This distinguishes criminal forfeiture, which is imposed as part of the defendant's sentence, from civil forfeiture which may be pursued as an action against the property in rem without regard to who the owner may be.) The other tenet of current law is that if a third party has notice of the forfeiture but fails to file a timely claim, his or her interests are extinguished, and may not be recognized when the court enters the final order of forfeiture. See United States v. Hentz, 1996 WL 355327 (E.D. Pa. June 20, 1996) (once third party fails to file a claim in the ancillary proceeding, government has clear title under 21 U.S.C. §853(n)(7) and can market the property notwithstanding third party's name on the deed). In the rare event that a third party claims that he or she was not afforded adequate notice of a criminal forfeiture action, the person may file a motion under Rule 60(b) of the Federal Rules of Civil Procedure to reopen the ancillary proceeding. See United States v. Bouler, 927 F. Supp. 911 (W.D.N.C. 1996) (Rule 60(b) is the proper means by which a third party may move to reopen an ancillary proceeding).

If no third parties assert their interests in the ancillary proceeding, the court must nonetheless determine that the defendant, or combination of defendants, had an interest in the property. Criminal defendants may be jointly and severally liable for the forfeiture of the entire proceeds of the criminal offense. See United States v. Hurley, 63 F.3d 1 (1st Cir. 1995) (government can collect the proceeds only once, but subject to that cap, it can collect from any defendant so much of the proceeds as was foreseeable to that defendant); United States v. Cleveland, 1997 WL 602186 (E.D. La. Sept. 29, 1997) (same); United States v. McCarroll, 1996 WL 355371 at *9 (N.D. Ill. June 25, 1996) (following Hurley), aff'd sub nom. United States v. Jarrett, 133 F.3d 519 (7th Cir. 1998); United States v. DeFries, 909 F. Supp. 13, 19–20 (D.D.C. 1995) (defendants are jointly and severally liable even where government is able to determine precisely how much each defendant benefitted from the scheme), rev'd on other grounds, 129 F.3d 1293 (D.C. Cir. 1997). Therefore, the conviction of any of the defendants is sufficient to support the forfeiture of the entire proceeds of the offense, even if the defendants have divided the money among themselves.

As noted in (c)(4), the ancillary proceeding is not considered a part of sentencing. Thus, the Federal Rules of Evidence would apply to the ancillary proceeding, as is the case currently.

Subdivision (d). Subdivision (d) replaces the forfeiture provisions of Rule 38(e) which provide that the court may stay an order of forfeiture pending appeal. The purpose of the provision is to ensure that the property remains intact and unencumbered so that it may be returned to the defendant in the event the appeal is successful. Subdivision (d) makes clear, however, that a district court is not divested of jurisdiction over an ancillary proceeding even if the defendant appeals his or her conviction. This allows the court to proceed with the resolution of third party claims even as the appellate court considers the appeal. Otherwise, third parties would have to await the conclusion of the appellate process even to begin to have their claims heard. See United States v. Messino, 907 F. Supp. 1231 (N.D. Ill. 1995) (the district court retains jurisdiction over forfeiture matters while an appeal is pending).

Finally, subdivision (d) provides a rule to govern what happens if the court determines that a third-party claim should be granted but the defendant's appeal is still pending. The defendant is barred from filing a claim in the ancillary proceeding. See 18 U.S.C. §1963(l)(2); 21 U.S.C. §853(n)(2). Thus, the court's determination, in the ancillary proceeding, that a third party has an interest in the property superior to that of the defendant cannot be binding on the defendant. So, in the event that the court finds in favor of the third party, that determination is final only with respect to the government's alleged interest. If the defendant prevails on appeal, he or she recovers the property as if no conviction or forfeiture ever took place. But if the order of forfeiture is affirmed, the amendment to the order of forfeiture in favor of the third party becomes effective.

Subdivision (e). Subdivision (e) makes clear, as courts have found, that the court retains jurisdiction to amend the order of forfeiture at any time to include subsequently located property which was originally included in the forfeiture order and any substitute property. See United States v. Hurley, 63 F.3d 1 (1st Cir. 1995) (court retains authority to order forfeiture of substitute assets after appeal is filed); United States v. Voigt, 89 F.3d 1050 (3rd Cir. 1996) (following Hurley). Third parties, of course, may contest the forfeiture of substitute assets in the ancillary proceeding. See United States v. Lester, 85 F.3d 1409 (9th Cir. 1996).

Subdivision (e)(1) makes clear that the right to a bifurcated jury trial to determine whether the government has established the requisite nexus between the property and the offense, see (b)(4), does not apply to the forfeiture of substitute assets or to the addition of newly-discovered property to an existing order of forfeiture. It is well established in the case law that the forfeiture of substitute assets is solely an issue for the court. See United States v. Hurley, 63 F.3d 1 (1st Cir. 1995) (court retains authority to order forfeiture of substitute assets after appeal is filed); United States v. Voigt, 89 F.3d 1050 (3d Cir. 1996) (following Hurley; court may amend order of forfeiture at any time to include substitute assets); United States v. Thompson, 837 F. Supp. 585 (S.D.N.Y. 1993) (court, not jury, orders forfeiture of substitute assets). As a practical matter, courts have also determined that they, not the jury, must determine the forfeitability of assets discovered after the trial is over and the jury has been dismissed. See United States v. Saccoccia, 898 F. Supp. 53 (D.R.I. 1995) (government may conduct post-trial discovery to determine location and identity of forfeitable assets; post-trial discovery resulted in discovery of gold bars buried in defendant's mother's backyard several years after the entry of an order directing the defendant to forfeit all property, up to $137 million, involved in his money laundering offense).

GAP Report—Rule 32.2. The Committee amended the rule to clarify several key points. First, subdivision (b) was redrafted to make it clear that if no third party files a petition to assert property rights, the trial court must determine whether the defendant has an interest in the property to be forfeited and the extent of that interest. As published, the rule would have permitted the trial judge to order the defendant to forfeit the property in its entirety if no third party filed a claim.

Second, Rule 32.2(c)(4) was added to make it clear that the ancillary proceeding is not a part of sentencing.

Third, the Committee clarified the procedures to be used if the government (1) discovers property subject to forfeiture after the court has entered an order of forfeiture and (2) seeks the forfeiture of "substitute" property under a statute authorizing such substitution.

COMMITTEE NOTES ON RULES—2002 AMENDMENT

The language of Rule 32.2 has been amended as part of the general restyling of the Criminal Rules to make them more easily understood and to make style and terminology consistent throughout the rules. These changes are intended to be stylistic only.

COMMITTEE NOTES ON RULES—2009 AMENDMENT

Subdivision (a). The amendment responds to some uncertainty regarding the form of the required notice that the government will seek forfeiture as part of the sentence, making it clear that the notice should not be designated as a separate count in an indictment or information. The amendment also makes it clear that the indictment or information need only provide general notice that the government is seeking forfeiture, without identifying the specific property being sought. This is consistent with the 2000 Committee Note, as well as many lower court decisions.

Although forfeitures are not charged as counts, the federal judiciary's Case Management and Electronic Case Files system should note that forfeiture has been alleged so as to assist the parties and the court in tracking the subsequent status of forfeiture allegations.

The court may direct the government to file a bill of particulars to inform the defendant of the identity of the property that the government is seeking to forfeit or the amount of any money judgment sought if necessary to enable the defendant to prepare a defense or to avoid unfair surprise. See, e.g., United States v. Moffitt, Zwerdling, & Kemler, P.C., 83 F.3d 660, 665 (4th Cir. 1996) (holding that the government need not list each asset subject to forfeiture in the indictment because notice can be provided in a bill of particulars); United States v. Vasquez-Ruiz, 136 F. Supp. 2d 941, 944 (N.D. Ill. 2001) (directing the government to identify in a bill of particulars, at least 30 days before trial, the specific items of property, including substitute assets, that it claims are subject to forfeiture); United States v. Best, 657 F. Supp. 1179, 1182 (N.D. Ill. 1987) (directing the government to provide a bill of particulars apprising the defendants as to the time periods during which they obtained the specified classes of property through their alleged racketeering activity and the interest in each of these properties that was allegedly obtained unlawfully). See also United States v. Columbo, 2006 WL 2012511 * 5 & n.13 (S.D. N.Y. 2006) (denying motion for bill of particulars and noting that government proposed sending letter detailing basis for forfeiture allegations).

Subdivision (b)(1). Rule 32.2(b)(1) sets forth the procedure for determining if property is subject to forfeiture. Subparagraph (A) is carried forward from the current Rule without change.

Subparagraph (B) clarifies that the parties may submit additional evidence relating to the forfeiture in the forfeiture phase of the trial, which may be necessary even if the forfeiture is not contested. Subparagraph (B) makes it clear that in determining what evidence or information should be accepted, the court should consider relevance and reliability. Finally, subparagraph (B) requires the court to hold a hearing when forfeiture is contested. The Committee foresees that in some instances live testimony will be needed to determine the reliability of proffered information. Cf. Rule 32.1(b)(1)(B)(iii) (providing the defendant in a proceeding for revocation of probation or supervised release with the opportunity, upon request, to question any adverse witness unless the judge determines this is not in the interest of justice).

Subdivision (b)(2)(A). Current Rule 32.2(b) provides the procedure for issuing a preliminary forfeiture order once the court finds that the government has established the nexus between the property and the offense (or the amount of the money judgment). The amendment makes clear that the preliminary order may include substitute assets if the government has met the statutory criteria.

Subdivision (b)(2)(B). This new subparagraph focuses on the timing of the preliminary forfeiture order, stating that the court should issue the order "sufficiently in advance of sentencing to allow the parties to suggest revisions or modifications before the order becomes final." Many courts have delayed entry of the preliminary order until the time of sentencing. This is undesirable because the parties have no opportunity to advise the court of omissions or errors in the order before it becomes final as to the defendant (which occurs upon oral announcement of the sentence and the entry of the criminal judgment). Once the sentence has been announced, the rules give the sentencing court only very limited authority to correct errors or omissions in the preliminary forfeiture order. Pursuant to Rule 35(a), the district court may correct a sentence, including an incorporated forfeiture order, within seven days after oral announcement of the sentence. During the seven-day period, corrections are limited to those necessary to correct "arithmetical, technical, or other clear error." See United States v. King, 368 F. Supp. 2d 509, 512–13 (D.S.C. 2005). Corrections of clerical errors may also be made pursuant to Rule 36. If the order contains errors or omissions that do not fall within Rules 35(a) or 36, and the court delays entry of the preliminary forfeiture order until the time of sentencing, the parties may be left with no alternative to an appeal, which is a waste of judicial resources. The amendment requires the court to enter the preliminary order in advance of sentencing to permit time for corrections, unless it is not practical to do so in an individual case.

Subdivision (b)(2)(C). The amendment explains how the court is to reconcile the requirement that it make the forfeiture order part of the sentence with the fact that in some cases the government will not have completed its post-conviction investigation to locate the forfeitable property by the time of sentencing. In that case the court is authorized to issue a forfeiture order describing the property in "general" terms, which order may be amended pursuant to Rule 32.2(e)(1) when additional specific property is identified.

The authority to issue a general forfeiture order should be used only in unusual circumstances and not as a matter of course. For cases in which a general order was properly employed, see United States v. BCCI Holdings (Luxembourg), 69 F. Supp. 2d 36 (D.D.C. 1999) (ordering forfeiture of all of a large, complex corporation's assets in the United States, permitting the government to continue discovery necessary to identify and trace those assets); United States v. Saccoccia, 898 F. Supp. 53 (D.R.I. 1995) (ordering forfeiture of up to a specified amount of laundered drug proceeds so that the government could continue investigation which led to the discovery and forfeiture of gold bars buried by the defendant in his mother's back yard).

Subdivisions (b)(3) and (4). The amendment moves the language explaining when the forfeiture order becomes final as to the defendant to new subparagraph (b)(4)(A), where it is coupled with new language explaining that the order is not final as to third parties until the completion of the ancillary proceedings provided for in Rule 32.2(c).

New subparagraphs (B) and (C) are intended to clarify what the district court is required to do at sentencing, and to respond to conflicting decisions in the courts regarding the application of Rule 36 to correct clerical errors. The new subparagraphs add considerable detail regarding the oral announcement of the forfeiture at sentencing, the reference to the forfeiture order in the judgment and commitment order, the availability of Rule 36 to correct the failure to include the forfeiture order in the judgment and commitment order, and the time to appeal.

New subparagraph (C) clarifies the time for appeals concerning forfeiture by the defendant or government from two kinds of orders: the original judgment of conviction and later orders amending or refusing to amend the judgment under Rule 32.2(e) to add additional property. This provision does not address appeals by the government or a third party from orders in ancillary proceedings under Rule 32.2(c).

Subdivision (b)(5)(A). The amendment clarifies the procedure for requesting a jury determination of forfeiture. The goal is to avoid an inadvertent waiver of the right to a jury determination, while also providing timely notice to the court and to the jurors themselves if they will be asked to make the forfeiture determination. The amendment requires that the court determine whether either party requests a jury determination of forfeiture in cases where the government has given notice that it is seeking forfeiture and a jury has been empaneled to determine guilt or innocence. The rule requires the court to make this determination before the jury retires. Jurors who know that they may face an additional task after they return their verdict will be more accepting of the additional responsibility in the forfeiture proceeding, and the court will be better able to plan as well.

Although the rule permits a party to make this request just before the jury retires, it is desirable, when possible, to make the request earlier, at the time when the jury is empaneled. This allows the court to plan, and also allows the court to tell potential jurors what to expect in terms of their service.

Subdivision (b)(5)(B) explains that "the government must submit a proposed Special Verdict Form listing each property subject to forfeiture." Use of such a form is desirable, and the government is in the best position to draft the form.

Subdivisions (b)(6) and (7). These provisions are based upon the civil forfeiture provisions in Supplemental Rule G of the Federal Rules of Civil Procedure, which are also incorporated by cross reference. The amendment governs such mechanical and technical issues as the manner of publishing notice of forfeiture to third parties and the interlocutory sale of property, bringing practice under the Criminal Rules into conformity with the Civil Rules.

Changes Made to Proposed Amendment Released for Public Comment. The proposed amendment to Rule 32.2 was modified to use the term "property" throughout. As published, the proposed amendment used the terms property and asset(s) interchangeably. No difference in meaning was intended, and in order to avoid confusion, a single term was used consistently throughout. The term "forfeiture order" was substituted, where possible, for the wordier "order of forfeiture." Other small stylistic changes (such as the insertion of "the" in subpart titles) were also made to conform to the style conventions.

In new subpart (b)(4)(C), dealing with the time for appeals, the words "the defendant or the government" were substituted for the phrase "a party." This portion of the rule addresses only appeals from the original judgment of conviction and later orders amending or refusing to amend the judgment under Rule 32.2(e) to add additional property. Only the defendant and the government are parties at this stage of the proceedings. This portion of the rule does not address appeals by the government or a third party from orders in ancillary proceedings under Rule 32.2(c). This point was also clarified in the Committee note.

Additionally, two other changes were made to the Committee Note: a reference to the use of the ECF system to aid the court and parties in tracking the status of forfeiture allegations, and an additional illustrative case.

REFERENCES IN TEXT

The Supplemental Rules of the Federal Rules of Civil Procedure, referred to in subd. (b)(6)(C), (D), (7), are set out in the Appendix to Title 28, Judiciary and Judicial Procedure.

The Federal Rules of Civil Procedure, referred to in subd. (c)(1)(B), are set out in the Appendix to Title 28, Judiciary and Judicial Procedure.

Rule 33. New Trial

(a) Defendant's Motion. Upon the defendant's motion, the court may vacate any judgment and grant a new trial if the interest of justice so requires. If the case was tried without a jury, the court may take additional testimony and enter a new judgment.

(b) Time to File.

(1) Newly Discovered Evidence. Any motion for a new trial grounded on newly discovered evidence must be filed within 3 years after the verdict or finding of guilty. If an appeal is pending, the court may not grant a motion for a new trial until the appellate court remands the case.

(2) Other Grounds. Any motion for a new trial grounded on any reason other than newly discovered evidence must be filed within 14 days after the verdict or finding of guilty.

(As amended Feb. 28, 1966, eff. July 1, 1966; Mar. 9, 1987, eff. Aug. 1, 1987; Apr. 24, 1998, eff. Dec. 1, 1998; Apr. 29, 2002, eff. Dec. 1, 2002; Apr. 25, 2005, eff. Dec. 1, 2005; Mar. 26, 2009, eff. Dec. 1, 2009.)

NOTES OF ADVISORY COMMITTEE ON RULES—1944

This rule enlarges the time limit for motions for new trial on the ground of newly discovered evidence, from 60 days to two years; and for motions for new trial on other grounds from three to five days. Otherwise, it substantially continues existing practice. See Rule II of the Criminal Appeals Rules of 1933, 292 U.S. 661. Cf. Rule 59(a) of the Federal Rules of Civil Procedure [28 U.S.C., Appendix].

NOTES OF ADVISORY COMMITTEE ON RULES—1966 AMENDMENT

The amendments to the first two sentences make it clear that a judge has no power to order a new trial on his own motion, that he can act only in response to a motion timely made by a defendant. Problems of double jeopardy arise when the court acts on its own motion. See United States v. Smith, 331 U.S. 469 (1947). These amendments do not, of course, change the power which the court has in certain circumstances, prior to verdict or finding of guilty, to declare a mistrial and order a new trial on its own motion. See e.g., Gori v. United States, 367 U.S. 364 (1961); Downum v. United States, 372 U.S. 734 (1963); United States v. Tateo, 377 U.S. 463 (1964). The amendment to the last sentence changes the time in which the motion may be made to 7 days. See the Advisory Committee's Note to Rule 29.

The amendments are technical. No substantive change is intended.

As currently written, the time for filing a motion for new trial on the ground of newly discovered evidence runs from the "final judgment." The courts, in interpreting that language, have uniformly concluded that that language refers to the action of the Court of Appeals. See, e.g., United States v. Reyes, 49 F.3d 63, 66 (2d Cir. 1995)(citing cases). It is less clear whether that action is the appellate court's judgment or the issuance of its mandate. In Reyes, the court concluded that it was the latter event. In either case, it is clear that the present approach of using the appellate court's final judgment as the triggering event can cause great disparity in the amount of time available to a defendant to file timely a motion for new trial. This would be especially true if, as noted by the Court in Reyes, supra at 67, an appellate court stayed its mandate pending review by the Supreme Court. See also Herrera v. Collins, 506 U.S. 390, 410–412 (1993) (noting divergent treatment by States of time for filing motions for new trial).

It is the intent of the Committee to remove that element of inconsistency by using the trial court's verdict or finding of guilty as the triggering event. The change also furthers internal consistency within the rule itself; the time for filing a motion for new trial on any other ground currently runs from that same event.

Finally, the time to file a motion for new trial based upon newly discovered evidence is increased to three years to compensate for what would have otherwise resulted in less time than that currently contemplated in the rule for filing such motions.

Changes Made to Rule 33 After Publication ("GAP Report"). The Advisory Committee changed the proposed amendment to require that any motions for new trials based upon newly discovered evidence must be filed within three years, instead of two years, from the date of the verdict. The Committee also incorporated changes offered by the Style Subcommittee.

The language of Rule 33 has been amended as part of the general restyling of the Criminal Rules to make them more easily understood and to make style and terminology consistent throughout the rules. These changes are intended to be stylistic only.

Rule 33(b)(2) has been amended to remove the requirement that the court must act within seven days after a verdict or finding of guilty if it sets another time for filing a motion for a new trial. This amendment parallels similar changes to Rules 29 and 34. Further, a conforming amendment has been made to Rule 45(b)(2).

Currently, Rule 33(b)(2) requires the defendant to move for a new trial within seven days after the verdict or the finding of guilty verdict, or within some other time set by the court in an order issued during that same seven-day period. Similar provisions exist in Rules 29 and 34. Courts have held that the seven-day rule is jurisdictional. Thus, if a defendant files a request for an extension of time to file a motion for a new trial within the seven-day period, the court must rule on that motion or request within the same seven-day period. If for some reason the court does not rule on the request within the seven days, it loses jurisdiction to act on the underlying substantive motion. See, e.g., United States v. Smith, 331 U.S. 469, 473–474 (1947) (rejecting argument that trial court had power to grant new trial on its own motion after expiration of time in Rule 33); United States v. Marquez, 291 F.3d 23, 27–28 (D.C. Cir. 2002) (citing language of Rule 33, and holding that "district court forfeited the power to act when it failed to . . . fix a new time for a filing a motion for new trial [sic] within seven days of the verdict").

Assuming that the current rule was intended to promote finality, there is nothing to prevent the court from granting the defendant a significant extension of time, so long as it does so within the seven-day period. Thus, the Committee believed that the rule should be amended to be consistent with all of the other timing requirements in the rules, which do not force the court to act on a motion to extend the time for filing within a particular period of time or lose jurisdiction to do so.

Accordingly, the amendment deletes the language regarding the court's acting within seven days to set the time for filing. Read in conjunction with the conforming amendment to Rule 45(b), the defendant is still required to file a timely motion for a new trial under Rule 33(b)(2) within the seven-day period specified. The defendant may, under Rule 45, seek an extension of time to file the underlying motion as long as the defendant does so within the seven-day period. But the court itself is not required to act on that motion within any particular time. Further, under Rule 45(b)(1)(B), if for some reason the defendant fails to file the underlying motion for new trial within the specified time, the court may nonetheless consider that untimely underlying motion if the court determines that the failure to file it on time was the result of excusable neglect.

Changes Made After Publication and Comment. The Committee made no substantive changes to Rule 33 following publication.

Former Rules 29, 33, and 34 adopted 7-day periods for their respective motions. This period has been expanded to 14 days. Experience has proved that in many cases it is not possible to prepare a satisfactory motion in 7 days, even under the former rule that excluded intermediate Saturdays, Sundays, and legal holidays. This led to frequent requests for continuances, and the filing of bare bones motions that required later supplementation. The 14-day period—including intermediate Saturdays, Sundays, and legal holidays as provided by Rule 45(a)—sets a more realistic time for the filing of these motions.

Rule 34. Arresting Judgment

(a) In General. Upon the defendant's motion or on its own, the court must arrest judgment if the court does not have jurisdiction of the charged offense.

(b) Time to File. The defendant must move to arrest judgment within 14 days after the court accepts a verdict or finding of guilty, or after a plea of guilty or nolo contendere.

(As amended Feb. 28, 1966, eff. July 1, 1966; Apr. 29, 2002, eff. Dec. 1, 2002; Apr. 25, 2005, eff. Dec. 1, 2005; Mar. 26, 2009, eff. Dec. 1, 2009; Apr. 25, 2014, eff. Dec. 1, 2014.)

This rule continues existing law except that it enlarges the time for making motions in arrest of judgment from 3 days to 5 days. See Rule II (2) of Criminal Appeals Rules of 1933, 292 U.S.C. 661.

The words "on motion of a defendant" are added to make clear here, as in Rule 33, that the court may act only pursuant to a timely motion by the defendant.

The amendment to the second sentence is designed to clarify an ambiguity in the rule as originally drafted. In Lott v. United States, 367 U.S. 421 (1961) the Supreme Court held that when a defendant pleaded nolo contendere the time in which a motion could be made under this rule did not begin to run until entry of the judgment. The Court held that such a plea was not a "determination of guilty." No reason of policy appears to justify having the time for making this motion commence with the verdict or finding of guilt but not with the acceptance of the plea of nolo contendere or the plea of guilty. The amendment changes the result in the Lott case and makes the periods uniform. The amendment also changes the time in which the motion may be made to 7 days. See the Advisory Committee's Note to Rule 29.

COMMITTEE NOTES ON RULES—2002 AMENDMENT

The language of Rule 34 has been amended as part of the general restyling of the Criminal Rules to make them more easily understood and to make style and terminology consistent throughout the rules. These changes are intended to be stylistic only.

COMMITTEE NOTES ON RULES—2005 AMENDMENT

Rule 34(b) has been amended to remove the requirement that the court must act within seven days after the court accepts a verdict or finding of guilty, or after a plea of guilty or nolo contendere if it sets another time for filing a motion to arrest a judgment. The amendment parallels similar amendments to Rules 29 and 33. Further, a conforming amendment has been made to Rule 45(b).

Currently, Rule 34(b) requires the defendant to move to arrest judgment within seven days after the court accepts a verdict or finding of guilty, or after a plea of guilty or nolo contendere, or within some other time set by the court in an order issued by the court within that same seven-day period. Similar provisions exist in Rules 29 and 33. Courts have held that the seven-day rule is jurisdictional. Thus, if a defendant files a request for an extension of time to file a motion to arrest judgment within the seven-day period, the judge must rule on that motion or request within the same seven-day period. If for some reason the court does not rule on the request within the seven days, the court loses jurisdiction to act on the underlying substantive motion, if it is not filed within the seven days. See, e.g., United States v. Smith, 331 U.S. 469, 473–474 (1947) (rejecting argument that trial court had power to grant new trial on its own motion after expiration of time in Rule 33); United States v. Marquez, 291 F.3d 23, 27–28 (D.C. Cir. 2002) (citing language of Rule 33, and holding that "district court forfeited the power to act when it failed to . . . fix a new time for filing a motion for a new trial within seven days of the verdict").

Assuming that the current rule was intended to promote finality, there is nothing to prevent the court from granting the defendant a significant extension of time, so long as it does so within the seven-day period. Thus, the Committee believed that the rule should be amended to be consistent with all of the other timing requirements in the rules, which do not force the court to rule on a motion to extend the time for filing within a particular period of time or lose jurisdiction to do so.

Accordingly, the amendment deletes the language regarding the court's acting within seven days to set the time for filing. Read in conjunction with the conforming amendment to Rule 45(b), the defendant is still required to file a timely motion to arrest judgment under Rule 34 within the seven-day period specified. The defendant may, under Rule 45, seek an extension of time to file the underlying motion as long as the defendant does so within the seven-day period. But the court itself is not required to act on that motion within any particular time. Further, under Rule 45(b)(1)(B), if for some reason the defendant fails to file the underlying motion within the specified time, the court may nonetheless consider that untimely motion if the court determines that the failure to file it on time was the result of excusable neglect.

Changes Made After Publication and Comment. The Committee made no substantive changes to Rule 34 following publication.

COMMITTEE NOTES ON RULES—2009 AMENDMENT

Former Rules 29, 33, and 34 adopted 7-day periods for their respective motions. This period has been expanded to 14 days. Experience has proved that in many cases it is not possible to prepare a satisfactory motion in 7 days, even under the former rule that excluded intermediate Saturdays, Sundays, and legal holidays. This led to frequent requests for continuances, and the filing of bare bones motions that required later supplementation. The 14-day period—including intermediate Saturdays, Sundays, and legal holidays as provided by Rule 45(a)—sets a more realistic time for the filing of these motions.

COMMITTEE NOTES ON RULES—2014 AMENDMENT

Rule 34(a). This amendment conforms Rule 34 to Rule 12(b) which has been amended to remove language that the court at any time while the case is pending may hear a claim that the "indictment or information fails . . . to state an offense." The amended Rule 12 instead requires that such a defect be raised before trial.

Changes Made After Publication and Comment. No changes were made after publication and comment.

Rule 35. Correcting or Reducing a Sentence

(a) Correcting Clear Error. Within 14 days after sentencing, the court may correct a sentence that resulted from arithmetical, technical, or other clear error.
(b) Reducing a Sentence for Substantial Assistance.
(1) In General. Upon the government's motion made within one year of sentencing, the court may reduce a sentence if the defendant, after sentencing, provided substantial assistance in investigating or prosecuting another person.
(2) Later Motion. Upon the government's motion made more than one year after sentencing, the court may reduce a sentence if the defendant's substantial assistance involved:
(A) information not known to the defendant until one year or more after sentencing;
(B) information provided by the defendant to the government within one year of sentencing, but which did not become useful to the government until more than one year after sentencing; or
(C) information the usefulness of which could not reasonably have been anticipated by the defendant until more than one year after sentencing and which was promptly provided to the government after its usefulness was reasonably apparent to the defendant.

(3) Evaluating Substantial Assistance. In evaluating whether the defendant has provided substantial assistance, the court may consider the defendant's presentence assistance.
(4) Below Statutory Minimum. When acting under Rule 35(b), the court may reduce the sentence to a level below the minimum sentence established by statute.

(c) "Sentencing" Defined. As used in this rule, "sentencing" means the oral announcement of the sentence.

(As amended Feb. 28, 1966, eff. July 1, 1966; Apr. 30, 1979, eff. Aug. 1, 1979; Apr. 28, 1983, eff. Aug. 1, 1983; Pub. L. 98–473, title II, §215(b), Oct. 12, 1984, 98 Stat. 2015; Apr. 29, 1985, eff. Aug. 1, 1985; Pub. L. 99–570, title I, §1009(a), Oct. 27, 1986, 100 Stat. 3207–8; Apr. 30, 1991, eff. Dec. 1, 1991; Apr. 24, 1998, eff. Dec. 1, 1998; Apr. 29, 2002, eff. Dec. 1, 2002; Apr. 26, 2004, eff. Dec. 1, 2004; Apr. 30, 2007, eff. Dec. 1, 2007; Mar. 26, 2009, eff. Dec. 1, 2009.)

NOTES OF ADVISORY COMMITTEE ON RULES—1944

The first sentence of the rule continues existing law. The second sentence introduces a flexible time limitation on the power of the court to reduce a sentence, in lieu of the present limitation of the term of court. Rule 45(c) abolishes the expiration of a term of court as a time limitation, thereby necessitating the introduction of a specific time limitation as to all proceedings now governed by the term of court as a limitation. The Federal Rules of Civil Procedure (Rule 6(c)) [28 U.S.C., Appendix], abolishes the term of court as a time limitation in respect to civil actions. The two rules together thus do away with the significance of the expiration of a term of court which has largely become an anachronism.

NOTES OF ADVISORY COMMITTEE ON RULES—1966 AMENDMENT

The amendment to the first sentence gives the court power to correct a sentence imposed in an illegal manner within the same time limits as those provided for reducing a sentence. In Hill v. United States, 368 U.S. 424 (1962) the court held that a motion to correct an illegal sentence was not an appropriate way for a defendant to raise the question whether when he appeared for sentencing the court had afforded him an opportunity to make a statement in his own behalf as required by Rule 32(a). The amendment recognizes the distinction between an illegal sentence, which may be corrected at any time, and a sentence imposed in an illegal manner, and provides a limited time for correcting the latter.

The second sentence has been amended to increase the time within which the court may act from 60 days to 120 days. The 60-day period is frequently too short to enable the defendant to obtain and file the evidence, information and argument to support a reduction in sentence. Especially where a defendant has been committed to an institution at a distance from the sentencing court, the delays involved in institutional mail inspection procedures and the time required to contact relatives, friends and counsel may result in the 60-day period passing before the court is able to consider the case.

The other amendments to the second sentence clarify ambiguities in the timing provisions. In those cases in which the mandate of the court of appeals is issued prior to action by the Supreme Court on the defendant's petition for certiorari, the rule created problems in three situations: (1) If the writ were denied, the last phrase of the rule left obscure the point at which the period began to run because orders of the Supreme Court denying applications for writs are not sent to the district courts. See Johnson v. United States, 235 F.2d 459 (5th Cir. 1956). (2) If the writ were granted but later dismissed as improvidently granted, the rule did not provide any time period for reduction of sentence. (3) If the writ were granted and later the Court affirmed a judgment of the court of appeals which had affirmed the conviction, the rule did not provide any time period for reduction of sentence. The amendment makes it clear that in each of these three situations the 120-period commences to run with the entry of the order or judgment of the Supreme Court.

The third sentence has been added to make it clear that the time limitation imposed by Rule 35 upon the reduction of a sentence does not apply to such reduction upon the revocation of probation as authorized by 18 U.S.C. §3653.

NOTES OF ADVISORY COMMITTEE ON RULES—1979 AMENDMENT

Rule 35 is amended in order to make it clear that a judge may, in his discretion, reduce a sentence of incarceration to probation. To the extent that this permits the judge to grant probation to a defendant who has already commenced service of a term of imprisonment, it represents a change in the law. See United States v. Murray, 275 U.S. 347 (1928) (Probation Act construed not to give power to district court to grant probation to convict after beginning of service of sentence, even in the same term of court); Affronti v. United States, 350 U.S. 79 (1955) (Probation Act construed to mean that after a sentence of consecutive terms on multiple counts of an indictment has been imposed and service of sentence for the first such term has commenced, the district court may not suspend sentence and grant probation as to the remaining term or terms). In construing the statute in Murray and Affronti, the Court concluded Congress could not have intended to make the probation provisions applicable during the entire period of incarceration (the only other conceivable interpretation of the statute), for this would result in undue duplication of the three methods of mitigating a sentence—probation, pardon and parole—and would impose upon district judges the added burden of responding to probation applications from prisoners throughout the service of their terms of imprisonment. Those concerns do not apply to the instant provisions, for the reduction may occur only within the time specified in subdivision (b). This change gives "meaningful effect" to the motion-to-reduce remedy by allowing the court "to consider all alternatives that were available at the time of imposition of the original sentence." United States v. Golphin, 362 F.Supp. 698 (W.D.Pa. 1973).

Should the reduction to a sentence of probation occur after the defendant has been incarcerated more than six months, this would put into issue the applicability of 18 U.S.C. §3651, which provides that initially the court "may impose a sentence in excess of six months and provide that the defendant be confined in a jail-type institution for a period not exceeding six months and that the execution of the remainder of the sentence be suspended and the defendant placed on probation for such period and upon such terms and conditions as the court deems best."

NOTES OF ADVISORY COMMITTEE ON RULES—1983 AMENDMENT

Note to Subdivision (b). There is currently a split of authority on the question of whether a court may reduce a sentence within 120 days after revocation of probation when the sentence was imposed earlier but execution of the sentence had in the interim been suspended in part or in its entirety. Compare United States v. Colvin, 644 F.2d 703 (8th Cir. 1981) (yes); United States v. Johnson, 634 F.2d 94 (3d Cir. 1980) (yes); with United States v. Rice, 671 F.2d 455 (11th Cir. 1982) (no); United States v. Kahane, 527 F.2d 491 (2d Cir. 1975) (no). The Advisory Committee believes that the rule should be clarified in light of this split, and has concluded that as a policy matter the result reached in Johnson is preferable.

The Supreme Court declared in Korematsu v. United States, 319 U.S. 432, 435 (1943), that "the difference to the probationer between imposition of sentence followed by probation . . . and suspension of the imposition of sentence [followed by probation]" is not a meaningful one. When imposition of sentence is suspended entirely at the time a defendant is placed on probation, that defendant has 120 days after revocation of probation and imposition of sentence to petition for leniency. The amendment to subdivision (b) makes it clear that similar treatment is to be afforded probationers for whom execution, rather than imposition, of sentence was originally suspended.

The change facilitates the underlying objective of rule 35, which is to "give every convicted defendant a second round before the sentencing judge, and [afford] the judge an opportunity to reconsider the sentence in the light of any further information about the defendant or the case which may have been presented to him in the interim." United States v. Ellenbogan, 390 F.2d 537, 543 (2d Cir. 1968). It is only technically correct that a reduction may be sought when a suspended sentence is imposed. As noted in Johnson, supra, at 96:

It frequently will be unrealistic for a defendant whose sentence has just been suspended to petition the court for the further relief of a reduction of that suspended sentence.

Just as significant, we doubt that sentencing judges would be very receptive to Rule 35 motions proffered at the time the execution of a term of imprisonment is suspended in whole or in part and the defendant given a term of probation. Moreover, the sentencing judge cannot know of events that might occur later and that might bear on what would constitute an appropriate term of imprisonment should the defendant violate his probation. . . . In particular, it is only with the revocation hearing that the judge is in a position to consider whether a sentence originally suspended pending probation should be reduced. The revocation hearing is thus the first point at which an offender can be afforded a realistic opportunity to plead for a light sentence. If the offender is to be provided two chances with the sentencing judge, to be meaningful this second sentence must occur subsequent to the revocation hearing.

NOTES OF ADVISORY COMMITTEE ON RULES—1985 AMENDMENT

Note to Subdivision (b). This amendment to Rule 35(b) conforms its language to the nonliteral interpretation which most courts have already placed upon the rule, namely, that it suffices that the defendant's motion was made within the 120 days and that the court determines the motion within a reasonable time thereafter. United States v. DeMier, 671 F.2d 1200 (8th Cir. 1982); United States v. Smith, 650 F.2d 206 (9th Cir. 1981); United States v. Johnson, 634 F.2d 94 (3d Cir. 1980); United States v. Mendoza, 581 F.2d 89 (5th Cir. 1978); United States V. Stollings, 516 F.2d 1287 (4th Cir. 1975). Despite these decisions, a change in the language is deemed desirable to remove any doubt which might arise from dictum in some cases, e.g., United States v. Addonizio, 442 U.S. 178, 189 (1979), that Rule 35 only "authorizes District Courts to reduce a sentence within 120 days" and that this time period "is jurisdictional, and may not be extended." See United States v. Kajevic, 711 F.2d 767 (7th Cir. 1983), following the Addonizio dictum.

As for the "reasonable time" limitation, reasonableness in this context "must be evaluated in light of the policies supporting the time limitations and the reasons for the delay in each case." United States v. Smith, supra, at 209. The time runs "at least for so long as the judge reasonably needs time to consider and act upon the motion." United States v. Stollings, supra, at 1288.

In some instances the court may decide to reduce a sentence even though no motion seeking such action is before the court. When that is the case, the amendment makes clear, the reduction must actually occur within the time specified.

This amendment does not preclude the filing of a motion by a defendant for further reduction of sentence after the court has reduced a sentence on its own motion, if filed within the 120 days specified in this rule.

NOTES OF ADVISORY COMMITTEE ON RULES——1991 AMENDMENT

Rule 35(b), as amended in 1987 as part of the Sentencing Reform Act of 1984, reflects a method by which the government may obtain valuable assistance from defendants in return for an agreement to file a motion to reduce the sentence, even if the reduction would reduce the sentence below the mandatory minimum sentence.

The title of subsection (b) has been amended to reflect that there is a difference between correcting an illegal or improper sentence, as in subsection (a), and reducing an otherwise legal sentence for special reasons under subsection (b).

Under the 1987 amendment, the trial court was required to rule on the government's motion to reduce a defendant's sentence within one year after imposition of the sentence. This caused problems, however, in situations where the defendant's assistance could not be fully assessed in time to make a timely motion which could be ruled upon before one year had elapsed. The amendment requires the government to make its motion to reduce the sentence before one year has elapsed but does not require the court to rule on the motion within the one year limit. This change should benefit both the government and the defendant and will permit completion of the defendant's anticipated cooperation with the government. Although no specific time limit is set on the court's ruling on the motion to reduce the sentence, the burden nonetheless rests on the government to request and justify a delay in the court's ruling.

The amendment also recognizes that there may be those cases where the defendant's assistance or cooperation may not occur until after one year has elapsed. For example, the defendant may not have obtained information useful to the government until after the time limit had passed. In those instances the trial court in its discretion may consider what would otherwise be an untimely motion if the government establishes that the cooperation could not have been furnished within the one-year time limit. In deciding whether to consider an untimely motion, the court may, for example, consider whether the assistance was provided as early as possible.

Subdivision (c) is intended to adopt, in part, a suggestion from the Federal Courts Study Committee 1990 that Rule 35 be amended to recognize explicitly the ability of the sentencing court to correct a sentence imposed as a result of an obvious arithmetical, technical or other clear error, if the error is discovered shortly after the sentence is imposed. At least two courts of appeals have held that the trial court has the inherent authority, notwithstanding the repeal of former Rule 35(a) by the Sentencing Reform Act of 1984, to correct a sentence within the time allowed for sentence appeal by any party under 18 U.S.C. 3742. See United States v. Cook, 890 F.2d 672 (4th Cir. 1989) (error in applying sentencing guidelines); United States v. Rico, 902 F.2d 1065 (2nd Cir. 1990) (failure to impose prison sentence required by terms of plea agreement). The amendment in effect codifies the result in those two cases but provides a more stringent time requirement. The Committee believed that the time for correcting such errors should be narrowed within the time for appealing the sentence to reduce the likelihood of jurisdictional questions in the event of an appeal and to provide the parties with an opportunity to address the court's correction of the sentence, or lack thereof, in any appeal of the sentence. A shorter period of time would also reduce the likelihood of abuse of the rule by limiting its application to acknowledged and obvious errors in sentencing.

The authority to correct a sentence under this subdivision is intended to be very narrow and to extend only to those cases in which an obvious error or mistake has occurred in the sentence, that is, errors which would almost certainly result in a remand of the case to the trial court for further action under Rule 35(a). The subdivision is not intended to afford the court the opportunity to reconsider the application or interpretation of the sentencing guidelines or for the court simply to change its mind about the appropriateness of the sentence. Nor should it be used to reopen issues previously resolved at the sentencing hearing through the exercise of the court's discretion with regard to the application of the sentencing guidelines. Furthermore, the Committee did not intend that the rule relax any requirement that the parties state all objections to a sentence at or before the sentencing hearing. See, e.g., United States v. Jones, 899 F.2d 1097 (11th Cir. 1990).

The subdivision does not provide for any formalized method of bringing the error to the attention of the court and recognizes that the court could sua sponte make the correction. Although the amendment does not expressly address the issue of advance notice to the parties or whether the defendant should be present in court for resentencing, the Committee contemplates that the court will act in accordance with Rules 32 and 43 with regard to any corrections in the sentence. Compare United States v. Cook, supra (court erred in correcting sentence sua sponte in absence of defendant) with United States v. Rico, supra (court heard arguments on request by government to correct sentence). The Committee contemplates that the court would enter an order correcting the sentence and that such order must be entered within the seven (7) day period so that the appellate process (if a timely appeal is taken) may proceed without delay and without jurisdictional confusion.

Rule 35(c) provides an efficient and prompt method for correcting obvious technical errors that are called to the court's attention immediately after sentencing. But the addition of this subdivision is not intended to preclude a defendant from obtaining statutory relief from a plainly illegal sentence. The Committee's assumption is that a defendant detained pursuant to such a sentence could seek relief under 28 U.S.C. §2255 if the seven day period provided in Rule 35(c) has elapsed. Rule 35(c) and §2255 should thus provide sufficient authority for a district court to correct obvious sentencing errors.

The Committee considered, but rejected, a proposal from the Federal Courts Study Committee to permit modification of a sentence, within 120 days of sentencing, based upon new factual information not known to the defendant at the time of sentencing. Unlike the proposed subdivision (c) which addresses obvious technical mistakes, the ability of the defendant (and perhaps the government) to come forward with new evidence would be a significant step toward returning Rule 35 to its former state. The Committee believed that such a change would inject into Rule 35 a degree of postsentencing discretion which would raise doubts about the finality of determinate sentencing that Congress attempted to resolve by eliminating former Rule 35(a). It would also tend to confuse the jurisdiction of the courts of appeals in those cases in which a timely appeal is taken with respect to the sentence. Finally, the Committee was not persuaded by the available evidence that a problem of sufficient magnitude existed at this time which would warrant such an amendment.

COMMITTEE NOTES ON RULES——1998 AMENDMENT

The amendment to Rule 35(b) is intended to fill a gap in current practice. Under the Sentencing Reform Act and the applicable guidelines, a defendant who has provided "substantial" assistance to the Government before sentencing may receive a reduced sentence under United States Sentencing Guideline §5K1.1. In addition, a defendant who provides substantial assistance after the sentence has been imposed may receive a reduction of the sentence if the Government files a motion under Rule 35(b). In theory, a defendant who has provided substantial assistance both before and after sentencing could benefit from both §5K1.1 and Rule 35(b). But a defendant who has provided, on the whole, substantial assistance may not be able to benefit from either provision because each provision requires "substantial assistance." As one court has noted, those two provisions contain distinct "temporal boundaries." United States v. Drown, 942 F.2d 55, 59 (1st Cir. 1991).

Although several decisions suggest that a court may aggregate the defendant's pre-sentencing and post-sentencing assistance in determining whether the "substantial assistance" requirement of Rule 35(b) has been met, United States v. Speed, 53 F.3d 643, 647—649 (4th Cir. 1995) (Ellis, J. concurring), there is no formal mechanism for doing so. The amendment to Rule 35(b) is designed to fill that need. Thus, the amendment permits the court to consider, in determining the substantiality of post-sentencing assistance, the defendant's pre-sentencing assistance, irrespective of whether that assistance, standing alone, was substantial.

The amendment, however, is not intended to provide a double benefit to the defendant. Thus, if the defendant has already received a reduction of sentence under U.S.S.G. §5K1.1 for substantial pre-sentencing assistance, he or she may not have that assistance counted again in a post-sentence Rule 35(b) motion.

Changes Made After Publication ("GAP Report"). The Committee incorporated the Style Subcommittee's suggested changes.

127

The language of Rule 35 has been amended as part of the general restyling of the Criminal Rules to make them more easily understood and to make style and terminology consistent throughout the rules. These changes are intended to be stylistic only, except as noted below.

The Committee deleted current Rule 35(a) (Correction on Remand). Congress added that rule, which currently addresses the issue of the district court's actions following a remand on the issue of sentencing, in the Sentencing Reform Act of 1984. Pub. L. No. 98–473. The rule cross-references 18 U.S.C. §3742, also enacted in 1984, which provides detailed guidance on the various options available to the appellate courts in addressing sentencing errors. In reviewing both provisions, the Committee concluded that Rule 35(a) was no longer needed. First, the statute clearly covers the subject matter and second, it is not necessary to address an issue that would be very clear to a district court following a decision by a court of appeals.

Former Rule 35(c), which addressed the authority of the court to correct certain errors in the sentence, is now located in Rule 35(a). In the current version of Rule 35(c), the sentencing court is authorized to correct errors in the sentence if the correction is made within seven days of the imposition of the sentence. The revised rule uses the term "sentencing." No change in practice is intended by using that term.

A substantive change has been made in revised Rule 35(b). Under current Rule 35(b), if the government believes that a sentenced defendant has provided substantial assistance in investigating or prosecuting another person, it may move the court to reduce the original sentence; ordinarily, the motion must be filed within one year of sentencing. In 1991, the rule was amended to permit the government to file such motions after more than one year had elapsed if the government could show that the defendant's substantial assistance involved "information or evidence not known by the defendant" until more than one year had elapsed. The current rule, however, did not address the question whether a motion to reduce a sentence could be filed and granted in those instances when the defendant's substantial assistance involved information provided by the defendant within one year of sentence but that did not become useful to the government until more than one year after sentencing (e.g., when the government starts an investigation to which the information is pertinent). The courts were split on the issue. Compare United States v. Morales, 52 F.3d 7 (1st Cir. 1995) (permitting filing and granting of motion) with United States v. Orozco, 160 F.3d 1309 (11th Cir. 1998) (denying relief and citing cases). Although the court in Orozco felt constrained to deny relief under Rule 35(b), the court urged an amendment of the rule to:

address the apparent unforeseen situation presented in this case where a convicted defendant provides information to the government prior to the expiration of the jurisdictional, one-year period from sentence imposition, but that information does not become useful to the government until more than one year after sentence imposition. Id. at 1316, n. 13.

Nor does the existing rule appear to allow a substantial assistance motion under equally deserving circumstances where a defendant, who fails to provide information within one year of sentencing because its usefulness could not reasonably have been anticipated, later provides the information to the government promptly upon its usefulness becoming apparent.

Revised Rule 35(b) is intended to address both of those situations. First, Rule 35(b)(2)(B) makes clear that a sentence reduction motion is permitted in those instances identified by the court in Orozco. Second, Rule 35(b)(2)(C) recognizes that a post-sentence motion is also appropriate in those instances where the defendant did not provide any information within one year of sentencing, because its usefulness was not reasonably apparent to the defendant during that period. But the rule requires that once the defendant realizes the importance of the information the defendant promptly provide the information to the government. What constitutes "prompt" notification will depend on the circumstances of the case.

The rule's one-year restriction generally serves the important interests of finality and of creating an incentive for defendants to provide promptly what useful information they might have. Thus, the proposed amendment would not eliminate the one-year requirement as a generally operative element. But where the usefulness of the information is not reasonably apparent until a year or more after sentencing, no sound purpose is served by the current rule's removal of any incentive to provide that information to the government one year or more after the sentence (or if previously provided, for the government to seek to reward the defendant) when its relevance and substantiality become evident.

By using the term "involves" in Rule 35(b)(2) in describing the sort of information that may result in substantial assistance, the Committee recognizes that a court does not lose jurisdiction to consider a Rule 35(b)(2) motion simply because other information, not covered by any of the three provisions in Rule 35(b)(2), is presented in the motion.

Rule 35(c) is a new provision, which defines sentencing for purposes of Rule 35 as the oral announcement of the sentence.

Originally, the language in Rule 35 had used the term "imposition of sentence." The term "imposition of sentence" was not defined in the rule and the courts addressing the meaning of the term were split. The majority view was that the term meant the oral announcement of the sentence and the minority view was that it meant the entry of the judgment. See United States v. Aguirre, 214 F.3d 1122, 1124–25 (9th Cir. 2000) (discussion of original Rule 35(c) and citing cases). During the restyling of all of the Criminal Rules in 2000 and 2001, the Committee determined that the uniform term "sentencing" throughout the entire rule was the more appropriate term. After further reflection, and with the recognition that some ambiguity may still be present in using the term "sentencing," the Committee believes that the better approach is to make clear in the rule itself that the term "sentencing" in Rule 35 means the oral announcement of the sentence. That is the meaning recognized in the majority of the cases addressing the issue.

Changes Made to Rule 35 After Publication and Comment. The Committee changed the definition of the triggering event for the timing requirements in Rule 35 to conform to the majority view in the circuit courts and adopted a special definitional section, Rule 35(c), to define sentencing as the "oral announcement of the sentence."

Subdivision (b)(1). The amendment conforms Rule 35(b)(1) to the Supreme Court's decision in United States v. Booker, 543 U.S. 220 (2005). In Booker the Court held that the provision of the federal sentencing statute that makes the Guidelines mandatory, 18 U.S.C. §3553(b)(1), violates the Sixth Amendment right to jury trial. With this provision severed and excised, the Court held, the Sentencing Reform Act "makes the Guidelines effectively advisory," and "requires a sentencing court to consider Guidelines ranges, see 18 U.S.C.A. §3553(a)(4) (Supp. 2004), but it permits the court to tailor the sentence in light of other statutory concerns as well, see §3553(a) (Supp. 2004)." Id. at 245–46. Subdivision (b)(1)(B) has been deleted because it treats the guidelines as mandatory.

Changes Made to Proposed Amendment Released for Public Comment. No changes were made to the text of the proposed amendment as released for public comment, but one change was made in the Committee Note. Here—as in the other Booker rules—the Committee deleted the reference to the Fifth Amendment from the description of the Supreme Court's decision in Booker.

Former Rule 35 permitted the correction of arithmetic, technical, or clear errors within 7 days of sentencing. In light of the increased complexity of the sentencing process, the Committee concluded it would be beneficial to expand this period to 14 days, including intermediate Saturdays, Sundays, and legal holidays as provided by Rule 45(a). Extension of the period in this fashion will cause no jurisdictional problems if an appeal has been filed, because Federal Rule of Appellate Procedure 4(b)(5) expressly provides that the filing of a notice of appeal does not divest the district court of jurisdiction to correct a sentence under Rule 35(a).

1986—Subd. (b). Pub. L. 99–570 substituted "in accordance with the guidelines and policy statements issued by the Sentencing Commission pursuant to section 994 of title 28, United States Code. The court's authority to lower a sentence under this subdivision includes the authority to lower such sentence to a level below that established by statute as a minimum sentence" for "to the extent that such assistance is a factor in applicable guidelines or policy statements issued by the Sentencing Commission pursuant to 28 U.S.C. 994(a)".

1984—Pub. L. 98–473 amended Rule 35 generally. Prior to amendment, rule read as follows:

"RULE 35. CORRECTION OR REDUCTION OF SENTENCE

"(a) Correction of Sentence. The court may correct an illegal sentence at any time and may correct a sentence imposed in an illegal manner within the time provided herein for the reduction of sentence.

"(b) Reduction of Sentence. A motion to reduce a sentence may be made, or the court may reduce a sentence without motion, within 120 days after the sentence is imposed or probation is revoked, or within 120 days after receipt by the court of a mandate issued upon affirmance of the judgment or dismissal of the appeal, or within 120 days after entry of any order or judgment of the Supreme Court denying review of, or having the effect of upholding, a judgment of conviction or probation revocation. The court shall determine the motion within a reasonable time. Changing a sentence from a sentence of incarceration to a grant of probation shall constitute a permissible reduction of sentence under this subdivision."

EFFECTIVE DATE OF 1986 AMENDMENT

Pub. L. 99–570, title I, §1009(b), Oct. 27, 1986, 100 Stat. 3207–8, provided that: "The amendment made by this section [amending this rule] shall take effect on the date of the taking effect of rule 35(b) of the Federal Rules of Criminal Procedure, as amended by section 215(b) of the Comprehensive Crime Control Act of 1984 [section 215(b) of Pub. L. 98–473, effective Nov. 1, 1987]."

EFFECTIVE AND TERMINATION DATES OF 1985 AMENDMENTS

Section 2 of the Order of the Supreme Court dated Apr. 29, 1985, provided: "That the foregoing amendments to the Federal Rules of Criminal Procedure [amending Rules 6, 11, 12.1, 12.2, 35, 45, 49, and 57] shall take effect on August 1, 1985 and shall govern all proceedings in criminal cases thereafter commenced and, insofar as just and practicable, all proceedings in criminal cases then pending. The amendment to Rule 35(b) shall be effective until November 1, 1986, when Section 215(b) of the Comprehensive Crime Control Act of 1984, Pub. L. 98–473, approved October 12, 1984, 98 Stat. 2015, goes into effect." See section 22 of Pub. L. 100–182, set out below, for application of Rule 35(b) to conduct occurring before effective date of sentencing guidelines.

Pub. L. 98–473, title II, §235(a)(1), Oct. 12, 1984, 98 Stat. 2031, which originally provided for an effective date of Nov. 1, 1986 for the amendment to Rule 35 by section 215(b) of Pub. L. 98–473, was later amended to provide for an effective date of Nov. 1, 1987, with applicability only to offenses committed after the taking effect of such amendment. See Effective Date note set out under section 3551 of this title.

EFFECTIVE DATE OF 1984 AMENDMENT

Amendment by Pub. L. 98–473 effective Nov. 1, 1987, and applicable only to offenses committed after the taking effect of such amendment, see section 235(a)(1) of Pub. L. 98–473, set out as an Effective Date note under section 3551 of this title.

APPLICATION OF RULE 35(B) TO CONDUCT OCCURRING BEFORE EFFECTIVE DATE OF SENTENCING GUIDELINES

Pub. L. 100–182, §22, Dec. 7, 1987, 101 Stat. 1271, provided that: "The amendment to rule 35(b) of the Federal Rules of Criminal Procedure made by the order of the Supreme Court on April 29, 1985, shall apply with respect to all offenses committed before the taking effect of section 215(b) of the Comprehensive Crime Control Act of 1984 [section 215(b) of Pub. L. 98–473, effective Nov. 1, 1987]."

AUTHORITY TO LOWER A SENTENCE BELOW STATUTORY MINIMUM FOR OLD OFFENSES

Subd. (b) of this rule as amended by section 215(b) of Pub. L. 98–473 and subd. (b) of this rule as in effect before the taking effect of the initial set of guidelines promulgated by the United States Sentencing Commission pursuant to chapter 58 (§991 et seq.) of Title 28, Judiciary and Judicial Procedure, applicable in the case of an offense committed before the taking effect of such guidelines notwithstanding section 235 of Pub. L. 98–473, see section 24 of Pub. L. 100–182, set out as a note under section 3553 of this title.

Rule 36. Clerical Error

After giving any notice it considers appropriate, the court may at any time correct a clerical error in a judgment, order, or other part of the record, or correct an error in the record arising from oversight or omission.

(As amended Apr. 29, 2002, eff. Dec. 1, 2002.)

NOTES OF ADVISORY COMMITTEE ON RULES—1944

This rule continues existing law. Rupinski v. United States, 4 F.2d 17 (C.C.A. 6th). The rule is similar to Rule 60(a) of the Federal Rules of Civil Procedure [28 U.S.C., Appendix].

COMMITTEE NOTES ON RULES—2002 AMENDMENT

The language of Rule 36 has been amended as part of the general restyling of the Criminal Rules to make them more easily understood and to make style and terminology consistent throughout the rules. These changes are intended to be stylistic only.

Rule 37. Indicative Ruling on a Motion for Relief That Is Barred by a Pending Appeal

(a) Relief Pending Appeal. If a timely motion is made for relief that the court lacks authority to grant because of an appeal that has been docketed and is pending, the court may:
(1) defer considering the motion;
(2) deny the motion; or
(3) state either that it would grant the motion if the court of appeals remands for that purpose or that the motion raises a substantial issue.

(b) Notice to the Court of Appeals. The movant must promptly notify the circuit clerk under Federal Rule of Appellate Procedure 12.1 if the district court states that it would grant the motion or that the motion raises a substantial issue.
(c) Remand. The district court may decide the motion if the court of appeals remands for that purpose.

(Added Apr. 23, 2012, eff. Dec. 1, 2012.)

COMMITTEE NOTES ON RULES—2012

This new rule adopts for any motion that the district court cannot grant because of a pending appeal the practice that most courts follow when a party makes a motion under Rule 60(b) of the Federal Rules of Civil Procedure to vacate a judgment that is pending on appeal. After an appeal has been docketed and while it remains pending, the district court cannot grant a Rule 60(b) motion without a remand. But it can entertain the motion and deny it, defer consideration, or state that it would grant the motion if the court of appeals remands for that purpose or state that the motion raises a substantial issue. Experienced lawyers often refer to the suggestion for remand as an "indicative ruling." (Federal Rule of Appellate Procedure 4(b)(3) lists three motions that, if filed within the relevant time limit, suspend the effect of a notice of appeal filed before or after the motion is filed until the judgment of conviction is entered and the last such motion is ruled upon. The district court has authority to grant the motion without resorting to the indicative ruling procedure.)

The procedure formalized by Federal Rule of Appellate Procedure 12.1 is helpful when relief is sought from an order that the court cannot reconsider because the order is the subject of a pending appeal. In the criminal context, the Committee anticipates that Criminal Rule 37 will be used primarily if not exclusively for newly discovered evidence motions under Criminal Rule 33(b)(1) (see United States v. Cronic, 466 U.S. 648, 667 n.42 (1984)), reduced sentence motions under Criminal Rule 35(b), and motions under 18 U.S.C. §3582(c). Rule 37 does not attempt to define the circumstances in which an appeal limits or defeats the district court's authority to act in the face of a pending appeal. The rules that govern the relationship between trial courts and appellate courts may be complex, depending in part on the nature of the order and the source of appellate jurisdiction. Rule 37 applies only when those rules deprive the district court of authority to grant relief without appellate permission. If the district court concludes that it has authority to grant relief without appellate permission, it can act without falling back on the indicative ruling procedure.

To ensure proper coordination of proceedings in the district court and in the appellate court, the movant must notify the circuit clerk under Federal Rule of Appellate Procedure 12.1 if the district court states that it would grant the motion or that the motion raises a substantial issue. Remand is in the court of appeals' discretion under Federal Rule of Appellate Procedure 12.1.

Often it will be wise for the district court to determine whether it in fact would grant the motion if the court of appeals remands for that purpose. But a motion may present complex issues that require extensive litigation and that may either be mooted or be presented in a different context by decision of the issues raised on appeal. In such circumstances the district court may prefer to state that the motion raises a substantial issue, and to state the reasons why it prefers to decide only if the court of appeals agrees that it would be useful to decide the motion before decision of the pending appeal. The district court is not bound to grant the motion after stating that the motion raises a substantial issue; further proceedings on remand may show that the motion ought not be granted.

Changes Made to Proposed Amendment Released for Public Comment. No changes were made in the amendment as published.

Rule 38. Staying a Sentence or a Disability

(a) Death Sentence. The court must stay a death sentence if the defendant appeals the conviction or sentence.

(b) Imprisonment.

(1) Stay Granted. If the defendant is released pending appeal, the court must stay a sentence of imprisonment.

(2) Stay Denied; Place of Confinement. If the defendant is not released pending appeal, the court may recommend to the Attorney General that the defendant be confined near the place of the trial or appeal for a period reasonably necessary to permit the defendant to assist in preparing the appeal.

(c) Fine. If the defendant appeals, the district court, or the court of appeals under Federal Rule of Appellate Procedure 8, may stay a sentence to pay a fine or a fine and costs. The court may stay the sentence on any terms considered appropriate and may require the defendant to:

(1) deposit all or part of the fine and costs into the district court's registry pending appeal;

(2) post a bond to pay the fine and costs; or

(3) submit to an examination concerning the defendant's assets and, if appropriate, order the defendant to refrain from dissipating assets.

(d) Probation. If the defendant appeals, the court may stay a sentence of probation. The court must set the terms of any stay.

(e) Restitution and Notice to Victims.

(1) In General. If the defendant appeals, the district court, or the court of appeals under Federal Rule of Appellate Procedure 8, may stay—on any terms considered appropriate—any sentence providing for restitution under 18 U.S.C. §3556 or notice under 18 U.S.C. §3555.

(2) Ensuring Compliance. The court may issue any order reasonably necessary to ensure compliance with a restitution order or a notice order after disposition of an appeal, including:

(A) a restraining order;

(B) an injunction;

(C) an order requiring the defendant to deposit all or part of any monetary restitution into the district court's registry; or

(D) an order requiring the defendant to post a bond.

(f) Forfeiture. A stay of a forfeiture order is governed by Rule 32.2(d).

(g) Disability. If the defendant's conviction or sentence creates a civil or employment disability under federal law, the district court, or the court of appeals under Federal Rule of Appellate Procedure 8, may stay the disability pending appeal on any terms considered appropriate. The court may issue any order reasonably necessary to protect the interest represented by the disability pending appeal, including a restraining order or an injunction.

(As amended Dec. 27, 1948, eff. Jan. 1, 1949; Feb. 28, 1966, eff. July 1, 1966; Dec. 4, 1967, eff. July 1, 1968; Apr. 24, 1972, eff. Oct. 1, 1972; Pub. L. 98–473, title II, §215(c), Oct. 12, 1984, 98 Stat. 2016; Mar. 9, 1987, eff. Aug. 1, 1987; Apr. 17, 2000, eff. Dec. 1, 2000; Apr. 29, 2002, eff. Dec. 1, 2002.)

NOTES OF ADVISORY COMMITTEE ON RULES—1944

This rule substantially continues existing law except that it provides that in case an appeal is taken from a judgment imposing a sentence of imprisonment, a stay shall be granted only if the defendant so elects, or is admitted to bail. Under the present rule the sentence is automatically stayed unless the defendant elects to commence service of the sentence pending appeal. The new rule merely changes the burden of making the election. See Rule V of the Criminal Appeals Rules, 1933, 292 U.S. 661.

NOTES OF ADVISORY COMMITTEE ON RULES—1966 AMENDMENT

A defendant sentenced to a term of imprisonment is committed to the custody of the Attorney General who is empowered by statute to designate the place of his confinement. 18 U.S.C. §4082. The sentencing court has no authority to designate the place of imprisonment. See, e.g., Hogue v. United States, 287 F.2d 99 (5th Cir. 1961), cert. den., 368 U.S. 932 (1961).

When the place of imprisonment has been designated, and notwithstanding the pendency of an appeal, the defendant is usually transferred from the place of his temporary detention within the district of his conviction unless he has elected "not to commence service of the sentence." This transfer can be avoided only if the defendant makes the election, a course sometimes advised by counsel who may deem it necessary to consult with the defendant from time to time before the appeal is finally perfected. However, the election deprives the defendant of a right to claim credit for the time spent in jail pending the disposition of the appeal because 18 U.S.C. §3568 provides that the sentence of imprisonment commences, to run only from "the date on which such person is received at the penitentiary, reformatory, or jail for service of said sentence." See, e.g., Shelton v. United States, 234 F.2d 132 (5th Cir. 1956).

The amendment eliminates the procedure for election not to commence service of sentence. In lieu thereof it is provided that the court may recommend to the Attorney General that the defendant be retained at or transferred to a place of confinement near the place of trial or the place where the appeal is to be heard for the period reasonably necessary to permit the defendant to assist in the preparation of his appeal to the court of appeals. Under this procedure the defendant would no longer be required to serve dead time in a local jail in order to assist in preparation of his appeal.

NOTES OF ADVISORY COMMITTEE ON RULES—1968 AMENDMENT

Subdivisions (b) and (c) of this rule relate to appeals, the provisions of which are transferred to and covered by the Federal Rules of Appellate Procedure. See Advisory Committee Note under rule 37.

NOTES OF ADVISORY COMMITTEE ON RULES—1972 AMENDMENT

Rule 38(a)(2) is amended to reflect rule 9(b), Federal Rules of Appellate Procedure. The criteria for the stay of a sentence of imprisonment pending disposition of an appeal are those specified in rule 9(c) which incorporates 18 U.S.C. §3148 by reference.

The last sentence of subdivision (a)(2) is retained although easy access to the defendant has become less important with the passage of the Criminal Justice Act which provides for compensation to the attorney to travel to the place at which the defendant is confined. Whether the court will recommend confinement near the place of trial or place where the appeal is to be heard will depend upon a balancing of convenience against the possible advantage of confinement at a more remote correctional institution where facilities and program may be more adequate.

The amendment to subdivision (a)(4) gives the court discretion in deciding whether to stay the order placing the defendant on probation. It also makes mandatory the fixing of conditions for the stay if a stay is granted. The court cannot release the defendant pending appeal without either placing him on probation or fixing the conditions for the stay under the Bail Reform Act, 18 U.S.C. §3148.

Former rule 38(a)(4) makes mandatory a stay of an order placing the defendant on probation whenever an appeal is noted. The court may or may not impose conditions upon the stay. See rule 46, Federal Rules of Criminal Procedure; and the Bail Reform Act, 18 U.S.C. §3148.

Having the defendant on probation during the period of appeal may serve the objectives of both community protection and defendant rehabilitation. In current practice, the order of probation is sometimes stayed for an appeal period as long as two years. In a situation where the appeal is unsuccessful, the defendant must start under probation supervision after so long a time that the conditions of probation imposed at the time of initial sentencing may no longer appropriately relate either to the defendant's need for rehabilitation or to the community's need for protection. The purposes of probation are more likely to be served if the judge can exercise discretion, in appropriate cases, to require the defendant to be under probation during the period of appeal. The American Bar Association Project on Standards for Criminal Justice takes the position that prompt imposition of sentence aids in the rehabilitation of defendants, ABA Standards Relating to Pleas of Guilty §1.8(a)(i), Commentary p. 40 (Approved Draft, 1968). See also Sutherland and Cressey, Principles of Criminology 336 (1966).

Under 18 U.S.C. §3148 the court now has discretion to impose conditions of release which are necessary to protect the community against danger from the defendant. This is in contrast to release prior to conviction, where the only appropriate criterion is insuring the appearance of the defendant. 18 U.S.C. §3146. Because the court may impose conditions of release to insure community protection, it seems appropriate to enable the court to do so by ordering the defendant to submit to probation supervision during the period of appeal, thus giving the probation service responsibility for supervision.

A major difference between probation and release under 18 U.S.C. §3148 exists if the defendant violates the conditions imposed upon his release. In the event that release is under 18 U.S.C. §3148, the violation of the condition may result in his being placed in custody pending the decision on appeal. If the appeal were unsuccessful, the order placing him on probation presumably would become effective at that time, and he would then be released under probation supervision. If the defendant were placed on probation, his violation of a condition could result in the imposition of a jail or prison sentence. If the appeal were unsuccessful, the jail or prison sentence would continue to be served.

NOTES OF ADVISORY COMMITTEE ON RULES—1987 AMENDMENT

The amendments are technical. No substantive change is intended.

COMMITTEE NOTES ON RULES—2000 AMENDMENT

The rule is amended to reflect the creation of new Rule 32.2 which now governs criminal forfeiture procedures.

GAP Report—Rule 38. The Committee made no changes to the published draft.

COMMITTEE NOTES ON RULES—2002 AMENDMENT

The language of Rule 38 has been amended as part of the general restyling of the Criminal Rules to make them more easily understood and to make style and terminology consistent throughout the rules. These changes are intended to be stylistic only.

The reference to Appellate Rule 9(b) is deleted. The Committee believed that the reference was unnecessary and its deletion was not intended to be substantive in nature.

REFERENCES IN TEXT

The Federal Rules of Appellate Procedure, referred to in subds. (c), (e)(1), and (g), are set out in the Appendix to Title 28, Judiciary and Judicial Procedure.

AMENDMENT BY PUBLIC LAW

1984—Pub. L. 98–473, §215(c)(1), substituted "Stay of Execution" for "Stay of Execution, and Relief Pending Review" in rule catchline.

Subd. (a). Pub. L. 98–473, §215(c)(1), struck out subd. heading "(a) Stay of Execution".

Pub. L. 98–473, §215(c)(3), (4), redesignated subd. (a)(1) as (a), and inserted "from the conviction or sentence" after "is taken".

Subd. (b). Pub. L. 98–473, §215(c)(3), (5), redesignated subd. (a)(2) as (b), and inserted "from the conviction or sentence" after "is taken".

Pub. L. 98–473, §215(c)(2), struck out subd. (b) relating to bail, which had been abrogated Dec. 4, 1967, eff. July 1, 1968.

Subd. (c). Pub. L. 98–473, §215(c)(3), redesignated subd. (a)(3) as (c).

Pub. L. 98–473, §215(c)(2), struck out subd. (c) relating to application for relief pending review, which had been abrogated Dec. 4, 1967, eff. July 1, 1968.

Subd. (d). Pub. L. 98–473, §215(c)(3), (6), redesignated subd. (a)(4) as (d) and amended it generally. Prior to amendment, subd. (a)(4) read as follows: "An order placing the defendant on probation may be stayed if an appeal is taken. If not stayed, the court shall specify when the term of probation shall commence. If the order is stayed the court shall fix the terms of the stay."

Subds. (e), (f). Pub. L. 98–473, §215(c)(7), added subds. (e) and (f).

EFFECTIVE DATE OF 1984 AMENDMENT

Amendment by Pub. L. 98–473 effective Nov. 1, 1987, and applicable only to offenses committed after the taking effect of such amendment, see section 235(a)(1) of Pub. L. 98–473, set out as an Effective Date note under section 3551 of this title.

Rule 39. [Reserved]

TITLE VIII. SUPPLEMENTARY AND SPECIAL PROCEEDINGS

Rule 40. Arrest for Failing to Appear in Another District or for Violating Conditions of Release Set in Another District

(a) In General. A person must be taken without unnecessary delay before a magistrate judge in the district of arrest if the person has been arrested under a warrant issued in another district for:

(i) failing to appear as required by the terms of that person's release under 18 U.S.C. §§3141–3156 or by a subpoena; or

(ii) violating conditions of release set in another district.

(b) Proceedings. The judge must proceed under Rule 5(c)(3) as applicable.

(c) Release or Detention Order. The judge may modify any previous release or detention order issued in another district, but must state in writing the reasons for doing so.

(d) Video Teleconferencing. Video teleconferencing may be used to conduct an appearance under this rule if the defendant consents.

(As amended Feb. 28, 1966, eff. July 1, 1966; Apr. 24, 1972, eff. Oct. 1, 1972; Apr. 30, 1979, eff. Aug. 1, 1979; Pub. L. 96–42, §1(2), July 31, 1979, 93 Stat. 326; Apr. 28, 1982, eff. Aug. 1, 1982; Pub. L. 98–473, title II, §§209(c), 215(d), Oct. 12, 1984, 98 Stat. 1986, 2016; Mar. 9, 1987, eff. Aug. 1, 1987; Apr. 25, 1989, eff. Dec. 1, 1989; Apr. 22, 1993, eff. Dec. 1, 1993; Apr. 29, 1994, eff. Dec. 1, 1994; Apr. 27, 1995, eff. Dec. 1, 1995; Apr. 29, 2002, eff. Dec. 1, 2002; Apr. 12, 2006, eff. Dec. 1, 2006; Apr. 26, 2011, eff. Dec. 1, 2011.)

NOTES OF ADVISORY COMMITTEE ON RULES——1944

1. This rule modifies and revamps existing procedure. The present practice has developed as a result of a series of judicial decisions, the only statute dealing with the subject being exceedingly general, 18 U.S.C. 591 [now 3041] (Arrest and removal for trial):

For any crime or offense against the United States, the offender may, by any justice or judge of the United States, or by any United States commissioner, or by any chancellor, judge of a supreme or superior court, chief or first judge of common pleas, mayor of a city, justice of the peace, or other magistrate, of any State where he may be found, and agreeably to the usual mode of process against offenders in such State, and at the expense of the United States, be arrested and imprisoned, or bailed, as the case may be, for trial before such court of the United States as by law has cognizance of the offense. * * * Where any offender or witness is committed in any district other than that where the offense is to be tried, it shall be the duty of the judge of the district where such offender or witness is imprisoned, seasonably to issue, and of the marshal to execute, a warrant for his removal to the district where the trial is to be had.

The scope of a removal hearing, the issues to be considered, and other similar matters are governed by judicial decisions, Beavers v. Henkel, 194 U.S. 73; Tinsley v. Treat, 205 U.S. 20; Henry v. Henkel, 235 U.S. 219; Rodman v. Pothier, 264 U.S. 399; Morse v. United States, 267 U.S. 80; Fetters v. United States ex rel. Cunningham, 283 U.S. 638; United States ex rel. Kassin v. Mulligan, 295 U.S. 396; see, also, 9 Edmunds, Cyclopedia of Federal Procedure 39053, et seq.

2. The purpose of removal proceedings is to accord safeguards to a defendant against an improvident removal to a distant point for trial. On the other hand, experience has shown that removal proceedings have at times been used by defendants for dilatory purposes and in attempting to frustrate prosecution by preventing or postponing transportation even as between adjoining districts and between places a few miles apart. The object of the rule is adequately to meet each of these two situations.

3. For the purposes of removal, all cases in which the accused is apprehended in a district other than that in which the prosecution is pending have been divided into two groups: first, those in which the place of arrest is either in another district of the same State, or if in another State, then less than 100 miles from the place where the prosecution is pending; and second, cases in which the arrest occurs in a State other than that in which the prosecution is pending and the place of arrest is 100 miles or more distant from the latter place.

In the first group of cases, removal proceedings are abolished. The defendant's right to the usual preliminary hearing is, of course, preserved, but the committing magistrate, if he holds defendant would bind him over to the district court in which the prosecution is pending. As ordinarily there are no removal proceedings in State prosecutions as between different parts of the same State, but the accused is transported by virtue of the process under which he was arrested, it seems reasonable that no removal proceedings should be required in the Federal courts as between districts in the same State. The provision as to arrest in another State but at a place less than 100 miles from the place where the prosecution is pending was added in order to preclude obstruction against bringing the defendant a short distance for trial.

In the second group of cases mentioned in the first paragraph, removal proceedings are continued. The practice to be followed in removal hearings will depend on whether the demand for removal is based upon an indictment or upon an information or complaint. In the latter case, proof of identity and proof of reasonable cause to believe the defendant guilty will have to be adduced in order to justify the issuance of a warrant of removal. In the former case, proof of identity coupled with a certified copy of the indictment will be sufficient, as the indictment will be conclusive proof of probable cause. The distinction is based on the fact that in case of an indictment, the grand jury, which is an arm of the court, has already found probable cause. Since the action of the grand jury is not subject to review by a district judge in the district in which the grand jury sits, it seems illogical to permit such review collaterally in a removal proceeding by a judge in another district.

4. For discussions of this rule see, Homer Cummings, 29 A.B.A.Jour. 654, 656; Holtzoff, 3 F.R.D. 445, 450–452; Holtzoff, 12 George Washington L.R. 119, 127–130; Holtzoff, The Federal Bar Journal, October 1944, 18–37; Berge, 42 Mich.L.R. 353, 374; Medalie, 4 Lawyers Guild R. (3)1, 4.

Note to Subdivision (b). The rule provides that all removal hearings shall take place before a United States commissioner or a Federal judge. It does not confer such jurisdiction on State or local magistrates. While theoretically under existing law State and local magistrates have authority to conduct removal hearings, nevertheless as a matter of universal practice, such proceedings are always conducted before a United States commissioner or a Federal judge, 9 Edmunds, Cyclopedia of Federal Procedure 3919.

The amendment conforms to the change made in the corresponding procedure in Rule 5(b).

Subdivision (a) is amended to make clear that the person shall be taken before the federal magistrate "without unnecessary delay." Although the former rule was silent in this regard, it probably would have been interpreted to require prompt appearance, and there is therefore advantage in making this explicit in the rule itself. See C. Wright, Federal Practice and Procedure: Criminal §652 (1969, Supp. 1971). Subdivision (a) is amended to also make clear that the person is to be brought before a "federal magistrate" rather than a state or local magistrate authorized by 18 U.S.C. §3041. The former rules were inconsistent in this regard. Although rule 40(a) provided that the person may be brought before a state or local officer authorized by former rule 5(a), such state or local officer lacks authority to conduct a preliminary examination under rule 5(c), and a principal purpose of the appearance is to hold a preliminary examination where no prior indictment or information has issued. The Federal Magistrates Act should make it possible to bring a person before a federal magistrate. See C. Wright, Federal Practice and Procedure: Criminal §653, especially n.35 (1969, Supp. 1971).

Subdivision (b)(2) is amended to provide that the federal magistrate should inform the defendant of the fact that he may avail himself of the provisions of rule 20 if applicable in the particular case. However, the failure to so notify the defendant should not invalidate the removal procedure. Although the old rule is silent in this respect, it is current practice to so notify the defendant, and it seems desirable, therefore, to make this explicit in the rule itself.

The requirement that an order of removal under subdivision (b)(3) can be made only by a judge of the United States and cannot be made by a United States magistrate is retained. However, subdivision (b)(5) authorizes issuance of the warrant of removal by a United States magistrate if he is authorized to do so by a rule of district court adopted in accordance with 28 U.S.C. §636(b):

Any district court * * * by the concurrence of a majority of all the judges * * * may establish rules pursuant to which any full-time United States magistrate * * * may be assigned * * * such additional duties as are not inconsistent with the Constitution and laws of the United States.

Although former rule 40(b)(3) required that the warrant of removal be issued by a judge of the United States, there appears no constitutional or statutory prohibition against conferring this authority upon a United States magistrate in accordance with 28 U.S.C. §636(b). The background history is dealt with in detail in 8A J. Moore, Federal Practice 40.01 and 40.02 (2d ed. Cipes 1970, Supp. 1971).

Subdivision (b)(4) makes explicit reference to provisions of the Bail Reform Act of 1966 by incorporating a cross-reference to 18 U.S.C. §3146 and §3148.

This substantial revision of rule 40 abolishes the present distinction between arrest in a nearby district and arrest in a distant district, clarifies the authority of the magistrate with respect to the setting of bail where bail had previously been fixed in the other district, adds a provision dealing with arrest of a probationer in a district other than the district of supervision, and adds a provision dealing with arrest of a defendant or witness for failure to appear in another district.

Note to Subdivision (a). Under subdivision (a) of the present rule, if a person is arrested in a nearby district (another district in the same state, or a place less than 100 miles away), the usual rule 5 and 5.1 preliminary proceedings are conducted. But under subdivision (b) of the present rule, if a person is arrested in a distant district, then a hearing leading to a warrant of removal is held. New subdivision (a) would make no distinction between these two situations and would provide for rule 5 and 5.1 proceedings in all instances in which the arrest occurs outside the district where the warrant issues or where the offense is alleged to have been committed.

This abolition of the distinction between arrest in a nearby district and arrest in a distant district rests upon the conclusion that the procedures prescribed in rules 5 and 5.1 are adequate to protect the rights of an arrestee wherever he might be arrested. If the arrest is without a warrant, it is necessary under rule 5 that a complaint be filed forthwith complying with the requirements of rule 4(a) with respect to the showing of probable cause. If the arrest is with a warrant, that warrant will have been issued upon the basis of an indictment or of a complaint or information showing probable cause, pursuant to rules 4(a) and 9(a). Under rule 5.1 dealing with the preliminary examination, the defendant is to be held to answer only upon a showing of probable cause that an offense has been committed and that the defendant committed it.

Under subdivision (a), there are two situations in which no preliminary examination will be held. One is where "an indictment has been returned or an information filed," which pursuant to rule 5(c) obviates the need for a preliminary examination. The order is where "the defendant elects to have the preliminary examination conducted in the district in which the prosecution is pending." A defendant might wish to elect that alternative when, for example, the law in that district is that the complainant and other material witnesses may be required to appear at the preliminary examination and give testimony. See Washington v. Clemmer, 339 F.2d 715 (D.C. Cir. 1964).

New subdivision (a) continues the present requirement that if the arrest was without a warrant a warrant must thereafter issue in the district in which the offense is alleged to have been committed. This will ensure that in the district of anticipated prosecution there will have been a probable cause determination by a magistrate or grand jury.

Note to Subdivision (b). New subdivision (b) follows existing subdivision (b)(2) in requiring the magistrate to inform the defendant of the provisions of rule 20 applicable in the particular case. Failure to so notify the defendant should not invalidate the proceedings.

Note to Subdivision (c). New subdivision (c) follows existing subdivision (b)(4) as to transmittal of papers.

Note to Subdivision (d). New subdivision (d) has no counterpart in the present rule. It provides a procedure for dealing with the situation in which a probationer is arrested in a district other than the district of supervision, consistent with 18 U.S.C. §3653, which provides in part:

If the probationer shall be arrested in any district other than that in which he was last supervised, he shall be returned to the district in which the warrant was issued, unless jurisdiction over him is transferred as above provided to the district in which he is found, and in that case he shall be detained pending further proceedings in such district.

One possibility, provided for in subdivision (d)(1), is that of transferring jurisdiction over the probationer to the district in which he was arrested. This is permissible under the aforementioned statute, which provides in part:

Whenever during the period of his probation, a probationer heretofore or hereafter placed on probation, goes from the district in which he is being supervised to another district, jurisdiction over him may be transferred, in the discretion of the court, from the court for the district from which he goes to the court for the other district, with the concurrence of the latter court. Thereupon the court for the district to which jurisdiction is transferred shall have all power with respect to the probationer that was previously possessed by the court for the district from which the transfer is made, except that the period of probation shall not be changed without the consent of the sentencing court. This process under the same conditions may be repeated whenever during the period of this probation the probationer goes from the district in which he is being supervised to another district.

Such transfer may be particularly appropriate when it is found that the probationer has now taken up residence in the district where he was arrested or where the alleged occurrence deemed to constitute a violation of probation took place in the district of arrest. In current practice, probationers arrested in a district other than that of their present supervision are sometimes unnecessarily returned to the district of their supervision, at considerable expense and loss of time, when the more appropriate course of action would have been transfer of probation jurisdiction.

Subdivision (d)(2) and (3) deal with the situation in which there is not a transfer of probation jurisdiction to the district of arrest. If the alleged probation violation occurred in the district of arrest, then, under subdivision (d)(2), the preliminary hearing provided for in rule 32.1(a)(1) is to be held in that district. This is consistent with the reasoning in Morrissey v. Brewer, 408 U.S. 471 (1972), made applicable to probation cases in Gagnon v. Scarpelli, 411 U.S. 778 (1973), where the Court stressed that often a parolee "is arrested at a place distant from the state institution, to which he may be returned before the final decision is made concerning revocation," and cited this as a factor contributing to the conclusion that due process requires "that some minimal inquiry be conducted at or reasonably near the place of the alleged parole violation or arrest and as promptly as convenient after arrest while information is fresh and sources are available." As later noted in Gerstein v. Pugh, 420 U.S. 103 (1975):

> In Morrissey v. Brewer * * * and Gagnon v. Scarpelli * * * we held that a parolee or probationer arrested prior to revocation is entitled to an informal preliminary hearing at the place of arrest, with some provision for live testimony. * * * That preliminary hearing, more than the probable cause determination required by the Fourth Amendment, serves the purpose of gathering and preserving live testimony, since the final revocation hearing frequently is held at some distance from the place where the violation occurred.

However, if the alleged violation did not occur in that district, then first-hand testimony concerning the violation is unlikely to be available there, and thus the reasoning of Morrissey and Gerstein does not call for holding the preliminary hearing in that district. In such a case, as provided in subdivision (d)(3), the probationer should be held to answer in the district court of the district having probation jurisdiction. The purpose of the proceeding there provided for is to ascertain the identity of the probationer and provide him with copies of the warrant and the application for the warrant. A probationer is subject to the reporting condition at all times and is also subject to the continuing power of the court to modify such conditions. He therefore stands subject to return back to the jurisdiction district without the necessity of conducting a hearing in the district of arrest to determine whether there is probable cause to revoke his probation.

Note to Subdivision (e). New subdivision (e) has no counterpart in the present rule. It has been added because some confusion currently exists as to whether present rule 40(b) is applicable to the case in which a bench warrant has issued for the return of a defendant or witness who has absented himself and that person is apprehended in a distant district. In Bandy v. United States, 408 F.2d 518 (8th Cir. 1969), a defendant, who had been released upon his personal recognizance after conviction and while petitioning for certiorari and who failed to appear as required after certiorari was denied, objected to his later arrest in New York and removal to Leavenworth without compliance with the rule 40 procedures. The court concluded:

> The short answer to Bandy's first argument is found in Rush v. United States, 290 F.2d 709, 710 (5 Cir. 1961): "The provisions of Rules 5 and 40, Federal Rules of Criminal Procedure, 18 U.S.C.A. may not be availed of by a prisoner in escape status * * *." As noted by Holtzoff, "Removal of Defendants in Federal Criminal Procedure", 4 F.R.D. 455, 458 (1946):
>
> > "Resort need not be had, however, to this [removal] procedure for the purpose of returning a prisoner who has been recaptured after an escape from custody. It has been pointed out that in such a case the court may summarily direct his return under its general power to issue writs not specifically provided for by statute, which may be necessary for the exercise of its jurisdiction and agreeable to the usages and principles of law. In fact, in such a situation no judicial process appears necessary. The prisoner may be retaken and administratively returned to the custody from which he escaped."

Bandy's arrest in New York was pursuant to a bench warrant issued by the United States District Court for the District of North Dakota on May 1, 1962, when Bandy failed to surrender himself to commence service of his sentence on the conviction for filing false income tax refunds. As a fugitive from justice, Bandy was not entitled upon apprehension to a removal hearing, and he was properly removed to the United States Penitentiary at Leavenworth, Kansas to commence service of sentence. Consistent with Bandy, new subdivision (e) does not afford such a person all of the protections provided for in subdivision (a). However, subdivision (e) does ensure that a determination of identity will be made before that person is held to answer in the district of arrest.

Note to Subdivision (f). Although the matter of bail is dealt with in rule 46 and 18 U.S.C. §§3146 and 3148, new subdivision (f) has been added to clarify the situation in which a defendant makes his initial appearance before the United States magistrate and there is a warrant issued by a judge of a different district who has endorsed the amount of bail on the warrant. The present ambiguity of the rule is creating practical administrative problems. If the United States magistrate concludes that a lower bail is appropriate, the judge who fixed the original bail on the warrant has, on occasion, expressed the view that this is inappropriate conduct by the magistrate. If the magistrate, in such circumstances, does not reduce the bail to the amount supported by all of the facts, there may be caused unnecessary inconvenience to the defendant, and there would arguably be a violation of at least the spirit of the Bail Reform Act and the Eighth Amendment.

The Procedures Manual for United States Magistrates, issued under the authority of the Judicial Conference of the United States, provides in ch. 6, pp. 8–9:

> Where the arrest occurs in a "distant" district, the rules do not expressly limit the discretion of the magistrate in the setting of conditions of release. However, whether or not the magistrate in the district of arrest has authority to set his own bail under Rule 40, considerations of propriety and comity would dictate that the magistrate should not attempt to set bail in a lower amount than that fixed by a judge in another district. If an unusual situation should arise where it appears from all the information available to the magistrate that the amount of bail endorsed on the warrant is excessive, he should consult with a judge of his own district or with the judge in the other district who fixed the bail in order to resolve any difficulties. (Where an amount of bail is merely recommended on the indictment by the United States attorney, the magistrate has complete discretion in setting conditions of release.)

Rule 40 as amended would encourage the above practice and hopefully would eliminate the present confusion and misunderstanding.

The last sentence of subdivision (f) requires that the magistrate set forth the reasons for his action in writing whenever he fixes bail in an amount different from that previously fixed. Setting forth the reasons for the amount of bail fixed, certainly a sound practice in all circumstances, is particularly appropriate when the bail differs from that previously fixed in another district. The requirement that reasons be set out will ensure that the "considerations of propriety and comity" referred to above will be specifically taken into account.

CONGRESSIONAL MODIFICATION OF PROPOSED 1979 AMENDMENT

Pub. L. 96–42, §1(2), July 31, 1979, 93 Stat. 326 [set out as a note under section 2074 of Title 28, Judiciary and Judicial Procedure], provided in part that the amendment proposed by the Supreme Court [in its order of Apr. 30, 1979] affecting rule 40 of the Federal Rules of Criminal Procedure [this rule] would take effect on Aug. 1, 1979, as amended by that section. See 1979 Amendment note below.

NOTES OF ADVISORY COMMITTEE ON RULES——1982 AMENDMENT

The amendment to 40(d) is intended to make it clear that the transfer provisions therein apply whenever the arrest occurs other than in the district of probation jurisdiction, and that if probable cause is found at a preliminary hearing held pursuant to Rule 40(d)(2) the probationer should be held to answer in the district having probation jurisdiction.

On occasion, the district of probation supervision and the district of probation jurisdiction will not be the same. See, e.g., Cupp v. Byington, 179 F.Supp. 669 (S.D.Ind. 1960) (supervision in Southern District of Indiana, but jurisdiction never transferred from District of Nevada). In such circumstances, it is the district having jurisdiction which may revoke the defendant's probation. Cupp v. Byington, supra; 18 U.S.C. §3653 ("the court for the district having jurisdiction over him * * * may revoke the probation"; if probationer goes to another district, "jurisdiction over him may be transferred," and only then does "the court for the district to which jurisdiction is transferred * * * have all the power with respect to the probationer that was previously possessed by the court for the district from which the transfer was made"). That being the case, that is the jurisdiction to which the probationer should be transferred as provided in Rule 40(d).

Because Rule 32.1 has now taken effect, a cross-reference to those provisions has been made in subdivision (d)(1) so as to clarify how the magistrate is to proceed if jurisdiction is transferred.

NOTES OF ADVISORY COMMITTEE ON RULES—1987 AMENDMENT

The amendments are technical. No substantive change is intended.

NOTES OF ADVISORY COMMITTEE ON RULES—1989 AMENDMENT

The amendments recognize that convicted defendants may be on supervised release as well as on probation. See 18 U.S.C. §§3583, and 3624(e).

NOTES OF ADVISORY COMMITTEE ON RULES—1993 AMENDMENT

The amendment to subdivision (a) is intended to expedite determining where a defendant will be held to answer by permitting facsimile transmission of a warrant or a certified copy of the warrant. The amendment recognizes an increased reliance by the public in general, and the legal profession in particular, on accurate and efficient transmission of important legal documents by facsimile machines.

The Rule is also amended to conform to the Judicial Improvements Act of 1990 [P.L. 101–650, Title III, Section 321] which provides that each United States magistrate appointed under section 631 of title 28, United States Code, shall be known as a United States magistrate judge.

NOTES OF ADVISORY COMMITTEE ON RULES—1994 AMENDMENT

The amendment to subdivision (d) is intended to clarify the authority of a magistrate judge to set conditions of release in those cases where a probationer or supervised releasee is arrested in a district other than the district having jurisdiction. As written, there appeared to be a gap in Rule 40, especially under (d)(1) where the alleged violation occurs in a jurisdiction other than the district having jurisdiction.

A number of rules contain references to pretrial, trial, and post-trial release or detention of defendants, probationers and supervised releasees. Rule 46, for example, addresses the topic of release from custody. Although Rule 46(c) addresses custody pending sentencing and notice of appeal, the rule makes no explicit provision for detaining or releasing probationers or supervised releasees who are later arrested for violating terms of their probation or release. Rule 32.1 provides guidance on proceedings involving revocation of probation or supervised release. In particular, Rule 32.1(a)(1) recognizes that when a person is held in custody on the ground that the person violated a condition of probation or supervised release, the judge or United States magistrate judge may release the person under Rule 46(c), pending the revocation proceeding. But no other explicit reference is made in Rule 32.1 to the authority of a judge or magistrate judge to determine conditions of release for a probationer or supervised releasee who is arrested in a district other than the district having jurisdiction.

The amendment recognizes that a judge or magistrate judge considering the case of a probationer or supervised releasee under Rule 40(d) has the same authority vis a vis decisions regarding custody as a judge or magistrate judge proceeding under Rule 32.1(a)(1). Thus, regardless of the ultimate disposition of an arrested probationer or supervised releasee under Rule 40(d), a judge or magistrate judge acting under that rule may rely upon Rule 46(c) in determining whether custody should be continued and if not, what conditions, if any, should be placed upon the person.

NOTES OF ADVISORY COMMITTEE ON RULES—1995 AMENDMENT

The amendment to Rule 40(a) is a technical, conforming change to reflect an amendment to Rule 5, which recognizes a limited exception to the general rule that all arrestees must be taken before a federal magistrate judge.

COMMITTEE NOTES ON RULES—2002 AMENDMENT

The language of Rule 40 has been amended as part of the general restyling of the Criminal Rules to make them more easily understood and to make style and terminology consistent throughout the rules. These changes are intended to be stylistic only.

Rule 40 has been completely revised. The Committee believed that it would be much clearer and more helpful to locate portions of Rule 40 in Rules 5 (initial appearances), 5.1 (preliminary hearings), and 32.1 (revocation or modification of probation or supervised release). Accordingly, current Rule 40(a) has been relocated in Rules 5 and 5.1. Current Rule 40(b) has been relocated in Rule 5(c)(2)(B) and current Rule 40(c) has been moved to Rule 5(c)(2)(F).

Current Rule 40(d) has been relocated in Rule 32.1(a)(5). The first sentence of current Rule 40(e) is now located in revised Rule 40(a). The second sentence of current Rule 40(e) is now in revised Rule 40(b) and current Rule 40(f) is revised Rule 40(c).

COMMITTEE NOTES ON RULES—2006 AMENDMENT

Subdivision (a). Rule 40 currently refers only to a person arrested for failing to appear in another district. The amendment is intended to fill a perceived gap in the rule that a magistrate judge in the district of arrest lacks authority to set release conditions for a person arrested only for violation of conditions of release. See, e.g., United States v. Zhu, 215 F.R.D. 21, 26 (D. Mass. 2003). The Committee believes that it would be inconsistent for the magistrate judge to be empowered to release an arrestee who had failed to appear altogether, but not to release one who only violated conditions of release in a minor way. Rule 40(a) is amended to expressly cover not only failure to appear, but also violation of any other condition of release.

Changes Made After Publication and Comment. The Committee made minor clarifying changes in the published rule at the suggestion of the Style Committee.

COMMITTEE NOTES ON RULES—2011 AMENDMENT

Subdivision (d). The amendment provides for video teleconferencing in order to bring the rule into conformity with Rule 5(f).

Changes Made to Proposed Amendment Released for Public Comment. The amendment was rephrased to track precisely the language of Rule 5(f), on which it was modeled.

AMENDMENT BY PUBLIC LAW

1984—Subd. (d)(1). Pub. L. 98–473, §215(d), substituted "3605" for "3653".

Subd. (f). Pub. L. 98–473, §209(c), substituted "Release or Detention" for "Bail" as the subdivision heading and, in text, substituted "If a person was previously detained or conditionally released, pursuant to chapter 207 of title 18, United States Code," for "If bail was previously fixed", "decision previously made" for "amount of bail previously fixed", "by that decision" for "by the amount of bail previously fixed", and "amends the release or detention decision or alters the conditions of release" for "fixes bail different from that previously fixed".

1979—Subd. (d)(1). Pub. L. 96–42, §1(2)(A), struck out "in accordance with Rule 32.1(a)" after "Proceed in".

135

Subd. (d)(2). Pub. L. 96—42, §1(2)(B), struck out "in accordance with Rule 32.1(a)(1)" after "Hold a prompt preliminary hearing".

EFFECTIVE DATE OF 1984 AMENDMENT

Amendment by section 215(d) of Pub. L. 98—473 effective Nov. 1, 1987, and applicable only to offenses committed after the taking effect of such amendment, see section 235(a)(1) of Pub. L. 98—473, set out as an Effective Date note under section 3551 of this title.

Rule 41. Search and Seizure

(a) Scope and Definitions.
   (1) Scope. This rule does not modify any statute regulating search or seizure, or the issuance and execution of a search warrant in special circumstances.
   (2) Definitions. The following definitions apply under this rule:
      (A) "Property" includes documents, books, papers, any other tangible objects, and information.
      (B) "Daytime" means the hours between 6:00 a.m. and 10:00 p.m. according to local time.
      (C) "Federal law enforcement officer" means a government agent (other than an attorney for the government) who is engaged in enforcing the criminal laws and is within any category of officers authorized by the Attorney General to request a search warrant.
      (D) "Domestic terrorism" and "international terrorism" have the meanings set out in 18 U.S.C. §2331.
      (E) "Tracking device" has the meaning set out in 18 U.S.C. §3117(b).

(b) Venue for a Warrant Application. At the request of a federal law enforcement officer or an attorney for the government:
   (1) a magistrate judge with authority in the district—or if none is reasonably available, a judge of a state court of record in the district—has authority to issue a warrant to search for and seize a person or property located within the district;
   (2) a magistrate judge with authority in the district has authority to issue a warrant for a person or property outside the district if the person or property is located within the district when the warrant is issued but might move or be moved outside the district before the warrant is executed;
   (3) a magistrate judge—in an investigation of domestic terrorism or international terrorism—with authority in any district in which activities related to the terrorism may have occurred has authority to issue a warrant for a person or property within or outside that district;
   (4) a magistrate judge with authority in the district has authority to issue a warrant to install within the district a tracking device; the warrant may authorize use of the device to track the movement of a person or property located within the district, outside the district, or both; and
   (5) a magistrate judge having authority in any district where activities related to the crime may have occurred, or in the District of Columbia, may issue a warrant for property that is located outside the jurisdiction of any state or district, but within any of the following:
      (A) a United States territory, possession, or commonwealth;
      (B) the premises—no matter who owns them—of a United States diplomatic or consular mission in a foreign state, including any appurtenant building, part of a building, or land used for the mission's purposes; or
      (C) a residence and any appurtenant land owned or leased by the United States and used by United States personnel assigned to a United States diplomatic or consular mission in a foreign state.

   (6) a magistrate judge with authority in any district where activities related to a crime may have occurred has authority to issue a warrant to use remote access to search electronic storage media and to seize or copy electronically stored information located within or outside that district if:
      (A) the district where the media or information is located has been concealed through technological means; or
      (B) in an investigation of a violation of 18 U.S.C. §1030(a)(5), the media are protected computers that have been damaged without authorization and are located in five or more districts.

(c) Persons or Property Subject to Search or Seizure. A warrant may be issued for any of the following:
   (1) evidence of a crime;
   (2) contraband, fruits of crime, or other items illegally possessed;
   (3) property designed for use, intended for use, or used in committing a crime; or
   (4) a person to be arrested or a person who is unlawfully restrained.

(d) Obtaining a Warrant.
   (1) In General. After receiving an affidavit or other information, a magistrate judge—or if authorized by Rule 41(b), a judge of a state court of record—must issue the warrant if there is probable cause to search for and seize a person or property or to install and use a tracking device.
   (2) Requesting a Warrant in the Presence of a Judge.
      (A) Warrant on an Affidavit. When a federal law enforcement officer or an attorney for the government presents an affidavit in support of a warrant, the judge may require the affiant to appear personally and may examine under oath the affiant and any witness the affiant produces.
      (B) Warrant on Sworn Testimony. The judge may wholly or partially dispense with a written affidavit and base a warrant on sworn testimony if doing so is reasonable under the circumstances.
      (C) Recording Testimony. Testimony taken in support of a warrant must be recorded by a court reporter or by a suitable recording device, and the judge must file the transcript or recording with the clerk, along with any affidavit.

   (3) Requesting a Warrant by Telephonic or Other Reliable Electronic Means. In accordance with Rule 4.1, a magistrate judge may issue a warrant based on information communicated by telephone or other reliable electronic means.

(e) Issuing the Warrant.
   (1) In General. The magistrate judge or a judge of a state court of record must issue the warrant to an officer authorized to execute it.
   (2) Contents of the Warrant.
      (A) Warrant to Search for and Seize a Person or Property. Except for a tracking-device warrant, the warrant must identify the person or property to be searched, identify any person or property to be seized, and designate the magistrate judge to whom it must be returned. The warrant must command the officer to:
         (i) execute the warrant within a specified time no longer than 14 days;
         (ii) execute the warrant during the daytime, unless the judge for good cause expressly authorizes execution at another time; and
         (iii) return the warrant to the magistrate judge designated in the warrant.

      (B) Warrant Seeking Electronically Stored Information. A warrant under Rule 41(e)(2)(A) may authorize the seizure of electronic storage media or the seizure or copying of electronically stored information. Unless otherwise specified, the warrant authorizes a later review of the media or information consistent with the warrant. The time for executing the warrant in Rule 41(e)(2)(A) and (f)(1)(A) refers to the seizure or on-site copying of the media or information, and not to any later off-site copying or review.
      (C) Warrant for a Tracking Device. A tracking-device warrant must identify the person or property to be tracked, designate the magistrate judge to whom it must be returned, and specify a reasonable length of time that the device may be used. The time must not exceed 45 days from the date the warrant was issued. The court may, for good cause, grant one or more extensions for a reasonable period not to exceed 45 days each. The warrant must command the officer to:
         (i) complete any installation authorized by the warrant within a specified time no longer than 10 days;

136

(ii) perform any installation authorized by the warrant during the daytime, unless the judge for good cause expressly authorizes installation at another time; and

(iii) return the warrant to the judge designated in the warrant.

(f) Executing and Returning the Warrant.

(1) Warrant to Search for and Seize a Person or Property.

(A) Noting the Time. The officer executing the warrant must enter on it the exact date and time it was executed.

(B) Inventory. An officer present during the execution of the warrant must prepare and verify an inventory of any property seized. The officer must do so in the presence of another officer and the person from whom, or from whose premises, the property was taken. If either one is not present, the officer must prepare and verify the inventory in the presence of at least one other credible person. In a case involving the seizure of electronic storage media or the seizure or copying of electronically stored information, the inventory may be limited to describing the physical storage media that were seized or copied. The officer may retain a copy of the electronically stored information that was seized or copied.

(C) Receipt. The officer executing the warrant must give a copy of the warrant and a receipt for the property taken to the person from whom, or from whose premises, the property was taken or leave a copy of the warrant and receipt at the place where the officer took the property. For a warrant to use remote access to search electronic storage media and seize or copy electronically stored information, the officer must make reasonable efforts to serve a copy of the warrant and receipt on the person whose property was searched or who possessed the information that was seized or copied. Service may be accomplished by any means, including electronic means, reasonably calculated to reach that person.

(D) Return. The officer executing the warrant must promptly return it—together with a copy of the inventory—to the magistrate judge designated on the warrant. The officer may do so by reliable electronic means. The judge must, on request, give a copy of the inventory to the person from whom, or from whose premises, the property was taken and to the applicant for the warrant.

(2) Warrant for a Tracking Device.

(A) Noting the Time. The officer executing a tracking-device warrant must enter on it the exact date and time the device was installed and the period during which it was used.

(B) Return. Within 10 days after the use of the tracking device has ended, the officer executing the warrant must return it to the judge designated in the warrant. The officer may do so by reliable electronic means.

(C) Service. Within 10 days after the use of the tracking device has ended, the officer executing a tracking-device warrant must serve a copy of the warrant on the person who was tracked or whose property was tracked. Service may be accomplished by delivering a copy to the person who, or whose property, was tracked; or by leaving a copy at the person's residence or usual place of abode with an individual of suitable age and discretion who resides at that location and by mailing a copy to the person's last known address. Upon request of the government, the judge may delay notice as provided in Rule 41(f)(3).

(3) Delayed Notice. Upon the government's request, a magistrate judge—or if authorized by Rule 41(b), a judge of a state court of record—may delay any notice required by this rule if the delay is authorized by statute.

(g) Motion to Return Property. A person aggrieved by an unlawful search and seizure of property or by the deprivation of property may move for the property's return. The motion must be filed in the district where the property was seized. The court must receive evidence on any factual issue necessary to decide the motion. If it grants the motion, the court must return the property to the movant, but may impose reasonable conditions to protect access to the property and its use in later proceedings.

(h) Motion to Suppress. A defendant may move to suppress evidence in the court where the trial will occur, as Rule 12 provides.

(i) Forwarding Papers to the Clerk. The magistrate judge to whom the warrant is returned must attach to the warrant a copy of the return, of the inventory, and of all other related papers and must deliver them to the clerk in the district where the property was seized.

(As amended Dec. 27, 1948, eff. Oct. 20, 1949; Apr. 9, 1956, eff. July 8, 1956; Apr. 24, 1972, eff. Oct. 1, 1972; Mar. 18, 1974, eff. July 1, 1974; Apr. 26 and July 8, 1976, eff. Aug. 1, 1976; Pub. L. 95–78, §2(e), July 30, 1977, 91 Stat. 320, eff. Oct. 1, 1977; Apr. 30, 1979, eff. Aug. 1, 1979; Mar. 9, 1987, eff. Aug. 1, 1987; Apr. 25, 1989, eff. Dec. 1, 1989; May 1, 1990, eff. Dec. 1, 1990; Apr. 22, 1993, eff. Dec. 1, 1993; Pub. L. 107–56, title II, §219, Oct. 26, 2001, 115 Stat. 291; Apr. 29, 2002, eff. Dec. 1, 2002; Apr. 12, 2006, eff. Dec. 1, 2006; Apr. 23, 2008, eff. Dec. 1, 2008; Mar. 26, 2009, eff. Dec. 1, 2009; Apr. 26, 2011, eff. Dec. 1, 2011; Apr. 28, 2016, eff. Dec. 1, 2016.)

NOTES OF ADVISORY COMMITTEE ON RULES—1944

This rule is a codification of existing law and practice.

Note to Subdivision (a). This rule is a restatement of existing law, 18 U.S.C. [former] 611.

Note to Subdivision (b). This rule is a restatement of existing law, 18 U.S.C. [former] 612; Conyer v. United States, 80 F.2d 292 (C.C.A. 6th). This provision does not supersede or repeal special statutory provisions permitting the issuance of search warrants in specific circumstances. See Subdivision (g) and Note thereto, infra.

Note to Subdivision (c). This rule is a restatement of existing law, 18 U.S.C. [former] 613–616, 620; Dumbra v. United States, 268 U.S. 435.

Note to Subdivision (d). This rule is a restatement of existing law, 18 U.S.C. [former] 621–624.

Note to Subdivision (e). This rule is a restatement of existing law and practice, with the exception hereafter noted, 18 U.S.C. [former] 625, 626; Weeks v. United States, 232 U.S. 383; Silverthorne Lumber Co. v. United States, 251 U.S. 385; Agello v. United States, 269 U.S. 20; Gouled v. United States, 255 U.S. 298. While under existing law a motion to suppress evidence or to compel return of property obtained by an illegal search and seizure may be made either before a commissioner subject to review by the court on motion, or before the court, the rule provides that such motion may be made only before the court. The purpose is to prevent multiplication of proceedings and to bring the matter before the court in the first instance. While during the life of the Eighteenth Amendment when such motions were numerous it was a common practice in some districts for commissioners to hear such motions, the prevailing practice at the present time is to make such motions before the district court. This practice, which is deemed to be preferable, is embodied in the rule.

Note to Subdivision (f). This rule is a restatement of existing law, 18 U.S.C. [former] 627; Cf. Rule 5(c) (last sentence).

Note to Subdivision (g). While Rule 41 supersedes the general provisions of 18 U.S.C. 611–626 [now 18 U.S.C. 3105, 3109], relating to search warrants, it does not supersede, but preserves, all other statutory provisions permitting searches and seizures in specific situations. Among such statutes are the following:

U.S.C., Title 18:
Section 287 [former] (Search warrant for suspected counterfeiture)

U.S.C., Title 19:
Section 1595 (Customs duties; searches and seizures)

U.S.C., Title 26:

Section 3117 [now 5557] (Officers and agents authorized to investigate, issue search warrants, and prosecute for violations)

For statutes which incorporate by reference 18 U.S.C. [former] 98, and therefore are now controlled by this rule, see, e. g.:

U.S.C., Title 18:

Section 12 [former] (Subversive activities; undermining loyalty, discipline, or morale of armed forces; searches and seizures)

U.S.C., Title 26:

Section 3116 [now 7302] (Forfeitures and seizures)

Statutory provision for a warrant for detention of war materials seized under certain circumstances is found in 22 U.S.C. 402 [see 401] (Seizure of war materials intended for unlawful export.)

Other statutes providing for searches and seizures or entry without warrants are the following:

U.S.C., Title 19:

Section 482 (Search of vehicles and persons)

U.S.C., Title 25:

Section 246 [now 18 U.S.C. 3113] (Searches and seizures)

U.S.C., Title 26:

Section 3601 [now 7606] (Entry of premises for examination of taxable objects)

U.S.C., Title 29:

Section 211 (Investigations, inspections, and records)

U.S.C., Title 49:

Section 781 [now 80302] (Unlawful use of vessels, vehicles, and aircrafts; contraband article defined)
Section 782 [now 80303] (Seizure and forfeiture)
Section 784 [now 80306] (Application of related laws)

NOTES OF ADVISORY COMMITTEE ON RULES—1948 AMENDMENT

Subdivision (b)(3).—The amendment is to substitute proper reference to Title 18 in place of the repealed acts.

Subdivision (g).—To eliminate reference to sections of the Act of June 15, 1917, c. 30, which have been repealed by the Act of June 25, 1948, c. 645, which enacted Title 18.

NOTES OF ADVISORY COMMITTEE ON RULES—1972 AMENDMENT

Subdivision (a) is amended to provide that a search warrant may be issued only upon the request of a federal law enforcement officer or an attorney for the government. The phrase "federal law enforcement officer" is defined in subdivision (h) in a way which will allow the Attorney General to designate the category of officers who are authorized to make application for a search warrant. The phrase "attorney for the government" is defined in rule 54.

The title to subdivision (b) is changed to make it conform more accurately to the content of the subdivision. Subdivision (b) is also changed to modernize the language used to describe the property which may be seized with a lawfully issued search warrant and to take account of a recent Supreme Court decision (Warden v. Haden, 387 U.S. 294 (1967)) and recent congressional action (18 U.S.C. §3103a) which authorize the issuance of a search warrant to search for items of solely evidential value. 18 U.S.C. §3103a provides that "a warrant may be issued to search for and seize any property that constitutes evidence of a criminal offense. . . ."

Recent state legislation authorizes the issuance of a search warrant for evidence of crime. See, e.g., Cal. Penal Code §1524(4) (West Supp. 1968); Ill.Rev.Stat. ch. 38, §108–3 (1965); LSA C.Cr.P. art. 161 (1967); N.Y. CPL §690.10(4) (McKinney, 1971); Ore.Rev.Stat. §141.010 (1969); Wis.Stat. §968.13(2) (1969).

The general weight of recent text and law review comment has been in favor of allowing a search for evidence. 8 Wigmore, Evidence §2184a. (McNaughton rev. 1961); Kamisar. The Wiretapping-Eavesdropping Problem: A professor's View, 44 Minn.L.Rev. 891 (1960); Kaplan, Search and Seizure: A No-Man's Land in the Criminal Law, 49 Calif.L.Rev. 474 (1961); Comments: 66 Colum.L.Rev. 355 (1966), 45 N.C.L.Rev. 512 (1967), 20 U.Chi.L.Rev. 319 (1953).

There is no intention to limit the protection of the fifth amendment against compulsory self-incrimination, so items which are solely "testimonial" or "communicative" in nature might well be inadmissible on those grounds. Schmerber v. California, 384 U.S. 757 (1966). The court referred to the possible fifth amendment limitation in Warden v. Hayden, supra:

This case thus does not require that we consider whether there are items of evidential value whose very nature precludes them from being the object of a reasonable search and seizure. [387 U.S. at 303].

See ALI Model Code of Pre-Arraignment Procedure §551.03(2) and commentary at pp. 3–5 (April 30, 1971).

It seems preferable to allow the fifth amendment limitation to develop as cases arise rather than attempt to articulate the constitutional doctrine as part of the rule itself.

The amendment to subdivision (c) is intended to make clear that a search warrant may properly be based upon a finding of probable cause based upon hearsay. That a search warrant may properly be issued on the basis of hearsay is current law. See, e.g., Jones v. United States, 362 U.S. 257 (1960); Spinelli v. United States, 393 U.S. 410 (1969). See also State v. Beal, 40 Wis.2d 607, 162 N.W.2d 640 (1968), reversing prior Wisconsin cases which held that a search warrant could not properly issue on the basis of hearsay evidence.

The provision in subdivision (c) that the magistrate may examine the affiant or witnesses under oath is intended to assure him an opportunity to make a careful decision as to whether there is probable cause. It seems desirable to do this as an incident to the issuance of the warrant rather than having the issue raised only later on a motion to suppress the evidence. See L. Tiffany, D. McIntyre, and D. Rotenberg, Detection of Crime 118 (1967). If testimony is taken it must be recorded, transcribed, and made part of the affidavit or affidavits. This is to insure an adequate basis for determining the sufficiency of the evidentiary grounds for the issuance of the search warrant if that question should later arise.

The requirement that the warrant itself state the grounds for its issuance and the names of any affiants, is eliminated as unnecessary paper work. There is no comparable requirement for an arrest warrant in rule 4. A person who wishes to challenge the validity of a search warrant has access to the affidavits upon which the warrant was issued.

The former requirement that the warrant require that the search be conducted "forthwith" is changed to read "within a specified period of time not to exceed 10 days." The former rule contained an inconsistency between subdivision (c) requiring that the search be conducted "forthwith" and subdivision (d) requiring execution "within 10 days after its date." The amendment resolves this ambiguity and confers discretion upon the issuing magistrate to specify the time within which the search may be conducted to meet the needs of the particular case.

The rule is also changed to allow the magistrate to authorize a search at a time other than "daytime," where there is "reasonable cause shown" for doing so. To make clear what "daytime" means, the term is defined in subdivision (h).

Subdivision (d) is amended to conform its language to the Federal Magistrates Act. The language "The warrant may be executed and returned only within 10 days after its date" is omitted as unnecessary. The matter is now covered adequately in proposed subdivision (c) which gives the issuing officer authority to fix the time within which the warrant is to be executed.

The amendment to subdivision (e) and the addition of subdivision (f) are intended to require the motion to suppress evidence to be made in the trial court rather than in the district in which the evidence was seized as now allowed by the rule. In DiBella v. United States, 369 U.S. 121 (1962), the court, in effect, discouraged motions to suppress in the district in which the property was seized:

There is a decision in the Second Circuit, United States v. Klapholz, 230 F.2d 494 (1956), allowing the Government an appeal from an order granting a post-indictment motion to suppress, apparently for the single reason that the motion was filed in the district of seizure rather than of trial; but the case was soon thereafter taken by a District Court to have counseled declining jurisdiction of such motions for reasons persuasive against allowing the appeal: "This course will avoid a needless duplication of effort by two courts and provide a more expeditious resolution of the controversy besides avoiding the risk of determining prematurely and inadequately the admissibility of evidence at the trial. . . . A piecemeal adjudication such as that which would necessarily follow from a disposition of the motion here might conceivably result in prejudice either to the Government or the defendants, or both." United States v. Lester, 21 F.R.D. 30, 31 (D.C.S.D.N.Y. 1957). Rule 41(e), of course, specifically provides for making of the motion in the district of seizure On a summary hearing, however, the ruling there is likely always to be tentative. We think it accords most satisfactorily with sound administration of the Rules to treat such rulings as interlocutory. [369 U.S. at 132–133.]

As amended, subdivision (e) provides for a return of the property if (1) the person is entitled to lawful possession and (2) the seizure was illegal. This means that the judge in the district of seizure does not have to decide the legality of the seizure in cases involving contraband which, even if seized illegally, is not to be returned.

The five grounds for returning the property, presently listed in the rule, are dropped for two reasons—(1) substantive grounds for objecting to illegally obtained evidence (e.g., Miranda) are not ordinarily codified in the rules and (2) the categories are not entirely accurate. See United States v. Howard, 138 F.Supp. 376, 380 (D.Md. 1956).

A sentence is added to subdivision (e) to provide that a motion for return of property, made in the district of trial, shall be treated also as a motion to suppress under rule 12. This change is intended to further the objective of rule 12 which is to have all pretrial motions disposed of in a single court appearance rather than to have a series of pretrial motions made on different dates, causing undue delay in administration.

Subdivision (f) is new and reflects the position that it is best to have the motion to suppress made in the court of the district of trial rather than in the court of the district in which the seizure occurred. The motion to suppress in the district of trial should be made in accordance with the provisions of rule 12.

Subdivision (g) is changed to conform to subdivision (c) which requires the return to be made before a federal judicial officer even though the search warrant may have been issued by a nonfederal magistrate.

Subdivision (h) is former rule 41(g) with the addition of a definition of the term "daytime" and the phrase "federal law enforcement officer."

NOTES OF ADVISORY COMMITTEE ON RULES——1974 AMENDMENT

The amendment restores the words "court of record" which were inadvertently omitted from the amended text of the subdivision which was transmitted by the Judicial Conference to the Supreme Court and prescribed by the Court on April 24, 1972.

NOTES OF ADVISORY COMMITTEE ON RULES——1977 AMENDMENT

Rule 41(c)(2) is added to establish a procedure for the issuance of a search warrant when it is not reasonably practicable for the person obtaining the warrant to present a written affidavit to a magistrate or a state judge as required by subdivision (c)(1). At least two states have adopted a similar procedure, Ariz.Rev.Stat. Ann. §§13–1444(c)–1445(c) (Supp. 1973); Cal.Pen. Code §§1526(b), 1528(b) (West Supp. 1974), and comparable amendments are under consideration in other jurisdictions. See Israel, Legislative Regulation of Searches and Seizures: The Michigan Proposals, 73 Mich.L.Rev. 221, 258–63 (1975); Nakell, Proposed Revisions of North Carolina's Search and Seizure Law, 52 N.Car.L.Rev. 277, 306–11 (1973). It has been strongly recommended that "every State enact legislation that provides for the issuance of search warrants pursuant to telephoned petitions and affidavits from police officers." National Advisory Commission on Criminal Justice Standards and Goals, Report on Police 95 (1973). Experience with the procedure has been most favorable. Miller, Telephonic Search Warrants: The San Diego Experience, 9 The Prosecutor 385 (1974).

The trend of recent Supreme Court decisions has been to give greater priority to the use of a search warrant as the proper way of making a lawful search:

It is a cardinal rule that, in seizing goods and articles, law enforcement agents must secure and use search warrants whenever reasonably practicable. . . . This rule rests upon the desirability of having magistrates rather than police officers determine when searches and seizures are permissible and what limitations should be placed upon such activities. Trupiano v. United States, 334 U.S. 699, 705 (1948), quoted with approval in Chimel v. California, 395 U.S. 752, 758 (1969).

See also Coolidge v. New Hampshire, 403 U.S. 443 (1971); Note, Chambers v. Maroney: New Dimensions in the Law of Search and Seizure, 46 Indiana L.J. 257, 262 (1971).

Use of search warrants can best be encouraged by making it administratively feasible to obtain a warrant when one is needed. One reason for the nonuse of the warrant has been the administrative difficulties involved in getting a warrant, particularly at times of the day when a judicial officer is ordinarily unavailable. See L. Tiffany, D. McIntyre, and D. Rotenberg, Detection of Crime 105–116 (1967); LaFave, Improving Police Performance Through the Exclusionary Rule, 30 Mo.L.Rev. 391, 411 (1965). Federal law enforcement officers are not infrequently confronted with situations in which the circumstances are not sufficiently "exigent" to justify the serious step of conducting a warrantless search of private premises, but yet there exists a significant possibility that critical evidence would be lost in the time it would take to obtain a search warrant by traditional means. See, e.g., United States v. Johnson,——F.2d——(D.C. Cir. June 16, 1975).

Subdivision (c)(2) provides that a warrant may be issued on the basis of an oral statement of a person not in the physical presence of the federal magistrate. Telephone, radio, or other electronic methods of communication are contemplated. For the warrant to properly issue, four requirements must be met:

(1) The applicant—a federal law enforcement officer or an attorney for the government, as required by subdivision (a)—must persuade the magistrate that the circumstances of time and place make it reasonable to request the magistrate to issue a warrant on the basis of oral testimony. This restriction on the issuance of a warrant recognizes the inherent limitations of an oral warrant procedure, the lack of demeanor evidence, and the lack of a written record for the reviewing magistrate to consider before issuing the warrant. See Comment, Oral Search Warrants: A New Standard of Warrant Availability, 21 U.C.L.A. Law Review 691, 701 (1974). Circumstances making it reasonable to obtain a warrant on oral testimony exist if delay in obtaining the warrant might result in the destruction or disappearance of the property [see Chimel v. California, 395 U.S. 752, 773–774 (1969) (White, dissenting); Landynski, The Supreme Court's Search for Fourth Amendment Standards: The Warrantless Search, 45 Conn.B.J. 2, 25 (1971)]; or because of the time when the warrant is sought, the distance from the magistrate of the person seeking the warrant, or both.

(2) The applicant must orally state facts sufficient to satisfy the probable cause requirement for the issuance of the search warrant. (See subdivision (c)(1).) This information may come from either the applicant federal law enforcement officer or the attorney for the government or a witness willing to make an oral statement. The oral testimony must be recorded at this time so that the transcribed affidavit will provide an adequate basis for determining the sufficiency of the evidence if that issue should later arise. See Kipperman. Inaccurate Search Warrant Affidavits as a Ground for Suppressing Evidence, 84 Harv.L.Rev. 825 (1971). It is contemplated that the recording of the oral testimony will be made by a court reporter, by a mechanical recording device, or by a verbatim contemporaneous writing by the magistrate. Recording a telephone conversation is no longer difficult with many easily operated recorders available. See 86:2 L.A. Daily Journal 1 (1973); Miller, Telephonic Search Warrants: The San Diego Experience, 9 The Prosecutor 385, 386 (1974).

(3) The applicant must read the contents of the warrant to the federal magistrate in order to enable the magistrate to know whether the requirements of certainty in the warrant are satisfied. The magistrate may direct that changes be made in the warrant. If the magistrate approves the warrant as requested or as modified by the magistrate, he then issues the warrant by directing the applicant to sign the magistrate's name to the duplicate original warrant. The magistrate then causes to be made a written copy of the approved warrant. This constitutes the original warrant. The magistrate enters the time of issuance of the duplicate original warrant on the face of the original warrant.

(4) Return of the duplicate original warrant and the original warrant must conform to subdivision (d). The transcript of the sworn oral testimony setting forth the grounds for issuance of the warrant must be signed by affiant in the presence of the magistrate and filed with the court.

Because federal magistrates are likely to be accessible through the use of the telephone or other electronic devices, it is unnecessary to authorize state judges to issue warrants under subdivision (c)(2).

Although the procedure set out in subdivision (c)(2) contemplates resort to technology which did not exist when the Fourth Amendment was adopted, the Advisory Committee is of the view that the procedure complies with all of the requirements of the Amendment. The telephonic search warrant process has been upheld as constitutional by the courts, e.g., People v. Peck, 38 Cal.App.3d 993, 113 Cal.Rptr. 806 (1974), and has consistently been so viewed by commentators. See Israel, Legislative Regulation of Searches and Seizures: The Michigan Proposals, 73 Mich.L.Rev. 221, 260 (1975); Nakell, Proposed Revisions of North Carolina's Search and Seizure Law, 52 N.Car.L.Rev. 277, 310 (1973); Comment, Oral Search Warrants: A New Standard of Warrant Availability, 21 U.C.L.A.Rev. 691, 697 (1973).

Reliance upon oral testimony as a basis for issuing a search warrant is permissible under the Fourth Amendment. Campbell v. Minnesota, 487 F.2d 1 (8th Cir. 1973); United States ex rel. Gaugler v. Brierley, 477 F.2d 516 (3d Cir. 1973); Tabasko v. Barton, 472 F.2d 871 (6th Cir. 1972); Frazier v. Roberts, 441 F.2d 1224 (8th Cir. 1971). Thus, the procedure authorized under subdivision (c)(2) is not objectionable on the ground that the oral statement is not transcribed in advance of the issuance of the warrant. People v. Peck, 38 Cal.App.3d 993, 113 Cal.Rptr. 806 (1974). Although it has been questioned whether oral testimony will suffice under the Fourth Amendment if some kind of contemporaneous record is not made of that testimony, see dissent from denial of certiorari in Christofferson v. Washington, 393 U.S. 1090 (1969), this problem is not present under the procedure set out in subdivision (c)(2).

The Fourth Amendment requires that warrants issue "upon probable cause, supported by Oath or affirmation." The significance of the oath requirement is "that someone must take the responsibility for the facts alleged, giving rise to the probable cause for the issuance of a warrant." United States ex rel. Pugh v. Pate, 401 F.2d 6 (7th Cir. 1968); See also Frazier v. Roberts, 441 F.2d 1224 (8th Cir. 1971). This is accomplished under the procedure required by subdivision (c)(2); the need for an oath under the Fourth Amendment does not "require a face to face confrontation between the magistrate and the affiant." People v. Chavez, 27 Cal.App.3d 883, 104 Cal.Rptr. 247 (1972). See also People v. Aguirre, 26 Cal.App.3d 7, 103 Cal.Rptr. 153 (1972), noting it is unnecessary that "oral statements [be] taken in the physical presence of the magistrate."

The availability of the procedure authorized by subdivision (c)(2) will minimize the necessity of federal law enforcement officers engaging in other practices which, at least on occasion, might threaten to a greater extent those values protected by the Fourth Amendment. Although it is permissible for an officer in the field to relay his information by radio or telephone to another officer who has more ready access to a magistrate and who will thus act as the affiant, Lopez v. United States, 370 F.2d 8 (5th Cir. 1966); State v. Banks, 250 N.C. 728, 110 S.E.2d 322 (1959), that procedure is less desirable than that permitted under subdivision (c)(2), for it deprives "the magistrate of the opportunity to examine the officer at the scene, who is in a much better position to answer questions relating to probable cause and the requisite scope of the search." Israel, Legislative Regulation of Searches and Seizures: The Michigan Proposals, 73 Mich.L.Rev. 221, 260 (1975). Or, in the absence of the subdivision (c)(2) procedure, officers might take "protective custody" of the premises and occupants for a significant period of time while a search warrant was sought by traditional means. The extent to which the "protective custody" procedure may be employed consistent with the Fourth Amendment is uncertain at best; see Griswold, Criminal Procedure, 1969—Is It a Means or an End?, 29 Md.L.Rev. 307, 317 (1969). The unavailability of the subdivision (c)(2) procedure also makes more tempting an immediate resort to a warrantless search in the hope that the circumstances will later be found to have been sufficiently "exigent" to justify such a step. See Miller, Telephonic Search Warrants: The San Diego Experience, 9 The Prosecutor 385, 386 (1974), noting a dramatic increase in police utilization of the warrant process following enactment of a telephonic warrant statute.

NOTES OF COMMITTEE ON THE JUDICIARY, SENATE REPORT NO. 95–354; 1977 AMENDMENTS PROPOSED BY THE SUPREME COURT

The committee agrees with the Supreme Court that it is desirable to encourage Federal law enforcement officers to seek search warrants in situations where they might otherwise conduct warrantless searches by providing for a telephone search warrant procedure with the basic characteristics suggested in the proposed Rule 41(c)(2). As the Supreme Court has observed, "It is a cardinal rule that, in seizing goods and articles, law enforcement agents must secure and use search warrants whenever reasonably practicable." After consideration of the Supreme Court version and a proposal set forth in H.R. 7888, the committee decided to use the language of the House bill as the vehicle, with certain modifications.

A new provision, as indicated in subparagraph (c)(2)(A), is added to establish a procedure for the issuance of a search warrant where the circumstances make it reasonable to dispense with a written affidavit to be presented in person to a magistrate. At least two States have adopted a similar procedure—Arizona and California—and comparable amendments are under consideration in other jurisdictions. Such a procedure has been strongly recommended by the National Advisory Commission on Criminal Justice Standards and Goals and State experience with the procedure has been favorable. The telephone search warrant process has been upheld as constitutional by the courts and has consistently been so viewed by commentators.

In recommending a telephone search warrant procedure, the Advisory Committee note on the Supreme Court proposal points out that the preferred method of conducting a search is with a search warrant. The note indicates that the rationale for the proposed change is to encourage Federal law enforcement officers to seek search warrants in situations when they might otherwise conduct warrantless searches. "Federal law enforcement officers are not infrequently confronted with situations in which the circumstances are not sufficiently 'exigent' to justify the serious step of conducting a warrantless search of private premises, but yet there exists a significant possibility that critical evidence would be lost in the time it would take to obtain a search warrant by traditional means."

Subparagraph (c)(2)(B) provides that the person requesting the warrant shall prepare a "duplicate original warrant" which will be read and recorded verbatim by the magistrate on an "original warrant." The magistrate may direct that the warrant be modified.

Subparagraph (c)(2)(C) provides that, if the magistrate is satisfied that the circumstances are such as to make it reasonable to dispense with a written affidavit and that grounds for the application exist or there is probable cause to believe that they exist, he shall order the issuance of the warrant by directing the requestor to sign the magistrate's name on the duplicate original warrant. The magistrate is required to sign the original warrant and enter the time of issuance thereon. The finding of probable cause may be based on the same type of evidence appropriate for a warrant upon affidavit.

Subparagraph (c)(2)(D) requires the magistrate to place the requestor and any witness under oath and, if a voice recording device is available, to record the proceeding. If a voice recording is not available, the proceeding must be recorded verbatim stenographically or in longhand. Verified copies must be filed with the court as specified.

Subparagraph (c)(2)(E) provides that the contents of the warrant upon oral testimony shall be the same as the contents of a warrant upon affidavit.

Subparagraph (c)(2)(F) provides that the person who executes the warrant shall enter the exact time of execution on the face of the duplicate original warrant. Unlike H.R. 7888, this subparagraph does not require the person who executes the warrant to have physical possession of the duplicate original warrant at the time of the execution of the warrant. The committee believes this would make an unwise and unnecessary distinction between execution of regular warrants issued on written affidavits and warrants issued by telephone that would limit the flexibility and utility of this procedure for no useful purpose.

Finally, subparagraph (c)(2)(G) makes it clear that, absent a finding of bad faith by the government, the magistrate's judgment that the circumstances made it reasonable to dispense with a written affidavit—a decision that does not go to the core question of whether there was probable cause to issue a warrant—is not a ground for granting a motion to suppress evidence.

CONGRESSIONAL MODIFICATION OF PROPOSED 1977 AMENDMENT

Pub. L. 95–78, §2(e), July 30, 1977, 91 Stat. 320, provided in part that the amendment by the Supreme Court [in its order of Apr. 26, 1976] to subdivision (c) of rule 41 of the Federal Rules of Criminal Procedure [subd. (c) of this rule] is approved in a modified form.

NOTES OF ADVISORY COMMITTEE ON RULES—1979 AMENDMENT

This amendment to Rule 41 is intended to make it possible for a search warrant to issue to search for a person under two circumstances: (i) when there is probable cause to arrest that person; or (ii) when that person is being unlawfully restrained. There may be instances in which a search warrant would be required to conduct a search in either of these circumstances. Even when a search warrant would not be required to enter a place to search for a person, a procedure for obtaining a warrant should be available so that law enforcement officers will be encouraged to resort to the preferred alternative of acquiring "an objective predetermination of probable cause" Katz v. United States, 389 U.S. 347, 88 S.Ct. 507, 19 L.Ed.2d 576 (1967), in this instance, that the person sought is at the place to be searched.

That part of the amendment which authorizes issuance of a search warrant to search for a person unlawfully restrained is consistent with ALI Model Code of Pre-Arraignment Procedure §SS 210.3(1)(d) (Proposed Official Draft, 1975), which specifies that a search warrant may issue to search for "an individual * * * who is unlawfully held in confinement or other restraint." As noted in the Commentary thereto, id. at p. 507:

Ordinarily such persons will be held against their will and in that case the persons are, of course, not subject to "seizure." But they are, in a sense, "evidence" of crime, and the use of search warrants for these purposes presents no conceptual difficulties.
Some state search warrant provisions also provide for issuance of a warrant in these circumstances. See, e. g., Ill.Rev.Stat. ch. 38, §108–3 ("Any person who has been kidnapped in violation of the laws of this State, or who has been kidnapped in another jurisdiction and is now concealed within this State").

It may be that very often exigent circumstances, especially the need to act very promptly to protect the life or well-being of the kidnap victim, would justify an immediate warrantless search for the person restrained. But this is not inevitably the case. Moreover, as noted above there should be available a process whereby law enforcement agents may acquire in advance a judicial determination that they have cause to intrude upon the privacy of those at the place where the victim is thought to be located.

That part of the amendment which authorizes issuance of a search warrant to search for a person to be arrested is also consistent with ALI Model Code of Pre-Arraignment Procedure §SS 210.3(1)(d) (Proposed Official Draft, 1975), which states that a search warrant may issue to search for "an individual for whose arrest there is reasonable cause." As noted in the Commentary thereto, id. at p. 507, it is desirable that there be "explicit statutory authority for such searches." Some state search warrant provisions also expressly provide for the issuance of a search warrant to search for a person to be arrested. See, e. g., Del.Code Ann. tit. 11, §2305 ("Persons for whom a warrant of arrest has been issued"). This part of the amendment to Rule 41 covers a defendant or witness for whom an arrest warrant has theretofore issued, or a defendant for whom grounds to arrest exist even though no arrest warrant has theretofore issued. It also covers the arrest of a deportable alien under 8 U.S.C. §1252, whose presence at a certain place might be important evidence of criminal conduct by another person, such as the harboring of undocumented aliens under 8 U.S.C. §1324(a)(3).

In United States v. Watson, 423 U.S. 411, 96 S.Ct. 820, 46 L.Ed.2d 598 (1976), the Court once again alluded to "the still unsettled question" of whether, absent exigent circumstances, officers acting without a warrant may enter private premises to make an arrest. Some courts have indicated that probable cause alone ordinarily is sufficient to support an arrest entry. United States v. Fernandez, 480 F.2d 726 (2d Cir. 1973); United States ex rel. Wright v. Woods, 432 F.2d 1143 (7th Cir. 1970). There exists some authority, however, that except under exigent circumstances a warrant is required to enter the defendant's own premises, United States v. Calhoun, 542 F.2d 1094 (9th Cir. 1976); United States v. Lindsay, 506 F.2d 166 (D.C.Cir. 1974); Dorman v. United States, 435 F.2d 385 (D.C.Cir. 1970), or, at least, to enter the premises of a third party, Virgin Islands v. Gereau, 502 F.2d 914 (3d Cir. 1974); Fisher v. Volz, 496 F.2d 333 (3d Cir. 1974); Huotari v. Vanderport, 380 F.Supp. 645 (D.Minn. 1974).

It is also unclear, assuming a need for a warrant, what kind of warrant is required, although it is sometimes assumed that an arrest warrant will suffice, e. g., United States v. Calhoun, supra; United States v. James, 528 F.2d 999 (5th Cir. 1976). There is a growing body of authority, however, that what is needed to justify entry of the premises of a third party to arrest is a search warrant, e. g., Virgin Islands v. Gereau, supra; Fisher v. Volz, supra. The theory is that if the privacy of this third party is to be protected adequately, what is needed is a probable cause determination by a magistrate that the wanted person is presently within that party's premises. "A warrant for the arrest of a suspect may indicate that the police officer has probable cause to believe the suspect committed the crime; it affords no basis to believe the suspect is in some stranger's home." Fisher v. Volz, supra.

It has sometimes been contended that a search warrant should be required for a nonexigent entry to arrest even when the premises to be entered are those of the person to be arrested. Rotenberg & Tanzer, Searching for the Person to be Seized, 35 Ohio St.L.J. 56, 69 (1974). Case authority in support is lacking, and it may be that the protections of a search warrant are less important in such a situation because ordinarily "rudimentary police procedure dictates that a suspect's residence be eliminated as a possible hiding place before a search is conducted elsewhere." People v. Sprovieri, 95 Ill.App.2d 10, 238 N.E.2d 115 (1968).

Despite these uncertainties, the fact remains that in some circuits under some circumstances a search warrant is required to enter private premises to arrest. Moreover, the law on this subject is in a sufficient state of uncertainty that this position may be taken by other courts. It is thus important that Rule 41 clearly express that a search warrant for this purpose may issue. And even if future decisions head the other direction, the need for the amendment would still exist. It is clear that law enforcement officers "may not constitutionally enter the home of a private individual to search for another person, though he be named in a valid arrest warrant in their

141

possession, absent probable cause to believe that the named suspect is present within at the time." Fisher v. Volz, supra. The cautious officer is entitled to a procedure whereby he may have this probable cause determination made by a neutral and detached magistrate in advance of the entry.

NOTES OF ADVISORY COMMITTEE ON RULES—1987 AMENDMENT

The amendments are technical. No substantive change is intended.

NOTES OF ADVISORY COMMITTEE ON RULES—1989 AMENDMENT

The amendment to Rule 41(e) conforms the rule to the practice in most districts and eliminates language that is somewhat confusing. The Supreme Court has upheld warrants for the search and seizure of property in the possession of persons who are not suspected of criminal activity. See, e.g., Zurcher v. Stanford Daily, 436 U.S. 547 (1978). Before the amendment, Rule 41(e) permitted such persons to seek return of their property if they were aggrieved by an unlawful search and seizure. But, the rule failed to address the harm that may result from the interference with the lawful use of property by persons who are not suspected of wrongdoing. Courts have recognized that once the government no longer has a need to use evidence, it should be returned. See, e.g., United States v. Wilson, 540 F.2d 1100 (D.C. Cir. 1976). Prior to the amendment, Rule 41(e) did not explicitly recognize a right of a property owner to obtain return of lawfully seized property even though the government might be able to protect its legitimate law enforcement interests in the property despite its return—e.g., by copying documents or by conditioning the return on government access to the property at a future time. As amended, Rule 41(e) provides that an aggrieved person may seek return of property that has been unlawfully seized, and a person whose property has been lawfully seized may seek return of property when aggrieved by the government's continued possession of it.

No standard is set forth in the rule to govern the determination of whether property should be returned to a person aggrieved either by an unlawful seizure or by deprivation of the property. The fourth amendment protects people from unreasonable seizures as well as unreasonable searches, United States v. Place, 462 U.S. 696, 701 (1983), and reasonableness under all of the circumstances must be the test when a person seeks to obtain the return of property. If the United States has a need for the property in an investigation or prosecution, its retention of the property generally is reasonable. But, if the United States' legitimate interests can be satisfied even if the property is returned, continued retention of the property would become unreasonable.

The amendment deletes language dating from 1944 stating that evidence shall not be admissible at a hearing or at a trial if the court grants the motion to return property under Rule 41(e). This language has not kept pace with the development of exclusionary rule doctrine and is currently only confusing. The Supreme Court has now held that evidence seized in violation of the fourth amendment, but in good faith pursuant to a warrant, may be used even against a person aggrieved by the constitutional violation. United States v. Leon, 468 U.S. 897 (1984). The Court has also held that illegally seized evidence may be admissible against persons who are not personally aggrieved by an illegal search or seizure. Rakas v. Illinois, 439 U.S. 128 (1978). Property that is inadmissible for one purpose (e.g., as part of the government's case-in-chief) may be admissible for another purpose (e.g., impeachment, United States v. Havens, 446 U.S. 620 (1980)). Federal courts have relied upon these decisions and permitted the government to retain and to use evidence as permitted by the fourth amendment.

Rule 41(e) is not intended to deny the United States the use of evidence permitted by the fourth amendment and federal statutes, even if the evidence might have been unlawfully seized. See, e.g., United States v. Calandra, 414 U.S. 338, 349 n.6 (1978) ("Rule 41(e) does not constitute a statutory expansion of the exclusionary rule."); United States v. Roberts, 852 F.2d 671 (2nd Cir. 1988) (exceptions to exclusionary rule applicable to Rule 41(e)). Thus, the exclusionary provision is deleted, and the scope of the exclusionary rule is reserved for judicial decisions.

In opting for a reasonableness approach and in deleting the exclusionary language, the Committee rejects the analysis of Sovereign News Co. v. United States, 690 F.2d 569 (6th Cir. 1982), cert. denied, 464 U.S. 814 (1983), which held that the United States must return photocopies of lawfully seized business records unless it could demonstrate that the records were "necessary for a specific investigation." As long as the government has a law enforcement purpose in copying records, there is no reason why it should be saddled with a heavy burden of justifying the copying. Although some cases have held that the government must return copies of records where the originals were illegally seized—See, e.g., United States v. Wallace & Tiernan Co., 336 U.S. 793, 801 (1948); Goodman v. United States, 369 F.2d 166 (9th Cir. 1966)—these holdings are questionable in situations in which the government is permitted under Supreme Court decisions to use illegally seized evidence, and their reasoning does not apply to legally seized evidence.

As amended, Rule 41(e) avoids an all or nothing approach whereby the government must either return records and make no copies or keep originals notwithstanding the hardship to their owner. The amended rule recognizes that reasonable accommodations might protect both the law enforcement interests of the United States and the property rights of property owners and holders. In many instances documents and records that are relevant to ongoing or contemplated investigations and prosecutions may be returned to their owner as long as the government preserves a copy for future use. In some circumstances, however, equitable considerations might justify an order requiring the government to return or destroy all copies of records that it has seized. See, e.g., Paton v. LaPrade, 524 F.2d 862, 867–69 (3rd Cir. 1975). The amended rule contemplates judicial action that will respect both possessory and law enforcement interests.

The word "judge" is changed to "court" in the second sentence of subdivision (e) to clarify that a magistrate may receive evidence in the course of making a finding or a proposed finding for consideration by the district judge.

NOTES OF ADVISORY COMMITTEE ON RULES—1990 AMENDMENT

Rule 41(a). The amendment to Rule 41(a) serves several purposes. First, it furthers the constitutional preference for warrants by providing a mechanism whereby a warrant may be issued in a district for a person or property that is moving into or through a district or might move outside the district while the warrant is sought or executed. Second, it clarifies the authority of federal magistrates to issue search warrants for property that is relevant to criminal investigation being conducted in a district and, although located outside the United States, that is in a place where the United States may lawfully conduct a search.

The amendment is not intended to expand the class of persons authorized to request a warrant and the language "upon request of a federal law enforcement officer," modifies all warrants covered by Rule 41. The amendment is intended to make clear that judges of state courts of record within a federal district may issue search warrants for persons or property located within that district. The amendment does not prescribe the circumstances in which a warrant is required and is not intended to change the law concerning warrant requirements. Rather the rule provides a mechanism for the issuance of a warrant when one is required, or when a law enforcement officer desires to seek a warrant even though warrantless activity is permissible.

Rule 41(a)(1) permits anticipatory warrants by omitting the words "is located," which in the past required that in all instances the object of the search had to be located within the district at the time the warrant was issued. Now a search for property or a person within the district, or expected to be within the district, is valid if it otherwise complies with the rule.

Rule 41(a)(2) authorizes execution of search warrants in another district under limited circumstances. Because these searches are unusual, the rule limits to federal magistrates the authority to issue such warrants. The rule permits a federal magistrate to issue a search warrant for property within the district which is moving or may move outside the district. The amendment recognizes that there are inevitable delays between the application for a warrant and its authorization, on the one hand, and the execution of the warrant, on the other hand. The amendment also recognizes that when property is in motion, there may be good reason to delay execution until the property comes to rest. The amendment provides a practical tool for federal law enforcement officers that avoids the necessity of their either seeking several warrants in different districts for the same property or their relying on an exception to the warrant requirement for search of property or a person that has moved outside a district.

The amendment affords a useful warrant procedure to cover familiar fact patterns, like the one typified by United States v. Chadwick, 433 U.S. 1 (1976). In Chadwick, agents in San Diego observed suspicious activities involving a footlocker carried onto a train. When the train arrived in Boston, the agents made an arrest and conducted a warrantless search of the footlocker (which the Supreme Court held was invalid). Under the amended rule, agents who have probable cause in San Diego would be able to obtain a warrant for a search of the footlocker even though it is moving outside the district. Agents, who will not be sure exactly where the footlocker will be unloaded from the train, may execute the warrant when the journey ends. See also United States v. Karo, 468 U.S. 705 (1984) (rejecting argument that obtaining warrant to monitor beeper would not comply with requirement of particularity because its final destination may not be known); United States v. Knotts, 460 U.S. 276 (1983) (agents followed beeper across state lines). The Supreme Court's holding in Chadwick permits law enforcement officers to seize and hold an object like a footlocker while seeking a warrant. Although the amended rule would not disturb this holding, it provides a mechanism for agents to seek a probable cause determination and a warrant before interfering with the property and seizing it. It encourages reliance on warrants.

The amendment is not intended to abrogate the requirements of probable cause and prompt execution. At some point, a warrant issued in one district might become stale when executed in another district. But staleness can be a problem even when a warrant is executed in the district in which it was issued. See generally United States v. Harris, 403 U.S. 573, 579, 589 (1971). And at some point, an intervening event might make execution of a warrant unreasonable. Cf. Illinois v. Andreas, 463 U.S. 765, 772 (1983). Evaluations of the execution of a warrant must, in the nature of things, be made after the warrant is issued.

Nor does the amendment abrogate the requirement of particularity. Thus, it does not authorize searches of premises other than a particular place. As recognized by the Supreme Court in Karo, supra, although agents may not know exactly where moving property will come to rest, they can still describe with particularity the object to be searched.

The amendment would authorize the search of a particular object or container provided that law enforcement officials were otherwise in a lawful position to execute the search without making an impermissible intrusion. For example, it would authorize the search of luggage moving aboard a plane.

Rule 41(a)(3) [The Supreme Court did not adopt the addition of a subsection (3) to Rule 41(a)] provides for warrants to search property outside the United States. No provision for search warrants for persons is made lest the rule be read as a substitute for extradition proceedings. As with the provision for searches outside a district, supra, this provision is limited to search warrants issued by federal magistrates. The phrase "relevant to criminal investigation" is intended to encompass all of the types of property that are covered by Rule 41(b), which is unchanged by the amendment. That phrase also is intended to include those investigations which begin with the request for the search warrant.

Some searches and seizures by federal officers outside the territory of the United States may be governed by the fourth amendment. See generally Saltzburg, the Reach of the Bill of Rights Beyond the Terra Firma of the United States, 20 Va. J. Int'l L. 741 (1980). Prior to the amendment of the rule, it was unclear how federal officers might obtain warrants authorizing searches outside the district of the issuing magistrate. Military Rule of Evidence 315 provided guidance for searches of military personnel and property and nonmilitary property in a foreign country. But it had no civilian counterpart. See generally S. Saltzburg, L. Schinasi, & D. Schlueter, Military Rules of Evidence Manual 274–95 (2d ed. 1986).

Although the amendment rests on the assumption that the Constitution applies to some extraterritorial searches, cf United States v. Verdugo-Urquidez, 110 S. Ct. 1056, 494 U.S. 259 (1990) (fourth amendment inapplicable to extraterritorial searches of property owned by nonresident aliens), it does not address the question of when the Constitution requires a warrant. Nor does it address the issue of whether international agreements or treaties or the law of a foreign nation might be applicable. See United States v. Patterson, 812 F. 2d 486 (9th Cir. 1987). Instead, the amendment is intended to provide necessary clarification as to how a warrant may be obtained when law enforcement officials are required, or find it desirable, to do so.

Notes of Advisory Committee on Rules—1993 Amendment

The amendment to Rule 41(c)(2)(A) is intended to expand the authority of magistrates and judges in considering oral requests for search warrants. It also recognizes the value of, and the public's increased dependence on facsimile machines to transmit written information efficiently and accurately. As amended, the Rule should thus encourage law enforcement officers to seek a warrant, especially when it is necessary, or desirable, to supplement oral telephonic communications by written materials which may now be transmitted electronically as well. The magistrate issuing the warrant may require that the original affidavit be ultimately filed. The Committee considered, but rejected, amendments to the Rule which would have permitted other means of electronic transmission, such as the use of computer modems. In its view, facsimile transmissions provide some method of assuring the authenticity of the writing transmitted by the affiant.

The Committee considered amendments to Rule 41(c)(2)(B), Application, Rule 41(c)(2)(C), Issuance, and Rule 41(g), Return of Papers to Clerk, but determined that allowing use of facsimile transmissions in those instances would not save time and would present problems and questions concerning the need to preserve facsimile copies.

The Rule is also amended to conform to the Judicial Improvements Act of 1990 [P.L. 101–650, Title III, Section 321] which provides that each United States magistrate appointed under section 631 of title 28, United States Code, shall be known as a United States magistrate judge.

Committee Notes on Rules—2002 Amendment

The language of Rule 41 has been amended as part of the general restyling of the Criminal Rules to make them more easily understood and to make style and terminology consistent throughout the rules. These changes are intended to be stylistic only, except as otherwise noted below. Rule 41 has been completely reorganized to make it easier to read and apply its key provisions.

Rule 41(b)(3) is a new provision that incorporates a congressional amendment to Rule 41 as a part of the Uniting and Strengthening America by Providing Appropriate Tools Required to Intercept and Obstruct Terrorism (USA PATRIOT ACT) Act of 2001. The provision explicitly addresses the authority of a magistrate judge to issue a search warrant in an investigation of domestic or international terrorism. As long as the magistrate judge has authority in a district where activities related to terrorism may have occurred, the magistrate judge may issue a warrant for persons or property not only within the district, but outside the district as well.

Current Rule 41(c)(1), which refers to the fact that hearsay evidence may be used to support probable cause, has been deleted. That language was added to the rule in 1972, apparently to reflect emerging federal case law. See Advisory Committee Note to 1972 Amendments to Rule 41 (citing cases). Similar language was added to Rule 4 in 1974. In the intervening years, however, the case law has become perfectly clear on that proposition. Thus, the Committee believed that the reference to hearsay was no longer necessary. Furthermore, the limited reference to hearsay evidence was misleading to the extent that it might have suggested that other forms of inadmissible evidence could not be considered. For example, the rule made no reference to considering a defendant's prior criminal record, which clearly may be considered in deciding whether probable cause exists. See, e.g., Brinegar v. United States, 338 U.S. 160 (1949) (officer's knowledge of defendant's prior criminal activity). Rather than address that issue, or any other similar issues, the Committee believed that the matter was best addressed in Rule 1101(d)(3), Federal Rules of Evidence. That rule explicitly provides that the Federal Rules of Evidence do not apply to "preliminary examinations in criminal cases, . . . issuance of warrants for arrest, criminal summonses, and search warrants . . . ." The Advisory Committee Note accompanying that rule recognizes that: "The nature of the proceedings makes application of the formal rules of evidence inappropriate and impracticable." The Committee did not intend to make any substantive changes in practice by deleting the reference to hearsay evidence.

Current Rule 41(d) provides that the officer taking the property under the warrant must provide a receipt for the property and complete an inventory. The revised rule indicates that the inventory may be completed by an officer present during the execution of the warrant, and not necessarily the officer actually executing the warrant.

Committee Notes on Rules—2006 Amendment

143

The amendments to Rule 41 address three issues: first, procedures for issuing tracking device warrants; second, a provision for delaying any notice required by the rule; and third, a provision permitting a magistrate judge to use reliable electronic means to issue warrants.

Subdivision (a). Amended Rule 41(a)(2) includes two new definitional provisions. The first, in Rule 41(a)(2)(D), addresses the definitions of "domestic terrorism" and "international terrorism," terms used in Rule 41(b)(2). The second, in Rule 41(a)(2)(E), addresses the definition of "tracking device."

Subdivision (b). Amended Rule 41(b)(4) is a new provision, designed to address the use of tracking devices. Such searches are recognized both by statute, see 18 U.S.C. §3117(a) and by caselaw, see, e.g., United States v. Karo, 468 U.S. 705 (1984); United States v. Knotts, 460 U.S. 276 (1983). Warrants may be required to monitor tracking devices when they are used to monitor persons or property in areas where there is a reasonable expectation of privacy. See, e.g., United States v. Karo, supra (although no probable cause was required to install beeper, officers' monitoring of its location in defendant's home raised Fourth Amendment concerns). Nonetheless, there is no procedural guidance in current Rule 41 for those judicial officers who are asked to issue tracking device warrants. As with traditional search warrants for persons or property, tracking device warrants may implicate law enforcement interests in multiple districts.

The amendment provides that a magistrate judge may issue a warrant, if he or she has the authority to do so in the district, to install and use a tracking device, as that term is defined in 18 U.S.C. §3117(b). The magistrate judge's authority under this rule includes the authority to permit entry into an area where there is a reasonable expectation of privacy, installation of the tracking device, and maintenance and removal of the device. The Committee did not intend by this amendment to expand or contract the definition of what might constitute a tracking device. The amendment is based on the understanding that the device will assist officers only in tracking the movements of a person or property. The warrant may authorize officers to track the person or property within the district of issuance, or outside the district.

Because the authorized tracking may involve more than one district or state, the Committee believes that only federal judicial officers should be authorized to issue this type of warrant. Even where officers have no reason to believe initially that a person or property will move outside the district of issuance, issuing a warrant to authorize tracking both inside and outside the district avoids the necessity of obtaining multiple warrants if the property or person later crosses district or state lines.

The amendment reflects the view that if the officers intend to install or use the device in a constitutionally protected area, they must obtain judicial approval to do so. If, on the other hand, the officers intend to install and use the device without implicating any Fourth Amendment rights, there is no need to obtain the warrant. See, e.g., United States v. Knotts, supra, where the officers' actions in installing and following tracking device did not amount to a search under the Fourth Amendment.

Subdivision (d). Amended Rule 41(d) includes new language on tracking devices. The tracking device statute, 18 U.S.C. §3117, does not specify the standard an applicant must meet to install a tracking device. The Supreme Court has acknowledged that the standard for installation of a tracking device is unresolved, and has reserved ruling on the issue until it is squarely presented by the facts of a case. See United States v. Karo, 468 U.S. 705, 718 n. 5 (1984). The amendment to Rule 41 does not resolve this issue or hold that such warrants may issue only on a showing of probable cause. Instead, it simply provides that if probable cause is shown, the magistrate judge must issue the warrant. And the warrant is only needed if the device is installed (for example, in the trunk of the defendant's car) or monitored (for example, while the car is in the defendant's garage) in an area in which the person being monitored has a reasonable expectation of privacy.

Subdivision (e). Rule 41(e) has been amended to permit magistrate judges to use reliable electronic means to issue warrants. Currently, the rule makes no provision for using such media. The amendment parallels similar changes to Rules 5 and 32.1(a)(5)(B)(i).

The amendment recognizes the significant improvements in technology. First, more counsel, courts, and magistrate judges now routinely use facsimile transmissions of documents. And many courts and magistrate judges are now equipped to receive filings by electronic means. Indeed, some courts encourage or require that certain documents be filed by electronic means. Second, the technology has advanced to the state where such filings may be sent from, and received at, locations outside the courthouse. Third, electronic media can now provide improved quality of transmission and security measures. In short, in a particular case, using facsimiles and electronic media to transmit a warrant can be both reliable and efficient use of judicial resources.

The term "electronic" is used to provide some flexibility to the rule and make allowance for further technological advances in transmitting data. Although facsimile transmissions are not specifically identified, the Committee envisions that facsimile transmissions would fall within the meaning of "electronic means."

While the rule does not impose any special requirements on use of facsimile transmissions, neither does it presume that those transmissions are reliable. The rule treats all electronic transmissions in a similar fashion. Whatever the mode, the means used must be "reliable." While the rule does not further define that term, the Committee envisions that a court or magistrate judge would make that determination as a local matter. In deciding whether a particular electronic means, or media, would be reliable, the court might consider first, the expected quality and clarity of the transmission. For example, is it possible to read the contents of the warrant in its entirety, as though it were the original or a clean photocopy? Second, the court may consider whether security measures are available to insure that the transmission is not compromised. In this regard, most courts are now equipped to require that certain documents contain a digital signature, or some other similar system for restricting access. Third, the court may consider whether there are reliable means of preserving the document for later use.

Amended Rule 41(e)(2)(B) is a new provision intended to address the contents of tracking device warrants. To avoid open-ended monitoring of tracking devices, the revised rule requires the magistrate judge to specify in the warrant the length of time for using the device. Although the initial time stated in the warrant may not exceed 45 days, extensions of time may be granted for good cause. The rule further specifies that any installation of a tracking device authorized by the warrant must be made within ten calendar days and, unless otherwise provided, that any installation occur during daylight hours.

Subdivision (f). Current Rule 41(f) has been completely revised to accommodate new provisions dealing with tracking device warrants. First, current Rule 41(f)(1) has been revised to address execution and delivery of warrants to search for and seize a person or property; no substantive change has been made to that provision. New Rule 41(f)(2) addresses execution and delivery of tracking device warrants. That provision generally tracks the structure of revised Rule 41(f)(1), with appropriate adjustments for the particular requirements of tracking device warrants. Under Rule 41(f)(2)(A) the officer must note on the warrant the time the device was installed and the period during which the device was used. And under new Rule 41(f)(2)(B), the officer must return the tracking device warrant to the magistrate judge designated in the warrant, within 10 calendar days after use of the device has ended.

Amended Rule 41(f)(2)(C) addresses the particular problems of serving a copy of a tracking device warrant on the person who has been tracked, or whose property has been tracked. In the case of other warrants, current Rule 41 envisions that the subjects of the search typically know that they have been searched, usually within a short period of time after the search has taken place. Tracking device warrants, on the other hand, are by their nature covert intrusions and can be successfully used only when the person being investigated is unaware that a tracking device is being used. The amendment requires that the officer must serve a copy of the tracking device warrant on the person within 10 calendar days after the tracking has ended. That service may be accomplished by either personally serving the person, or both by leaving a copy at the person's residence or usual abode and by sending a copy by mail. The Rule also provides, however, that the officer may (for good cause) obtain the court's permission to delay further service of the warrant. That might be appropriate, for example, where the owner of the tracked property is undetermined, or where the officer establishes that the investigation is ongoing and that disclosure of the warrant will compromise that investigation.

Use of a tracking device is to be distinguished from other continuous monitoring or observations that are governed by statutory provisions or caselaw. See Title III, Omnibus Crime Control and Safe Streets Act of 1968, as amended by Title I of the 1986 Electronic Communications Privacy Act [Electronic Communications Privacy Act of 1986], 18 U.S.C. §§2510–2520 [sic]; United States v. Biasucci, 786 F.2d 504 (2d Cir. 1986) (video camera); United States v. Torres, 751 F.2d 875 (7th Cir. 1984) (television surveillance).

Finally, amended Rule 41(f)(3) is a new provision that permits the government to request, and the magistrate judge to grant, a delay in any notice required in Rule 41. The amendment is co-extensive with 18 U.S.C. §3103a(b). That new provision, added as part of the Uniting and Strengthening America by Providing Appropriate Tools Required to Intercept and Obstruct Terrorism (USA PATRIOT) Act of 2001, authorizes a court to delay any notice required in conjunction with the issuance of any search warrants.

Changes Made After Publication and Comment. The Committee agreed with the NADCL [sic] proposal that the words "has authority" should be inserted in Rule 41(c)(3), and (4) to parallel similar language in Rule 41(c)(1) and (2). The Committee also considered, but rejected, a proposal from NADCL [sic] to completely redraft Rule 41(d), regarding the finding of probable cause. The Committee also made minor clarifying changes in the Committee Note.

COMMITTEE NOTES ON RULES—2008 AMENDMENT

Subdivision (b)(5). Rule 41(b)(5) authorizes a magistrate judge to issue a search warrant for property located within certain delineated parts of United States jurisdiction that are outside of any State or any federal judicial district. The locations covered by the rule include United States territories, possessions, and commonwealths not within a federal judicial district as well as certain premises associated with United States diplomatic and consular missions. These are locations in which the United States has a legally cognizable interest or in which it exerts lawful authority and control. The rule is intended to authorize a magistrate judge to issue a search warrant in any of the locations for which 18 U.S.C. §7(9) provides jurisdiction. The difference between the language in this rule and the statute reflect the style conventions used in these rules, rather than any intention to alter the scope of the legal authority conferred. Under the rule, a warrant may be issued by a magistrate judge in any district in which activities related to the crime under investigation may have occurred, or in the District of Columbia, which serves as the default district for venue under 18 U.S.C. §3238.

Rule 41(b)(5) provides the authority to issue warrants for the seizure of property in the designated locations when law enforcement officials are required or find it desirable to obtain such warrants. The Committee takes no position on the question whether the Constitution requires a warrant for searches covered by the rule, or whether any international agreements, treaties, or laws of a foreign nation might be applicable. The rule does not address warrants for persons, which could be viewed as inconsistent with extradition requirements.

Changes Made to Proposed Amendment Released for Public Comment. With the assistance of the Style Consultant, the Committee revised (b)(5)(B) and (C) for greater clarity and compliance with the style conventions governing these rules. Because the language no longer tracks precisely the statute, the Committee Note was revised to state that the proposed rule is intended to have the same scope as the jurisdictional provision upon which it was based, 18 U.S.C. §7(9).

COMMITTEE NOTES ON RULES—2009 AMENDMENT

The time set in the former rule at 10 days has been revised to 14 days. See the Committee Note to Rule 45(a).

Subdivision (e)(2). Computers and other electronic storage media commonly contain such large amounts of information that it is often impractical for law enforcement to review all of the information during execution of the warrant at the search location. This rule acknowledges the need for a two-step process: officers may seize or copy the entire storage medium and review it later to determine what electronically stored information falls within the scope of the warrant.

The term "electronically stored information" is drawn from Rule 34(a) of the Federal Rules of Civil Procedure, which states that it includes "writings, drawings, graphs, charts, photographs, sound recordings, images, and other data or data compilations stored in any medium from which information can be obtained." The 2006 Committee Note to Rule 34(a) explains that the description is intended to cover all current types of computer-based information and to encompass future changes and developments. The same broad and flexible description is intended under Rule 41.

In addition to addressing the two-step process inherent in searches for electronically stored information, the Rule limits the 10 [14] day execution period to the actual execution of the warrant and the on-site activity. While consideration was given to a presumptive national or uniform time period within which any subsequent off-site copying or review of the media or electronically stored information would take place, the practical reality is that there is no basis for a "one size fits all" presumptive period. A substantial amount of time can be involved in the forensic imaging and review of information. This is due to the sheer size of the storage capacity of media, difficulties created by encryption and booby traps, and the workload of the computer labs. The rule does not prevent a judge from imposing a deadline for the return of the storage media or access to the electronically stored information at the time the warrant is issued. However, to arbitrarily set a presumptive time period for the return could result in frequent petitions to the court for additional time.

It was not the intent of the amendment to leave the property owner without an expectation of the timing for return of the property, excluding contraband or instrumentalities of crime, or a remedy. Current Rule 41(g) already provides a process for the "person aggrieved" to seek an order from the court for a return of the property, including storage media or electronically stored information, under reasonable circumstances.

Where the "person aggrieved" requires access to the storage media or the electronically stored information earlier than anticipated by law enforcement or ordered by the court, the court on a case by case basis can fashion an appropriate remedy, taking into account the time needed to image and search the data and any prejudice to the aggrieved party.

The amended rule does not address the specificity of description that the Fourth Amendment may require in a warrant for electronically stored information, leaving the application of this and other constitutional standards concerning both the seizure and the search to ongoing case law development.

Subdivision (f)(1). Current Rule 41(f)(1) does not address the question of whether the inventory should include a description of the electronically stored information contained in the media seized. Where it is impractical to record a description of the electronically stored information at the scene, the inventory may list the physical storage media seized. Recording a description of the electronically stored information at the scene is likely to be the exception, and not the rule, given the large amounts of information contained on electronic storage media and the impracticality for law enforcement to image and review all of the information during the execution of the warrant. This is consistent with practice in the "paper world." In circumstances where filing cabinets of documents are seized, routine practice is to list the storage devices, i.e., the cabinets, on the inventory, as opposed to making a document by document list of the contents.

Changes Made to Proposed Amendment Released for Public Comment. The words "copying or" were added to the last line of Rule 41(e)(2)(B) to clarify that copying as well as review may take place off-site.

The Committee Note was amended to reflect the change to the text and to clarify that the amended Rule does not speak to constitutional questions concerning warrants for electronic information. Issues of particularity and search protocol are presently working their way through the courts. Compare United States v. Carey, 172 F.3d 1268 (10th Cir. 1999) (finding warrant authorizing search for "documentary evidence pertaining to the sale and distribution of controlled substances" to prohibit opening of files with a .jpg suffix) and United States v. Fleet Management Ltd., 521 F. Supp. 2d 436 (E.D. Pa. 2007) (warrant invalid when it "did not even attempt to differentiate between data that there was probable cause to seize and data that was completely unrelated to any relevant criminal activity") with United States v. Comprehensive Drug Testing, Inc., 513 F.3d 1085 (9th Cir. 2008) (the government had no reason to confine its search to key words; "computer files are easy to disguise or rename, and were we to limit the warrant to such a specific search protocol, much evidence could escape discovery simply because of [the defendants'] labeling of the files"); United States v. Brooks, 427 F.3d 1246 (10th Cir. 2005) (rejecting requirement that warrant describe specific search methodology).

Minor changes were also made to conform to style conventions.

145

Subdivisions (d)(3) and (e)(3). The amendment deletes the provisions that govern the application for and issuance of warrants by telephone or other reliable electronic means. These provisions have been transferred to new Rule 4.1, which governs complaints and warrants under Rules 3, 4, 9, and 41.

Subdivision (e)(2). The amendment eliminates unnecessary references to "calendar" days. As amended effective December 1, 2009, Rule 45(a)(1) provides that all periods of time stated in days include "every day, including intermediate Saturdays, Sundays, and legal holidays[.]"

Subdivisions (f)(1) and (2). The amendment permits any warrant return to be made by reliable electronic means. Requiring an in-person return can be burdensome on law enforcement, particularly in large districts when the return can require a great deal of time and travel. In contrast, no interest of the accused is affected by allowing what is normally a ministerial act to be done electronically. Additionally, in subdivision (f)(2) the amendment eliminates unnecessary references to "calendar" days. As amended effective December 1, 2009, Rule 45(a)(1) provides that all periods of time stated in days include "every day, including intermediate Saturdays, Sundays, and legal holidays[.]"

Changes Made to Proposed Amendment Released for Public Comment. Obsolescent references to "calendar" days were deleted by a technical and conforming amendment not included in the rule as published. No other changes were made after publication.

Subdivision (b). The revision to the caption is not substantive. Adding the word "venue" makes clear that Rule 41(b) identifies the courts that may consider an application for a warrant, not the constitutional requirements for the issuance of a warrant, which must still be met.

Subdivision (b)(6). The amendment provides that in two specific circumstances a magistrate judge in a district where activities related to a crime may have occurred has authority to issue a warrant to use remote access to search electronic storage media and seize or copy electronically stored information even when that media or information is or may be located outside of the district.

First, subparagraph (b)(6)(A) provides authority to issue a warrant to use remote access within or outside that district when the district in which the media or information is located is not known because of the use of technology such as anonymizing software.

Second, (b)(6)(B) allows a warrant to use remote access within or outside the district in an investigation of a violation of 18 U.S.C. §1030(a)(5) if the media to be searched are protected computers that have been damaged without authorization, and they are located in many districts. Criminal activity under 18 U.S.C. §1030(a)(5) (such as the creation and control of "botnets") may target multiple computers in several districts. In investigations of this nature, the amendment would eliminate the burden of attempting to secure multiple warrants in numerous districts, and allow a single judge to oversee the investigation.

As used in this rule, the terms "protected computer" and "damage" have the meaning provided in 18 U.S.C. §1030(e)(2) & (8).

The amendment does not address constitutional questions, such as the specificity of description that the Fourth Amendment may require in a warrant for remotely searching electronic storage media or seizing or copying electronically stored information, leaving the application of this and other constitutional standards to ongoing case law development.

Subdivision (f)(1)(C). The amendment is intended to ensure that reasonable efforts are made to provide notice of the search, seizure, or copying, as well as a receipt for any information that was seized or copied, to the person whose property was searched or who possessed the information that was seized or copied. Rule 41(f)(3) allows delayed notice only "if the delay is authorized by statute." See 18 U.S.C. §3103a (authorizing delayed notice in limited circumstances).

2001—Subd. (a). Pub. L. 107–56 inserted before period at end "and (3) in an investigation of domestic terrorism or international terrorism (as defined in section 2331 of title 18, United States Code), by a Federal magistrate judge in any district in which activities related to the terrorism may have occurred, for a search of property or for a person within or outside the district".

Amendment of this rule by order of the United States Supreme Court on Apr. 26, 1976, modified and approved by Pub. L. 95–78, effective Oct. 1, 1977, see section 4 of Pub. L. 95–78, set out as an Effective Date of Pub. L. 95–78 note under section 2074 of Title 28, Judiciary and Judicial Procedure.

Amendment of subd. (c)(1) by order of the United States Supreme Court of Apr. 26, 1976, effective Aug. 1, 1976, see section 1 of Pub. L. 94–349, set out as a note under section 2074 of Title 28, Judiciary and Judicial Procedure.

Amendment by Order of April 9, 1956, became effective 90 days thereafter.

Rule 42. Criminal Contempt

(a) Disposition After Notice. Any person who commits criminal contempt may be punished for that contempt after prosecution on notice.

    (1) Notice. The court must give the person notice in open court, in an order to show cause, or in an arrest order. The notice must:

        (A) state the time and place of the trial;

        (B) allow the defendant a reasonable time to prepare a defense; and

        (C) state the essential facts constituting the charged criminal contempt and describe it as such.

    (2) Appointing a Prosecutor. The court must request that the contempt be prosecuted by an attorney for the government, unless the interest of justice requires the appointment of another attorney. If the government declines the request, the court must appoint another attorney to prosecute the contempt.

    (3) Trial and Disposition. A person being prosecuted for criminal contempt is entitled to a jury trial in any case in which federal law so provides and must be released or detained as Rule 46 provides. If the criminal contempt involves disrespect toward or criticism of a judge, that judge is disqualified from presiding at the contempt trial or hearing unless the defendant consents. Upon a finding or verdict of guilty, the court must impose the punishment.

(b) Summary Disposition. Notwithstanding any other provision of these rules, the court (other than a magistrate judge) may summarily punish a person who commits criminal contempt in its presence if the judge saw or heard the contemptuous conduct and so certifies; a magistrate judge may summarily punish a person as provided in 28 U.S.C. §636(e). The contempt order must recite the facts, be signed by the judge, and be filed with the clerk.

(As amended Mar. 9, 1987, eff. Aug. 1, 1987; Apr. 29, 2002, eff. Dec. 1, 2002.)

The rule-making power of the Supreme Court with respect to criminal proceedings was extended to proceedings to punish for criminal contempt of court by the Act of November 21, 1941 (55 Stat. 779), 18 U.S.C. 689.

Note to Subdivision (a). This rule is substantially a restatement of existing law, Ex parte Terry, 128 U.S. 289; Cooke v. United States, 267 U.S. 517, 534.

Note to Subdivision (b). 1. This rule is substantially a restatement of the procedure prescribed in 28 U.S.C. 386–390 [now 18 U.S.C. 401, 402, 3285, 3691], and 29 U.S.C. 111 [now 18 U.S.C. 3692].

2. The requirement in the second sentence that the notice shall describe the criminal contempt as such is intended to obviate the frequent confusion between criminal and civil contempt proceedings and follows the suggestion made in McCann v. New York Stock Exchange, 80 F.2d 211 (C.C.A. 2d). See also Nye v. United States, 313 U.S. 33, 42–43.

3. The fourth sentence relating to trial by jury preserves the right to a trial by jury in those contempt cases in which it is granted by statute, but does not enlarge the right or extend it to additional cases. The respondent in a contempt proceeding may demand a trial by jury as of right if the proceeding is brought under the Act of March 23, 1932, c. 90, sec. 11, 47 Stat. 72, 29 U.S.C. 111 [now 18 U.S.C. 3692] (Norris-La Guardia Act), or the Act of October 15, 1914, c. 323, sec. 22, 38 Stat. 738, 28 U.S.C. 387 (Clayton Act).

4. The provision in the sixth sentence disqualifying the judge affected by the contempt if the charge involves disrespect to or criticism of him, is based, in part, on 29 U.S.C. former §112 (Contempts; demand for retirement of judge sitting in proceeding) and the observations of Chief Justice Taft in Cooke v. United States, 267 U.S. 517, 539, 45 S.Ct. 390, 69 L.Ed. 767.

5. Among the statutory provisions defining criminal contempts are the following:

U.S.C., Title 7:
Section 499m (Perishable Agricultural Commodities Act; investigation of complaints; procedure; penalties; etc.—(c) Disobedience to subpenas; remedy; contempt)

U.S.C., Title 9:
Section 7 (Witnesses before arbitrators; fees, compelling attendance)

U.S.C., Title 11:
Section 69 [former] (Referees; contempts before)

U.S.C., Title 15:
Section 49 (Federal Trade Commission; documentary evidence; depositions; witnesses)
Section 78u (Regulation of Securities Exchanges; investigation; injunctions and prosecution of offenses)
Section 100 (Trademarks; destruction of infringing labels; service of injunction, and proceedings for enforcement)
Section 155 (China Trade Act; authority of registrar in obtaining evidence)

U.S.C., Title 17:
Section 36 [now 502] (Injunctions; service and enforcement)

U.S.C., Title 19:
Section 1333 (Tariff Commission; testimony and production of papers—(b) Witnesses and evidence)

U.S.C., Title 22:
Section 270f (International Bureaus; Congresses, etc.; perjury; contempts; penalties)

U.S.C., Title 28:
Section 385 [now 459; 18 U.S.C. 401] (Administration of oaths; contempts)
Section 386 [now 18 U.S.C. 402, 3691] (Contempts; when constituting also criminal offense)
Section 387 [now 18 U.S.C. 402] (Same; procedure; bail; attachment; trial; punishment) (Clayton Act; jury trial; section)
Section 388 [former] (Same; review of conviction)
Section 389 [now 18 U.S.C. 402, 3691] (Same; not specifically enumerated)
Section 390 [now 18 U.S.C. 3285] (Same; limitations)
Section 390a [now 18 U.S.C. 402] ("Person" or "persons" defined)
Section 648 [now Rule 17(f), FRCP, 18 U.S.C., Appendix; Rule 45(d), FRCP, 28 U.S.C., Appendix] (Depositions under dedimus potestatem; witnesses; when required to attend)
Section 703 [former] (Punishment of witness for contempt)
Section 714 [now 1784] (Failure of witness to obey subpena; order to show cause in contempt proceedings)
Section 715 [now 1784] (Direction in order to show cause for seizure of property of witness in contempt)
Section 716 [now 1784] (Service of order to show cause)
Section 717 [now 1784] (Hearing on order to show cause; judgment; satisfaction)
Section 750 [now 2405] (Garnishees in suits by United States against a corporation; garnishee failing to appear)

U.S.C., Title 29:
Section 111 [now 18 U.S.C. 3692] (Contempts; speedy and public trial; jury) (Norris-La Guardia Act)
Section 112 [now Rule 42, FRCP, 18 U.S.C., Appendix] (Contempts; demands for retirement of judge sitting in proceeding)
Section 160 (Prevention of unfair labor practices—(h) Jurisdiction of courts unaffected by limitations prescribed in sections 101–115 of Title 29)
Section 161 (Investigatory powers of Board—(2) Court aid in compelling production of evidence and attendance of witnesses)
Section 209 (Fair Labor Standards Act; attendance of witnesses)

U.S.C., Title 33:
Section 927 (Longshoremen's and Harbor Workers' Compensation Act; powers of deputy commissioner)

U.S.C., Title 35:
Section 56 [now 24] (Failing to attend or testify)

U.S.C., Title 47:
Section 409 (Federal Communications Commission; hearing; subpenas; oaths; witnesses; production of books and papers; contempts; depositions; penalties)

U.S.C., Title 48:

Section 1345a (Canal Zone; general jurisdiction of district court; issue of process at request of officials; witnesses; contempt)

U.S.C., Title 49:

Section 12 [see 721(c)(2), 13301(c)(2)] (Interstate Commerce Commission; authority and duties of commission; witnesses; depositions—(3) Compelling attendance and testimony of witnesses, etc.)

Federal Rules of Civil Procedure:

Rule 45 (Subpoena) subdivision (f) (Contempt)

NOTES OF ADVISORY COMMITTEE ON RULES——1987 AMENDMENT

The amendments are technical. No substantive change is intended.

COMMITTEE NOTES ON RULES——2002 AMENDMENT

The language of Rule 42 has been amended as part of the general restyling of the Criminal Rules to make them more easily understood and to make style and terminology consistent throughout the rules. These changes are intended to be stylistic only, except as noted below.

The revised rule is intended to more clearly set out the procedures for conducting a criminal contempt proceeding. The current rule implicitly recognizes that an attorney for the government may be involved in the prosecution of such cases. Revised Rule 42(a)(2) now explicitly addresses the appointment of a "prosecutor" and adopts language to reflect the holding in Young v. United States ex rel. Vuitton, 481 U.S. 787 (1987). In that case the Supreme Court indicated that ordinarily the court should request that an attorney for the government prosecute the contempt; only if that request is denied, should the court appoint a private prosecutor. The rule envisions that a disinterested counsel should be appointed to prosecute the contempt.

Rule 42(b) has been amended to make it clear that a court may summarily punish a person for committing contempt in the court's presence without regard to whether other rules, such as Rule 32 (sentencing procedures), might otherwise apply. See, e.g., United States v. Martin-Trigona, 759 F.2d 1017 (2d Cir. 1985). Further, Rule 42(b) has been amended to recognize the contempt powers of a court (other than a magistrate judge) and a magistrate judge.

TITLE IX. GENERAL PROVISIONS

Rule 43. Defendant's Presence

(a) When Required. Unless this rule, Rule 5, or Rule 10 provides otherwise, the defendant must be present at:

(1) the initial appearance, the initial arraignment, and the plea;

(2) every trial stage, including jury impanelment and the return of the verdict; and

(3) sentencing.

(b) When Not Required. A defendant need not be present under any of the following circumstances:

(1) Organizational Defendant. The defendant is an organization represented by counsel who is present.

(2) Misdemeanor Offense. The offense is punishable by fine or by imprisonment for not more than one year, or both, and with the defendant's written consent, the court permits arraignment, plea, trial, and sentencing to occur by video teleconferencing or in the defendant's absence.

(3) Conference or Hearing on a Legal Question. The proceeding involves only a conference or hearing on a question of law.

(4) Sentence Correction. The proceeding involves the correction or reduction of sentence under Rule 35 or 18 U.S.C. §3582(c).

(c) Waiving Continued Presence.

(1) In General. A defendant who was initially present at trial, or who had pleaded guilty or nolo contendere, waives the right to be present under the following circumstances:

(A) when the defendant is voluntarily absent after the trial has begun, regardless of whether the court informed the defendant of an obligation to remain during trial;

(B) in a noncapital case, when the defendant is voluntarily absent during sentencing; or

(C) when the court warns the defendant that it will remove the defendant from the courtroom for disruptive behavior, but the defendant persists in conduct that justifies removal from the courtroom.

(2) Waiver's Effect. If the defendant waives the right to be present, the trial may proceed to completion, including the verdict's return and sentencing, during the defendant's absence.

(As amended Apr. 22, 1974, eff. Dec. 1, 1975; Pub. L. 94–64, §3(35), July 31, 1975, 89 Stat. 376; Mar. 9, 1987, eff. Aug. 1, 1987; Apr. 27, 1995, eff. Dec. 1, 1995; Apr. 24, 1998, eff. Dec. 1, 1998; Apr. 29, 2002, eff. Dec. 1, 2002; Apr. 26, 2011, eff. Dec. 1, 2011.)

NOTES OF ADVISORY COMMITTEE ON RULES——1944

1. The first sentence of the rule setting forth the necessity of the defendant's presence at arraignment and trial is a restatement of existing law, Lewis v. United States, 146 U.S. 370; Diaz v. United States, 223 U.S. 442, 455. This principle does not apply to hearings on motions made prior to or after trial, United States v. Lynch, 132 F.2d 111 (C.C.A. 3d).

2. The second sentence of the rule is a restatement of existing law that, except in capital cases, the defendant may not defeat the proceedings by voluntarily absenting himself after the trial has been commenced in his presence, Diaz v. United States, 223 U.S. 442, 455; United States v. Noble, 294 F. 689 (D.Mont.)—affirmed, 300 F. 689 (C.C.A. 9th); United States v. Barracota, 45 F.Supp. 38 (S.D.N.Y.); United States v. Vassalo, 52 F.2d 699 (E.D.Mich.).

3. The fourth sentence of the rule empowering the court in its discretion, with the defendant's written consent, to conduct proceedings in misdemeanor cases in defendant's absence adopts a practice prevailing in some districts comprising very large areas. In such districts appearance in court may require considerable travel, resulting in expense and hardship not commensurate with the gravity of the charge, if a minor infraction is involved and a small fine is eventually imposed. The rule, which is in the interest of defendants in such situations, leaves it discretionary with the court to permit defendants in misdemeanor cases to absent themselves and, if so, to determine in what types of misdemeanors and to what extent. Similar provisions are found in the statutes of a number of States. See A.L.I. Code of Criminal Procedure, pp. 881–882.

4. The purpose of the last sentence of the rule is to resolve a doubt that at times has arisen as to whether it is necessary to bring the defendant to court from an institution in which he is confined, possibly at a distant point, if the court determines to reduce the sentence previously imposed. It seems in the interest of both the Government and the defendant not to require such presence, because of the delay and expense that are involved.

NOTES OF ADVISORY COMMITTEE ON RULES——1974 AMENDMENT

The revision of rule 43 is designed to reflect Illinois v. Allen, 397 U.S. 337, 90 S.Ct. 1057, 25 L.Ed. 2d 353 (1970). In Allen, the court held that "there are at least three constitutionally permissible ways for a trial judge to handle an obstreperous defendant like Allen: (1) bind and gag him, thereby keeping him present; (2) cite him for contempt; (3) take him out of the courtroom until he promises to conduct himself properly." 397 U.S. at 343–344, 90 S.Ct. 1057.

Since rule 43 formerly limited trial in absentia to situations in which there is a "voluntary absence after the trial has been commenced," it could be read as precluding a federal judge from exercising the third option held to be constitutionally permissible in Allen. The amendment is designed to make clear that the judge does have the power to exclude the defendant from the courtroom when the circumstances warrant such action.

The decision in Allen, makes no attempt to spell out standards to guide a judge in selecting the appropriate method to ensure decorum in the courtroom and there is no attempt to do so in the revision of the rule.

The concurring opinion of Mr. Justice Brennan stresses that the trial judge should make a reasonable effort to enable an excluded defendant "to communicate with his attorney and, if possible, to keep apprised of the progress of the trial." 397 U.S. at 351, 90 S.Ct. 1057. The Federal Judicial Center is presently engaged in experimenting with closed circuit television in courtrooms. The experience gained from these experiments may make closed circuit television readily available in federal courtrooms through which an excluded defendant would be able to hear and observe the trial.

The defendant's right to be present during the trial on a capital offense has been said to be so fundamental that it may not be waived. Diaz v. United States, 223 U.S. 442, 455, 32 S.Ct. 250, 56 L.Ed. 500 (1912) (dictum); Near v. Cunningham, 313 F.2d 929, 931 (4th Cir. 1963); C. Wright, Federal Practice and Procedure: Criminal §723 at 199 (1969, Supp.1971).

However, in Illinois v. Allen, supra the court's opinion suggests that sanctions such as contempt may be least effective where the defendant is ultimately facing a far more serious sanction such as the death penalty. 397 U.S. at 345, 90 S.Ct. 1057. The ultimate determination of when a defendant can waive his right to be present in a capital case (assuming a death penalty provision is held constitutional, see Furman v. Georgia, 408 U.S. 238, 92 S.Ct. 2726, 33 L.Ed.2d 346 (1972)) is left for further clarification by the courts.

Subdivision (b)(1) makes clear that voluntary absence may constitute a waiver even if the defendant has not been informed by the court of his obligation to remain during the trial. Of course, proof of voluntary absence will require a showing that the defendant knew of the fact that the trial or other proceeding was going on. C. Wright, Federal Practice and Procedure: Criminal §723 n. 35 (1969). But it is unnecessary to show that he was specifically warned of his obligation to be present; a warning seldom is thought necessary in current practice. [See Taylor v. United States, 414 U.S. 17, 94 S.Ct. 194, 38 L.Ed.2d 174 (1973).]

Subdivision (c)(3) makes clear that the defendant need not be present at a conference held by the court and counsel where the subject of the conference is an issue of law.

The other changes in the rule are editorial in nature. In the last phrase of the first sentence, "these rules" is changed to read "this rule," because there are no references in any of the other rules to situations where the defendant is not required to be present. The phrase "at the time of the plea," is added to subdivision (a) to make perfectly clear that defendant must be present at the time of the plea. See rule 11(c)(5) which provides that the judge may set a time, other than arraignment, for the holding of a plea agreement procedure.

NOTES OF COMMITTEE ON THE JUDICIARY, HOUSE REPORT No. 94–247; 1975 AMENDMENT

A. Amendments Proposed by the Supreme Court. Rule 43 of the Federal Rules of Criminal Procedure deals with the presence of the defendant during the proceedings against him. It presently permits a defendant to be tried in absentia only in non-capital cases where the defendant has voluntarily absented himself after the trial has begun.

The Supreme Court amendments provide that a defendant has waived his right to be present at the trial of a capital or noncapital case in two circumstances: (1) when he voluntarily absents himself after the trial has begun; and (2) where he "engages in conduct which is such as to justify his being excluded from the courtroom."

B. Committee Action. The Committee added language to subdivision (b)(2), which deals with excluding a disruptive defendant from the courtroom. The Advisory Committee Note indicates that the rule proposed by the Supreme Court was drafted to reflect the decision in Illinois v. Allen, 397 U.S. 337 (1970). The Committee found that subdivision (b)(2) as proposed did not full track the Allen decision. Consequently, language was added to that subsection to require the court to warn a disruptive defendant before excluding him from the courtroom.

NOTES OF ADVISORY COMMITTEE ON RULES——1987 AMENDMENT

The amendments are technical. No substantive change is intended.

NOTES OF ADVISORY COMMITTEE ON RULES——1995 AMENDMENT

The revisions to Rule 43 focus on two areas. First, the amendments make clear that a defendant who, initially present at trial or who has entered a plea of guilty or nolo contendere, but who voluntarily flees before sentencing, may nonetheless be sentenced in absentia. Second, the rule is amended to extend to organizational defendants. In addition, some stylistic changes have been made.

Subdivision (a). The changes to subdivision (a) are stylistic in nature and the Committee intends no substantive change in the operation of that provision.

Subdivision (b). The changes in subdivision (b) are intended to remedy the situation where a defendant voluntarily flees before sentence is imposed. Without the amendment, it is doubtful that a court could sentence a defendant who had been present during the entire trial but flees before sentencing. Delay in conducting the sentencing hearing under such circumstances may result in difficulty later in gathering and presenting the evidence necessary to formulate a guideline sentence.

The right to be present at court, although important, is not absolute. The caselaw, and practice in many jurisdictions, supports the proposition that the right to be present at trial may be waived through, inter alia, the act of fleeing. See generally Crosby v. United States, 113 S.Ct. 748, 506 U.S. 255 (1993). The amendment extends only to noncapital cases and applies only where the defendant is voluntarily absent after the trial has commenced or where the defendant has entered a plea of guilty or nolo contendere. The Committee envisions that defense counsel will continue to represent the interests of the defendant at sentencing.

The words "at trial, or having pleaded guilty or nolo contendere" have been added at the end of the first sentence to make clear that the trial of an absent defendant is possible only if the defendant was previously present at the trial or has entered a plea of guilty or nolo contendere. See Crosby v. United States, supra.

Subdivision (c). The change to subdivision (c) is technical in nature and replaces the word "corporation" with a reference to "organization," as that term is defined in 18 U.S.C. §18 to include entities other than corporations.

COMMITTEE NOTES ON RULES—1998 AMENDMENT

The amendment to Rule 43(c)(4) is intended to address two issues. First, the rule is rewritten to clarify whether a defendant is entitled to be present at resentencing proceedings conducted under Rule 35. As a result of amendments over the last several years to Rule 35, implementation of the Sentencing Reform Act, and caselaw interpretations of Rules 35 and 43, questions had been raised whether the defendant had to be present at those proceedings. Under the present version of the rule, it could be possible to require the defendant's presence at a "reduction" of sentence hearing conducted under Rule 35(b), but not a "correction" of sentence hearing conducted under Rule 35(a). That potential result seemed at odds with sound practice. As amended, Rule 43(c)(4) would permit a court to reduce or correct a sentence under Rule 35(b) or (c), respectively, without the defendant being present. But a sentencing proceeding being conducted on remand by an appellate court under Rule 35(a) would continue to require the defendant's presence. See, e.g., United States v. Moree, 928 F.2d 654, 655–656 (5th Cir. 1991) (noting distinction between presence of defendant at modification of sentencing proceedings and those hearings that impose new sentence after original sentence has been set aside).

The second issue addressed by the amendment is the applicability of Rule 43 to resentencing hearings conducted under 18 U.S.C. §3582(c). Under that provision, a resentencing may be conducted as a result of retroactive changes to the Sentencing Guidelines by the United States Sentencing Commission or as a result of a motion by the Bureau of Prisons to reduce a sentence based on "extraordinary and compelling reasons." The amendment provides that a defendant's presence is not required at such proceedings. In the Committee's view, those proceedings are analogous to Rule 35(b) as it read before the Sentencing Reform Act of 1984, where the defendant's presence was not required. Further, the court may only reduce the original sentence under these proceedings.

Changes Made to Rule 43 After Publication ("GAP Report"). The Committee made no changes to the draft amendment as published.

COMMITTEE NOTES ON RULES—2002 AMENDMENT

The language of Rule 43 has been amended as part of the general restyling of the Criminal Rules to make them more easily understood and to make style and terminology consistent throughout the rules. These changes are intended to be stylistic only, except as noted below.

The first substantive change is reflected in Rule 43(a), which recognizes several exceptions to the requirement that a defendant must be present in court for all proceedings. In addition to referring to exceptions that might exist in Rule 43 itself, the amendment recognizes that a defendant need not be present when the court has permitted video teleconferencing procedures under Rules 5 and 10 or when the defendant has waived the right to be present for the arraignment under Rule 10. Second, by inserting the word "initial" before "arraignment," revised Rule 43(a)(1) reflects the view that a defendant need not be present for subsequent arraignments based upon a superseding indictment.

The Rule has been reorganized to make it easier to read and apply; revised Rule 43(b) is former Rule 43(c).

COMMITTEE NOTES ON RULES—2011 AMENDMENT

Subdivision (b). This rule currently allows proceedings in a misdemeanor case to be conducted in the defendant's absence with the defendant's written consent and the court's permission. The amendment allows participation through video teleconference as an alternative to appearing in person or not appearing. Participation by video teleconference is permitted only when the defendant has consented in writing and received the court's permission.

The Committee reiterates the concerns expressed in the 2002 Committee Notes to Rules 5 and 10, when those rules were amended to permit video teleconferencing. The Committee recognized the intangible benefits and impact of requiring a defendant to appear before a federal judicial officer in a federal courtroom, and what is lost when virtual presence is substituted for actual presence. These concerns are particularly heightened when a defendant is not present for the determination of guilt and sentencing. However, the Committee concluded that the use of video teleconferencing may be valuable in circumstances where the defendant would otherwise be unable to attend and the rule now authorizes proceedings in absentia.

Changes Made to Proposed Amendment Released for Public Comment. Because the Advisory Committee withdrew its proposal to amend Rule 32.1 to allow for video teleconferencing, the cross reference to Rule 32.1 in Rule 43(a) was deleted.

AMENDMENT BY PUBLIC LAW

1975—Pub. L. 94–64 amended subd. (b)(2) generally.

EFFECTIVE DATE OF AMENDMENTS PROPOSED APRIL 22, 1974; EFFECTIVE DATE OF 1975 AMENDMENTS

Amendments of this rule embraced in the order of the United States Supreme Court on Apr. 22, 1974 and the amendments of this rule made by section 3 of Pub. L. 94–64, effective Dec. 1, 1975, see section 2 of Pub. L. 94–64, set out as a note under rule 4 of these rules.

Rule 44. Right to and Appointment of Counsel

(a) Right to Appointed Counsel. A defendant who is unable to obtain counsel is entitled to have counsel appointed to represent the defendant at every stage of the proceeding from initial appearance through appeal, unless the defendant waives this right.

(b) Appointment Procedure. Federal law and local court rules govern the procedure for implementing the right to counsel.

(c) Inquiry Into Joint Representation.

(1) Joint Representation. Joint representation occurs when:

(A) two or more defendants have been charged jointly under Rule 8(b) or have been joined for trial under Rule 13; and

(B) the defendants are represented by the same counsel, or counsel who are associated in law practice.

(2) Court's Responsibilities in Cases of Joint Representation. The court must promptly inquire about the propriety of joint representation and must personally advise each defendant of the right to the effective assistance of counsel, including separate representation. Unless there is good cause to believe that no conflict of interest is likely to arise, the court must take appropriate measures to protect each defendant's right to counsel.

(As amended Feb. 28, 1966, eff. July 1, 1966; Apr. 24, 1972, eff. Oct. 1, 1972; Apr. 30, 1979, eff. Dec. 1, 1980; Mar. 9, 1987, eff. Aug. 1, 1987; Apr. 22, 1993, eff. Dec. 1, 1993; Apr. 29, 2002, eff. Dec. 1, 2002.)

NOTES OF ADVISORY COMMITTEE ON RULES—1944

1. This rule is a restatement of existing law in regard to the defendant's constitutional right of counsel as defined in recent judicial decisions. The Sixth Amendment provides:

"In all criminal prosecutions, the accused shall enjoy the right * * * to have the Assistance of Counsel for his defense."

28 U.S.C. former §394 (now §1654) provides:

"In all the courts of the United States the parties may plead and manage their own causes personally, or by the assistance of such counsel or attorneys at law as, by the rules of the said courts, respectively, are permitted to manage and conduct causes therein."

18 U.S.C. former §563 (now §3005), which is derived from the act of April 30, 1790 (1 Stat. 118), provides:

"Every person who is indicted of treason or other capital crime, shall be allowed to make his full defense by counsel learned in the law; and the court before which he is tried or some judge thereof, shall immediately, upon his request, assign to him such counsel, not exceeding two, as he may desire, and they shall have free access to him at all seasonable hours."

The present extent of the right of counsel has been defined recently in Johnson v. Zerbst, 304 U.S. 458; Walker v. Johnston, 312 U.S. 275; and Glasser v. United States, 315 U.S. 60. The rule is a restatement of the principles enunciated in these decisions. See, also, Holtzoff, 20 N.Y.U.L.Q.R. 1.

2. The rule is intended to indicate that the right of the defendant to have counsel assigned by the court relates only to proceedings in court and, therefore, does not include preliminary proceedings before a committing magistrate. Although the defendant is not entitled to have counsel assigned to him in connection with preliminary proceedings, he is entitled to be represented by counsel retained by him, if he so chooses, Rule 5(b) (Proceedings before the Commissioner; Statement by the Commissioner) and Rule 40(b)(2) (Commitment to Another District; Removal——Arrest in Distant District——Statement by Commissioner or Judge). As to defendant's right of counsel in connection with the taking of depositions, see Rule 15(c) (Depositions——Defendant's Counsel and Payment of Expenses).

A new rule is provided as a substitute for the old to provide for the assignment of counsel to defendants unable to obtain counsel during all stages of the proceeding. The Supreme Court has recently made clear the importance of providing counsel both at the earliest possible time after arrest and on appeal. See Crooker v. California, 357 U.S. 433 (1958); Cicenia v. LaGay, 357 U.S. 504 (1958); White v. Maryland, 373 U.S. 59 (1963); Gideon v. Wainwright, 372 U.S. 335 (1963); Douglas v. California, 372 U.S. 353 (1963). See also Association of the Bar of the City of New York, Special Committee to Study the Defender System, Equal Justice for the Accused (1959); Report of the Attorney General's Committee on Poverty and the Administration of Justice (1963); Beaney, Right to Counsel Before Arraignment, 45 Minn.L.Rev. 771 (1961); Boskey, The Right to Counsel in Appellate Proceedings, 45 Minn.L.Rev. 783 (1961); Douglas, The Right to Counsel——A Foreword, 45 Minn.L.Rev. 693 (1961); Kamisar, The Right to Counsel and the Fourteenth Amendment; A Dialogue on "The Most Pervasive Right" of an Accused, 30 U.Chi.L.Rev. 1 (1962); Kamisar, Betts v. Brady Twenty Years Later: The Right to Counsel and Due Process Values, 61 Mich.L.Rev. 219 (1962); Symposium, The Right to Counsel, 22 Legal Aid Briefcase 4–48 (1963). Provision has been made by law for a Legal Aid Agency in the District of Columbia which is charged with the duty of providing counsel and courts are admonished to assign such counsel "as early in the proceeding as practicable." D.C. Code §2–2202. Congress has now made provision for assignment of counsel and their compensation in all of the districts. Criminal Justice Act of 1964 (78 Stat. 552).

Like the original rule the amended rule provides a right to counsel which is broader in two respects than that for which compensation is provided in the Criminal Justice Act of 1964: (1) the right extends to petty offenses to be tried in the district courts, and (2) the right extends to defendants unable to obtain counsel for reasons other than financial. These rules do not cover procedures other than those in the courts of the United States and before United States commissioners. See Rule 1. Hence, the problems relating to the providing of counsel prior to the initial appearance before a court or commissioner are not dealt with in this rule. Cf. Escobedo v. United States, 378 U.S. 478 (1964); Enker and Elsen, Counsel for the Suspect: Massiah v. United States and Escobedo v. Illinois, 49 Minn.L.Rev. 47 (1964).

Subdivision (a).——This subdivision expresses the right of the defendant unable to obtain counsel to have such counsel assigned at any stage of the proceedings from his initial appearance before the commissioner or court through the appeal, unless he waives such right. The phrase "from his initial appearance before the commissioner or court" is intended to require the assignment of counsel as promptly as possible after it appears that the defendant is unable to obtain counsel. The right to assignment of counsel is not limited to those financially unable to obtain counsel. If a defendant is able to compensate counsel but still cannot obtain counsel, he is entitled to the assignment of counsel even though not to free counsel.

Subdivision (b).——This new subdivision reflects the adoption of the Criminal Justice Act of 1964. See Report of the Judicial Conference of the United States on the Criminal Justice Act of 1964, 36 F.R.D. 277 (1964).

Subdivision (a) is amended to reflect the Federal Magistrates Act of 1968. The phrase "federal magistrate" is defined in rule 54.

Note to Subdivision (c). Rule 44(c) establishes a procedure for avoiding the occurrence of events which might otherwise give rise to a plausible post-conviction claim that because of joint representation the defendants in a criminal case were deprived of their Sixth Amendment right to the effective assistance of counsel. Although "courts have differed with respect to the scope and nature of the affirmative duty of the trial judge to assure that criminal defendants are not deprived of their right to the effective assistance of counsel by joint representation of conflicting interests," Holloway v. Arkansas, 98 S.Ct. 1173 (1978) (where the Court found it unnecessary to reach this issue), this amendment is generally consistent with the current state of the law in several circuits. As held in United States v. Carrigan, 543 F.2d 1053 (2d Cir. 1976):

When a potential conflict of interest arises, either where a court has assigned the same counsel to represent several defendants or where the same counsel has been retained by co-defendants in a criminal case, the proper course of action for the trial judge is to conduct a hearing to determine whether a conflict exists to the degree that a defendant may be prevented from receiving advice and assistance sufficient to afford him the quality of representation guaranteed by the Sixth Amendment. The defendant should be fully advised by the trial court of the facts underlying the potential conflict and be given the opportunity to express his views.

See also United States v. Lawriw, 568 F.2d 98 (8th Cir. 1977) (duty on trial judge to make inquiry where joint representation by appointed or retained counsel, and "without such an inquiry a finding of knowing and intelligent waiver will seldom, if ever, be sustained by this Court"); Abraham v. United States, 549 F.2d 236 (2d Cir. 1977); United States v. Mari, 526 F.2d 117 (2d Cir. 1975); United States v. Truglio, 493 F.2d 574 (4th Cir. 1974) (joint representation should cause trial judge "to inquire whether the defenses to be presented in any way conflict"); United States v. DeBerry, 487 F.2d 488 (2d Cir. 1973); United States ex rel. Hart v. Davenport, 478 F.2d 203 (3d Cir. 1973) (noting there "is much to be said for the rule . . . which assumes prejudice and nonwaiver if there has been no on-the-record inquiry by the court as to the hazards to defendants from joint representation"; United States v. Alberti, 470 F.2d 878 (2d Cir. 1973); United States v. Foster, 469 F.2d 1 (1st Cir. 1972) (lack of sufficient inquiry shifts the burden of proof on the question of prejudice to the government); Campbell v. United States, 352 F.2d 359 (D.C. Cir. 1965) (where joint representation, court "has a duty to ascertain whether each defendant has an awareness of the potential risks of that course and nevertheless has knowingly chosen it"). Some states have taken a like position; see, e.g., State v. Olsen, —— Minn. ——, 258 N.W.2d 898 (1977).

This procedure is also consistent with that recommended in the ABA Standards Relating to the Function of the Trial Judge (Approved Draft, 1972), which provide in §3.4(b):

Whenever two or more defendants who have been jointly charged, or whose cases have been consolidated, are represented by the same attorney, the trial judge should inquire into potential conflicts which may jeopardize the right of each defendant to the fidelity of his counsel.

Avoiding a conflict-of-interest situation is in the first instance a responsibility of the attorney. If a lawyer represents "multiple clients having potentially differing interests, he must weigh carefully the possibility that his judgment may be impaired or his loyalty divided if he accepts or continues the employment," and he is to "resolve all doubts against the propriety of the representation." Code of Professional Responsibility, Ethical Consideration 5–15. See also ABA Standards Relating to the Defense Function §3.5(b) (Approved Draft, 1971), concluding that the "potential for conflict of interest in representing multiple defendants is so grave that ordinarily a lawyer should decline

151

to act for more than one of several co-defendants except in unusual situations when, after careful investigation, it is clear that no conflict is likely to develop and when the several defendants give an informed consent to such multiple representation."

It by no means follows that the inquiry provided for by rule 44(c) is unnecessary. For one thing, even the most diligent attorney may be unaware of facts giving rise to a potential conflict. Often "counsel must operate somewhat in the dark and feel their way uncertainly to an understanding of what their clients may be called upon to meet upon a trial" and consequently "are frequently unable to foresee developments which may require changes in strategy." United States v. Carrigan, supra (concurring opinion). "Because the conflicts are often subtle it is not enough to rely upon counsel, who may not be totally disinterested, to make sure that each of his joint clients has made an effective waiver." United States v. Lawriw, supra.

Moreover, it is important that the trial judge ascertain whether the effective and fair administration of justice would be adversely affected by continued joint representation, even when an actual conflict is not then apparent. As noted in United States v. Mari, supra (concurring opinion):

> Trial court insistence that, except in extraordinary circumstances, codefendants retain separate counsel will in the long run . . . prove salutary not only to the administration of justice and the appearance of justice but the cost of justice; habeas corpus petitions, petitions for new trials, appeals and occasionally retrials . . . can be avoided. Issues as to whether there is an actual conflict of interest, whether the conflict has resulted in prejudice, whether there has been a waiver, whether the waiver is intelligent and knowledgeable, for example, can all be avoided. Where a conflict that first did not appear subsequently arises in or before trial, . . . continuances or mistrials can be saved. Essentially by the time a case . . . gets to the appellate level the harm to the appearance of justice has already been done, whether or not reversal occurs; at the trial level it is a matter which is so easy to avoid.

A rule 44(c) inquiry is required whether counsel is assigned or retained. It "makes no difference whether counsel is appointed by the court or selected by the defendants; even where selected by the defendants the same dangers of potential conflict exist, and it is also possible that the rights of the public to the proper administration of justice may be affected adversely." United States v. Mari, supra (concurring opinion). See also United States v. Lawriw, supra. When there has been "no discussion as to possible conflict initiated by the court," it cannot be assumed that the choice of counsel by the defendants "was intelligently made with knowledge of any possible conflict." United States v. Carrigan, supra. As for assigned counsel, it is provided by statute that "the court shall appoint separate counsel for defendants having interests that cannot properly be represented by the same counsel, or when other good cause is shown." 18 U.S.C. §3006(A)(b). Rule 44(c) is not intended to prohibit the automatic appointment of separate counsel in the first instance, see Ford v. United States, 379 F.2d 123 (D.C. Cir. 1967); Lollar v. United States, 376 F.2d 243 (D.C. Cir. 1967), which would obviate the necessity for an inquiry.

Under rule 44(c), an inquiry is called for when the joined defendants are represented by the same attorney and also when they are represented by attorneys "associated in the practice of law." This is consistent with Code of Professional Responsibility, Disciplinary Rule 5–105(D) (providing that if "a lawyer is required to decline employment or to withdraw from employment" because of a potential conflict, "no partner or associate of his or his firm may accept or continue such employment"); and ABA Standards Relating to the Defense Function §3.5(b) (Approved Draft, 1971) (applicable to "a lawyer or lawyers who are associated in practice"). Attorneys representing joined defendants should so advise the court if they are associated in the practice of law.

The rule 44(c) procedure is not limited to cases expected to go to trial. Although the more dramatic conflict situations, such as when the question arises as to whether the several defendants should take the stand, Morgan v. United States, 396 F.2d 110 (2d Cir. 1968), tend to occur in a trial context, serious conflicts may also arise when one or more of the jointly represented defendants pleads guilty.

> The problem is that even where as here both codefendants pleaded guilty there are frequently potential conflicts of interest . . . [T]he prosecutor may be inclined to accept a guilty plea from one codefendant which may harm the interests of the other. The contrast in the dispositions of the cases may have a harmful impact on the codefendant who does not initially plead guilty; he may be pressured into pleading guilty himself rather than face his codefendant's bargained-for testimony at a trial. And it will be his own counsel's recommendation to the initially pleading codefendant which will have contributed to this harmful impact upon him . . . [I]n a given instance it would be at least conceivable that the prosecutor would be willing to accept pleas to lesser offenses from two defendants in preference to a plea of guilty by one defendant to a greater offense.

United States v. Mari, supra (concurring opinion). To the same effect is ABA Standards Relating to the Defense Function at 213–14.

It is contemplated that under rule 44(c) the court will make appropriate inquiry of the defendants and of counsel regarding the possibility of a conflict of interest developing. Whenever it is necessary to make a more particularized inquiry into the nature of the contemplated defense, the court should "pursue the inquiry with defendants and their counsel on the record but in chambers" so as "to avoid the possibility of prejudicial disclosures to the prosecution." United States v. Foster, supra. It is important that each defendant be "fully advised of the facts underlying the potential conflict and is given an opportunity to express his or her views." United States v. Alberti, supra. The rule specifically requires that the court personally advise each defendant of his right to effective assistance of counsel, including separate representation. See United States v. Foster, supra, requiring that the court make a determination that jointly represented defendants "understand that they may retain separate counsel, or if qualified, may have such counsel appointed by the court and paid for by the government."

Under rule 44(c), the court is to take appropriate measures to protect each defendant's right to counsel unless it appears "there is good cause to believe no conflict of interest is likely to arise" as a consequence of the continuation of such joint representation. A less demanding standard would not adequately protect the Sixth Amendment right to effective assistance of counsel or the effective administration of criminal justice. Although joint representation "is not per se violative of constitutional guarantees of effective assistance of counsel, Holloway v. Arkansas, supra, it would not suffice to require the court to act only when a conflict of interest is then apparent, for it is not possible "to anticipate with complete accuracy the course that a criminal trial may take." Fryar v. United States, 404 F.2d 1071 (10th Cir. 1968). This is particularly so in light of the fact that if a conflict later arises and a defendant thereafter raises a Sixth Amendment objection, a court must grant relief without indulging "in nice calculations as to the amount of prejudice arising from its denial." Glasser v. United States, 315 U.S. 60 (1942). This is because, as the Supreme Court more recently noted in Holloway v. Arkansas, supra, "in a case of joint representation of conflicting interests the evil . . . is in what the advocate finds himself compelled to refrain from doing," and this makes it "virtually impossible" to assess the impact of the conflict.

Rule 44(c) does not specify what particular measures must be taken. It is appropriate to leave this within the court's discretion, for the measures which will best protect each defendant's right to counsel may well vary from case to case. One possible course of action is for the court to obtain a knowing, intelligent and voluntary waiver of the right to separate representation, for, as noted in Holloway v. Arkansas, supra, "a defendant may waive his right to the assistance of an attorney unhindered by a conflict of interests." See United States v. DeBerry, supra, holding that defendants should be jointly represented only if "the court has ascertained that . . . each understands clearly the possibilities of a conflict of interest and waives any rights in connection with it." It must be emphasized that a "waiver of the right to separate representation should not be accepted by the court unless the defendants have each been informed of the probable hazards; and the voluntary character of their waiver is apparent." ABA Standards Relating to the Function of the Trial Judge at 45. United States v. Garcia, supra, spells out in significant detail what should be done to assure an adequate waiver:

> As in Rule 11 procedures, the district court should address each defendant personally and forthrightly advise him of the potential dangers of representation by counsel with a conflict of interest. The defendant must be at liberty to question the district court as to the nature and consequences of his legal representation. Most significantly, the court should seek to elicit a narrative response from each defendant that he has been advised of his right to effective representation, that he understands the details of his attorney's possible conflict of interest and the potential perils of such a conflict, that he has discussed the matter with his attorney or if he wishes with outside counsel, and that he voluntarily waives his Sixth Amendment protections. It is, of course, vital that the waiver be established by "clear, unequivocal, and unambiguous language." . . . Mere assent in response to a series of questions from the bench may in some circumstances constitute an adequate

waiver, but the court should nonetheless endeavor to have each defendant personally articulate in detail his intent to forego this significant constitutional protection. Recordation of the waiver colloquy between defendant and judge, will also serve the government's interest by assisting in shielding any potential conviction from collateral attack, either on Sixth Amendment grounds or on a Fifth or Fourteenth Amendment "fundamental fairness" basis.

See also Hyman, Joint Representation of Multiple Defendants in a Criminal Trial: The Court's Headache, 5 Hofstra L.Rev. 315, 334 (1977).

Another possibility is that the court will order that the defendants be separately represented in subsequent proceedings in the case. Though the court must remain alert to and take account of the fact that "certain advantages might accrue from joint representation," Holloway v. Arkansas, supra, it need not permit the joint representation to continue merely because the defendants express a willingness to so proceed. That is,

there will be cases where the court should require separate counsel to represent certain defendants despite the expressed wishes of such defendants. Indeed, failure of the trial court to require separate representation may . . . require a new trial, even though the defendants have expressed a desire to continue with the same counsel. The right to effective representation by counsel whose loyalty is undivided is so paramount in the proper administration of criminal justice that it must in some cases take precedence over all other considerations, including the expressed preference of the defendants concerned and their attorney.

United States v. Carrigan, supra (concurring opinion). See also United States v. Lawriw, supra; Abraham v. United States, supra; ABA Standards Relating to the Defense Function at 213, concluding that in some circumstances "even full disclosure and consent of the client may not be an adequate protection." As noted in United States v. Dolan, 570 F.2d 1177 (3d Cir. 1978), such an order may be necessary where the trial judge is

not satisfied that the waiver is proper. For example, a defendant may be competent enough to stand trial, but not competent enough to understand the complex, subtle, and sometimes unforeseeable dangers inherent in multiple representation. More importantly, the judge may find that the waiver cannot be intelligently made simply because he is not in a position to inform the defendant of the foreseeable prejudices multiple representation might entail for him.

As concluded in Dolan, "exercise of the court's supervisory powers by disqualifying an attorney representing multiple criminal defendants in spite of the defendants' express desire to retain that attorney does not necessarily abrogate defendant's sixth amendment rights". It does not follow from the absolute right of self-representation recognized in Faretta v. California, 422 U.S. 806 (1975), that there is an absolute right to counsel of one's own choice. Thus,

when a trial court finds an actual conflict of interest which impairs the ability of a criminal defendant's chosen counsel to conform with the ABA Code of Professional Responsibility, the court should not be required to tolerate an inadequate representation of a defendant. Such representation not only constitutes a breach of professional ethics and invites disrespect for the integrity of the court, but it is also detrimental to the independent interest of the trial judge to be free from future attacks over the adequacy of the waiver or the fairness of the proceedings in his own court and the subtle problems implicating the defendant's comprehension of the waiver. Under such circumstances, the court can elect to exercise its supervisory authority over members of the bar to enforce the ethical standard requiring an attorney to decline multiple representation.

United States v. Dolan, supra. See also Geer, Conflict of Interest and Multiple Defendants in a Criminal Case: Professional Responsibilities of the Defense Attorney, 62 Minn.L.Rev. 119 (1978); Note, Conflict of Interests in Multiple Representation of Criminal Co-Defendants, 68 J.Crim.L.&C. 226 (1977).

The failure in a particular case to conduct a rule 44(c) inquiry would not, standing alone, necessitate the reversal of a conviction of a jointly represented defendant. However, as is currently the case, a reviewing court is more likely to assume a conflict resulted from the joint representation when no inquiry or an inadequate inquiry was conducted. United States v. Carrigan, supra; United States v. DeBerry, supra. On the other hand, the mere fact that a rule 44(c) inquiry was conducted in the early stages of the case does not relieve the court of all responsibility in this regard thereafter. The obligation placed upon the court by rule 44(c) is a continuing one, and thus in a particular case further inquiry may be necessary on a later occasion because of new developments suggesting a potential conflict of interest.

Notes of Advisory Committee on Rules——1987 Amendment

The amendments are technical. No substantive change is intended.

Notes of Advisory Committee on Rules——1993 Amendment

The Rule is amended to conform to the Judicial Improvements Act of 1990 [P.L. 101–650, Title III, Section 321] which provides that each United States magistrate appointed under section 631 of title 28, United States Code, shall be known as a United States magistrate judge.

Committee Notes on Rules——2002 Amendment

The language of Rule 44 has been amended as part of the general restyling of the Criminal Rules to make them more easily understood and to make style and terminology consistent throughout the rules. These changes are intended to be stylistic only.

Revised Rule 44 now refers to the "appointment" of counsel, rather than the assignment of counsel; the Committee believed the former term was more appropriate. See 18 U.S.C. §3006A. In Rule 44(c), the term "retained or assigned" has been deleted as being unnecessary, without changing the court's responsibility to conduct an inquiry where joint representation occurs.

Effective Date of 1979 Amendment

Amendment of this rule by addition of subd. (c) by order of the United States Supreme Court of Apr. 30, 1979, effective Dec. 1, 1980, see section 1(1) of Pub. L. 96–42, July 31, 1979, 93 Stat. 326, set out as a note under section 2074 of Title 28, Judiciary and Judicial Procedure.

Rule 45. Computing and Extending Time

(a) Computing Time. The following rules apply in computing any time period specified in these rules, in any local rule or court order, or in any statute that does not specify a method of computing time.

(1) Period Stated in Days or a Longer Unit. When the period is stated in days or a longer unit of time:

(A) exclude the day of the event that triggers the period;

(B) count every day, including intermediate Saturdays, Sundays, and legal holidays; and

(C) include the last day of the period, but if the last day is a Saturday, Sunday, or legal holiday, the period continues to run until the end of the next day that is not a Saturday, Sunday, or legal holiday.

(2) Period Stated in Hours. When the period is stated in hours:

(A) begin counting immediately on the occurrence of the event that triggers the period;

(B) count every hour, including hours during intermediate Saturdays, Sundays, and legal holidays; and

(C) if the period would end on a Saturday, Sunday, or legal holiday, the period continues to run until the same time on the next day that is not a Saturday, Sunday, or legal holiday.

(3) Inaccessibility of the Clerk's Office. Unless the court orders otherwise, if the clerk's office is inaccessible:

(A) on the last day for filing under Rule 45(a)(1), then the time for filing is extended to the first accessible day that is not a Saturday, Sunday, or legal holiday; or

(B) during the last hour for filing under Rule 45(a)(2), then the time for filing is extended to the same time on the first accessible day that is not a Saturday, Sunday, or legal holiday.

(4) "Last Day" Defined. Unless a different time is set by a statute, local rule, or court order, the last day ends:

    (A) for electronic filing, at midnight in the court's time zone; and

    (B) for filing by other means, when the clerk's office is scheduled to close.

(5) "Next Day" Defined. The "next day" is determined by continuing to count forward when the period is measured after an event and backward when measured before an event.

(6) "Legal Holiday" Defined. "Legal holiday" means:

    (A) the day set aside by statute for observing New Year's Day, Martin Luther King Jr.'s Birthday, Washington's Birthday, Memorial Day, Independence Day, Labor Day, Columbus Day, Veterans' Day, Thanksgiving Day, or Christmas Day;

    (B) any day declared a holiday by the President or Congress; and

    (C) for periods that are measured after an event, any other day declared a holiday by the state where the district court is located.

(b) Extending Time.

(1) In General. When an act must or may be done within a specified period, the court on its own may extend the time, or for good cause may do so on a party's motion made:

    (A) before the originally prescribed or previously extended time expires; or

    (B) after the time expires if the party failed to act because of excusable neglect.

(2) Exception. The court may not extend the time to take any action under Rule 35, except as stated in that rule.

(c) Additional Time After Certain Kinds of Service. Whenever a party must or may act within a specified time after being served and service is made under Rule 49(a)(4)(C), (D), and (E), 3 days are added after the period would otherwise expire under subdivision (a).

(As amended Feb. 28, 1966, eff. July 1, 1966; Dec. 4, 1967, eff. July 1, 1968; Mar. 1, 1971, eff. July 1, 1971; Apr. 28, 1982, eff. Aug. 1, 1982; Apr. 29, 1985, eff. Aug. 1, 1985; Mar. 9, 1987, eff. Aug. 1, 1987; Apr. 29, 2002, eff. Dec. 1, 2002; Apr. 25, 2005, eff. Dec. 1, 2005; Apr. 30, 2007, eff. Dec. 1, 2007; Apr. 23, 2008, eff. Dec. 1, 2008; Mar. 26, 2009, eff. Dec. 1, 2009; Apr. 28, 2016, eff. Dec. 1, 2016; Apr. 26, 2018, eff. Dec. 1, 2018.)

NOTES OF ADVISORY COMMITTEE ON RULES—1944

The rule is in substance the same as Rule 6 of the Federal Rules of Civil Procedure [28 U.S.C., Appendix]. It seems desirable that matters covered by this rule should be regulated in the same manner for civil and criminal cases, in order to preclude possibility of confusion.

Note to Subdivision (a). This rule supersedes the method of computing time prescribed by Rule 13 of the Criminal Appeals Rules, promulgated on May 7, 1934, 292 U.S. 661.

Note to Subdivision (c). This rule abolishes the expiration of a term of court as a time limitation for the taking of any step in a criminal proceeding, as is done for civil cases by Rule 6(c) of the Federal Rules of Civil Procedure [28 U.S.C., Appendix]. In view of the fact that the duration of terms of court varies among the several districts and the further fact that the length of time for the taking of any step limited by a term of court depends on the stage within the term when the time begins to run, specific time limitations have been substituted for the taking of any step which previously had to be taken within the term of court.

Note to Subdivision (d). Cf. Rule 47 (Motions) and Rule 49 (Service and filing of papers).

NOTES OF ADVISORY COMMITTEE ON RULES—1966 AMENDMENT

Subdivision (a).—This amendment conforms the subdivision with the amendments made effective on July 1, 1963, to the comparable provision in Civil Rule 6(a). The only major change is to treat Saturdays as legal holidays for the purpose of computing time.

Subdivision (b).—The amendment conforms the subdivision to the amendments made effective in 1948 to the comparable provision in Civil Rule 6(b). One of these conforming changes, substituting the words "extend the time" for the words "enlarge the period" clarifies the ambiguity which gave rise to the decision in United States v. Robinson, 361 U.S. 220 (1960). The amendment also, in connection with the amendments to Rules 29 and 37, makes it clear that the only circumstances under which extensions can be granted under Rules 29, 33, 34, 35, 37(a)(2) and 39(c) are those stated in them.

Subdivision (c).—Subdivision (c) of Rule 45 is rescinded as unnecessary in view of the 1963 amendment to 28 U.S.C. §138 eliminating terms of court.

NOTES OF ADVISORY COMMITTEE ON RULES—1968 AMENDMENT

The amendment eliminates inappropriate references to Rules 37 and 39 which are to be abrogated.

NOTES OF ADVISORY COMMITTEE ON RULES—1971 AMENDMENT

The amendment adds Columbus Day to the list of legal holidays to conform the subdivision to the Act of June 28, 1968, 82 Stat. 250, which constituted Columbus Day a legal holiday effective after January 1, 1971.

The Act, which amended Title 5, U.S.C., §6103(a), changes the day on which certain holidays are to be observed. Washington's Birthday, Memorial Day and Veterans Day are to be observed on the third Monday in February, the last Monday in May and the fourth Monday in October, respectively, rather than, as heretofore, on February 22, May 30, and November 11, respectively. Columbus Day is to be observed on the second Monday in October. New Year's Day, Independence Day, Thanksgiving Day and Christmas continue to be observed on the traditional days.

NOTES OF ADVISORY COMMITTEE ON RULES—1982 AMENDMENT

The amendment to subdivision (a) takes account of the fact that on rare occasion severe weather conditions or other circumstances beyond control will make it impossible to meet a filing deadline under Rule 45(a). Illustrative is an incident which occurred in Columbus, Ohio during the "great blizzard of 1978," in which weather conditions deteriorated to the point where personnel in the clerk's office found it virtually impossible to reach the courthouse, and where the GSA Building Manager found it necessary to close and secure the entire building. The amendment covers that situation and also similar situations in which weather or other conditions made the clerk's office, though open, not readily accessible to the lawyer. Whether the clerk's office was in fact "inaccessible" on a given date is to be determined by the district court. Some state time computation statutes contain language somewhat similar to that in the amendment; see, e.g., Md.Code Ann. art. 94, §2.

NOTES OF ADVISORY COMMITTEE ON RULES—1985 AMENDMENT

The rule is amended to extend the exclusion of intermediate Saturdays, Sundays, and legal holidays to the computation of time periods less than 11 days. Under the current version of the Rule, parties bringing motions under rules with 10-day periods could have as few as 5 working days to prepare their motions. This change corresponds to the change being made in the comparable provision in Fed.R.Civ.P. 6(a).

The Birthday of Martin Luther King, Jr., which becomes a legal holiday effective January 1986, has been added to the list of legal holidays enumerated in the Rule.

The amendments are technical. No substantive change is intended.

COMMITTEE NOTES ON RULES—2002 AMENDMENT

The language of Rule 45 has been amended as part of the general restyling of the Criminal Rules to make them more easily understood and to make style and terminology consistent throughout the rules. These changes are intended to be stylistic only.

The additional three days provided by Rule 45(c) is extended to the means of service authorized by the new paragraph (D) added to Rule 5(b) of the Federal Rules of Civil Procedure, including—with the consent of the person served—service by electronic means. The means of service authorized in civil actions apply to criminal cases under Rule 49(b).

Rule 45(d), which governs the timing of written motions and affidavits, has been moved to Rule 47.

COMMITTEE NOTES ON RULES—2005 AMENDMENT

Rule 45(b) has been amended to conform to amendments to Rules 29, 33, and 34, which have been amended to remove the requirement that the court must act within the seven-day period specified in each of those rules if it sets another time for filing a motion under those rules.

Currently, Rules 29(c)(1), 33(b)(2), and 34(b) require the defendant to move for relief under those rules within the seven-day periods specified in those rules or within some other time set by the court in an order issued during that same seven-day period. Courts have held that the seven-day rule is jurisdictional. Thus, for example, if a defendant files a request for an extension of time to file a motion for a judgment of acquittal or a motion for new trial within the seven-day period, the court must rule on that motion or request within the same seven-day period. If for some reason the court does not rule on the request for an extension of time within the seven days, the court loses jurisdiction to act on the underlying substantive motion. See, e.g., United States v. Smith, 331 U.S. 469, 473–474 (1947) (rejecting argument that trial court had power to grant new trial on its own motion after expiration of time in Rule 33); United States v. Marquez, 291 F.3d 23, 27–28 (D.C. Cir. 2002) (citing language of Rule 33, and holding that "district court forfeited the power to act when it failed to . . . fix a new time for filing a motion for a new trial within seven days of the verdict").

Rule 45(b)(2) currently specifies that a court may not extend the time for taking action under Rules 29, 33, or 34, except as provided in those rules.

Assuming that the current provisions in Rules 29, 33, and 34 were intended to promote finality, there is nothing to prevent the court from granting the defendant a significant extension of time, under those rules, as long as it does so within the seven-day period. Thus, the Committee believed that those rules should be amended to be consistent with all of the other timing requirements in the rules, which do not force the court to rule on a motion to extend the time for filing, within a particular period of time or lose jurisdiction to do so. The change to Rule 45(b)(2) is thus a conforming amendment.

The defendant is still required to file motions under Rules 29, 33, and 34 within the seven-day period specified in those rules. The defendant, however, may consistently with Rule 45, seek an extension of time to file the underlying motion as long as the defendant does so within the seven-day period. But the court itself is not required to act on that motion within any particular time. Further, under Rule 45(b)(1)(B), if for some reason the defendant fails to file the underlying motion within the specified time, the court may nonetheless consider that untimely motion if the court determines that the failure to file it on time was the result of excusable neglect.

Changes Made After Publication and Comment. The Committee made no substantive changes to Rule 45 following publication.

COMMITTEE NOTES ON RULES—2007 AMENDMENT

Subdivision (c). Rule 45(c) is amended to remove any doubt as to the method for extending the time to respond after service by mail, leaving with the clerk of court, electronic means, or other means consented to by the party served. This amendment parallels the change in Federal Rule of Civil Procedure 6(e). Three days are added after the prescribed period otherwise expires under Rule 45(a). Intermediate Saturdays, Sundays, and legal holidays are included in counting these added three days. If the third day is a Saturday, Sunday, or legal holiday, the last day to act is the next day that is not a Saturday, Sunday, or legal holiday. The effect of invoking the day that the rule would otherwise expire under Rule 45(a) can be illustrated by assuming that the thirtieth day of a thirty-day period is a Saturday. Under Rule 45(a) the period expires on the next day that is not a Sunday or legal holiday. If the following Monday is a legal holiday, under Rule 45(a) the period expires on Tuesday. Three days are then added—Wednesday, Thursday, and Friday as the third and final day to act unless that is a legal holiday. If the prescribed period ends on a Friday, the three added days are Saturday, Sunday, and Monday, which is the third and final day to act unless it is a legal holiday. If Monday is a legal holiday, the next day that is not a legal holiday is the third and final day to act.

Application of Rule 45(c) to a period that is less than eleven days can be illustrated by a paper that is served by mailing on a Friday. If ten days are allowed to respond, intermediate Saturdays, Sundays, and legal holidays are excluded in determining when the period expires under Rule 45(a). If there is no legal holiday, the period expires on the Friday two weeks after the paper was mailed. The three added Rule 45(c) days are Saturday, Sunday, and Monday, which is the third and final day to act unless it is a legal holiday. If Monday is a legal holiday, the next day that is not a legal holiday is the final day to act.

Changes Made to Proposed Amendment Released for Public Comment. No change was made in the rule as published for public comment.

COMMITTEE NOTES ON RULES—2008 AMENDMENT

This amendment revises the cross references to Civil Rule 5, which have been renumbered as part of a general restyling of the Federal Rules of Civil Procedure. No substantive change is intended.

COMMITTEE NOTES ON RULES—2009 AMENDMENT

Subdivision (a). Subdivision (a) has been amended to simplify and clarify the provisions that describe how deadlines are computed. Subdivision (a) governs the computation of any time period found in a statute that does not specify a method of computing time, a Federal Rule of Criminal Procedure, a local rule, or a court order. In accordance with Rule 57(a)(1), a local rule may not direct that a deadline be computed in a manner inconsistent with subdivision (a). In making these time computation rules applicable to statutory time periods, subdivision (a) is consistent with Civil Rule 6(a). It is also consistent with the language of Rule 45 prior to restyling, when the rule applied to "computing any period of time." Although the restyled Rule 45(a) referred only to time periods "specified in these rules, any local rule, or any court order," some courts nonetheless applied the restyled Rule 45(a) when computing various statutory periods.

The time-computation provisions of subdivision (a) apply only when a time period must be computed. They do not apply when a fixed time to act is set. The amendments thus carry forward the approach taken in Violette v. P.A. Days, Inc., 427 F.3d 1015, 1016 (6th Cir. 2005) (holding that Civil Rule 6(a) "does not apply to situations where the court has established a specific calendar day as a deadline"), and reject the contrary holding of In re American Healthcare Management, Inc., 900 F.2d 827, 832 (5th Cir. 1990) (holding that Bankruptcy Rule 9006(a) governs treatment of a date-certain deadline set by court order). If, for example, the date for filing is "no later than November 1, 2007," subdivision (a) does not govern. But if a filing is required to be made "within 10 days" or "within 72 hours," subdivision (a) describes how that deadline is computed.

Subdivision (a) does not apply when computing a time period set by a statute if the statute specifies a method of computing time. See, e.g., 18 U.S.C. §3142(d) (excluding Saturdays, Sundays, and holidays from 10 day period). In addition, because the time period in Rule 46(h) is derived from 18 U.S.C. §§3142(d) and 3144, the Committee concluded that Rule 45(a) should not be applied to Rule 46(h).

Subdivision (a)(1). New subdivision (a)(1) addresses the computation of time periods that are stated in days. It also applies to time periods that are stated in weeks, months, or years. See, e.g., Rule 35(b)(1). Subdivision (a)(1)(B)'s directive to "count every day" is relevant only if the period is stated in days (not weeks, months or years).

Under former Rule 45(a), a period of 11 days or more was computed differently than a period of less than 11 days. Intermediate Saturdays, Sundays, and legal holidays were included in computing the longer periods, but excluded in computing the shorter periods. Former Rule 45(a) thus made computing deadlines unnecessarily complicated and led to counterintuitive results. For example, a 10-day period and a 14-day period that started on the same day usually ended on the same day—and the 10-day period not infrequently ended later than the 14-day period. See Miltimore Sales, Inc. v. Int'l Rectifier, Inc., 412 F.3d 685, 686 (6th Cir. 2005).

Under new subdivision (a)(1), all deadlines stated in days (no matter the length) are computed in the same way. The day of the event that triggers the deadline is not counted. All other days—including intermediate Saturdays, Sundays, and legal holidays—are counted, with only one exception: if the period ends on a Saturday, Sunday, or legal holiday, then the deadline falls on the next day that is not a Saturday, Sunday, or legal holiday. An illustration is provided below in the discussion of subdivision (a)(5). Subdivision (a)(3) addresses filing deadlines that expire on a day when the clerk's office is inaccessible.

Where subdivision (a) formerly referred to the "act, event, or default" that triggers the deadline, the new subdivision (a) refers simply to the "event" that triggers the deadline; this change in terminology is adopted for brevity and simplicity, and is not intended to change the meaning.

Periods previously expressed as less than 11 days will be shortened as a practical matter by the decision to count intermediate Saturdays, Sundays, and legal holidays in computing all periods. Many of those periods have been lengthened to compensate for the change. See, e.g., Rules 29(c)(1), 33(b)(2), 34, and 35(a).

Most of the 10-day periods were adjusted to meet the change in computation method by setting 14 days as the new period. A 14-day period corresponds to the most frequent result of a 10-day period under the former computation method—two Saturdays and two Sundays were excluded, giving 14 days in all. A 14-day period has an additional advantage. The final day falls on the same day of the week as the event that triggered the period—the 14th day after a Monday, for example, is a Monday. This advantage of using weeklong periods led to adopting 7-day periods to replace some of the periods set at less than 10 days, and 21-day periods to replace 20-day periods. Thirty-day and longer periods, however, were generally retained without change.

Subdivision (a)(2). New subdivision (a)(2) addresses the computation of time periods that are stated in hours. No such deadline currently appears in the Federal Rules of Criminal Procedure. But some statutes contain deadlines stated in hours, as do some court orders issued in expedited proceedings.

Under subdivision (a)(2), a deadline stated in hours starts to run immediately on the occurrence of the event that triggers the deadline. The deadline generally ends when the time expires. If, however, the time period expires at a specific time (say, 2:17 p.m.) on a Saturday, Sunday, or legal holiday, then the deadline is extended to the same time (2:17 p.m.) on the next day that is not a Saturday, Sunday, or legal holiday. Periods stated in hours are not to be "rounded up" to the next whole hour. Subdivision (a)(3) addresses situations when the clerk's office is inaccessible during the last hour before a filing deadline expires.

Subdivision (a)(2)(B) directs that every hour be counted. Thus, for example, a 72-hour period that commences at 10:23 a.m. on Friday, November 2, 2007, will run until 9:23 a.m. on Monday, November 5; the discrepancy in start and end times in this example results from the intervening shift from daylight saving time to standard time.

Subdivision (a)(3). When determining the last day of a filing period stated in days or a longer unit of time, a day on which the clerk's office is not accessible because of the weather or another reason is treated like a Saturday, Sunday, or legal holiday. When determining the end of a filing period stated in hours, if the clerk's office is inaccessible during the last hour of the filing period computed under subdivision (a)(2) then the period is extended to the same time on the next day that is not a weekend, holiday or day when the clerk's office is inaccessible.

Subdivision (a)(3)'s extensions apply "[u]nless the court orders otherwise." In some circumstances, the court might not wish a period of inaccessibility to trigger a full 24-hour extension; in those instances, the court can specify a briefer extension.

The text of the rule no longer refers to "weather or other conditions" as the reason for the inaccessibility of the clerk's office. The reference to "weather" was deleted from the text to underscore that inaccessibility can occur for reasons unrelated to weather, such as an outage of the electronic filing system. Weather can still be a reason for inaccessibility of the clerk's office. The rule does not attempt to define inaccessibility. Rather, the concept will continue to develop through caselaw, see, e.g., William G. Phelps, When Is Office of Clerk of Court Inaccessible Due to Weather or Other Conditions for Purpose of Computing Time Period for Filing Papers under Rule 6(a) of Federal Rules of Civil Procedure, 135 A.L.R. Fed. 259 (1996) (collecting cases). In addition, many local provisions address inaccessibility for purposes of electronic filing, see, e.g., D. Kan. Rule CR49.11 ("A Filing User whose filing is made untimely as the result of a technical failure may seek appropriate relief from the court.").

Subdivision (a)(4). New subdivision (a)(4) defines the end of the last day of a period for purposes of subdivision (a)(1). Subdivision (a)(4) does not apply in computing periods stated in hours under subdivision (a)(2), and does not apply if a different time is set by a statute, local rule, or order in the case. A local rule may, for example, address the problems that might arise if a single district has clerk's offices in different time zones, or provide that papers filed in a drop box after the normal hours of the clerk's office are filed as of the day that is date-stamped on the papers by a device in the drop box.

28 U.S.C. §452 provides that "[a]ll courts of the United States shall be deemed always open for the purpose of filing proper papers, issuing and returning process, and making motions and orders." A corresponding provision exists in Rule 56(a). Some courts have held that these provisions permit an after-hours filing by handing the papers to an appropriate official. See, e.g., Casalduc v. Diaz, 117 F.2d 915, 917 (1st Cir. 1941). Subdivision (a)(4) does not address the effect of the statute on the question of after-hours filing; instead, the rule is designed to deal with filings in the ordinary course without regard to Section 452.

Subdivision (a)(5). New subdivision (a)(5) defines the "next" day for purposes of subdivisions (a)(1)(C) and (a)(2)(C). The Federal Rules of Criminal Procedure contain both forward-looking time periods and backward-looking time periods. A forward-looking time period requires something to be done within a period of time after an event. See, e.g., Rule 35(a) (stating that a court may correct an arithmetic or technical error in a sentence "[w]ithin 14 days after sentencing"). A backward-looking time period requires something to be done within a period of time before an event. See, e.g., Rule 47(c) (stating that a party must serve a written motion "at least 7 days before the hearing date"). In determining what is the "next" day for purposes of subdivisions (a)(1)(C) and (a)(2)(C), one should continue counting in the same direction—that is, forward when computing a forward-looking period and backward when computing a backward-looking period. If, for example, a filing is due within 10 days after an event, and the tenth day falls on Saturday, September 1, 2007, then the filing is due on Tuesday, September 4, 2007 (Monday, September 3, is Labor Day). But if a filing is due 10 days before an event, and the tenth day falls on Saturday, September 1, then the filing is due on Friday, August 31. If the clerk's office is inaccessible on August 31, then subdivision (a)(3) extends the filing deadline forward to the next accessible day that is not a Saturday, Sunday, or legal holiday—no earlier than Tuesday, September 4.

Subdivision (a)(6). New subdivision (a)(6) defines "legal holiday" for purposes of the Federal Rules of Criminal Procedure, including the time-computation provisions of subdivision (a). Subdivision (a)(6) continues to include within the definition of "legal holiday" days that are declared a holiday by the President or Congress.

For forward-counted periods—i.e., periods that are measured after an event—subdivision (a)(6)(C) includes certain state holidays within the definition of legal holidays. However, state legal holidays are not recognized in computing backward-counted periods. For both forward- and backward-counted periods, the rule thus protects those who may be unsure of the effect of state holidays. For forward-counted deadlines, treating state holidays the same as federal holidays extends the deadline. Thus, someone who thought that the federal courts might be closed on a state holiday would be safeguarded against an inadvertent late filing. In contrast, for backward-counted deadlines, not giving state holidays the treatment of federal holidays allows filing on the state holiday itself rather than the day before. Take, for example, Monday, April 21, 2008 (Patriot's Day, a legal holiday in the relevant state). If a filing is due 14 days after an event, and the fourteenth day is April 21, then the filing is due on Tuesday, April 22 because Monday, April 21 counts as a legal holiday. But if a filing is due 14 days before an event, and the fourteenth day is April 21, the filing is due on Monday, April 21; the fact that April 21 is a state holiday does not make April 21 a legal holiday for purposes of computing this backward-counted deadline. But note that if the clerk's office is inaccessible on Monday, April 21, then subdivision (a)(3) extends the April 21 filing deadline forward to the next accessible day that is not a Saturday, Sunday or legal holiday—no earlier than Tuesday, April 22.

Changes Made to Proposed Amendment Released for Public Comment. The Standing Committee changed Rule 45(a)(6) to exclude state holidays from the definition of "legal holiday" for purposes of computing backward-counted periods; conforming changes were made to the Committee Note to subdivision (a)(6).

COMMITTEE NOTES ON RULES—2016 AMENDMENT

Subdivision (c). Rule 45(c) and Rule 6(d) of the Federal Rules of Civil Procedure contain parallel provisions providing additional time for actions after certain modes of service, identifying those modes by reference to Civil Rule 5(b)(2). Rule 45(c)—like Civil Rule 6(d)—is amended to remove service by electronic means under Rule 5(b)(2)(E) from the forms of service that allow 3 added days to act after being served. The amendment also adds clarifying parentheticals identifying the forms of service for which 3 days will still be added.

Civil Rule 5 was amended in 2001 to allow service by electronic means with the consent of the person served, and a parallel amendment to Rule 45(c) was adopted in 2002. Although electronic transmission seemed virtually instantaneous even then, electronic service was included in the modes of service that allow 3 added days to act after being served. There were concerns that the transmission might be delayed for some time, and particular concerns that incompatible systems might make it difficult or impossible to open attachments. Those concerns have been substantially alleviated by advances in technology and widespread skill in using electronic transmission.

A parallel reason for allowing the 3 added days was that electronic service was authorized only with the consent of the person to be served. Concerns about the reliability of electronic transmission might have led to refusals of consent; the 3 added days were calculated to alleviate these concerns.

Diminution of the concerns that prompted the decision to allow the 3 added days for electronic transmission is not the only reason for discarding this indulgence. Many rules have been changed to ease the task of computing time by adopting 7-, 14-, 21-, and 28-day periods that allow "day-of-the-week" counting. Adding 3 days at the end complicated the counting, and increased the occasions for further complication by invoking the provisions that apply when the last day is a Saturday, Sunday, or legal holiday.

Eliminating Rule 5(b) subparagraph (2)(E) from the modes of service that allow 3 added days means that the 3 added days cannot be retained by consenting to service by electronic means. Consent to electronic service in registering for electronic case filing, for example, does not count as consent to service "by any other means of delivery" under subparagraph (F).

Electronic service after business hours, or just before or during a weekend or holiday, may result in a practical reduction in the time available to respond. Extensions of time may be warranted to prevent prejudice.

COMMITTEE NOTES ON RULES—2018 AMENDMENT

Rule 49 previously required service and filing in a "manner provided" in the Civil Rules, and the time counting provisions in Criminal Rule 45(c) referred to certain means of service under Civil Rule 5. A contemporaneous amendment moves the instructions for filing and service in criminal cases from Civil Rule 5 into Criminal Rule 49. This amendment revises the cross references in Rule 45(c) to reflect this change.

Rule 46. Release from Custody; Supervising Detention

(a) Before Trial. The provisions of 18 U.S.C. §§3142 and 3144 govern pretrial release.

(b) During Trial. A person released before trial continues on release during trial under the same terms and conditions. But the court may order different terms and conditions or terminate the release if necessary to ensure that the person will be present during trial or that the person's conduct will not obstruct the orderly and expeditious progress of the trial.

(c) Pending Sentencing or Appeal. The provisions of 18 U.S.C. §3143 govern release pending sentencing or appeal. The burden of establishing that the defendant will not flee or pose a danger to any other person or to the community rests with the defendant.

(d) Pending Hearing on a Violation of Probation or Supervised Release. Rule 32.1(a)(6) governs release pending a hearing on a violation of probation or supervised release.

(e) Surety. The court must not approve a bond unless any surety appears to be qualified. Every surety, except a legally approved corporate surety, must demonstrate by affidavit that its assets are adequate. The court may require the affidavit to describe the following:

(1) the property that the surety proposes to use as security;

(2) any encumbrance on that property;

(3) the number and amount of any other undischarged bonds and bail undertakings the surety has issued; and

(4) any other liability of the surety.

(f) Bail Forfeiture.

(1) Declaration. The court must declare the bail forfeited if a condition of the bond is breached.

(2) Setting Aside. The court may set aside in whole or in part a bail forfeiture upon any condition the court may impose if:

(A) the surety later surrenders into custody the person released on the surety's appearance bond; or

(B) it appears that justice does not require bail forfeiture.

(3) Enforcement.

(A) Default Judgment and Execution. If it does not set aside a bail forfeiture, the court must, upon the government's motion, enter a default judgment.

(B) Jurisdiction and Service. By entering into a bond, each surety submits to the district court's jurisdiction and irrevocably appoints the district clerk as its agent to receive service of any filings affecting its liability.

(C) Motion to Enforce. The court may, upon the government's motion, enforce the surety's liability without an independent action. The government must serve any motion, and notice as the court prescribes, on the district clerk. If so served, the clerk must promptly mail a copy to the surety at its last known address.

(4) Remission. After entering a judgment under Rule 46(f)(3), the court may remit in whole or in part the judgment under the same conditions specified in Rule 46(f)(2).

(g) Exoneration. The court must exonerate the surety and release any bail when a bond condition has been satisfied or when the court has set aside or remitted the forfeiture. The court must exonerate a surety who deposits cash in the amount of the bond or timely surrenders the defendant into custody.

(h) Supervising Detention Pending Trial.

    (1) In General. To eliminate unnecessary detention, the court must supervise the detention within the district of any defendants awaiting trial and of any persons held as material witnesses.

    (2) Reports. An attorney for the government must report biweekly to the court, listing each material witness held in custody for more than 10 days pending indictment, arraignment, or trial. For each material witness listed in the report, an attorney for the government must state why the witness should not be released with or without a deposition being taken under Rule 15(a).

(i) Forfeiture of Property. The court may dispose of a charged offense by ordering the forfeiture of 18 U.S.C. §3142(c)(1)(B)(xi) property under 18 U.S.C. §3146(d), if a fine in the amount of the property's value would be an appropriate sentence for the charged offense.

(j) Producing a Statement.

    (1) In General. Rule 26.2(a)–(d) and (f) applies at a detention hearing under 18 U.S.C. §3142, unless the court for good cause rules otherwise.

    (2) Sanctions for Not Producing a Statement. If a party disobeys a Rule 26.2 order to produce a witness's statement, the court must not consider that witness's testimony at the detention hearing.

(As amended Apr. 9, 1956, eff. July 8, 1956; Feb. 28, 1966, eff. July 1, 1966; Apr. 24, 1972, eff. Oct. 1, 1972; Pub. L. 98–473, title II, §209(d), Oct. 12, 1984, 98 Stat. 1987; Mar. 9, 1987, eff. Aug. 1, 1987; Apr. 30, 1991, eff. Dec. 1, 1991; Apr. 22, 1993, eff. Dec. 1, 1993; Pub. L. 103–322, title XXXIII, §330003(h), Sept. 13, 1994, 108 Stat. 2141; Apr. 29, 2002, eff. Dec. 1, 2002.)

Notes of Advisory Committee on Rules——1944

Note to Subdivision (a)(1). This rule is substantially a restatement of existing law, 18 U.S.C. 596, 597 [now 3141].

Note to Subdivision (a)(2). This rule is substantially a restatement of Rule 6 of Criminal Appeals Rules, with the addition of a reference to bail pending certiorari. This rule does not supersede 18 U.S.C. 682 [now 3731] (Appeals; on behalf of the United States; rules of practice and procedure), which provides for the admission of the defendant to bail on his own recognizance pending an appeal taken by the Government.

Note to Subdivision (b). This rule is substantially a restatement of existing law, 28 U.S.C. [former] 657.

Note to Subdivision (d). This rule is a restatement of existing practice, and is based in part on 6 U.S.C. 15 [now 31 U.S.C. 9103] (Bonds or notes of United States in lieu of recognizance, stipulation, bond, guaranty, or undertaking; place of deposit; return to depositor; contractors' bonds).

Note to Subdivision (e). This rule is similar to Sec. 79 of A.L.I. Code of Criminal Procedure introducing, however, an element of flexibility. Corporate sureties are regulated by 6 U.S.C. 6–14 [now 31 U.S.C. 9304–9308].

Note to Subdivision (f). 1. With the exception hereafter noted, this rule is substantially a restatement of existing law in somewhat greater detail than contained in 18 U.S.C. [former] 601 (Remission of penalty of recognizance).

2. Subdivision (f)(2) changes existing law in that it increases the discretion of the court to set aside a forfeiture. The present power of the court is limited to cases in which the defendant's default had not been willful.

3. The second sentence of paragraph (3) is similar to Rule 73(f) of the Federal Rules of Civil Procedure [28 U.S.C., Appendix]. This paragraph also substitutes simple motion procedure for enforcing forfeited bail bonds for the procedure by scire facias, which was abolished by Rule 81(b) of the Federal Rules of Civil Procedure.

Note to Subdivision (g). This rule is a restatement of existing law and practice. It is based in part on 18 U.S.C. 599 [now 3142] (Surrender by bail).

Notes of Advisory Committee on Rules——1966 Amendment

Subdivision (c).——The more inclusive word "terms" is substituted for "amount" in view of the amendment to subdivision (d) authorizing releases without security on such conditions as are necessary to insure the appearance of the defendant. The phrase added at the end of this subdivision is designed to encourage commissioners and judges to set the terms of bail so as to eliminate unnecessary detention. See Stack v. Boyle, 342 U.S. 1 (1951); Bandy v. United States, 81 S.Ct. 197 (1960); Bandy v. United States, 82 S.Ct. 11 (1961); Carbo v. United States, 82 S.Ct. 662 (1962); review den. 369 U.S. 868 (1962).

Subdivision (d).——The amendments are designed to make possible (and to encourage) the release on bail of a greater percentage of indigent defendants than now are released. To the extent that other considerations make it reasonably likely that the defendant will appear it is both good practice and good economics to release him on bail even though he cannot arrange for cash or bonds in even small amounts. In fact it has been suggested that it may be a denial of constitutional rights to hold indigent prisoners in custody for no other reason than their inability to raise the money for a bond. Bandy v. United States, 81 S.Ct. 197 (1960).

The first change authorizes the acceptance as security of a deposit of cash or government securities in an amount less than the face amount of the bond. Since a defendant typically purchases a bail bond for a cash payment of a certain percentage of the face of the bond, a direct deposit with the court of that amount (returnable to the defendant upon his appearance) will often be equally adequate as a deterrent to flight. Cf. Ill.CodeCrim.Proc. §110–7 (1963).

The second change authorizes the release of the defendant without financial security on his written agreement to appear when other deterrents appear reasonably adequate. See the discussion of such deterrents in Bandy v. United States, 81 S.Ct. 197 (1960). It also permits the imposition of nonfinancial conditions as the price of dispensing with security for the bond. Such conditions are commonly used in England. Devin, The Criminal Prosecution in England, 89 (1958). See the suggestion in Note, Bail: An Ancient Practice Reexamined, 70 Yale L.J. 966, 975 (1961) that such conditions "* * * might include release in custody of a third party, such as the accused's employer, minister, attorney, or a private organization; release subject to a duty to report periodically to the court or other public official; or even release subject to a duty to return to jail each night." Willful failure to appear after forfeiture of bail is a separate criminal offense and hence an added deterrent to flight. 18 U.S.C. §3146.

For full discussion and general approval of the changes made here see Report of the Attorney General's Committee on Poverty and the Administration of Criminal Justice 58–89 (1963).

Subdivision (h).——The purpose of this new subdivision is to place upon the court in each district the responsibility for supervising the detention of defendants and witnesses and for eliminating all unnecessary detention. The device of the report by the attorney for the government is used because in many districts defendants will be held in custody in places where the court sits only at infrequent intervals and hence they cannot be brought personally before the court without substantial delay. The magnitude of the problem is suggested by the facts that during the fiscal year ending June 30, 1960, there were 23,811 instances in which persons were held in custody pending trial and that the average length of detention prior to disposition (i.e., dismissal, acquittal, probation, sentence to imprisonment, or any other method of removing the case from the court docket) was 25.3 days. Federal Prisons 1960, table 22, p. 60. Since 27,645 of the 38,855 defendants whose cases were terminated during the fiscal year ending June 30, 1960, pleaded guilty (United States Attorneys Statistical Report, October 1960, p. 1 and table 2), it would appear that the greater part of the detention reported occurs prior to the initial appearance of the defendant before the court.

The amendments are intended primarily to bring rule 46 into general conformity with the Bail Reform Act of 1966 and to deal in the rule with some issues not now included within the rule.

Subdivision (a) makes explicit that the Bail Reform Act of 1966 controls release on bail prior to trial. 18 U.S.C. §3146 refers to release of a defendant. 18 U.S.C. §3149 refers to release of a material witness.

Subdivision (b) deals with an issue not dealt with by the Bail Reform Act of 1966 or explicitly in former rule 46, that is, the issue of bail during trial. The rule gives the trial judge discretion to continue the prior conditions of release or to impose such additional conditions as are adequate to insure presence at trial or to insure that his conduct will not obstruct the orderly and expeditious progress of the trial.

Subdivision (c) provides for release during the period between a conviction and sentencing and for the giving of a notice of appeal or of the expiration of the time allowed for filing notice of appeal. There are situations in which defense counsel may informally indicate an intention to appeal but not actually give notice of appeal for several days. To deal with this situation the rule makes clear that the district court has authority to release under the terms of 18 U.S.C. §3148 pending notice of appeal (e.g., during the ten days after entry of judgment; see rule 4(b) of the Rules of Appellate Procedure). After the filing of notice of appeal, release by the district court shall be in accordance with the provisions of rule 9(b) of the Rules of Appellate Procedure. The burden of establishing that grounds for release exist is placed upon the defendant in the view that the fact of conviction justifies retention in custody in situations where doubt exists as to whether a defendant can be safely released pending either sentence or the giving of notice of appeal.

Subdivisions (d), (e), (f), and (g) remain unchanged. They were formerly lettered (e), (f), (g), and (h).

The amendments are technical. No substantive change is intended.

The amendment is technical. No substantive change is intended.

The addition of subdivision (i) is one of a series of similar amendments to Rules 26.2, 32, 32.1, and Rule 8 of the Rules Governing Proceedings Under 28 U.S.C. §2255 which extend Rule 26.2 to other proceedings and hearings. As pointed out in the Committee Note to the amendment to Rule 26.2, there is continuing and compelling need to assess the credibility and reliability of information relied upon by the court, whether the witness's testimony is being considered at a pretrial proceeding, at trial, or a post-trial proceeding. Production of a witness's prior statements directly furthers that goal.

The need for reliable information is no less crucial in a proceeding to determine whether a defendant should be released from custody. The issues decided at pretrial detention hearings are important to both a defendant and the community. For example, a defendant charged with criminal acts may be incarcerated prior to an adjudication of guilt without bail on grounds of future dangerousness which is not subject to proof beyond a reasonable doubt. Although the defendant clearly has an interest in remaining free prior to trial, the community has an equally compelling interest in being protected from potential criminal activity committed by persons awaiting trial.

In upholding the constitutionality of pretrial detention based upon dangerousness, the Supreme Court in United States v. Salerno, 481 U.S. 739 (1986), stressed the existence of procedural safeguards in the Bail Reform Act. The Act provides for the right to counsel and the right to cross-examine adverse witnesses. See, e.g., 18 U.S.C. §3142(f) (right of defendant to cross-examine adverse witness). Those safeguards, said the Court, are "specifically designed to further the accuracy of that determination." 481 U.S. at 751. The Committee believes that requiring the production of a witness's statement will further enhance the fact-finding process.

The Committee recognized that pretrial detention hearings are often held very early in a prosecution, and that a particular witness's statement may not yet be on file, or even known about. Thus, the amendment recognizes that in a particular case, the court may decide that good cause exists for not applying the rule.

The language of Rule 46 has been amended as part of the general restyling of the Criminal Rules to make them more easily understood and to make style and terminology consistent throughout the rules. These changes are intended to be stylistic only, except as noted below.

Although the general rule is that an appeal to a circuit court deprives the district court of jurisdiction, Rule 46(c) recognizes the apparent exception to that rule——that the district court retains jurisdiction to decide whether the defendant should be detained, even if a notice of appeal has been filed. See, e.g., United States v. Meyers, 95 F.3d 1475 (10th Cir. 1996), cert. denied, 522 U.S. 1006 (1997) (initial decision of whether to release defendant pending appeal is to be made by district court); United States v. Affleck, 765 F.2d 944 (10th Cir. 1985); Jago v. United States District Court, 570 F.2d 618 (6th Cir. 1978) (release of defendant pending appeal must first be sought in district court). See also Federal Rule of Appellate Procedure 9(b) and the accompanying Committee Note.

Revised Rule 46(h) deletes the requirement that the attorney for the government file bi-weekly reports with the court concerning the status of any defendants in pretrial detention. The Committee believed that the requirement was no longer necessary in light of the Speedy Trial Act provisions. 18 U.S.C. §§3161, et seq. On the other hand, the requirement that the attorney for the government file reports regarding detained material witnesses has been retained in the rule.

Rule 46(i) addresses the ability of a court to order forfeiture of property where a defendant has failed to appear as required by the court. The language in the current rule, Rule 46(h), was originally included by Congress. The new language has been restyled with no change in substance or practice intended. Under this provision, the court may only forfeit property as permitted under 18 U.S.C. §§3146(d) and 3142(c)(1)(B)(xi). The term "appropriate sentence" means a sentence that is consistent with the Sentencing Guidelines.

1994——Subd. (i)(1). Pub. L. 103–322 substituted "3142" for "3144".

1984——Subd. (a). Pub. L. 98–473, §209(d)(1), substituted "§§3142 and 3144" for "§3146, §3148, or §3149".

Subd. (c). Pub. L. 98–473, §209(d)(2), substituted "3143" for "3148".

Subd. (e)(2). Pub. L. 98–473, §209(d)(3), substituted "be set aside in whole or in part upon such conditions as the court may impose, if a person released upon execution of an appearance bond with a surety is subsequently surrendered by the surety into custody or if it otherwise appears that justice does not require the forfeiture" for "set aside, upon such conditions as the court may impose, if it appears that justice does not require the enforcement of the forfeiture".

Subd. (h). Pub. L. 98–473, §209(d)(4), added subd. (h).

Amendment by Order of April 9, 1956, became effective 90 days thereafter.

Rule 47. Motions and Supporting Affidavits

(a) In General. A party applying to the court for an order must do so by motion.

(b) Form and Content of a Motion. A motion—except when made during a trial or hearing—must be in writing, unless the court permits the party to make the motion by other means. A motion must state the grounds on which it is based and the relief or order sought. A motion may be supported by affidavit.

(c) Timing of a Motion. A party must serve a written motion—other than one that the court may hear ex parte—and any hearing notice at least 7 days before the hearing date, unless a rule or court order sets a different period. For good cause, the court may set a different period upon ex parte application.

(d) Affidavit Supporting a Motion. The moving party must serve any supporting affidavit with the motion. A responding party must serve any opposing affidavit at least one day before the hearing, unless the court permits later service.

(As amended Apr. 29, 2002, eff. Dec. 1, 2002; Mar. 26, 2009, eff. Dec. 1, 2009.)

NOTES OF ADVISORY COMMITTEE ON RULES—1944

1. This rule is substantially the same as the corresponding civil rule (first sentence of Rule 7(b)(1), Federal Rules of Civil Procedure) [28 U.S.C., Appendix], except that it authorizes the court to permit motions to be made orally and does not require that the grounds upon which a motion is made shall be stated "with particularity," as is the case with the civil rule.

2. This rule is intended to state general requirements for all motions. For particular provisions applying to specific motions, see Rules 6(b)(2), 12, 14, 15, 16, 17(b) and (c), 21, 22, 29 and Rule 41(e). See also Rule 49.

3. The last sentence providing that a motion may be supported by affidavit is not intended to permit "speaking motions" (e.g. motion to dismiss an indictment for insufficiency supported by affidavits), but to authorize the use of affidavits when affidavits are appropriate to establish a fact (e.g. authority to take a deposition or former jeopardy).

COMMITTEE NOTES ON RULES—2002 AMENDMENT

The language of Rule 47 has been amended as part of the general restyling of the Criminal Rules to make them more easily understood and to make style and terminology consistent throughout the rules. These changes are intended to be stylistic only, except as noted below.

In Rule 47(b), the word "orally" has been deleted. The Committee believed, first, that the term should not act as a limitation on those who are not able to speak orally and, second, a court may wish to entertain motions through electronic or other reliable means. Deletion of the term also comports with a similar change in Rule 26, regarding the taking of testimony during trial. In place of that word, the Committee substituted the broader phrase "by other means."

COMMITTEE NOTES ON RULES—2009 AMENDMENT

The time set in the former rule at 5 days, which excluded intermediate Saturdays, Sundays, and legal holidays, has been expanded to 7 days. See the Committee Note to Rule 45(a).

Rule 48. Dismissal

(a) By the Government. The government may, with leave of court, dismiss an indictment, information, or complaint. The government may not dismiss the prosecution during trial without the defendant's consent.

(b) By the Court. The court may dismiss an indictment, information, or complaint if unnecessary delay occurs in:

(1) presenting a charge to a grand jury;

(2) filing an information against a defendant; or

(3) bringing a defendant to trial.

(As amended Apr. 29, 2002, eff. Dec. 1, 2002.)

NOTES OF ADVISORY COMMITTEE ON RULES—1944

Note to Subdivision (a). 1. The first sentence of this rule will change existing law. The common-law rule that the public prosecutor may enter a nolle prosequi in his discretion, without any action by the court, prevails in the Federal courts, Confiscation Cases, 7 Wall. 454, 457; United States v. Woody, 2 F.2d 262 (D.Mont.). This provision will permit the filing of a nolle prosequi only by leave of court. This is similar to the rule now prevailing in many States. A.L.I. Code of Criminal Procedure, Commentaries, pp. 895–897.

2. The rule confers the power to file a dismissal by leave of court on the Attorney General, as well as on the United States attorney, since under existing law the Attorney General exercises "general superintendence and direction" over the United States attorneys "as to the manner of discharging their respective duties," 5 U.S.C. 317 [now 28 U.S.C. 509, 547]. Moreover it is the administrative practice for the Attorney General to supervise the filing of a nolle prosequi by United States attorneys. Consequently it seemed appropriate that the Attorney General should have such power directly.

3. The rule permits the filing of a dismissal of an indictment, information or complaint. The word "complaint" was included in order to resolve a doubt prevailing in some districts as to whether the United States attorney may file a nolle prosequi between the time when the defendant is bound over by the United States commissioner and the finding of an indictment. It has been assumed in a few districts that the power does not exist and that the United States attorney must await action of the grand jury, even if he deems it proper to dismiss the prosecution. This situation is an unnecessary hardship to some defendants.

4. The second sentence is a restatement of existing law, Confiscation Cases, 7 Wall. 454–457; United States v. Shoemaker, 27 Fed. Cases No. 16, 279 (C.C.Ill.). If the trial has commenced, the defendant has a right to insist on a disposition on the merits and may properly object to the entry of a nolle prosequi.

Note to Subdivision (b). This rule is a restatement of the inherent power of the court to dismiss a case for want of prosecution. Ex parte Altman, 34 F.Supp. 106 (S.D.Cal.).

COMMITTEE NOTES ON RULES—2002 AMENDMENT

The language of Rule 48 has been amended as part of the general restyling of the Criminal Rules to make them more easily understood and to make style and terminology consistent throughout the rules. These changes are intended to be stylistic only.

The Committee considered the relationship between Rule 48(b) and the Speedy Trial Act. See 18 U.S.C. §§3161, et seq. Rule 48(b), of course, operates independently from the Act. See, e.g., United States v. Goodson, 204 F.3d 508 (4th Cir. 2000) (noting purpose of Rule 48(b)); United States v. Carlone, 666 F.2d 1112, 1116 (7th Cir. 1981) (suggesting that Rule 48(b) could provide an alternate basis in an extreme case to dismiss an indictment, without reference to Speedy Trial Act); United States v.

Balochi, 527 F.2d 562, 563–64 (4th Cir. 1976) (per curiam) (Rule 48(b) is broader in compass). In re-promulgating Rule 48(b), the Committee intends no change in the relationship between that rule and the Speedy Trial Act.

Rule 49. Serving and Filing Papers

(a) Service on a Party.

(1) What is Required. Each of the following must be served on every party: any written motion (other than one to be heard ex parte), written notice, designation of the record on appeal, or similar paper.

(2) Serving a Party's Attorney. Unless the court orders otherwise, when these rules or a court order requires or permits service on a party represented by an attorney, service must be made on the attorney instead of the party.

(3) Service by Electronic Means.

(A) Using the Court's Electronic-Filing System. A party represented by an attorney may serve a paper on a registered user by filing it with the court's electronic-filing system. A party not represented by an attorney may do so only if allowed by court order or local rule. Service is complete upon filing, but is not effective if the serving party learns that it did not reach the person to be served.

(B) Using Other Electronic Means. A paper may be served by any other electronic means that the person consented to in writing. Service is complete upon transmission, but is not effective if the serving party learns that it did not reach the person to be served.

(4) Service by Nonelectronic Means. A paper may be served by:

(A) handing it to the person;

(B) leaving it:

(i) at the person's office with a clerk or other person in charge or, if no one is in charge, in a conspicuous place in the office; or

(ii) if the person has no office or the office is closed, at the person's dwelling or usual place of abode with someone of suitable age and discretion who resides there;

(C) mailing it to the person's last known address—in which event service is complete upon mailing;

(D) leaving it with the court clerk if the person has no known address; or

(E) delivering it by any other means that the person consented to in writing—in which event service is complete when the person making service delivers it to the agency designated to make delivery.

(b) Filing.

(1) When Required; Certificate of Service. Any paper that is required to be served must be filed no later than a reasonable time after service. No certificate of service is required when a paper is served by filing it with the court's electronic-filing system. When a paper is served by other means, a certificate of service must be filed with it or within a reasonable time after service or filing.

(2) Means of Filing.

(A) Electronically. A paper is filed electronically by filing it with the court's electronic-filing system. A filing made through a person's electronic-filing account and authorized by that person, together with the person's name on a signature block, constitutes the person's signature. A paper filed electronically is written or in writing under these rules.

(B) Nonelectronically. A paper not filed electronically is filed by delivering it:

(i) to the clerk; or

(ii) to a judge who agrees to accept it for filing, and who must then note the filing date on the paper and promptly send it to the clerk.

(3) Means Used by Represented and Unrepresented Parties.

(A) Represented Party. A party represented by an attorney must file electronically, unless nonelectronic filing is allowed by the court for good cause or is allowed or required by local rule.

(B) Unrepresented Party. A party not represented by an attorney must file nonelectronically, unless allowed to file electronically by court order or local rule.

(4) Signature. Every written motion and other paper must be signed by at least one attorney of record in the attorney's name—or by a person filing a paper if the person is not represented by an attorney. The paper must state the signer's address, e-mail address, and telephone number. Unless a rule or statute specifically states otherwise, a pleading need not be verified or accompanied by an affidavit. The court must strike an unsigned paper unless the omission is promptly corrected after being called to the attorney's or person's attention.

(5) Acceptance by the Clerk. The clerk must not refuse to file a paper solely because it is not in the form prescribed by these rules or by a local rule or practice.

(c) Service and Filing by Nonparties. A nonparty may serve and file a paper only if doing so is required or permitted by law. A nonparty must serve every party as required by Rule 49(a), but may use the court's electronic-filing system only if allowed by court order or local rule.

(d) Notice of a Court Order. When the court issues an order on any post-arraignment motion, the clerk must serve notice of the entry on each party as required by Rule 49(a). A party also may serve notice of the entry by the same means. Except as Federal Rule of Appellate Procedure 4(b) provides otherwise, the clerk's failure to give notice does not affect the time to appeal, or relieve—or authorize the court to relieve—a party's failure to appeal within the allowed time.

(As amended Feb. 28, 1966, eff. July 1, 1966; Dec. 4, 1967, eff. July 1, 1968; Apr. 29, 1985, eff. Aug. 1, 1985; Mar. 9, 1987, eff. Aug. 1, 1987; Apr. 22, 1993, eff. Dec. 1, 1993; Apr. 27, 1995, eff. Dec. 1, 1995; Apr. 29, 2002, eff. Dec. 1, 2002; Apr. 26, 2011, eff. Dec. 1, 2011; Apr. 26, 2018, eff. Dec. 1, 2018.)

Notes of Advisory Committee on Rules—1944

Note to Subdivision (a). This rule is substantially the same as Rule 5(a) of the Federal Rules of Civil Procedure [28 U.S.C., Appendix] with such adaptations as are necessary for criminal cases.

Note to Subdivision (b). The first sentence of this rule is in substance the same as the first sentence of Rule 5(b) of the Federal Rules of Civil Procedure [28 U.S.C., Appendix]. The second sentence incorporates by reference the second and third sentences of Rule 5(b) of the Federal Rules of Civil Procedure.

Note to Subdivision (c). This rule is an adaptation for criminal proceedings of Rule 77(d) of the Federal Rules of Civil Procedure [28 U.S.C., Appendix]. No consequence attaches to the failure of the clerk to give the prescribed notice, but in a case in which the losing party in reliance on the clerk's obligation to send a notice failed to file a timely notice of appeal, it was held competent for the trial judge, in the exercise of sound discretion, to vacate the judgment because of clerk's failure to give notice and to enter a new judgment, the term of court not having expired. Hill v. Hawes, 320 U.S. 520.

Note to Subdivision (d). This rule incorporates by reference Rule 5(d) and (e) of the Federal Rules of Civil Procedure [28 U.S.C., Appendix].

Notes of Advisory Committee on Rules—1966 Amendment

Subdivision (a).—The words "adverse parties" in the original rule introduced a question of interpretation. When, for example, is a co-defendant an adverse party? The amendment requires service on each of the parties thus avoiding the problem of interpretation and promoting full exchange of information among the parties. No restriction is intended, however, upon agreements among co-defendants or between the defendants and the government restricting exchange of papers in the interest of eliminating unnecessary expense. Cf. the amendment made effective July 1, 1963, to Civil Rule 5(a).

Subdivision (c).——The words "affected thereby" are deleted in order to require notice to all parties. Cf. the similar change made effective July 1, 1963, to Civil Rule 77(d).

The sentence added at the end of the subdivision eliminates the possibility of extension of the time to appeal beyond the provision for a 30 day extension on a showing or "excusable neglect" provided in Rule 37(a)(2). Cf. the similar change made in Civil Rule 77(d) effective in 1948. The question has arisen in a number of cases whether failure or delay in giving notice on the part of the clerk results in an extension of the time for appeal. The "general rule" has been said to be that in the event of such failure or delay "the time for taking an appeal runs from the date of later actual notice or receipt of the clerk's notice rather than from the date of entry of the order." Lohman v. United States, 237 F.2d 645, 646 (6th Cir. 1956). See also Rosenbloom v. United States, 355 U.S. 80 (1957) (permitting an extension). In two cases it has been held that no extension results from the failure to give notice of entry of judgments (as opposed to orders) since such notice is not required by Rule 49(d). Wilkinson v. United States, 278 F.2d 604 (10th Cir. 1960), cert. den. 363 U.S. 829; Hyche v. United States, 278 F.2d 915 (5th Cir. 1960), cert. den. 364 U.S. 881. The excusable neglect extension provision in Rule 37(a)(2) will cover most cases where failure of the clerk to give notice of judgments or orders has misled the defendant. No need appears for an indefinite extension without time limit beyond the 30 day period.

NOTES OF ADVISORY COMMITTEE ON RULES——1968 AMENDMENT

The amendment corrects the reference to Rule 37(a)(2), the pertinent provisions of which are contained in Rule 4(b) of the Federal Rules of Appellate Procedure.

NOTES OF ADVISORY COMMITTEE ON RULES——1985 AMENDMENT

18 U.S.C. §3575(a) and 21 U.S.C. §849(a), dealing respectively with dangerous special offender sentencing and dangerous special drug offender sentencing, provide for the prosecutor to file notice of such status "with the court" and for the court to "order the notice sealed" under specified circumstances, but also declare that disclosure of this notice shall not be made "to the presiding judge without the consent of the parties" before verdict or plea of guilty or nolo contendere. It has been noted that these provisions are "regrettably unclear as to where, in fact, such notice is to be filed" and that possibly filing with the chief judge is contemplated. United States v. Tramunti, 377 F.Supp. 6 (S.D.N.Y. 1974). But such practice has been a matter of dispute when the chief judge would otherwise have been the presiding judge in the case, United States v. Gaylor, No. 80–5016 (4th Cir. 1981), and "it does not solve the problem in those districts where there is only one federal district judge appointed," United States v. Tramunti, supra.

The first sentence of subdivision (e) clarifies that the filing of such notice with the court is to be accomplished by filing with the clerk of the court, which is generally the procedure for filing with the court; see subdivision (d) of this rule. Except in a district having a single judge and no United States magistrate, the clerk will then, as provided in the second sentence, transmit the notice to the chief judge or to some other judge or a United States magistrate if the chief judge is scheduled to be the presiding judge in the case, so that the determination regarding sealing of the notice may be made without the disclosure prohibited by the aforementioned statutes. But in a district having a single judge and no United States magistrate this prohibition means the clerk may not disclose the notice to the court at all until the time specified by statute. The last sentence of subdivision (e) contemplates that in such instances the clerk will seal the notice if the case falls within the local rule describing when "a public record may prejudice fair consideration of a pending criminal matter," the determination called for by the aforementioned statutes. The local rule might provide, for example, that the notice is to be sealed upon motion by any party.

NOTES OF ADVISORY COMMITTEE ON RULES——1987 AMENDMENT

The amendments are technical. No substantive change is intended.

NOTES OF ADVISORY COMMITTEE ON RULES——1993 AMENDMENT

The Rule is amended to conform to the Judicial Improvements Act of 1990 [P.L. 101–650, Title III, Section 321] which provides that each United States magistrate appointed under section 631 of title 28, United States Code, shall be known as a United States magistrate judge.

NOTES OF ADVISORY COMMITTEE ON RULES——1995 AMENDMENT

Subdivision (e) has been deleted because both of the statutory provisions cited in the rule have been abrogated.

COMMITTEE NOTES ON RULES——2002 AMENDMENT

The language of Rule 49 has been amended as part of the general restyling of the Criminal Rules to make them more easily understood and to make style and terminology consistent throughout the rules.

Rule 49(c) has been amended to reflect proposed changes in the Federal Rules of Civil Procedure that permit (but do not require) a court to provide notice of its orders and judgments through electronic means. See Federal Rules of Civil Procedure 5(b) and 77(d). As amended, Rule 49(c) now parallels a similar extant provision in Rule 49(b), regarding service of papers.

COMMITTEE NOTES ON RULES——2011 AMENDMENT

Subdivision (e). Filing papers by electronic means is added as new subdivision (e), which is drawn from Civil Rule 5(d)(3). It makes it clear that a paper filed electronically in compliance with the Court's local rule is a written paper.

Changes Made to Proposed Amendment Released for Public Comment. No changes were made in the rule as published.

COMMITTEE NOTES ON RULES——2018 AMENDMENT

Rule 49 previously required service and filing in a "manner provided" in "a civil action." The amendments to Rule 49 move the instructions for filing and service from the Civil Rules into Rule 49. Placing instructions for filing and service in the criminal rule avoids the need to refer to two sets of rules, and permits independent development of those rules. Except where specifically noted, the amendments are intended to carry over the existing law on filing and service and to preserve parallelism with the Civil Rules.

Additionally, the amendments eliminate the provision permitting electronic filing only when authorized by local rules, moving—with the Rules governing Appellate, Civil, and Bankruptcy proceedings—to a national rule that mandates electronic filing for parties represented by an attorney with certain exceptions. Electronic filing has matured. Most districts have adopted local rules that require electronic filing by represented parties, and allow reasonable exceptions as required by the former rule. The time has come to seize the advantages of electronic filing by making it mandatory in all districts for a party represented by an attorney, except that nonelectronic filing may be allowed by the court for good cause, or allowed or required by local rule.

Rule 49(a)(1). The language from former Rule 49(a) is retained in new Rule 49(a)(1), except for one change. The new phrase, "Each of the following must be served on every party" restores to this part of the rule the passive construction that it had prior to restyling in 2002. That restyling revised the language to apply to parties only, inadvertently ending its application to nonparties who, on occasion, file motions in criminal cases. Additional guidance for nonparties appears in new subdivision (c).

Rule 49(a)(2). The language from former Rule 49(b) concerning service on the attorney of a represented party is retained here, with the "unless" clause moved to the beginning for reasons of style only.

Rule 49(a)(3) and (4). Subsections (a)(3) and (4) list the permissible means of service. These new provisions duplicate the description of permissible means from Civil Rule 5, carrying them into the criminal rule.

By listing service by filing with the court's electronic-filing system first, in (3)(A), the rule now recognizes the advantages of electronic filing and service and its widespread use in criminal cases by represented defendants and government attorneys.

But the e-filing system is designed for attorneys, and its use can pose many challenges for pro se parties. In the criminal context, the rules must ensure ready access to the courts by all pro se defendants and incarcerated individuals, filers who often lack reliable access to the internet or email. Although access to electronic-filing systems may expand with time, presently many districts do not allow e-filing by unrepresented defendants or prisoners. Accordingly, subsection (3)(A) provides that represented parties may serve registered users by filing with the court's electronic-filing system, but unrepresented parties may do so only if allowed by court order or local rule.

Subparagraph (3)(B) permits service by "other electronic means," such as email, that the person served consented to in writing.

Both subparagraphs (3)(A) and (B) include the direction from Civil Rule 5 that service is complete upon e-filing or transmission, but is not effective if the serving party learns that the person to be served did not receive the notice of e-filing or the paper transmitted by other electronic means. The language mirrors Civil Rule 5(b)(2)(E). But unlike Civil Rule 5, Criminal Rule 49 contains a separate provision for service by use of the court's electronic-filing system. The rule does not make the court responsible for notifying a person who filed the paper with the court's electronic-filing system that an attempted transmission by the court's system failed.

Subsection (a)(4) lists a number of traditional, nonelectronic means of serving papers, identical to those provided in Civil Rule 5.

Rule 49(b)(1). Filing rules in former Rule 49 appeared in subdivision (d), which provided that a party must file a copy of any paper the party is required to serve, and required in a manner provided in a civil action. These requirements now appear in subdivision (b).

The language requiring filing of papers that must be served is retained from former subdivision (d), but has been moved to subsection (1) of subdivision (b), and revised to restore the passive phrasing prior to the restyling in 2002. That restyling departed from the phrasing in Civil Rule 5(d)(1) and inadvertently limited this requirement to filing by parties.

The language in former subdivision (d) that required filing "in a manner provided for in a civil action" has been replaced in new subsection (b)(1) by language drawn from Civil Rule 5(d)(1). That provision used to state "Any paper . . . that is required to be served—together with a certificate of service—must be filed within a reasonable time after service." A contemporaneous amendment to Civil Rule 5(d)(1) has subdivided this provision into two parts, one of which addresses the Certificate of Service. Although the Criminal Rules version is not subdivided in the same way, it parallels the Civil Rules provision from which it was drawn. Because "within" might be read as barring filing before the paper is served, "no later than" is substituted to ensure that it is proper to file a paper before it is served.

The second sentence of subsection (b)(1), which states that no certificate of service is required when service is made using the court's electronic-filing system, mirrors the contemporaneous amendment to Civil Rule 5. When service is not made by filing with the court's electronic-filing system, a certificate of service must be filed.

Rule 49(b)(2). New subsection (b)(2) lists the three ways papers can be filed. (A) provides for electronic filing using the court's electronic-filing system and includes a provision, drawn from the Civil Rule, stating that a filing made through a person's electronic-filing account and authorized by that person, together with the person's name on a signature block, constitutes the person's signature. The last sentence of subsection (b)(2)(A) contains the language of former Rule 49(e), providing that e-filed papers are "written or in writing," deleting the words "in compliance with a local rule" as no longer necessary.

Subsection (b)(2)(B) carries over from the Civil Rule two nonelectronic methods of filing a paper: delivery to the court clerk and delivery to a judge who agrees to accept it for filing.

Rule 49(b)(3). New subsection (b)(3) provides instructions for parties regarding the means of filing to be used, depending upon whether the party is represented by an attorney. Subsection (b)(3)(A) requires represented parties to use the court's electronic-filing system, but provides that nonelectronic filing may be allowed for good cause, and may be required or allowed for other reasons by local rule. This language is identical to that adopted in the contemporaneous amendment to Civil Rule 5.

Subsection (b)(3)(B) requires unrepresented parties to file nonelectronically, unless allowed to file electronically by court order or local rule. This language differs from that of the amended Civil Rule, which provides that an unrepresented party may be "required" to file electronically by a court order or local rule that allows reasonable exceptions. A different approach to electronic filing by unrepresented parties is needed in criminal cases, where electronic filing by pro se prisoners presents significant challenges. Pro se parties filing papers under the criminal rules generally lack the means to e-file or receive electronic confirmations, yet must be provided access to the courts under the Constitution.

Rule 49(b)(4). This new language requiring a signature and additional information was drawn from Civil Rule 11(a). The language has been restyled (with no intent to change the meaning) and the word "party" changed to "person" in order to accommodate filings by nonparties.

Rule 49(b)(5). This new language prohibiting a clerk from refusing a filing for improper form was drawn from Civil Rule 5(d)(4).

Rule 49(c). This provision is new. It recognizes that in limited circumstances nonparties may file motions in criminal cases. Examples include representatives of the media challenging the closure of proceedings, material witnesses requesting to be deposed under Rule 15, or victims asserting rights under Rule 60. Subdivision (c) permits nonparties to file a paper in a criminal case, but only when required or permitted by law to do so. It also requires nonparties who file to serve every party and to use means authorized by subdivision (a).

The rule provides that nonparties, like unrepresented parties, may use the court's electronic-filing system only when permitted to do so by court order or local rule.

Rule 49(d). This provision carries over the language formerly in Rule 49(c) with one change. The former language requiring that notice be provided "in a manner provided for in a civil action" has been replaced by a requirement that notice be served as required by Rule 49(a). This parallels Civil Rule 77(d)(1), which requires that the clerk give notice as provided in Civil Rule 5(b).

REFERENCES IN TEXT

The Federal Rules of Appellate Procedure, referred to in subd. (d), are set out in the Appendix to Title 28, Judiciary and Judicial Procedure.

Rule 49.1. Privacy Protection For Filings Made with the Court

(a) Redacted Filings. Unless the court orders otherwise, in an electronic or paper filing with the court that contains an individual's social-security number, taxpayer-identification number, or birth date, the name of an individual known to be a minor, a financial-account number, or the home address of an individual, a party or nonparty making the filing may include only:

    (1) the last four digits of the social-security number and taxpayer-identification number;

    (2) the year of the individual's birth;

    (3) the minor's initials;

    (4) the last four digits of the financial-account number; and

    (5) the city and state of the home address.

(b) Exemptions from the Redaction Requirement. The redaction requirement does not apply to the following:

    (1) a financial-account number or real property address that identifies the property allegedly subject to forfeiture in a forfeiture proceeding;

    (2) the record of an administrative or agency proceeding;

    (3) the official record of a state-court proceeding;

    (4) the record of a court or tribunal, if that record was not subject to the redaction requirement when originally filed;

    (5) a filing covered by Rule 49.1(d);

    (6) a pro se filing in an action brought under 28 U.S.C. §§2241,[1] 2254, or 2255;

    (7) a court filing that is related to a criminal matter or investigation and that is prepared before the filing of a criminal charge or is not filed as part of any docketed criminal case;

    (8) an arrest or search warrant; and

    (9) a charging document and an affidavit filed in support of any charging document.

(c) Immigration Cases. A filing in an action brought under 28 U.S.C. §2241 that relates to the petitioner's immigration rights is governed by Federal Rule of Civil Procedure 5.2.

(d) Filings Made Under Seal. The court may order that a filing be made under seal without redaction. The court may later unseal the filing or order the person who made the filing to file a redacted version for the public record.

(e) Protective Orders. For good cause, the court may by order in a case:

    (1) require redaction of additional information; or

    (2) limit or prohibit a nonparty's remote electronic access to a document filed with the court.

(f) Option for Additional Unredacted Filing Under Seal. A person making a redacted filing may also file an unredacted copy under seal. The court must retain the unredacted copy as part of the record.

(g) Option for Filing a Reference List. A filing that contains redacted information may be filed together with a reference list that identifies each item of redacted information and specifies an appropriate identifier that uniquely corresponds to each item listed. The list must be filed under seal and may be amended as of right. Any reference in the case to a listed identifier will be construed to refer to the corresponding item of information.

(h) Waiver of Protection of Identifiers. A person waives the protection of Rule 49.1(a) as to the person's own information by filing it without redaction and not under seal.

(Added Apr. 30, 2007, eff. Dec. 1, 2007.)

COMMITTEE NOTES ON RULES—2007

The rule is adopted in compliance with section 205(c)(3) of the E-Government Act of 2002, Public Law No. 107–347. Section 205(c)(3) requires the Supreme Court to prescribe rules "to protect privacy and security concerns relating to electronic filing of documents and the public availability . . . of documents filed electronically." The rule goes further than the E-Government Act in regulating paper filings even when they are not converted to electronic form. But the number of filings that remain in paper form is certain to diminish over time. Most districts scan paper filings into the electronic case file, where they become available to the public in the same way as documents initially filed in electronic form. It is electronic availability, not the form of the initial filing, that raises the privacy and security concerns addressed in the E-Government Act.

The rule is derived from and implements the policy adopted by the Judicial Conference in September 2001 to address the privacy concerns resulting from public access to electronic case files. See http://www.privacy.uscourts.gov/Policy.htm. The Judicial Conference policy is that documents in case files generally should be made available electronically to the same extent they are available at the courthouse, provided that certain "personal data identifiers" are not included in the public file.

While providing for the public filing of some information, such as the last four digits of an account number, the rule does not intend to establish a presumption that this information never could or should be protected. For example, it may well be necessary in individual cases to prevent remote access by nonparties to any part of an account number or social security number. It may also be necessary to protect information not covered by the redaction requirement—such as driver's license numbers and alien registration numbers—in a particular case. In such cases, protection may be sought under subdivision (d) or (e). Moreover, the Rule does not affect the protection available under other rules, such as Criminal Rule 16(d) and Civil Rules 16 and 26(c), or under other sources of protective authority.

Parties must remember that any personal information not otherwise protected by sealing or redaction will be made available over the internet. Counsel should notify clients of this fact so that an informed decision may be made on what information is to be included in a document filed with the court.

The clerk is not required to review documents filed with the court for compliance with this rule. The responsibility to redact filings rests with counsel and the party or nonparty making the filing.

Subdivision (e) provides that the court can order in a particular case more extensive redaction than otherwise required by the Rule, where necessary to protect against disclosure to nonparties of sensitive or private information. Nothing in this subdivision is intended to affect the limitations on sealing that are otherwise applicable to the court.

Subdivision (f) allows a person who makes a redacted filing to file an unredacted document under seal. This provision is derived from section 205(c)(3)(iv) of the E-Government Act. Subdivision (g) allows the option to file a register of redacted information. This provision is derived from section 205(c)(3)(v) of the E-Government Act, as amended in 2004.

In accordance with the E-Government Act, subdivision (f) of the rule refers to "redacted" information. The term "redacted" is intended to govern a filing that is prepared with abbreviated identifiers in the first instance, as well as a filing in which a personal identifier is edited after its preparation.

Subdivision (h) allows a person to waive the protections of the rule as to that person's own personal information by filing it unsealed and in unredacted form. One may wish to waive the protection if it is determined that the costs of redaction outweigh the benefits to privacy. If a person files an unredacted identifier by mistake, that person may seek relief from the court.

Trial exhibits are subject to the redaction requirements of Rule 49.1 to the extent they are filed with the court. Trial exhibits that are not initially filed with the court must be redacted in accordance with the rule if and when they are filed as part of an appeal or for other reasons.

The Judicial Conference Committee on Court Administration and Case Management has issued "Guidance for Implementation of the Judicial Conference Policy on Privacy and Public Access to Electronic Criminal Case Files" (March 2004). This document sets out limitations on remote electronic access to certain sensitive materials in criminal cases. It provides in part as follows:

The following documents shall not be included in the public case file and should not be made available to the public at the courthouse or via remote electronic access:

- unexecuted summonses or warrants of any kind (e.g., search warrants, arrest warrants);
- pretrial bail or presentence investigation reports;
- statements of reasons in the judgment of conviction;
- juvenile records;
- documents containing identifying information about jurors or potential jurors;
- financial affidavits filed in seeking representation pursuant to the Criminal Justice Act;
- ex parte requests for authorization of investigative, expert or other services pursuant to the Criminal Justice Act; and
- sealed documents (e.g., motions for downward departure for substantial assistance, plea agreements indicating cooperation).

To the extent that the Rule does not exempt these materials from disclosure, the privacy and law enforcement concerns implicated by the above documents in criminal cases can be accommodated under the rule through the sealing provision of subdivision (d) or a protective order provision of subdivision (e).

Changes Made to Proposed Amendment Released for Public Comment. Numerous changes were made in the rule after publication in response to the public comments as well as continued consultation among the reporters and chairs of the advisory committees as each committee reviewed its own rule.

A number of revisions were made in all of the e-government rules. These include: (1) using of the term "individual" rather than "person" where possible, (2) clarifying that the responsibility for redaction lies with the person making the filing, (3) rewording the exemption from redaction for information necessary to identify property subject to forfeiture, so that it is clearly applicable in ancillary proceedings related to forfeiture, and (4) rewording the exemption from redaction for judicial decisions that were not subject to redaction when originally filed. Additionally, some changes of a technical or stylistic nature (involving matters such as hyphenation and the use of "a" or "the") were made to achieve clarity as well as consistency among the various e-government rules.

Two changes were made to the provisions concerning actions under §§2241, 2254, and 2255, which the published rule exempted from the redaction requirement. First, in response to criticism that the original exemption was unduly broad, the Committee limited the exemption to pro se filings in these actions. Second, a new subdivision (c) was added to provide that all actions under §2241 in which immigration claims were made would be governed exclusively by Civil Rule 5.2. This change (which was made after the Advisory Committee meeting) was deemed necessary to ensure consistency in the treatment of redaction and public access to records in immigration cases. The addition of the new subdivision required renumbering of the subdivisions designated as (c) to (g) at the time of publication.

The provision governing protective orders was revised to employ the flexible "cause shown" standard that governs protective orders under the Federal Rules of Civil Procedure.

Finally, language was added to the Note clarifying the impact of the CACM policy that is reprinted in the Note: if the materials enumerated in the CACM policy are not exempt from disclosure under the rule, the sealing and protective order provisions of the rule are applicable.

REFERENCES IN TEXT

The Federal Rules of Civil Procedure, referred to in subd. (c), are set out in the Appendix to Title 28, Judiciary and Judicial Procedure.

___

¹ So in original. Probably should be only one section symbol.

Rule 50. Prompt Disposition

Scheduling preference must be given to criminal proceedings as far as practicable.

(As amended Apr. 24, 1972, eff. Oct. 1, 1972; Mar. 18, 1974, eff. July 1, 1974; Apr. 26 and July 8, 1976, eff. Aug. 1, 1976; Apr. 22, 1993, eff. Dec. 1, 1993; Apr. 29, 2002, eff. Dec. 1, 2002.)

NOTES OF ADVISORY COMMITTEE ON RULES——1944

This rule is a restatement of the inherent residual power of the court over its own calendars, although as a matter of practice in most districts the assignment of criminal cases for trial is handled by the United States attorney. Cf. Federal Rules of Civil Procedure, Rules 40 and 78 [28 U.S.C., Appendix]. The direction that preference shall be given to criminal proceedings as far as practicable is generally recognized as desirable in the orderly administration of justice.

NOTES OF ADVISORY COMMITTEE ON RULES——1972 AMENDMENT

The addition to the rule proposed by subdivision (b) is designed to achieve the more prompt disposition of criminal cases.

Preventing undue delay in the administration of criminal justice has become an object of increasing interest and concern. This is reflected in the Congress. See, e.g., 116 Cong.Rec. S7291–97 (daily ed. May 18, 1970) (remarks of Senator Ervin). Bills have been introduced fixing specific time limits. See S. 3936, H.R. 14822, H.R. 15888, 91st Cong., 2d Sess. (1970).

Proposals for dealing with the problem of delay have also been made by the President's Commission on Law Enforcement and Administration of Justice, Task Force Report: The Courts (1967) especially pp. 84–90, and by the American Bar Association Project on Standards for Criminal Justice, Standards Relating to Speedy Trial (Approved Draft, 1968). Both recommend specific time limits for each stage in the criminal process as the most effective way of achieving prompt disposition of criminal cases. See also Note, Nevada's 1967 Criminal Procedure Law from Arrest to Trial: One State's Response to a Widely Recognized Need, 1969 Utah L.Rev. 520, 542 no. 114.

Historically, the right to a speedy trial has been thought of as a protection for the defendant. Delay can cause a hardship to a defendant who is in custody awaiting trial. Even if afforded the opportunity for pretrial release, a defendant nonetheless is likely to suffer anxiety during a period of unwanted delay, and he runs the risk that his memory and those of his witnesses may suffer as time goes on.

Delay can also adversely affect the prosecution. Witnesses may lose interest or disappear or their memories may fade thus making them more vulnerable to cross-examination. See Note, The Right to a Speedy Criminal Trial, 57 Colum.L.Rev. 846 (1957).

There is also a larger public interest in the prompt disposition of criminal cases which may transcend the interest of the particular prosecutor, defense counsel, and defendant. Thus there is need to try to expedite criminal cases even when both prosecution and defense may be willing to agree to a continuance or continuances. It has long been said that it is the certain and prompt imposition of a criminal sanction rather than its severity that has a significant deterring effect upon potential criminal conduct. See Banfield and Anderson, Continuances in the Cook County Criminal Courts, 35 U.Chi.L.Rev. 259, 259–63 (1968).

165

Providing specific time limits for each stage of the criminal justice system is made difficult, particularly in federal courts, by the widely varying conditions which exist between the very busy urban districts on the one hand and the far less busy rural districts on the other hand. In the former, account must be taken of the extremely heavy caseload, and the prescription of relatively short time limits is realistic only if there is provided additional prosecutorial and judicial manpower. In some rural districts, the availability of a grand jury only twice a year makes unrealistic the provision of short time limits within which an indictment must be returned. This is not to say that prompt disposition of criminal cases cannot be achieved. It means only that the achieving of prompt disposition may require solutions which vary from district to district. Finding the best methods will require innovation and experimentation. To encourage this, the proposed draft mandates each district court to prepare a plan to achieve the prompt disposition of criminal cases in the district. The method prescribed for the development and approval of the district plans is comparable to that prescribed in the Jury Selection and Service Act of 1968, 28 U.S.C. §1863(a).

Each plan shall include rules which specify time limits and a means for reporting the status of criminal cases. The appropriate length of the time limits is left to the discretion of the individual district courts. This permits each district court to establish time limits that are appropriate in light of its criminal caseload, frequency of grand jury meetings, and any other factors which affect the progress of criminal actions. Where local conditions exist which contribute to delay, it is contemplated that appropriate efforts will be made to eliminate those conditions. For example, experience in some rural districts demonstrates that grand juries can be kept on call thus eliminating the grand jury as a cause for prolonged delay. Where manpower shortage is a major cause for delay, adequate solutions will require congressional action. But the development and analysis of the district plans should disclose where manpower shortages exist; how large the shortages are; and what is needed, in the way of additional manpower, to achieve the prompt disposition of criminal cases.

The district court plans must contain special provision for prompt disposition of cases in which there is reason to believe that the pretrial liberty of a defendant poses danger to himself, to any other person, or to the community. Prompt disposition of criminal cases may provide an alternative to the pretrial detention of potentially dangerous defendants. See 116 Cong.Rec. S7291–97 (daily ed. May 18, 1970) (remarks of Senator Ervin). Prompt disposition of criminal cases in which the defendant is held in pretrial detention would ensure that the deprivation of liberty prior to conviction would be minimized.

Approval of the original plan and any subsequent modification must be obtained from a reviewing panel made up of one judge from the district submitting the plan (either the chief judge or another active judge appointed by him) and the members of the judicial council of the circuit. The makeup of this reviewing panel is the same as that provided by the Jury Selection and Service Act of 1968, 28 U.S.C. §1863(a). This reviewing panel is also empowered to direct the modification of a district court plan.

The Circuit Court of Appeals for the Second Circuit recently adopted a set of rules for the prompt disposition of criminal cases. See 8 Cr.L. 2251 (Jan. 13, 1971). These rules, effective July 5, 1971, provide time limits for the early trial of high risk defendants, for court control over the granting of continuances, for criteria to control continuance practice, and for sanction against the prosecution or defense in the event of noncompliance with prescribed time limits.

NOTES OF ADVISORY COMMITTEE ON RULES——1974 AMENDMENT

The amendment designates the first paragraph of Rule 50 as subdivision (a) entitled "Calendars," in view of the recent addition of subdivision (b) to the rule.

NOTES OF ADVISORY COMMITTEE ON RULES——1976 AMENDMENT

This amendment to rule 50(b) takes account of the enactment of The Speedy Trial Act of 1974, 18 U.S.C. §§3152–3156, 3161–3174. As the various provisions of the Act take effect, see 18 U.S.C. §3163, they and the district plans adopted pursuant thereto will supplant the plans heretofore adopted under rule 50(b). The first such plan must be prepared and submitted by each district court before July 1, 1976. 18 U.S.C. §3165(e)(1).

That part of rule 50(b) which sets out the necessary contents of district plans has been deleted, as the somewhat different contents of the plans required by the Act are enumerated in 18 U.S.C. §3166. That part of rule 50(b) which describes the manner in which district plans are to be submitted, reviewed, modified and reported upon has also been deleted, for these provisions now appear in 18 U.S.C. §3165(c) and (d).

NOTES OF ADVISORY COMMITTEE ON RULES——1993 AMENDMENT

The Rule is amended to conform to the Judicial Improvements Act of 1990 [P.L. 101–650, Title III, Section 321] which provides that each United States magistrate appointed under section 631 of title 28, United States Code, shall be known as a United States magistrate judge.

COMMITTEE NOTES ON RULES——2002 AMENDMENT

The language of Rule 50 has been amended as part of the general restyling of the Criminal Rules to make them more easily understood and to make style and terminology consistent throughout the rules. These changes are intended to be stylistic only, except as noted below.

The first sentence in current Rule 50(a), which says that a court may place criminal proceedings on a calendar, has been deleted. The Committee believed that the sentence simply stated a truism and was no longer necessary.

Current Rule 50(b), which simply mirrors 18 U.S.C. §3165, has been deleted in its entirety. The rule was added in 1971 to meet congressional concerns in pending legislation about deadlines in criminal cases. Provisions governing deadlines were later enacted by Congress and protections were provided in the Speedy Trial Act. The Committee concluded that in light of those enactments, Rule 50(b) was no longer necessary.

EFFECTIVE DATE OF 1976 AMENDMENT

Amendment of subd. (b) by the order of the United States Supreme Court of Apr. 26, 1976, effective Aug. 1, 1976, see section 1 of Pub. L. 94–349, July 8, 1976, 90 Stat. 822, set out as a note under section 2074 of Title 28, Judiciary and Judicial Procedure.

Rule 51. Preserving Claimed Error

(a) Exceptions Unnecessary. Exceptions to rulings or orders of the court are unnecessary.

(b) Preserving a Claim of Error. A party may preserve a claim of error by informing the court—when the court ruling or order is made or sought—of the action the party wishes the court to take, or the party's objection to the court's action and the grounds for that objection. If a party does not have an opportunity to object to a ruling or order, the absence of an objection does not later prejudice that party. A ruling or order that admits or excludes evidence is governed by Federal Rule of Evidence 103.

(As amended Mar. 9, 1987, eff. Aug. 1, 1987; Apr. 29, 2002, eff. Dec. 1, 2002.)

NOTES OF ADVISORY COMMITTEE ON RULES——1944

1. This rule is practically identical with Rule 46 of the Federal Rules of Civil Procedure [28 U.S.C., Appendix]. It relates to a matter of trial practice which should be the same in civil and criminal cases in the interest of avoiding confusion. The corresponding civil rule has been construed in Ulm v. Moore-McCormack Lines, Inc., 115 F.2d 492 (C.C.A. 2d), and Bucy v. Nevada Construction Company, 125 F.2d 213, 218 (C.C.A. 9th). See, also, Orfield, 22 Texas L.R. 194, 221. As to the method of taking objections to instructions to the jury, see Rule 30.

2. Many States have abolished the use of exceptions in criminal and civil cases. See, e.g., Cal.Pen. Code (Deering, 1941), sec. 1259; Mich.Stat.Ann. (Henderson, 1938), secs. 28.1046, 28.1053; Ohio Gen Code Ann. (Page, 1938), secs. 11560, 13442–7; Oreg.Comp. Laws Ann. (1940), secs. 5–704, 26–1001.

The amendments are technical. No substantive change is intended.

The language of Rule 51 has been amended as part of the general restyling of the Criminal Rules to make them more easily understood and to make style and terminology consistent throughout the rules. These changes are intended to be stylistic only.

The Rule includes a new sentence that explicitly states that any rulings regarding evidence are governed by Federal Rule of Evidence 103. The sentence was added because of concerns about the Supersession Clause, 28 U.S.C. §2072(b), of the Rules Enabling Act, and the possibility that an argument might have been made that Congressional approval of this rule would supersede that Rule of Evidence.

The Federal Rules of Evidence, referred to in subd. (b), are set out in the Appendix to Title 28, Judiciary and Judicial Procedure.

Rule 52. Harmless and Plain Error

(a) Harmless Error. Any error, defect, irregularity, or variance that does not affect substantial rights must be disregarded.
(b) Plain Error. A plain error that affects substantial rights may be considered even though it was not brought to the court's attention.

(As amended Apr. 29, 2002, eff. Dec. 1, 2002.)

Note to Subdivision (a). This rule is a restatement of existing law, 28 U.S.C. [former] 391 (second sentence): "On the hearing of any appeal, certiorari, writ of error, or motion for a new trial, in any case, civil or criminal, the court shall give judgment after an examination of the entire record before the court, without regard to technical errors, defects, or exceptions which do not affect the substantial rights of the parties"; 18 U.S.C. [former] 556; "No indictment found and presented by a grand jury in any district or other court of the United States shall be deemed insufficient, nor shall the trial, judgment, or other proceeding thereon be affected by reason of any defect or imperfection in matter of form only, which shall not tend to the prejudice of the defendant, * * *." A similar provision is found in Rule 61 of the Federal Rules of Civil Procedure [28 U.S.C., Appendix].

Note to Subdivision (b). This rule is a restatement of existing law, Wiborg v. United States, 163 U.S. 632, 658; Hemphill v. United States, 112 F.2d 505 (C.C.A. 9th), reversed 312 U.S. 657. Rule 27 of the Rules of the Supreme Court provides that errors not specified will be disregarded, "save as the court, at its option, may notice a plain error not assigned or specified." Similar provisions are found in the rules of several circuit courts of appeals.

The language of Rule 52 has been amended as part of the general restyling of the Criminal Rules to make them more easily understood and to make style and terminology consistent throughout the rules. These changes are intended to be stylistic only.

Rule 52(b) has been amended by deleting the words "or defect" after the words "plain error". The change is intended to remove any ambiguity in the rule. As noted by the Supreme Court, the language "plain error or defect" was misleading to the extent that it might be read in the disjunctive. See United States v. Olano, 507 U.S. 725, 732 (1993) (incorrect to read Rule 52(b) in the disjunctive); United States v. Young, 470 U.S. 1, 15 n. 12 (1985) (use of disjunctive in Rule 52(b) is misleading).

Rule 53. Courtroom Photographing and Broadcasting Prohibited

Except as otherwise provided by a statute or these rules, the court must not permit the taking of photographs in the courtroom during judicial proceedings or the broadcasting of judicial proceedings from the courtroom.

(As amended Apr. 29, 2002, eff. Dec. 1, 2002.)

While the matter to which the rule refers has not been a problem in the Federal courts as it has been in some State tribunals, the rule was nevertheless included with a view to giving expression to a standard which should govern the conduct of judicial proceedings, Orfield, 22 Texas L.R. 194, 222–3; Robbins, 21 A.B.A.Jour. 301, 304. See, also, Report of the Special Committee on Cooperation between Press, Radio and Bar, as to Publicity Interfering with Fair Trial of Judicial and Quasi-Judicial Proceedings (1937), 62 A.B.A.Rep. 851, 862–865; (1932) 18 A.B.A.Jour. 762; (1926) 12 Id. 488; (1925) 11 Id. 64.

The language of Rule 53 has been amended as part of the general restyling of the Criminal Rules to make them more easily understood and to make style and terminology consistent throughout the rules. These changes are intended to be stylistic only, except as noted below.

Although the word "radio" has been deleted from the rule, the Committee does not believe that the amendment is a substantive change but rather one that accords with judicial interpretation applying the current rule to other forms of broadcasting and functionally equivalent means. See, e.g., United States v. Hastings, 695 F.2d 1278, 1279, n. 5 (11th Cir. 1983) (television proceedings prohibited); United States v. McVeigh, 931 F. Supp. 753 (D. Colo. 1996) (release of tape recordings of proceedings prohibited). Given modern technology capabilities, the Committee believed that a more generalized reference to "broadcasting" is appropriate.

Also, although the revised rule does not explicitly recognize exceptions within the rules themselves, the restyled rule recognizes that other rules might permit, for example, video teleconferencing, which clearly involves "broadcasting" of the proceedings, even if only for limited purposes.

Rule 54. [Transferred] [1]

Certain provisions in current Rule 54 have been moved to revised Rule 1 as part of a general restyling of the Criminal Rules to make them more easily understood and to make style and terminology consistent throughout the rules. Other provisions in Rule 54 have been deleted as being unnecessary.

[1] All of Rule 54 was moved to Rule 1.

Rule 55. Records

The clerk of the district court must keep records of criminal proceedings in the form prescribed by the Director of the Administrative Office of the United States Courts. The clerk must enter in the records every court order or judgment and the date of entry.

(As amended Dec. 27, 1948, eff. Oct. 20, 1949; Feb. 28, 1966, eff. July 1, 1966; Apr. 24, 1972, eff. Oct. 1, 1972; Apr. 28, 1983, eff. Aug. 1, 1983; Apr. 22, 1993, eff. Dec. 1, 1993; Apr. 29, 2002, eff. Dec. 1, 2002.)

NOTES OF ADVISORY COMMITTEE ON RULES—1944

The Federal Rules of Civil Procedure Rule 79 [28 U.S.C., Appendix], prescribed in detail the books and records to be kept by the clerk in civil cases. Subsequently to the effective date of the civil rules, however, the Act establishing the Administrative Office of the United States Courts became law (Act of August 7, 1939; 53 Stat. 1223; 28 U.S.C. 444–450 [now 332–333, 456, 601–610]). One of the duties of the Director of that Office is to have charge, under the supervision and direction of the Conference of Senior Circuit Judges, of all administrative matters relating to the offices of the clerks and other clerical and administrative personnel of the courts, 28 U.S.C. 446 [now 604, 609]. In view of this circumstance it seemed best not to prescribe the records to be kept by the clerks of the district courts and by the United States commissioners, in criminal proceedings, but to vest the power to do so in the Director of the Administrative Office of the United States Courts with the approval of the Conference of Senior Circuit Judges.

NOTES OF ADVISORY COMMITTEE ON RULES—1948 AMENDMENT

To incorporate nomenclature provided for by Revised Title 28 U.S.C., §331.

NOTES OF ADVISORY COMMITTEE ON RULES—1966 AMENDMENT

Rule 37(a)(2) provides that for the purpose of commencing the running of the time for appeal a judgment or order is entered "when it is entered in the criminal docket." The sentence added here requires that such a docket be kept and that it show the dates on which judgments or orders are entered therein. Cf. Civil Rule 79(a).

NOTES OF ADVISORY COMMITTEE ON RULES—1983 AMENDMENT

The Advisory Committee Note to original Rule 55 observes that, in light of the authority which the Director and Judicial Conference have over the activities of clerks, "it seems best not to prescribe the records to be kept by clerks." Because of current experimentation with automated record-keeping, this approach is more appropriate than ever before. The amendment will make it possible for the Director to permit use of more sophisticated record-keeping techniques, including those which may obviate the need for a "criminal docket" book. The reference to the Judicial Conference has been stricken as unnecessary. See 28 U.S.C. §604.

NOTES OF ADVISORY COMMITTEE ON RULES—1993 AMENDMENT

The Rule is amended to conform to the Judicial Improvements Act of 1990 [P.L. 101–650, Title III, Section 321] which provides that each United States magistrate appointed under section 631 of title 28, United States Code, shall be known as a United States magistrate judge.

COMMITTEE NOTES ON RULES—2002 AMENDMENT

The language of Rule 55 has been amended as part of the general restyling of the Criminal Rules to make them more easily understood and to make style and terminology consistent throughout the rules. These changes are intended to be stylistic only.

Rule 56. When Court Is Open

(a) In General. A district court is considered always open for any filing, and for issuing and returning process, making a motion, or entering an order.

(b) Office Hours. The clerk's office—with the clerk or a deputy in attendance—must be open during business hours on all days except Saturdays, Sundays, and legal holidays.

(c) Special Hours. A court may provide by local rule or order that its clerk's office will be open for specified hours on Saturdays or legal holidays other than those set aside by statute for observing New Year's Day, Martin Luther King, Jr.'s Birthday, Washington's Birthday, Memorial Day, Independence Day, Labor Day, Columbus Day, Veterans' Day, Thanksgiving Day, and Christmas Day.

(As amended Dec. 27, 1948, eff. Oct. 20, 1949; Feb. 28, 1966, eff. July 1, 1966; Dec. 4, 1967, eff. July 1, 1968; Mar. 1, 1971, eff. July 1, 1971; Apr. 25, 1988, eff. Aug. 1, 1988; Apr. 29, 2002, eff. Dec. 1, 2002.)

NOTES OF ADVISORY COMMITTEE ON RULES—1944

1. The first sentence of this rule is substantially the same as Rule 77(a) of the Federal Rules of Civil Procedure [28 U.S.C., Appendix], except that it is applicable to circuit courts of appeals as well as to district courts.

2. In connection with this rule, see 28 U.S.C. [former] 14 (Monthly adjournments for trial of criminal causes) and sec. 15 [now 141] (Special terms). These sections "indicate a policy of avoiding the hardships consequent upon a closing of the court during vacations," Abbott v. Brown, 241 U.S. 606, 611.

3. The second sentence of the rule is identical with the first sentence of Rule 77(c) of the Federal Rules of Civil Procedure [28 U.S.C., Appendix].

4. The term "legal holidays" includes Federal holidays as well as holidays prescribed by the laws of the State where the clerk's office is located.

NOTES OF ADVISORY COMMITTEE ON RULES—1948 AMENDMENT

To incorporate nomenclature provided for by Revised Title 28, U.S.C. §43(a).

NOTES OF ADVISORY COMMITTEE ON RULES—1966 AMENDMENT

The change is in conformity with the changes made in Rule 45. See the similar changes in Civil Rule 77(c) made effective July 1, 1963.

NOTES OF ADVISORY COMMITTEE ON RULES—1968 AMENDMENT

The provisions relating to courts of appeals are included in Rule 47 of the Federal Rules of Appellate Procedure.

NOTES OF ADVISORY COMMITTEE ON RULES—1971 AMENDMENT

The amendment adds Columbus Day to the list of legal holidays. See the Note accompanying the amendment of Rule 45(a).

NOTES OF ADVISORY COMMITTEE ON RULES—1988 AMENDMENT

The amendment is technical. No substantive change is intended.

COMMITTEE NOTES ON RULES—2002 AMENDMENT

The language of Rule 56 has been amended as part of the general restyling of the Criminal Rules to make them more easily understood and to make style and terminology consistent throughout the rules. These changes are intended to be stylistic only.

Rule 57. District Court Rules

(a) In General.

(1) Adopting Local Rules. Each district court acting by a majority of its district judges may, after giving appropriate public notice and an opportunity to comment, make and amend rules governing its practice. A local rule must be consistent with—but not duplicative of—federal statutes and rules adopted under 28 U.S.C. §2072 and must conform to any uniform numbering system prescribed by the Judicial Conference of the United States.

(2) Limiting Enforcement. A local rule imposing a requirement of form must not be enforced in a manner that causes a party to lose rights because of an unintentional failure to comply with the requirement.

(b) Procedure When There Is No Controlling Law. A judge may regulate practice in any manner consistent with federal law, these rules, and the local rules of the district. No sanction or other disadvantage may be imposed for noncompliance with any requirement not in federal law, federal rules, or the local district rules unless the alleged violator was furnished with actual notice of the requirement before the noncompliance.

(c) Effective Date and Notice. A local rule adopted under this rule takes effect on the date specified by the district court and remains in effect unless amended by the district court or abrogated by the judicial council of the circuit in which the district is located. Copies of local rules and their amendments, when promulgated, must be furnished to the judicial council and the Administrative Office of the United States Courts and must be made available to the public.

(As amended Dec. 27, 1948, eff. Oct. 20, 1949; Dec. 4, 1967, eff. July 1, 1968; Apr. 29, 1985, eff. Aug. 1, 1985; Apr. 22, 1993, eff. Dec. 1, 1993; Apr. 27, 1995, eff. Dec. 1, 1995; Apr. 29, 2002, eff. Dec. 1, 2002.)

NOTES OF ADVISORY COMMITTEE ON RULES——1944

Note to Subdivision (a). This rule is substantially a restatement of 28 U.S.C. 731 [now 2071] (Rules of practice in district courts). A similar provision is found in Rule 83 of the Federal Rules of Civil Procedure [28 U.S.C., Appendix].

Note to Subdivision (b). 1. One of the purposes of this rule is to abrogate any existing requirement of conformity to State procedure on any point whatsoever. The Federal Rules of Civil Procedure [28 U.S.C., Appendix] have been held to repeal the Conformity Act, Sibbach v. Wilson, 312 U.S. 1, 10.

2. While the rules are intended to constitute a comprehensive procedural code for criminal cases in the Federal courts, nevertheless it seemed best not to endeavor to prescribe a uniform practice as to some matters of detail, but to leave the individual courts free to regulate them, either by local rules or by usage. Among such matters are the mode of impaneling a jury, the manner and order of interposing challenges to jurors, the manner of selecting the foreman of a trial jury, the matter of sealed verdicts, the order of counsel's arguments to the jury, and other similar details.

NOTES OF ADVISORY COMMITTEE ON RULES——1948 AMENDMENT

To incorporate nomenclature provided for by Revised Title 28, U.S.C., §43(a).

NOTES OF ADVISORY COMMITTEE ON RULES——1968 AMENDMENT

The provisions relating to the court of appeals are included in Rule 47 of the Federal Rules of Appellate Procedure.

NOTES OF ADVISORY COMMITTEE ON RULES——1985 AMENDMENT

Rule 57 has been reformulated to correspond to Fed.R.Civ.P. 83, including the proposed amendments thereto. The purpose of the reformulation is to emphasize that the procedures for adoption of local rules by a district court are the same under both the civil and the criminal rules. In particular, the major purpose of the reformulation is to enhance the local rulemaking process by requiring appropriate public notice of proposed rules and an opportunity to comment on them. See Committee Note to Fed.R.Civ.P. 83.

NOTES OF ADVISORY COMMITTEE ON RULES——1993 AMENDMENT

The Rule is amended to conform to the Judicial Improvements Act of 1990 [P.L. 101–650, Title III, Section 321] which provides that each United States magistrate appointed under section 631 of title 28, United States Code, shall be known as a United States magistrate judge.

NOTES OF ADVISORY COMMITTEE ON RULES——1995 AMENDMENT

Subdivision (a). This rule is amended to reflect the requirement that local rules be consistent not only with the national rules but also with Acts of Congress. The amendment also states that local rules should not repeat national rules and Acts of Congress.

The amendment also requires that the numbering of local rules conform with any numbering system that may be prescribed by the Judicial Conference. Lack of uniform numbering might create unnecessary traps for counsel and litigants. A uniform numbering system would make it easier for an increasingly national bar to locate a local rule that applies to a particular procedural issue.

Paragraph (2) is new. Its aim is to protect against loss of rights in the enforcement of local rules relating to matters of form. The proscription of paragraph (2) is narrowly drawn——covering only nonwillful violations and only those involving local rules directed to matters of form. It does not limit the court's power to impose substantive penalties upon a party if it or its attorney stubbornly or repeatedly violates a local rule, even one involving merely a matter of form. Nor does it affect the court's power to enforce local rules that involve more than mere matters of form——for example, a local rule requiring that the defendant waive a jury trial within a specified time.

Subdivision (b). This rule provides flexibility to the court in regulating practice when there is no controlling law. Specifically, it permits the court to regulate practice in any manner consistent with Acts of Congress, with rules adopted under 28 U.S.C. §2072, and with the district's local rules. This rule recognizes that courts rely on multiple directives to control practice. Some courts regulate practice through the published Federal Rules and the local rules of the court. Some courts also have used internal operating procedures, standing orders, and other internal directives. Although such directives continue to be authorized, they can lead to problems. Counsel or litigants may be unaware of the various directives. In addition, the sheer volume of directives may impose an unreasonable barrier. For example, it may be difficult to obtain copies of the directives. Finally, counsel or litigants may be unfairly sanctioned for failing to comply with a directive. For these reasons, the amendment disapproves imposing any sanction or other disadvantage on a person for noncompliance with such an internal directive, unless the alleged violator has been furnished in a particular case with actual notice of the requirement.

There should be no adverse consequence to a party or attorney for violating special requirements relating to practice before a particular judge unless the party or attorney has actual notice of those requirements. Furnishing litigants with a copy outlining the judge's practices——or attaching instructions to a notice setting a case for conference or trial——would suffice to give actual notice, as would an order in a case specifically adopting by reference a judge's standing order and indicating how copies can be obtained.

COMMITTEE NOTES ON RULES——2002 AMENDMENT

The language of Rule 57 has been amended as part of the general restyling of the Criminal Rules to make them more easily understood and to make style and terminology consistent throughout the rules. These changes are intended to be stylistic only.

Rule 58. Petty Offenses and Other Misdemeanors

(a) Scope.

(1) In General. These rules apply in petty offense and other misdemeanor cases and on appeal to a district judge in a case tried by a magistrate judge, unless this rule provides otherwise.

(2) Petty Offense Case Without Imprisonment. In a case involving a petty offense for which no sentence of imprisonment will be imposed, the court may follow any provision of these rules that is not inconsistent with this rule and that the court considers appropriate.

(3) Definition. As used in this rule, the term "petty offense for which no sentence of imprisonment will be imposed" means a petty offense for which the court determines that, in the event of conviction, no sentence of imprisonment will be imposed.

(b) Pretrial Procedure.

(1) Charging Document. The trial of a misdemeanor may proceed on an indictment, information, or complaint. The trial of a petty offense may also proceed on a citation or violation notice.

(2) Initial Appearance. At the defendant's initial appearance on a petty offense or other misdemeanor charge, the magistrate judge must inform the defendant of the following:

(A) the charge, and the minimum and maximum penalties, including imprisonment, fines, any special assessment under 18 U.S.C. §3013, and restitution under 18 U.S.C. §3556;

(B) the right to retain counsel;

(C) the right to request the appointment of counsel if the defendant is unable to retain counsel—unless the charge is a petty offense for which the appointment of counsel is not required;

(D) the defendant's right not to make a statement, and that any statement made may be used against the defendant;

(E) the right to trial, judgment, and sentencing before a district judge—unless:

(i) the charge is a petty offense; or

(ii) the defendant consents to trial, judgment, and sentencing before a magistrate judge;

(F) the right to a jury trial before either a magistrate judge or a district judge—unless the charge is a petty offense;

(G) any right to a preliminary hearing under Rule 5.1, and the general circumstances, if any, under which the defendant may secure pretrial release; and

(H) that a defendant who is not a United States citizen may request that an attorney for the government or a federal law enforcement official notify a consular officer from the defendant's country of nationality that the defendant has been arrested—but that even without the defendant's request, a treaty or other international agreement may require consular notification.

(3) Arraignment.

(A) Plea Before a Magistrate Judge. A magistrate judge may take the defendant's plea in a petty offense case. In every other misdemeanor case, a magistrate judge may take the plea only if the defendant consents either in writing or on the record to be tried before a magistrate judge and specifically waives trial before a district judge. The defendant may plead not guilty, guilty, or (with the consent of the magistrate judge) nolo contendere.

(B) Failure to Consent. Except in a petty offense case, the magistrate judge must order a defendant who does not consent to trial before a magistrate judge to appear before a district judge for further proceedings.

(c) Additional Procedures in Certain Petty Offense Cases. The following procedures also apply in a case involving a petty offense for which no sentence of imprisonment will be imposed:

(1) Guilty or Nolo Contendere Plea. The court must not accept a guilty or nolo contendere plea unless satisfied that the defendant understands the nature of the charge and the maximum possible penalty.

(2) Waiving Venue.

(A) Conditions of Waiving Venue. If a defendant is arrested, held, or present in a district different from the one where the indictment, information, complaint, citation, or violation notice is pending, the defendant may state in writing a desire to plead guilty or nolo contendere; to waive venue and trial in the district where the proceeding is pending; and to consent to the court's disposing of the case in the district where the defendant was arrested, is held, or is present.

(B) Effect of Waiving Venue. Unless the defendant later pleads not guilty, the prosecution will proceed in the district where the defendant was arrested, is held, or is present. The district clerk must notify the clerk in the original district of the defendant's waiver of venue. The defendant's statement of a desire to plead guilty or nolo contendere is not admissible against the defendant.

(3) Sentencing. The court must give the defendant an opportunity to be heard in mitigation and then proceed immediately to sentencing. The court may, however, postpone sentencing to allow the probation service to investigate or to permit either party to submit additional information.

(4) Notice of a Right to Appeal. After imposing sentence in a case tried on a not-guilty plea, the court must advise the defendant of a right to appeal the conviction and of any right to appeal the sentence. If the defendant was convicted on a plea of guilty or nolo contendere, the court must advise the defendant of any right to appeal the sentence.

(d) Paying a Fixed Sum in Lieu of Appearance.

(1) In General. If the court has a local rule governing forfeiture of collateral, the court may accept a fixed-sum payment in lieu of the defendant's appearance and end the case, but the fixed sum may not exceed the maximum fine allowed by law.

(2) Notice to Appear. If the defendant fails to pay a fixed sum, request a hearing, or appear in response to a citation or violation notice, the district clerk or a magistrate judge may issue a notice for the defendant to appear before the court on a date certain. The notice may give the defendant an additional opportunity to pay a fixed sum in lieu of appearance. The district clerk must serve the notice on the defendant by mailing a copy to the defendant's last known address.

(3) Summons or Warrant. Upon an indictment, or upon a showing by one of the other charging documents specified in Rule 58(b)(1) of probable cause to believe that an offense has been committed and that the defendant has committed it, the court may issue an arrest warrant or, if no warrant is requested by an attorney for the government, a summons. The showing of probable cause must be made under oath or under penalty of perjury, but the affiant need not appear before the court. If the defendant fails to appear before the court in response to a summons, the court may summarily issue a warrant for the defendant's arrest.

(e) Recording the Proceedings. The court must record any proceedings under this rule by using a court reporter or a suitable recording device.

(f) New Trial. Rule 33 applies to a motion for a new trial.

(g) Appeal.

(1) From a District Judge's Order or Judgment. The Federal Rules of Appellate Procedure govern an appeal from a district judge's order or a judgment of conviction or sentence.

(2) From a Magistrate Judge's Order or Judgment.

(A) Interlocutory Appeal. Either party may appeal an order of a magistrate judge to a district judge within 14 days of its entry if a district judge's order could similarly be appealed. The party appealing must file a notice with the clerk specifying the order being appealed and must serve a copy on the adverse party.

(B) Appeal from a Conviction or Sentence. A defendant may appeal a magistrate judge's judgment of conviction or sentence to a district judge within 14 days of its entry. To appeal, the defendant must file a notice with the clerk specifying the judgment being appealed and must serve a copy on an attorney for the government.

(C) Record. The record consists of the original papers and exhibits in the case; any transcript, tape, or other recording of the proceedings; and a certified copy of the docket entries. For purposes of the appeal, a copy of the record of the proceedings must be made available to a defendant who establishes by affidavit an inability to pay or give security for the record. The Director of the Administrative Office of the United States Courts must pay for those copies.

(D) Scope of Appeal. The defendant is not entitled to a trial de novo by a district judge. The scope of the appeal is the same as in an appeal to the court of appeals from a judgment entered by a district judge.

(3) Stay of Execution and Release Pending Appeal. Rule 38 applies to a stay of a judgment of conviction or sentence. The court may release the defendant pending appeal under the law relating to release pending appeal from a district court to a court of appeals.

(Added May 1, 1990, eff. Dec. 1, 1990; amended Apr. 30, 1991, eff. Dec. 1, 1991; Apr. 22, 1993, eff. Dec. 1, 1993; Apr. 11, 1997, eff. Dec. 1, 1997; Apr. 29, 2002, eff. Dec. 1, 2002; Apr. 12, 2006, eff. Dec. 1, 2006; Mar. 26, 2009, eff. Dec. 1, 2009; Apr. 25, 2014, eff. Dec. 1, 2014.)

NOTES OF ADVISORY COMMITTEE ON RULES——1990

This new rule is largely a restatement of the Rules of Procedure for the Trial of Misdemeanors before United States Magistrates which were promulgated in 1980 to replace the Rules for the Trial of Minor Offenses before United States Magistrates (1970). The Committee believed that a new single rule should be incorporated into the Rules of Criminal Procedure where those charged with its execution could readily locate it and realize its relationship with the other Rules. A number of technical changes have been made throughout the rule and unless otherwise noted, no substantive changes were intended in those amendments. The Committee envisions no major changes in the way in which the trial of misdemeanors and petty offenses are currently handled.

The title of the rule has been changed by deleting the phrase "Before United States Magistrates" to indicate that this rule may be used by district judges as well as magistrates. The phrase "and Petty Offenses" has been added to the title and elsewhere throughout the rule because the term "misdemeanor" does not include an "infraction." See 18 U.S.C. §3559(a). A petty offense, however, is defined in 18 U.S.C. §19 as a Class B misdemeanor, a Class C misdemeanor, or an infraction, with limitations on fines of no more than $5,000 for an individual and $10,000 for an organization.

Subdivision (a) is an amended version of current Magistrates Rule 1. Deletion of the phrase "before United States Magistrates under 18 U.S.C. §3401" in Rule 1(a) will enable district judges to use the abbreviated procedures of this rule. Consistent with that change, the term "magistrate" is amended to read "the court," wherever appropriate throughout the rule, to indicate that both judges and magistrates may use the rule. The last sentence in (a)(1) has been amended to reflect that the rule also governs an appeal from a magistrate's decision to a judge of the district court. An appeal from a district judge's decision would be governed by the Federal Rules of Appellate Procedure. Subdivision (a)(2) rephrases prior language in Magistrate Rule 1(b). Subdivision (a)(3) adds a statutory reference to 18 U.S.C. §19, which defines a petty offense as a "Class B misdemeanor, a Class C misdemeanor, or an infraction" with the $5,000 and $10,000 fine limitations noted supra. The phrase "regardless of the penalty authorized by law" has been deleted.

Subdivision (b) is an amended version of current Magistrates Rule 2. The last sentence in current Rule 2(a) has been deleted because 18 U.S.C. §3401(a), provides that a magistrate will have jurisdiction to try misdemeanor cases when specially designated to do so by the district court or courts served by the Magistrate.

Subdivision (b)(2) reflects the standard rights advisements currently included in Magistrates Rule 2 with several amendments. Subdivision (b)(2)(A) specifically requires that the defendant be advised of all penalties which may be imposed upon conviction, including specifically a special assessment and restitution. A number of technical, nonsubstantive, changes have been made in the contents of advisement of rights. A substantive change is reflected in subdivision (b)(2)(G), currently Magistrates Rule 2(b)(7), and (8). That rule currently provides that, unless the prosecution is on an indictment or information, a defendant who is charged with a misdemeanor other than a petty offense has a right to a preliminary hearing, if the defendant does not consent to be tried by the magistrate. As amended, only a defendant in custody has a right to a preliminary hearing.

Subdivision (b)(3)(A) is based upon Magistrates Rule 2(c) and has been amended by deleting the last sentence, which provides that trial may occur within 30 days "upon written consent of the defendant." The change is warranted because the Speedy Trial Act does not apply to petty offenses. See 18 U.S.C. §3172(2). Subdivision (b)(3)(B), "Failure to Consent," currently appears in Magistrates Rule 3(a). The first sentence has been amended to make it applicable to all misdemeanor and petty offense defendants who fail to consent. The last sentence of Rule 3(a) has been deleted entirely. Because the clerk is responsible for all district court case files, including those for misdemeanor and petty offense cases tried by magistrates, it is not necessary to state that the file be transmitted to the clerk of court.

Subdivision (c) is an amended version of current Magistrates Rule 3 with the exception of Rule 3(a), which, as noted supra is now located in subdivision (b)(3)(B) of the new rule. The phrase "petty offense for which no sentence of imprisonment will be imposed" has been deleted because the heading for subdivision (c) limits its application to those petty offenses. The Committee recognizes that subdivision (c)(2) might result in attempted forum shopping. See, e.g., United States v. Shaw, 467 F. Supp. 86 (W.D. La. 1979), affm'd, 615 F. 2d 251 (5th Cir. 1980). In order to maintain a streamlined and less formal procedure which is consistent with the remainder of the Rule, subdivision (c)(2) does not require the formal "consent" of the United States Attorneys involved before a waiver of venue may be accomplished. Cf. Rule 20 (Transfer From the District for Plea and Sentence). The Rule specifically envisions that there will be communication and coordination between the two districts involved. To that end, reasonable efforts should be made to contact the United States Attorney in the district in which the charges were instituted. Subdivision (c)(4), formerly Rule 3(d), now specifically provides that the defendant be advised of the right to appeal the sentence. This subdivision is also amended to provide for advising the defendant of the right to appeal a sentence under the Sentencing Reform Act when the defendant is sentenced following a plea of guilty. Both amendments track the language of Rule 32(a)(2), as amended by the Sentencing Reform Act.

Subdivision (d) is an amended version of Magistrates Rule 4. The amendments are technical in nature and no substantive change is intended.

Subdivision (e) consists of the first sentence of Magistrates Rule 5. The second sentence of that Rule was deleted as being inconsistent with 28 U.S.C. §753(b) which gives the court discretion to decide how the proceedings will be recorded. The third sentence is deleted to preclude routine waivers of a verbatim record and to insure that all petty offenses are recorded.

Subdivision (f) replaces Magistrates Rule 6 and simply incorporates by reference Rule 33.

Subdivision (g) is an amended version of Magistrates Rule 7. Because the new rule may be used by both magistrates and judges, subdivision (g)(1) was added to make it clear that the Federal Rules of Appellate Procedure govern any appeal in a case tried by a district judge pursuant to the new rule. Subdivision (g)(2)(B), based upon Magistrates Rule 7(b), now provides for appeal of a sentence by a magistrate and is thus consistent with the provisions of 18 U.S.C. §3742(f). Finally, subdivision (g)(3) is based upon Magistrates Rule 7(d) but has been amended to provide that a stay of execution is applicable, if an appeal is taken from a sentence as well as from a conviction. This change is consistent with the recent amendment of Rule 38 by the Sentencing Reform Act.

The new rule does not include Magistrates Rules 8 and 9. Rule 8 has been deleted because the subject of local rules is covered in Rule 57. Rule 9, which defined a petty offense, is now covered in 18 U.S.C. §19.

NOTES OF ADVISORY COMMITTEE ON RULES——1991 AMENDMENT

The amendments are technical. No substantive changes are intended.

NOTES OF ADVISORY COMMITTEE ON RULES——1993 AMENDMENT

The Rule is amended to conform to the Judicial Improvements Act of 1990 [P.L. 101—650, Title III, Section 321] which provides that each United States magistrate appointed under section 631 of title 28, United States Code, shall be known as a United States magistrate judge.

The Federal Courts Improvement Act of 1996, Sec. 202, amended 18 U.S.C. §3401(b) and 28 U.S.C. §636(a) to remove the requirement that a defendant must consent to a trial before a magistrate judge in a petty offense that is a class B misdemeanor charging a motor vehicle offense, a class C misdemeanor, or an infraction. Section 202 also changed 18 U.S.C. §3401(b) to provide that in all other misdemeanor cases, the defendant may consent to trial either orally on the record or in writing. The amendments to Rule 58(b)(2) and (3) conform the rule to the new statutory language and include minor stylistic changes.

COMMITTEE NOTES ON RULES——2002 AMENDMENT

The language of Rule 58 has been amended as part of the general restyling of the Criminal Rules to make them more easily understood and to make style and terminology consistent throughout the rules. These changes are intended to be stylistic only.

The title of the rule has been changed to "Petty Offenses and Other Misdemeanors." In Rule 58(c)(2)(B) (regarding waiver of venue), the Committee amended the rule to require that the "district clerk," instead of the magistrate judge, inform the original district clerk if the defendant waives venue and the prosecution proceeds in the district where the defendant was arrested. The Committee intends no change in practice.

In Rule 58(g)(1) and (g)(2)(A), the Committee deleted as unnecessary the word "decision" because its meaning is covered by existing references to an "order, judgment, or sentence" by a district judge or magistrate judge. In the Committee's view, deletion of that term does not amount to a substantive change.

COMMITTEE NOTES ON RULES——2006 AMENDMENT

Subdivision (b)(2)(G). Rule 58(b)(2)(G) sets out the advice to be given to defendants at an initial appearance on a misdemeanor charge, other than a petty offense. As currently written, the rule is restricted to those cases where the defendant is held in custody, thus creating a conflict and some confusion when compared to Rule 5.1(a) concerning the right to a preliminary hearing. Paragraph (G) is incomplete in its description of the circumstances requiring a preliminary hearing. In contrast, Rule 5.1(a) is a correct statement of the law concerning the defendant's entitlement to a preliminary hearing and is consistent with 18 U.S.C. §3060 in this regard. Rather than attempting to define, or restate, in Rule 58 when a defendant may be entitled to a Rule 5.1 preliminary hearing, the rule is amended to direct the reader to Rule 5.1.

Changes Made After Publication and Comment. The Committee [made] no changes to the Rule or Committee note after publication.

COMMITTEE NOTES ON RULES——2009 AMENDMENT

The times set in the former rule at 10 days have been revised to 14 days. See the Committee Note to Rule 45(a).

COMMITTEE NOTES ON RULES——2014 AMENDMENT

Rule 58(b)(2)(H). Article 36 of the Vienna Convention on Consular Relations provides that detained foreign nationals shall be advised that they may have the consulate of their home country notified of their arrest and detention, and bilateral agreements with numerous countries require consular notification whether or not the detained foreign national requests it. Article 36 requires consular notification advice to be given "without delay," and arresting officers are primarily responsible for providing this advice.

Providing this advice at the initial appearance is designed, not to relieve law enforcement officers of that responsibility, but to provide additional assurance that U.S. treaty obligations are fulfilled, and to create a judicial record of that action. The Committee concluded that the most effective and efficient method of conveying this information is to provide it to every defendant, without attempting to determine the defendant's citizenship.

At the time of this amendment, many questions remain unresolved by the courts concerning Article 36, including whether it creates individual rights that may be invoked in a judicial proceeding and what, if any, remedy may exist for a violation of Article 36. Sanchez-Llamas v. Oregon, 548 U.S. 331 (2006). This amendment does not address those questions. More particularly, it does not create any such rights or remedies.

Changes Made After Publication and Comment. In response to public comments the amendment was rephrased to state that the information regarding consular notification should be provided to all defendants who are arraigned. Although it is anticipated that ordinarily only defendants who are held in custody will ask the government to notify a consular official of their arrest, it is appropriate to provide this information to all defendants at the initial appearance. The new phrasing also makes it clear that the advice should be provided to every defendant, without any attempt to determine the defendant's citizenship. A conforming change was made to the Committee Note.

REFERENCES IN TEXT

The Federal Rules of Appellate Procedure, referred to in subd. (g)(1), are set out in the Appendix to Title 28, Judiciary and Judicial Procedure.

Rule 59. Matters Before a Magistrate Judge

(a) Nondispositive Matters. A district judge may refer to a magistrate judge for determination any matter that does not dispose of a charge or defense. The magistrate judge must promptly conduct the required proceedings and, when appropriate, enter on the record an oral or written order stating the determination. A party may serve and file objections to the order within 14 days after being served with a copy of a written order or after the oral order is stated on the record, or at some other time the court sets. The district judge must consider timely objections and modify or set aside any part of the order that is contrary to law or clearly erroneous. Failure to object in accordance with this rule waives a party's right to review.

(b) Dispositive Matters.

(1) Referral to Magistrate Judge. A district judge may refer to a magistrate judge for recommendation a defendant's motion to dismiss or quash an indictment or information, a motion to suppress evidence, or any matter that may dispose of a charge or defense. The magistrate judge must promptly conduct the required proceedings. A record must be made of any evidentiary proceeding and of any other proceeding if the magistrate judge considers it necessary. The magistrate judge must enter on the record a recommendation for disposing of the matter, including any proposed findings of fact. The clerk must immediately serve copies on all parties.

(2) Objections to Findings and Recommendations. Within 14 days after being served with a copy of the recommended disposition, or at some other time the court sets, a party may serve and file specific written objections to the proposed findings and recommendations. Unless the district judge directs otherwise, the objecting party must promptly arrange for transcribing the record, or whatever portions of it the parties agree to or the magistrate judge considers sufficient. Failure to object in accordance with this rule waives a party's right to review.

(3) De Novo Review of Recommendations. The district judge must consider de novo any objection to the magistrate judge's recommendation. The district judge may accept, reject, or modify the recommendation, receive further evidence, or resubmit the matter to the magistrate judge with instructions.

(Added Apr. 25, 2005, eff. Dec. 1, 2005; amended Mar. 26, 2009, eff. Dec. 1, 2009.)

COMMITTEE NOTES ON RULES—2002

Rule 59, which dealt with the effective date of the Federal Rules of Criminal Procedure, is no longer necessary and has been deleted.

COMMITTEE NOTES ON RULES—2005

Rule 59 is a new rule that creates a procedure for a district judge to review nondispositive and dispositive decisions by magistrate judges. The rule is derived in part from Federal Rule of Civil Procedure 72.

The Committee's consideration of a new rule on the subject of review of a magistrate judge's decisions resulted from United States v. Abonce-Barrera, 257 F.3d 959 (9th Cir. 2001). In that case the Ninth Circuit held that the Criminal Rules do not require appeals from nondispositive decisions by magistrate judges to district judges as a requirement for review by a court of appeals. The court suggested that Federal Rule of Civil Procedure 72 could serve as a suitable model for a criminal rule.

Rule 59(a) sets out procedures to be used in reviewing nondispositive matters, that is, those matters that do not dispose of the case. The rule requires that if the district judge has referred a matter to a magistrate judge, the magistrate judge must issue an oral or written order on the record. To preserve the issue for further review, a party must object to that order within 10 days after being served with a copy of the order or after the oral order is stated on the record or at some other time set by the court. If an objection is made, the district court is required to consider the objection. If the court determines that the magistrate judge's order, or a portion of the order, is contrary to law or is clearly erroneous, the court must set aside the order, or the affected part of the order. See also 28 U.S.C. §636(b)(1)(A).

Rule 59(b) provides for assignment and review of recommendations made by magistrate judges on dispositive matters, including motions to suppress or quash an indictment or information. The rule directs the magistrate judge to consider the matter promptly, hold any necessary evidentiary hearings, and enter his or her recommendation on the record. After being served with a copy of the magistrate judge's recommendation, under Rule 59(b)(2), the parties have a period of 10 days to file any objections. If any objections are filed, the district court must consider the matter de novo and accept, reject, or modify the recommendation, or return the matter to the magistrate judge for further consideration.

Both Rule 59(a) and (b) contain a provision that explicitly states that failure to file an objection in accordance with the rule amounts to a waiver of the issue. This waiver provision is intended to establish the requirements for objecting in a district court in order to preserve appellate review of magistrate judges' decisions. In Thomas v. Arn, 474 U.S. 140, 155 (1985), the Supreme Court approved the adoption of waiver rules on matters for which a magistrate judge had made a decision or recommendation. The Committee believes that the waiver provisions will enhance the ability of a district court to review a magistrate judge's decision or recommendation by requiring a party to promptly file an objection to that part of the decision or recommendation at issue. Further, the Supreme Court has held that a de novo review of a magistrate judge's decision or recommendation is required to satisfy Article III concerns only where there is an objection. Peretz v. United States, 501 U.S. 293 (1991).

Despite the waiver provisions, the district judge retains the authority to review any magistrate judge's decision or recommendation whether or not objections are timely filed. This discretionary review is in accord with the Supreme Court's decision in Thomas v. Arn, supra, at 154. See also Matthews v. Weber, 423 U.S. 261, 270–271 (1976).

Although the rule distinguishes between "dispositive" and "nondispositive" matters, it does not attempt to define or otherwise catalog motions that may fall within either category. Instead, that task is left to the case law.

Changes Made After Publication and Comment. The Committee adopted almost all of the style suggestions by the Style Subcommittee, and several of the suggestions by the Federal Magistrate Judges' Association. In particular the Committee adopted a variation of the language suggested by the Association concerning matters disposing of a "charge or defense." The committee also addressed the issue in Rule 59(a) of clarifying the starting point for the 10 days in which to file objections by changing the word "made" in line 9 to read "stated." In Rule 59(b)(1) the Committee rearranged the order of the sample motions that would be considered "dispositive." Finally, the Committee included a paragraph at the end of the Committee Note, addressing the decision not to further specify in the rule, or the Note, what matters might be dispositive or nondispositive.

COMMITTEE NOTES ON RULES——2009 AMENDMENT

The times set in the former rule at 10 days have been revised to 14 days. See the Committee Note to Rule 45(a).

Rule 60. Victim's Rights

(a) In General.

(1) Notice of a Proceeding. The government must use its best efforts to give the victim reasonable, accurate, and timely notice of any public court proceeding involving the crime.

(2) Attending the Proceeding. The court must not exclude a victim from a public court proceeding involving the crime, unless the court determines by clear and convincing evidence that the victim's testimony would be materially altered if the victim heard other testimony at that proceeding. In determining whether to exclude a victim, the court must make every effort to permit the fullest attendance possible by the victim and must consider reasonable alternatives to exclusion. The reasons for any exclusion must be clearly stated on the record.

(3) Right to Be Heard on Release, a Plea, or Sentencing. The court must permit a victim to be reasonably heard at any public proceeding in the district court concerning release, plea, or sentencing involving the crime.

(b) Enforcement and Limitations.

(1) Time for Deciding a Motion. The court must promptly decide any motion asserting a victim's rights described in these rules.

(2) Who May Assert the Rights. A victim's rights described in these rules may be asserted by the victim, the victim's lawful representative, the attorney for the government, or any other person as authorized by 18 U.S.C. §3771(d) and (e).[1]

(3) Multiple Victims. If the court finds that the number of victims makes it impracticable to accord all of them their rights described in these rules, the court must fashion a reasonable procedure that gives effect to these rights without unduly complicating or prolonging the proceedings.

(4) Where Rights May Be Asserted. A victim's rights described in these rules must be asserted in the district where a defendant is being prosecuted for the crime.

(5) Limitations on Relief. A victim may move to reopen a plea or sentence only if:

(A) the victim asked to be heard before or during the proceeding at issue, and the request was denied;

(B) the victim petitions the court of appeals for a writ of mandamus within 10 days after the denial, and the writ is granted; and

(C) in the case of a plea, the accused has not pleaded to the highest offense charged.

(6) No New Trial. A failure to afford a victim any right described in these rules is not grounds for a new trial.

(Added Apr. 23, 2008, eff. Dec. 1, 2008.)

COMMITTEE NOTES ON RULES——2008

This rule implements several provisions of the Crime Victims' Rights Act, codified at 18 U.S.C. §3771, in judicial proceedings in the federal courts.

Subdivision (a)(1). This subdivision incorporates 18 U.S.C. §3771(a)(2), which provides that a victim has a "right to reasonable, accurate, and timely notice of any public court proceeding. . . ." The enactment of 18 U.S.C. §3771(a)(2) supplemented an existing statutory requirement that all federal departments and agencies engaged in the detection, investigation, and prosecution of crime identify victims at the earliest possible time and inform those victims of various rights, including the right to notice of the status of the investigation, the arrest of a suspect, the filing of charges against a suspect, and the scheduling of judicial proceedings. See 42 U.S.C. §10607(b) & (c)(3)(A)–(D).

173

Subdivision (a)(2). This subdivision incorporates 18 U.S.C. §3771(a)(3), which provides that the victim shall not be excluded from public court proceedings unless the court finds by clear and convincing evidence that the victim's testimony would be materially altered by attending and hearing other testimony at the proceeding, and 18 U.S.C. §3771(b), which provides that the court shall make every effort to permit the fullest possible attendance by the victim.

Rule 615 of the Federal Rules of Evidence addresses the sequestration of witnesses. Although Rule 615 requires the court upon the request of a party to order the witnesses to be excluded so they cannot hear the testimony of other witnesses, it contains an exception for "a person authorized by statute to be present." Accordingly, there is no conflict between Rule 615 and this rule, which implements the provisions of the Crime Victims' Rights Act.

Subdivision (a)(3). This subdivision incorporates 18 U.S.C. §3771(a)(4), which provides that a victim has the "right to be reasonably heard at any public proceeding in the district court involving release, plea, [or] sentencing. . . ."

Subdivision (b). This subdivision incorporates the provisions of 18 U.S.C. §3771(d)(1), (2), (3), and (5). The statute provides that the victim, the victim's lawful representative, and the attorney for the government, and any other person as authorized by 18 U.S.C. §3771(d) and (e) may assert the victim's rights. In referring to the victim and the victim's lawful representative, the committee intends to include counsel. 18 U.S.C. §3771(e) makes provision for the rights of victims who are incompetent, incapacitated, or deceased, and 18 U.S.C. §3771(d)(1) provides that "[a] person accused of the crime may not obtain any form of relief under this chapter."

The statute provides that those rights are to be asserted in the district court where the defendant is being prosecuted (or if no prosecution is underway, in the district where the crime occurred). Where there are too many victims to accord each the rights provided by the statute, the district court is given the authority to fashion a reasonable procedure to give effect to the rights without unduly complicating or prolonging the proceedings.

Finally, the statute and the rule make it clear that failure to provide relief under the rule never provides a basis for a new trial. Failure to afford the rights provided by the statute and implementing rules may provide a basis for re-opening a plea or a sentence, but only if the victim can establish all of the following: the victim asserted the right before or during the proceeding, the right was denied, the victim petitioned for mandamus within 10 days as provided by 18 U.S.C. §3771(d)(5)(B), and—in the case of a plea—the defendant did not plead guilty to the highest offense charged.

Changes Made to Proposed Amendment Released for Public Comment. Subdivision (a)(2) was revised to make it clear that the duty to permit fullest attendance arises in the context of the victim's possible exclusion.

Subdivision(b)(2) was revised to respond to concerns that the amendments did not clearly state that the victim's lawful representative could assert the victim's rights. The Committee Note makes it clear that a victim or the lawful representative of a victim may generally participate through counsel, and provides that any other person authorized by 18 U.S.C. §3771(d) and (e) may assert the victim's rights, such as persons authorized to raise the rights of victims who are minors or are incompetent.

References throughout subdivision (b) were revised to indicate that they were applicable to the victim's rights described in the Federal Rules of Criminal Procedure, not merely subdivision (a) of Rule 60.

Other minor changes were made at the suggestion of the Style Consultant to improve clarity.

REFERENCES IN TEXT

18 U.S.C. §3771(e), referred to in subd. (b)(2), was redesignated 18 U.S.C. §3771(e)(2) by Pub. L. 114–22, title I, §113(a)(3)(A), May 29, 2015, 129 Stat. 240.

[1] See References in Text note below.

Rule 61. Title

These rules may be known and cited as the Federal Rules of Criminal Procedure.

(As amended Apr. 29, 2002, eff. Dec. 1, 2002; Apr. 23, 2008, eff. Dec. 1, 2008.)

SHORT TITLE OF 1975 AMENDMENT

Pub. L. 94–64, §1, July 31, 1975, 89 Stat. 370, provided: "That this Act [amending rules 4, 9, 11, 12, 12.1, 12.2, 15, 16, 17, 20, 32 and 43 of these rules and enacting provisions set out as a note under rule 4] may be cited as the 'Federal Rules of Criminal Procedure Amendments Act of 1975'."

NOTES OF ADVISORY COMMITTEE ON RULES—1944

This rule is similar to Rule 85 of the Federal Rules of Civil Procedure [28 U.S.C., Appendix], which reads as follows:

These rules may be known and cited as the Federal Rules of Civil Procedure.

COMMITTEE NOTES ON RULES—2002 AMENDMENT

No changes have been made to Rule 60, as a result of the general restyling of the Criminal Rules.

COMMITTEE NOTES ON RULES—2008 AMENDMENT

Excerpt from Report of the Advisory Committee on Federal Rules of Criminal Procedure. This amendment renumbers current Rule 60 as Rule 61 to accommodate the new victims' rights rule.

Changes Made to Proposed Amendment Released for Public Comment. No changes were made.

175

Table of Contents

FEDERAL RULES OF APPELLATE PROCEDURE
(As amended to December 1, 2019)

HISTORICAL NOTE

The Federal Rules of Appellate Procedure were adopted by order of the Supreme Court on Dec. 4, 1967, transmitted to Congress by the Chief Justice on Jan. 15, 1968, and became effective on July 1, 1968.

The Rules have been amended Mar. 30, 1970, eff. July 1, 1970; Mar. 1, 1971, eff. July 1, 1971; Apr. 24, 1972, eff. Oct. 1, 1972; Apr. 30, 1979, eff. Aug. 1, 1979; Oct. 12, 1984, Pub. L. 98–473, title II, §210, 98 Stat 1987; Mar. 10, 1986, eff. July 1, 1986; Nov. 18, 1988, Pub. L. 100–690, title VII, §7111, 102 Stat. 4419; Apr. 25, 1989, eff. Dec. 1, 1989; Apr. 30, 1991, eff. Dec. 1, 1991; Apr. 22, 1993, eff. Dec. 1, 1993; Apr. 29, 1994, eff. Dec. 1, 1994; Apr. 27, 1995, eff. Dec. 1, 1995; Apr. 23, 1996, eff. Dec. 1, 1996; Apr. 24, 1996, Pub. L. 104–132, title I, §103, 110 Stat. 1218; Apr. 24, 1998, eff. Dec. 1, 1998; Apr. 29, 2002, eff. Dec. 1, 2002; Mar. 27, 2003, eff. Dec. 1, 2003; Apr. 25, 2005, eff. Dec. 1, 2005; Apr. 12, 2006, eff. Dec. 1, 2006; Apr. 30, 2007, eff. Dec. 1, 2007; Mar. 26, 2009, eff. Dec. 1, 2009; Apr. 28, 2010, eff. Dec. 1, 2010; Apr. 26, 2011, eff. Dec. 1, 2011; Apr. 16, 2013, eff. Dec. 1, 2013; Apr. 25, 2014, eff. Dec. 1, 2014; Apr. 28, 2016, eff. Dec. 1, 2016; Apr. 27, 2017, eff. Dec. 1, 2017; Apr. 26, 2018, eff. Dec. 1, 2018; Apr. 25, 2019, eff. Dec. 1, 2019.

APPENDIX OF FORMS

APPENDIX: LENGTH LIMITS STATED IN THE FEDERAL RULES OF APPELLATE PROCEDURE

EFFECTIVE DATE AND APPLICATION OF RULES

Section 2 of the Order of the Supreme Court, dated Dec. 4, 1967, provided: "That the foregoing rules shall take effect on July 1, 1968, and shall govern all proceedings in appeals and petitions for review or enforcement of orders thereafter brought in and in all such proceedings then pending, except to the extent that in the opinion of the court of appeals their application in a particular proceeding then pending would not be feasible or would work injustice, in which case the former procedure may be followed."

TITLE I. APPLICABILITY OF RULES

Rule 1. Scope of Rules; Definition; Title

(a) Scope of Rules.
    (1) These rules govern procedure in the United States courts of appeals.
    (2) When these rules provide for filing a motion or other document in the district court, the procedure must comply with the practice of the district court.

(b) Definition. In these rules, 'state' [1] includes the District of Columbia and any United States commonwealth or territory.
(c) Title. These rules are to be known as the Federal Rules of Appellate Procedure.

(As amended Apr. 30, 1979, eff. Aug. 1, 1979; Apr. 25, 1989, eff. Dec. 1, 1989; Apr. 29, 1994, eff. Dec. 1, 1994; Apr. 24, 1998, eff. Dec. 1, 1998; Apr. 29, 2002, eff. Dec. 1, 2002; Apr. 28, 2010, eff. Dec. 1, 2010.)

NOTES OF ADVISORY COMMITTEE ON RULES—1967

These rules are drawn under the authority of 28 U.S.C. §2072, as amended by the Act of November 6, 1966, 80 Stat. 1323 (1 U.S. Code Cong. & Ad. News, p. 1546 (1966)) (Rules of Civil Procedure); 28 U.S.C. §2075 (Bankruptcy Rules); and 18 U.S.C. §§3771 (Procedure to and including verdict) and 3772 (Procedure after verdict). Those statutes combine to give to the Supreme Court power to make rules of practice and procedure for all cases within the jurisdiction of the courts of appeals. By the terms of the statutes, after the rules have taken effect all laws in conflict with them are of no further force or effect. Practice and procedure in the eleven courts of appeals are now regulated by rules promulgated by each court under the authority of 28 U.S.C. §2071. Rule 47 expressly authorizes the courts of appeals to make rules of practice not inconsistent with these rules.

As indicated by the titles under which they are found, the following rules are of special application: Rules 3 through 12 apply to appeals from judgments and orders of the district courts; Rules 13 and 14 apply to appeals from decisions of the Tax Court (Rule 13 establishes an appeal as the mode of review of decisions of the Tax Court in place of the present petition for review); Rules 15 through 20 apply to proceedings for review or enforcement of orders of administrative agencies, boards, commissions and officers. Rules 22 through 24 regulate habeas corpus proceedings and appeals in forma pauperis. All other rules apply to all proceedings in the courts of appeals.

NOTES OF ADVISORY COMMITTEE ON RULES—1979 AMENDMENT

The Federal Rules of Appellate Procedure were designed as an integrated set of rules to be followed in appeals to the courts of appeals, covering all steps in the appellate process, whether they take place in the district court or in the court of appeals, and with their adoption Rules 72–76 of the F.R.C.P. were abrogated. In some instances, however, the F.R.A.P. provide that a motion or application for relief may, or must, be made in the district court. See Rules 4(a), 10(b), and 24. The proposed amendment would make it clear that when this is so the motion or application is to be made in the form and manner prescribed by the F.R.C.P. or F.R.Cr.P. and local rules relating to the form and presentation of motions and is not governed by Rule 27 of the F.R.A.P. See Rule 7(b) of the F.R.C.P. and Rule 47 of the F.R.Cr.P.

The amendment is technical. No substantive change is intended.

Subdivision (c). A new subdivision is added to the rule. The text of new subdivision (c) has been moved from Rule 48 to Rule 1 to allow the addition of new rules at the end of the existing set of appellate rules without burying the title provision among other rules. In a similar fashion the Bankruptcy Rules combine the provisions governing the scope of the rules and the title in the first rule.

The language and organization of the rule are amended to make the rule more easily understood. In addition to changes made to improve the understanding, the Advisory Committee has changed language to make style and terminology consistent throughout the appellate rules. These changes are intended to be stylistic only. The Advisory Committee recommends deleting the language in subdivision (a) that describes the different types of proceedings that may be brought in a court of appeals. The Advisory Committee believes that the language is unnecessary and that its omission does not work any substantive change.

Subdivision (b). Two recent enactments make it likely that, in the future, one or more of the Federal Rules of Appellate Procedure ("FRAP") will extend or limit the jurisdiction of the courts of appeals. In 1990, Congress amended the Rules Enabling Act to give the Supreme Court authority to use the federal rules of practice and procedure to define when a ruling of a district court is final for purposes of 28 U.S.C. §1291. See 28 U.S.C. §2072(c). In 1992, Congress amended 28 U.S.C. §1292 to give the Supreme Court authority to use the federal rules of practice and procedure to provide for appeals of interlocutory decisions that are not already authorized by 28 U.S.C. §1292. See 28 U.S.C. §1292(e). Both §1291 and §1292 are unquestionably jurisdictional statutes, and thus, as soon as FRAP is amended to define finality for purposes of the former or to authorize interlocutory appeals not provided for by the latter, FRAP will "extend or limit the jurisdiction of the courts of appeals," and subdivision (b) will become obsolete. For that reason, subdivision (b) has been abrogated.

Changes Made After Publication and Comments. No changes were made to the text of the proposed amendment or to the Committee Note.

Subdivision (b). New subdivision (b) defines the term "state" to include the District of Columbia and any commonwealth or territory of the United States. Thus, as used in these Rules, "state" includes the District of Columbia, Guam, American Samoa, the U.S. Virgin Islands, the Commonwealth of Puerto Rico, and the Commonwealth of the Northern Mariana Islands.

Changes Made After Publication and Comment. No changes were made after publication and comment.

¹ So in original.

Rule 2. Suspension of Rules

On its own or a party's motion, a court of appeals may——to expedite its decision or for other good cause——suspend any provision of these rules in a particular case and order proceedings as it directs, except as otherwise provided in Rule 26(b).

(As amended Apr. 24, 1998, eff. Dec. 1, 1998.)

The primary purpose of this rule is to make clear the power of the courts of appeals to expedite the determination of cases of pressing concern to the public or to the litigants by prescribing a time schedule other than that provided by the rules. The rule also contains a general authorization to the courts to relieve litigants of the consequences of default where manifest injustice would otherwise result. Rule 26(b) prohibits a court of appeals from extending the time for taking appeal or seeking review.

The language of the rule is amended to make the rule more easily understood. In addition to changes made to improve the understanding, the Advisory Committee has changed language to make style and terminology consistent throughout the appellate rules. These changes are intended to be stylistic only.

TITLE II. APPEAL FROM A JUDGMENT OR ORDER OF A DISTRICT COURT

Rule 3. Appeal as of Right——How Taken

(a) Filing the Notice of Appeal.

(1) An appeal permitted by law as of right from a district court to a court of appeals may be taken only by filing a notice of appeal with the district clerk within the time allowed by Rule 4. At the time of filing, the appellant must furnish the clerk with enough copies of the notice to enable the clerk to comply with Rule 3(d).

(2) An appellant's failure to take any step other than the timely filing of a notice of appeal does not affect the validity of the appeal, but is ground only for the court of appeals to act as it considers appropriate, including dismissing the appeal.

(3) An appeal from a judgment by a magistrate judge in a civil case is taken in the same way as an appeal from any other district court judgment.

(4) An appeal by permission under 28 U.S.C. §1292(b) or an appeal in a bankruptcy case may be taken only in the manner prescribed by Rules 5 and 6, respectively.

(b) Joint or Consolidated Appeals.

(1) When two or more parties are entitled to appeal from a district-court judgment or order, and their interests make joinder practicable, they may file a joint notice of appeal. They may then proceed on appeal as a single appellant.

(2) When the parties have filed separate timely notices of appeal, the appeals may be joined or consolidated by the court of appeals.

(c) Contents of the Notice of Appeal.

 (1) The notice of appeal must:

  (A) specify the party or parties taking the appeal by naming each one in the caption or body of the notice, but an attorney representing more than one party may describe those parties with such terms as "all plaintiffs," "the defendants," "the plaintiffs A, B, et al.," or "all defendants except X";

  (B) designate the judgment, order, or part thereof being appealed; and

  (C) name the court to which the appeal is taken.

 (2) A pro se notice of appeal is considered filed on behalf of the signer and the signer's spouse and minor children (if they are parties), unless the notice clearly indicates otherwise.

 (3) In a class action, whether or not the class has been certified, the notice of appeal is sufficient if it names one person qualified to bring the appeal as representative of the class.

 (4) An appeal must not be dismissed for informality of form or title of the notice of appeal, or for failure to name a party whose intent to appeal is otherwise clear from the notice.

 (5) Form 1 in the Appendix of Forms is a suggested form of a notice of appeal.

(d) Serving the Notice of Appeal.

 (1) The district clerk must serve notice of the filing of a notice of appeal by sending a copy to each party's counsel of record—excluding the appellant's—or, if a party is proceeding pro se, to the party's last known address. When a defendant in a criminal case appeals, the clerk must also serve a copy of the notice of appeal on the defendant. The clerk must promptly send a copy of the notice of appeal and of the docket entries—and any later docket entries—to the clerk of the court of appeals named in the notice. The district clerk must note, on each copy, the date when the notice of appeal was filed.

 (2) If an inmate confined in an institution files a notice of appeal in the manner provided by Rule 4(c), the district clerk must also note the date when the clerk docketed the notice.

 (3) The district clerk's failure to serve notice does not affect the validity of the appeal. The clerk must note on the docket the names of the parties to whom the clerk sends copies, with the date of sending. Service is sufficient despite the death of a party or the party's counsel.

(e) Payment of Fees. Upon filing a notice of appeal, the appellant must pay the district clerk all required fees. The district clerk receives the appellate docket fee on behalf of the court of appeals.

(As amended Apr. 30, 1979, eff. Aug. 1, 1979; Mar. 10, 1986, eff. July 1, 1986; Apr. 25, 1989, eff. Dec. 1, 1989; Apr. 22, 1993, eff. Dec. 1, 1993; Apr. 29, 1994, eff. Dec. 1, 1994; Apr. 24, 1998, eff. Dec. 1, 1998; Apr. 25, 2019, eff. Dec. 1, 2019.)

NOTES OF ADVISORY COMMITTEE ON RULES—1967

General Note. Rule 3 and Rule 4 combine to require that a notice of appeal be filed with the clerk of the district court within the time prescribed for taking an appeal. Because the timely filing of a notice of appeal is "mandatory and jurisdictional," United States v. Robinson, 361 U.S. 220, 224, 80 S.Ct. 282, 4 L.Ed.2d 259 (1960), compliance with the provisions of those rules is of the utmost importance. But the proposed rules merely restate, in modified form, provisions now found in the civil and criminal rules (FRCP 5(e), 73; FRCrP 37), and decisions under the present rules which dispense with literal compliance in cases in which it cannot fairly be exacted should control interpretation of these rules. Illustrative decisions are: Fallen v. United States, 378 U.S. 139, 84 S.Ct. 1689, 12 L.Ed.2d 760 (1964) (notice of appeal by a prisoner, in the form of a letter delivered, well within the time fixed for appeal, to prison authorities for mailing to the clerk of the district court held timely filed notwithstanding that it was received by the clerk after expiration of the time for appeal; the appellant "did all he could" to effect timely filing); Richey v. Wilkins, 335 F.2d 1 (2d Cir. 1964) (notice filed in the court of appeals by a prisoner without assistance of counsel held sufficient); Halfen v. United States, 324 F.2d 52 (10th Cir. 1963) (notice mailed to district judge in time to have been received by him in normal course held sufficient); Riffle v. United States, 299 F.2d 802 (5th Cir. 1962) (letter of prisoner to judge of court of appeals held sufficient). Earlier cases evidencing "a liberal view of papers filed by indigent and incarcerated defendants" are listed in Coppedge v. United States, 369 U.S. 438, 442, n. 5, 82 S.Ct. 917, 8 L.Ed.2d 21 (1962).

Subdivision (a). The substance of this subdivision is derived from FRCP 73(a) and FRCrP 37(a)(1). The proposed rule follows those rules in requiring nothing other than the filing of a notice of appeal in the district court for the perfection of the appeal. The petition for allowance (except for appeals governed by Rules 5 and 6), citations, assignments of error, summons and severance—all specifically abolished by earlier modern rules—are assumed to be sufficiently obsolete as no longer to require pointed abolition.

Subdivision (b). The first sentence is derived from FRCP 74. The second sentence is added to encourage consolidation of appeals whenever feasible.

Subdivision (c). This subdivision is identical with corresponding provisions in FRCP 73(b) and FRCrP 37(a)(1).

Subdivision (d). This subdivision is derived from FRCP 73(b) and FRCrP 37(a)(1). The duty of the clerk to forward a copy of the notice of appeal and of the docket entries to the court of appeals in a criminal case extended to habeas corpus and 28 U.S.C. §2255 proceedings.

NOTES OF ADVISORY COMMITTEE ON RULES—1979 AMENDMENT

Subdivision (c). The proposed amendment would add the last sentence. Because of the fact that the timely filing of the notice of appeal has been characterized as jurisdictional (See, e.g., Brainerd v. Beal (C.A. 7th, 1974) 498 F.2d 901, in which the filing of a notice of appeal one day late was fatal), it is important that the right to appeal not be lost by mistakes of mere form. In a number of decided cases it has been held that so long as the function of notice is met by the filing of a paper indicating an intention to appeal, the substance of the rule has been complied with. See, e.g., Cobb v. Lewis (C.A. 5th, 1974) 488 F.2d 41; Holley v. Capps (C.A. 5th, 1972) 468 F.2d 1366. The proposed amendment would give recognition to this practice.

When a notice of appeal is filed, the clerk should ascertain whether any judgment designated therein has been entered in compliance with Rules 58 and 79(a) of the F.R.C.P. See Note to Rule 4(a)(6), infra.

Subdivision (d). The proposed amendment would extend to civil cases the present provision applicable to criminal cases, habeas corpus cases, and proceedings under 28 U.S.C. §2255, requiring the clerk of the district court to transmit to the clerk of the court of appeals a copy of the notice of appeal and of the docket entries, which should include reference to compliance with the requirements for payment of fees. See Note to (e), infra.

This requirement is the initial step in proposed changes in the rules to place in the court of appeals an increased practical control over the early steps in the appeal.

Subdivision (e). Proposed new Rule 3(e) represents the second step in shifting to the court of appeals the control of the early stages of an appeal. See Note to Rule 3(d) above. Under the present rules the payment of the fee prescribed by 28 U.S.C. 1917 is not covered. Under the statute, however, this fee is paid to the clerk of the district court at the time the notice of appeal is filed. Under present Rule 12, the "docket fee" fixed by the Judicial Conference of the United States under 28 U.S.C. §1913 must be paid to the clerk of the court of appeals within the time fixed for transmission of the record, ". . . and the clerk shall thereupon enter the appeal upon the docket."

Under the proposed new Rule 3(e) both fees would be paid to the clerk of the district court at the time the notice of appeal is filed, the clerk of the district court receiving the docket fee on behalf of the court of appeals.

In view of the provision in Rule 3(a) that "[f]ailure of an appellant to take any step other than the timely filing of a notice of appeal does not affect the validity of the appeal, but is ground only for such action as the court of appeals deems appropriate, which may include dismissal of the appeal," the case law indicates that the failure to prepay the statutory filing fee does not constitute a jurisdictional defect. See Parissi v. Telechron, 349 U.S. 46 (1955); Gould v. Members of N. J. Division of Water Policy & Supply, 555 F.2d 340 (3d Cir. 1977). Similarly, under present Rule 12, failure to pay the docket fee within the time prescribed may be excused by the court of appeals. See, e. g., Walker v. Mathews, 546 F.2d 814 (9th Cir. 1976). Proposed new Rule 3(e) adopts the view of these cases, requiring that both fees be paid at the time the notice of appeal is filed, but subject to the provisions of Rule 26(b) preserving the authority of the court of appeals to permit late payment.

NOTES OF ADVISORY COMMITTEE ON RULES——1986 AMENDMENT

The amendments to Rule 3(d) are technical. No substantive change is intended.

NOTES OF ADVISORY COMMITTEE ON RULES——1989 AMENDMENT

The amendment is technical. No substantive change is intended.

NOTES OF ADVISORY COMMITTEE ON RULES——1993 AMENDMENT

Note to subdivision (c). The amendment is intended to reduce the amount of satellite litigation spawned by the Supreme Court's decision in Torres v. Oakland Scavenger Co., 487 U.S. 312 (1988). In Torres the Supreme Court held that the language in Rule 3(c) requiring a notice of appeal to "specify the party or parties taking the appeal" is a jurisdictional requirement and that naming the first named party and adding "et al.," without any further specificity is insufficient to identify the appellants. Since the Torres decision, there has been a great deal of litigation regarding whether a notice of appeal that contains some indication of the appellants' identities but does not name the appellants is sufficiently specific.

The amendment states a general rule that specifying the parties should be done by naming them. Naming an appellant in an otherwise timely and proper notice of appeal ensures that the appellant has perfected an appeal. However, in order to prevent the loss of a right to appeal through inadvertent omission of a party's name or continued use of such terms as "et al.," which are sufficient in all district court filings after the complaint, the amendment allows an attorney representing more than one party the flexibility to indicate which parties are appealing without naming them individually. The test established by the rule for determining whether such designations are sufficient is whether it is objectively clear that a party intended to appeal. A notice of appeal filed by a party proceeding pro se is filed on behalf of the party signing the notice and the signer's spouse and minor children, if they are parties, unless the notice clearly indicates a contrary intent.

In class actions, naming each member of a class as an appellant may be extraordinarily burdensome or even impossible. In class actions if class certification has been denied, named plaintiffs may appeal the order denying the class certification on their own behalf and on behalf of putative class members, United States Parole Comm'n v. Geraghty, 445 U.S. 388 (1980); or if the named plaintiffs choose not to appeal the order denying the class certification, putative class members may appeal, United Airlines, Inc. v. McDonald, 432 U.S. 385 (1977). If no class has been certified, naming each of the putative class members as an appellant would often be impossible. Therefore the amendment provides that in class actions, whether or not the class has been certified, it is sufficient for the notice to name one person qualified to bring the appeal as a representative of the class.

Finally, the rule makes it clear that dismissal of an appeal should not occur when it is otherwise clear from the notice that the party intended to appeal. If a court determines it is objectively clear that a party intended to appeal, there are neither administrative concerns nor fairness concerns that should prevent the appeal from going forward.

Note to subdivision (d). The amendment requires the district court clerk to send to the clerk of the court of appeals a copy of every docket entry in a case after the filing of a notice of appeal. This amendment accompanies the amendment to Rule 4(a)(4), which provides that when one of the posttrial motions enumerated in Rule 4(a)(4) is filed, a notice of appeal filed before the disposition of the motion becomes effective upon disposition of the motion. The court of appeals needs to be advised that the filing of a posttrial motion has suspended a notice of appeal. The court of appeals also needs to know when the district court has ruled on the motion. Sending copies of all docket entries after the filing of a notice of appeal should provide the courts of appeals with the necessary information.

NOTES OF ADVISORY COMMITTEE ON RULES——1994 AMENDMENT

Subdivision (a). The amendment requires a party filing a notice of appeal to provide the court with sufficient copies of the notice for service on all other parties.

COMMITTEE NOTES ON RULES——1998 AMENDMENT

The language and organization of the rule are amended to make the rule more easily understood. In addition to changes made to improve the understanding, the Advisory Committee has changed language to make style and terminology consistent throughout the appellate rules. These changes are generally intended to be stylistic only; in this rule, however, substantive changes are made in subdivisions (a), (b), and (d).

Subdivision (a). The provision in paragraph (a)(3) is transferred from former Rule 3.1(b). The Federal Courts Improvement Act of 1996, Pub. L. No. 104–317, repealed paragraphs (4) and (5) of 28 U.S.C. §636(c). That statutory change made the continued separate existence of Rule 3.1 unnecessary. New paragraph (a)(3) of this rule simply makes it clear that an appeal from a judgment by a magistrate judge is taken in identical fashion to any other appeal from a district-court judgment.

Subdivision (b). A joint appeal is authorized only when two or more persons may appeal from a single judgment or order. A joint appeal is treated as a single appeal and the joint appellants file a single brief. Under existing Rule 3(b) parties decide whether to join their appeals. They may do so by filing a joint notice of appeal or by joining their appeals after filing separate notices of appeal.

In consolidated appeals the separate appeals do not merge into one. The parties do not proceed as a single appellant. Under existing Rule 3(b) it is unclear whether appeals may be consolidated without court order if the parties stipulate to consolidation. The language resolves that ambiguity by requiring court action.

183

The language also requires court action to join appeals after separate notices of appeal have been filed.

Subdivision (d). Paragraph (d)(2) has been amended to require that when an inmate files a notice of appeal by depositing the notice in the institution's internal mail system, the clerk must note the docketing date—rather than the receipt date—on the notice of appeal before serving copies of it. This change conforms to a change in Rule 4(c). Rule 4(c) is amended to provide that when an inmate files the first notice of appeal in a civil case by depositing the notice in an institution's internal mail system, the time for filing a cross-appeal runs from the date the district court dockets the inmate's notice of appeal. Existing Rule 4(c) says that in such a case the time for filing a cross-appeal runs from the date the district court receives the inmate's notice of appeal. A court may "receive" a paper when its mail is delivered to it even if the mail is not processed for a day or two, making the date of receipt uncertain. "Docketing" is an easily identified event. The change is made to eliminate the uncertainty.

COMMITTEE NOTES ON RULES—2019 AMENDMENT

Amendments to Subdivision (d) change the words "mailing" and "mails" to "sending" and "sends," and delete language requiring certain forms of service, to allow for electronic service. Other rules determine when a party or the clerk may or must send a notice electronically or non-electronically.

[Rule 3.1. Appeal from a Judgment of a Magistrate Judge in a Civil Case] (Abrogated Apr. 24, 1998, eff. Dec. 1, 1998)

COMMITTEE NOTES ON RULES—1998 AMENDMENT

The Federal Courts Improvement Act of 1996, Pub. L. No. 104–317, repealed paragraphs (4) and (5) of 28 U.S.C. §636(c). That statutory change means that when parties consent to trial before a magistrate judge, appeal lies directly, and as a matter of right, to the court of appeals under §636(c)(3). The parties may not choose to appeal first to a district judge and thereafter seek discretionary review in the court of appeals.

As a result of the statutory amendments, subdivision (a) of Rule 3.1 is no longer necessary. Since Rule 3.1 existed primarily because of the provisions in subdivision (a), subdivision (b) has been moved to Rule 3(a)(3) and Rule 3.1 has been abrogated.

Rule 4. Appeal as of Right—When Taken

(a) Appeal in a Civil Case.
    (1) Time for Filing a Notice of Appeal.
        (A) In a civil case, except as provided in Rules 4(a)(1)(B), 4(a)(4), and 4(c), the notice of appeal required by Rule 3 must be filed with the district clerk within 30 days after entry of the judgment or order appealed from.
        (B) The notice of appeal may be filed by any party within 60 days after entry of the judgment or order appealed from if one of the parties is:
            (i) the United States;
            (ii) a United States agency;
            (iii) a United States officer or employee sued in an official capacity; or
            (iv) a current or former United States officer or employee sued in an individual capacity for an act or omission occurring in connection with duties performed on the United States' behalf—including all instances in which the United States represents that person when the judgment or order is entered or files the appeal for that person.

        (C) An appeal from an order granting or denying an application for a writ of error coram nobis is an appeal in a civil case for purposes of Rule 4(a).

    (2) Filing Before Entry of Judgment. A notice of appeal filed after the court announces a decision or order—but before the entry of the judgment or order—is treated as filed on the date of and after the entry.
    (3) Multiple Appeals. If one party timely files a notice of appeal, any other party may file a notice of appeal within 14 days after the date when the first notice was filed, or within the time otherwise prescribed by this Rule 4(a), whichever period ends later.
    (4) Effect of a Motion on a Notice of Appeal.
        (A) If a party files in the district court any of the following motions under the Federal Rules of Civil Procedure—and does so within the time allowed by those rules—the time to file an appeal runs for all parties from the entry of the order disposing of the last such remaining motion:
            (i) for judgment under Rule 50(b);
            (ii) to amend or make additional factual findings under Rule 52(b), whether or not granting the motion would alter the judgment;
            (iii) for attorney's fees under Rule 54 if the district court extends the time to appeal under Rule 58;
            (iv) to alter or amend the judgment under Rule 59;
            (v) for a new trial under Rule 59; or
            (vi) for relief under Rule 60 if the motion is filed no later than 28 days after the judgment is entered.

        (B)(i) If a party files a notice of appeal after the court announces or enters a judgment—but before it disposes of any motion listed in Rule 4(a)(4)(A)—the notice becomes effective to appeal a judgment or order, in whole or in part, when the order disposing of the last such remaining motion is entered.
        (ii) A party intending to challenge an order disposing of any motion listed in Rule 4(a)(4)(A), or a judgment's alteration or amendment upon such a motion, must file a notice of appeal, or an amended notice of appeal—in compliance with Rule 3(c)—within the time prescribed by this Rule measured from the entry of the order disposing of the last such remaining motion.
        (iii) No additional fee is required to file an amended notice.

    (5) Motion for Extension of Time.
        (A) The district court may extend the time to file a notice of appeal if:
            (i) a party so moves no later than 30 days after the time prescribed by this Rule 4(a) expires; and
            (ii) regardless of whether its motion is filed before or during the 30 days after the time prescribed by this Rule 4(a) expires, that party shows excusable neglect or good cause.

        (B) A motion filed before the expiration of the time prescribed in Rule 4(a)(1) or (3) may be ex parte unless the court requires otherwise. If the motion is filed after the expiration of the prescribed time, notice must be given to the other parties in accordance with local rules.
        (C) No extension under this Rule 4(a)(5) may exceed 30 days after the prescribed time or 14 days after the date when the order granting the motion is entered, whichever is later.

(6) Reopening the Time to File an Appeal. The district court may reopen the time to file an appeal for a period of 14 days after the date when its order to reopen is entered, but only if all the following conditions are satisfied:

    (A) the court finds that the moving party did not receive notice under Federal Rule of Civil Procedure 77(d) of the entry of the judgment or order sought to be appealed within 21 days after entry;

    (B) the motion is filed within 180 days after the judgment or order is entered or within 14 days after the moving party receives notice under Federal Rule of Civil Procedure 77(d) of the entry, whichever is earlier; and

    (C) the court finds that no party would be prejudiced.

(7) Entry Defined.

    (A) A judgment or order is entered for purposes of this Rule 4(a):

        (i) if Federal Rule of Civil Procedure 58(a) does not require a separate document, when the judgment or order is entered in the civil docket under Federal Rule of Civil Procedure 79(a); or

        (ii) if Federal Rule of Civil Procedure 58(a) requires a separate document, when the judgment or order is entered in the civil docket under Federal Rule of Civil Procedure 79(a) and when the earlier of these events occurs:

            • the judgment or order is set forth on a separate document, or

            • 150 days have run from entry of the judgment or order in the civil docket under Federal Rule of Civil Procedure 79(a).

    (B) A failure to set forth a judgment or order on a separate document when required by Federal Rule of Civil Procedure 58(a) does not affect the validity of an appeal from that judgment or order.

(b) Appeal in a Criminal Case.

    (1) Time for Filing a Notice of Appeal.

        (A) In a criminal case, a defendant's notice of appeal must be filed in the district court within 14 days after the later of:

            (i) the entry of either the judgment or the order being appealed; or

            (ii) the filing of the government's notice of appeal.

        (B) When the government is entitled to appeal, its notice of appeal must be filed in the district court within 30 days after the later of:

            (i) the entry of the judgment or order being appealed; or

            (ii) the filing of a notice of appeal by any defendant.

    (2) Filing Before Entry of Judgment. A notice of appeal filed after the court announces a decision, sentence, or order—but before the entry of the judgment or order—is treated as filed on the date of and after the entry.

    (3) Effect of a Motion on a Notice of Appeal.

        (A) If a defendant timely makes any of the following motions under the Federal Rules of Criminal Procedure, the notice of appeal from a judgment of conviction must be filed within 14 days after the entry of the order disposing of the last such remaining motion, or within 14 days after the entry of the judgment of conviction, whichever period ends later. This provision applies to a timely motion:

            (i) for judgment of acquittal under Rule 29;

            (ii) for a new trial under Rule 33, but if based on newly discovered evidence, only if the motion is made no later than 14 days after the entry of the judgment; or

            (iii) for arrest of judgment under Rule 34.

        (B) A notice of appeal filed after the court announces a decision, sentence, or order—but before it disposes of any of the motions referred to in Rule 4(b)(3)(A)—becomes effective upon the later of the following:

            (i) the entry of the order disposing of the last such remaining motion; or

            (ii) the entry of the judgment of conviction.

        (C) A valid notice of appeal is effective—without amendment—to appeal from an order disposing of any of the motions referred to in Rule 4(b)(3)(A).

    (4) Motion for Extension of Time. Upon a finding of excusable neglect or good cause, the district court may—before or after the time has expired, with or without motion and notice—extend the time to file a notice of appeal for a period not to exceed 30 days from the expiration of the time otherwise prescribed by this Rule 4(b).

    (5) Jurisdiction. The filing of a notice of appeal under this Rule 4(b) does not divest a district court of jurisdiction to correct a sentence under Federal Rule of Criminal Procedure 35(a), nor does the filing of a motion under 35(a) affect the validity of a notice of appeal filed before entry of the order disposing of the motion. The filing of a motion under Federal Rule of Criminal Procedure 35(a) does not suspend the time for filing a notice of appeal from a judgment of conviction.

    (6) Entry Defined. A judgment or order is entered for purposes of this Rule 4(b) when it is entered on the criminal docket.

(c) Appeal by an Inmate Confined in an Institution.

    (1) If an institution has a system designed for legal mail, an inmate confined there must use that system to receive the benefit of this Rule 4(c)(1). If an inmate files a notice of appeal in either a civil or a criminal case, the notice is timely if it is deposited in the institution's internal mail system on or before the last day for filing and:

        (A) it is accompanied by:

            (i) a declaration in compliance with 28 U.S.C. §1746—or a notarized statement—setting out the date of deposit and stating that first-class postage is being prepaid; or

            (ii) evidence (such as a postmark or date stamp) showing that the notice was so deposited and that postage was prepaid; or

        (B) the court of appeals exercises its discretion to permit the later filing of a declaration or notarized statement that satisfies Rule 4(c)(1)(A)(i).

    (2) If an inmate files the first notice of appeal in a civil case under this Rule 4(c), the 14-day period provided in Rule 4(a)(3) for another party to file a notice of appeal runs from the date when the district court dockets the first notice.

    (3) When a defendant in a criminal case files a notice of appeal under this Rule 4(c), the 30-day period for the government to file its notice of appeal runs from the entry of the judgment or order appealed from or from the district court's docketing of the defendant's notice of appeal, whichever is later.

(d) Mistaken Filing in the Court of Appeals. If a notice of appeal in either a civil or a criminal case is mistakenly filed in the court of appeals, the clerk of that court must note on the notice the date when it was received and send it to the district clerk. The notice is then considered filed in the district court on the date so noted.

(As amended Apr. 30, 1979, eff. Aug. 1, 1979; Pub. L. 100–690, title VII, §7111, Nov. 18, 1988, 102 Stat. 4419; Apr. 30, 1991, eff. Dec. 1, 1991; Apr. 22, 1993, eff. Dec. 1, 1993; Apr. 27, 1995, eff. Dec. 1, 1995; Apr. 24, 1998, eff. Dec. 1, 1998; Apr. 29, 2002, eff. Dec. 1, 2002; Apr. 25, 2005, eff. Dec. 1, 2005; Mar. 26, 2009, eff. Dec. 1, 2009; Apr. 28, 2010, eff. Dec. 1, 2010; Apr. 26, 2011, eff. Dec. 1, 2011; Apr. 28, 2016, eff. Dec. 1, 2016; Apr. 27, 2017, eff. Dec. 1, 2017.)

NOTES OF ADVISORY COMMITTEE ON RULES——1967

Subdivision (a). This subdivision is derived from FRCP 73(a) without any change of substance. The requirement that a request for an extension of time for filing the notice of appeal made after expiration of the time be made by motion and on notice codifies the result reached under the present provisions of FRCP 73(a) and 6(b). North Umberland Mining Co. v. Standard Accident Ins. Co., 193 F.2d 951 (9th Cir., 1952); Cohen v. Plateau Natural Gas Co., 303 F.2d 273 (10th Cir., 1962); Plant Economy, Inc. v. Mirror Insulation Co., 308 F.2d 275 (3d Cir., 1962).

Since this subdivision governs appeals in all civil cases, it supersedes the provisions of section 25 of the Bankruptcy Act (11 U.S.C. §48). Except in cases to which the United States or an officer or agency thereof is a party, the change is a minor one, since a successful litigant in a bankruptcy proceeding may, under section 25, oblige an aggrieved party to appeal within 30 days after entry of judgment—the time fixed by this subdivision in cases involving private parties only—by serving him with notice of entry on the day thereof, and by the terms of section 25 an aggrieved party must in any event appeal within 40 days after entry of judgment. No reason appears why the time for appeal in bankruptcy should not be the same as that in civil cases generally. Furthermore, section 25 is a potential trap for the uninitiated. The time for appeal which it provides is not applicable to all appeals which may fairly be termed appeals in bankruptcy. Section 25 governs only those cases referred to in section 24 as "proceedings in bankruptcy" and "controversies arising in proceedings in bankruptcy." Lowenstein v. Reikes, 54 F.2d 481 (2d Cir., 1931), cert. den., 285 U.S. 539, 52 S.Ct. 311, 76 L.Ed. 932 (1932). The distinction between such cases and other cases which arise out of bankruptcy is often difficult to determine. See 2 Moore's Collier on Bankruptcy 24.12 through 24.36 (1962). As a result it is not always clear whether an appeal is governed by section 25 or by FRCP 73(a), which is applicable to such appeals in bankruptcy as are not governed by section 25.

In view of the unification of the civil and admiralty procedure accomplished by the amendments of the Federal Rules of Civil Procedure effective July 1, 1966, this subdivision governs appeals in those civil actions which involve admiralty or maritime claims and which prior to that date were known as suits in admiralty.

The only other change possibly effected by this subdivision is in the time for appeal from a decision of a district court on a petition for impeachment of an award of a board of arbitration under the Act of May 20, 1926, c. 347, §9 (44 Stat. 585), 45 U.S.C. §159. The act provides that a notice of appeal from such a decision shall be filed within 10 days of the decision. This singular provision was apparently repealed by the enactment in 1948 of 28 U.S.C. §2107, which fixed 30 days from the date of entry of judgment as the time for appeal in all actions of a civil nature except actions in admiralty or bankruptcy matters or those in which the United States is a party. But it was not expressly repealed, and its status is in doubt. See 7 Moore's Federal Practice 73.09[2] (1966). The doubt should be resolved, and no reason appears why appeals in such cases should not be taken within the time provided for civil cases generally.

Subdivision (b). This subdivision is derived from FRCrP 37(a)(2) without change of substance.

NOTES OF ADVISORY COMMITTEE ON RULES——1979 AMENDMENT

Subdivision (a)(1). The words "(including a civil action which involves an admiralty or maritime claim and a proceeding in bankruptcy or a controversy arising therein)," which appear in the present rule are struck out as unnecessary and perhaps misleading in suggesting that there may be other categories that are not either civil or criminal within the meaning of Rule 4(a) and (b).

The phrases "within 30 days of such entry" and "within 60 days of such entry" have been changed to read "after" instead of "or." The change is for clarity only, since the word "of" in the present rule appears to be used to mean "after." Since the proposed amended rule deals directly with the premature filing of a notice of appeal, it was thought useful to emphasize the fact that except as provided, the period during which a notice of appeal may be filed is the 30 days, or 60 days as the case may be, following the entry of the judgment or order appealed from. See Notes to Rule 4(a)(2) and (4), below.

Subdivision (a)(2). The proposed amendment to Rule 4(a)(2) would extend to civil cases the provisions of Rule 4(b), dealing with criminal cases, designed to avoid the loss of the right to appeal by filing the notice of appeal prematurely. Despite the absence of such a provision in Rule 4(a) the courts of appeals quite generally have held premature appeals effective. See, e. g., Matter of Grand Jury Empanelled Jan. 21, 1975, 541 F.2d 373 (3d Cir. 1976); Hodge v. Hodge, 507 F.2d 87 (3d Cir. 1976); Song Jook Suh v. Rosenberg, 437 F.2d 1098 (9th Cir. 1971); Ruby v. Secretary of the Navy, 365 F.2d 385 (9th Cir. 1966); Firchau v. Diamond Nat'l Corp., 345 F.2d 469 (9th Cir. 1965).

The proposed amended rule would recognize this practice but make an exception in cases in which a post trial motion has destroyed the finality of the judgment. See Note to Rule 4(a)(4) below.

Subdivision (a)(4). The proposed amendment would make it clear that after the filing of the specified post trial motions, a notice of appeal should await disposition of the motion. Since the proposed amendments to Rules 3, 10, and 12 contemplate that immediately upon the filing of the notice of appeal the fees will be paid and the case docketed in the court of appeals, and the steps toward its disposition set in motion, it would be undesirable to proceed with the appeal while the district court has before it a motion the granting of which would vacate or alter the judgment appealed from. See, e. g., Kieth v. Newcourt, 530 F.2d 826 (8th Cir. 1976). Under the present rule, since docketing may not take place until the record is transmitted, premature filing is much less likely to involve waste effort. See, e. g., Stokes v. Peyton's Inc., 508 F.2d 1287 (5th Cir. 1975). Further, since a notice of appeal filed before the disposition of a post trial motion, even if it were treated as valid for purposes of jurisdiction, would not embrace objections to the denial of the motion, it is obviously preferable to postpone the notice of appeal until after the motion is disposed of.

The present rule, since it provides for the "termination" of the "running" of the appeal time, is ambiguous in its application to a notice of appeal filed prior to a post trial motion filed within the 10 day limit. The amendment would make it clear that in such circumstances the appellant should not proceed with the appeal during pendency of the motion but should file a new notice of appeal after the motion is disposed of.

Subdivision (a)(5). Under the present rule it is provided that upon a showing of excusable neglect the district court at any time may extend the time for the filing of a notice of appeal for a period not to exceed 30 days from the expiration of the time otherwise prescribed by the rule, but that if the application is made after the original time has run, the order may be made only on motion with such notice as the court deems appropriate.

A literal reading of this provision would require that the extension be ordered and the notice of appeal filed within the 30 day period, but despite the surface clarity of the rule, it has produced considerable confusion. See the discussion by Judge Friendly in In re Orbitek, 520 F.2d 358 (2d Cir. 1975). The proposed amendment would make it clear that a motion to extend the time must be filed no later than 30 days after the expiration of the original appeal time, and that if the motion is timely filed the district court may act upon the motion at a later date, and may extend the time not in excess of 10 days measured from the date on which the order granting the motion is entered.

Under the present rule there is a possible implication that prior to the time the initial appeal time has run, the district court may extend the time on the basis of an informal application. The amendment would require that the application must be made by motion, though the motion may be made ex parte. After the expiration of the initial time a motion for the extension of the time must be made in compliance with the F.R.C.P. and local rules of the district court. See Note to proposed amended Rule 1, supra. And see Rules 6(d), 7(b) of the F.R.C.P.

The proposed amended rule expands to some extent the standard for the grant of an extension of time. The present rule requires a "showing of excusable neglect." While this was an appropriate standard in cases in which the motion is made after the time for filing the notice of appeal has run, and remains so, it has never fit exactly the situation in which the appellant seeks an extension before the expiration of the initial time. In such a case "good cause," which is the standard that is applied in the granting of other extensions of time under Rule 26(b) seems to be more appropriate.

Subdivision (a)(6). The proposed amendment would call attention to the requirement of Rule 58 of the F.R.C.P. that the judgment constitute a separate document. See United States v. Indrelunas, 411 U.S. 216 (1973). When a notice of appeal is filed, the clerk should ascertain whether any judgment designated therein has been entered in compliance with Rules 58 and 79(a) and if not, so advise all parties and the district judge. While the requirement of Rule 48 is not jurisdictional (see Bankers Trust Co. v. Mallis, 431 U.S. 928 (1977)), compliance is important since the time for the filing of a notice of appeal by other parties is measured by the time at which the judgment is properly entered.

NOTES OF ADVISORY COMMITTEE ON RULES—1991 AMENDMENT

The amendment provides a limited opportunity for relief in circumstances where the notice of entry of a judgment or order, required to be mailed by the clerk of the district court pursuant to Rule 77(d) of the Federal Rules of Civil Procedure, is either not received by a party or is received so late as to impair the opportunity to file a timely notice of appeal. The amendment adds a new subdivision (6) allowing a district court to reopen for a brief period the time for appeal upon a finding that notice of entry of a judgment or order was not received from the clerk or a party within 21 days of its entry and that no party would be prejudiced. By "prejudice" the Committee means some adverse consequence other than the cost of having to oppose the appeal and encounter the risk of reversal, consequences that are present in every appeal. Prejudice might arise, for example, if the appellee had taken some action in reliance on the expiration of the normal time period for filing a notice of appeal.

Reopening may be ordered only upon a motion filed within 180 days of the entry of a judgment or order or within 7 days of receipt of notice of such entry, whichever is earlier. This provision establishes an outer time limit of 180 days for a party who fails to receive timely notice of entry of a judgment to seek additional time to appeal and enables any winning party to shorten the 180-day period by sending (and establishing proof of receipt of) its own notice of entry of a judgment, as authorized by Fed. R. Civ. P. 77(d). Winning parties are encouraged to send their own notice in order to lessen the chance that a judge will accept a claim of non-receipt in the face of evidence that notices were sent by both the clerk and the winning party. Receipt of a winning party's notice will shorten only the time for reopening the time for appeal under this subdivision, leaving the normal time periods for appeal unaffected.

If the motion is granted, the district court may reopen the time for filing a notice of appeal only for a period of 14 days from the date of entry of the order reopening the time for appeal.

NOTES OF ADVISORY COMMITTEE ON RULES—1993 AMENDMENT

Note to Paragraph (a)(1). The amendment is intended to alert readers to the fact that paragraph (a)(4) extends the time for filing an appeal when certain posttrial motions are filed. The Committee hopes that awareness of the provisions of paragraph (a)(4) will prevent the filing of a notice of appeal when a posttrial tolling motion is pending.

Note to Paragraph (a)(2). The amendment treats a notice of appeal filed after the announcement of a decision or order, but before its formal entry, as if the notice had been filed after entry. The amendment deletes the language that made paragraph (a)(2) inapplicable to a notice of appeal filed after announcement of the disposition of a posttrial motion enumerated in paragraph (a)(4) but before the entry of the order, see Acosta v. Louisiana Dep't of Health & Human Resources, 478 U.S. 251 (1986) (per curiam); Alerte v. McGinnis, 898 F.2d 69 (7th Cir. 1990). Because the amendment of paragraph (a)(4) recognizes all notices of appeal filed after announcement or entry of judgment—even those that are filed while the posttrial motions enumerated in paragraph (a)(4) are pending—the amendment of this paragraph is consistent with the amendment of paragraph (a)(4).

Note to Paragraph (a)(3). The amendment is technical in nature; no substantive change is intended.

Note to Paragraph (a)(4). The 1979 amendment of this paragraph created a trap for an unsuspecting litigant who files a notice of appeal before a posttrial motion, or while a posttrial motion is pending. The 1979 amendment requires a party to file a new notice of appeal after the motion's disposition. Unless a new notice is filed, the court of appeals lacks jurisdiction to hear the appeal. Griggs v. Provident Consumer Discount Co., 459 U.S. 56 (1982). Many litigants, especially pro se litigants, fail to file the second notice of appeal, and several courts have expressed dissatisfaction with the rule. See, e.g., Averhart v. Arrendondo, 773 F.2d 919 (7th Cir. 1985); Harcon Barge Co. v. D & G Boat Rentals, Inc., 746 F.2d 278 (5th Cir. 1984), cert. denied, 479 U.S. 930 (1986).

The amendment provides that a notice of appeal filed before the disposition of a specified posttrial motion will become effective upon disposition of the motion. A notice filed before the filing of one of the specified motions or after the filing of a motion but before disposition of the motion is, in effect, suspended until the motion is disposed of, whereupon, the previously filed notice effectively places jurisdiction in the court of appeals.

Because a notice of appeal will ripen into an effective appeal upon disposition of a posttrial motion, in some instances there will be an appeal from a judgment that has been altered substantially because the motion was granted in whole or in part. Many such appeals will be dismissed for want of prosecution when the appellant fails to meet the briefing schedule. But, the appellee may also move to strike the appeal. When responding to such a motion, the appellant would have an opportunity to state that, even though some relief sought in a posttrial motion was granted, the appellant still plans to pursue the appeal. Because the appellant's response would provide the appellee with sufficient notice of the appellant's intentions, the Committee does not believe that an additional notice of appeal is needed.

The amendment provides that a notice of appeal filed before the disposition of a posttrial tolling motion is sufficient to bring the underlying case, as well as any orders specified in the original notice, to the court of appeals. If the judgment is altered upon disposition of a posttrial motion, however, and if a party wishes to appeal from the disposition of the motion, the party must amend the notice to so indicate. When a party files an amended notice, no additional fees are required because the notice is an amendment of the original and not a new notice of appeal.

Paragraph (a)(4) is also amended to include, among motions that extend the time for filing a notice of appeal, a Rule 60 motion that is served within 10 days after entry of judgment. This eliminates the difficulty of determining whether a posttrial motion made within 10 days after entry of a judgment is a Rule 59(e) motion, which tolls the time for filing an appeal, or a Rule 60 motion, which historically has not tolled the time. The amendment comports with the practice in several circuits of treating all motions to alter or amend judgments that are made within 10 days after entry of judgment as Rule 59(e) motions for purposes of Rule 4(a)(4). See, e.g., Finch v. City of Vernon, 845 F.2d 256 (11th Cir. 1988); Rados v. Celotex Corp., 809 F.2d 170 (2d Cir. 1986); Skagerberg v. Oklahoma, 797 F.2d 881 (10th Cir. 1986). To conform to a recent Supreme Court decision, however—Budinich v. Becton Dickinson and Co., 486 U.S. 196 (1988)—the amendment excludes motions for attorney's fees from the class of motions that extend the filing time unless a district court, acting under Rule 58, enters an order extending the time for appeal. This amendment is to be read in conjunction with the amendment of Fed. R. Civ. P. 58.

Note to subdivision (b). The amendment grammatically restructures the portion of this subdivision that lists the types of motions that toll the time for filing an appeal. This restructuring is intended to make the rule easier to read. No substantive change is intended other than to add a motion for judgment of acquittal under Criminal Rule 29 to the list of tolling motions. Such a motion is the equivalent of a Fed. R. Civ. P. 50(b) motion for judgment notwithstanding the verdict, which tolls the running of time for an appeal in a civil case.

The proposed amendment also eliminates an ambiguity from the third sentence of this subdivision. Prior to this amendment, the third sentence provided that if one of the specified motions was filed, the time for filing an appeal would run from the entry of an order denying the motion. That sentence, like the parallel provision in Rule 4(a)(4), was intended to toll the running of time for appeal if one of the posttrial motions is timely filed. In a criminal case, however, the time for filing the motions runs not from entry of judgment (as it does in civil cases), but from the verdict or finding of guilt. Thus, in a criminal case, a posttrial motion may be disposed of more than 10 days before sentence is imposed, i.e. before the entry of judgment. United States v. Hashagen, 816 F.2d 899, 902 n.5 (3d Cir. 1987). To make it clear that a notice of appeal need not be filed before entry of judgment, the amendment states that an appeal may be taken within 10 days after the entry of an order disposing of the motion, or within 10 days after the entry of judgment, whichever is later. The amendment also changes the language in the third sentence providing that an appeal may be taken within 10 days after the entry of an order denying the motion; the amendment says instead that an appeal may be taken within 10 days after the entry of an order disposing of the last such motion outstanding. (Emphasis added) The change recognizes that there may be multiple posttrial motions filed and that, although one or more motions may be granted in whole or in part, a defendant may still wish to pursue an appeal.

The amendment also states that a notice of appeal filed before the disposition of any of the posttrial tolling motions becomes effective upon disposition of the motions. In most circuits this language simply restates the current practice. See United States v. Cortes, 895 F.2d 1245 (9th Cir.), cert. denied, 495 U.S. 939 (1990). Two circuits, however, have questioned that practice in light of the language of the rule, see United States v. Gargano, 826 F.2d 610 (7th Cir. 1987), and United States v. Jones, 669 F.2d 559 (8th Cir. 1982), and the Committee wishes to clarify the rule. The amendment is consistent with the proposed amendment of Rule 4(a)(4).

Subdivision (b) is further amended in light of new Fed. R. Crim. P. 35(c), which authorizes a sentencing court to correct any arithmetical, technical, or other clear errors in sentencing within 7 days after imposing the sentence. The Committee believes that a sentencing court should be able to act under Criminal Rule 35(c) even if a notice of appeal has already been filed; and that a notice of appeal should not be affected by the filing of a Rule 35(c) motion or by correction of a sentence under Rule 35(c).

Note to subdivision (c). In Houston v. Lack, 487 U.S. 266 (1988), the Supreme Court held that a pro se prisoner's notice of appeal is "filed" at the moment of delivery to prison authorities for forwarding to the district court. The amendment reflects that decision. The language of the amendment is similar to that in Supreme Court Rule 29.2.

Permitting an inmate to file a notice of appeal by depositing it in an institutional mail system requires adjustment of the rules governing the filing of cross-appeals. In a civil case, the time for filing a cross-appeal ordinarily runs from the date when the first notice of appeal is filed. If an inmate's notice of appeal is filed by depositing it in an institution's mail system, it is possible that the notice of appeal will not arrive in the district court until several days after the "filing" date and perhaps even after the time for filing a cross-appeal has expired. To avoid that problem, subdivision (c) provides that in a civil case when an institutionalized person files a notice of appeal by depositing it in the institution's mail system, the time for filing a cross-appeal runs from the district court's receipt of the notice. The amendment makes a parallel change regarding the time for the government to appeal in a criminal case.

NOTES OF ADVISORY COMMITTEE ON RULES—1995 AMENDMENT

Subdivision (a). Fed. R. Civ. P. 50, 52, and 59 were previously inconsistent with respect to whether certain postjudgment motions had to be filed or merely served no later than 10 days after entry of judgment. As a consequence Rule 4(a)(4) spoke of making or serving such motions rather than filing them. Civil Rules 50, 52, and 59, are being revised to require filing before the end of the 10-day period. As a consequence, this rule is being amended to provide that "filing" must occur within the 10 day period in order to affect the finality of the judgment and extend the period for filing a notice of appeal.

The Civil Rules require the filing of postjudgment motions "no later than 10 days after entry of judgment"—rather than "within" 10 days—to include postjudgment motions that are filed before actual entry of the judgment by the clerk. This rule is amended, therefore, to use the same terminology.

The rule is further amended to clarify the fact that a party who wants to obtain review of an alteration or amendment of a judgment must file a notice of appeal or amend a previously filed notice to indicate intent to appeal from the altered judgment.

COMMITTEE NOTES ON RULES—1998 AMENDMENT

The language and organization of the rule are amended to make the rule more easily understood. In addition to changes made to improve the understanding, the Advisory Committee has changed language to make style and terminology consistent throughout the appellate rules. These changes are intended to be stylistic only; in this rule, however, substantive changes are made in paragraphs (a)(6) and (b)(4), and in subdivision (c).

Subdivision (a), paragraph (1). Although the Advisory Committee does not intend to make any substantive changes in this paragraph, cross-references to Rules 4(a)(1)(B) and 4(c) have been added to subparagraph (a)(1)(A).

Subdivision (a), paragraph (4). Item (vi) in subparagraph (A) of Rule 4(a)(4) provides that filing a motion for relief under Fed. R. Civ. P. 60 will extend the time for filing a notice of appeal if the Rule 60 motion is filed no later than 10 days after judgment is entered. Again, the Advisory Committee does not intend to make any substantive change in this paragraph. But because Fed. R. Civ. P. 6(a) and Fed. R. App. P. 26(a) have different methods for computing time, one might be uncertain whether the 10-day period referred to in Rule 4(a)(4) is computed using Civil Rule 6(a) or Appellate Rule 26(a). Because the Rule 60 motion is filed in the district court, and because Fed. R. App. P. 1(a)(2) says that when the appellate rules provide for filing a motion in the district court, "the procedure must comply with the practice of the district court," the rule provides that the 10-day period is computed using Fed. R. Civ. P. 6(a).

Subdivision (a), paragraph (6). Paragraph (6) permits a district court to reopen the time for appeal if a party has not received notice of the entry of judgment and no party would be prejudiced by the reopening. Before reopening the time for appeal, the existing rule requires the district court to find that the moving party was entitled to notice of the entry of judgment and did not receive it "from the clerk or any party within 21 days of its entry." The Advisory Committee makes a substantive change. The finding must be that the movant did not receive notice "from the district court or any party within 21 days after entry." This change broadens the type of notice that can preclude reopening the time for appeal. The existing rule provides that only notice from a party or from the clerk bars reopening. The new language precludes reopening if the movant has received notice from "the court."

Subdivision (b). Two substantive changes are made in what will be paragraph (b)(4). The current rule permits an extension of time to file a notice of appeal if there is a "showing of excusable neglect." First, the rule is amended to permit a court to extend the time for "good cause" as well as for excusable neglect. Rule 4(a) permits extensions for both reasons in civil cases and the Advisory Committee believes that "good cause" should be sufficient in criminal cases as well. The amendment does not limit extensions for good cause to instances in which the motion for extension of time is filed before the original time has expired. The rule gives the district court discretion to grant extensions for good cause whenever the court believes it appropriate to do so provided that the extended period does not exceed 30 days after the expiration of the time otherwise prescribed by Rule 4(b). Second, paragraph (b)(4) is amended to require only a "finding" of excusable neglect or good cause and not a "showing" of them. Because the rule authorizes the court to provide an extension without a motion, a "showing" is obviously not required; a "finding" is sufficient.

Subdivision (c). Substantive amendments are made in this subdivision. The current rule provides that if an inmate confined in an institution files a notice of appeal by depositing it in the institution's internal mail system, the notice is timely filed if deposited on or before the last day for filing. Some institutions have special internal mail systems for handling legal mail; such systems often record the date of deposit of mail by an inmate, the date of delivery of mail to an inmate, etc. The Advisory Committee amends the rule to require an inmate to use the system designed for legal mail, if there is one, in order to receive the benefit of this subdivision.

When an inmate uses the filing method authorized by subdivision (c), the current rule provides that the time for other parties to appeal begins to run from the date the district court "receives" the inmate's notice of appeal. The rule is amended so that the time for other parties begins to run when the district court "dockets" the inmate's appeal. A court may "receive" a paper when its mail is delivered to it even if the mail is not processed for a day or two, making the date of receipt uncertain. "Docketing" is an easily identified event. The change eliminates uncertainty. Paragraph (c)(3) is further amended to make it clear that the time for the government to file its appeal runs from the later of the entry of the judgment or order appealed from or the district court's docketing of a defendant's notice filed under this paragraph (c).

COMMITTEE NOTES ON RULES—2002 AMENDMENT

Subdivision (a)(1)(C). The federal courts of appeals have reached conflicting conclusions about whether an appeal from an order granting or denying an application for a writ of error coram nobis is governed by the time limitations of Rule 4(a) (which apply in civil cases) or by the time limitations of Rule 4(b) (which apply in criminal cases). Compare United States v. Craig, 907 F.2d 653, 655–57, amended 919 F.2d 57 (7th Cir. 1990); United States v. Cooper, 876 F.2d 1192, 1193–94 (5th Cir. 1989); and United States v. Keogh, 391 F.2d 138, 140 (2d Cir. 1968) (applying the time limitations of Rule 4(a)); with Yasui v. United States, 772 F.2d 1496, 1498–99 (9th Cir. 1985); and United States v. Mills, 430 F.2d 526, 527–28 (8th Cir. 1970) (applying the time limitations of Rule 4(b)). A new part (C) has been added to Rule 4(a)(1) to resolve this conflict by providing that the time limitations of Rule 4(a) will apply.

Subsequent to the enactment of Fed. R. Civ. P. 60(b) and 28 U.S.C. §2255, the Supreme Court has recognized the continued availability of a writ of error coram nobis in at least one narrow circumstance. In 1954, the Court permitted a litigant who had been convicted of a crime, served his full sentence, and been released from prison, but who was continuing to suffer a legal disability on account of the conviction, to seek a writ of error coram nobis to set aside the conviction. United States v. Morgan, 346 U.S. 502 (1954). As the Court recognized, in the Morgan situation an application for a writ of error coram nobis "is of the same general character as [a motion] under 28 U.S.C. §2255." Id. at 506 n.4. Thus, it seems appropriate that the time limitations of Rule 4(a), which apply when a district court grants or denies relief under 28 U.S.C. §2255, should also apply when a district court grants or denies a writ of error coram nobis. In addition, the strong public interest in the speedy resolution of criminal appeals that is reflected in the shortened deadlines of Rule 4(b) is not present in the Morgan situation, as the party seeking the writ of error coram nobis has already served his or her full sentence.

Notwithstanding Morgan, it is not clear whether the Supreme Court continues to believe that the writ of error coram nobis is available in federal court. In civil cases, the writ has been expressly abolished by Fed. R. Civ. P. 60(b). In criminal cases, the Supreme Court has recently stated that it has become " 'difficult to conceive of a situation' " in which the writ " 'would be necessary or appropriate.' " Carlisle v. United States, 517 U.S. 416, 429 (1996) (quoting United States v. Smith, 331 U.S. 469, 475 n.4 (1947)). The amendment to Rule 4(a)(1) is not intended to express any view on this issue; rather, it is merely meant to specify time limitations for appeals.

Rule 4(a)(1)(C) applies only to motions that are in substance, and not merely in form, applications for writs of error coram nobis. Litigants may bring and label as applications for a writ of error coram nobis what are in reality motions for a new trial under Fed. R. Crim. P. 33 or motions for correction or reduction of a sentence under Fed. R. Crim. P. 35. In such cases, the time limitations of Rule 4(b), and not those of Rule 4(a), should be enforced.

Changes Made After Publication and Comments. No changes were made to the text of the proposed amendment or to the Committee Note.

Subdivision (a)(4)(A)(vi). Rule 4(a)(4)(A)(vi) has been amended to remove a parenthetical that directed that the 10-day deadline be "computed using Federal Rule of Civil Procedure 6(a)." That parenthetical has become superfluous because Rule 26(a)(2) has been amended to require that all deadlines under 11 days be calculated as they are under Fed. R. Civ. P. 6(a).

Changes Made After Publication and Comments. No changes were made to the text of the proposed amendment or to the Committee Note.

Subdivision (a)(5)(A)(ii). Rule 4(a)(5)(A) permits the district court to extend the time to file a notice of appeal if two conditions are met. First, the party seeking the extension must file its motion no later than 30 days after the expiration of the time originally prescribed by Rule 4(a). Second, the party seeking the extension must show either excusable neglect or good cause. The text of Rule 4(a)(5)(A) does not distinguish between motions filed prior to the expiration of the original deadline and those filed after the expiration of the original deadline. Regardless of whether the motion is filed before or during the 30 days after the original deadline expires, the district court may grant an extension if a party shows either excusable neglect or good cause.

Despite the text of Rule 4(a)(5)(A), most of the courts of appeals have held that the good cause standard applies only to motions brought prior to the expiration of the original deadline and that the excusable neglect standard applies only to motions brought during the 30 days following the expiration of the original deadline. See Pontarelli v. Stone, 930 F.2d 104, 109–10 (1st Cir. 1991) (collecting cases from the Second, Fifth, Sixth, Seventh, Eighth, Ninth, and Eleventh Circuits). These courts have relied heavily upon the Advisory Committee Note to the 1979 amendment to Rule 4(a)(5). But the Advisory Committee Note refers to a draft of the 1979 amendment that was ultimately rejected. The rejected draft directed that the good cause standard apply only to motions filed prior to the expiration of the original deadline. Rule 4(a)(5), as actually amended, did not. See 16A Charles Alan Wright, et al., Federal Practice and Procedure §3950.3, at 148–49 (2d ed. 1996).

The failure of the courts of appeals to apply Rule 4(a)(5)(A) as written has also created tension between that rule and Rule 4(b)(4). As amended in 1998, Rule 4(b)(4) permits the district court to extend the time for filing a notice of appeal in a criminal case for an additional 30 days upon a finding of excusable neglect or good cause. Both Rule 4(b)(4) and the Advisory Committee Note to the 1998 amendment make it clear that an extension can be granted for either excusable neglect or good cause, regardless of whether a motion for an extension is filed before or during the 30 days following the expiration of the original deadline.

Rule 4(a)(5)(A)(ii) has been amended to correct this misunderstanding and to bring the rule in harmony in this respect with Rule 4(b)(4). A motion for an extension filed prior to the expiration of the original deadline may be granted if the movant shows either excusable neglect or good cause. Likewise, a motion for an extension filed during the 30 days following the expiration of the original deadline may be granted if the movant shows either excusable neglect or good cause.

The good cause and excusable neglect standards have "different domains." Lorenzen v. Employees Retirement Plan, 896 F.2d 228, 232 (7th Cir. 1990). They are not interchangeable, and one is not inclusive of the other. The excusable neglect standard applies in situations in which there is fault; in such situations, the need for an extension is usually occasioned by something within the control of the movant. The good cause standard applies in situations in which there is no fault—excusable or otherwise. In such situations, the need for an extension is usually occasioned by something that is not within the control of the movant.

Thus, the good cause standard can apply to motions brought during the 30 days following the expiration of the original deadline. If, for example, the Postal Service fails to deliver a notice of appeal, a movant might have good cause to seek a post-expiration extension. It may be unfair to make such a movant prove that its "neglect" was excusable, given that the movant may not have been neglectful at all. Similarly, the excusable neglect standard can apply to motions brought prior to the expiration of the original deadline. For example, a movant may bring a pre-expiration motion for an extension of time when an error committed by the movant makes it unlikely that the movant will be able to meet the original deadline.

Changes Made After Publication and Comments. No changes were made to the text of the proposed amendment. The stylistic changes to the Committee Note suggested by Judge Newman were adopted. In addition, two paragraphs were added at the end of the Committee Note to clarify the difference between the good cause and excusable neglect standards.

Subdivision (a)(7). Several circuit splits have arisen out of uncertainties about how Rule 4(a)(7)'s definition of when a judgment or order is "entered" interacts with the requirement in Fed. R. Civ. P. 58 that, to be "effective," a judgment must be set forth on a separate document. Rule 4(a)(7) and Fed. R. Civ. P. 58 have been amended to resolve those splits.

1. The first circuit split addressed by the amendments to Rule 4(a)(7) and Fed. R. Civ. P. 58 concerns the extent to which orders that dispose of post-judgment motions must be set forth on separate documents. Under Rule 4(a)(4)(A), the filing of certain post-judgment motions tolls the time to appeal the underlying judgment until the "entry" of the order disposing of the last such remaining motion. Courts have disagreed about whether such an order must be set forth on a separate document before it is treated as "entered." This disagreement reflects a broader dispute among courts about whether Rule 4(a)(7) independently imposes a separate document requirement (a requirement that is distinct from the separate document requirement that is imposed by the Federal Rules of Civil Procedure ("FRCP")) or whether Rule 4(a)(7) instead incorporates the separate document requirement as it exists in the FRCP. Further complicating the matter, courts in the former "camp" disagree among themselves about the scope of the separate document requirement that they interpret Rule 4(a)(7) as imposing, and courts in the latter "camp" disagree among themselves about the scope of the separate document requirement imposed by the FRCP.

Rule 4(a)(7) has been amended to make clear that it simply incorporates the separate document requirement as it exists in Fed. R. Civ. P. 58. If Fed. R. Civ. P. 58 does not require that a judgment or order be set forth on a separate document, then neither does Rule 4(a)(7); the judgment or order will be deemed entered for purposes of Rule 4(a) when it is entered in the civil docket. If Fed. R. Civ. P. 58 requires that a judgment or order be set forth on a separate document, then so does Rule 4(a)(7); the judgment or order will not be deemed entered for purposes of Rule 4(a) until it is so set forth and entered in the civil docket (with one important exception, described below).

In conjunction with the amendment to Rule 4(a)(7), Fed. R. Civ. P. 58 has been amended to provide that orders disposing of the post-judgment motions listed in new Fed. R. Civ. P. 58(a)(1) (which post-judgment motions include, but are not limited to, the post-judgment motions that can toll the time to appeal under Rule 4(a)(4)(A)) do not have to be set forth on separate documents. See Fed. R. Civ. P. 58(a)(1). Thus, such orders are entered for purposes of Rule 4(a) when they are entered in the civil docket pursuant to Fed. R. Civ. P. 79(a). See Rule 4(a)(7)(A)(1).

2. The second circuit split addressed by the amendments to Rule 4(a)(7) and Fed. R. Civ. P. 58 concerns the following question: When a judgment or order is required to be set forth on a separate document under Fed. R. Civ. P. 58 but is not, does the time to appeal the judgment or order—or the time to bring post-judgment motions, such as a motion for a new trial under Fed. R. Civ. P. 59—ever begin to run? According to every circuit except the First Circuit, the answer is "no." The First Circuit alone holds that parties will be deemed to have waived their right to have a judgment or order entered on a separate document three months after the judgment or order is entered in the civil docket. See Fiore v. Washington County Community Mental Health Ctr., 960 F.2d 229, 236 (1st Cir. 1992) (en banc). Other circuits have rejected this cap as contrary to the relevant rules. See, e.g., United States v. Haynes, 158 F.3d 1327, 1331 (D.C. Cir. 1998); Hammack v. Baroid Corp., 142 F.3d 266, 269–70 (5th Cir. 1998); Rubin v. Schottenstein, Zox & Dunn, 110 F.3d 1247, 1253 n.4 (6th Cir. 1997), vacated on other grounds, 143 F.3d 263 (6th Cir. 1998) (en banc). However, no court has questioned the wisdom of imposing such a cap as a matter of policy.

Both Rule 4(a)(7)(A) and Fed. R. Civ. P. 58 have been amended to impose such a cap. Under the amendments, a judgment or order is generally treated as entered when it is entered in the civil docket pursuant to Fed. R. Civ. P. 79(a). There is one exception: When Fed. R. Civ. P. 58(a)(1) requires the judgment or order to be set forth on a separate document, that judgment or order is not treated as entered until it is set forth on a separate document (in addition to being entered in the civil docket) or until the expiration of 150 days after its entry in the civil docket, whichever occurs first. This cap will ensure that parties will not be given forever to appeal (or to bring a post-judgment motion) when a court fails to set forth a judgment or order on a separate document in violation of Fed. R. Civ. P. 58(a)(1).

3. The third circuit split—this split addressed only by the amendment to Rule 4(a)(7)—concerns whether the appellant may waive the separate document requirement over the objection of the appellee. In Bankers Trust Co. v. Mallis, 435 U.S. 381, 387 (1978) (per curiam), the Supreme Court held that the "parties to an appeal may waive the separate-judgment requirement of Rule 58." Specifically, the Supreme Court held that when a district court enters an order and "clearly evidence[s] its intent that the . . . order . . . represent[s] the final decision in the case," the order is a "final decision" for purposes of 28 U.S.C. §1291, even if the order has not been set forth on a separate document for purposes of Fed. R. Civ. P. 58. Id. Thus, the parties can choose to appeal without waiting for the order to be set forth on a separate document.

Courts have disagreed about whether the consent of all parties is necessary to waive the separate document requirement. Some circuits permit appellees to object to attempted Mallis waivers and to force appellants to return to the trial court, request that judgment be set forth on a separate document, and appeal a second time. See, e.g., Selletti v. Carey, 173 F.3d 104, 109—10 (2d Cir. 1999); Williams v. Borg, 139 F.3d 737, 739—40 (9th Cir. 1998); Silver Star Enters., Inc. v. M/V Saramacca, 19 F.3d 1008, 1013 (5th Cir. 1994). Other courts disagree and permit Mallis waivers even if the appellee objects. See, e.g., Haynes, 158 F.3d at 1331; Miller v. Artistic Cleaners, 153 F.3d 781, 783—84 (7th Cir. 1998); Alvord-Polk, Inc. v. F. Schumacher & Co., 37 F.3d 996, 1006 n.8 (3d Cir. 1994).

New Rule 4(a)(7)(B) is intended both to codify the Supreme Court's holding in Mallis and to make clear that the decision whether to waive the requirement that the judgment or order be set forth on a separate document is the appellant's alone. It is, after all, the appellant who needs a clear signal as to when the time to file a notice of appeal has begun to run. If the appellant chooses to bring an appeal without waiting for the judgment or order to be set forth on a separate document, then there is no reason why the appellee should be able to object. All that would result from honoring the appellee's objection would be delay.

4. The final circuit split addressed by the amendment to Rule 4(a)(7) concerns the question whether an appellant who chooses to waive the separate document requirement must appeal within 30 days (60 days if the government is a party) from the entry in the civil docket of the judgment or order that should have been set forth on a separate document but was not. In Townsend v. Lucas, 745 F.2d 933 (5th Cir. 1984), the district court dismissed a 28 U.S.C. §2254 action on May 6, 1983, but failed to set forth the judgment on a separate document. The plaintiff appealed on January 10, 1984. The Fifth Circuit dismissed the appeal, reasoning that, if the plaintiff waived the separate document requirement, then his appeal would be from the May 6 order, and if his appeal was from the May 6 order, then it was untimely under Rule 4(a)(1). The Fifth Circuit stressed that the plaintiff could return to the district court, move that the judgment be set forth on a separate document, and appeal from that judgment within 30 days. Id. at 934. Several other cases have embraced the Townsend approach. See, e.g., Armstrong v. Ahitow, 36 F.3d 574, 575 (7th Cir. 1994) (per curiam); Hughes v. Halifax County Sch. Bd., 823 F.2d 832, 835—36 (4th Cir. 1987); Harris v. McCarthy, 790 F.2d 753, 756 n.1 (9th Cir. 1986).

Those cases are in the distinct minority. There are numerous cases in which courts have heard appeals that were not filed within 30 days (60 days if the government was a party) from the judgment or order that should have been set forth on a separate document but was not. See, e.g., Haynes, 158 F.3d at 1330—31; Clough v. Rush, 959 F.2d 182, 186 (10th Cir. 1992); McCalden v. California Library Ass'n, 955 F.2d 1214, 1218—19 (9th Cir. 1990). In the view of these courts, the remand in Townsend was "precisely the purposeless spinning of wheels abjured by the Court in the [Mallis] case." 15B Charles Alan Wright et al., Federal Practice and Procedure §3915, at 259 n.8 (3d ed. 1992).

The Committee agrees with the majority of courts that have rejected the Townsend approach. In drafting new Rule 4(a)(7)(B), the Committee has been careful to avoid phrases such as "otherwise timely appeal" that might imply an endorsement of Townsend.

Changes Made After Publication and Comments. No changes were made to the text of proposed Rule 4(a)(7)(B) or to the third or fourth numbered sections of the Committee Note, except that, in several places, references to a judgment being "entered" on a separate document were changed to references to a judgment being "set forth" on a separate document. This was to maintain stylistic consistency. The appellate rules and the civil rules consistently refer to "entering" judgments on the civil docket and to "setting forth" judgments on separate documents.

Two major changes were made to the text of proposed Rule 4(a)(7)(A)—one substantive and one stylistic. The substantive change was to increase the "cap" from 60 days to 150 days. The Appellate Rules Committee and the Civil Rules Committee had to balance two concerns that are implicated whenever a court fails to enter its final decision on a separate document. On the one hand, potential appellants need a clear signal that the time to appeal has begun to run, so that they do not unknowingly forfeit their rights. On the other hand, the time to appeal cannot be allowed to run forever. A party who receives no notice whatsoever of a judgment has only 180 days to move to reopen the time to appeal from that judgment. See Rule 4(a)(6)(A). It hardly seems fair to give a party who does receive notice of a judgment an unlimited amount of time to appeal, merely because that judgment was not set forth on a separate piece of paper. Potential appellees and the judicial system need some limit on the time within which appeals can be brought.

The 150-day cap properly balances these two concerns. When an order is not set forth on a separate document, what signals litigants that the order is final and appealable is a lack of further activity from the court. A 60-day period of inactivity is not sufficiently rare to signal to litigants that the court has entered its last order. By contrast, 150 days of inactivity is much less common and thus more clearly signals to litigants that the court is done with their case.

The major stylistic change to Rule 4(a)(7) requires some explanation. In the published draft, proposed Rule 4(a)(7)(A) provided that "[a] judgment or order is entered for purposes of this Rule 4(a) when it is entered for purposes of Rule 58(b) of the Federal Rules of Civil Procedure." In other words, Rule 4(a)(7)(A) told readers to look to FRCP 58(b) to ascertain when a judgment is entered for purposes of starting the running of time to appeal. Sending appellate lawyers to the civil rules to discover when time began to run for purposes of the appellate rules was itself somewhat awkward, but it was made more confusing by the fact that, when readers went to proposed FRCP 58(b), they found this introductory clause: "Judgment is entered for purposes of Rules 50, 52, 54(d)(2)(B), 59, 60, and 62 when . . ."

This introductory clause was confusing for both appellate lawyers and trial lawyers. It was confusing for appellate lawyers because Rule 4(a)(7) informed them that FRCP 58(b) would tell them when the time begins to run for purposes of the appellate rules, but when they got to FRCP 58(b) they found a rule that, by its terms, dictated only when the time begins to run for purposes of certain civil rules. The introductory clause was confusing for trial lawyers because FRCP 58(b) described when judgment is entered for some purposes under the civil rules, but then was completely silent about when judgment is entered for other purposes.

To avoid this confusion, the Civil Rules Committee, on the recommendation of the Appellate Rules Committee, changed the introductory clause in FRCP 58(b) to read simply: "Judgment is entered for purposes of these Rules when . . . ." In addition, Rule 4(a)(7)(A) was redrafted [A redraft of Rule 4(a)(7) was faxed to members of the Appellate Rules Committee two weeks after our meeting in New Orleans. The Committee consented to the redraft without objection.] so that the triggering events for the running of the time to appeal (entry in the civil docket, and being set forth on a separate document or passage of 150 days) were incorporated directly into Rule 4(a)(7), rather than indirectly through a reference to FRCP 58(b). This eliminates the need for appellate lawyers to examine Rule 58(b) and any chance that Rule 58(b)'s introductory clause (even as modified) might confuse them.

We do not believe that republication of Rule 4(a)(7) or FRCP 58 is necessary. In substance, rewritten Rule 4(a)(7)(A) and FRCP 58(b) operate identically to the published versions, except that the 60-day cap has been replaced with a 150-day cap—a change that was suggested by some of the commentators and that makes the cap more forgiving.

Subdivision (b)(5). Federal Rule of Criminal Procedure 35(a) permits a district court, acting within 7 days after the imposition of sentence, to correct an erroneous sentence in a criminal case. Some courts have held that the filing of a motion for correction of a sentence suspends the time for filing a notice of appeal from the judgment of conviction. See, e.g., United States v. Carmouche, 138 F.3d 1014, 1016 (5th Cir. 1998) (per curiam); United States v. Morillo, 8 F.3d 864, 869 (1st Cir. 1993). Those courts establish conflicting timetables for appealing a judgment of conviction after the filing of a motion to correct a sentence. In the First Circuit, the time to appeal is suspended only for the period provided by Fed. R. Crim. P. 35(a) for the district court to correct a sentence; the time to appeal begins to run again once 7 days have passed after sentencing, even if the motion is still pending. By contrast, in the Fifth Circuit, the time to appeal does not begin to run again until the district court actually issues an order disposing of the motion.

Rule 4(b)(5) has been amended to eliminate the inconsistency concerning the effect of a motion to correct a sentence on the time for filing a notice of appeal. The amended rule makes clear that the time to appeal continues to run, even if a motion to correct a sentence is filed. The amendment is consistent with Rule 4(b)(3)(A), which lists the motions that toll the time to appeal, and notably omits any mention of a Fed. R. Crim. P. 35(a) motion. The amendment also should promote certainty and minimize the likelihood of confusion concerning the time to appeal a judgment of conviction.

If a district court corrects a sentence pursuant to Fed. R. Crim. P. 35(a), the time for filing a notice of appeal of the corrected sentence under Rule 4(b)(1) would begin to run when the court enters a new judgment reflecting the corrected sentence.

Changes Made After Publication and Comments. The reference to Federal Rule of Criminal Procedure 35(c) was changed to Rule 35(a) to reflect the pending amendment of Rule 35. The proposed amendment to Criminal Rule 35, if approved, will take effect at the same time that the proposed amendment to Appellate Rule 4 will take effect, if approved.

Committee Notes on Rules—2005 Amendment

Rule 4(a)(6) has permitted a district court to reopen the time to appeal a judgment or order upon finding that four conditions were satisfied. First, the district court had to find that the appellant did not receive notice of the entry of the judgment or order from the district court or any party within 21 days after the judgment or order was entered. Second, the district court had to find that the appellant moved to reopen the time to appeal within 7 days after the appellant received notice of the entry of the judgment or order. Third, the district court had to find that the appellant moved to reopen the time to appeal within 180 days after the judgment or order was entered. Finally, the district court had to find that no party would be prejudiced by the reopening of the time to appeal.

Rule 4(a)(6) has been amended to specify more clearly what type of "notice" of the entry of a judgment or order precludes a party from later moving to reopen the time to appeal. In addition, Rule 4(a)(6) has been amended to address confusion about what type of "notice" triggers the 7-day period to bring a motion to reopen. Finally, Rule 4(a)(6) has been reorganized to set forth more logically the conditions that must be met before a district court may reopen the time to appeal.

Subdivision (a)(6)(A). Former subdivision (a)(6)(B) has been redesignated as subdivision (a)(6)(A), and one substantive change has been made. As amended, the subdivision will preclude a party from moving to reopen the time to appeal a judgment or order only if the party receives (within 21 days) formal notice of the entry of that judgment or order under Civil Rule 77(d). No other type of notice will preclude a party.

The reasons for this change take some explanation. Prior to 1998, former subdivision (a)(6)(B) permitted a district court to reopen the time to appeal if it found "that a party entitled to notice of the entry of a judgment or order did not receive such notice from the clerk or any party within 21 days of its entry." The rule was clear that the "notice" to which it referred was the notice required under Civil Rule 77(d), which must be served by the clerk pursuant to Civil Rule 5(b) and may also be served by a party pursuant to that same rule. In other words, prior to 1998, former subdivision (a)(6)(B) was clear that, if a party did not receive formal notice of the entry of a judgment or order under Civil Rule 77(d), that party could later move to reopen the time to appeal (assuming that the other requirements of subdivision (a)(6) were met).

In 1998, former subdivision (a)(6)(B) was amended to change the description of the type of notice that would preclude a party from moving to reopen. As a result of the amendment, former subdivision (a)(6)(B) no longer referred to the failure of the moving party to receive "such notice"—that is, the notice required by Civil Rule 77(d)—but instead referred to the failure of the moving party to receive "the notice." And former subdivision (a)(6)(B) no longer referred to the failure of the moving party to receive notice from "the clerk or any party," both of whom are explicitly mentioned in Civil Rule 77(d). Rather, former subdivision (a)(6)(B) referred to the failure of the moving party to receive notice from "the district court or any party."

The 1998 amendment meant, then, that the type of notice that precluded a party from moving to reopen the time to appeal was no longer limited to Civil Rule 77(d) notice. Under the 1998 amendment, some type of notice, in addition to Civil Rule 77(d) notice, precluded a party. But the text of the amended rule did not make clear what type of notice qualified. This was an invitation for litigation, confusion, and possible circuit splits.

To avoid such problems, former subdivision (a)(6)(B)—new subdivision (a)(6)(A)—has been amended to restore its pre-1998 simplicity. Under new subdivision (a)(6)(A), if the court finds that the moving party was not notified under Civil Rule 77(d) of the entry of the judgment or order that the party seeks to appeal within 21 days after that judgment or order was entered, then the court is authorized to reopen the time to appeal (if all of the other requirements of subdivision (a)(6) are met). Because Civil Rule 77(d) requires that notice of the entry of a Judgment or order be formally served under Civil Rule 5(b), any notice that is not so served will not operate to preclude the reopening of the time to appeal under new subdivision (a)(6)(A).

Subdivision (a)(6)(B). Former subdivision (a)(6)(A) required a party to move to reopen the time to appeal "within 7 days after the moving party receives notice of the entry [of the judgment or order sought to be appealed]." Former subdivision (a)(6)(A) has been redesignated as subdivision (a)(6)(B), and one important substantive change has been made: The subdivision now makes clear that only formal notice of the entry of a judgment or order under Civil Rule 77(d) will trigger the 7-day period to move to reopen the time to appeal.

The circuits have been split over what type of "notice" is sufficient to trigger the 7-day period. The majority of circuits that addressed the question held that only written notice was sufficient, although nothing in the text of the rule suggested such a limitation. See, e.g., Bass v. United States Dep't of Agric., 211 F.3d 959, 963 (5th Cir. 2000). By contrast, the Ninth Circuit held that while former subdivision (a)(6)(A) did not require written notice, "the quality of the communication [had to] rise to the functional equivalent of written notice." Nguyen v. Southwest Leasing & Rental, Inc., 282 F.3d 1061, 1066 (9th Cir. 2002). Other circuits suggested in dicta that former subdivision (a)(6)(A) required only "actual notice," which, presumably, could have included oral notice that was not "the functional equivalent of written notice." See, e.g., Lowry v. McDonnell Douglas Corp., 211 F.3d 457, 464 (8th Cir. 2000). And still other circuits read into former subdivision (a)(6)(A) restrictions that appeared only in former subdivision (a)(6)(B) (such as the requirement that notice be received "from the district court or any party," see Benavides v. Bureau of Prisons, 79 F.3d 1211, 1214 (D.C. Cir. 1996)) or that appeared in neither former subdivision (a)(6)(A) nor former subdivision (a)(6)(B) (such as the requirement that notice be served in the manner prescribed by Civil Rule 5, see Ryan v. First Unum Life Ins. Co., 174 F.3d 302, 304–05 (2d Cir. 1999)).

Former subdivision (a)(6)(A)—new subdivision (a)(6)(B)—has been amended to resolve this circuit split by providing that only formal notice of the entry of a judgment or order under Civil Rule 77(d) will trigger the 7-day period. Using Civil Rule 77(d) notice as the trigger has two advantages: First, because Civil Rule 77(d) is clear and familiar, circuit splits are unlikely to develop over its meaning. Second, because Civil Rule 77(d) notice must be served under Civil Rule 5(b), establishing whether and when such notice was provided should generally not be difficult.

Using Civil Rule 77(d) notice to trigger the 7-day period will not unduly delay appellate proceedings. Rule 4(a)(6) applies to only a small number of cases— cases in which a party was not notified of a judgment or order by either the clerk or another party within 21 days after entry. Even with respect to those cases, an appeal cannot be brought more than 180 days after entry, no matter what the circumstances. In addition, Civil Rule 77(d) permits parties to serve notice of the entry of a judgment or order. The winning party can prevent Rule 4(a)(6) from even coming into play simply by serving notice of entry within 21 days. Failing that, the winning party can always trigger the 7-day deadline to move to reopen by serving belated notice.

Changes Made After Publication and Comments. No change was made to the text of subdivision (A)—regarding the type of notice that precludes a party from later moving to reopen the time to appeal—and only minor stylistic changes were made to the Committee Note to subdivision (A).

A substantial change was made to subdivision (B)—regarding the type of notice that triggers the 7-day deadline for moving to reopen the time to appeal. Under the published version of subdivision (B), the 7-day deadline would have been triggered when "the moving party receives or observes written notice of the entry from any source." The Committee was attempting to implement an "eyes/ears" distinction: The 7-day period was triggered when a party learned of the entry of a judgment or order by reading about it (whether on a piece of paper or a computer screen), but was not triggered when a party merely heard about it.

Above all else, subdivision (B) should be clear and easy to apply; it should neither risk opening another circuit split over its meaning nor create the need for a lot of factfinding by district courts. After considering the public comments—and, in particular, the comments of two committees of the California bar—the Committee decided that subdivision (B) could do better on both counts. The published standard—"receives or observes written notice of the entry from any source"—was awkward and, despite the guidance of the Committee Note, was likely to give courts problems. Even if the standard had proved to be sufficiently clear, district courts would still have been left to make factual findings about whether a particular attorney or party "received" or "observed" notice that was written or electronic.

The Committee concluded that the solution suggested by the California bar—using Civil Rule 77(d) notice to trigger the 7-day period—made a lot of sense. The standard is clear; no one doubts what it means to be served with notice of the entry of judgment under Civil Rule 77(d). The standard is also unlikely to give rise to many factual disputes. Civil Rule 77(d) notice must be formally served under Civil Rule 5(b), so establishing the presence or absence of such notice should be relatively easy. And, for the reasons described in the Committee Note, using Civil Rule 77(d) as the trigger will not unduly delay appellate proceedings.

For these reasons, the Committee amended subdivision (B) so that the 7-day deadline will be triggered only by notice of the entry of a judgment or order that is served under Civil Rule 77(d). (Corresponding changes were made to the Committee Note.) The Committee does not believe that the amendment needs to be published again for comment, as the issue of what type of notice should trigger the 7-day deadline has already been addressed by commentators, the revised version of subdivision (B) is far more forgiving than the published version, and it is highly unlikely that the revised version will be found ambiguous in any respect.

COMMITTEE NOTES ON RULES—2009 AMENDMENT

Subdivision (a)(4)(B)(ii). Subdivision (a)(4)(B)(ii) is amended to address problems that stemmed from the adoption—during the 1998 restyling project— of language referring to "a judgment altered or amended upon" a post-trial motion.

Prior to the restyling, subdivision (a)(4) instructed that "[a]ppellate review of an order disposing of any of [the post-trial motions listed in subdivision (a)(4)] requires the party, in compliance with Appellate Rule 3(c), to amend a previously filed notice of appeal. A party intending to challenge an alteration or amendment of the judgment shall file a notice, or amended notice, of appeal within the time prescribed by this Rule 4 measured from the entry of the order disposing of the last such motion outstanding." After the restyling, subdivision (a)(4)(B)(ii) provided: "A party intending to challenge an order disposing of any motion listed in Rule 4(a)(4)(A), or a judgment altered or amended upon such a motion, must file a notice of appeal, or an amended notice of appeal—in compliance with Rule 3(c)—within the time prescribed by this Rule measured from the entry of the order disposing of the last such remaining motion."

One court has explained that the 1998 amendment introduced ambiguity into the Rule: "The new formulation could be read to expand the obligation to file an amended notice to circumstances where the ruling on the post-trial motion alters the prior judgment in an insignificant manner or in a manner favorable to the appellant, even though the appeal is not directed against the alteration of the judgment." Sorensen v. City of New York, 413 F.3d 292, 296 n.2 (2d Cir. 2005). The current amendment removes that ambiguous reference to "a judgment altered or amended upon" a post-trial motion, and refers instead to "a judgment's alteration or amendment" upon such a motion. Thus, subdivision (a)(4)(B)(ii) requires a new or amended notice of appeal when an appellant wishes to challenge an order disposing of a motion listed in Rule 4(a)(4)(A) or a judgment's alteration or amendment upon such a motion.

Changes Made After Publication and Comment. No changes were made to the proposal as published. Instead, the Committee has added the commentators' suggestions to its study agenda.

Subdivision (a)(4)(A)(vi). Subdivision (a)(4) provides that certain timely post-trial motions extend the time for filing an appeal. Lawyers sometimes move under Civil Rule 60 for relief that is still available under another rule such as Civil Rule 59. Subdivision (a)(4)(A)(vi) provides for such eventualities by extending the time for filing an appeal so long as the Rule 60 motion is filed within a limited time. Formerly, the time limit under subdivision (a)(4)(A)(vi) was 10 days, reflecting the 10-day limits for making motions under Civil Rules 50(b), 52(b), and 59. Subdivision (a)(4)(A)(vi) now contains a 28-day limit to match the revisions to the time limits in the Civil Rules.

Subdivision (a)(5)(C). The time set in the former rule at 10 days has been revised to 14 days. See the Note to Rule 26.

Subdivision (a)(6)(B). The time set in the former rule at 7 days has been revised to 14 days. Under the time-computation approach set by former Rule 26(a), "7 days" always meant at least 9 days and could mean as many as 11 or even 13 days. Under current Rule 26(a), intermediate weekends and holidays are counted. Changing the period from 7 to 14 days offsets the change in computation approach. See the Note to Rule 26.

Subdivisions (b)(1)(A) and (b)(3)(A). The times set in the former rule at 10 days have been revised to 14 days. See the Note to Rule 26.

193

Committee Notes on Rules—2010 Amendment

Subdivision (a)(7). Subdivision (a)(7) is amended to reflect the renumbering of Civil Rule 58 as part of the 2007 restyling of the Civil Rules. References to Civil Rule "58(a)(1)" are revised to refer to Civil Rule "58(a)." No substantive change is intended.

The amendments are technical and conforming. In accordance with established Judicial Conference procedures they were not published for public comment.

Committee Notes on Rules—2011 Amendment

Subdivision (a)(1)(B). Rule 4(a)(1)(B) has been amended to make clear that the 60-day appeal period applies in cases in which an officer or employee of the United States is sued in an individual capacity for acts or omissions occurring in connection with duties performed on behalf of the United States. (A concurrent amendment to Rule 40(a)(1) makes clear that the 45-day period to file a petition for panel rehearing also applies in such cases.)

The amendment to Rule 4(a)(1)(B) is consistent with a 2000 amendment to Civil Rule 12(a)(3), which specified an extended 60-day period to respond to complaints when "[a] United States officer or employee [is] sued in an individual capacity for an act or omission occurring in connection with duties performed on the United States' behalf." The Committee Note to the 2000 amendment explained: "Time is needed for the United States to determine whether to provide representation to the defendant officer or employee. If the United States provides representation, the need for an extended answer period is the same as in actions against the United States, a United States agency, or a United States officer sued in an official capacity." The same reasons justify providing additional time to the Solicitor General to decide whether to file an appeal.

However, because of the greater need for clarity of application when appeal rights are at stake, the amendment to Rule 4(a)(1)(B), and the corresponding legislative amendment to 28 U.S.C. §2107 that is simultaneously proposed, include safe harbor provisions that parties can readily apply and rely upon. Under new subdivision 4(a)(1)(B)(iv), a case automatically qualifies for the 60-day appeal period if (1) a legal officer of the United States has appeared in the case, in an official capacity, as counsel for the current or former officer or employee and has not withdrawn the appearance at the time of the entry of the judgment or order appealed from or (2) a legal officer of the United States appears on the notice of appeal as counsel, in an official capacity, for the current or former officer or employee. There will be cases that do not fall within either safe harbor but that qualify for the longer appeal period. An example would be a case in which a federal employee is sued in an individual capacity for an act occurring in connection with federal duties and the United States does not represent the employee either when the judgment is entered or when the appeal is filed but the United States pays for private counsel for the employee.

Changes Made After Publication and Comment. The Committee made two changes to the proposal after publication and comment.

First, the Committee inserted the words "current or former" before "United States officer or employee." This insertion causes the text of the proposed Rule to diverge slightly from that of Civil Rules 4(i)(3) and 12(a)(3), which refer simply to "a United States officer or employee [etc.]." This divergence, though, is only stylistic. The 2000 Committee Notes to Civil Rules 4(i)(3) and 12(a)(3) make clear that those rules are intended to encompass former as well as current officers or employees. It is desirable to make this clarification in the text of Rule 4(a)(1) because that Rule's appeal time periods are jurisdictional.

Second, the Committee added, at the end of Rule 4(a)(1)(B)(iv), the following new language: "—including all instances in which the United States represents that person when the judgment or order is entered or files the appeal for that person." During the public comment period, concerns were raised that a party might rely on the longer appeal period, only to risk the appeal being held untimely by a court that later concluded that the relevant act or omission had not actually occurred in connection with federal duties. The Committee decided to respond to this concern by adding two safe harbor provisions. These provisions make clear that the longer appeal periods apply in any case where the United States either represents the officer or employee at the time of entry of the relevant judgment or files the notice of appeal on the officer or employee's behalf.

Committee Notes on Rules—2016 Amendment

Subdivision (a)(4). A clarifying amendment is made to subdivision (a)(4). Former Rule 4(a)(4) provided that "[i]f a party timely files in the district court" certain post-judgment motions, "the time to file an appeal runs for all parties from the entry of the order disposing of the last such remaining motion." Responding to a circuit split concerning the meaning of "timely" in this provision, the amendment adopts the majority approach and rejects the approach taken in National Ecological Foundation v. Alexander, 496 F.3d 466 (6th Cir. 2007). A motion made after the time allowed by the Civil Rules will not qualify as a motion that, under Rule 4(a)(4)(A), re-starts the appeal time—and that fact is not altered by, for example, a court order that sets a due date that is later than permitted by the Civil Rules, another party's consent or failure to object to the motion's lateness, or the court's disposition of the motion without explicit reliance on untimeliness.

Subdivision (c)(1). Rule 4(c)(1) is revised to streamline and clarify the operation of the inmate-filing rule.

The Rule requires the inmate to show timely deposit and prepayment of postage. The Rule is amended to specify that a notice is timely if it is accompanied by a declaration or notarized statement stating the date the notice was deposited in the institution's mail system and attesting to the prepayment of first-class postage. The declaration must state that first-class postage "is being prepaid," not (as directed by the former Rule) that first-class postage "has been prepaid." This change reflects the fact that inmates may need to rely upon the institution to affix postage after the inmate has deposited the document in the institution's mail system. New Form 7 in the Appendix of Forms sets out a suggested form of the declaration.

The amended rule also provides that a notice is timely without a declaration or notarized statement if other evidence accompanying the notice shows that the notice was deposited on or before the due date and that postage was prepaid. If the notice is not accompanied by evidence that establishes timely deposit and prepayment of postage, then the court of appeals has discretion to accept a declaration or notarized statement at a later date. The Rule uses the phrase "exercises its discretion to permit"—rather than simply "permits"—to help ensure that pro se inmate litigants are aware that a court will not necessarily forgive a failure to provide the declaration initially.

Committee Notes on Rules—2017 Amendment

Subdivision (a)(4)(B)(iii). This technical amendment restores the former subdivision (a)(4)(B)(iii) that was inadvertently deleted in 2009.

References in Text

The Federal Rules of Civil Procedure, referred to in subd. (a)(4), (6), and (7), are set out in this Appendix.

The Federal Rules of Criminal Procedure, referred to in subd. (b)(3), (5), are set out in the Appendix to Title 18, Crimes and Criminal Procedure.

Amendment by Public Law

1988—Subd. (b). Pub. L. 100–690 inserted "(i)" and "or (ii) a notice of appeal by the Government" in first sentence, and "(i)" and "or (ii) a notice of appeal by any defendant" in fifth sentence.

Rule 5. Appeal by Permission

(a) Petition for Permission to Appeal.

(1) To request permission to appeal when an appeal is within the court of appeals' discretion, a party must file a petition with the circuit clerk and serve it on all other parties to the district-court action.

(2) The petition must be filed within the time specified by the statute or rule authorizing the appeal or, if no such time is specified, within the time provided by Rule 4(a) for filing a notice of appeal.

(3) If a party cannot petition for appeal unless the district court first enters an order granting permission to do so or stating that the necessary conditions are met, the district court may amend its order, either on its own or in response to a party's motion, to include the required permission or statement. In that event, the time to petition runs from entry of the amended order.

(b) Contents of the Petition; Answer or Cross-Petition; Oral Argument.

(1) The petition must include the following:

(A) the facts necessary to understand the question presented;

(B) the question itself;

(C) the relief sought;

(D) the reasons why the appeal should be allowed and is authorized by a statute or rule; and

(E) an attached copy of:

(i) the order, decree, or judgment complained of and any related opinion or memorandum, and

(ii) any order stating the district court's permission to appeal or finding that the necessary conditions are met.

(2) A party may file an answer in opposition or a cross-petition within 10 days after the petition is served.

(3) The petition and answer will be submitted without oral argument unless the court of appeals orders otherwise.

(c) Form of Papers; Number of Copies; Length Limits. All papers must conform to Rule 32(c)(2). An original and 3 copies must be filed unless the court requires a different number by local rule or by order in a particular case. Except by the court's permission, and excluding the accompanying documents required by Rule 5(b)(1)(E):

(1) a paper produced using a computer must not exceed 5,200 words; and

(2) a handwritten or typewritten paper must not exceed 20 pages.

(d) Grant of Permission; Fees; Cost Bond; Filing the Record.

(1) Within 14 days after the entry of the order granting permission to appeal, the appellant must:

(A) pay the district clerk all required fees; and

(B) file a cost bond if required under Rule 7.

(2) A notice of appeal need not be filed. The date when the order granting permission to appeal is entered serves as the date of the notice of appeal for calculating time under these rules.

(3) The district clerk must notify the circuit clerk once the petitioner has paid the fees. Upon receiving this notice, the circuit clerk must enter the appeal on the docket. The record must be forwarded and filed in accordance with Rules 11 and 12(c).

(As amended Apr. 30, 1979, eff. Aug. 1, 1979; Apr. 29, 1994, eff. Dec. 1, 1994; Apr. 24, 1998, eff. Dec. 1, 1998; Apr. 29, 2002, eff. Dec. 1, 2002; Mar. 26, 2009, eff. Dec. 1, 2009; Apr. 28, 2016, eff. Dec. 1, 2016; Apr. 25, 2019, eff. Dec. 1, 2019.)

NOTES OF ADVISORY COMMITTEE ON RULES—1967

This rule is derived in the main from Third Circuit Rule 11(2), which is similar to the rule governing appeals under 28 U.S.C. §1292(b) in a majority of the circuits. The second sentence of subdivision (a) resolves a conflict over the question of whether the district court can amend an order by supplying the statement required by §1292(b) at any time after entry of the order, with the result that the time fixed by the statute commences to run on the date of entry of the order as amended. Compare Milbert v. Bison Laboratories, 260 F.2d 431 (3d Cir., 1958) with Sperry Rand Corporation v. Bell Telephone Laboratories, 272 F.2d (2d Cir., 1959), Hadjipateras v. Pacifica, S.A., 290 F.2d 697 (5th Cir., 1961), and Houston Fearless Corporation v. Teter, 313 F.2d 91 (10th Cir., 1962). The view taken by the Second, Fifth and Tenth Circuits seems theoretically and practically sound, and the rule adopts it. Although a majority of the circuits now require the filing of a notice of appeal following the grant of permission to appeal, filing of the notice serves no function other than to provide a time from which the time for transmitting the record and docketing the appeal begins to run.

NOTES OF ADVISORY COMMITTEE ON RULES—1979 AMENDMENT

The proposed amendment adapts to the practice in appeals from interlocutory orders under 28 U.S.C. §1292(b) the provisions of proposed Rule 3(e) above, requiring payment of all fees in the district court upon the filing of the notice of appeal. See Note to proposed amended Rule 3(e), supra.

NOTES OF ADVISORY COMMITTEE ON RULES—1994 AMENDMENT

Subdivision (c). The amendment makes it clear that a court may require a different number of copies either by rule or by order in an individual case. The number of copies of any document that a court of appeals needs varies depending upon the way in which the court conducts business. The internal operation of the courts of appeals necessarily varies from circuit to circuit because of differences in the number of judges, the geographic area included within the circuit, and other such factors. Uniformity could be achieved only by setting the number of copies artificially high so that parties in all circuits file enough copies to satisfy the needs of the court requiring the greatest number. Rather than do that, the Committee decided to make it clear that local rules may require a greater or lesser number of copies and that, if the circumstances of a particular case indicate the need for a different number of copies in that case, the court may so order.

COMMITTEE NOTES ON RULES—1998 AMENDMENT

In 1992 Congress added subsection (e) to 28 U.S.C. §1292. Subsection (e) says that the Supreme Court has power to prescribe rules that "provide for an appeal of an interlocutory decision to the courts of appeals that is not otherwise provided for" in section 1292. The amendment of Rule 5 was prompted by the possibility of new rules authorizing additional interlocutory appeals. Rather than add a separate rule governing each such appeal, the Committee believes it is preferable to amend Rule 5 so that is will govern all such appeals.

In addition the Federal Courts Improvement Act of 1996, Pub. L. 104–317, abolished appeals by permission under 28 U.S.C. §636(c)(5), making Rule 5.1 obsolete.

This new Rule 5 is intended to govern all discretionary appeals from district-court orders, judgments, or decrees. At this time that includes interlocutory appeals under 28 U.S.C. §1292(b), (c)(1), and (d)(1) & (2). If additional interlocutory appeals are authorized under §1292(e), the new Rule is intended to govern them if the appeals are discretionary.

Subdivision (a). Paragraph (a)(1) says that when granting an appeal is within a court of appeals' discretion, a party may file a petition for permission to appeal. The time for filing provision states only that the petition must be filed within the time provided in the statute or rule authorizing the appeal or, if no such time is specified, within the time provided by Rule 4(a) for filing a notice of appeal.

Section 1292(b), (c), and (d) provide that the petition must be filed within 10 days after entry of the order containing the statement prescribed in the statute. Existing Rule 5(a) provides that if a district court amends an order to contain the prescribed statement, the petition must be filed within 10 days after entry of the amended order. The new rule similarly says that if a party cannot petition without the district court's permission or statement that necessary circumstances are present, the district court may amend its order to include such a statement and the time to petition runs from the entry of the amended order.

The provision that the Rule 4(a) time for filing a notice of appeal should apply if the statute or rule is silent about the filing time was drawn from existing Rule 5.1.

Subdivision (b). The changes made in the provisions in paragraph (b)(1) are intended only to broaden them sufficiently to make them appropriate for all discretionary appeals.

In paragraph (b)(2) a uniform time—7 days—is established for filing an answer in opposition or cross-petition. Seven days is the time for responding under existing Rule 5 and is an appropriate length of time when dealing with an interlocutory appeal. Although existing Rule 5.1 provides 14 days for responding, the Committee does not believe that the longer response time is necessary.

Subdivision (c). Subdivision (c) is substantively unchanged.

Subdivision (d). Paragraph (d)(2) is amended to state that "the date when the order granting permission to appeal is entered serves as the date of the notice of appeal" for purposes of calculating time under the rules. That language simply clarifies existing practice.

COMMITTEE NOTES ON RULES—2002 AMENDMENT

Subdivision (c). A petition for permission to appeal, a cross-petition for permission to appeal, and an answer to a petition or cross-petition for permission to appeal are all "other papers" for purposes of Rule 32(c)(2), and all of the requirements of Rule 32(a) apply to those papers, except as provided in Rule 32(c)(2). During the 1998 restyling of the Federal Rules of Appellate Procedure, Rule 5(c) was inadvertently changed to suggest that only the requirements of Rule 32(a)(1) apply to such papers. Rule 5(c) has been amended to correct that error.

Rule 5(c) has been further amended to limit the length of papers filed under Rule 5.

Changes Made After Publication and Comments. No changes were made to the text of the proposed amendment or to the Committee Note.

COMMITTEE NOTES ON RULES—2009 AMENDMENT

Subdivision (b)(2). Subdivision (b)(2) is amended in the light of the change in Rule 26(a)'s time computation rules. Subdivision (b)(2) formerly required that an answer in opposition to a petition for permission to appeal, or a cross-petition for permission to appeal, be filed "within 7 days after the petition is served." Under former Rule 26(a), "7 days" always meant at least 9 days and could mean as many as 11 or even 13 days. Under current Rule 26(a), intermediate weekends and holidays are counted. Changing the period from 7 to 10 days offsets the change in computation approach. See the Note to Rule 26.

Subdivision (d)(1). The time set in the former rule at 10 days has been revised to 14 days. See the Note to Rule 26.

COMMITTEE NOTES ON RULES—2016 AMENDMENT

The page limits previously employed in Rules 5, 21, 27, 35, and 40 have been largely overtaken by changes in technology. For papers produced using a computer, those page limits are now replaced by word limits. The word limits were derived from the current page limits using the assumption that one page is equivalent to 260 words. Papers produced using a computer must include the certificate of compliance required by Rule 32(g); Form 6 in the Appendix of Forms suffices to meet that requirement. Page limits are retained for papers prepared without the aid of a computer (i.e., handwritten or typewritten papers). For both the word limit and the page limit, the calculation excludes the accompanying documents required by Rule 5(b)(1)(E) and any items listed in Rule 32(f).

COMMITTEE NOTES ON RULES—2019 AMENDMENT

Subdivision (a)(1) is amended to delete the reference to "proof of service" to reflect amendments to Rule 25(d) that eliminate the requirement of a proof of service when service is completed using a court's electronic filing system.

[Rule 5.1. Appeal by Leave under 28 U.S.C. §636(c)(5)] (Abrogated Apr. 24, 1998, eff. Dec. 1, 1998)

COMMITTEE NOTES ON RULES—1998 AMENDMENT

The Federal Courts Improvement Act of 1996, Pub. L. No. 104–317, abolished appeals by permission under 28 U.S.C. §636(c)(5), making Rule 5.1 obsolete. Rule 5.1 is, therefore, abrogated.

Rule 6. Appeal in a Bankruptcy Case

(a) Appeal From a Judgment, Order, or Decree of a District Court Exercising Original Jurisdiction in a Bankruptcy Case. An appeal to a court of appeals from a final judgment, order, or decree of a district court exercising jurisdiction under 28 U.S.C. §1334 is taken as any other civil appeal under these rules.

(b) Appeal From a Judgment, Order, or Decree of a District Court or Bankruptcy Appellate Panel Exercising Appellate Jurisdiction in a Bankruptcy Case.

(1) Applicability of Other Rules. These rules apply to an appeal to a court of appeals under 28 U.S.C. §158(d)(1) from a final judgment, order, or decree of a district court or bankruptcy appellate panel exercising appellate jurisdiction under 28 U.S.C. §158(a) or (b), but with these qualifications:

(A) Rules 4(a)(4), 4(b), 9, 10, 11, 12(c), 13–20, 22–23, and 24(b) do not apply;

(B) the reference in Rule 3(c) to "Form 1 in the Appendix of Forms" must be read as a reference to Form 5;

(C) when the appeal is from a bankruptcy appellate panel, "district court," as used in any applicable rule, means "appellate panel"; and

(D) in Rule 12.1, "district court" includes a bankruptcy court or bankruptcy appellate panel.

(2) Additional Rules. In addition to the rules made applicable by Rule 6(b)(1), the following rules apply:

(A) Motion for Rehearing.

(i) If a timely motion for rehearing under Bankruptcy Rule 8022 is filed, the time to appeal for all parties runs from the entry of the order disposing of the motion. A notice of appeal filed after the district court or bankruptcy appellate panel announces or enters a judgment, order, or decree—but before disposition of the motion for rehearing—becomes effective when the order disposing of the motion for rehearing is entered.

(ii) If a party intends to challenge the order disposing of the motion—or the alteration or amendment of a judgment, order, or decree upon the motion—then the party, in compliance with Rules 3(c) and 6(b)(1)(B), must file a notice of appeal or amended notice of appeal. The notice or amended notice must be filed within the time prescribed by Rule 4—excluding Rules 4(a)(4) and 4(b)—measured from the entry of the order disposing of the motion.

(iii) No additional fee is required to file an amended notice.

(B) The Record on Appeal.

(i) Within 14 days after filing the notice of appeal, the appellant must file with the clerk possessing the record assembled in accordance with Bankruptcy Rule 8009—and serve on the appellee—a statement of the issues to be presented on appeal and a designation of the record to be certified and made available to the circuit clerk.

(ii) An appellee who believes that other parts of the record are necessary must, within 14 days after being served with the appellant's designation, file with the clerk and serve on the appellant a designation of additional parts to be included.

(iii) The record on appeal consists of:

• the redesignated record as provided above;

• the proceedings in the district court or bankruptcy appellate panel; and

• a certified copy of the docket entries prepared by the clerk under Rule 3(d).

(C) Making the Record Available.

(i) When the record is complete, the district clerk or bankruptcy-appellate-panel clerk must number the documents constituting the record and promptly make it available to the circuit clerk. If the clerk makes the record available in paper form, the clerk will not send documents of unusual bulk or weight, physical exhibits other than documents, or other parts of the record designated for omission by local rule of the court of appeals, unless directed to do so by a party or the circuit clerk. If unusually bulky or heavy exhibits are to be made available in paper form, a party must arrange with the clerks in advance for their transportation and receipt.

(ii) All parties must do whatever else is necessary to enable the clerk to assemble the record and make it available. When the record is made available in paper form, the court of appeals may provide by rule or order that a certified copy of the docket entries be made available in place of the redesignated record. But any party may request at any time during the pendency of the appeal that the redesignated record be made available.

(D) Filing the Record. When the district clerk or bankruptcy-appellate-panel clerk has made the record available, the circuit clerk must note that fact on the docket. The date noted on the docket serves as the filing date of the record. The circuit clerk must immediately notify all parties of the filing date.

(c) Direct Review by Permission Under 28 U.S.C. §158(d)(2).

(1) Applicability of Other Rules. These rules apply to a direct appeal by permission under 28 U.S.C. §158(d)(2), but with these qualifications:

(A) Rules 3–4, 5(a)(3), 6(a), 6(b), 8(a), 8(c), 9–12, 13–20, 22–23, and 24(b) do not apply;

(B) as used in any applicable rule, "district court" or "district clerk" includes—to the extent appropriate—a bankruptcy court or bankruptcy appellate panel or its clerk; and

(C) the reference to "Rules 11 and 12(c)" in Rule 5(d)(3) must be read as a reference to Rules 6(c)(2)(B) and (C).

(2) Additional Rules. In addition, the following rules apply:

(A) The Record on Appeal. Bankruptcy Rule 8009 governs the record on appeal.

(B) Making the Record Available. Bankruptcy Rule 8010 governs completing the record and making it available.

(C) Stays Pending Appeal. Bankruptcy Rule 8007 applies to stays pending appeal.

(D) Duties of the Circuit Clerk. When the bankruptcy clerk has made the record available, the circuit clerk must note that fact on the docket. The date noted on the docket serves as the filing date of the record. The circuit clerk must immediately notify all parties of the filing date.

(E) Filing a Representation Statement. Unless the court of appeals designates another time, within 14 days after entry of the order granting permission to appeal, the attorney who sought permission must file a statement with the circuit clerk naming the parties that the attorney represents on appeal.

(As amended Apr. 30, 1979, eff. Aug. 1, 1979; Apr. 25, 1989, eff. Dec. 1, 1989; Apr. 30, 1991, eff. Dec. 1, 1991; Apr. 22, 1993, eff. Dec. 1, 1993; Apr. 24, 1998, eff. Dec. 1, 1998; Mar. 26, 2009, eff. Dec. 1, 2009; Apr. 25, 2014, eff. Dec. 1, 2014.)

NOTES OF ADVISORY COMMITTEE ON RULES—1967

This rule is substantially a restatement of present procedure. See D.C. Cir. Rule 34; 6th Cir. Rule 11; 7th Cir. Rule 10(d); 10th Cir. Rule 13.

Present circuit rules commonly provide that the petition for allowance of an appeal shall be filed within the time allowed by Section 25 of the Bankruptcy Act for taking appeals of right. For the reasons explained in the Note accompanying Rule 4, that rule makes the time for appeal in bankruptcy cases the same as that which obtains in other civil cases and thus supersedes Section 25. Thus the present rule simply continues the former practice of making the time for filing the petition in appeals by allowance the same as that provided for filing the notice of appeal in appeals of right.

NOTES OF ADVISORY COMMITTEE ON RULES—1979 AMENDMENT

The proposed amendment adapts to the practice in appeals by allowance in bankruptcy proceedings the provisions of proposed Rule 3(e) above, requiring payment of all fees in the district court at the time of the filing of the notice of appeal. See Note to Rule 3(e), supra.

NOTES OF ADVISORY COMMITTEE ON RULES—1989 AMENDMENT

A new Rule 6 is proposed. The Bankruptcy Reform Act of 1978, Pub. L. No. 95—598, 92 Stat. 2549, the Supreme Court decision in Northern Pipeline Construction Co. v. Marathon Pipe Line Co., 458 U.S. 50 (1982), and the Bankruptcy Amendments and Federal Judgeship Act of 1984, Pub. L. No. 98—353, 98 Stat. 333, have made the existing Rule 6 obsolete.

Subdivision (a). Subdivision (a) provides that when a district court exercises original jurisdiction in a bankruptcy matter, rather than referring it to a bankruptcy judge for a final determination, the appeal should be taken in identical fashion as appeals from district court decisions in other civil actions. A district court exercises original jurisdiction and this subdivision applies when the district court enters a final order or judgment upon consideration of a bankruptcy judge's proposed findings of fact and conclusions of law in a non-core proceeding pursuant to 28 U.S.C. §157(c)(1) or when a district court withdraws a proceeding pursuant to 28 U.S.C. §157(d). This subdivision is included to avoid uncertainty arising from the question of whether a bankruptcy case is a civil case. The rules refer at various points to the procedure "in a civil case", see, e.g. Rule 4(a)(1). Subdivision (a) makes it clear that such rules apply to an appeal from a district court bankruptcy decision.

Subdivision (b). Subdivision (b) governs appeals that follow intermediate review of a bankruptcy judge's decision by a district court or a bankruptcy appellate panel.

Subdivision (b)(1). Subdivision (b)(1) provides for the general applicability of the Federal Rules of Appellate Procedure, with specified exceptions, to appeals covered by subdivision (b) and makes necessary word adjustments.

Subdivision (b)(2). Paragraph (i) provides that the time for filing a notice of appeal shall begin to run anew from the entry of an order denying a rehearing or from the entry of a subsequent judgment. The Committee deliberately omitted from the rule any provision governing the validity of a notice of appeal filed prior to the entry of an order denying a rehearing; the Committee intended to leave undisturbed the current state of the law on that issue. Paragraph (ii) calls for a redesignation of the appellate record assembled in the bankruptcy court pursuant to Rule 8006 of the Rules of Bankruptcy Procedure. After an intermediate appeal, a party may well narrow the focus of its efforts on the second appeal and a redesignation of the record may eliminate unnecessary material. The proceedings during the first appeal are included to cover the possibility that independent error in the intermediate appeal, for example failure to follow appropriate procedures, may be assigned in the court of appeals. Paragraph (iii) provides for the transmission of the record and tracks the appropriate subsections of Rule 11. Paragraph (iv) provides for the filing of the record and notices to the parties. Paragraph (ii) and Paragraph (iv) both refer to "a certified copy of the docket entries". The "docket entries" referred to are the docket entries in the district court or the bankruptcy appellate panel, not the entire docket in the bankruptcy court.

NOTES OF ADVISORY COMMITTEE ON RULES—1993 AMENDMENT

Note to Subparagraph (b)(2)(i). The amendment accompanies concurrent changes to Rule 4(a)(4). Although Rule 6 never included language such as that being changed in Rule 4(a)(4), language that made a notice of appeal void if it was filed before, or during the pendency of, certain posttrial motions, courts have found that a notice of appeal is premature if it is filed before the court disposes of a motion for rehearing. See, e.g., In re X-Cel, Inc., 823 F.2d 192 (7th Cir. 1987); In re Shah, 859 F.2d 1463 (10th Cir. 1988). The Committee wants to achieve the same result here as in Rule 4, the elimination of a procedural trap.

COMMITTEE NOTES ON RULES—1998 AMENDMENT

The language and organization of the rule are amended to make the rule more easily understood. In addition to changes made to improve the understanding, the Advisory Committee has changed language to make style and terminology consistent throughout the appellate rules. These changes are intended to be stylistic only.

Subdivision (b). Language is added to Rule 6(b)(2)(A)(ii) to conform with the corresponding provision in Rule 4(a)(4). The new language is clarifying rather than substantive. The existing rule states that a party intending to challenge an alteration or amendment of a judgment must file an amended notice of appeal. Of course if a party has not previously filed a notice of appeal, the party would simply file a notice of appeal not an amended one. The new language states that the party must file "a notice of appeal or amended notice of appeal."

COMMITTEE NOTES ON RULES—2009 AMENDMENT

Subdivision (b)(2)(B). The times set in the former rule at 10 days have been revised to 14 days. See the Note to Rule 26.

COMMITTEE NOTES ON RULES—2014 AMENDMENT

Subdivision (b)(1). Subdivision (b)(1) is updated to reflect the renumbering of 28 U.S.C. §158(d) as 28 U.S.C. §158(d)(1). Subdivision (b)(1)(A) is updated to reflect the renumbering of Rule 12(b) as Rule 12(c). New subdivision (b)(1)(D) provides that references in Rule 12.1 to the "district court" include—as appropriate—a bankruptcy court or bankruptcy appellate panel.

Subdivision (b)(2). Subdivision (b)(2)(A)(i) is amended to refer to Bankruptcy Rule 8022 (in accordance with the renumbering of Part VIII of the Bankruptcy Rules).

Subdivision (b)(2)(A)(ii) is amended to address problems that stemmed from the adoption—during the 1998 restyling project—of language referring to challenges to "an altered or amended judgment, order, or decree." Current Rule 6(b)(2)(A)(ii) states that "[a] party intending to challenge an altered or amended judgment, order, or decree must file a notice of appeal or amended notice of appeal . . . ." Before the 1998 restyling, the comparable subdivision of Rule 6 instead read "[a] party intending to challenge an alteration or amendment of the judgment, order, or decree shall file an amended notice of appeal . . . ." The 1998 restyling made a similar change in Rule 4(a)(4). One court has explained that the 1998 amendment introduced ambiguity into that Rule: "The new formulation could be read to expand the obligation to file an amended notice to circumstances where the ruling on the post-trial motion alters the prior judgment in an insignificant manner or in a manner favorable to the appellant, even though the appeal is not directed against the alteration of the judgment." Sorensen v. City of New York, 413 F.3d 292, 296 n.2 (2d Cir. 2005). Though the Sorensen court was writing of Rule 4(a)(4), a similar concern arises with respect to Rule 6(b)(2)(A)(ii). Rule 4(a)(4) was amended in 2009 to remove the ambiguity identified by the Sorensen court. The current amendment follows suit by removing Rule 6(b)(2)(A)(ii)'s reference to challenging "an altered or amended judgment, order, or decree," and referring instead to challenging "the alteration or amendment of a judgment, order, or decree."

Subdivision (b)(2)(B)(i) is amended to refer to Rule 8009 (in accordance with the renumbering of Part VIII of the Bankruptcy Rules).

Due to the shift to electronic filing, in some appeals the record will no longer be transmitted in paper form. Subdivisions (b)(2)(B)(i), (b)(2)(C), and (b)(2)(D) are amended to reflect the fact that the record sometimes will be made available electronically.

198

Subdivision (b)(2)(D) sets the duties of the circuit clerk when the record has been made available. Because the record may be made available in electronic form, subdivision (b)(2)(D) does not direct the clerk to "file" the record. Rather, it directs the clerk to note on the docket the date when the record was made available and to notify the parties of that date, which shall serve as the date of filing the record for purposes of provisions in these Rules that calculate time from that filing date.

Subdivision (c). New subdivision (c) is added to govern permissive direct appeals from the bankruptcy court to the court of appeals under 28 U.S.C. §158(d)(2). For further provisions governing such direct appeals, see Bankruptcy Rule 8006.

Subdivision (c)(1). Subdivision (c)(1) provides for the general applicability of the Federal Rules of Appellate Procedure, with specified exceptions, to appeals covered by subdivision (c) and makes necessary word adjustments.

Subdivision (c)(2). Subdivision (c)(2)(A) provides that the record on appeal is governed by Bankruptcy Rule 8009. Subdivision (c)(2)(B) provides that the record shall be made available as stated in Bankruptcy Rule 8010. Subdivision (c)(2)(C) provides that Bankruptcy Rule 8007 applies to stays pending appeal; in addition, Appellate Rule 8(b) applies to sureties on bonds provided in connection with stays pending appeal.

Subdivision (c)(2)(D), like subdivision (b)(2)(D), directs the clerk to note on the docket the date when the record was made available and to notify the parties of that date, which shall serve as the date of filing the record for purposes of provisions in these Rules that calculate time from that filing date.

Subdivision (c)(2)(E) is modeled on Rule 12(b), with appropriate adjustments.

Changes Made After Publication and Comment. No changes were made after publication and comment.

REFERENCES IN TEXT

The Bankruptcy Rules, referred to in subd. (b)(2)(A)(i), (B)(i), (c)(2)(A)—(C), are set out in the Appendix to Title 11, Bankruptcy.

Rule 7. Bond for Costs on Appeal in a Civil Case

In a civil case, the district court may require an appellant to file a bond or provide other security in any form and amount necessary to ensure payment of costs on appeal. Rule 8(b) applies to a surety on a bond given under this rule.

(As amended Apr. 30, 1979, eff. Aug. 1, 1979; Apr. 24, 1998, eff. Dec. 1, 1998.)

NOTES OF ADVISORY COMMITTEE ON RULES—1967

This rule is derived from FRCP 73(c) without change in substance.

NOTES OF ADVISORY COMMITTEE ON RULES—1979 AMENDMENT

The amendment would eliminate the provision of the present rule that requires the appellant to file a $250 bond for costs on appeal at the time of filing his notice of appeal. The $250 provision was carried forward in the F.R.App.P. from former Rule 73(c) of the F.R.Civ.P., and the $250 figure has remained unchanged since the adoption of that rule in 1937. Today it bears no relationship to actual costs. The amended rule would leave the question of the need for a bond for costs and its amount in the discretion of the court.

COMMITTEE NOTES ON RULES—1998 AMENDMENT

The language of the rule is amended to make the rule more easily understood. In addition to changes made to improve the understanding, the Advisory Committee has changed language to make style and terminology consistent throughout the appellate rules. These changes are intended to be stylistic only.

Rule 8. Stay or Injunction Pending Appeal

(a) Motion for Stay.
    (1) Initial Motion in the District Court. A party must ordinarily move first in the district court for the following relief:
        (A) a stay of the judgment or order of a district court pending appeal;
        (B) approval of a bond or other security provided to obtain a stay of judgment; or
        (C) an order suspending, modifying, restoring, or granting an injunction while an appeal is pending.

    (2) Motion in the Court of Appeals; Conditions on Relief. A motion for the relief mentioned in Rule 8(a)(1) may be made to the court of appeals or to one of its judges.
        (A) The motion must:
            (i) show that moving first in the district court would be impracticable; or
            (ii) state that, a motion having been made, the district court denied the motion or failed to afford the relief requested and state any reasons given by the district court for its action.

        (B) The motion must also include:
            (i) the reasons for granting the relief requested and the facts relied on;
            (ii) originals or copies of affidavits or other sworn statements supporting facts subject to dispute; and
            (iii) relevant parts of the record.

        (C) The moving party must give reasonable notice of the motion to all parties.
        (D) A motion under this Rule 8(a)(2) must be filed with the circuit clerk and normally will be considered by a panel of the court. But in an exceptional case in which time requirements make that procedure impracticable, the motion may be made to and considered by a single judge.
        (E) The court may condition relief on a party's filing a bond or other security in the district court.

    (b) Proceeding Against a Security Provider. If a party gives security with one or more security providers, each provider submits to the jurisdiction of the district court and irrevocably appoints the district clerk as its agent on whom any papers affecting its liability on the security may be served. On motion, a security provider's liability may be enforced in the district court without the necessity of an independent action. The motion and any notice that the district court prescribes may be served on the district clerk, who must promptly send a copy to each security provider whose address is known.
    (c) Stay in a Criminal Case. Rule 38 of the Federal Rules of Criminal Procedure governs a stay in a criminal case.

(As amended Mar. 10, 1986, eff. July 1, 1986; Apr. 27, 1995, eff. Dec. 1, 1995; Apr. 24, 1998, eff. Dec. 1, 1998; Apr. 26, 2018, eff. Dec. 1, 2018.)

NOTES OF ADVISORY COMMITTEE ON RULES—1967

Subdivision (a). While the power of a court of appeals to stay proceedings in the district court during the pendency of an appeal is not explicitly conferred by statute, it exists by virtue of the all writs statute, 28 U.S.C. §1651. Eastern Greyhound Lines v. Fusco, 310 F.2d 632 (6th Cir., 1962); United States v. Lynd, 301 F.2d 818 (5th Cir., 1962); Public Utilities Commission of Dist. of Col. v. Capital Transit Co., 94 U.S.App.D.C. 140, 214 F.2d 242 (1954). And the Supreme Court has termed the power "inherent" (In re McKenzie, 180 U.S. 536, 551, 21 S.Ct. 468, 45 L.Ed. 657 (1901)) and "part of its (the court of appeals) traditional equipment for the administration of justice." (Scripps-Howard Radio v. F.C.C., 316 U.S. 4, 9–10, 62 S.Ct. 875, 86 L.Ed. 1229 (1942)). The power of a single judge of the court of appeals to grant a stay pending appeal was recognized in In re McKenzie, supra. Alexander v. United States, 173 F.2d 865 (9th Cir., 1949) held that a single judge could not stay the judgment of a district court, but it noted the absence of a rule of court authorizing the practice. FRCP 62(g) adverts to the grant of a stay by a single judge of the appellate court. The requirement that application be first made to the district court is the case law rule. Cumberland Tel. & Tel. Co. v. Louisiana Public Service Commission, 260 U.S. 212, 219, 43 S.Ct. 75, 67 L.Ed. 217 (1922); United States v. El-O-Pathic Pharmacy, 192 F.2d 62 (9th Cir., 1951); United States v. Hansell, 109 F.2d 613 (2d Cir., 1940). The requirement is explicitly stated in FRCrP 38(c) and in the rules of the First, Third, Fourth and Tenth Circuits. See also Supreme Court Rules 18 and 27.

The statement of the requirement in the proposed rule would work a minor change in present practice. FRCP 73(e) requires that if a bond for costs on appeal or a supersedeas bond is offered after the appeal is docketed, leave to file the bond must be obtained from the court of appeals. There appears to be no reason why matters relating to supersedeas and cost bonds should not be initially presented to the district court whenever they arise prior to the disposition of the appeal. The requirement of FRCP 73(e) appears to be a concession to the view that once an appeal is perfected, the district court loses all power over its judgment. See In re Federal Facilities Trust, 227 F.2d 651 (7th Cir., 1955) and cases—cited at 654–655. No reason appears why all questions related to supersedeas or the bond for costs on appeal should not be presented in the first instance to the district court in the ordinary case.

Subdivision (b). The provisions respecting a surety upon a bond or other undertaking are based upon FRCP 65.1.

NOTES OF ADVISORY COMMITTEE ON RULES—1986 AMENDMENT

The amendments to Rule 8(b) are technical. No substantive change is intended.

NOTES OF ADVISORY COMMITTEE ON RULES—1995 AMENDMENT

Subdivision (c). The amendment conforms subdivision (c) to previous amendments to Fed. R. Crim. P. 38. This amendment strikes the reference to subdivision (a) of Fed. R. Crim. P. 38 so that Fed. R. App. P. 8(c) refers instead to all of Criminal Rule 38. When Rule 8(c) was adopted Fed. R. Crim. P. 38(a) included the procedures for obtaining a stay of execution when the sentence in question was death, imprisonment, a fine, or probation. Criminal Rule 38 was later amended and now addresses those topics in separate subdivisions. Subdivision 38(a) now addresses only stays of death sentences. The proper cross reference is to all of Criminal Rule 38.

COMMITTEE NOTES ON RULES—1998 AMENDMENT

The language and organization of the rule are amended to make the rule more easily understood. In addition to changes made to improve the understanding, the Advisory Committee has changed language to make style and terminology consistent throughout the appellate rules. These changes are intended to be stylistic only.

COMMITTEE NOTES ON RULES—2018 AMENDMENT

The amendments to subdivisions (a) and (b) conform this rule with the amendment of Federal Rule of Civil Procedure 62. Rule 62 formerly required a party to provide a "supersedeas bond" to obtain a stay of the judgment and proceedings to enforce the judgment. As amended, Rule 62(b) allows a party to obtain a stay by providing a "bond or other security." The word "mail" is changed to "send" to avoid restricting the method of serving security providers. Other rules specify the permissible manners of service.

REFERENCES IN TEXT

Rule 38 of the Federal Rules of Criminal Procedure, referred to in subd. (c), are set out in the Appendix to Title 18, Crimes and Criminal Procedure.

Rule 9. Release in a Criminal Case

(a) Release Before Judgment of Conviction.

(1) The district court must state in writing, or orally on the record, the reasons for an order regarding the release or detention of a defendant in a criminal case. A party appealing from the order must file with the court of appeals a copy of the district court's order and the court's statement of reasons as soon as practicable after filing the notice of appeal. An appellant who questions the factual basis for the district court's order must file a transcript of the release proceedings or an explanation of why a transcript was not obtained.

(2) After reasonable notice to the appellee, the court of appeals must promptly determine the appeal on the basis of the papers, affidavits, and parts of the record that the parties present or the court requires. Unless the court so orders, briefs need not be filed.

(3) The court of appeals or one of its judges may order the defendant's release pending the disposition of the appeal.

(b) Release After Judgment of Conviction. A party entitled to do so may obtain review of a district-court order regarding release after a judgment of conviction by filing a notice of appeal from that order in the district court, or by filing a motion in the court of appeals if the party has already filed a notice of appeal from the judgment of conviction. Both the order and the review are subject to Rule 9(a). The papers filed by the party seeking review must include a copy of the judgment of conviction.

(c) Criteria for Release. The court must make its decision regarding release in accordance with the applicable provisions of 18 U.S.C. §§3142, 3143, and 3145(c).

(As amended Apr. 24, 1972, eff. Oct. 1, 1972; Pub. L. 98–473, title II, §210, Oct. 12, 1984, 98 Stat. 1987; Apr. 29, 1994, eff. Dec. 1, 1994; Apr. 24, 1998, eff. Dec. 1, 1998.)

NOTES OF ADVISORY COMMITTEE ON RULES—1967

Subdivision (a). The appealability of release orders entered prior to a judgment of conviction is determined by the provisions of 18 U.S.C. §3147, as qualified by 18 U.S.C. §3148, and by the rule announced in Stack v. Boyle, 342 U.S. 1, 72 S.Ct. 1, 96 L.Ed. 3 (1951), holding certain orders respecting release appealable as final orders under 28 U.S.C. §1291. The language of the rule, "(an)n appeal authorized by law from an order refusing or imposing conditions of release," is intentionally broader than that used in 18 U.S.C. §3147 in describing orders made appealable by that section. The summary procedure ordained by the rule is intended to apply to all appeals from orders respecting release, and it would appear that at least some orders not made appealable by 18 U.S.C. §3147 are nevertheless appealable under the Stack v. Boyle rationale. See, for example, United States v. Foster, 278 F.2d 567 (2d Cir., 1960), holding appealable an order refusing to extend bail limits. Note also the provisions of 18 U.S.C. §3148, which after withdrawing from persons charged with an offense punishable by death and from those who have been convicted of an offense the right of appeal granted by 18 U.S.C. §3147, expressly preserves "other rights to judicial review of conditions of release or orders of detention."

The purpose of the subdivision is to insure the expeditious determination of appeals respecting release orders, an expedition commanded by 18 U.S.C. §3147 and by the Court in Stack v. Boyle, supra. It permits such appeals to be heard on an informal record without the necessity of briefs and on reasonable notice. Equally important to the just and speedy disposition of these appeals is the requirement that the district court state the reasons for its decision. See Jones v. United States, 358 F.2d 543 (D.C. Cir., 1966); Rhodes v. United States, 275 F.2d 78 (4th Cir., 1960); United States v. Williams, 253 F.2d 144 (7th Cir., 1958).

Subdivision (b). This subdivision regulates procedure for review of an order respecting release at a time when the jurisdiction of the court of appeals has already attached by virtue of an appeal from the judgment of conviction. Notwithstanding the fact that jurisdiction has passed to the court of appeals, both 18 U.S.C. §3148 and FRCrP 38(c) contemplate that the initial determination of whether a convicted defendant is to be released pending the appeal is to be made by the district court. But at this point there is obviously no need for a separate appeal from the order of the district court respecting release. The court of appeals or a judge thereof has power to effect release on motion as an incident to the pending appeal. See FRCrP 38(c) and 46(a)(2). But the motion is functionally identical with the appeal regulated by subdivision (a) and requires the same speedy determination if relief is to be effective. Hence the similarity of the procedure outlined in the two subdivisions.

NOTES OF ADVISORY COMMITTEE ON RULES—1972 AMENDMENT

Subdivision (c) is intended to bring the rule into conformity with 18 U.S.C. §3148 and to allocate to the defendant the burden of establishing that he will not flee and that he poses no danger to any other person or to the community. The burden is placed upon the defendant in the view that the fact of his conviction justifies retention in custody in situations where doubt exists as to whether he can be safely released pending disposition of his appeal. Release pending appeal may also be denied if "it appears that an appeal is frivolous or taken for delay." 18 U.S.C. §3148. The burden of establishing the existence of these criteria remains with the government.

NOTES OF ADVISORY COMMITTEE ON RULES—1994 AMENDMENT

Rule 9 has been entirely rewritten. The basic structure of the rule has been retained. Subdivision (a) governs appeals from bail decisions made before the judgment of conviction is entered at the time of sentencing. Subdivision (b) governs review of bail decisions made after sentencing and pending appeal.

Subdivision (a). The subdivision applies to appeals from "an order regarding release or detention" of a criminal defendant before judgment of conviction, i.e., before sentencing. See Fed.R.Crim.P. 32. The old rule applied only to a defendant's appeal from an order "refusing or imposing conditions of release." The new broader language is needed because the government is now permitted to appeal bail decisions in certain circumstances. 18 U.S.C. §§3145 and 3731. For the same reason, the rule now requires a district court to state reasons for its decision in all instances, not only when it refuses release or imposes conditions on release.

The rule requires a party appealing from a district court's decision to supply the court of appeals with a copy of the district court's order and its statement of reasons. In addition, an appellant who questions the factual basis for the district court's decision must file a transcript of the release proceedings, if possible. The rule also permits a court to require additional papers. A court must act promptly to decide these appeals; lack of pertinent information can cause delays. The old rule left the determination of what should be filed entirely within the party's discretion; it stated that the court of appeals would hear the appeal "upon such papers, affidavits, and portions of the record as the parties shall present."

Subdivision (b). This subdivision applies to review of a district court's decision regarding release made after judgment of conviction. As in subdivision (a), the language has been changed to accommodate the government's ability to seek review.

The word "review" is used in this subdivision, rather than "appeal" because review may be obtained, in some instances, upon motion. Review may be obtained by motion if the party has already filed a notice of appeal from the judgment of conviction. If the party desiring review of the release decision has not filed such a notice of appeal, review may be obtained only by filing a notice of appeal from the order regarding release.

The requirements of subdivision (a) apply to both the order and the review. That is, the district court must state its reasons for the order. The party seeking review must supply the court of appeals with the same information required by subdivision (a). In addition, the party seeking review must also supply the court with information about the conviction and the sentence.

Subdivision (c). This subdivision has been amended to include references to the correct statutory provisions.

COMMITTEE NOTES ON RULES—1998 AMENDMENT

The language and organization of the rule are amended to make the rule more easily understood. In addition to changes made to improve the understanding, the Advisory Committee has changed language to make style and terminology consistent throughout the appellate rules. These changes are intended to be stylistic only.

AMENDMENT BY PUBLIC LAW

1984—Subd. (c). Pub. L. 98–473 substituted "3143" for "3148" and inserted "and that the appeal is not for purpose of delay and raises a substantial question of law or fact likely to result in reversal or in an order for a new trial" after "community".

Rule 10. The Record on Appeal

    (a) Composition of the Record on Appeal. The following items constitute the record on appeal:
        (1) the original papers and exhibits filed in the district court;
        (2) the transcript of proceedings, if any; and
        (3) a certified copy of the docket entries prepared by the district clerk.

    (b) The Transcript of Proceedings.

(1) Appellant's Duty to Order. Within 14 days after filing the notice of appeal or entry of an order disposing of the last timely remaining motion of a type specified in Rule 4(a)(4)(A), whichever is later, the appellant must do either of the following:

(A) order from the reporter a transcript of such parts of the proceedings not already on file as the appellant considers necessary, subject to a local rule of the court of appeals and with the following qualifications:

(i) the order must be in writing;

(ii) if the cost of the transcript is to be paid by the United States under the Criminal Justice Act, the order must so state; and

(iii) the appellant must, within the same period, file a copy of the order with the district clerk; or

(B) file a certificate stating that no transcript will be ordered.

(2) Unsupported Finding or Conclusion. If the appellant intends to urge on appeal that a finding or conclusion is unsupported by the evidence or is contrary to the evidence, the appellant must include in the record a transcript of all evidence relevant to that finding or conclusion.

(3) Partial Transcript. Unless the entire transcript is ordered:

(A) the appellant must—within the 14 days provided in Rule 10(b)(1)—file a statement of the issues that the appellant intends to present on the appeal and must serve on the appellee a copy of both the order or certificate and the statement;

(B) if the appellee considers it necessary to have a transcript of other parts of the proceedings, the appellee must, within 14 days after the service of the order or certificate and the statement of the issues, file and serve on the appellant a designation of additional parts to be ordered; and

(C) unless within 14 days after service of that designation the appellant has ordered all such parts, and has so notified the appellee, the appellee may within the following 14 days either order the parts or move in the district court for an order requiring the appellant to do so.

(4) Payment. At the time of ordering, a party must make satisfactory arrangements with the reporter for paying the cost of the transcript.

(c) Statement of the Evidence When the Proceedings Were Not Recorded or When a Transcript Is Unavailable. If the transcript of a hearing or trial is unavailable, the appellant may prepare a statement of the evidence or proceedings from the best available means, including the appellant's recollection. The statement must be served on the appellee, who may serve objections or proposed amendments within 14 days after being served. The statement and any objections or proposed amendments must then be submitted to the district court for settlement and approval. As settled and approved, the statement must be included by the district clerk in the record on appeal.

(d) Agreed Statement as the Record on Appeal. In place of the record on appeal as defined in Rule 10(a), the parties may prepare, sign, and submit to the district court a statement of the case showing how the issues presented by the appeal arose and were decided in the district court. The statement must set forth only those facts averred and proved or sought to be proved that are essential to the court's resolution of the issues. If the statement is truthful, it—together with any additions that the district court may consider necessary to a full presentation of the issues on appeal—must be approved by the district court and must then be certified to the court of appeals as the record on appeal. The district clerk must then send it to the circuit clerk within the time provided by Rule 11. A copy of the agreed statement may be filed in place of the appendix required by Rule 30.

(e) Correction or Modification of the Record.

(1) If any difference arises about whether the record truly discloses what occurred in the district court, the difference must be submitted to and settled by that court and the record conformed accordingly.

(2) If anything material to either party is omitted from or misstated in the record by error or accident, the omission or misstatement may be corrected and a supplemental record may be certified and forwarded:

(A) on stipulation of the parties;

(B) by the district court before or after the record has been forwarded; or

(C) by the court of appeals.

(3) All other questions as to the form and content of the record must be presented to the court of appeals.

(As amended Apr. 30, 1979, eff. Aug. 1, 1979; Mar. 10, 1986, eff. July 1, 1986; Apr. 30, 1991, eff. Dec. 1, 1991; Apr. 22, 1993, eff. Dec. 1, 1993; Apr. 27, 1995, eff. Dec. 1, 1995; Apr. 24, 1998, eff. Dec. 1, 1998; Mar. 26, 2009, eff. Dec. 1, 2009.)

Notes of Advisory Committee on Rules—1967

This rule is derived from FRCP 75(a), (b), (c) and (d) and FRCP 76, without change in substance.

Notes of Advisory Committee on Rules—1979 Amendment

The proposed amendments to Rule 10(b) would require the appellant to place with the reporter a written order for the transcript of proceedings and file a copy with the clerk, and to indicate on the order if the transcript is to be provided under the Criminal Justice Act. If the appellant does not plan to order a transcript of any of the proceedings, he must file a certificate to that effect. These requirements make the appellant's steps in readying the appeal a matter of record and give the district court notice of requests for transcripts at the expense of the United States under the Criminal Justice Act. They are also the third step in giving the court of appeals some control over the production and transmission of the record. See Note to Rules 3(d)(e) above and Rule 11 below.

In the event the appellant orders no transcript, or orders a transcript of less than all the proceedings, the procedure under the proposed amended rule remains substantially as before. The appellant must serve on the appellee a copy of his order or in the event no order is placed, of the certificate to that effect, and a statement of the issues he intends to present on appeal, and the appellee may thereupon designate additional parts of the transcript to be included, and upon appellant's refusal to order the additional parts, may either order them himself or seek an order requiring the appellant to order them. The only change proposed in this procedure is to place a 10 day time limit on motions to require the appellant to order the additional portions.

Rule 10(b) is made subject to local rules of the courts of appeals in recognition of the practice in some circuits in some classes of cases, e. g., appeals by indigents in criminal cases after a short trial, of ordering immediate preparation of a complete transcript, thus making compliance with the rule unnecessary.

Notes of Advisory Committee on Rules—1986 Amendment

The amendments to Rules 10(b) and (c) are technical. No substantive change is intended.

Notes of Advisory Committee on Rules—1993 Amendment

The amendment is technical and no substantive change is intended.

Notes of Advisory Committee on Rules—1995 Amendment

Subdivision (b)(1). The amendment conforms this rule to amendments made in Rule 4(a)(4) in 1993. The amendments to Rule 4(a)(4) provide that certain postjudgment motions have the effect of suspending a filed notice of appeal until the disposition of the last of such motions. The purpose of this amendment is to suspend the 10-day period for ordering a transcript if a timely postjudgment motion is made and a notice of appeal is suspended under Rule 4(a)(4). The 10-day period set forth in the first sentence of this rule begins to run when the order disposing of the last of such postjudgment motions outstanding is entered.

COMMITTEE NOTES ON RULES—1998 AMENDMENT

The language and organization of the rule are amended to make the rule more easily understood. In addition to changes made to improve the understanding, the Advisory Committee has changed language to make style and terminology consistent throughout the appellate rules. These changes are intended to be stylistic only.

COMMITTEE NOTES ON RULES—2009 AMENDMENT

Subdivisions (b)(1), (b)(3), and (c). The times set in the former rule at 10 days have been revised to 14 days. See the Note to Rule 26.

REFERENCES IN TEXT

The Criminal Justice Act, referred to in subd. (b)(1)(A)(ii), probably means the Criminal Justice Act of 1964, Pub. L. 88–455, Aug. 20, 1964, 78 Stat. 552, as amended, which enacted section 3006A of Title 18, Crimes and Criminal Procedure, and provisions set out as notes under section 3006A of Title 18. For complete classification of this Act to the Code, see Short Title note set out under section 3006A of Title 18 and Tables.

Rule 11. Forwarding the Record

(a) Appellant's Duty. An appellant filing a notice of appeal must comply with Rule 10(b) and must do whatever else is necessary to enable the clerk to assemble and forward the record. If there are multiple appeals from a judgment or order, the clerk must forward a single record.

(b) Duties of Reporter and District Clerk.

(1) Reporter's Duty to Prepare and File a Transcript. The reporter must prepare and file a transcript as follows:

(A) Upon receiving an order for a transcript, the reporter must enter at the foot of the order the date of its receipt and the expected completion date and send a copy, so endorsed, to the circuit clerk.

(B) If the transcript cannot be completed within 30 days of the reporter's receipt of the order, the reporter may request the circuit clerk to grant additional time to complete it. The clerk must note on the docket the action taken and notify the parties.

(C) When a transcript is complete, the reporter must file it with the district clerk and notify the circuit clerk of the filing.

(D) If the reporter fails to file the transcript on time, the circuit clerk must notify the district judge and do whatever else the court of appeals directs.

(2) District Clerk's Duty to Forward. When the record is complete, the district clerk must number the documents constituting the record and send them promptly to the circuit clerk together with a list of the documents correspondingly numbered and reasonably identified. Unless directed to do so by a party or the circuit clerk, the district clerk will not send to the court of appeals documents of unusual bulk or weight, physical exhibits other than documents, or other parts of the record designated for omission by local rule of the court of appeals. If the exhibits are unusually bulky or heavy, a party must arrange with the clerks in advance for their transportation and receipt.

(c) Retaining the Record Temporarily in the District Court for Use in Preparing the Appeal. The parties may stipulate, or the district court on motion may order, that the district clerk retain the record temporarily for the parties to use in preparing the papers on appeal. In that event the district clerk must certify to the circuit clerk that the record on appeal is complete. Upon receipt of the appellee's brief, or earlier if the court orders or the parties agree, the appellant must request the district clerk to forward the record.

(d) [Abrogated.]

(e) Retaining the Record by Court Order.

(1) The court of appeals may, by order or local rule, provide that a certified copy of the docket entries be forwarded instead of the entire record. But a party may at any time during the appeal request that designated parts of the record be forwarded.

(2) The district court may order the record or some part of it retained if the court needs it while the appeal is pending, subject, however, to call by the court of appeals.

(3) If part or all of the record is ordered retained, the district clerk must send to the court of appeals a copy of the order and the docket entries together with the parts of the original record allowed by the district court and copies of any parts of the record designated by the parties.

(f) Retaining Parts of the Record in the District Court by Stipulation of the Parties. The parties may agree by written stipulation filed in the district court that designated parts of the record be retained in the district court subject to call by the court of appeals or request by a party. The parts of the record so designated remain a part of the record on appeal.

(g) Record for a Preliminary Motion in the Court of Appeals. If, before the record is forwarded, a party makes any of the following motions in the court of appeals:

• for dismissal;

• for release;

• for a stay pending appeal;

• for additional security on the bond on appeal or on a bond or other security provided to obtain a stay of judgment; or

• for any other intermediate order—

the district clerk must send the court of appeals any parts of the record designated by any party.

(As amended Apr. 30, 1979, eff. Aug. 1, 1979; Mar. 10, 1986, eff. July 1, 1986; Apr. 24, 1998, eff. Dec. 1, 1998; Apr. 26, 2018, eff. Dec. 1, 2018.)

NOTES OF ADVISORY COMMITTEE ON RULES—1967

Subdivisions (a) and (b). These subdivisions are derived from FRCP 73(g) and FRCP 75(e). FRCP 75(e) presently directs the clerk of the district court to transmit the record within the time allowed or fixed for its filing, which, under the provisions of FRCP 73(g) is within 40 days from the date of filing the notice of appeal, unless an extension is obtained from the district court. The precise time at which the record must be transmitted thus depends upon the time required for delivery of the record from the district court to the court of appeals, since, to permit its timely filing, it must reach the court of appeals before expiration of the 40-day period of an extension thereof. Subdivision (a) of this rule provides that the record is to be transmitted within the 40-day period, or any extension thereof; subdivision (b) provides that transmission is effected when the clerk of the district court mails or otherwise forwards the record to the clerk of the court of appeals; Rule 12(b) directs the clerk of the court of appeals to file the record upon its receipt following timely docketing and transmittal. It can thus be determined with certainty precisely when the clerk of the district court must forward the record to the clerk of the court of appeals in order to effect timely filing: the final day of the 40-day period or of any extension thereof.

Subdivision (c). This subdivision is derived from FRCP 75(e) without change of substance.

Subdivision (d). This subdivision is derived from FRCP 73(g) and FRCrP 39(c). Under present rules the district court is empowered to extend the time for filing the record and docketing the appeal. Since under the proposed rule timely transmission now insures timely filing (see note to subdivisions (a) and (b) above) the power of the district court is expressed in terms of its power to extend the time for transmitting the record. Restriction of that power to a period of 90 days after the filing of the notice of appeal represents a change in the rule with respect to appeals in criminal cases. FRCrP 39(c) now permits the district court to extend the time for filing and docketing without restriction. No good reason appears for a difference between the civil and criminal rule in this regard, and subdivision (d) limits the power of the district court to extend the time for transmitting the record in all cases to 90 days from the date of filing the notice of appeal, just as its power is now limited with respect to docketing and filing in civil cases. Subdivision (d) makes explicit the power of the court of appeals to permit the record to be filed at any time. See Pyramid Motor Freight Corporation v. Ispass, 330, U.S. 695, 67 S.Ct. 954, 91 L.Ed. 1184 (1947).

Subdivisions (e), (f) and (g). These subdivisions are derived from FRCP 75(f), (a) and (g), respectively, without change of substance.

Under present Rule 11(a) it is provided that the record shall be transmitted to the court of appeals within 40 days after the filing of the notice of appeal. Under present Rule 11(d) the district court, on request made during the initial time or any extension thereof, and cause shown, may extend the time for the transmission of the record to a point not more than 90 days after the filing of the first notice of appeal. If the district court is without authority to grant a request to extend the time, or denies a request for extension, the appellant may make a motion for extension of time in the court of appeals. Thus the duty to see that the record is transmitted is placed on the appellant. Aside from ordering the transcript within the time prescribed the appellant has no control over the time at which the record is transmitted, since all steps beyond this point are in the hands of the reporter and the clerk. The proposed amendments recognize this fact and place the duty directly on the reporter and the clerk. After receiving the written order for the transcript (See Note to Rule 10(b) above), the reporter must acknowledge its receipt, indicate when he expects to have it completed, and mail the order so endorsed to the clerk of the court of appeals. Requests for extensions of time must be made by the reporter to the clerk of the court of appeals and action on such requests is entered on the docket. Thus from the point at which the transcript is ordered the clerk of the court of appeals is made aware of any delays. If the transcript is not filed on time, the clerk of the court of appeals will notify the district judge.

Present Rule 11(b) provides that the record shall be transmitted when it is "complete for the purposes of the appeal." The proposed amended rule continues this requirement. The record is complete for the purposes of the appeal when it contains the original papers on file in the clerk's office, all necessary exhibits, and the transcript, if one is to be included. Cf. present Rule 11(c). The original papers will be in the custody of the clerk of the district court at the time the notice of appeal is filed. See Rule 5(e) of the F.R.C.P. The custody of exhibits is often the subject of local rules. Some of them require that documentary exhibits must be deposited with the clerk. See Local Rule 13 of the Eastern District of Virginia. Others leave exhibits with counsel, subject to order of the court. See Local Rule 33 of the Northern District of Illinois. If under local rules the custody of exhibits is left with counsel, the district court should make adequate provision for their preservation during the time during which an appeal may be taken, the prompt deposit with the clerk of such as under Rule 11(b) are to be transmitted to the court of appeals, and the availability of others in the event that the court of appeals should require their transmission. Cf. Local Rule 11 of the Second Circuit.

Usually the record will be complete with the filing of the transcript. While the proposed amendment requires transmission "forthwith" when the record is complete, it was not designed to preclude a local requirement by the court of appeals that the original papers and exhibits be transmitted when complete without awaiting the filing of the transcript.

The proposed amendments continue the provision in the present rule that documents of unusual bulk or weight and physical exhibits other than documents shall not be transmitted without direction by the parties or by the court of appeals, and the requirement that the parties make special arrangements for transmission and receipt of exhibits of unusual bulk or weight. In addition, they give recognition to local rules that make transmission of other record items subject to order of the court of appeals. See Local Rule 4 of the Seventh Circuit.

The amendments to Rule 11(b) are technical. No substantive change is intended.

The language and organization of the rule are amended to make the rule more easily understood. In addition to changes made to improve the understanding, the Advisory Committee has changed language to make style and terminology consistent throughout the appellate rules. These changes are intended to be stylistic only.

The amendment of subdivision (g) conforms this rule with the amendment of Federal Rule of Civil Procedure 62. Rule 62 formerly required a party to provide a "supersedeas bond" to obtain a stay of the judgment and proceedings to enforce the judgment. As amended, Rule 62(b) allows a party to obtain a stay by providing a "bond or other security."

Rule 12. Docketing the Appeal; Filing a Representation Statement; Filing the Record

(a) Docketing the Appeal. Upon receiving the copy of the notice of appeal and the docket entries from the district clerk under Rule 3(d), the circuit clerk must docket the appeal under the title of the district-court action and must identify the appellant, adding the appellant's name if necessary.

(b) Filing a Representation Statement. Unless the court of appeals designates another time, the attorney who filed the notice of appeal must, within 14 days after filing the notice, file a statement with the circuit clerk naming the parties that the attorney represents on appeal.

(c) Filing the Record, Partial Record, or Certificate. Upon receiving the record, partial record, or district clerk's certificate as provided in Rule 11, the circuit clerk must file it and immediately notify all parties of the filing date.

(As amended Apr. 1, 1979, eff. Aug. 1, 1979; Mar. 10, 1986, eff. July 1, 1986; Apr. 22, 1993, eff. Dec. 1, 1993; Apr. 24, 1998, eff. Dec. 1, 1998; Mar. 26, 2009, eff. Dec. 1, 2009.)

Subdivision (a). All that is involved in the docketing of an appeal is the payment of the docket fee. In practice, after the clerk of the court of appeals receives the record from the clerk of the district court he notifies the appellant of its receipt and requests payment of the fee. Upon receipt of the fee, the clerk enters the appeal upon the docket and files the record. The appellant is allowed to pay the fee at any time within the time allowed or fixed for transmission of the record and thereby to discharge his responsibility for docketing. The final sentence is added in the interest of facilitating future reference and citation and location of cases in indexes. Compare 3d Cir. Rule 10(2); 4th Cir. Rule 9(8); 6th Cir. Rule 14(1).

Subdivision (c). The rules of the circuits generally permit the appellee to move for dismissal in the event the appellant fails to effect timely filing of the record. See 1st Cir. Rule 21(3); 3d Cir. Rule 21(4); 5th Cir. Rule 16(1); 8th Cir. Rule 7(d).

NOTES OF ADVISORY COMMITTEE ON RULES—1979 AMENDMENT

Subdivision (a). Under present Rule 12(a) the appellant must pay the docket fee within the time fixed for the transmission of the record, and upon timely payment of the fee, the appeal is docketed. The proposed amendment takes the docketing out of the hands of the appellant. The fee is paid at the time the notice of appeal is filed and the appeal is entered on the docket upon receipt of a copy of the notice of appeal and of the docket entries, which are sent to the court of appeals under the provisions of Rule 3(d). This is designed to give the court of appeals control of its docket at the earliest possible time so that within the limits of its facilities and personnel it can screen cases for appropriately different treatment, expedite the proceedings through prehearing conferences or otherwise, and in general plan more effectively for the prompt disposition of cases.

Subdivision (b). The proposed amendment conforms the provision to the changes in Rule 11.

NOTES OF ADVISORY COMMITTEE ON RULES—1986 AMENDMENT

The amendment to Rule 12(a) is technical. No substantive change is intended.

NOTES OF ADVISORY COMMITTEE ON RULES—1993 AMENDMENT

Note to new subdivision (b). This amendment is a companion to the amendment of Rule 3(c). The Rule 3(c) amendment allows an attorney who represents more than one party on appeal to "specify" the appellants by general description rather than by naming them individually. The requirement added here is that whenever an attorney files a notice of appeal, the attorney must soon thereafter file a statement indicating all parties represented on the appeal by that attorney. Although the notice of appeal is the jurisdictional document and it must clearly indicate who is bringing the appeal, the representation statement will be helpful especially to the court of appeals in identifying the individual appellants.

The rule allows a court of appeals to require the filing of the representation statement at some time other than specified in the rule so that if a court of appeals requires a docketing statement or appearance form the representation statement may be combined with it.

COMMITTEE NOTES ON RULES—1998 AMENDMENT

The language of the rule is amended to make the rule more easily understood. In addition to changes made to improve the understanding, the Advisory Committee has changed language to make style and terminology consistent throughout the appellate rules. These changes are intended to be stylistic only.

COMMITTEE NOTES ON RULES—2009 AMENDMENT

Subdivision (b). The time set in the former rule at 10 days has been revised to 14 days. See the Note to Rule 26.

Rule 12.1. Remand After an Indicative Ruling by the District Court on a Motion for Relief That Is Barred by a Pending Appeal

(a) Notice to the Court of Appeals. If a timely motion is made in the district court for relief that it lacks authority to grant because of an appeal that has been docketed and is pending, the movant must promptly notify the circuit clerk if the district court states either that it would grant the motion or that the motion raises a substantial issue.

(b) Remand After an Indicative Ruling. If the district court states that it would grant the motion or that the motion raises a substantial issue, the court of appeals may remand for further proceedings but retains jurisdiction unless it expressly dismisses the appeal. If the court of appeals remands but retains jurisdiction, the parties must promptly notify the circuit clerk when the district court has decided the motion on remand.

(As added Mar. 26, 2009, eff. Dec. 1, 2009.)

COMMITTEE NOTES ON RULES—2009

This new rule corresponds to Federal Rule of Civil Procedure 62.1, which adopts for any motion that the district court cannot grant because of a pending appeal the practice that most courts follow when a party moves under Civil Rule 60(b) to vacate a judgment that is pending on appeal. After an appeal has been docketed and while it remains pending, the district court cannot grant relief under a rule such as Civil Rule 60(b) without a remand. But it can entertain the motion and deny it, defer consideration, state that it would grant the motion if the court of appeals remands for that purpose, or state that the motion raises a substantial issue. Experienced lawyers often refer to the suggestion for remand as an "indicative ruling." (Appellate Rule 4(a)(4) lists six motions that, if filed within the relevant time limit, suspend the effect of a notice of appeal filed before or after the motion is filed until the last such motion is disposed of. The district court has authority to grant the motion without resorting to the indicative ruling procedure.)

The procedure formalized by Rule 12.1 is helpful when relief is sought from an order that the court cannot reconsider because the order is the subject of a pending appeal. In the criminal context, the Committee anticipates that Rule 12.1 will be used primarily if not exclusively for newly discovered evidence motions under Criminal Rule 33(b)(1) (see United States v. Cronic, 466 U.S. 648, 667 n.42 (1984)), reduced sentence motions under Criminal Rule 35(b), and motions under 18 U.S.C. §3582(c).

Rule 12.1 does not attempt to define the circumstances in which an appeal limits or defeats the district court's authority to act in the face of a pending appeal. The rules that govern the relationship between trial courts and appellate courts may be complex, depending in part on the nature of the order and the source of appeal jurisdiction. Appellate Rule 12.1 applies only when those rules deprive the district court of authority to grant relief without appellate permission.

To ensure proper coordination of proceedings in the district court and in the court of appeals, the movant must notify the circuit clerk if the district court states that it would grant the motion or that the motion raises a substantial issue. The "substantial issue" standard may be illustrated by the following hypothetical: The district court grants summary judgment dismissing a case. While the plaintiff's appeal is pending, the plaintiff moves for relief from the judgment, claiming newly discovered evidence and also possible fraud by the defendant during the discovery process. If the district court reviews the motion and indicates that the motion "raises a substantial issue," the court of appeals may well wish to remand rather than proceed to determine the appeal.

If the district court states that it would grant the motion or that the motion raises a substantial issue, the movant may ask the court of appeals to remand so that the district court can make its final ruling on the motion. In accordance with Rule 47(a)(1), a local rule may prescribe the format for the litigants' notifications and the district court's statement.

Remand is in the court of appeals' discretion. The court of appeals may remand all proceedings, terminating the initial appeal. In the context of postjudgment motions, however, that procedure should be followed only when the appellant has stated clearly its intention to abandon the appeal. The danger is that if the initial appeal is terminated and the district court then denies the requested relief, the time for appealing the initial judgment will have run out and a court might rule that the appellant is limited to appealing the denial of the postjudgment motion. The latter appeal may well not provide the appellant with the opportunity to raise all the challenges that could have been raised on appeal from the underlying judgment. See, e.g., Browder v. Dir., Dep't of Corrections of Ill., 434 U.S. 257, 263 n.7 (1978) ("[A]n appeal from denial of Rule 60(b) relief does not bring up the underlying judgment for review."). The Committee does not endorse the notion that a court of appeals should decide that the initial appeal was abandoned—despite the absence of any clear statement of intent to abandon the appeal—merely because an unlimited remand occurred, but the possibility that a court might take that troubling view underscores the need for caution in delimiting the scope of the remand.

The court of appeals may instead choose to remand for the sole purpose of ruling on the motion while retaining jurisdiction to proceed with the appeal after the district court rules on the motion (if the appeal is not moot at that point and if any party wishes to proceed). This will often be the preferred course in the light of the concerns expressed above. It is also possible that the court of appeals may wish to proceed to hear the appeal even after the district court has granted relief on remand; thus, even when the district court indicates that it would grant relief, the court of appeals may in appropriate circumstances choose a limited rather than unlimited remand.

If the court of appeals remands but retains jurisdiction, subdivision (b) requires the parties to notify the circuit clerk when the district court has decided the motion on remand. This is a joint obligation that is discharged when the required notice is given by any litigant involved in the motion in the district court.

When relief is sought in the district court during the pendency of an appeal, litigants should bear in mind the likelihood that a new or amended notice of appeal will be necessary in order to challenge the district court's disposition of the motion. See, e.g., Jordan v. Bowen, 808 F.2d 733, 736–37 (10th Cir. 1987) (viewing district court's response to appellant's motion for indicative ruling as a denial of appellant's request for relief under Rule 60(b), and refusing to review that denial because appellant had failed to take an appeal from the denial); TAAG Linhas Aereas de Angola v. Transamerica Airlines, Inc., 915 F.2d 1351, 1354 (9th Cir. 1990) ("[W]here a 60(b) motion is filed subsequent to the notice of appeal and considered by the district court after a limited remand, an appeal specifically from the ruling on the motion must be taken if the issues raised in that motion are to be considered by the Court of Appeals.").

Changes Made After Publication and Comment. No changes were made to the text of Rule 12.1. The Appellate Rules Committee made two changes to the Note in response to public comments, and made additional changes in consultation with the Civil Rules Committee and in response to some Appellate Rules Committee members' suggestions. The Standing Committee made two further changes to the Note.

As published for comment, the second paragraph of the Note read: "[Appellate Rule 12.1 is not limited to the Civil Rule 62.1 context; Rule 12.1 may also be used, for example, in connection with motions under Criminal Rule 33. See United States v. Cronic, 466 U.S. 648, 667 n.42 (1984).] The procedure formalized by Rule 12.1 is helpful whenever relief is sought from an order that the court cannot reconsider because the order is the subject of a pending appeal." The Appellate Rules Committee discussed the Solicitor General's concern that Appellate Rule 12.1 might be misused in the criminal context. In response, the Appellate Rules Committee deleted the second paragraph as published and substituted the following language: "The procedure formalized by Rule 12.1 is helpful when relief is sought from an order that the court cannot reconsider because the order is the subject of a pending appeal. In the criminal context, the Committee anticipates that Rule 12.1's use will be limited to newly discovered evidence motions under Criminal Rule 33(b)(1) (see United States v. Cronic, 466 U.S. 648, 667 n.42 (1984)), reduced sentence motions under Criminal Rule 35(b), and motions under 18 U.S.C. §3582(c)." The Standing Committee further revised the latter sentence to read: "In the criminal context, the Committee anticipates that Rule 12.1 will be used primarily if not exclusively for newly discovered evidence motions under Criminal Rule 33(b)(1) (see United States v. Cronic, 466 U.S. 648, 667 n.42 (1984)), reduced sentence motions under Criminal Rule 35(b), and motions under 18 U.S.C. §3582(c)."

As published for comment, the first sentence of the Note's last paragraph read: "When relief is sought in the district court during the pendency of an appeal, litigants should bear in mind the likelihood that a separate notice of appeal will be necessary in order to challenge the district court's disposition of the motion." In response to a suggestion by Public Citizen, the Appellate Rules Committee revised this sentence to refer to a "new or amended" notice of appeal rather than a "separate" notice of appeal.

The Appellate Rules Committee, in consultation with the Civil Rules Committee, added the following parenthetical at the end of the Note's first paragraph: "(The effect of a notice of appeal on district-court authority is addressed by Appellate Rule 4(a)(4), which lists six motions that, if filed within the relevant time limit, suspend the effect of a notice of appeal filed before or after the motion is filed until the last such motion is disposed of. The district court has authority to grant the motion without resorting to the indicative ruling procedure.)" This parenthetical is designed to forestall confusion concerning the effect of tolling motions on a district court's power to act. The Standing Committee approved a change to the first sentence of the parenthetical; it now reads: "Appellate Rule 4(a)(4) lists six motions that, if filed within the relevant time limit, suspend the effect of a notice of appeal filed before or after the motion is filed until the last such motion is disposed of."

The Appellate Rules Committee, acting at the suggestion of the Civil Rules Committee, altered the wording of one sentence in the first paragraph and one sentence in the fifth paragraph of the Note. The changes are designed to remove references to remands of "the action," since those references would be in tension with the Note's advice concerning the advisability of limited remands. Thus, in the Note's first paragraph "if the action is remanded" became "if the court of appeals remands for that purpose," and in the Note's fifth paragraph "may ask the court of appeals to remand the action" became "may ask the court of appeals to remand."

The Appellate Rules Committee also made stylistic changes to the Note's first and third paragraphs. "Experienced appeal lawyers" became "Experienced lawyers," and "act in face of a pending appeal" became "act in the face of a pending appeal."

TITLE III. APPEALS FROM THE UNITED STATES TAX COURT

Rule 13. Appeals from the Tax Court

(a) Appeal as of Right.

(1) How Obtained; Time for Filing a Notice of Appeal.

(A) An appeal as of right from the United States Tax Court is commenced by filing a notice of appeal with the Tax Court clerk within 90 days after the entry of the Tax Court's decision. At the time of filing, the appellant must furnish the clerk with enough copies of the notice to enable the clerk to comply with Rule 3(d). If one party files a timely notice of appeal, any other party may file a notice of appeal within 120 days after the Tax Court's decision is entered.

(B) If, under Tax Court rules, a party makes a timely motion to vacate or revise the Tax Court's decision, the time to file a notice of appeal runs from the entry of the order disposing of the motion or from the entry of a new decision, whichever is later.

(2) Notice of Appeal; How Filed. The notice of appeal may be filed either at the Tax Court clerk's office in the District of Columbia or by sending it to the clerk. If sent by mail the notice is considered filed on the postmark date, subject to §7502 of the Internal Revenue Code, as amended, and the applicable regulations.

(3) Contents of the Notice of Appeal; Service; Effect of Filing and Service. Rule 3 prescribes the contents of a notice of appeal, the manner of service, and the effect of its filing and service. Form 2 in the Appendix of Forms is a suggested form of a notice of appeal.

(4) The Record on Appeal; Forwarding; Filing.

(A) Except as otherwise provided under Tax Court rules for the transcript of proceedings, the appeal is governed by the parts of Rules 10, 11, and 12 regarding the record on appeal from a district court, the time and manner of forwarding and filing, and the docketing in the court of appeals.

(B) If an appeal is taken to more than one court of appeals, the original record must be sent to the court named in the first notice of appeal filed. In an appeal to any other court of appeals, the appellant must apply to that other court to make provision for the record.

(b) Appeal by Permission. An appeal by permission is governed by Rule 5.

(As amended Apr. 1, 1979, eff. Aug. 1, 1979; Apr. 29, 1994, eff. Dec. 1, 1994; Apr. 24, 1998, eff. Dec. 1, 1998; Apr. 16, 2013, eff. Dec. 1, 2013; Apr. 25, 2019, eff. Dec. 1, 2019.)

NOTES OF ADVISORY COMMITTEE ON RULES—1967

Subdivision (a). This subdivision effects two changes in practice respecting review of Tax Court decisions: (1) Section 7483 of the Internal Revenue Code, 68A Stat. 891, 26 U.S.C. §7483, provides that review of a Tax Court decision may be obtained by filing a petition for review. The subdivision provides for review by the filing of the simple and familiar notice of appeal used to obtain review of district court judgments; (2) Section 7483, supra, requires that a petition for review be filed within 3 months after a decision is rendered, and provides that if a petition is so filed by one party, any other party may file a petition for review within 4 months after the decision is rendered. In the interest of fixing the time for review with precision, the proposed rule substitutes "90 days" and "120 days" for the statutory "3 months" and "4 months", respectively. The power of the Court to regulate these details of practice is clear. Title 28 U.S.C. §2072, as amended by the Act of November 6, 1966, 80 Stat. 1323 (1 U.S. Code Cong. & Ad. News, p. 1546 (1966)), authorizes the Court to regulate ". . . practice and procedure in proceedings for the review by the courts of appeals of decisions of the Tax Court of the United States. . . ."

The second paragraph states the settled teaching of the case law. See Robert Louis Stevenson Apartments, Inc. v. C.I.R., 337 F.2d 681, 10 A.L.R.3d 112 (8th Cir., 1964); Denholm & McKay Co. v. C.I.R., 132 F.2d 243 (1st Cir., 1942); Helvering v. Continental Oil Co., 63 App.D.C. 5, 68 F.2d 750 (1934); Burnet v. Lexington Ice & Coal Co., 62 F.2d 906 (4th Cir., 1933); Griffiths v. C.I.R., 50 F.2d 782 (7th Cir., 1931).

Subdivision (b). The subdivision incorporates the statutory provision (Title 26, U.S.C. §7502) that timely mailing is to be treated as timely filing. The statute contains special provisions respecting other than ordinary mailing. If the notice of appeal is sent by registered mail, registration is deemed prima facie evidence that the notice was delivered to the clerk of the Tax Court, and the date of registration is deemed the postmark date. If the notice of appeal is sent by certified mail, the effect of certification with respect to prima facie evidence of delivery and the postmark date depends upon regulations of the Secretary of the Treasury. The effect of a postmark made other than by the United States Post Office likewise depends upon regulations of the Secretary. Current regulations are found in 26 CFR §301.7502–1.

NOTES OF ADVISORY COMMITTEE ON RULES—1979 AMENDMENT

The proposed amendment reflects the change in the title of the Tax Court to "United States Tax Court." See 26 U.S.C. §7441.

NOTES OF ADVISORY COMMITTEE ON RULES—1994 AMENDMENT

Subdivision (a). The amendment requires a party filing a notice of appeal to provide the court with sufficient copies of the notice for service on all other parties.

COMMITTEE NOTES ON RULES—1998 AMENDMENT

The language and organization of the rule are amended to make the rule more easily understood. In addition to changes made to improve the understanding, the Advisory Committee has changed language to make style and terminology consistent throughout the appellate rules. These changes are intended to be stylistic only.

COMMITTEE NOTES ON RULES—2013 AMENDMENT

Rules 13 and 14 are amended to address the treatment of permissive interlocutory appeals from the Tax Court under 26 U.S.C. §7482(a)(2). Rules 13 and 14 do not currently address such appeals; instead, those Rules address only appeals as of right from the Tax Court. The existing Rule 13—governing appeals as of right—is revised and becomes Rule 13(a). New subdivision (b) provides that Rule 5 governs appeals by permission. The definition of district court and district clerk in current subdivision (d)(1) is deleted; definitions are now addressed in Rule 14. The caption of Title III is amended to reflect the broadened application of this Title.

Changes Made After Publication and Comment. No changes were made after publication and comment.

COMMITTEE NOTES ON RULES—2019 AMENDMENT

The amendment to subdivision (a)(2) will allow an appellant to send a notice of appeal to the Tax Court clerk by means other than mail. Other rules determine when a party must send a notice electronically or non-electronically.

REFERENCES IN TEXT

Section 7502 of the Internal Revenue Code, referred to in subd. (b), is classified to section 112 of Title 26, Internal Revenue Code.

Rule 14. Applicability of Other Rules to Appeals from the Tax Court

All provisions of these rules, except Rules 4, 6–9, 15–20, and 22–23, apply to appeals from the Tax Court. References in any applicable rule (other than Rule 24(a)) to the district court and district clerk are to be read as referring to the Tax Court and its clerk.

(As amended Apr. 24, 1998, eff. Dec. 1, 1998; Apr. 16, 2013, eff. Dec. 1, 2013.)

TITLE IV. REVIEW OR ENFORCEMENT OF AN ORDER OF AN ADMINISTRATIVE AGENCY, BOARD, COMMISSION, OR OFFICER

Rule 15. Review or Enforcement of an Agency Order—How Obtained; Intervention

(a) Petition for Review; Joint Petition.

(1) Review of an agency order is commenced by filing, within the time prescribed by law, a petition for review with the clerk of a court of appeals authorized to review the agency order. If their interests make joinder practicable, two or more persons may join in a petition to the same court to review the same order.

(2) The petition must:

(A) name each party seeking review either in the caption or the body of the petition—using such terms as "et al.," "petitioners," or "respondents" does not effectively name the parties;

(B) name the agency as a respondent (even though not named in the petition, the United States is a respondent if required by statute); and

(C) specify the order or part thereof to be reviewed.

(3) Form 3 in the Appendix of Forms is a suggested form of a petition for review.

(4) In this rule "agency" includes an agency, board, commission, or officer; "petition for review" includes a petition to enjoin, suspend, modify, or otherwise review, or a notice of appeal, whichever form is indicated by the applicable statute.

(b) Application or Cross-Application to Enforce an Order; Answer; Default.

(1) An application to enforce an agency order must be filed with the clerk of a court of appeals authorized to enforce the order. If a petition is filed to review an agency order that the court may enforce, a party opposing the petition may file a cross-application for enforcement.

(2) Within 21 days after the application for enforcement is filed, the respondent must serve on the applicant an answer to the application and file it with the clerk. If the respondent fails to answer in time, the court will enter judgment for the relief requested.

(3) The application must contain a concise statement of the proceedings in which the order was entered, the facts upon which venue is based, and the relief requested.

(c) Service of the Petition or Application. The circuit clerk must serve a copy of the petition for review, or an application or cross-application to enforce an agency order, on each respondent as prescribed by Rule 3(d), unless a different manner of service is prescribed by statute. At the time of filing, the petitioner must:

(1) serve, or have served, a copy on each party admitted to participate in the agency proceedings, except for the respondents;

(2) file with the clerk a list of those so served; and

(3) give the clerk enough copies of the petition or application to serve each respondent.

(d) Intervention. Unless a statute provides another method, a person who wants to intervene in a proceeding under this rule must file a motion for leave to intervene with the circuit clerk and serve a copy on all parties. The motion—or other notice of intervention authorized by statute—must be filed within 30 days after the petition for review is filed and must contain a concise statement of the interest of the moving party and the grounds for intervention.

(e) Payment of Fees. When filing any separate or joint petition for review in a court of appeals, the petitioner must pay the circuit clerk all required fees.

(As amended Apr. 22, 1993, eff. Dec. 1, 1993; Apr. 24, 1998, eff. Dec. 1, 1998; Mar. 26, 2009, eff. Dec. 1, 2009.)

is now in effect in all circuits. Third Circuit Rule 18 is a typical circuit rule, and for convenience it is referred to as the uniform rule in the notes which accompany rules under this Title.

Subdivision (a). The uniform rule (see General Note above) requires that the petition for review contain "a concise statement, in barest outline, of the nature of the proceedings as to which relief is sought, the facts upon which venue is based, the grounds upon which relief is sought, and the relief prayed." That language is derived from Section 4 of the Hobbs Administrative Orders Review Act of 1950, 64 Stat. 1130, reenacted as 28 U.S.C. §2344 (28 U.S.C.A. §2344 (Suppl. 1966)). A few other statutes also prescribe the content of the petition, but the great majority are silent on the point. The proposed rule supersedes 28 U.S.C. §2344 and other statutory provisions prescribing the form of the petition for review and permits review to be initiated by the filing of a simple petition similar in form to the notice of appeal used in appeals from judgments of district courts. The more elaborate form of petition for review now required is rarely useful either to the litigants or to the courts. There is no effective, reasonable way of obliging petitioners to come to the real issues before those issues are formulated in the briefs. Other provisions of this subdivision are derived from sections 1 and 2 of the uniform rule.

Subdivision (b). This subdivision is derived from sections 3, 4 and 5 of the uniform rule.

Subdivision (c). This subdivision is derived from section 1 of the uniform rule.

Subdivision (d). This subdivision is based upon section 6 of the uniform rule. Statutes occasionally permit intervention by the filing of a notice of intention to intervene. The uniform rule does not fix a time limit for intervention, and the only time limits fixed by statute are the 30–day periods found in the Communications Act Amendments, 1952, §402(e), 66 Stat. 719, 47 U.S.C. §402(e), and the Sugar Act of 1948, §205(d), 61 Stat. 927, 7 U.S.C. §1115(d).

NOTES OF ADVISORY COMMITTEE ON RULES——1993 AMENDMENT

Subdivision (a). The amendment is a companion to the amendment of Rule 3(c). Both Rule 3(c) and Rule 15(a) state that a notice of appeal or petition for review must name the parties seeking appellate review. Rule 3(c), however, provides an attorney who represents more than one party on appeal the flexibility to describe the parties in general terms rather than naming them individually. Rule 15(a) does not allow that flexibility; each petitioner must be named. A petition for review of an agency decision is the first filing in any court and, therefore, is analogous to a complaint in which all parties must be named.

Subdivision (e). The amendment adds subdivision (e). Subdivision (e) parallels Rule 3(e) that requires the payment of fees when filing a notice of appeal. The omission of such a requirement from Rule 15 is an apparent oversight. Five circuits have local rules requiring the payment of such fees, see, e.g., Fifth Cir. Loc. R. 15.1, and Fed. Cir. Loc. R. 15(a)(2).

COMMITTEE NOTES ON RULES——1998 AMENDMENT

The language and organization of the rule are amended to make the rule more easily understood. In addition to changes made to improve the understanding, the Advisory Committee has changed language to make style and terminology consistent throughout the appellate rules. These changes are intended to be stylistic only.

COMMITTEE NOTES ON RULES——2009 AMENDMENT

Subdivision (b)(2). The time set in the former rule at 20 days has been revised to 21 days. See the Note to Rule 26.

Rule 15.1. Briefs and Oral Argument in a National Labor Relations Board Proceeding

In either an enforcement or a review proceeding, a party adverse to the National Labor Relations Board proceeds first on briefing and at oral argument, unless the court orders otherwise.

(As added Mar. 10, 1986, eff. July 1, 1986; amended Apr. 24, 1998, eff. Dec. 1, 1998.)

NOTES OF ADVISORY COMMITTEE ON RULES——1986

This rule simply confirms the existing practice in most circuits.

COMMITTEE NOTES ON RULES——1998 AMENDMENT

The language of the rule is amended to make the rule more easily understood. In addition to changes made to improve the understanding, the Advisory Committee has changed language to make style and terminology consistent throughout the appellate rules. These changes are intended to be stylistic only.

Rule 16. The Record on Review or Enforcement

(a) Composition of the Record. The record on review or enforcement of an agency order consists of:
    (1) the order involved;
    (2) any findings or report on which it is based; and
    (3) the pleadings, evidence, and other parts of the proceedings before the agency.

(b) Omissions From or Misstatements in the Record. The parties may at any time, by stipulation, supply any omission from the record or correct a misstatement, or the court may so direct. If necessary, the court may direct that a supplemental record be prepared and filed.

(As amended Apr. 24, 1998, eff. Dec. 1, 1998.)

NOTES OF ADVISORY COMMITTEE ON RULES——1967

Subdivision (a) is based upon 28 U.S.C. §2112(b). There is no distinction between the record compiled in the agency proceeding and the record on review; they are one and the same. The record in agency cases is thus the same as that in appeals from the district court—the original papers, transcripts and exhibits in the proceeding below. Subdivision (b) is based upon section 8 of the uniform rule (see General Note following Rule 15).

COMMITTEE NOTES ON RULES——1998 AMENDMENT

The language and organization of the rule are amended to make the rule more easily understood. In addition to changes made to improve the understanding, the Advisory Committee has changed language to make style and terminology consistent throughout the appellate rules. These changes are intended to be stylistic only.

Rule 17. Filing the Record

(a) Agency to File; Time for Filing; Notice of Filing. The agency must file the record with the circuit clerk within 40 days after being served with a petition for review, unless the statute authorizing review provides otherwise, or within 40 days after it files an application for enforcement unless the respondent fails to answer or the court orders otherwise. The court may shorten or extend the time to file the record. The clerk must notify all parties of the date when the record is filed.

(b) Filing—What Constitutes.

(1) The agency must file:

(A) the original or a certified copy of the entire record or parts designated by the parties; or

(B) a certified list adequately describing all documents, transcripts of testimony, exhibits, and other material constituting the record, or describing those parts designated by the parties.

(2) The parties may stipulate in writing that no record or certified list be filed. The date when the stipulation is filed with the circuit clerk is treated as the date when the record is filed.

(3) The agency must retain any portion of the record not filed with the clerk. All parts of the record retained by the agency are a part of the record on review for all purposes and, if the court or a party so requests, must be sent to the court regardless of any prior stipulation.

(As amended Apr. 24, 1998, eff. Dec. 1, 1998.)

NOTES OF ADVISORY COMMITTEE ON RULES—1967

Subdivision (a). This subdivision is based upon section 7 of the uniform rule (see General Note following Rule 15). That rule does not prescribe a time for filing the record in enforcement cases. Forty days are allowed in order to avoid useless preparation of the record or certified list in cases where the application for enforcement is not contested.

Subdivision (b). This subdivision is based upon 28 U.S.C. §2112 and section 7 of the uniform rule. It permits the agency to file either the record itself or a certified list of its contents. It also permits the parties to stipulate against transmission of designated parts of the record without the fear that an inadvertent stipulation may "diminish" the record. Finally, the parties may, in cases where consultation of the record is unnecessary, stipulate that neither the record nor a certified list of its contents be filed.

COMMITTEE NOTES ON RULES—1998 AMENDMENT

The language and organization of the rule are amended to make the rule more easily understood. In addition to changes made to improve the understanding, the Advisory Committee has changed language to make style and terminology consistent throughout the appellate rules. These changes are intended to be stylistic only; a substantive change is made, however, in subdivision (b).

Subdivision (b). The current rule provides that when a court of appeals is asked to review or enforce an agency order, the agency must file either "the entire record or such parts thereof as the parties may designate by stipulation filed with the agency" or a certified list describing the documents, transcripts, exhibits, and other material constituting the record. If the agency is not filing a certified list, the current rule requires the agency to file the entire record unless the parties file a "stipulation" designating only parts of the record. Such a "stipulation" presumably requires agreement of the parties as to the parts to be filed. The amended language in subparagraph (b)(1)(A) permits the agency to file the entire record or "parts designated by the parties." The new language permits the filing of less than the entire record even when the parties do not agree as to which parts should be filed. Each party can designate the parts that it wants filed; the agency can then forward the parts designated by each party. In contrast, paragraph (b)(2) continues to require stipulation, that is agreement of the parties, that the agency need not file either the record or a certified list.

Rule 18. Stay Pending Review

(a) Motion for a Stay.

(1) Initial Motion Before the Agency. A petitioner must ordinarily move first before the agency for a stay pending review of its decision or order.

(2) Motion in the Court of Appeals. A motion for a stay may be made to the court of appeals or one of its judges.

(A) The motion must:

(i) show that moving first before the agency would be impracticable; or

(ii) state that, a motion having been made, the agency denied the motion or failed to afford the relief requested and state any reasons given by the agency for its action.

(B) The motion must also include:

(i) the reasons for granting the relief requested and the facts relied on;

(ii) originals or copies of affidavits or other sworn statements supporting facts subject to dispute; and

(iii) relevant parts of the record.

(C) The moving party must give reasonable notice of the motion to all parties.

(D) The motion must be filed with the circuit clerk and normally will be considered by a panel of the court. But in an exceptional case in which time requirements make that procedure impracticable, the motion may be made to and considered by a single judge.

(b) Bond. The court may condition relief on the filing of a bond or other appropriate security.

(As amended Apr. 24, 1998, eff. Dec. 1, 1998.)

NOTES OF ADVISORY COMMITTEE ON RULES—1967

While this rule has no counterpart in present rules regulating review of agency proceedings, it merely assimilates the procedure for obtaining stays in agency proceedings with that for obtaining stays in appeals from the district courts. The same considerations which justify the requirement of an initial application to the district court for a stay pending appeal support the requirement of an initial application to the agency pending review. See Note accompanying Rule 8. Title 5, U.S.C. §705 (5 U.S.C.A. §705 (1966 Pamphlet)) confers general authority on both agencies and reviewing courts to stay agency action pending review. Many of the statutes authorizing review of agency action by the courts of appeals deal with the question of stays, and at least one, the Act of June 15, 1936, 49 Stat. 1499 (7 U.S.C. §10a), prohibits a stay pending review. The proposed rule in nowise affects such statutory provisions respecting stays. By its terms, it simply indicates the procedure to be followed when a stay is sought.

COMMITTEE NOTES ON RULES—1998 AMENDMENT

The language and organization of the rule are amended to make the rule more easily understood. In addition to changes made to improve the understanding, the Advisory Committee has changed language to make style and terminology consistent throughout the appellate rules. These changes are intended to be stylistic only.

Rule 19. Settlement of a Judgment Enforcing an Agency Order in Part

When the court files an opinion directing entry of judgment enforcing the agency's order in part, the agency must within 14 days file with the clerk and serve on each other party a proposed judgment conforming to the opinion. A party who disagrees with the agency's proposed judgment must within 10 days file with the clerk and serve the agency with a proposed judgment that the party believes conforms to the opinion. The court will settle the judgment and direct entry without further hearing or argument.

(As amended Mar. 10, 1986, eff. July 1, 1986; Apr. 24, 1998, eff. Dec. 1, 1998; Mar. 26, 2009, eff. Dec. 1, 2009.)

Notes of Advisory Committee on Rules—1967

This is section 12 of the uniform rule (see General Note following Rule 15) with changes in phraseology.

Notes of Advisory Committee on Rules—1986 Amendment

The deletion of the words "in whole or" is designed to eliminate delay in the issuance of a judgment when the court of appeals has either enforced completely the order of an agency or denied completely such enforcement. In such a clear-cut situation, it serves no useful purpose to delay the issuance of the judgment until a proposed judgment is submitted by the agency and reviewed by the respondent. This change conforms the Rule to the existing practice in most circuits. Other amendments are technical and no substantive change is intended.

Committee Notes on Rules—1998 Amendment

The language of the rule is amended to make the rule more easily understood. In addition to changes made to improve the understanding, the Advisory Committee has changed language to make style and terminology consistent throughout the appellate rules. These changes are intended to be stylistic only.

Committee Notes on Rules—2009 Amendment

Rule 19 formerly required a party who disagreed with the agency's proposed judgment to file a proposed judgment "within 7 days." Under former Rule 26(a), "7 days" always meant at least 9 days and could mean as many as 11 or even 13 days. Under current Rule 26(a), intermediate weekends and holidays are counted. Changing the period from 7 to 10 days offsets the change in computation approach. See the Note to Rule 26.

Rule 20. Applicability of Rules to the Review or Enforcement of an Agency Order

All provisions of these rules, except Rules 3–14 and 22–23, apply to the review or enforcement of an agency order. In these rules, "appellant" includes a petitioner or applicant, and "appellee" includes a respondent.

(As amended Apr. 24, 1998, eff. Dec. 1, 1998.)

Notes of Advisory Committee on Rules—1967

The proposed rule continues the present uniform practice of the circuits of regulating agency review or enforcement proceedings by the general rules applicable to appeals from judgments of the district courts.

Committee Notes on Rules—1998 Amendment

The language of the rule is amended to make the rule more easily understood. In addition to changes made to improve the understanding, the Advisory Committee has changed language to make style and terminology consistent throughout the appellate rules. These changes are intended to be stylistic only.

TITLE V. EXTRAORDINARY WRITS

Rule 21. Writs of Mandamus and Prohibition, and Other Extraordinary Writs

(a) Mandamus or Prohibition to a Court: Petition, Filing, Service, and Docketing.
(1) A party petitioning for a writ of mandamus or prohibition directed to a court must file the petition with the circuit clerk and serve it on all parties to the proceeding in the trial court. The party must also provide a copy to the trial-court judge. All parties to the proceeding in the trial court other than the petitioner are respondents for all purposes.
(2)(A) The petition must be titled "In re [name of petitioner]."
(B) The petition must state:
(i) the relief sought;
(ii) the issues presented;
(iii) the facts necessary to understand the issue presented by the petition; and
(iv) the reasons why the writ should issue.

(C) The petition must include a copy of any order or opinion or parts of the record that may be essential to understand the matters set forth in the petition.
(3) Upon receiving the prescribed docket fee, the clerk must docket the petition and submit it to the court.

(b) Denial; Order Directing Answer; Briefs; Precedence.
(1) The court may deny the petition without an answer. Otherwise, it must order the respondent, if any, to answer within a fixed time.
(2) The clerk must serve the order to respond on all persons directed to respond.
(3) Two or more respondents may answer jointly.
(4) The court of appeals may invite or order the trial-court judge to address the petition or may invite an amicus curiae to do so. The trial-court judge may request permission to address the petition but may not do so unless invited or ordered to do so by the court of appeals.
(5) If briefing or oral argument is required, the clerk must advise the parties, and when appropriate, the trial-court judge or amicus curiae.
(6) The proceeding must be given preference over ordinary civil cases.

(7) The circuit clerk must send a copy of the final disposition to the trial-court judge.

(c) Other Extraordinary Writs. An application for an extraordinary writ other than one provided for in Rule 21(a) must be made by filing a petition with the circuit clerk and serving it on the respondents. Proceedings on the application must conform, so far as is practicable, to the procedures prescribed in Rule 21(a) and (b).

(d) Form of Papers; Number of Copies; Length Limits. All papers must conform to Rule 32(c)(2). An original and 3 copies must be filed unless the court requires the filing of a different number by local rule or by order in a particular case. Except by the court's permission, and excluding the accompanying documents required by Rule 21(a)(2)(C):

(1) a paper produced using a computer must not exceed 7,800 words; and

(2) a handwritten or typewritten paper must not exceed 30 pages.

(As amended Apr. 29, 1994, eff. Dec. 1, 1994; Apr. 23, 1996, eff. Dec. 1, 1996; Apr. 24, 1998, eff. Dec. 1, 1998; Apr. 29, 2002, eff. Dec. 1, 2002; Apr. 28, 2016, eff. Dec. 1, 2016; Apr. 25, 2019, eff. Dec. 1, 2019.)

NOTES OF ADVISORY COMMITTEE ON RULES—1967

The authority of courts of appeals to issue extraordinary writs is derived from 28 U.S.C. §1651. Subdivisions (a) and (b) regulate in detail the procedure surrounding the writs most commonly sought—mandamus or prohibition directed to a judge or judges. Those subdivisions are based upon Supreme Court Rule 31, with certain changes which reflect the uniform practice among the circuits (Seventh Circuit Rule 19 is a typical circuit rule). Subdivision (c) sets out a very general procedure to be followed in applications for the variety of other writs which may be issued under the authority of 28 U.S.C. §1651.

NOTES OF ADVISORY COMMITTEE ON RULES—1994 AMENDMENT

Subdivision (d). The amendment makes it clear that a court may require a different number of copies either by rule or by order in an individual case. The number of copies of any document that a court of appeals needs varies depending upon the way in which the court conducts business. The internal operation of the courts of appeals necessarily varies from circuit to circuit because of differences in the number of judges, the geographic area included within the circuit, and other such factors. Uniformity could be achieved only by setting the number of copies artificially high so that parties in all circuits file enough copies to satisfy the needs of the court requiring the greatest number. Rather than do that, the Committee decided to make it clear that local rules may require a greater or lesser number of copies and that, if the circumstances of a particular case indicate the need for a different number of copies in that case, the court may so order.

NOTES OF ADVISORY COMMITTEE ON RULES—1996 AMENDMENT

In most instances, a writ of mandamus or prohibition is not actually directed to a judge in any more personal way than is an order reversing a court's judgment. Most often a petition for a writ of mandamus seeks review of the intrinsic merits of a judge's action and is in reality an adversary proceeding between the parties. See, e.g., Walker v. Columbia Broadcasting System, Inc., 443 F.2d 33 (7th Cir. 1971). In order to change the tone of the rule and of mandamus proceedings generally, the rule is amended so that the judge is not treated as a respondent. The caption and subdivision (a) are amended by deleting the reference to the writs as being "directed to a judge or judges."

Subdivision (a). Subdivision (a) applies to writs of mandamus or prohibition directed to a court, but it is amended so that a petition for a writ of mandamus or prohibition does not bear the name of the judge. The amendments to subdivision (a) speak, however, about mandamus or prohibition "directed to a court." This language is inserted to distinguish subdivision (a) from subdivision (c). Subdivision (c) governs all other extraordinary writs, including a writ of mandamus or prohibition directed to an administrative agency rather than to a court and a writ of habeas corpus.

The amendments require the petitioner to provide a copy of the petition to the trial court judge. This will alert the judge to the filing of the petition. This is necessary because the trial court judge is not treated as a respondent and, as a result, is not served. A companion amendment is made in subdivision (b). It requires the circuit clerk to send a copy of the disposition of the petition to the trial court judge.

Subdivision (b). The amendment provides that even if relief is requested of a particular judge, although the judge may request permission to respond, the judge may not do so unless the court invites or orders a response.

The court of appeals ordinarily will be adequately informed not only by the opinions or statements made by the trial court judge contemporaneously with the entry of the challenged order but also by the arguments made on behalf of the party opposing the relief. The latter does not create an attorney-client relationship between the party's attorney and the judge whose action is challenged, nor does it give rise to any right to compensation from the judge.

If the court of appeals desires to hear from the trial court judge, however, the court may invite or order the judge to respond. In some instances, especially those involving court administration or the failure of a judge to act, it may be that no one other than the judge can provide a thorough explanation of the matters at issue. Because it is ordinarily undesirable to place the trial court judge, even temporarily, in an adversarial posture with a litigant, the rule permits a court of appeals to invite an amicus curiae to provide a response to the petition. In those instances in which the respondent does not oppose issuance of the writ or does not have sufficient perspective on the issue to provide an adequate response, participation of an amicus may avoid the need for the trial judge to participate.

Subdivision (c). The changes are stylistic only. No substantive changes are intended.

COMMITTEE NOTES ON RULES—1998 AMENDMENT

The language and organization of the rule are amended to make the rule more easily understood. In addition to changes made to improve the understanding, the Advisory Committee has changed language to make style and terminology consistent throughout the appellate rules. These changes are intended to be stylistic only.

COMMITTEE NOTES ON RULES—2002 AMENDMENT

Subdivision (d). A petition for a writ of mandamus or prohibition, an application for another extraordinary writ, and an answer to such a petition or application are all "other papers" for purposes of Rule 32(c)(2), and all of the requirements of Rule 32(a) apply to those papers, except as provided in Rule 32(c)(2). During the 1998 restyling of the Federal Rules of Appellate Procedure, Rule 21(d) was inadvertently changed to suggest that only the requirements of Rule 32(a)(1) apply to such papers. Rule 21(d) has been amended to correct that error.

Rule 21(d) has been further amended to limit the length of papers filed under Rule 21.

Changes Made After Publication and Comments. No changes were made to the text of the proposed amendment or to the Committee Note, except that the page limit was increased from 20 pages to 30 pages. The Committee was persuaded by some commentators that petitions for extraordinary writs closely resemble principal briefs on the merits and should be allotted more than 20 pages.

COMMITTEE NOTES ON RULES—2016 AMENDMENT

The page limits previously employed in Rules 5, 21, 27, 35, and 40 have been largely overtaken by changes in technology. For papers produced using a computer, those page limits are now replaced by word limits. The word limits were derived from the current page limits using the assumption that one page is equivalent to 260 words. Papers produced using a computer must include the certificate of compliance required by Rule 32(g); Form 6 in the Appendix of Forms suffices to meet that requirement. Page limits are retained for papers prepared without the aid of a computer (i.e., handwritten or typewritten papers). For both the word limit and the page limit, the calculation excludes the accompanying documents required by Rule 21(a)(2)(C) and any items listed in Rule 32(f).

COMMITTEE NOTES ON RULES—2019 AMENDMENT

The term "proof of service" in subdivisions (a)(1) and (c) is deleted to reflect amendments to Rule 25(d) that eliminate the requirement of a proof of service when service is completed using a court's electronic filing system.

TITLE VI. HABEAS CORPUS; PROCEEDINGS IN FORMA PAUPERIS

Rule 22. Habeas Corpus and Section 2255 Proceedings

(a) Application for the Original Writ. An application for a writ of habeas corpus must be made to the appropriate district court. If made to a circuit judge, the application must be transferred to the appropriate district court. If a district court denies an application made or transferred to it, renewal of the application before a circuit judge is not permitted. The applicant may, under 28 U.S.C. §2253, appeal to the court of appeals from the district court's order denying the application.

(b) Certificate of Appealability.

(1) In a habeas corpus proceeding in which the detention complained of arises from process issued by a state court, or in a 28 U.S.C. §2255 proceeding, the applicant cannot take an appeal unless a circuit justice or a circuit or district judge issues a certificate of appealability under 28 U.S.C. §2253(c). If an applicant files a notice of appeal, the district clerk must send to the court of appeals the certificate (if any) and the statement described in Rule 11(a) of the Rules Governing Proceedings Under 28 U.S.C. §2254 or §2255 (if any), along with the notice of appeal and the file of the district-court proceedings. If the district judge has denied the certificate, the applicant may request a circuit judge to issue it.

(2) A request addressed to the court of appeals may be considered by a circuit judge or judges, as the court prescribes. If no express request for a certificate is filed, the notice of appeal constitutes a request addressed to the judges of the court of appeals.

(3) A certificate of appealability is not required when a state or its representative or the United States or its representative appeals.

(As amended Pub. L. 104–132, title I, §103, Apr. 24, 1996, 110 Stat. 1218; Apr. 24, 1998, eff. Dec. 1, 1998; Mar. 26, 2009, eff. Dec. 1, 2009.)

NOTES OF ADVISORY COMMITTEE ON RULES—1967

Subdivision (a). Title 28 U.S.C. §2241(a) authorizes circuit judges to issue the writ of habeas corpus. Section 2241(b), however, authorizes a circuit judge to decline to entertain an application and to transfer it to the appropriate district court, and this is the usual practice. The first two sentences merely make present practice explicit. Title 28 U.S.C. §2253 seems clearly to contemplate that once an application is presented to a district judge and is denied by him, the remedy is an appeal from the order of denial. But the language of 28 U.S.C. §2241 seems to authorize a second original application to a circuit judge following a denial by a district judge. In re Gersing, 79 U.S.App.D.C. 245, 145 F.2d 481 (D.C. Cir., 1944) and Chapman v. Teets, 241 F.2d 186 (9th Cir., 1957) acknowledge the availability of such a procedure. But the procedure is ordinarily a waste of time for all involved, and the final sentence attempts to discourage it.

A court of appeals has no jurisdiction as a court to grant an original writ of habeas corpus, and courts of appeals have dismissed applications addressed to them. Loum v. Alvis, 263 F.2d 836 (6th Cir., 1959); In re Berry, 221 F.2d 798 (9th Cir., 1955); Posey v. Dowd, 134 F.2d 613 (7th Cir., 1943). The fairer and more expeditious practice is for the court of appeals to regard an application addressed to it as being addressed to one of its members, and to transfer the application to the appropriate district court in accordance with the provisions of this rule. Perhaps such a disposition is required by the rationale of In re Burwell, 350 U.S. 521, 76 S.Ct. 539, 100 L.Ed. 666 (1956).

Subdivision (b). Title 28 U.S.C. §2253 provides that an appeal may not be taken in a habeas corpus proceeding where confinement is under a judgment of a state court unless the judge who rendered the order in the habeas corpus proceeding, or a circuit justice or judge, issues a certificate of probable cause. In the interest of insuring that the matter of the certificate will not be overlooked and that, if the certificate is denied, the reasons for denial in the first instance will be available on any subsequent application, the proposed rule requires the district judge to issue the certificate or to state reasons for its denial.

While 28 U.S.C. §2253 does not authorize the court of appeals as a court to grant a certificate of probable cause, In re Burwell, 350 U.S. 521, 76 S.Ct. 539, 100 L.Ed. 666 (1956) makes it clear that a court of appeals may not decline to consider a request for the certificate addressed to it as a court but must regard the request as made to the judges thereof. The fourth sentence incorporates the Burwell rule.

Although 28 U.S.C. §2253 appears to require a certificate of probable cause even when an appeal is taken by a state or its representative, the legislative history strongly suggests that the intention of Congress was to require a certificate only in the case in which an appeal is taken by an applicant for the writ. See United States ex rel. Tillery v. Cavell, 294 F.2d 12 (3d Cir., 1960). Four of the five circuits which have ruled on the point have so interpreted section 2253. United States ex rel. Tillery v. Cavell, supra; Buder v. Bell, 306 F.2d 71 (6th Cir., 1962); United States ex rel. Calhoun v. Pate, 341 F.2d 885 (7th Cir., 1965); State of Texas v. Graves, 352 F.2d 514 (5th Cir., 1965). Cf. United States ex rel. Carrol v. LaVallee, 342 F.2d 641 (2d Cir., 1965). The final sentence makes it clear that a certificate of probable cause is not required of a state or its representative.

COMMITTEE NOTES ON RULES—1998 AMENDMENT

The language and organization of the rule are amended to make the rule more easily understood. In addition to changes made to improve the understanding, the Advisory Committee has changed language to make style and terminology consistent throughout the appellate rules. These changes are intended to be stylistic only; in this rule, however, substantive changes are made in paragraphs (b)(1) and (b)(3).

Subdivision (b), paragraph (1). Two substantive changes are made in this paragraph. First, the paragraph is made applicable to 28 U.S.C. §2255 proceedings. This brings the rule into conformity with 28 U.S.C. §2253 as amended by the Anti-Terrorism and Effective Death Penalty Act of 1996, Pub. L. No.

213

104–132. Second, the rule states that a certificate of appealability may be issued by "a circuit justice or a circuit or district judge." That language adds a reference to the circuit justice which also brings the rule into conformity with section 2253. The language continues to state that in addition to the circuit justice, both a circuit and a district judge may issue a certificate of appealability. The language of section 2253 is ambiguous; it states that a certificate of appealability may be issued by "a circuit justice or judge." Since the enactment of the Anti-Terrorism and Effective Death Penalty Act, three circuits have held that both district and circuit judges, as well as the circuit justice, may issue a certificate of appealability. Else v. Johnson, 104 F.3d 82 (5th Cir. 1997); Lyons v. Ohio Adult Parole Authority, 105 F.3d 1063 (6th Cir. 1997); and Hunter v. United States, 101 F.3d 1565 (11th Cir. 1996). The approach taken by the rule is consistent with those decisions.

Subdivision (b), paragraph (3). The Anti-Terrorism and Effective Death Penalty Act of 1996, Pub. L. No. 104–132, amended 28 U.S.C. §2253 to make it applicable to §2255 proceedings. Accordingly, paragraph (3) is amended to provide that when the United States or its representative appeals, a certificate of appealability is not required.

COMMITTEE NOTES ON RULES—2009 AMENDMENT

Subdivision (b)(1). The requirement that the district judge who rendered the judgment either issue a certificate of appealability or state why a certificate should not issue has been deleted from subdivision (b)(1). Rule 11(a) of the Rules Governing Proceedings under 28 U.S.C. §2254 or §2255 now delineates the relevant requirement. When an applicant has filed a notice of appeal, the district clerk must transmit the record to the court of appeals; if the district judge has issued a certificate of appealability, the district clerk must include in this transmission the certificate and the statement of reasons for grant of the certificate.

Changes Made After Publication and Comment. The Appellate Rules Committee approved the proposed amendment to Appellate Rule 22(b) with the style changes (described below) [omitted] which were suggested by Professor Kimble. As detailed in the report of the Criminal Rules Committee, a number of changes were made to the proposals concerning Rule 11 of the habeas and Section 2255 rules in response to public comment.

At the Standing Committee's direction, the language proposed for Appellate Rule 22(b) was circulated to the circuit clerks for their comment. Pursuant to comments received from the circuit clerks, the second sentence of Rule 22(b) was revised to make clear that the Rule requires the transmission of the record by the district court when an appeal is filed, regardless of whether the certificate of appealability was granted or denied by the district judge; a conforming change was made to the last sentence of the Committee Note.

AMENDMENT BY PUBLIC LAW

1996—Pub. L. 104–132 inserted "and section 2255" after "corpus" in catchline and amended text generally. Prior to amendment, text read as follows:

"(a) Application for the original writ.—An application for a writ of habeas corpus shall be made to the appropriate district court. If application is made to a circuit judge, the application will ordinarily be transferred to the appropriate district court. If an application is made to or transferred to the district court and denied, renewal of the application before a circuit judge is not favored; the proper remedy is by appeal to the court of appeals from the order of the district court denying the writ.

"(b) Necessity of certificate of probable cause for appeal.—In a habeas corpus proceeding in which the detention complained of arises out of process issued by a state court, an appeal by the applicant for the writ may not proceed unless a district or a circuit judge issues a certificate of probable cause. If an appeal is taken by the applicant, the district judge who rendered the judgment shall either issue a certificate of probable cause or state the reasons why such a certificate should not issue. The certificate or the statement shall be forwarded to the court of appeals with the notice of appeal and the file of the proceedings in the district court. If the district judge has denied the certificate, the applicant for the writ may then request issuance of the certificate by a circuit judge. If such a request is addressed to the court of appeals, it shall be deemed addressed to the judges thereof and shall be considered by a circuit judge or judges as the court deems appropriate. If no express request for a certificate is filed, the notice of appeal shall be deemed to constitute a request addressed to the judges of the court of appeals. If an appeal is taken by a state or its representative, a certificate of probable cause is not required."

Rule 23. Custody or Release of a Prisoner in a Habeas Corpus Proceeding

(a) Transfer of Custody Pending Review. Pending review of a decision in a habeas corpus proceeding commenced before a court, justice, or judge of the United States for the release of a prisoner, the person having custody of the prisoner must not transfer custody to another unless a transfer is directed in accordance with this rule. When, upon application, a custodian shows the need for a transfer, the court, justice, or judge rendering the decision under review may authorize the transfer and substitute the successor custodian as a party.

(b) Detention or Release Pending Review of Decision Not to Release. While a decision not to release a prisoner is under review, the court or judge rendering the decision, or the court of appeals, or the Supreme Court, or a judge or justice of either court, may order that the prisoner be:
    (1) detained in the custody from which release is sought;
    (2) detained in other appropriate custody; or
    (3) released on personal recognizance, with or without surety.

(c) Release Pending Review of Decision Ordering Release. While a decision ordering the release of a prisoner is under review, the prisoner must—unless the court or judge rendering the decision, or the court of appeals, or the Supreme Court, or a judge or justice of either court orders otherwise—be released on personal recognizance, with or without surety.

(d) Modification of the Initial Order on Custody. An initial order governing the prisoner's custody or release, including any recognizance or surety, continues in effect pending review unless for special reasons shown to the court of appeals or the Supreme Court, or to a judge or justice of either court, the order is modified or an independent order regarding custody, release, or surety is issued.

(As amended Mar. 10, 1986, eff. July 1, 1986; Apr. 24, 1998, eff. Dec. 1, 1998.)

NOTES OF ADVISORY COMMITTEE ON RULES—1967

The rule is the same as Supreme Court Rule 49, as amended on June 12, 1967, effective October 2, 1967.

NOTES OF ADVISORY COMMITTEE ON RULES—1986 AMENDMENT

The amendments to Rules 23(b) and (c) are technical. No substantive change is intended.

COMMITTEE NOTES ON RULES—1998 AMENDMENT

The language and organization of the rule are amended to make the rule more easily understood. In addition to changes made to improve the understanding, the Advisory Committee has changed language to make style and terminology consistent throughout the appellate rules. These changes are intended to be stylistic only.

Subdivison (d). The current rule states that the initial order governing custody or release "shall govern review" in the court of appeals. The amended language says that the initial order generally "continues in effect" pending review.

When Rule 23 was adopted it used the same language as Supreme Court Rule 49, which then governed custody of prisoners in habeas corpus proceedings. The "shall govern review" language was drawn from the Supreme Court Rule. The Supreme Court has since amended its rule, now Rule 36, to say that the initial order "shall continue in effect" unless for reasons shown it is modified or a new order is entered. Rule 23 is amended to similarly state that the initial order "continues in effect." The new language is clearer. It removes the possible implication that the initial order created law of the case, a strange notion to attach to an order regarding custody or release.

Rule 24. Proceeding in Forma Pauperis

(a) Leave to Proceed in Forma Pauperis.
(1) Motion in the District Court. Except as stated in Rule 24(a)(3), a party to a district-court action who desires to appeal in forma pauperis must file a motion in the district court. The party must attach an affidavit that:
(A) shows in the detail prescribed by Form 4 of the Appendix of Forms the party's inability to pay or to give security for fees and costs;
(B) claims an entitlement to redress; and
(C) states the issues that the party intends to present on appeal.

(2) Action on the Motion. If the district court grants the motion, the party may proceed on appeal without prepaying or giving security for fees and costs, unless a statute provides otherwise. If the district court denies the motion, it must state its reasons in writing.
(3) Prior Approval. A party who was permitted to proceed in forma pauperis in the district-court action, or who was determined to be financially unable to obtain an adequate defense in a criminal case, may proceed on appeal in forma pauperis without further authorization, unless:
(A) the district court—before or after the notice of appeal is filed—certifies that the appeal is not taken in good faith or finds that the party is not otherwise entitled to proceed in forma pauperis and states in writing its reasons for the certification or finding; or
(B) a statute provides otherwise.

(4) Notice of District Court's Denial. The district clerk must immediately notify the parties and the court of appeals when the district court does any of the following:
(A) denies a motion to proceed on appeal in forma pauperis;
(B) certifies that the appeal is not taken in good faith; or
(C) finds that the party is not otherwise entitled to proceed in forma pauperis.

(5) Motion in the Court of Appeals. A party may file a motion to proceed on appeal in forma pauperis in the court of appeals within 30 days after service of the notice prescribed in Rule 24(a)(4). The motion must include a copy of the affidavit filed in the district court and the district court's statement of reasons for its action. If no affidavit was filed in the district court, the party must include the affidavit prescribed by Rule 24(a)(1).

(b) Leave to Proceed in Forma Pauperis on Appeal from the United States Tax Court or on Appeal or Review of an Administrative-Agency Proceeding. A party may file in the court of appeals a motion for leave to proceed on appeal in forma pauperis with an affidavit prescribed by Rule 24(a)(1):
(1) in an appeal from the United States Tax Court; and
(2) when an appeal or review of a proceeding before an administrative agency, board, commission, or officer proceeds directly in the court of appeals.

(c) Leave to Use Original Record. A party allowed to proceed on appeal in forma pauperis may request that the appeal be heard on the original record without reproducing any part.

(As amended Apr. 1, 1979, eff. Aug. 1, 1979; Mar. 10, 1986, eff. July 1, 1986; Apr. 24, 1998, eff. Dec. 1, 1998; Apr. 29, 2002, eff. Dec. 1, 2002; Apr. 16, 2013, eff. Dec. 1, 2013.)

NOTES OF ADVISORY COMMITTEE ON RULES—1967

Subdivision (a). Authority to allow prosecution of an appeal in forma pauperis is vested in "[a]ny court of the United States" by 28 U.S.C. §1915(a). The second paragraph of section 1915(a) seems to contemplate initial application to the district court for permission to proceed in forma pauperis, and although the circuit rules are generally silent on the question, the case law requires initial application to the district court. Hayes v. United States, 258 F.2d 400 (5th Cir., 1958), cert. den. 358 U.S. 856, 79 S.Ct. 87, 3 L.Ed.2d 89 (1958); Elkins v. United States, 250 F.2d 145 (9th Cir., 1957) see 364 U.S. 206, 80 S.Ct. 1437, 4 L.Ed.2d 1669 (1960); United States v. Farley, 238 F.2d 575 (2d Cir., 1956) see 354 U.S. 521, 77 S.Ct. 1371, 1 L.Ed.2d 1529 (1957). D.C. Cir. Rule 41(a) requires initial application to the district court. The content of the affidavit follows the language of the statute; the requirement of a statement of the issues comprehends the statutory requirement of a statement of "the nature of the . . . appeal. . . ." The second sentence is in accord with the decision in McGann v. United States, 362 U.S. 309, 80 S.Ct. 725, 4 L.Ed.2d 734 (1960). The requirement contained in the third sentence has no counterpart in present circuit rules, but it has been imposed by decision in at least two circuits. Ragan v. Cox, 305 F.2d 58 (10th Cir., 1962); United States ex rel. Breedlove v. Dowd, 269 F.2d 693 (7th Cir., 1959).

The second paragraph permits one whose indigency has been previously determined by the district court to proceed on appeal in forma pauperis without the necessity of a redetermination of indigency, while reserving to the district court its statutory authority to certify that the appeal is not taken in good faith, 28 U.S.C. §1915(a), and permitting an inquiry into whether the circumstances of the party who was originally entitled to proceed in forma pauperis have changed during the course of the litigation. Cf. Sixth Circuit Rule 26.

The final paragraph establishes a subsequent motion in the court of appeals, rather than an appeal from the order of denial or from the certification of lack of good faith, as the proper procedure for calling in question the correctness of the action of the district court. The simple and expeditious motion procedure seems clearly preferable to an appeal. This paragraph applies only to applications for leave to appeal in forma pauperis. The order of a district court refusing leave to initiate an action in the district court in forma pauperis is reviewable on appeal. See Roberts v. United States District Court, 339 U.S. 844, 70 S.Ct. 954, 94 L.Ed. 1326 (1950).

Subdivision (b). Authority to allow prosecution in forma pauperis is vested only in a "court of the United States" (see Note to subdivision (a), above). Thus in proceedings brought directly in a court of appeals to review decisions of agencies or of the Tax Court, authority to proceed in forma pauperis should be sought in the court of appeals. If initial review of agency action is had in a district court, an application to appeal to a court of appeals in forma pauperis from the judgment of the district court is governed by the provisions of subdivision (a).

NOTES OF ADVISORY COMMITTEE ON RULES—1979 AMENDMENT

The proposed amendment reflects the change in the title of the Tax Court to "United States Tax Court." See 26 U.S.C. §7441.

NOTES OF ADVISORY COMMITTEE ON RULES—1986 AMENDMENT

The amendments to Rule 24(a) are technical. No substantive change is intended.

COMMITTEE NOTES ON RULES—1998 AMENDMENT

The language and organization of the rule are amended to make the rule more easily understood. In addition to changes made to improve the understanding, the Advisory Committee has changed language to make style and terminology consistent throughout the appellate rules. These changes are intended to be stylistic only. The Advisory Committee deletes the language in subdivision (c) authorizing a party proceeding in forma pauperis to file papers in typewritten form because the authorization is unnecessary. The rules permit all parties to file typewritten documents.

COMMITTEE NOTES ON RULES—2002 AMENDMENT

Subdivision (a)(2). Section 804 of the Prison Litigation Reform Act of 1995 ("PLRA") amended 28 U.S.C. §1915 to require that prisoners who bring civil actions or appeals from civil actions must "pay the full amount of a filing fee." 28 U.S.C. §1915(b)(1). Prisoners who are unable to pay the full amount of the filing fee at the time that their actions or appeals are filed are generally required to pay part of the fee and then to pay the remainder of the fee in installments. 28 U.S.C. §1915(b). By contrast, Rule 24(a)(2) has provided that, after the district court grants a litigant's motion to proceed on appeal in forma pauperis, the litigant may proceed "without prepaying or giving security for fees and costs." Thus, the PLRA and Rule 24(a)(2) appear to be in conflict.

Rule 24(a)(2) has been amended to resolve this conflict. Recognizing that future legislation regarding prisoner litigation is likely, the Committee has not attempted to incorporate into Rule 24 all of the requirements of the current version of 28 U.S.C. §1915. Rather, the Committee has amended Rule 24(a)(2) to clarify that the rule is not meant to conflict with anything required by the PLRA or any other statute.

Subdivision (a)(3). Rule 24(a)(3) has also been amended to eliminate an apparent conflict with the PLRA. Rule 24(a)(3) has provided that a party who was permitted to proceed in forma pauperis in the district court may continue to proceed in forma pauperis in the court of appeals without further authorization, subject to certain conditions. The PLRA, by contrast, provides that a prisoner who was permitted to proceed in forma pauperis in the district court and who wishes to continue to proceed in forma pauperis on appeal may not do so "automatically," but must seek permission. See, e.g., Morgan v. Haro, 112 F.3d 788, 789 (5th Cir. 1997) ("A prisoner who seeks to proceed IFP on appeal must obtain leave to so proceed despite proceeding IFP in the district court.").

Rule 24(a)(3) has been amended to resolve this conflict. Again, recognizing that future legislation regarding prisoner litigation is likely, the Committee has not attempted to incorporate into Rule 24 all of the requirements of the current version of 28 U.S.C. §1915. Rather, the Committee has amended Rule 24(a)(3) to clarify that the rule is not meant to conflict with anything required by the PLRA or any other statute.

Changes Made After Publication and Comments. No changes were made to the text of the proposed amendment or to the Committee Note, except that "a statute provides otherwise" was substituted in place of "the law requires otherwise" in the text of the rule and conforming changes (as well as a couple of minor stylistic changes) were made to the Committee Note.

COMMITTEE NOTES ON RULES—2013 AMENDMENT

Rule 24(b) currently refers to review of proceedings "before an administrative agency, board, commission, or officer (including for the purpose of this rule the United States Tax Court)." Experience suggests that Rule 24(b) contributes to confusion by fostering the impression that the Tax Court is an executive branch agency rather than a court. (As a general example of that confusion, appellate courts have returned Tax Court records to the Internal Revenue Service, believing the Tax Court to be part of that agency.) To remove this possible source of confusion, the quoted parenthetical is deleted from subdivision (b) and appeals from the Tax Court are separately listed in subdivision (b)'s heading and in new subdivision (b)(1).

Changes Made After Publication and Comment. No changes were made after publication and comment.

TITLE VII. GENERAL PROVISIONS

Rule 25. Filing and Service

(a) Filing.

(1) Filing with the Clerk. A paper required or permitted to be filed in a court of appeals must be filed with the clerk.

(2) Filing: Method and Timeliness.

(A) Nonelectronic Filing.

(i) In General. For a paper not filed electronically, filing may be accomplished by mail addressed to the clerk, but filing is not timely unless the clerk receives the papers within the time fixed for filing.

(ii) A Brief or Appendix. A brief or appendix not filed electronically is timely filed, however, if on or before the last day for filing, it is:

• mailed to the clerk by first-class mail, or other class of mail that is at least as expeditious, postage prepaid; or

• dispatched to a third-party commercial carrier for delivery to the clerk within 3 days.

(iii) Inmate Filing. If an institution has a system designed for legal mail, an inmate confined there must use that system to receive the benefit of this Rule 25(a)(2)(A)(iii). A paper not filed electronically by an inmate is timely if it is deposited in the institution's internal mail system on or before the last day for filing and:

• it is accompanied by: a declaration in compliance with 28 U.S.C. §1746—or a notarized statement—setting out the date of deposit and stating that first-class postage is being prepaid; or evidence (such as a postmark or date stamp) showing that the paper was so deposited and that postage was prepaid; or

• the court of appeals exercises its discretion to permit the later filing of a declaration or notarized statement that satisfies Rule 25(a)(2)(A)(iii).

(B) Electronic Filing and Signing.

(i) By a Represented Person—Generally Required; Exceptions. A person represented by an attorney must file electronically, unless nonelectronic filing is allowed by the court for good cause or is allowed or required by local rule.

(ii) By an Unrepresented Person—When Allowed or Required. A person not represented by an attorney:
- may file electronically only if allowed by court order or by local rule; and
- may be required to file electronically only by court order, or by a local rule that includes reasonable exceptions.

(iii) Signing. A filing made through a person's electronic-filing account and authorized by that person, together with that person's name on a signature block, constitutes the person's signature.

(iv) Same as a Written Paper. A paper filed electronically is a written paper for purposes of these rules.

(3) Filing a Motion with a Judge. If a motion requests relief that may be granted by a single judge, the judge may permit the motion to be filed with the judge; the judge must note the filing date on the motion and give it to the clerk.

(4) Clerk's Refusal of Documents. The clerk must not refuse to accept for filing any paper presented for that purpose solely because it is not presented in proper form as required by these rules or by any local rule or practice.

(5) Privacy Protection. An appeal in a case whose privacy protection was governed by Federal Rule of Bankruptcy Procedure 9037, Federal Rule of Civil Procedure 5.2, or Federal Rule of Criminal Procedure 49.1 is governed by the same rule on appeal. In all other proceedings, privacy protection is governed by Federal Rule of Civil Procedure 5.2, except that Federal Rule of Criminal Procedure 49.1 governs when an extraordinary writ is sought in a criminal case.

(b) Service of All Papers Required. Unless a rule requires service by the clerk, a party must, at or before the time of filing a paper, serve a copy on the other parties to the appeal or review. Service on a party represented by counsel must be made on the party's counsel.

(c) Manner of Service.

(1) Nonelectronic service may be any of the following:

(A) personal, including delivery to a responsible person at the office of counsel;

(B) by mail; or

(C) by third-party commercial carrier for delivery within 3 days.

(2) Electronic service of a paper may be made (A) by sending it to a registered user by filing it with the court's electronic-filing system or (B) by sending it by other electronic means that the person to be served consented to in writing.

(3) When reasonable considering such factors as the immediacy of the relief sought, distance, and cost, service on a party must be by a manner at least as expeditious as the manner used to file the paper with the court.

(4) Service by mail or by commercial carrier is complete on mailing or delivery to the carrier. Service by electronic means is complete on filing or sending, unless the party making service is notified that the paper was not received by the party served.

(d) Proof of Service.

(1) A paper presented for filing must contain either of the following if it was served other than through the court's electronic-filing system:

(A) an acknowledgment of service by the person served; or

(B) proof of service consisting of a statement by the person who made service certifying:

(i) the date and manner of service;

(ii) the names of the persons served; and

(iii) their mail or electronic addresses, facsimile numbers, or the addresses of the places of delivery, as appropriate for the manner of service.

(2) When a brief or appendix is filed by mailing or dispatch in accordance with Rule 25(a)(2)(A)(ii), the proof of service must also state the date and manner by which the document was mailed or dispatched to the clerk.

(3) Proof of service may appear on or be affixed to the papers filed.

(e) Number of Copies. When these rules require the filing or furnishing of a number of copies, a court may require a different number by local rule or by order in a particular case.

(As amended Mar. 10, 1986, eff. July 1, 1986; Apr. 30, 1991, eff. Dec. 1, 1991; Apr. 22, 1993, eff. Dec. 1, 1993; Apr. 29, 1994, eff. Dec. 1, 1994; Apr. 23, 1996, eff. Dec. 1, 1996; Apr. 24, 1998, eff. Dec. 1, 1998; Apr. 29, 2002, eff. Dec. 1, 2002; Apr. 12, 2006, eff. Dec. 1, 2006; Apr. 30, 2007, eff. Dec. 1, 2007; Mar. 26, 2009, eff. Dec. 1, 2009; Apr. 28, 2016, eff. Dec. 1, 2016; Apr. 26, 2018, eff. Dec. 1, 2018; Apr. 25, 2019, eff. Dec. 1, 2019.)

NOTES OF ADVISORY COMMITTEE ON RULES—1967

The rule that filing is not timely unless the papers filed are received within the time allowed is the familiar one. Ward v. Atlantic Coast Line R.R. Co., 265 F.2d 75 (5th Cir., 1959), rev'd on other grounds 362 U.S. 396, 80 S.Ct. 789, 4 L.Ed.2d 820 (1960); Kahler-Ellis Co. v. Ohio Turnpike Commission, 225 F.2d 922 (6th Cir., 1955). An exception is made in the case of briefs and appendices in order to afford the parties the maximum time for their preparation. By the terms of the exception, air mail delivery must be used whenever it is the most expeditious manner of delivery.

A majority of the circuits now require service of all papers filed with the clerk. The usual provision in present rules is for service on "adverse" parties. In view of the extreme simplicity of service by mail, there seems to be no reason why a party who files a paper should not be required to serve all parties to the proceeding in the court of appeals, whether or not they may be deemed adverse. The common requirement of proof of service is retained, but the rule permits it to be made by simple certification, which may be endorsed on the copy which is filed.

NOTES OF ADVISORY COMMITTEE ON RULES—1986 AMENDMENT

The amendments to Rules 25(a) and (b) are technical. No substantive change is intended.

NOTES OF ADVISORY COMMITTEE ON RULES—1991 AMENDMENT

Subdivision (a). The amendment permits, but does not require, courts of appeals to adopt local rules that allow filing of papers by electronic means. However, courts of appeals cannot adopt such local rules until the Judicial Conference of the United States authorizes filing by facsimile or other electronic means.

NOTES OF ADVISORY COMMITTEE ON RULES—1993 AMENDMENT

The amendment accompanies new subdivision (c) of Rule 4 and extends the holding in Houston v. Lack, 487 U.S. 266 (1988), to all papers filed in the courts of appeals by persons confined in institutions.

Subdivision (a). Several circuits have local rules that authorize the office of the clerk to refuse to accept for filing papers that are not in the form required by these rules or by local rules. This is not a suitable role for the office of the clerk and the practice exposes litigants to the hazards of time bars; for these reasons, such rules are proscribed by this rule. This provision is similar to Fed.R.Civ.P. 5(e) and Fed.R.Bankr.P. 5005.

The Committee wishes to make it clear that the provision prohibiting a clerk from refusing a document does not mean that a clerk's office may no longer screen documents to determine whether they comply with the rules. A court may delegate to the clerk authority to inform a party about any noncompliance with the rules and, if the party is willing to correct the document, to determine a date by which the corrected document must be resubmitted. If a party refuses to take the steps recommended by the clerk or if in the clerk's judgment the party fails to correct the noncompliance, the clerk must refer the matter to the court for a ruling.

Subdivision (d). Two changes have been made in this subdivision. Subdivision (d) provides that a paper presented for filing must contain proof of service.

The last sentence of subdivision (d) has been deleted as unnecessary. That sentence stated that a clerk could permit papers to be filed without acknowledgment or proof of service but must require that it be filed promptly thereafter. In light of the change made in subdivision (a) which states that a clerk may not refuse to accept for filing a document because it is not in the proper form, there is no further need for a provision stating that a clerk may accept a paper lacking a proof of service. The clerk must accept such a paper. That portion of the deleted sentence stating that the clerk must require that proof of service be filed promptly after the filing of the document if the proof is not filed concurrently with the document is also unnecessary.

The second amendment requires that the certificate of service must state the addresses to which the papers were mailed or at which they were delivered. The Federal Circuit has a similar local rule, Fed.Cir.R. 25.

Subdivision (e). Subdivision (e) is a new subdivision. It makes it clear that whenever these rules require a party to file or furnish a number of copies a court may require a different number of copies either by rule or by order in an individual case. The number of copies of any document that a court of appeals needs varies depending upon the way in which the court conducts business. The internal operation of the courts of appeals necessarily varies from circuit to circuit because of differences in the number of judges, the geographic area included within the circuit, and other such factors. Uniformity could be achieved only by setting the number of copies artificially high so that parties in all circuits file enough copies to satisfy the needs of the court requiring the greatest number. Rather than do that, the Committee decided to make it clear that local rules may require a greater or lesser number of copies and that, if the circumstances of a particular case indicate the need for a different number of copies in that case, the court may so order.

A party must consult local rules to determine whether the court requires a different number than that specified in these national rules. The Committee believes it would be helpful if each circuit either: 1) included a chart at the beginning of its local rules showing the number of copies of each document required to be filed with the court along with citation to the controlling rule; or 2) made available such a chart to each party upon commencement of an appeal; or both. If a party fails to file the required number of copies, the failure does not create a jurisdictional defect. Rule 3(a) states: "Failure of an appellant to take any step other than the timely filing of a notice of appeal does not affect the validity of the appeal, but is ground only for such action as the court of appeals deems appropriate. . . ."

Subdivision (a). The amendment deletes the language requiring a party to use "the most expeditious form of delivery by mail, except special delivery" in order to file a brief using the mailbox rule. That language was adopted before the Postal Service offered Express Mail and other expedited delivery services. The amendment makes it clear that it is sufficient to use First-Class Mail. Other equally or more expeditious classes of mail service, such as Express Mail, also may be used. In addition, the amendment permits the use of commercial carriers. The use of private, overnight courier services has become commonplace in law practice. Expedited services offered by commercial carriers often provide faster delivery than First-Class Mail; therefore, there should be no objection to the use of commercial carriers as long as they are reliable. In order to make use of the mailbox rule when using a commercial carrier, the amendment requires that the filer employ a carrier who undertakes to deliver the document in no more than three calendar days. The three-calendar-day period coordinates with the three-day extension provided by Rule 26(c).

Subdivision (c). The amendment permits service by commercial carrier if the carrier is to deliver the paper to the party being served within three days of the carrier's receipt of the paper. The amendment also expresses a desire that when reasonable, service on a party be accomplished by a manner as expeditious as the manner used to file the paper with the court. When a brief or motion is filed with the court by hand delivering the paper to the clerk's office, or by overnight courier, the copies should be served on the other parties by an equally expeditious manner—meaning either by personal service, if distance permits, or by overnight courier, if mail delivery to the party is not ordinarily accomplished overnight. The reasonableness standard is included so that if a paper is hand delivered to the clerk's office for filing but the other parties must be served in a different city, state, or region, personal service on them ordinarily will not be expected. If use of an equally expeditious manner of service is not reasonable, use of the next most expeditious manner may be. For example, if the paper is filed by hand delivery to the clerk's office but the other parties reside in distant cities, service on them need not be personal but in most instances should be by overnight courier. Even that may not be required, however, if the number of parties that must be served would make the use of overnight service too costly. A factor that bears upon the reasonableness of serving parties expeditiously is the immediacy of the relief requested.

Subdivision (d). The amendment adds a requirement that when a brief or appendix is filed by mail or commercial carrier, the certificate of service state the date and manner by which the document was mailed or dispatched to the clerk. Including that information in the certificate of service avoids the necessity for a separate certificate concerning the date and manner of filing.

The language and organization of the rule are amended to make the rule more easily understood. In addition to changes made to improve the understanding, the Advisory Committee has changed language to make style and terminology consistent throughout the appellate rules. These changes are intended to be stylistic only; a substantive amendment is made, however, in subdivision (a).

Subdivision (a). The substantive amendment in this subdivision is in subparagraph (a)(2)(C) and is a companion to an amendment in Rule 4(c). Currently Rule 25(a)(2)(C) provides that if an inmate confined in an institution files a document by depositing it in the institution's internal mail system, the document is timely filed if deposited on or before the last day for filing. Some institutions have special internal mail systems for handling legal mail; such systems often record the date of deposit of mail by an inmate, the date of delivery of mail to an inmate, etc. The Advisory Committee amends the rule to require an inmate to use the system designed for legal mail, if there is one, in order to receive the benefit of this subparagraph.

Rule 25(a)(2)(D) presently authorizes the courts of appeals to permit papers to be filed by electronic means. Rule 25 has been amended in several respects to permit papers also to be served electronically. In addition, Rule 25(c) has been reorganized and subdivided to make it easier to understand.

Subdivision (c)(1)(D). New subdivision (c)(1)(D) has been added to permit service to be made electronically, such as by e-mail or fax. No party may be served electronically, either by the clerk or by another party, unless the party has consented in writing to such service.

A court of appeals may not, by local rule, forbid the use of electronic service on a party that has consented to its use. At the same time, courts have considerable discretion to use local rules to regulate electronic service. Difficult and presently unforeseeable questions are likely to arise as electronic service becomes more common. Courts have the flexibility to use their local rules to address those questions. For example, courts may use local rules to set forth specific procedures that a party must follow before the party will be deemed to have given written consent to electronic service.

Parties also have the flexibility to define the terms of their consent; a party's consent to electronic service does not have to be "all-or-nothing." For example, a party may consent to service by facsimile transmission, but not by electronic mail; or a party may consent to electronic service only if "courtesy" copies of all transmissions are mailed within 24 hours; or a party may consent to electronic service of only documents that were created with Corel WordPerfect.

Subdivision (c)(2). The courts of appeals are authorized under Rule 25(a)(2)(D) to permit papers to be filed electronically. Technological advances may someday make it possible for a court to forward an electronically filed paper to all parties automatically or semi-automatically. When such court-facilitated service becomes possible, courts may decide to permit parties to use the courts' transmission facilities to serve electronically filed papers on other parties who have consented to such service. Court personnel would use the court's computer system to forward the papers, but the papers would be considered served by the filing parties, just as papers that are carried from one address to another by the United States Postal Service are considered served by the sending parties. New subdivision (c)(2) has been added so that the courts of appeals may use local rules to authorize such use of their transmission facilities, as well as to address the many questions that court-facilitated electronic service is likely to raise.

Subdivision (c)(4). The second sentence of new subdivision (c)(4) has been added to provide that electronic service is complete upon transmission. Transmission occurs when the sender performs the last act that he or she must perform to transmit a paper electronically; typically, it occurs when the sender hits the "send" or "transmit" button on an electronic mail program. There is one exception to the rule that electronic service is complete upon transmission: If the sender is notified—by the sender's e-mail program or otherwise—that the paper was not received, service is not complete, and the sender must take additional steps to effect service. A paper has been "received" by the party on which it has been served as long as the party has the ability to retrieve it. A party cannot defeat service by choosing not to access electronic mail on its server.

Changes Made After Publication and Comments. No changes were made to the text of the proposed amendment. A paragraph was added to the Committee Note to clarify that consent to electronic service is not an "all-or-nothing" matter.

Subdivision (d)(1)(B)(iii). Subdivision (d)(1)(B)(iii) has been amended to require that, when a paper is served electronically, the proof of service of that paper must include the electronic address or facsimile number to which the paper was transmitted.

Changes Made After Publication and Comments. The text of the proposed amendment was changed to refer to "electronic" addresses (instead of to "e-mail" addresses), to include "facsimile numbers," and to add the concluding phrase "as appropriate for the manner of service." Conforming changes were made to the Committee Note.

COMMITTEE NOTES ON RULES—2006 AMENDMENT

Subdivision (a)(2)(D). Amended Rule 25(a)(2)(D) acknowledges that many courts have required electronic filing by means of a standing order, procedures manual, or local rule. These local practices reflect the advantages that courts and most litigants realize from electronic filing. Courts that mandate electronic filing recognize the need to make exceptions when requiring electronic filing imposes a hardship on a party. Under Rule 25(a)(2)(D), a local rule that requires electronic filing must include reasonable exceptions, but Rule 25(a)(2)(D) does not define the scope of those exceptions. Experience with the local rules that have been adopted and that will emerge will aid in drafting new local rules and will facilitate gradual convergence on uniform exceptions, whether in local rules or in an amended Rule 25(a)(2)(D).

A local rule may require that both electronic and "hard" copies of a paper be filed. Nothing in the last sentence of Rule 25(a)(2)(D) is meant to imply otherwise.

Changes Made After Publication and Comment. Rule 25(a)(2)(D) has been changed in one significant respect: It now authorizes the courts of appeals to require electronic filing only "if reasonable exceptions are allowed." [1] The published version of Rule 25(a)(2)(D) did not require "reasonable exceptions." The change was made in response to the argument of many commentators that the national rule should require that the local rules include exceptions for those for whom mandatory electronic filing would pose a hardship.

Although Rule 25(a)(2)(D) requires that hardship exceptions be included in any local rules that mandate electronic filing, it does not attempt to define the scope of those exceptions. Commentators were largely in agreement that the local rules should include hardship exceptions of some type. But commentators did not agree about the perimeters of those exceptions. The Advisory Committee believes that, at this point, it does not have enough experience with mandatory electronic filing to impose specific hardship exceptions on the circuits. Rather, the Advisory Committee believes that the circuits should be free for the time being to experiment with different formulations.

The Committee Note has been changed to reflect the addition of the "reasonable exceptions" clause to the text of the rule. The Committee Note has also been changed to add the final two sentences. Those sentences were added at the request of Judge Sandra L. Lynch, a member of CACM [the Court Administration and Case Management Committee]. Judge Lynch believes that there will be few appellate judges who will want to receive only electronic copies of briefs, but there will be many who will want to receive electronic copies in addition to hard copies. Thus, the local rules of most circuits are likely to require a "written" copy or "paper" copy, in addition to an electronic copy. The problem is that the last sentence of Rule 25(a)(2)(D) provides that "[a] paper filed by electronic means in compliance with a local rule constitutes a written paper for the purpose of applying these rules." Judge Lynch's concern is that this sentence may leave attorneys confused as to whether a local rule requiring a "written" or "paper" copy of a brief requires anything in addition to the electronic copy. The final two sentences of the Committee Note are intended to clarify the matter.

COMMITTEE NOTES ON RULES—2007 AMENDMENT

Subdivision (a)(5). Section 205(c)(3)(A)(i) of the E-Government Act of 2002 (Public Law 107–347, as amended by Public Law 108–281) requires that the rules of practice and procedure be amended "to protect privacy and security concerns relating to electronic filing of documents and the public availability . . . of

219

documents filed electronically." In response to that directive, the Federal Rules of Bankruptcy, Civil, and Criminal Procedure have been amended, not merely to address the privacy and security concerns raised by documents that are filed electronically, but also to address similar concerns raised by documents that are filed in paper form. See Fed. R. Bankr. P. 9037; Fed. R. Civ. P. 5.2; and Fed. R. Crim. P. 49.1.

Appellate Rule 25(a)(5) requires that, in cases that arise on appeal from a district court, bankruptcy appellate panel, or bankruptcy court, the privacy rule that applied to the case below will continue to apply to the case on appeal. With one exception, all other cases—such as cases involving the review or enforcement of an agency order, the review of a decision of the tax court, or the consideration of a petition for an extraordinary writ—will be governed by Civil Rule 5.2. The only exception is when an extraordinary writ is sought in a criminal case—that is, a case in which the related trial-court proceeding is governed by Criminal Rule 49.1. In such a case, Criminal Rule 49.1 will govern in the court of appeals as well.

Changes Made After Publication and Comment. The rule is a modified version of the provision as published. The changes from the published proposal implement suggestions by the Style Subcommittee of the Standing Committee on Rules of Practice and Procedure.

COMMITTEE NOTES ON RULES—2009 AMENDMENT

Under former Rule 26(a), short periods that span weekends or holidays were computed without counting those weekends or holidays. To specify that a period should be calculated by counting all intermediate days, including weekends or holidays, the Rules used the term "calendar days." Rule 26(a) now takes a "days-are-days" approach under which all intermediate days are counted, no matter how short the period. Accordingly, "3 calendar days" in subdivisions (a)(2)(B)(ii) and (c)(1)(C) is amended to read simply "3 days."

COMMITTEE NOTES ON RULES—2016 AMENDMENT

Rule 25(a)(2)(C) is revised to streamline and clarify the operation of the inmate-filing rule.

The Rule requires the inmate to show timely deposit and prepayment of postage. The Rule is amended to specify that a paper is timely if it is accompanied by a declaration or notarized statement stating the date the paper was deposited in the institution's mail system and attesting to the prepayment of first-class postage. The declaration must state that first-class postage "is being prepaid," not (as directed by the former Rule) that first-class postage "has been prepaid." This change reflects the fact that inmates may need to rely upon the institution to affix postage after the inmate has deposited the document in the institution's mail system. New Form 7 in the Appendix of Forms sets out a suggested form of the declaration.

The amended rule also provides that a paper is timely without a declaration or notarized statement if other evidence accompanying the paper shows that the paper was deposited on or before the due date and that postage was prepaid. If the paper is not accompanied by evidence that establishes timely deposit and prepayment of postage, then the court of appeals has discretion to accept a declaration or notarized statement at a later date. The Rule uses the phrase "exercises its discretion to permit"—rather than simply "permits"—to help ensure that pro se inmate litigants are aware that a court will not necessarily forgive a failure to provide the declaration initially.

COMMITTEE NOTES ON RULES—2018 AMENDMENT

The amendments conform Rule 25 to the amendments to Federal Rule of Civil Procedure 5 on electronic filing, signature, and service. They establish, in Rule 25(a)(2)(B), a new national rule that generally makes electronic filing mandatory. The rule recognizes exceptions for persons proceeding without an attorney, exceptions for good cause, and variations established by local rule. The amendments establish national rules regarding the methods of signing and serving electronic documents in Rule 25(a)(2)(B)(iii) and (c)(2).

COMMITTEE NOTES ON RULES—2019 AMENDMENT

The amendment conforms Rule 25 to other federal rules regarding proof of service. As amended, subdivision (d) eliminates the requirement of proof of service or acknowledgment of service when service is made through a court's electronic-filing system. The notice of electronic filing generated by the court's system serves that purpose.

REFERENCES IN TEXT

The Federal Rules of Bankruptcy Procedure, referred to in subd. (a)(5), are set out in the Appendix to Title 11, Bankruptcy.

The Federal Rules of Civil Procedure, referred to in subd. (a)(5), are set out in this Appendix.

The Federal Rules of Criminal Procedure, referred to in subd. (a)(5), are set out in the Appendix to Title 18, Crimes and Criminal Procedure.

[1] At its June 15–16, 2005, meeting, the Standing Rules Committee with the concurrence of the advisory committee chair agreed to set out the "reasonable exception" clause as a separate sentence in the rule, consistent with drafting conventions of the Style Project.

Rule 26. Computing and Extending Time

(a) Computing Time. The following rules apply in computing any time period specified in these rules, in any local rule or court order, or in any statute that does not specify a method of computing time.

(1) Period Stated in Days or a Longer Unit. When the period is stated in days or a longer unit of time:

(A) exclude the day of the event that triggers the period;

(B) count every day, including intermediate Saturdays, Sundays, and legal holidays; and

(C) include the last day of the period, but if the last day is a Saturday, Sunday, or legal holiday, the period continues to run until the end of the next day that is not a Saturday, Sunday, or legal holiday.

(2) Period Stated in Hours. When the period is stated in hours:

(A) begin counting immediately on the occurrence of the event that triggers the period;

(B) count every hour, including hours during intermediate Saturdays, Sundays, and legal holidays; and

(C) if the period would end on a Saturday, Sunday, or legal holiday, the period continues to run until the same time on the next day that is not a Saturday, Sunday, or legal holiday.

(3) Inaccessibility of the Clerk's Office. Unless the court orders otherwise, if the clerk's office is inaccessible:

(A) on the last day for filing under Rule 26(a)(1), then the time for filing is extended to the first accessible day that is not a Saturday, Sunday, or legal holiday; or

(B) during the last hour for filing under Rule 26(a)(2), then the time for filing is extended to the same time on the first accessible day that is not a Saturday, Sunday, or legal holiday.

(4) "Last Day" Defined. Unless a different time is set by a statute, local rule, or court order, the last day ends:

(A) for electronic filing in the district court, at midnight in the court's time zone;

(B) for electronic filing in the court of appeals, at midnight in the time zone of the circuit clerk's principal office;

(C) for filing under Rules 4(c)(1), 25(a)(2)(A)(ii), and 25(a)(2)(A)(iii)—and filing by mail under Rule 13(a)(2)—at the latest time for the method chosen for delivery to the post office, third-party commercial carrier, or prison mailing system; and

(D) for filing by other means, when the clerk's office is scheduled to close.

(5) "Next Day" Defined. The "next day" is determined by continuing to count forward when the period is measured after an event and backward when measured before an event.

(6) "Legal Holiday" Defined. "Legal holiday" means:

(A) the day set aside by statute for observing New Year's Day, Martin Luther King Jr.'s Birthday, Washington's Birthday, Memorial Day, Independence Day, Labor Day, Columbus Day, Veterans' Day, Thanksgiving Day, or Christmas Day;

(B) any day declared a holiday by the President or Congress; and

(C) for periods that are measured after an event, any other day declared a holiday by the state where either of the following is located: the district court that rendered the challenged judgment or order, or the circuit clerk's principal office.

(b) Extending Time. For good cause, the court may extend the time prescribed by these rules or by its order to perform any act, or may permit an act to be done after that time expires. But the court may not extend the time to file:

(1) a notice of appeal (except as authorized in Rule 4) or a petition for permission to appeal; or

(2) a notice of appeal from or a petition to enjoin, set aside, suspend, modify, enforce, or otherwise review an order of an administrative agency, board, commission, or officer of the United States, unless specifically authorized by law.

(c) Additional Time After Certain Kinds of Service. When a party may or must act within a specified time after being served, and the paper is not served electronically on the party or delivered to the party on the date stated in the proof of service, 3 days are added after the period would otherwise expire under Rule 26(a).

(As amended Mar. 1, 1971, eff. July 1, 1971; Mar. 10, 1986, eff. July 1, 1986; Apr. 25, 1989, eff. Dec. 1, 1989; Apr. 30, 1991, eff. Dec. 1, 1991; Apr. 23, 1996, eff. Dec. 1, 1996; Apr. 24, 1998, eff. Dec. 1, 1998; Apr. 29, 2002, eff. Dec. 1, 2002; Apr. 25, 2005, eff. Dec. 1, 2005; Mar. 26, 2009, eff. Dec. 1, 2009; Apr. 28, 2016, eff. Dec. 1, 2016; Apr. 26, 2018, eff. Dec. 1, 2018; Apr. 25, 2019, eff. Dec. 1, 2019.)

NOTES OF ADVISORY COMMITTEE ON RULES—1967

The provisions of this rule are based upon FRCP 6(a), (b) and (e). See also Supreme Court Rule 34 and FRCrP 45. Unlike FRCP 6(b), this rule, read with Rule 27, requires that every request for enlargement of time be made by motion, with proof of service on all parties. This is the simplest, most convenient way of keeping all parties advised of developments. By the terms of Rule 27(b) a motion for enlargement of time under Rule 26(b) may be entertained and acted upon immediately, subject to the right of any party to seek reconsideration. Thus the requirement of motion and notice will not delay the granting of relief of a kind which a court is inclined to grant as of course. Specifically, if a court is of the view that an extension of time sought before expiration of the period originally prescribed or as extended by a previous order ought to be granted in effect ex parte, as FRCP 6(b) permits, it may grant motions seeking such relief without delay.

NOTES OF ADVISORY COMMITTEE ON RULES—1971 AMENDMENT

The amendment adds Columbus Day to the list of legal holidays to conform the subdivision to the Act of June 28, 1968, 82 Stat. 250, which constituted Columbus Day a legal holiday effective after January 1, 1971.

The Act, which amended Title 5, U.S.C. §6103(a), changes the day on which certain holidays are to be observed. Washington's Birthday, Memorial Day and Veterans Day are to be observed on the third Monday in February, the last Monday in May and the fourth Monday in October, respectively, rather than, as heretofore, on February 22, May 30, and November 11, respectively. Columbus Day is to be observed on the second Monday in October. New Year's Day, Independence Day, Thanksgiving Day and Christmas continue to be observed on the traditional days.

NOTES OF ADVISORY COMMITTEE ON RULES—1986 AMENDMENT

The Birthday of Martin Luther King, Jr., is added to the list of national holidays in Rule 26(a). The amendment to Rule 26(c) is technical. No substantive change is intended.

NOTES OF ADVISORY COMMITTEE ON RULES—1989 AMENDMENT

The proposed amendment brings Rule 26(a) into conformity with the provisions of Rule 6(a) of the Rules of Civil Procedure, Rule 45(a) of the Rules of Criminal Procedure, and Rule 9006(a) of the Rules of Bankruptcy Procedure which allow additional time for filing whenever a clerk's office is inaccessible on the last day for filing due to weather or other conditions.

NOTES OF ADVISORY COMMITTEE ON RULES—1996 AMENDMENT

The amendment is a companion to the proposed amendments to Rule 25 that permit service on a party by commercial carrier. The amendments to subdivision (c) of this rule make the three-day extension applicable not only when service is accomplished by mail, but whenever delivery to the party being served occurs later than the date of service stated in the proof of service. When service is by mail or commercial carrier, the proof of service recites the date of mailing or delivery to the commercial carrier. If the party being served receives the paper on a later date, the three-day extension applies. If the party being served receives the paper on the same date as the date of service recited in the proof of service, the three-day extension is not available.

The amendment also states that the three-day extension is three calendar days. Rule 26(a) states that when a period prescribed or allowed by the rules is less than seven days, intermediate Saturdays, Sundays, and legal holidays do not count. Whether the three-day extension in Rule 26(c) is such a period, meaning that three-days could actually be five or even six days, is unclear. The D.C. Circuit recently held that the parallel three-day extension provided in the Civil Rules is not such a period and that weekends and legal holidays do count. CNPq v. Inter-Trade, 50 F.3d 56 (D.C. Cir. 1995). The Committee believes that is the right result and that the issue should be resolved. Providing that the extension is three calendar days means that if a period would otherwise end on Thursday but the three-day extension applies, the paper must be filed on Monday. Friday, Saturday, and Sunday are the extension days. Because the last day of the period as extended is Sunday, the paper must be filed the next day, Monday.

COMMITTEE NOTES ON RULES—1998 AMENDMENT

The language and organization of the rule are amended to make the rule more easily understood. In addition to changes made to improve the understanding, the Advisory Committee has changed language to make style and terminology consistent throughout the appellate rules. These changes are intended to be stylistic only; two substantive changes are made, however, in subdivision (a).

Subdivision (a). First, the amendments make the computation method prescribed in this rule applicable to any time period imposed by a local rule. This means that if a local rule establishing a time limit is permitted, the national rule will govern the computation of that period.

Second, paragraph (a)(2) includes language clarifying that whenever the rules establish a time period in "calendar days," weekends and legal holidays are counted.

COMMITTEE NOTES ON RULES—2002 AMENDMENT

Subdivision (a)(2). The Federal Rules of Civil Procedure and the Federal Rules of Criminal Procedure compute time differently than the Federal Rules of Appellate Procedure. Fed. R. Civ. P. 6(a) and Fed. R. Crim. P. 45(a) provide that, in computing any period of time, "[w]hen the period of time prescribed or allowed is less than 11 days, intermediate Saturdays, Sundays, and legal holidays shall be excluded in the computation." By contrast, Rule 26(a)(2) provides that, in computing any period of time, a litigant should "[e]xclude intermediate Saturdays, Sundays, and legal holidays when the period is less than 7 days, unless stated in calendar days." Thus, deadlines of 7, 8, 9, and 10 days are calculated differently under the rules of civil and criminal procedure than they are under the rules of appellate procedure. This creates a trap for unwary litigants. No good reason for this discrepancy is apparent, and thus Rule 26(a)(2) has been amended so that, under all three sets of rules, intermediate Saturdays, Sundays, and legal holidays will be excluded when computing deadlines under 11 days but will be counted when computing deadlines of 11 days and over.

Changes Made After Publication and Comments. No changes were made to the text of the proposed amendment or to the Committee Note.

Subdivision (c). Rule 26(c) has been amended to provide that when a paper is served on a party by electronic means, and that party is required or permitted to respond to that paper within a prescribed period, 3 calendar days are added to the prescribed period. Electronic service is usually instantaneous, but sometimes it is not, because of technical problems. Also, if a paper is electronically transmitted to a party on a Friday evening, the party may not realize that he or she has been served until two or three days later. Finally, extending the "3-day rule" to electronic service will encourage parties to consent to such service under Rule 25(c).

Changes Made After Publication and Comments. No changes were made to the text of the proposed amendment or to the Committee Note.

COMMITTEE NOTES ON RULES—2005 AMENDMENT

Subdivision (a)(4). Rule 26(a)(4) has been amended to refer to the third Monday in February as "Washington's Birthday." A federal statute officially designates the holiday as "Washington's Birthday," reflecting the desire of Congress specially to honor the first president of the United States. See 5 U.S.C. §6103(a). During the 1998 restyling of the Federal Rules of Appellate Procedure, references to "Washington's Birthday" were mistakenly changed to "Presidents' Day." The amendment corrects that error.

Changes Made After Publication and Comments. No changes were made to the text of the proposed amendment or to the Committee Note.

COMMITTEE NOTES ON RULES—2009 AMENDMENT

Subdivision (a). Subdivision (a) has been amended to simplify and clarify the provisions that describe how deadlines are computed. Subdivision (a) governs the computation of any time period found in a statute that does not specify a method of computing time, a Federal Rule of Appellate Procedure, a local rule, or a court order. In accordance with Rule 47(a)(1), a local rule may not direct that a deadline be computed in a manner inconsistent with subdivision (a).

The time-computation provisions of subdivision (a) apply only when a time period must be computed. They do not apply when a fixed time to act is set. The amendments thus carry forward the approach taken in Violette v. P.A. Days, Inc., 427 F.3d 1015, 1016 (6th Cir. 2005) (holding that Civil Rule 6(a) "does not apply to situations where the court has established a specific calendar day as a deadline"), and reject the contrary holding of In re American Healthcare Management, Inc., 900 F.2d 827, 832 (5th Cir. 1990) (holding that Bankruptcy Rule 9006(a) governs treatment of date-certain deadline set by court order). If, for example, the date for filing is "no later than November 1, 2007," subdivision (a) does not govern. But if a filing is required to be made "within 10 days" or "within 72 hours," subdivision (a) describes how that deadline is computed.

Subdivision (a) does not apply when computing a time period set by a statute if the statute specifies a method of computing time. See, e.g., 20 U.S.C. §7711(b)(1) (requiring certain petitions for review by a local educational agency or a state to be filed "within 30 working days (as determined by the local educational agency or State) after receiving notice of" federal agency decision).

Subdivision (a)(1). New subdivision (a)(1) addresses the computation of time periods that are stated in days. It also applies to time periods that are stated in weeks, months, or years; though no such time period currently appears in the Federal Rules of Appellate Procedure, such periods may be set by other covered provisions such as a local rule. See, e.g., Third Circuit Local Appellate Rule 46.3(c)(1). Subdivision (a)(1)(B)'s directive to "count every day" is relevant only if the period is stated in days (not weeks, months, or years).

Under former Rule 26(a), a period of 11 days or more was computed differently than a period of less than 11 days. Intermediate Saturdays, Sundays, and legal holidays were included in computing the longer periods, but excluded in computing the shorter periods. Former Rule 26(a) thus made computing deadlines unnecessarily complicated and led to counterintuitive results. For example, a 10-day period and a 14-day period that started on the same day usually ended on the same day—and the 10-day period not infrequently ended later than the 14-day period. See Miltimore Sales, Inc. v. Int'l Rectifier, Inc., 412 F.3d 685, 686 (6th Cir. 2005).

Under new subdivision (a)(1), all deadlines stated in days (no matter the length) are computed in the same way. The day of the event that triggers the deadline is not counted. All other days—including intermediate Saturdays, Sundays, and legal holidays—are counted, with only one exception: If the period ends on a Saturday, Sunday, or legal holiday, then the deadline falls on the next day that is not a Saturday, Sunday, or legal holiday. An illustration is provided below in the discussion of subdivision (a)(5). Subdivision (a)(3) addresses filing deadlines that expire on a day when the clerk's office is inaccessible.

Where subdivision (a) formerly referred to the "act, event, or default" that triggers the deadline, new subdivision (a) refers simply to the "event" that triggers the deadline; this change in terminology is adopted for brevity and simplicity, and is not intended to change meaning.

Periods previously expressed as less than 11 days will be shortened as a practical matter by the decision to count intermediate Saturdays, Sundays, and legal holidays in computing all periods. Many of those periods have been lengthened to compensate for the change. See, e.g., Rules 5(b)(2), 5(d)(1), 28.1(f), & 31(a).

Most of the 10-day periods were adjusted to meet the change in computation method by setting 14 days as the new period. A 14-day period corresponds to the most frequent result of a 10-day period under the former computation method—two Saturdays and two Sundays were excluded, giving 14 days in all. A 14-day period has an additional advantage. The final day falls on the same day of the week as the event that triggered the period—the 14th day after a Monday, for example, is a Monday. This advantage of using week-long periods led to adopting 7-day periods to replace some of the periods set at less than 10 days, and 21-day periods to replace 20-day periods. Thirty-day and longer periods, however, were retained without change.

Subdivision (a)(2). New subdivision (a)(2) addresses the computation of time periods that are stated in hours. No such deadline currently appears in the Federal Rules of Appellate Procedure. But some statutes contain deadlines stated in hours, as do some court orders issued in expedited proceedings.

Under subdivision (a)(2), a deadline stated in hours starts to run immediately on the occurrence of the event that triggers the deadline. The deadline generally ends when the time expires. If, however, the time period expires at a specific time (say, 2:17 p.m.) on a Saturday, Sunday, or legal holiday, then the deadline is extended to the same time (2:17 p.m.) on the next day that is not a Saturday, Sunday, or legal holiday. Periods stated in hours are not to be "rounded up" to the next whole hour. Subdivision (a)(3) addresses situations when the clerk's office is inaccessible during the last hour before a filing deadline expires.

Subdivision (a)(2)(B) directs that every hour be counted. Thus, for example, a 72-hour period that commences at 10:00 a.m. on Friday, November 2, 2007, will run until 9:00 a.m. on Monday, November 5; the discrepancy in start and end times in this example results from the intervening shift from daylight saving time to standard time.

Subdivision (a)(3). When determining the last day of a filing period stated in days or a longer unit of time, a day on which the clerk's office is not accessible because of the weather or another reason is treated like a Saturday, Sunday, or legal holiday. When determining the end of a filing period stated in hours, if the clerk's office is inaccessible during the last hour of the filing period computed under subdivision (a)(2) then the period is extended to the same time on the next day that is not a weekend, holiday or day when the clerk's office is inaccessible.

Subdivision (a)(3)'s extensions apply "[u]nless the court orders otherwise." In some circumstances, the court might not wish a period of inaccessibility to trigger a full 24-hour extension; in those instances, the court can specify a briefer extension.

The text of the rule no longer refers to "weather or other conditions" as the reason for the inaccessibility of the clerk's office. The reference to "weather" was deleted from the text to underscore that inaccessibility can occur for reasons unrelated to weather, such as an outage of the electronic filing system. Weather can still be a reason for inaccessibility of the clerk's office. The rule does not attempt to define inaccessibility. Rather, the concept will continue to develop through caselaw, see, e.g., Tchakmakjian v. Department of Defense, 57 Fed. Appx. 438, 441 (Fed. Cir. 2003) (unpublished per curiam opinion) (inaccessibility "due to anthrax concerns"); cf. William G. Phelps, When Is Office of Clerk of Court Inaccessible Due to Weather or Other Conditions for Purpose of Computing Time Period for Filing Papers under Rule 6(a) of Federal Rules of Civil Procedure, 135 A.L.R. Fed. 259 (1996) (collecting cases). In addition, local provisions may address inaccessibility for purposes of electronic filing.

Subdivision (a)(4). New subdivision (a)(4) defines the end of the last day of a period for purposes of subdivision (a)(1). Subdivision (a)(4) does not apply in computing periods stated in hours under subdivision (a)(2), and does not apply if a different time is set by a statute, local rule, or order in the case. A local rule may, for example, address the problems that might arise under subdivision (a)(4)(A) if a single district has clerk's offices in different time zones, or provide that papers filed in a drop box after the normal hours of the clerk's office are filed as of the day that is date-stamped on the papers by a device in the drop box.

28 U.S.C. §452 provides that "[a]ll courts of the United States shall be deemed always open for the purpose of filing proper papers, issuing and returning process, and making motions and orders." A corresponding provision exists in Rule 45(a)(2). Some courts have held that these provisions permit an after-hours filing by handing the papers to an appropriate official. See, e.g., Casalduc v. Diaz, 117 F.2d 915, 917 (1st Cir. 1941). Subdivision (a)(4) does not address the effect of the statute on the question of after-hours filing; instead, the rule is designed to deal with filings in the ordinary course without regard to Section 452.

Subdivision (a)(4)(A) addresses electronic filings in the district court. For example, subdivision (a)(4)(A) would apply to an electronically-filed notice of appeal. Subdivision (a)(4)(B) addresses electronic filings in the court of appeals.

Subdivision (a)(4)(C) addresses filings by mail under Rules 25(a)(2)(B)(i) and 13(b), filings by third-party commercial carrier under Rule 25(a)(2)(B)(ii), and inmate filings under Rules 4(c)(1) and 25(a)(2)(C). For such filings, subdivision (a)(4)(C) provides that the "last day" ends at the latest time (prior to midnight in the filer's time zone) that the filer can properly submit the filing to the post office, third-party commercial carrier, or prison mail system (as applicable) using the filer's chosen method of submission. For example, if a correctional institution's legal mail system's rules of operation provide that items may only be placed in the mail system between 9:00 a.m. and 5:00 p.m., then the "last day" for filings under Rules 4(c)(1) and 25(a)(2)(C) by inmates in that institution ends at 5:00 p.m. As another example, if a filer uses a drop box maintained by a third-party commercial carrier, the "last day" ends at the time of that drop box's last scheduled pickup. Filings by mail under Rule 13(b) continue to be subject to §7502 of the Internal Revenue Code, as amended, and the applicable regulations.

Subdivision (a)(4)(D) addresses all other non-electronic filings; for such filings, the last day ends under (a)(4)(D) when the clerk's office in which the filing is made is scheduled to close.

Subdivision (a)(5). New subdivision (a)(5) defines the "next" day for purposes of subdivisions (a)(1)(C) and (a)(2)(C). The Federal Rules of Appellate Procedure contain both forward-looking time periods and backward-looking time periods. A forward-looking time period requires something to be done within a period of time after an event. See, e.g., Rule 4(a)(1)(A) (subject to certain exceptions, notice of appeal in a civil case must be filed "within 30 days after the judgment or order appealed from is entered"). A backward-looking time period requires something to be done within a period of time before an event. See, e.g., Rule 31(a)(1) ("[A] reply brief must be filed at least 7 days before argument, unless the court, for good cause, allows a later filing."). In determining what is the "next" day for purposes of subdivisions (a)(1)(C) and (a)(2)(C), one should continue counting in the same direction—that is, forward when computing a forward-looking period and backward when computing a backward-looking period. If, for example, a filing is due within 10 days after an event, and the tenth day falls on Saturday, September 1, 2007, then the filing is due on Tuesday, September 4, 2007 (Monday, September 3, is Labor Day). But if a filing is due 10 days before an event, and the tenth day falls on Saturday, September 1, then the filing is due on Friday, August 31. If the clerk's office is inaccessible on August 31, then subdivision (a)(3) extends the filing deadline forward to the next accessible day that is not a Saturday, Sunday or legal holiday—no earlier than Tuesday, September 4.

Subdivision (a)(6). New subdivision (a)(6) defines "legal holiday" for purposes of the Federal Rules of Appellate Procedure, including the time-computation provisions of subdivision (a). Subdivision (a)(6) continues to include within the definition of "legal holiday" days that are declared a holiday by the President or Congress.

For forward-counted periods—i.e., periods that are measured after an event—subdivision (a)(6)(C) includes certain state holidays within the definition of legal holidays. However, state legal holidays are not recognized in computing backward-counted periods. For both forward- and backward-counted periods, the rule thus protects those who may be unsure of the effect of state holidays. For forward-counted deadlines, treating state holidays the same as federal holidays extends the deadline. Thus, someone who thought that the federal courts might be closed on a state holiday would be safeguarded against an inadvertent late filing. In contrast, for backward-counted deadlines, not giving state holidays the treatment of federal holidays allows filing on the state holiday itself rather than the day before. Take, for example, Monday, April 21, 2008 (Patriot's Day, a legal holiday in the relevant state). If a filing is due 14 days after an event, and the fourteenth day is April 21, then the filing is due on Tuesday, April 22 because Monday, April 21 counts as a legal holiday. But if a filing is due 14 days before an event, and the fourteenth day is Monday, April 21; the filing is due on Monday, April 21; the fact that April 21 is a state holiday does not make April 21 a legal holiday for purposes of computing this backward-counted deadline. But note that if the clerk's office is inaccessible on Monday, April 21, then subdivision (a)(3) extends the April 21 filing deadline forward to the next accessible day that is not a Saturday, Sunday or legal holiday—no earlier than Tuesday, April 22.

Subdivision (c). To specify that a period should be calculated by counting all intermediate days, including weekends or holidays, the Rules formerly used the term "calendar days." Because new subdivision (a) takes a "days-are-days" approach under which all intermediate days are counted, no matter how short the period, "3 calendar days" in subdivision (c) is amended to read simply "3 days."

Rule 26(c) has been amended to eliminate uncertainty about application of the 3-day rule. Civil Rule 6(e) was amended in 2004 to eliminate similar uncertainty in the Civil Rules.

Under the amendment, a party that is required or permitted to act within a prescribed period should first calculate that period, without reference to the 3-day rule provided by Rule 26(c), but with reference to the other time computation provisions of the Appellate Rules. After the party has identified the date on which the prescribed period would expire but for the operation of Rule 26(c), the party should add 3 calendar days. The party must act by the third day of the extension, unless that day is a Saturday, Sunday, or legal holiday, in which case the party must act by the next day that is not a Saturday, Sunday, or legal holiday.

To illustrate: A paper is served by mail on Thursday, November 1, 2007. The prescribed time to respond is 30 days. The prescribed period ends on Monday, December 3 (because the 30th day falls on a Saturday, the prescribed period extends to the following Monday). Under Rule 26(c), three calendar days are added—Tuesday, Wednesday, and Thursday—and thus the response is due on Thursday, December 6.

Changes Made After Publication and Comment. No changes were made after publication and comment, except for the style changes (described below) [omitted] which were suggested by Professor Kimble.

COMMITTEE NOTES ON RULES—2016 AMENDMENT

Subdivision (a)(4)(C). The reference to Rule 13(b) is revised to refer to Rule 13(a)(2) in light of a 2013 amendment to Rule 13. The amendment to subdivision (a)(4)(C) is technical and no substantive change is intended.

Subdivision (c). Rule 26(c) is amended to remove service by electronic means under Rule 25(c)(1)(D) from the modes of service that allow 3 added days to act after being served.

Rule 25(c) was amended in 2002 to provide for service by electronic means. Although electronic transmission seemed virtually instantaneous even then, electronic service was included in the modes of service that allow 3 added days to act after being served. There were concerns that the transmission might be delayed for some time, and particular concerns that incompatible systems might make it difficult or impossible to open attachments. Those concerns have been substantially alleviated by advances in technology and widespread skill in using electronic transmission.

A parallel reason for allowing the 3 added days was that electronic service was authorized only with the consent of the person to be served. Concerns about the reliability of electronic transmission might have led to refusals of consent; the 3 added days were calculated to alleviate these concerns.

Diminution of the concerns that prompted the decision to allow the 3 added days for electronic transmission is not the only reason for discarding this indulgence. Many rules have been changed to ease the task of computing time by adopting 7-, 14-, 21-, and 28-day periods that allow "day-of-the-week" counting. Adding 3 days at the end complicated the counting, and increased the occasions for further complication by invoking the provisions that apply when the last day is a Saturday, Sunday, or legal holiday.

Electronic service after business hours, or just before or during a weekend or holiday, may result in a practical reduction in the time available to respond. Extensions of time may be warranted to prevent prejudice.

Rule 26(c) has also been amended to refer to instances when a party "may or must act . . . after being served" rather than to instances when a party "may or must act . . . after service." If, in future, an Appellate Rule sets a deadline for a party to act after that party itself effects service on another person, this change in language will clarify that Rule 26(c)'s three added days are not accorded to the party who effected service.

COMMITTEE NOTES ON RULES—2018 AMENDMENT

The amendments adjust references to subdivisions of Rule 25 that have been renumbered.

COMMITTEE NOTES ON RULES—2019 AMENDMENT

The amendment in subdivision (c) simplifies the expression of the current rules for when three days are added. In addition, the amendment revises the subdivision to conform to the amendments to Rule 25(d).

Rule 26.1. Disclosure Statement

(a) Nongovernmental Corporations. Any nongovernmental corporation that is a party to a proceeding in a court of appeals must file a statement that identifies any parent corporation and any publicly held corporation that owns 10% or more of its stock or states that there is no such corporation. The same requirement applies to a nongovernmental corporation that seeks to intervene.

(b) Organizational Victims in Criminal Cases. In a criminal case, unless the government shows good cause, it must file a statement that identifies any organizational victim of the alleged criminal activity. If the organizational victim is a corporation, the statement must also disclose the information required by Rule 26.1(a) to the extent it can be obtained through due diligence.

(c) Bankruptcy Cases. In a bankruptcy case, the debtor, the trustee, or, if neither is a party, the appellant must file a statement that:
    (1) identifies each debtor not named in the caption; and
    (2) for each debtor that is a corporation, discloses the information required by Rule 26.1(a).

(d) Time for Filing; Supplemental Filing. The Rule 26.1 statement must:
    (1) be filed with the principal brief or upon filing a motion, response, petition, or answer in the court of appeals, whichever occurs first, unless a local rule requires earlier filing;
    (2) be included before the table of contents in the principal brief; and
    (3) be supplemented whenever the information required under Rule 26.1 changes.

(e) Number of Copies. If the Rule 26.1 statement is filed before the principal brief, or if a supplemental statement is filed, an original and 3 copies must be filed unless the court requires a different number by local rule or by order in a particular case.

(As added Apr. 25, 1989, eff. Dec. 1, 1989; amended Apr. 30, 1991, eff. Dec. 1, 1991; Apr. 29, 1994, eff. Dec. 1, 1994; Apr. 24, 1998, eff. Dec. 1, 1998; Apr. 29, 2002, eff. Dec. 1, 2002; Apr. 25, 2019, eff. Dec. 1, 2019.)

NOTES OF ADVISORY COMMITTEE ON RULES—1989

The purpose of this rule is to assist judges in making a determination of whether they have any interests in any of a party's related corporate entities that would disqualify the judges from hearing the appeal. The committee believes that this rule represents minimum disclosure requirements. If a Court of Appeals wishes to require additional information, a court is free to do so by local rule. However, the committee requests the courts to consider the desirability of uniformity and the burden that varying circuit rules creates on attorneys who practice in many circuits.

NOTES OF ADVISORY COMMITTEE ON RULES—1994 AMENDMENT

The amendment requires a party to file three copies of the disclosure statement whenever the statement is filed before the party's principal brief. Because the statement is included in each copy of the party's brief, there is no need to require the filing of additional copies at that time. A court of appeals may require the filing of a different number of copies by local rule or by order in a particular case.

COMMITTEE NOTES ON RULES—1998 AMENDMENT

The language and organization of the rule are amended to make the rule more easily understood. In addition to changes made to improve the understanding, the Advisory Committee has changed language to make style and terminology consistent throughout the appellate rules. These changes are intended to be stylistic only; a substantive change is made, however, in subdivision (a).

Subdivison [sic] (a). The amendment deletes the requirement that a corporate party identify subsidiaries and affiliates that have issued shares to the public. Although several circuit rules require identification of such entities, the Committee believes that such disclosure is unnecessary.

A disclosure statement assists a judge in ascertaining whether or not the judge has an interest that should cause the judge to recuse himself or herself from the case. Given that purpose, disclosure of entities that would not be adversely affected by a decision in the case is unnecessary.

Disclosure of a party's parent corporation is necessary because a judgment against a subsidiary can negatively impact the parent. A judge who owns stock in the parent corporation, therefore, has an interest in litigation involving the subsidiary. The rule requires disclosure of all of a party's parent corporations meaning grandparent and great grandparent corporations as well. For example, if a party is a closely held corporation, the majority shareholder of which is a corporation formed by a publicly traded corporation for the purpose of acquiring and holding the shares of the party, the publicly traded grandparent corporation should be disclosed. Conversely, disclosure of a party's subsidiaries or affiliated corporations is ordinarily unnecessary. For example, if a party is a part owner of a corporation in which a judge owns stock, the possibility is quite remote that the judge might be biased by the fact that the judge and the litigant are co-owners of a corporation.

The amendment, however, adds a requirement that the party lists all its stockholders that are publicly held companies owning 10% or more of the stock of the party. A judgment against a corporate party can adversely affect the value of the company's stock and, therefore, persons owning stock in the party have an interest in the outcome of the litigation. A judge owning stock in a corporate party ordinarily recuses himself or herself. The new requirement takes the analysis one step further and assumes that if a judge owns stock in a publicly held corporation which in turn owns 10% or more of the stock in the party, the judge may have sufficient interest in the litigation to require recusal. The 10% threshold ensures that the corporation in which the judge may own stock is itself sufficiently invested in the party that a judgment adverse to the party could have an adverse impact upon the investing corporation in which the judge may own stock. This requirement is modeled on the Seventh Circuit's disclosure requirement.

Subdivision (b). The language requiring inclusion of the disclosure statement in a party's principal brief is moved to this subdivision because it deals with the time for filing the statement.

COMMITTEE NOTES ON RULES—2002 AMENDMENT

a. Alternative One [At its June 7–8, 2001, meeting, the Committee on Rules of Practice and Procedure voted to reject Alternative One.]

Subdivision (a). Rule 26.1(a) presently requires nongovernmental corporate parties to file a "corporate disclosure statement." In that statement, a nongovernmental corporate party is required to identify all of its parent corporations and all publicly held corporations that own 10% or more of its stock. The corporate disclosure statement is intended to assist judges in determining whether they must recuse themselves by reason of "a financial interest in the subject matter in controversy." Code of Judicial Conduct, Canon 3C(1)(c) (1972).

Rule 26.1(a) has been amended to require that nongovernmental corporate parties who currently do not have to file a corporate disclosure statement—that is, nongovernmental corporate parties who do not have any parent corporations and at least 10% of whose stock is not owned by any publicly held corporation—inform the court of that fact. At present, when a corporate disclosure statement is not filed, courts do not know whether it has not been filed because there was nothing to report or because of ignorance of Rule 26.1(a).

Rule 26.1(a) does not require the disclosure of all information that could conceivably be relevant to a judge who is trying to decide whether he or she has a "financial interest" in a case. Experience with divergent disclosure practices and improving technology may provide the foundation for more comprehensive disclosure requirements. The Judicial Conference, supported by the committees that work regularly with the Code of Judicial Conduct and by the Administrative Office of the United States Courts, is in the best position to develop any additional requirements and to adjust those requirements as technology and other developments warrant. Thus, Rule 26.1(a) has been amended to authorize the Judicial Conference to promulgate more detailed financial disclosure requirements—requirements that might apply beyond nongovernmental corporate parties.

As has been true in the past, Rule 26.1(a) does not forbid the promulgation of local rules that require disclosures in addition to those required by Rule 26.1(a) itself. However, along with the authority provided to the Judicial Conference to require additional disclosures is the authority to preempt any local rulemaking on the topic of financial disclosure.

Subdivision (b). Rule 26.1(b) has been amended to require parties to file supplemental disclosure statements whenever there is a change in the information that Rule 26.1(a) requires the parties to disclose. For example, if a publicly held corporation acquires 10% or more of a party's stock after the party has filed its disclosure statement, the party should file a supplemental statement identifying that publicly held corporation.

Subdivision (c). Rule 26.1(c) has been amended to provide that a party who is required to file a supplemental disclosure statement must file an original and 3 copies, unless a local rule or an order entered in a particular case provides otherwise.

b. Alternative Two [At its June 7–8, 2001, meeting, the Committee on Rules of Practice and Procedure voted to approve Alternative Two.]

Subdivision (a). Rule 26.1(a) requires nongovernmental corporate parties to file a "corporate disclosure statement." In that statement, a nongovernmental corporate party is required to identify all of its parent corporations and all publicly held corporations that own 10% or more of its stock. The corporate disclosure statement is intended to assist judges in determining whether they must recuse themselves by reason of "a financial interest in the subject matter in controversy." Code of Judicial Conduct, Canon 3C(1)(c) (1972).

Rule 26.1(a) has been amended to require that nongovernmental corporate parties who have not been required to file a corporate disclosure statement—that is, nongovernmental corporate parties who do not have any parent corporations and at least 10% of whose stock is not owned by any publicly held corporation—inform the court of that fact. At present, when a corporate disclosure statement is not filed, courts do not know whether it has not been filed because there was nothing to report or because of ignorance of Rule 26.1.

Subdivision (b). Rule 26.1(b) has been amended to require parties to file supplemental disclosure statements whenever there is a change in the information that Rule 26.1(a) requires the parties to disclose. For example, if a publicly held corporation acquires 10% or more of a party's stock after the party has filed its disclosure statement, the party should file a supplemental statement identifying that publicly held corporation.

Subdivision (c). Rule 26.1(c) has been amended to provide that a party who is required to file a supplemental disclosure statement must file an original and 3 copies, unless a local rule or an order entered in a particular case provides otherwise.

Changes Made After Publication and Comments. The Committee is submitting two versions of proposed Rule 26.1 for the consideration of the Standing Committee.

The first version—"Alternative One"—is the same as the version that was published, except that the rule has been amended to refer to "any information that may be publicly designated by the Judicial Conference" instead of to "any information that may be required by the Judicial Conference." At its April meeting, the Committee gave unconditional approval to all of "Alternative One," except the Judicial Conference provisions. The Committee conditioned its approval of the Judicial Conference provisions on the Standing Committee's assuring itself that lawyers would have ready access to any standards promulgated by the Judicial Conference and that the Judicial Conference provisions were consistent with the Rules Enabling Act.

The second version—"Alternative Two"—is the same as the version that was published, except that the Judicial Conference provisions have been eliminated. The Civil Rules Committee met several days after the Appellate Rules Committee and joined the Bankruptcy Rules Committee in disapproving the Judicial Conference provisions. Given the decreasing likelihood that the Judicial Conference provisions will be approved by the Standing Committee, I asked Prof. Schiltz to draft, and the Appellate Rules Committee to approve, a version of Rule 26.1 that omitted those provisions. "Alternative Two" was circulated to and approved by the Committee in late April.

I should note that, at its April meeting, the Appellate Rules Committee discussed the financial disclosure provision that was approved by the Bankruptcy Rules Committee. That provision defines the scope of the financial disclosure obligation much differently than the provisions approved by the Appellate, Civil, and Criminal Rules Committees, which are based on existing Rule 26.1. For example, the bankruptcy provision requires disclosure when a party "directly or indirectly" owns 10 percent or more of "any class" of a publicly or privately held corporation's "equity interests." Members of the Appellate Rules Committee expressed several concerns about the provision approved by the Bankruptcy Rules Committee, objecting both to its substance and to its ambiguity.

COMMITTEE NOTES ON RULES—2019 AMENDMENT

These amendments are designed to help judges determine whether they must recuse themselves because of an "interest that could be affected substantially by the outcome of the proceeding." Code of Judicial Conduct, Canon 3(C)(1)(c) (2009).

Subdivision (a) is amended to encompass nongovernmental corporations that seek to intervene on appeal.

New subdivision (b) corresponds to the disclosure requirement in Criminal Rule 12.4(a)(2). Like Criminal Rule 12.4(a)(2), subdivision (b) requires the government to identify organizational victims to help judges comply with their obligations under the Code of Judicial Conduct. In some cases, there are many organizational victims, but the effect of the crime on each one is relatively small. In such cases, the amendment allows the government to show good cause to be relieved of making the disclosure statements because the organizations' interests could not be "affected substantially by the outcome of the proceedings."

New subdivision (c) requires disclosure of the names of all the debtors in bankruptcy cases, because the names of the debtors are not always included in the caption in appeals. Subdivision (c) also imposes disclosure requirements concerning the ownership of corporate debtors.

Subdivisions (d) and (e) (formerly subdivisions (b) and (c)) apply to all the disclosure requirements in Rule 26.1.

Rule 27. Motions

(a) In General.

(1) Application for Relief. An application for an order or other relief is made by motion unless these rules prescribe another form. A motion must be in writing unless the court permits otherwise.

(2) Contents of a Motion.

(A) Grounds and Relief Sought. A motion must state with particularity the grounds for the motion, the relief sought, and the legal argument necessary to support it.

(B) Accompanying Documents.

(i) Any affidavit or other paper necessary to support a motion must be served and filed with the motion.

(ii) An affidavit must contain only factual information, not legal argument.

(iii) A motion seeking substantive relief must include a copy of the trial court's opinion or agency's decision as a separate exhibit.

(C) Documents Barred or Not Required.

(i) A separate brief supporting or responding to a motion must not be filed.

(ii) A notice of motion is not required.

(iii) A proposed order is not required.

(3) Response.

(A) Time to file. Any party may file a response to a motion; Rule 27(a)(2) governs its contents. The response must be filed within 10 days after service of the motion unless the court shortens or extends the time. A motion authorized by Rules 8, 9, 18, or 41 may be granted before the 10-day period runs only if the court gives reasonable notice to the parties that it intends to act sooner.

(B) Request for Affirmative Relief. A response may include a motion for affirmative relief. The time to respond to the new motion, and to reply to that response, are governed by Rule 27(a)(3)(A) and (a)(4). The title of the response must alert the court to the request for relief.

(4) Reply to Response. Any reply to a response must be filed within 7 days after service of the response. A reply must not present matters that do not relate to the response.

(b) Disposition of a Motion for a Procedural Order. The court may act on a motion for a procedural order—including a motion under Rule 26(b)—at any time without awaiting a response, and may, by rule or by order in a particular case, authorize its clerk to act on specified types of procedural motions. A party adversely affected by the court's, or the clerk's, action may file a motion to reconsider, vacate, or modify that action. Timely opposition filed after the motion is granted in whole or in part does not constitute a request to reconsider, vacate, or modify the disposition; a motion requesting that relief must be filed.

(c) Power of a Single Judge to Entertain a Motion. A circuit judge may act alone on any motion, but may not dismiss or otherwise determine an appeal or other proceeding. A court of appeals may provide by rule or by order in a particular case that only the court may act on any motion or class of motions. The court may review the action of a single judge.

(d) Form of Papers; Length Limits; Number of Copies.

(1) Format.

(A) Reproduction. A motion, response, or reply may be reproduced by any process that yields a clear black image on light paper. The paper must be opaque and unglazed. Only one side of the paper may be used.

(B) Cover. A cover is not required, but there must be a caption that includes the case number, the name of the court, the title of the case, and a brief descriptive title indicating the purpose of the motion and identifying the party or parties for whom it is filed. If a cover is used, it must be white.

(C) Binding. The document must be bound in any manner that is secure, does not obscure the text, and permits the document to lie reasonably flat when open.

(D) Paper Size, Line Spacing, and Margins. The document must be on 8½ by 11 inch paper. The text must be double-spaced, but quotations more than two lines long may be indented and single-spaced. Headings and footnotes may be single-spaced. Margins must be at least one inch on all four sides. Page numbers may be placed in the margins, but no text may appear there.

(E) Typeface and Type Styles. The document must comply with the typeface requirements of Rule 32(a)(5) and the type-style requirements of Rule 32(a)(6).

(2) Length Limits. Except by the court's permission, and excluding the accompanying documents authorized by Rule 27(a)(2)(B):

(A) a motion or response to a motion produced using a computer must not exceed 5,200 words;

(B) a handwritten or typewritten motion or response to a motion must not exceed 20 pages;

(C) a reply produced using a computer must not exceed 2,600 words; and

(D) a handwritten or typewritten reply to a response must not exceed 10 pages.

(3) Number of Copies. An original and 3 copies must be filed unless the court requires a different number by local rule or by order in a particular case.

(e) Oral Argument. A motion will be decided without oral argument unless the court orders otherwise.

(As amended Apr. 1, 1979, eff. Aug. 1, 1979; Apr. 25, 1989, eff. Dec. 1, 1989; Apr. 29, 1994, eff. Dec. 1, 1994; Apr. 24, 1998, eff. Dec. 1, 1998; Apr. 29, 2002, eff. Dec. 1, 2002; Apr. 25, 2005, eff. Dec. 1, 2005; Mar. 26, 2009, eff. Dec. 1, 2009; Apr. 28, 2016, eff. Dec. 1, 2016.)

NOTES OF ADVISORY COMMITTEE ON RULES—1967

Subdivisions (a) and (b). Many motions seek relief of a sort which is ordinarily unopposed or which is granted as of course. The provision of subdivision (a) which permits any party to file a response in opposition to a motion within 7 days after its service upon him assumes that the motion is one of substance which ought not be acted upon without affording affected parties an opportunity to reply. A motion to dismiss or otherwise determine an appeal is clearly such a motion. Motions authorized by Rules 8, 9, 18 and 41 are likewise motions of substance; but in the nature of the relief sought, to afford an adversary an automatic delay of at least 7 days is undesirable, thus such motions may be acted upon after notice which is reasonable under the circumstances.

The term "motions for procedural orders" is used in subdivision (b) to describe motions which do not substantially affect the rights of the parties or the ultimate disposition of the appeal. To prevent delay in the disposition of such motions, subdivision (b) provides that they may be acted upon immediately without awaiting a response, subject to the right of any party who is adversely affected by the action to seek reconsideration.

Subdivision (c). Within the general consideration of procedure on motions is the problem of the power of a single circuit judge. Certain powers are granted to a single judge of a court of appeals by statute. Thus, under 28 U.S.C. §2101(f) a single judge may stay execution and enforcement of a judgment to enable a party aggrieved to obtain certiorari; under 28 U.S.C. §2251 a judge before whom a habeas corpus proceeding involving a person detained by state authority is pending may stay any proceeding against the person; under 28 U.S.C. §2253 a single judge may issue a certificate of probable cause. In addition, certain of these rules expressly grant power to a single judge. See Rules 8, 9 and 18.

This subdivision empowers a single circuit judge to act upon virtually all requests for intermediate relief which may be made during the course of an appeal or other proceeding. By its terms he may entertain and act upon any motion other than a motion to dismiss or otherwise determine an appeal or other proceeding. But the relief sought must be "relief which under these rules may properly be sought by motion."

Examples of the power conferred on a single judge by this subdivision are: to extend the time for transmitting the record or docketing the appeal (Rules 11 and 12); to permit intervention in agency cases (Rule 15), or substitution in any case (Rule 43); to permit an appeal in forma pauperis (Rule 24); to enlarge any time period fixed by the rules other than that for initiating a proceeding in the court of appeals (Rule 26(b)); to permit the filing of a brief by amicus curiae (Rule 29); to authorize the filing of a deferred appendix (Rule 30(c)), or dispense with the requirement of an appendix in a specific case (Rule 30(f)), or permit carbon copies of briefs or appendices to be used (Rule 32(a)); to permit the filing of additional briefs (Rule 28(c)), or the filing of briefs of extraordinary length (Rule 28(g)); to postpone oral argument (Rule 34(a)), or grant additional time therefor (Rule 34(b)).

Certain rules require that application for the relief or orders which they authorize be made by petition. Since relief under those rules may not properly be sought by motion, a single judge may not entertain requests for such relief. Thus a single judge may not act upon requests for permission to appeal (see Rules 5 and 6); or for mandamus or other extraordinary writs (see Rule 21), other than for stays or injunctions pendente lite, authority to grant which is "expressly conferred by these rules" on a single judge under certain circumstances (see Rules 8 and 18); or upon petitions for rehearing (see Rule 40).

A court of appeals may by order or rule abridge the power of a single judge if it is of the view that a motion or a class of motions should be disposed of by a panel. Exercise of any power granted a single judge is discretionary with the judge. The final sentence in this subdivision makes the disposition of any matter by a single judge subject to review by the court.

Notes of Advisory Committee on Rules—1979 Amendment

The proposed amendment would give sanction to local rules in a number of circuits permitting the clerk to dispose of specified types of procedural motions.

Notes of Advisory Committee on Rules—1989 Amendment

The amendment is technical. No substantive change is intended.

Notes of Advisory Committee on Rules—1994 Amendment

Subdivision (d). The amendment makes it clear that a court may require a different number of copies either by rule or by order in an individual case. The number of copies of any document that a court of appeals needs varies depending upon the way in which the court conducts business. The internal operation of the courts of appeals necessarily varies from circuit to circuit because of differences in the number of judges, the geographic area included within the circuit, and other such factors. Uniformity could be achieved only by setting the number of copies artificially high so that parties in all circuits file enough copies to satisfy the needs of the court requiring the greatest number. Rather than do that, the Committee decided to make it clear that local rules may require a greater or lesser number of copies and that, if the circumstances of a particular case indicate the need for a different number of copies in that case, the court may so order.

Committee Notes on Rules—1998 Amendment

In addition to amending Rule 27 to conform to uniform drafting standards, several substantive amendments are made. The Advisory Committee had been working on substantive amendments to Rule 27 just prior to completion of this larger project.

Subdivision (a). Paragraph (1) retains the language of the existing rule indicating that an application for an order or other relief is made by filing a motion unless another form is required by some other provision in the rules.

Paragraph (1) also states that a motion must be in writing unless the court permits otherwise. The writing requirement has been implicit in the rule; the Advisory Committee decided to make it explicit. There are, however, instances in which a court may permit oral motions. Perhaps the most common such instance would be a motion made during oral argument in the presence of opposing counsel; for example, a request for permission to submit a supplemental brief on an issue raised by the court for the first time at oral argument. Rather than limit oral motions to those made during oral argument or, conversely, assume the propriety of making even extremely complex motions orally during argument, the Advisory Committee decided that it is better to leave the determination of the propriety of an oral motion to the court's discretion. The provision does not disturb the practice in those circuits that permit certain procedural motions, such as a motion for extension of time for filing a brief, to be made by telephone and ruled upon by the clerk.

Paragraph (2) outlines the contents of a motion. It begins with the general requirement from the current rule that a motion must state with particularity the grounds supporting it and the relief requested. It adds a requirement that all legal arguments should be presented in the body of the motion; a separate brief or memorandum supporting or responding to a motion must not be filed. The Supreme Court uses this single document approach. Sup. Ct. R. 21.1. In furtherance of the requirement that all legal argument must be contained in the body of the motion, paragraph (2) also states that an affidavit that is attached to a motion should contain only factual information and not legal argument.

Paragraph (2) further states that whenever a motion requests substantive relief, a copy of the trial court's opinion or agency's decision must be attached.

Although it is common to present a district court with a proposed order along with the motion requesting relief, that is not the practice in the courts of appeals. A proposed order is not required and is not expected or desired. Nor is a notice of motion required.

Paragraph (3) retains the provisions of the current rule concerning the filing of a response to a motion except that the time for responding has been expanded to 10 days rather than 7 days. Because the time periods in the rule apply to a substantive motion as well as a procedural motion, the longer time period may help reduce the number of motions for extension of time, or at least provide a more realistic time frame within which to make and dispose of such a motion.

A party filing a response in opposition to a motion may also request affirmative relief. It is the Advisory Committee's judgment that it is permissible to combine the response and the new motion in the same document. Indeed, because there may be substantial overlap of arguments in the response and in the request for affirmative relief, a combined document may be preferable. If a request for relief is combined with a response, the caption of the document must alert the court to the request for relief. The time for a response to such a new request and for reply to that response are governed by the general rules regulating responses and replies.

Paragraph (4) is new. Two circuits currently have rules authorizing a reply. As a general matter, a reply should not reargue propositions presented in the motion or present matters that do not relate to the response. Sometimes matters relevant to the motion arise after the motion is filed; treatment of such matters in the reply is appropriate even though strictly speaking it may not relate to the response.

Subdivision (b). The material in this subdivision remains substantively unchanged except to clarify that one may file a motion for reconsideration, etc., of a disposition by either the court or the clerk. A new sentence is added indicating that if a motion is granted in whole or in part before the filing of timely opposition to the motion, the filing of the opposition is not treated as a request for reconsideration, etc. A party wishing to have the court reconsider, vacate, or modify the disposition must file a new motion that addresses the order granting the motion.

Although the rule does not require a court to do so, it would be helpful if, whenever a motion is disposed of before receipt of any response from the opposing party, the ruling indicates that it was issued without awaiting a response. Such a statement will aid the opposing party in deciding whether to request reconsideration. The opposing party may have mailed a response about the time of the ruling and be uncertain whether the court has considered it.

Subdivision (c). The changes in this subdivision are stylistic only. No substantive changes are intended.

Subdivision (d). This subdivision has been substantially revised.

The format requirements have been moved from Rule 32(b) to paragraph (1) of this subdivision. No cover is required, but a caption is needed as well as a descriptive title indicating the purpose of the motion and identifying the party or parties for whom it is filed. Spiral binding or secure stapling at the upper left-hand corner satisfies the binding requirement. But they are not intended to be the exclusive methods of binding.

Paragraph (2) establishes page limits; twenty pages for a motion or a response, and ten pages for a reply. Three circuits have established page limits by local rule. This rule does not establish special page limits for those instances in which a party combines a response to a motion with a new request for affirmative relief. Because a combined document most often will be used when there is substantial overlap in the argument in opposition to the motion and in the argument for the affirmative relief, twenty pages may be sufficient in most instances. If it is not, the party may request additional pages. If ten pages is insufficient for the original movant to both reply to the response, and respond to the new request for affirmative relief, two separate documents may be used or a request for additional pages may be made.

The changes in paragraph (4) are stylistic only. No substantive changes are intended.

Subdivision (e). This new provision makes it clear that there is no right to oral argument on a motion. Seven circuits have local rules stating that oral argument of motions will not be held unless the court orders it.

Committee Notes on Rules—2002 Amendment

Subdivision (a)(3)(A). Subdivision (a)(3)(A) presently requires that a response to a motion be filed within 10 days after service of the motion. Intermediate Saturdays, Sundays, and legal holidays are counted in computing that 10-day deadline, which means that, except when the 10-day deadline ends on a weekend or legal holiday, parties generally must respond to motions within 10 actual days.

Fed. R. App. P. 26(a)(2) has been amended to provide that, in computing any period of time, a litigant should "[e]xclude intermediate Saturdays, Sundays, and legal holidays when the period is less than 11 days, unless stated in calendar days." This change in the method of computing deadlines means that 10-day deadlines (such as that in subdivision (a)(3)(A)) have been lengthened as a practical matter. Under the new computation method, parties would never have less than 14 actual days to respond to motions, and legal holidays could extend that period to as much as 18 days.

Permitting parties to take two weeks or more to respond to motions would introduce significant and unwarranted delay into appellate proceedings. For that reason, the 10-day deadline in subdivision (a)(3)(A) has been reduced to 8 days. This change will, as a practical matter, ensure that every party will have at least 10 actual days—but, in the absence of a legal holiday, no more than 12 actual days—to respond to motions. The court continues to have discretion to shorten or extend that time in appropriate cases.

Changes Made After Publication and Comments. In response to the objections of commentators, the time to respond to a motion was increased from the proposed 7 days to 8 days. No other changes were made to the text of the proposed amendment or to the Committee Note.

Subdivision (a)(4). Subdivision (a)(4) presently requires that a reply to a response to a motion be filed within 7 days after service of the response. Intermediate Saturdays, Sundays, and legal holidays are counted in computing that 7-day deadline, which means that, except when the 7-day deadline ends on a weekend or legal holiday, parties generally must reply to responses to motions within one week.

Fed. R. App. P. 26(a)(2) has been amended to provide that, in computing any period of time, a litigant should "[e]xclude intermediate Saturdays, Sundays, and legal holidays when the period is less than 11 days, unless stated in calendar days." This change in the method of computing deadlines means that 7-day deadlines (such as that in subdivision (a)(4)) have been lengthened as a practical matter. Under the new computation method, parties would never have less than 9 actual days to reply to responses to motions, and legal holidays could extend that period to as much as 13 days.

Permitting parties to take 9 or more days to reply to a response to a motion would introduce significant and unwarranted delay into appellate proceedings. For that reason, the 7-day deadline in subdivision (a)(4) has been reduced to 5 days. This change will, as a practical matter, ensure that every party will have 7 actual days to file replies to responses to motions (in the absence of a legal holiday).

Changes Made After Publication and Comments. No changes were made to the text of the proposed amendment or to the Committee Note.

Subdivision (d)(1)(B). A cover is not required on motions, responses to motions, or replies to responses to motions. However, Rule 27(d)(1)(B) has been amended to provide that if a cover is nevertheless used on such a paper, the cover must be white. The amendment is intended to promote uniformity in federal appellate practice.

Changes Made After Publication and Comments. No changes were made to the text of the proposed amendment or to the Committee Note.

Subdivision (d)(1)(E). A new subdivision (E) has been added to Rule 27(d)(1) to provide that a motion, a response to a motion, and a reply to a response to a motion must comply with the typeface requirements of Rule 32(a)(5) and the type-style requirements of Rule 32(a)(6). The purpose of the amendment is to promote uniformity in federal appellate practice and to prevent the abuses that might occur if no restrictions were placed on the size of typeface used in motion papers.

Changes Made After Publication and Comments. No changes were made to the text of the proposed amendment or to the Committee Note.

Subdivision (a)(3)(A). Subdivision (a)(3)(A) formerly required that a response to a motion be filed "within 8 days after service of the motion unless the court shortens or extends the time." Prior to the 2002 amendments to Rule 27, subdivision (a)(3)(A) set this period at 10 days rather than 8 days. The period was changed in 2002 to reflect the change from a time-computation approach that counted intermediate weekends and holidays to an approach that did not. (Prior to the 2002 amendments, intermediate weekends and holidays were excluded only if the period was less than 7 days; after those amendments, such days were excluded if the period was less than 11 days.) Under current Rule 26(a), intermediate weekends and holidays are counted for all periods. Accordingly, revised subdivision (a)(3)(A) once again sets the period at 10 days.

Subdivision (a)(4). Subdivision (a)(4) formerly required that a reply to a response be filed "within 5 days after service of the response." Prior to the 2002 amendments, this period was set at 7 days; in 2002 it was shortened in the light of the 2002 change in time-computation approach (discussed above). Under current Rule 26(a), intermediate weekends and holidays are counted for all periods, and revised subdivision (a)(4) once again sets the period at 7 days.

The page limits previously employed in Rules 5, 21, 27, 35, and 40 have been largely overtaken by changes in technology. For papers produced using a computer, those page limits are now replaced by word limits. The word limits were derived from the current page limits using the assumption that one page is equivalent to 260 words. Papers produced using a computer must include the certificate of compliance required by Rule 32(g); Form 6 in the Appendix of Forms suffices to meet that requirement. Page limits are retained for papers prepared without the aid of a computer (i.e., handwritten or typewritten papers). For both the word limit and the page limit, the calculation excludes the accompanying documents required by Rule 27(a)(2)(B) and any items listed in Rule 32(f).

Rule 28. Briefs

(a) Appellant's Brief. The appellant's brief must contain, under appropriate headings and in the order indicated:
    (1) a disclosure statement if required by Rule 26.1;
    (2) a table of contents, with page references;
    (3) a table of authorities—cases (alphabetically arranged), statutes, and other authorities—with references to the pages of the brief where they are cited;
    (4) a jurisdictional statement, including:
        (A) the basis for the district court's or agency's subject-matter jurisdiction, with citations to applicable statutory provisions and stating relevant facts establishing jurisdiction;
        (B) the basis for the court of appeals' jurisdiction, with citations to applicable statutory provisions and stating relevant facts establishing jurisdiction;
        (C) the filing dates establishing the timeliness of the appeal or petition for review; and
        (D) an assertion that the appeal is from a final order or judgment that disposes of all parties' claims, or information establishing the court of appeals' jurisdiction on some other basis;

    (5) a statement of the issues presented for review;
    (6) a concise statement of the case setting out the facts relevant to the issues submitted for review, describing the relevant procedural history, and identifying the rulings presented for review, with appropriate references to the record (see Rule 28(e));
    (7) a summary of the argument, which must contain a succinct, clear, and accurate statement of the arguments made in the body of the brief, and which must not merely repeat the argument headings;
    (8) the argument, which must contain:
        (A) appellant's contentions and the reasons for them, with citations to the authorities and parts of the record on which the appellant relies; and
        (B) for each issue, a concise statement of the applicable standard of review (which may appear in the discussion of the issue or under a separate heading placed before the discussion of the issues);

    (9) a short conclusion stating the precise relief sought; and
    (10) the certificate of compliance, if required by Rule 32(g)(1).

(b) Appellee's Brief. The appellee's brief must conform to the requirements of Rule 28(a)(1)–(8) and (10), except that none of the following need appear unless the appellee is dissatisfied with the appellant's statement:
    (1) the jurisdictional statement;
    (2) the statement of the issues;
    (3) the statement of the case; and
    (4) the statement of the standard of review.

(c) Reply Brief. The appellant may file a brief in reply to the appellee's brief. Unless the court permits, no further briefs may be filed. A reply brief must contain a table of contents, with page references, and a table of authorities—cases (alphabetically arranged), statutes, and other authorities—with references to the pages of the reply brief where they are cited.

(d) References to Parties. In briefs and at oral argument, counsel should minimize use of the terms "appellant" and "appellee." To make briefs clear, counsel should use the parties' actual names or the designations used in the lower court or agency proceeding, or such descriptive terms as "the employee," "the injured person," "the taxpayer," "the ship," "the stevedore."

(e) References to the Record. References to the parts of the record contained in the appendix filed with the appellant's brief must be to the pages of the appendix. If the appendix is prepared after the briefs are filed, a party referring to the record must follow one of the methods detailed in Rule 30(c). If the original record is used under Rule 30(f) and is not consecutively paginated, or if the brief refers to an unreproduced part of the record, any reference must be to the page of the original document. For example:
    • Answer p. 7;
    • Motion for Judgment p. 2;

• Transcript p. 231.

Only clear abbreviations may be used. A party referring to evidence whose admissibility is in controversy must cite the pages of the appendix or of the transcript at which the evidence was identified, offered, and received or rejected.

(f) Reproduction of Statutes, Rules, Regulations, etc. If the court's determination of the issues presented requires the study of statutes, rules, regulations, etc., the relevant parts must be set out in the brief or in an addendum at the end, or may be supplied to the court in pamphlet form.

(g) [Reserved]

(h) [Reserved]

(i) Briefs in a Case Involving Multiple Appellants or Appellees. In a case involving more than one appellant or appellee, including consolidated cases, any number of appellants or appellees may join in a brief, and any party may adopt by reference a part of another's brief. Parties may also join in reply briefs.

(j) Citation of Supplemental Authorities. If pertinent and significant authorities come to a party's attention after the party's brief has been filed—or after oral argument but before decision—a party may promptly advise the circuit clerk by letter, with a copy to all other parties, setting forth the citations. The letter must state the reasons for the supplemental citations, referring either to the page of the brief or to a point argued orally. The body of the letter must not exceed 350 words. Any response must be made promptly and must be similarly limited.

(As amended Apr. 30, 1979, eff. Aug. 1, 1979; Mar. 10, 1986, eff. July 1, 1986; Apr. 25, 1989, eff. Dec. 1, 1989; Apr. 30, 1991, eff. Dec. 1, 1991; Apr. 22, 1993, eff. Dec. 1, 1993; Apr. 29, 1994, eff. Dec. 1, 1994; Apr. 24, 1998, eff. Dec. 1, 1998; Apr. 29, 2002, eff. Dec. 1, 2002; Apr. 25, 2005, eff. Dec. 1, 2005; Apr. 16, 2013, eff. Dec. 1, 2013; Apr. 28, 2016, eff. Dec. 1, 2016; Apr. 25, 2019, eff. Dec. 1, 2019.)

NOTES OF ADVISORY COMMITTEE ON RULES—1967

This rule is based upon Supreme Court Rule 40. For variations in present circuit rules on briefs see 2d Cir. Rule 17, 3d Cir. Rule 24, 5th Cir. Rule 24, and 7th Cir. Rule 17. All circuits now limit the number of pages of briefs, a majority limiting the brief to 50 pages of standard typographic printing. Fifty pages of standard typographic printing is the approximate equivalent of 70 pages of typewritten text, given the page sizes required by Rule 32 and the requirement set out there that text produced by a method other than standard typographic must be double spaced.

NOTES OF ADVISORY COMMITTEE ON RULES—1979 AMENDMENT

The proposed amendment eliminates the distinction appearing in the present rule between the permissible length in pages of printed and typewritten briefs, investigation of the matter having disclosed that the number of words on the printed page is little if any larger than the number on a page typed in standard elite type.

The provision is made subject to local rule to permit the court of appeals to require that typewritten briefs be typed in larger type and permit a correspondingly larger number of pages.

Subdivision (j). Proposed new Rule 28(j) makes provision for calling the court's attention to authorities that come to the party's attention after the brief has been filed. It is patterned after the practice under local rule in some of the circuits.

NOTES OF ADVISORY COMMITTEE ON RULES—1986 AMENDMENT

While Rule 28(g) can be read as requiring that tables of authorities be included in a reply brief, such tables are often not included. Their absence impedes efficient use of the reply brief to ascertain the appellant's response to a particular argument of the appellee or to the appellee's use of a particular authority. The amendment to Rule 28(c) is intended to make it clear that such tables are required in reply briefs.

The amendment to Rule 28(j) is technical. No substantive change is intended.

NOTES OF ADVISORY COMMITTEE ON RULES—1989 AMENDMENT

The amendment provides that the corporate disclosure statement required by new rule 26.1 shall be treated similarly to tables of contents and tables of citations and shall not be counted for purposes of the number of pages allowed in a brief.

NOTES OF ADVISORY COMMITTEE ON RULES—1991 AMENDMENT

Subdivision (a). The amendment adds a new subparagraph (2) that requires an appellant to include a specific jurisdictional statement in the appellant's brief to aid the court of appeals in determining whether it has both federal subject matter and appellate jurisdiction.

Subdivision (b). The amendment requires the appellee to include a jurisdictional statement in the appellee's brief except that the appellee need not include the statement if the appellee is satisfied with the appellant's jurisdictional statement.

Subdivision (h). The amendment provides that when more than one party appeals from a judgment or order, the party filing the first appeal is normally treated as the appellant for purposes of this rule and Rules 30 and 31. The party who first files an appeal usually is the principal appellant and should be treated as such. Parties who file a notice of appeal after the first notice often bring protective appeals and they should be treated as cross appellants. Local rules in the Fourth and Federal Circuits now take that approach. If notices of appeal are filed on the same day, the rule follows the old approach of treating the plaintiff below as the appellant. For purposes of this rule, in criminal cases "the plaintiff" means the United States. In those instances where the designations provided by the rule are inappropriate, they may be altered by agreement of the parties or by an order of the court.

NOTES OF ADVISORY COMMITTEE ON RULES—1993 AMENDMENT

Note to paragraph (a)(5). The amendment requires an appellant's brief to state the standard of review applicable to each issue on appeal. Five circuits currently require these statements. Experience in those circuits indicates that requiring a statement of the standard of review generally results in arguments that are properly shaped in light of the standard.

NOTES OF ADVISORY COMMITTEE ON RULES—1994 AMENDMENT

Subdivision (a). The amendment adds a requirement that an appellant's brief contain a summary of the argument. A number of circuits have local rules requiring a summary and the courts report that they find the summary useful. See, D.C. Cir. R. 11(a)(5); 5th Cir. R. 28.2.2; 8th Cir. R. 28A(i)(6); 11th Cir. R. 28–2(i); and Fed. Cir. R. 28.

Subdivision (b). The amendment adds a requirement that an appellee's brief contain a summary of the argument.

Subdivision (g). The amendment adds proof of service to the list of items in a brief that do not count for purposes of the page limitation. The concurrent amendment to Rule 25(d) requires a certificate of service to list the addresses to which a paper was mailed or at which it was delivered. When a number of parties must be served, the listing of addresses may run to several pages and those pages should not count for purposes of the page limitation.

COMMITTEE NOTES ON RULES—1998 AMENDMENT

The language and organization of the rule are amended to make the rule more easily understood. In additional to changes made to improve the understanding, the Advisory Committee has changed language to make style and terminology consistent throughout the appellate rules. These changes are intended to be stylistic only.

Several substantive changes are made in this rule, however. Most of them are necessary to conform Rule 28 with changes recommended in Rule 32.

Subdivision (a). The current rule requires a brief to include a statement of the case which includes a description of the nature of the case, the course of proceedings, the disposition of the case—all of which might be described as the procedural history—as well as a statement of the facts. The amendments separate this into two statements: one procedural, called the statement of the case; and one factual, called the statement of the facts. The Advisory Committee believes that the separation will be helpful to the judges. The table of contents and table of authorities have also been separated into two distinct items.

An additional amendment of subdivision (a) is made to conform it with an amendment being made to Rule 32. Rule 32(a)(7) generally requires a brief to include a certificate of compliance with type-volume limitations contained in that rule. (No certificate is required if a brief does not exceed 30 pages, or 15 pages for a reply brief.) Rule 28(a) is amended to include that certificate in the list of items that must be included in a brief whenever it is required by Rule 32.

Subdivision (g). The amendments delete subdivision (g) that limited a principal brief to 50 pages and a reply brief to 25 pages. The length limitations have been moved to Rule 32. Rule 32 deals generally with the format for a brief or appendix.

Subdivision (h). The amendment requires an appellee's brief to comply with Rule 28(a)(1) through (11) with regard to a cross-appeal. The addition of separate paragraphs requiring a corporate disclosure statement, table of authorities, statement of facts, and certificate of compliance increased the relevant paragraphs of subdivision (a) from (7) to (11). The other changes are stylistic; no substantive changes are intended.

COMMITTEE NOTES ON RULES—2002 AMENDMENT

Subdivision (j). In the past, Rule 28(j) has required parties to describe supplemental authorities "without argument." Enforcement of this restriction has been lax, in part because of the difficulty of distinguishing "state[ment] . . . [of] the reasons for the supplemental citations," which is required, from "argument" about the supplemental citations, which is forbidden.

As amended, Rule 28(j) continues to require parties to state the reasons for supplemental citations, with reference to the part of a brief or oral argument to which the supplemental citations pertain. But Rule 28(j) no longer forbids "argument." Rather, Rule 28(j) permits parties to decide for themselves what they wish to say about supplemental authorities. The only restriction upon parties is that the body of a Rule 28(j) letter—that is, the part of the letter that begins with the first word after the salutation and ends with the last word before the complimentary close—cannot exceed 350 words. All words found in footnotes will count toward the 350-word limit.

Changes Made After Publication and Comments. No changes were made to the text of the proposed amendment or to the Committee Note, except that the word limit was increased from 250 to 350 in response to the complaint of some commentators that parties would have difficulty bringing multiple supplemental authorities to the attention of the court in one 250-word letter.

COMMITTEE NOTES ON RULES—2005 AMENDMENT

Subdivision (c). Subdivision (c) has been amended to delete a sentence that authorized an appellee who had cross-appealed to file a brief in reply to the appellant's response. All rules regarding briefing in cases involving cross-appeals have been consolidated into new Rule 28.1.

Subdivision (h). Subdivision (h)—regarding briefing in cases involving cross-appeals—has been deleted. All rules regarding such briefing have been consolidated into new Rule 28.1.

COMMITTEE NOTES ON RULES—2013 AMENDMENT

Subdivision (a). Rule 28(a) is amended to remove the requirement of separate statements of the case and of the facts. Currently Rule 28(a)(6) provides that the statement of the case must "indicat[e] the nature of the case, the course of proceedings, and the disposition below," and it precedes Rule 28(a)(7)'s requirement that the brief include "a statement of facts." Experience has shown that these requirements have generated confusion and redundancy. Rule 28(a) is amended to consolidate subdivisions (a)(6) and (a)(7) into a new subdivision (a)(6) that provides for one "statement," much like Supreme Court Rule 24.1(g) (which requires "[a] concise statement of the case, setting out the facts material to the consideration of the questions presented, with appropriate references to the joint appendix. . . ."). This permits but does not require the lawyer to present the factual and procedural history chronologically. Conforming changes are made by renumbering Rules 28(a)(8) through (11) as Rules 28(a)(7) through (10).

The statement of the case should describe the nature of the case, which includes (1) the facts relevant to the issues submitted for review; (2) those aspects of the case's procedural history that are necessary to understand the posture of the appeal or are relevant to the issues submitted for review; and (3) the rulings presented for review. The statement should be concise, and can include subheadings, particularly for the purpose of highlighting the rulings presented for review.

Subdivision (b). Rule 28(b) is amended to accord with the amendment to Rule 28(a). Current Rules 28(b)(3) and (4) are consolidated into new Rule 28(b)(3), which refers to "the statement of the case." Rule 28(b)(5) becomes Rule 28(b)(4). And Rule 28(b)'s reference to certain subdivisions of Rule 28(a) is updated to reflect the renumbering of those subdivisions.

Changes Made After Publication and Comment. After publication and comment, the Committee made one change to the text of the proposal and two changes to the Committee Note.

During the comment period, concerns were raised that the deletion of current Rule 28(a)(6)'s reference to "the nature of the case, the course of proceedings, and the disposition below" might lead readers to conclude that those items may no longer be included in the statement of the case. The Committee rejected that concern with respect to the "nature of the case" and the "disposition below," because the Rule as published would naturally be read to permit continued inclusion of those items in the statement of the case. The Committee adhered to its view that the deletion of "course of proceedings" is useful because that phrase tends to elicit unnecessary detail; but to address the commenters' concerns, the Committee added, to the revised Rule text, the phrase "describing the relevant procedural history."

The Committee augmented the Note to Rule 28(a) in two respects. It added a reference to Supreme Court Rule 24.1(g), upon which the proposed revision to Rule 28(a)(6) is modeled. And it added—as a second paragraph in the Note—a discussion of the contents of the statement of the case.

COMMITTEE NOTES ON RULES—2016 AMENDMENT

Rule 28(a)(10) is revised to refer to Rule 32(g)(1) instead of Rule 32(a)(7), to reflect the relocation of the certificate-of-compliance requirement.

COMMITTEE NOTES ON RULES—2019 AMENDMENT

The phrase "corporate disclosure statement" is changed to "disclosure statement" to reflect the revision of Rule 26.1.

Rule 28.1. Cross-Appeals

(a) Applicability. This rule applies to a case in which a cross-appeal is filed. Rules 28(a)–(c), 31(a)(1), 32(a)(2), and 32(a)(7)(A)–(B) do not apply to such a case, except as otherwise provided in this rule.

(b) Designation of Appellant. The party who files a notice of appeal first is the appellant for the purposes of this rule and Rules 30 and 34. If notices are filed on the same day, the plaintiff in the proceeding below is the appellant. These designations may be modified by the parties' agreement or by court order.

(c) Briefs. In a case involving a cross-appeal:

(1) Appellant's Principal Brief. The appellant must file a principal brief in the appeal. That brief must comply with Rule 28(a).

(2) Appellee's Principal and Response Brief. The appellee must file a principal brief in the cross-appeal and must, in the same brief, respond to the principal brief in the appeal. That appellee's brief must comply with Rule 28(a), except that the brief need not include a statement of the case unless the appellee is dissatisfied with the appellant's statement.

(3) Appellant's Response and Reply Brief. The appellant must file a brief that responds to the principal brief in the cross-appeal and may, in the same brief, reply to the response in the appeal. That brief must comply with Rule 28(a)(2)–(8) and (10), except that none of the following need appear unless the appellant is dissatisfied with the appellee's statement in the cross-appeal:

(A) the jurisdictional statement;

(B) the statement of the issues;

(C) the statement of the case; and

(D) the statement of the standard of review.

(4) Appellee's Reply Brief. The appellee may file a brief in reply to the response in the cross-appeal. That brief must comply with Rule 28(a)(2)–(3) and (10) and must be limited to the issues presented by the cross-appeal.

(5) No Further Briefs. Unless the court permits, no further briefs may be filed in a case involving a cross-appeal.

(d) Cover. Except for filings by unrepresented parties, the cover of the appellant's principal brief must be blue; the appellee's principal and response brief, red; the appellant's response and reply brief, yellow; the appellee's reply brief, gray; an intervenor's or amicus curiae's brief, green; and any supplemental brief, tan. The front cover of a brief must contain the information required by Rule 32(a)(2).

(e) Length.

(1) Page Limitation. Unless it complies with Rule 28.1(e)(2), the appellant's principal brief must not exceed 30 pages; the appellee's principal and response brief, 35 pages; the appellant's response and reply brief, 30 pages; and the appellee's reply brief, 15 pages.

(2) Type-Volume Limitation.

(A) The appellant's principal brief or the appellant's response and reply brief is acceptable if it:

(i) contains no more than 13,000 words; or

(ii) uses a monospaced face and contains no more than 1,300 lines of text.

(B) The appellee's principal and response brief is acceptable if it:

(i) contains no more than 15,300 words; or

(ii) uses a monospaced face and contains no more than 1,500 lines of text.

(C) The appellee's reply brief is acceptable if it contains no more than half of the type volume specified in Rule 28.1(e)(2)(A).

(f) Time to Serve and File a Brief. Briefs must be served and filed as follows:

(1) the appellant's principal brief, within 40 days after the record is filed;

(2) the appellee's principal and response brief, within 30 days after the appellant's principal brief is served;

(3) the appellant's response and reply brief, within 30 days after the appellee's principal and response brief is served; and

(4) the appellee's reply brief, within 21 days after the appellant's response and reply brief is served, but at least 7 days before argument unless the court, for good cause, allows a later filing.

(As added Apr. 25, 2005, eff. Dec. 1, 2005; amended Mar. 26, 2009, eff. Dec. 1, 2009; Apr. 16, 2013, eff. Dec. 1, 2013; Apr. 28, 2016, eff. Dec. 1, 2016; Apr. 26, 2018, eff. Dec. 1, 2018.)

COMMITTEE NOTES ON RULES—2005

The Federal Rules of Appellate Procedure have said very little about briefing in cases involving cross-appeals. This vacuum has frustrated judges, attorneys, and parties who have sought guidance in the rules. More importantly, this vacuum has been filled by conflicting local rules regarding such matters as the number and length of briefs, the colors of the covers of briefs, and the deadlines for serving and filing briefs. These local rules have created a hardship for attorneys who practice in more than one circuit.

New Rule 28.1 provides a comprehensive set of rules governing briefing in cases involving cross-appeals. The few existing provisions regarding briefing in such cases have been moved into new Rule 28.1, and several new provisions have been added to fill the gaps in the existing rules. The new provisions reflect the practices of the large majority of circuits and, to a significant extent, the new provisions have been patterned after the requirements imposed by Rules 28, 31, and 32 on briefs filed in cases that do not involve cross-appeals.

Subdivision (a). Subdivision (a) makes clear that, in a case involving a cross-appeal, briefing is governed by new Rule 28.1, and not by Rules 28(a), 28(b), 28(c), 31(a)(1), 32(a)(2), 32(a)(7)(A), and 32(a)(7)(B), except to the extent that Rule 28.1 specifically incorporates those rules by reference.

233

Subdivision (b). Subdivision (b) defines who is the "appellant" and who is the "appellee" in a case involving a cross-appeal. Subdivision (b) is taken directly from former Rule 28(h), except that subdivision (b) refers to a party being designated as an appellant "for the purposes of this rule and Rules 30 and 34," whereas former Rule 28(h) also referred to Rule 31. Because the matter addressed by Rule 31(a)(1)—the time to serve and file briefs—is now addressed directly in new Rule 28.1(f), the cross-reference to Rule 31 is no longer necessary. In Rule 31 and in all rules other than Rules 28.1, 30, and 34, references to an "appellant" refer both to the appellant in an appeal and to the cross-appellant in a cross-appeal, and references to an "appellee" refer both to the appellee in an appeal and to the cross-appellee in a cross-appeal. Cf. Rule 31(c).

Subdivision (c). Subdivision (c) provides for the filing of four briefs in a case involving a cross-appeal. This reflects the practice of every circuit except the Seventh. See 7th Cir. R. 28(d)(1)(a).

The first brief is the "appellant's principal brief." That brief—like the appellant's principal brief in a case that does not involve a cross-appeal—must comply with Rule 28(a).

The second brief is the "appellee's principal and response brief." Because this brief serves as the appellee's principal brief on the merits of the cross-appeal, as well as the appellee's response brief on the merits of the appeal, it must also comply with Rule 28(a), with the limited exceptions noted in the text of the rule.

The third brief is the "appellant's response and reply brief." Like a response brief in a case that does not involve a cross-appeal—that is, a response brief that does not also serve as a principal brief on the merits of a cross-appeal—the appellant's response and reply brief must comply with Rule 28(a)(2)–(9) and (11), with the exceptions noted in the text of the rule. See Rule 28(b). The one difference between the appellant's response and reply brief, on the one hand, and a response brief filed in a case that does not involve a cross-appeal, on the other, is that the latter must include a corporate disclosure statement. See Rule 28(a)(1) and (b). An appellant filing a response and reply brief in a case involving a cross-appeal has already filed a corporate disclosure statement with its principal brief on the merits of the appeal.

The fourth brief is the "appellee's reply brief." Like a reply brief in a case that does not involve a cross-appeal, it must comply with Rule 28(c), which essentially restates the requirements of Rule 28(a)(2)–(3) and (11). (Rather than restating the requirements of Rule 28(a)(2)–(3) and (11), as Rule 28(c) does, Rule 28.1(c)(4) includes a direct cross-reference.) The appellee's reply brief must also be limited to the issues presented by the cross-appeal.

Subdivision (d). Subdivision (d) specifies the colors of the covers on briefs filed in a case involving a cross-appeal. It is patterned after Rule 32(a)(2), which does not specifically refer to cross-appeals.

Subdivision (e). Subdivision (e) sets forth limits on the length of the briefs filed in a case involving a cross-appeal. It is patterned after Rule 32(a)(7), which does not specifically refer to cross-appeals. Subdivision (e) permits the appellee's principal and response brief to be longer than a typical principal brief on the merits because this brief serves not only as the principal brief on the merits of the cross-appeal, but also as the response brief on the merits of the appeal. Likewise, subdivision (e) permits the appellant's response and reply brief to be longer than a typical reply brief because this brief serves not only as the reply brief in the appeal, but also as the response brief in the cross-appeal. For purposes of determining the maximum length of an amicus curiae's brief filed in a case involving a cross-appeal, Rule 29(d)'s reference to "the maximum length authorized by these rules for a party's principal brief" should be understood to refer to subdivision (e)'s limitations on the length of an appellant's principal brief.

Subdivision (f). Subdivision (f) provides deadlines for serving and filing briefs in a cross-appeal. It is patterned after Rule 31(a)(1), which does not specifically refer to cross-appeals.

Changes Made After Publication and Comments. The Committee adopted the recommendation of the Style Subcommittee that the text of Rule 28.1 be changed in a few minor respects to improve clarity. (That recommendation is described below.) The Committee also adopted three suggestions made by the Department of Justice: (1) A sentence was added to the Committee Note to Rule 28.1(b) to clarify that the term "appellant" (and "appellee") as used by rules other than Rules 28.1, 30, and 34, refers to both the appellant in an appeal and the cross-appellant in a cross-appeal (and to both the appellee in an appeal and the cross-appellee in a cross-appeal). (2) Rule 28.1(d) was amended to prescribe cover colors for supplemental briefs and briefs filed by an intervenor or amicus curiae. (3) A few words were added to the Committee Note to Rule 28.1(e) to clarify the length of an amicus curiae's brief.

COMMITTEE NOTES ON RULES—2009 AMENDMENT

Subdivision (f)(4). Subdivision (f)(4) formerly required that the appellee's reply brief be served "at least 3 days before argument unless the court, for good cause, allows a later filing." Under former Rule 26(a), "3 days" could mean as many as 5 or even 6 days. See the Note to Rule 26. Under revised Rule 26(a), intermediate weekends and holidays are counted. Changing "3 days" to "7 days" alters the period accordingly. Under revised Rule 26(a), when a period ends on a weekend or holiday, one must continue to count in the same direction until the next day that is not a weekend or holiday; the choice of the 7-day period for subdivision (f)(4) will minimize such occurrences.

COMMITTEE NOTES ON RULES—2013 AMENDMENT

Subdivision (c). Subdivision (c) is amended to accord with the amendments to Rule 28(a). Rule 28(a) is amended to consolidate subdivisions (a)(6) and (a)(7) into a new subdivision (a)(6) that provides for one "statement of the case setting out the facts relevant to the issues submitted for review, describing the relevant procedural history, and identifying the rulings presented for review. . . ." Rule 28.1(c) is amended to refer to that consolidated "statement of the case," and references to subdivisions of Rule 28(a) are revised to reflect the re-numbering of those subdivisions.

Changes Made After Publication and Comment. No changes were made to the text of the proposed amendment to Rule 28.1 after publication and comment. The Committee revised a quotation in the Committee Note to Rule 28.1(c) to conform to the changes (described above) to the text of proposed Rule 28(a)(6).

COMMITTEE NOTES ON RULES—2016 AMENDMENT

When Rule 28.1 was adopted in 2005, it modeled its type-volume limits on those set forth in Rule 32(a)(7) for briefs in cases that did not involve a cross-appeal. At that time, Rule 32(a)(7)(B) set word limits based on an estimate of 280 words per page.

In the course of adopting word limits for the length limits in Rules 5, 21, 27, 35, and 40, and responding to concern about the length of briefs, the Committee has reevaluated the conversion ratio (from pages to words) and decided to apply a conversion ratio of 260 words per page. Rules 28.1 and 32(a)(7)(B) are amended to reduce the word limits accordingly.

In a complex case, a party may need to file a brief that exceeds the type-volume limitations specified in these rules, such as to include unusually voluminous information explaining relevant background or legal provisions or to respond to multiple briefs by opposing parties or amici. The Committee expects that courts will accommodate those situations by granting leave to exceed the type-volume limitations as appropriate.

COMMITTEE NOTES ON RULES—2018 AMENDMENT

Subdivision (f)(4) is amended to extend the period for filing a reply brief from 14 days to 21 days. Before the elimination of the "three-day rule" in Rule 26(c), attorneys were accustomed to a period of 17 days within which to file a reply brief, and the committee concluded that shortening the period from 17 days to 14 days could adversely affect the preparation of useful reply briefs. Because time periods are best measured in increments of 7 days, the period is extended to 21 days.

Rule 29. Brief of an Amicus Curiae

(a) During Initial Consideration of a Case on the Merits.

(1) Applicability. This Rule 29(a) governs amicus filings during a court's initial consideration of a case on the merits.

(2) When Permitted. The United States or its officer or agency or a state may file an amicus brief without the consent of the parties or leave of court. Any other amicus curiae may file a brief only by leave of court or if the brief states that all parties have consented to its filing, but a court of appeals may prohibit the filing of or may strike an amicus brief that would result in a judge's disqualification.

(3) Motion for Leave to File. The motion must be accompanied by the proposed brief and state:

(A) the movant's interest; and

(B) the reason why an amicus brief is desirable and why the matters asserted are relevant to the disposition of the case.

(4) Contents and Form. An amicus brief must comply with Rule 32. In addition to the requirements of Rule 32, the cover must identify the party or parties supported and indicate whether the brief supports affirmance or reversal. An amicus brief need not comply with Rule 28, but must include the following:

(A) if the amicus curiae is a corporation, a disclosure statement like that required of parties by Rule 26.1;

(B) a table of contents, with page references;

(C) a table of authorities—cases (alphabetically arranged), statutes, and other authorities—with references to the pages of the brief where they are cited;

(D) a concise statement of the identity of the amicus curiae, its interest in the case, and the source of its authority to file;

(E) unless the amicus curiae is one listed in the first sentence of Rule 29(a)(2), a statement that indicates whether:

(i) a party's counsel authored the brief in whole or in part;

(ii) a party or a party's counsel contributed money that was intended to fund preparing or submitting the brief; and

(iii) a person—other than the amicus curiae, its members, or its counsel—contributed money that was intended to fund preparing or submitting the brief and, if so, identifies each such person;

(F) an argument, which may be preceded by a summary and which need not include a statement of the applicable standard of review; and

(G) a certificate of compliance under Rule 32(g)(1), if length is computed using a word or line limit.

(5) Length. Except by the court's permission, an amicus brief may be no more than one-half the maximum length authorized by these rules for a party's principal brief. If the court grants a party permission to file a longer brief, that extension does not affect the length of an amicus brief.

(6) Time for Filing. An amicus curiae must file its brief, accompanied by a motion for filing when necessary, no later than 7 days after the principal brief of the party being supported is filed. An amicus curiae that does not support either party must file its brief no later than 7 days after the appellant's or petitioner's principal brief is filed. A court may grant leave for later filing, specifying the time within which an opposing party may answer.

(7) Reply Brief. Except by the court's permission, an amicus curiae may not file a reply brief.

(8) Oral Argument. An amicus curiae may participate in oral argument only with the court's permission.

(b) During Consideration of Whether to Grant Rehearing.

(1) Applicability. This Rule 29(b) governs amicus filings during a court's consideration of whether to grant panel rehearing or rehearing en banc, unless a local rule or order in a case provides otherwise.

(2) When Permitted. The United States or its officer or agency or a state may file an amicus brief without the consent of the parties or leave of court. Any other amicus curiae may file a brief only by leave of court.

(3) Motion for Leave to File. Rule 29(a)(3) applies to a motion for leave.

(4) Contents, Form, and Length. Rule 29(a)(4) applies to the amicus brief. The brief must not exceed 2,600 words.

(5) Time for Filing. An amicus curiae supporting the petition for rehearing or supporting neither party must file its brief, accompanied by a motion for filing when necessary, no later than 7 days after the petition is filed. An amicus curiae opposing the petition must file its brief, accompanied by a motion for filing when necessary, no later than the date set by the court for the response.

(As amended Apr. 24, 1998, eff. Dec. 1, 1998; Apr. 28, 2010, eff. Dec. 1, 2010; Apr. 28, 2016, eff. Dec. 1, 2016; Apr. 26, 2018, eff. Dec. 1, 2018.)

NOTES OF ADVISORY COMMITTEE ON RULES—1967

Only five circuits presently regulate the filing of the brief of an amicus curiae. See D.C. Cir. Rule 18(j); 1st Cir. Rule 23(10); 6th Cir. Rule 17(4); 9th Cir. Rule 18(9); 10th Cir. Rule 20. This rule follows the practice of a majority of circuits in requiring leave of court to file an amicus brief except under the circumstances stated therein. Compare Supreme Court Rule 42.

COMMITTEE NOTES ON RULES—1998 AMENDMENT

The language and organization of the rule are amended to make the rule more easily understood. In addition to changes made to improve the understanding, the Advisory Committee has changed language to make style and terminology consistent throughout the appellate rules. These changes are intended to be stylistic only.

Several substantive changes are made in this rule, however.

Subdivision (a). The major change in this subpart is that when a brief is filed with the consent of all parties, it is no longer necessary to obtain the parties' written consent and to file the consents with the brief. It is sufficient to obtain the parties' oral consent and to state in the brief that all parties have consented. It is sometimes difficult to obtain all the written consents by the filing deadline and it is not unusual for counsel to represent that parties have consented; for example, in a motion for extension of time to file a brief it is not unusual for the movant to state that the other parties have been consulted and they do not object to the extension. If a party's consent has been misrepresented, the party will be able to take action before the court considers the amicus brief.

The District of Columbia is added to the list of entities allowed to file an amicus brief without consent of all parties. The other changes in this material are stylistic.

Subdivision (b). The provision in the former rule, granting permission to conditionally file the brief with the motion, is changed to one requiring that the brief accompany the motion. Sup. Ct. R. 37.4 requires that the proposed brief be presented with the motion.

The former rule only required the motion to identify the applicant's interest and to generally state the reasons why an amicus brief is desirable. The amended rule additionally requires that the motion state the relevance of the matters asserted to the disposition of the case. As Sup. Ct. R. 37.1 states:

An amicus curiae brief which brings relevant matter to the attention of the Court that has not already been brought to its attention by the parties is of considerable help to the Court. An amicus curiae brief which does not serve this purpose simply burdens the staff and facilities of the Court and its filing is not favored.
Because the relevance of the matters asserted by an amicus is ordinarily the most compelling reason for granting leave to file, the Committee believes that it is helpful to explicitly require such a showing.
Subdivision (c). The provisions in this subdivision are entirely new. Previously there was confusion as to whether an amicus brief must include all of the items listed in Rule 28. Out of caution practitioners in some circuits included all those items. Ordinarily that is unnecessary.

The requirement that the cover identify the party supported and indicate whether the amicus supports affirmance or reversal is an administrative aid.

Paragraph (c)(3) requires an amicus to state the source of its authority to file. The amicus simply must identify which of the provisions in Rule 29(a) provides the basis for the amicus to file its brief.

Subdivision (d). This new provision imposes a shorter page limit for an amicus brief than for a party's brief. This is appropriate for two reasons. First, an amicus may omit certain items that must be included in a party's brief. Second, an amicus brief is supplemental. It need not address all issues or all facets of a case. It should treat only matter not adequately addressed by a party.

Subdivision (e). The time limit for filing is changed. An amicus brief must be filed no later than 7 days after the principal brief of the party being supported is filed. Occasionally, an amicus supports neither party; in such instances, the amendment provides that the amicus brief must be filed no later than 7 days after the appellant's or petitioner's principal brief is filed. Note that in both instances the 7-day period runs from when a brief is filed. The passive voice—"is filed"—is used deliberately. A party or amicus can send its brief to a court for filing and, under Rule 25, the brief is timely if mailed within the filing period. Although the brief is timely if mailed within the filing period, it is not "filed" until the court receives it and file stamps it. "Filing" is done by the court, not by the party. It may be necessary for an amicus to contact the court to ascertain the filing date.

The 7-day stagger was adopted because it is long enough to permit an amicus to review the completed brief of the party being supported and avoid repetitious argument. A 7-day period also is short enough that no adjustment need be made in the opposing party's briefing schedule. The opposing party will have sufficient time to review arguments made by the amicus and address them in the party's responsive pleading. The timetable for filing the parties' briefs is unaffected by this change.

A court may grant permission to file an amicus brief in a context in which the party does not file a "principal brief"; for example, an amicus may be permitted to file in support of a party's petition for rehearing. In such instances the court will establish the filing time for the amicus.

The former rule's statement that a court may, for cause shown, grant leave for later filing is unnecessary. Rule 26(b) grants general authority to enlarge the time prescribed in these rules for good cause shown. This new rule, however, states that when a court grants permission for later filing, the court must specify the period within which an opposing party may answer the arguments of the amicus.

Subdivision (f). This subdivision generally prohibits the filing a a reply brief by an amicus curiae. Sup. Ct. R. 37 and local rules of the D.C., Ninth, and Federal Circuits state that an amicus may not file a reply brief. The role of an amicus should not require the use of a reply brief.

Subdivision (g). The language of this subdivision stating that an amicus will be granted permission to participate in oral argument "only for extraordinary reasons" has been deleted. The change is made to reflect more accurately the current practice in which it is not unusual for a court to permit an amicus to argue when a party is willing to share its argument time with the amicus. The Committee does not intend, however, to suggest that in other instances an amicus will be permitted to argue absent extraordinary circumstances.

COMMITTEE NOTES ON RULES—2010 AMENDMENT
Subdivision (a). New Rule 1(b) defines the term "state" to include "the District of Columbia and any United States commonwealth or territory." That definition renders subdivision (a)'s reference to a "Territory, Commonwealth, or the District of Columbia" redundant. Accordingly, subdivision (a) is amended to refer simply to "[t]he United States or its officer or agency or a state."

Subdivision (c). The subparts of subdivision (c) are renumbered due to the relocation of an existing provision in new subdivision (c)(1) and the addition of a new provision in new subdivision (c)(5). Existing subdivisions (c)(1) through (c)(5) are renumbered, respectively, (c)(2), (c)(3), (c)(4), (c)(6) and (c)(7). The new ordering of the subdivisions tracks the order in which the items should appear in the brief.

Subdivision (c)(1). The requirement that corporate amici include a disclosure statement like that required of parties by Rule 26.1 was previously stated in the third sentence of subdivision (c). The requirement has been moved to new subdivision (c)(1) for ease of reference.

Subdivision (c)(5). New subdivision (c)(5) sets certain disclosure requirements concerning authorship and funding. Subdivision (c)(5) exempts from the authorship and funding disclosure requirements entities entitled under subdivision (a) to file an amicus brief without the consent of the parties or leave of court. Subdivision (c)(5) requires amicus briefs to disclose whether counsel for a party authored the brief in whole or in part and whether a party or a party's counsel contributed money with the intention of funding the preparation or submission of the brief. A party's or counsel's payment of general membership dues to an amicus need not be disclosed. Subdivision (c)(5) also requires amicus briefs to state whether any other "person" (other than the amicus, its members, or its counsel) contributed money with the intention of funding the brief's preparation or submission, and, if so, to identify all such persons. "Person," as used in subdivision (c)(5), includes artificial persons as well as natural persons.

The disclosure requirement, which is modeled on Supreme Court Rule 37.6, serves to deter counsel from using an amicus brief to circumvent page limits on the parties' briefs. See Glassroth v. Moore, 347 F.3d 916, 919 (11th Cir. 2003) (noting the majority's suspicion "that amicus briefs are often used as a means of evading the page limitations on a party's briefs"). It also may help judges to assess whether the amicus itself considers the issue important enough to sustain the cost and effort of filing an amicus brief.

It should be noted that coordination between the amicus and the party whose position the amicus supports is desirable, to the extent that it helps to avoid duplicative arguments. This was particularly true prior to the 1998 amendments, when deadlines for amici were the same as those for the party whose position they supported. Now that the filing deadlines are staggered, coordination may not always be essential in order to avoid duplication. In any event, mere coordination—in the sense of sharing drafts of briefs—need not be disclosed under subdivision (c)(5). Cf. Eugene Gressman et al., Supreme Court Practice 739 (9th ed. 2007) (Supreme Court Rule 37.6 does not "require disclosure of any coordination and discussion between party counsel and amici counsel regarding their respective arguments....").

Changes Made After Publication and Comment. No changes were made to the proposed amendment to Rule 29(a). However, the Committee made a number of changes to Rule 29(c).

One change concerns the third subdivision of the authorship and funding disclosure requirement. As published, that third subdivision would have directed the filer to "identif[y] every person—other than the amicus curiae, its members, or its counsel—who contributed money that was intended to fund preparing or submitting the brief." A commentator criticized this language as ambiguous, because the commentator argued that the provision as drafted did not make clear whether it is necessary for the brief to state that no such persons exist (if that is the case). The Committee revised this portion of the requirement to require a statement that indicates whether "a person—other than the amicus curiae, its members, or its counsel—contributed money that was intended to fund preparing or submitting the brief and, if so, identifies each such person."

Another set of changes concerns the placement of the disclosure requirement. As published, the Rule 29(c) proposal would have placed the new authorship and funding disclosure requirement in a new subdivision (c)(7) and would have moved the requirement of a corporate disclosure statement from the initial block of text in Rule 29(c) to a new subdivision (c)(6). New subdivision (c)(7) would have directed that the authorship and funding disclosure be made "in the first footnote on the first page." Commentators criticized this directive as ambiguous and suggested that a better approach would be to direct that the authorship and funding disclosure follow the statement currently required by existing Rule 29(c)(3). The Committee found merit in these suggestions and decided to add the authorship and funding disclosure provision to existing subdivision (c)(3). However, a further revision to the structure of subdivision (c) was later made in response to style guidance from Professor Kimble, as discussed below.

Subsequent to the Appellate Rules Committee's meeting, the language adopted by the advisory committee was circulated to Professor Kimble for style review. Professor Kimble argued that the authorship and funding disclosure provision should be placed in a separate subdivision rather than being placed in existing subdivision (c)(3). In the light of the Appellate Rules Committee's goal of listing the required components in the order in which they should appear in the brief, the decision was made to place the authorship and funding disclosure provision in a new subdivision following existing subdivision (c)(3). Though this requires renumbering the subparts of Rule 29(c), those subparts have only existed for about a decade (since the 1998 restyling) and citations to the specific subparts of Rule 29(c) do not appear in the caselaw. Given that this change entails renumbering some subparts of Rule 29(c), it also seems advisable to move the corporate disclosure provision into a new subdivision (c)(1) and to renumber the subsequent subdivisions accordingly. Professor Kimble also suggested two stylistic changes to the language of what will now become new subdivision (c)(5). First, instead of using the language "unless filed by an amicus curiae listed in the first sentence of Rule 29(a)," the provision now reads "unless the amicus curiae is one listed in the first sentence of Rule 29(a)." Second, the words "indicates whether" have been moved up into the introductory text in 29(c)(5) instead of being repeated at the outset of the three subsections (29(c)(5)(A), (B) and (C)). Also, a comma has been added to what will become Rule 29(c)(3).

COMMITTEE NOTES ON RULES—2016 AMENDMENT
Rule 29 is amended to address amicus filings in connection with requests for panel rehearing and rehearing en banc.

Existing Rule 29 is renumbered Rule 29(a), and language is added to that subdivision (a) to state that its provisions apply to amicus filings during the court's initial consideration of a case on the merits. Rule 29(c)(7) becomes Rule 29(a)(4)(G) and is revised to accord with the relocation and revision of the certificate-of-compliance requirement. New Rule 32(g)(1) states that "[a] brief submitted under Rules 28.1(e)(2), 29(b)(4), or 32(a)(7)(B) . . . must include" a certificate of compliance. An amicus brief submitted during initial consideration of a case on the merits counts as a "brief submitted under Rule[] . . . 32(a)(7)(B)" if the amicus computes Rule 29(a)(5)'s length limit by taking half of a type-volume limit in Rule 32(a)(7)(B). Rule 29(a)(4)(G) restates Rule 32(g)(1)'s requirement functionally, by providing that a certificate of compliance is required if an amicus brief's length is computed using a word or line limit.

New subdivision (b) is added to address amicus filings in connection with a petition for panel rehearing or rehearing en banc. Subdivision (b) sets default rules that apply when a court does not provide otherwise by local rule or by order in a case. A court remains free to adopt different rules governing whether amicus filings are permitted in connection with petitions for rehearing, and governing the procedures when such filings are permitted.

COMMITTEE NOTES ON RULES—2018 AMENDMENT
The amendment to subdivision (a)(2) authorizes orders or local rules that prohibit the filing of or permit the striking of an amicus brief if the brief would result in a judge's disqualification. The amendment does not alter or address the standards for when an amicus brief requires a judge's disqualification. A comparable amendment to subdivision (b) is not necessary. Subdivision (b)(1) currently authorizes local rules and orders governing filings during a court's consideration of whether to grant panel rehearing or rehearing en banc. These local rules or orders may prohibit the filing of or permit the striking of an amicus brief that would result in a judge's disqualification. In addition, under subdivision (b)(2), a court may deny leave to file an amicus brief that would result in a judge's disqualification.

Rule 30. Appendix to the Briefs

(a) Appellant's Responsibility.
   (1) Contents of the Appendix. The appellant must prepare and file an appendix to the briefs containing:
      (A) the relevant docket entries in the proceeding below;
      (B) the relevant portions of the pleadings, charge, findings, or opinion;
      (C) the judgment, order, or decision in question; and
      (D) other parts of the record to which the parties wish to direct the court's attention.

   (2) Excluded Material. Memoranda of law in the district court should not be included in the appendix unless they have independent relevance. Parts of the record may be relied on by the court or the parties even though not included in the appendix.

(3) Time to File; Number of Copies. Unless filing is deferred under Rule 30(c), the appellant must file 10 copies of the appendix with the brief and must serve one copy on counsel for each party separately represented. An unrepresented party proceeding in forma pauperis must file 4 legible copies with the clerk, and one copy must be served on counsel for each separately represented party. The court may by local rule or by order in a particular case require the filing or service of a different number.

(b) All Parties' Responsibilities.

(1) Determining the Contents of the Appendix. The parties are encouraged to agree on the contents of the appendix. In the absence of an agreement, the appellant must, within 14 days after the record is filed, serve on the appellee a designation of the parts of the record the appellant intends to include in the appendix and a statement of the issues the appellant intends to present for review. The appellee may, within 14 days after receiving the designation, serve on the appellant a designation of additional parts to which it wishes to direct the court's attention. The appellant must include the designated parts in the appendix. The parties must not engage in unnecessary designation of parts of the record, because the entire record is available to the court. This paragraph applies also to a cross-appellant and a cross-appellee.

(2) Costs of Appendix. Unless the parties agree otherwise, the appellant must pay the cost of the appendix. If the appellant considers parts of the record designated by the appellee to be unnecessary, the appellant may advise the appellee, who must then advance the cost of including those parts. The cost of the appendix is a taxable cost. But if any party causes unnecessary parts of the record to be included in the appendix, the court may impose the cost of those parts on that party. Each circuit must, by local rule, provide for sanctions against attorneys who unreasonably and vexatiously increase litigation costs by including unnecessary material in the appendix.

(c) Deferred Appendix.

(1) Deferral Until After Briefs Are Filed. The court may provide by rule for classes of cases or by order in a particular case that preparation of the appendix may be deferred until after the briefs have been filed and that the appendix may be filed 21 days after the appellee's brief is served. Even though the filing of the appendix may be deferred, Rule 30(b) applies; except that a party must designate the parts of the record it wants included in the appendix when it serves its brief, and need not include a statement of the issues presented.

(2) References to the Record.

(A) If the deferred appendix is used, the parties may cite in their briefs the pertinent pages of the record. When the appendix is prepared, the record pages cited in the briefs must be indicated by inserting record page numbers, in brackets, at places in the appendix where those pages of the record appear.

(B) A party who wants to refer directly to pages of the appendix may serve and file copies of the brief within the time required by Rule 31(a), containing appropriate references to pertinent pages of the record. In that event, within 14 days after the appendix is filed, the party must serve and file copies of the brief, containing references to the pages of the appendix in place of or in addition to the references to the pertinent pages of the record. Except for the correction of typographical errors, no other changes may be made to the brief.

(d) Format of the Appendix. The appendix must begin with a table of contents identifying the page at which each part begins. The relevant docket entries must follow the table of contents. Other parts of the record must follow chronologically. When pages from the transcript of proceedings are placed in the appendix, the transcript page numbers must be shown in brackets immediately before the included pages. Omissions in the text of papers or of the transcript must be indicated by asterisks. Immaterial formal matters (captions, subscriptions, acknowledgments, etc.) should be omitted.

(e) Reproduction of Exhibits. Exhibits designated for inclusion in the appendix may be reproduced in a separate volume, or volumes, suitably indexed. Four copies must be filed with the appendix, and one copy must be served on counsel for each separately represented party. If a transcript of a proceeding before an administrative agency, board, commission, or officer was used in a district-court action and has been designated for inclusion in the appendix, the transcript must be placed in the appendix as an exhibit.

(f) Appeal on the Original Record Without an Appendix. The court may, either by rule for all cases or classes of cases or by order in a particular case, dispense with the appendix and permit an appeal to proceed on the original record with any copies of the record, or relevant parts, that the court may order the parties to file.

(As amended Mar. 30, 1970, eff. July 1, 1970; Mar. 10, 1986, eff. July 1, 1986; Apr. 30, 1991, eff. Dec. 1, 1991; Apr. 29, 1994, eff. Dec. 1, 1994; Apr. 24, 1998, eff. Dec. 1, 1998; Mar. 26, 2009, eff. Dec. 1, 2009.)

NOTES OF ADVISORY COMMITTEE ON RULES—1967

Subdivision (a). Only two circuits presently require a printed record (5th Cir. Rule 23(a); 8th Cir. Rule 10 (in civil appeals only)), and the rules and practice in those circuits combine to make the difference between a printed record and the appendix, which is now used in eight circuits and in the Supreme Court in lieu of the printed record, largely nominal. The essential characteristics of the appendix method are: (1) the entire record may not be reproduced; (2) instead, the parties are to set out in an appendix to the briefs those parts of the record which in their judgment the judges must consult in order to determine the issues presented by the appeal; (3) the appendix is not the record but merely a selection therefrom for the convenience of the judges of the court of appeals; the record is the actual trial court record, and the record itself is always available to supply inadvertent omissions from the appendix. These essentials are incorporated, either by rule or by practice, in the circuits that continue to require the printed record rather than the appendix. See 5th Cir. Rule 23(a)(9) and 8th Cir. Rule 10(a)–(d).

Subdivision (b). Under the practice in six of the eight circuits which now use the appendix method, unless the parties agree to use a single appendix, the appellant files with his brief an appendix containing the parts of the record which he deems it essential that the court read in order to determine the questions presented. If the appellee deems additional parts of the record necessary he must include such parts as an appendix to his brief. The proposed rules differ from that practice. By the new rule a single appendix is to be filed. It is to be prepared by the appellant, who must include therein those parts which he deems essential and those which the appellee designates as essential.

Under the practice by which each party files his own appendix the resulting reproduction of essential parts of the record is often fragmentary; it is not infrequently necessary to piece several appendices together to arrive at a usable reproduction. Too, there seems to be a tendency on the part of some appellants to reproduce less than what is necessary for a determination of the issues presented (see Moran Towing Corp. v. M. A. Gammino Construction Co., 363 F.2d 108 (1st Cir. 1966); Walters v. Shari Music Publishing Corp., 298 F.2d 206 (2d Cir. 1962) and cases cited therein; Morrison v. Texas Co., 289 F.2d 382 (7th Cir. 1961) and cases cited therein), a tendency which is doubtless encouraged by the requirement in present rules that the appellee reproduce in his separately prepared appendix such necessary parts of the record as are not included by the appellant.

Under the proposed rule responsibility for the preparation of the appendix is placed on the appellant. If the appellee feels that the appellant has omitted essential portions of the record, he may require the appellant to include such portions in the appendix. The appellant is protected against a demand that he reproduce parts which he considers unnecessary by the provisions entitling him to require the appellee to advance the costs of reproducing such parts and authorizing denial of costs for matter unnecessarily reproduced.

Subdivision (c). This subdivision permits the appellant to elect to defer the production of the appendix to the briefs until the briefs of both sides are written, and authorizes a court of appeals to require such deferred filing by rule or order. The advantage of this method of preparing the appendix is that it permits the parties to determine what parts of the record need to be reproduced in the light of the issues actually presented by the briefs. Often neither side is in a position to say precisely what is needed until the briefs are completed. Once the argument on both sides is known, it should be possible to confine the matter reproduced in the appendix to that which is essential to a determination of the appeal or review. This method of preparing the appendix is presently in use in the Tenth Circuit (Rule 17) and in other circuits in review of agency proceedings, and it has proven its value in reducing the volume required to be reproduced. When the record is long, use of this method is likely to result in substantial economy to the parties.

Subdivision (e). The purpose of this subdivision is to reduce the cost of reproducing exhibits. While subdivision (a) requires that 10 copies of the appendix be filed, unless the court requires a lesser number, subdivision (e) permits exhibits necessary for the determination of an appeal to be bound separately, and requires only 4 copies of such a separate volume or volumes to be filed and a single copy to be served on counsel.

Subdivision (f). This subdivision authorizes a court of appeals to dispense with the appendix method of reproducing parts of the record and to hear appeals on the original record and such copies of it as the court may require.

Since 1962 the Ninth Circuit has permitted all appeals to be heard on the original record and a very limited number of copies. Under the practice as adopted in 1962, any party to an appeal could elect to have the appeal heard on the original record and two copies thereof rather than on the printed record theretofore required. The resulting substantial saving of printing costs led to the election of the new practice in virtually all cases, and by 1967 the use of printed records had ceased. By a recent amendment, the Ninth Circuit has abolished the printed record altogether. Its rules now provide that all appeals are to be heard on the original record, and it has reduced the number of copies required to two sets of copies of the transmitted original papers (excluding copies of exhibits, which need not be filed unless specifically ordered). See 9 Cir. Rule 10, as amended June 2, 1967, effective September 1, 1967. The Eighth Circuit permits appeals in criminal cases and in habeas corpus and 28 U.S.C. §2255 proceedings to be heard on the original record and two copies thereof. See 8 Cir. Rule 8 (i)—(j). The Tenth Circuit permits appeals in all cases to be heard on the original record and four copies thereof whenever the record consists of two hundred pages or less. See 10 Cir. Rule 17(a). This subdivision expressly authorizes the continuation of the practices in the Eighth, Ninth and Tenth Circuits.

The judges of the Court of Appeals for the Ninth Circuit have expressed complete satisfaction with the practice there in use and have suggested that attention be called to the advantages which it offers in terms of reducing cost.

NOTES OF ADVISORY COMMITTEE ON RULES——1970 AMENDMENT

Subdivision (a). The amendment of subdivision (a) is related to the amendment of Rule 31(a), which authorizes a court of appeals to shorten the time for filing briefs. By virtue of this amendment, if the time for filing the brief of the appellant is shortened the time for filing the appendix is likewise shortened.

Subdivision (c). As originally written, subdivision (c) permitted the appellant to elect to defer filing of the appendix until 21 days after service of the brief of the appellee. As amended, subdivision (c) requires that an order of court be obtained before filing of the appendix can be deferred, unless a court permits deferred filing by local rule. The amendment should not cause use of the deferred appendix to be viewed with disfavor. In cases involving lengthy records, permission to defer filing of the appendix should be freely granted as an inducement to the parties to include in the appendix only matter that the briefs show to be necessary for consideration by the judges. But the Committee is advised that appellants have elected to defer filing of the appendix in cases involving brief records merely to obtain the 21 day delay. The subdivision is amended to prevent that practice.

NOTES OF ADVISORY COMMITTEE ON RULES——1986 AMENDMENT

Subdivision (a). During its study of the separate appendix [see Report on the Advisory Committee on the Federal Appellate Rules on the Operation of Rule 30, —— FRD —— (1985)], the Advisory Committee found that this document was frequently encumbered with memoranda submitted to the trial court. United States v. Noall, 587 F.2d 123, 125 n. 1 (2nd Cir. 1978). See generally Drewett v. Aetna Cas. & Sur. Co., 539 F.2d 496, 500 (5th Cir. 1976); Volkswagenwerk Aktiengesellschaft v. Church, 413 F.2d 1126, 1128 (9th Cir. 1969). Inclusion of such material makes the appendix more bulky and therefore less useful to the appellate panel. It also can increase significantly the costs of litigation.

There are occasions when such trial court memoranda have independent relevance in the appellate litigation. For instance, there may be a dispute as to whether a particular point was raised or whether a concession was made in the district court. In such circumstances, it is appropriate to include pertinent sections of such memoranda in the appendix.

Subdivision (b). The amendment to subdivision (b) is designed to require the circuits, by local rule, to establish a procedural mechanism for the imposition of sanctions against those attorneys who conduct appellate litigation in bad faith. Both 28 U.S.C. §1927 and the inherent power of the court authorized such sanctions. See Brennan v. Local 357, International Brotherhood of Teamsters, 709 F.2d 611 (9th Cir. 1983). See generally Roadway Express, Inc. v. Piper, 447 U.S. 752 (1980). While considerations of uniformity are important and doubtless will be taken into account by the judges of the respective circuits, the Advisory Committee believes that, at this time, the circuits need the flexibility to tailor their approach to the conditions of local practice. The local rule shall provide for notice and opportunity to respond before the imposition of any sanction.

Technical amendments also are made to subdivisions (a), (b) and (c) which are not intended to be substantive changes.

TAXATION OF FEES IN APPEALS IN WHICH THE REQUIREMENT OF AN APPENDIX IS DISPENSED WITH

The Judicial Conference of the United States at its session on October 28th and 29th approved the following resolution relating to fees to be taxed in the courts of appeals as submitted by the Judicial Council of the Ninth Circuit with the proviso that its application to any court of appeals shall be at the election of each such court:

For some time it has been the practice in the Ninth Circuit Court of Appeals to dispense with an appendix in an appellate record and to hear the appeal on the original record, with a number of copies thereof being supplied (Rule 30f, Federal Rules of Appellate Procedure). It has been the practice of the Court to tax a fee of $5 in small records and $10 in large records for the time of the clerk involved in preparing such appeals and by way of reimbursement for postage expense. Judicial Conference approval heretofore has not been secured and the Judicial Council of the Ninth Circuit now seeks to fix a flat fee of $15 to be charged as fees for costs to be charged by any court of appeals "in any appeal in which the requirement of an appendix is dispensed with pursuant to Rule 30f, Federal Rules of Appellate Procedure."

NOTES OF ADVISORY COMMITTEE ON RULES——1991 AMENDMENT

Subdivision (b). The amendment requires a cross appellant to serve the appellant with a statement of the issues that the cross appellant intends to pursue on appeal. No later than ten days after the record is filed, the appellant and cross appellant must serve each other with a statement of the issues each intends to present for review and with a designation of the parts of the record that each wants included in the appendix. Within the next ten days, both the appellee and the cross appellee may designate additional materials for inclusion in the appendix. The appellant must then include in the appendix the parts thus designated for both the appeal and any cross appeals. The Committee expects that simultaneous compliance with this subdivision by an appellant and a cross appellant will be feasible in most cases. If a cross appellant cannot fairly be expected to comply until receipt of the appellant's statement of issues, relief may be sought by motion in the court of appeals.

NOTES OF ADVISORY COMMITTEE ON RULES—1994 AMENDMENT

Subdivision (a). The only substantive change is to allow a court to require the filing of a greater number of copies of an appendix as well as a lesser number.

COMMITTEE NOTES ON RULES—1998 AMENDMENT

The language and organization of the rule are amended to make the rule more easily understood. In addition to changes made to improve the understanding, the Advisory Committee has changed language to make style and terminology consistent throughout the appellate rules. These changes are intended to be stylistic only.

Subdivision (a). Paragraph (a)(3) is amended so that it is consistent with Rule 31(b). An unrepresented party proceeding in forma pauperis is only required to file 4 copies of the appendix rather than 10.

Subdivision (c). When a deferred appendix is used, a brief must make reference to the original record rather than to the appendix because it does not exist when the briefs are prepared. Unless a party later files an amended brief with direct references to the pages of the appendix (as provided in subparagraph (c)(2)(B)), the material in the appendix must indicate the pages of the original record from which it was drawn so that a reader of the brief can make meaningful use of the appendix. The instructions in the current rule for cross-referencing the appendix materials to the original record are unclear. The language in paragraph (c)(2) has been amended to try to clarify the procedure.

Subdivision (d). In recognition of the fact that use of a typeset appendix is exceedingly rare in the courts of appeals, the last sentence—permitting a question and answer (as from a transcript) to be in a single paragraph—has been omitted.

COMMITTEE NOTES ON RULES—2009 AMENDMENT

Subdivision (b)(1). The times set in the former rule at 10 days have been revised to 14 days. See the Note to Rule 26.

Rule 31. Serving and Filing Briefs

(a) Time to Serve and File a Brief.
   (1) The appellant must serve and file a brief within 40 days after the record is filed. The appellee must serve and file a brief within 30 days after the appellant's brief is served. The appellant may serve and file a reply brief within 21 days after service of the appellee's brief but a reply brief must be filed at least 7 days before argument, unless the court, for good cause, allows a later filing.
   (2) A court of appeals that routinely considers cases on the merits promptly after the briefs are filed may shorten the time to serve and file briefs, either by local rule or by order in a particular case.

(b) Number of Copies. Twenty-five copies of each brief must be filed with the clerk and 2 copies must be served on each unrepresented party and on counsel for each separately represented party. An unrepresented party proceeding in forma pauperis must file 4 legible copies with the clerk, and one copy must be served on each unrepresented party and on counsel for each separately represented party. The court may by local rule or by order in a particular case require the filing or service of a different number.

(c) Consequence of Failure to File. If an appellant fails to file a brief within the time provided by this rule, or within an extended time, an appellee may move to dismiss the appeal. An appellee who fails to file a brief will not be heard at oral argument unless the court grants permission.

(As amended Mar. 30, 1970, eff. July 1, 1970; Mar. 10, 1986, eff. July 1, 1986; Apr. 29, 1994, eff. Dec. 1, 1994; Apr. 24, 1998, eff. Dec. 1, 1998; Apr. 29, 2002, eff. Dec. 1, 2002; Mar. 26, 2009, eff. Dec. 1, 2009; Apr. 26, 2018, eff. Dec. 1, 2018.)

NOTES OF ADVISORY COMMITTEE ON RULES—1967

A majority of the circuits now require the brief of the appellant to be filed within 30 days from the date on which the record is filed. But in those circuits an exchange of designations is unnecessary in the preparation of the appendix. The appellant files with his brief an appendix containing the parts of the record which he deems essential. If the appellee considers other parts essential, he includes those parts in his own appendix. Since the proposed rule requires the appellant to file with his brief an appendix containing necessary parts of the record as designated by both parties, the rule allows the appellant 40 days in order to provide time for the exchange of designations respecting the content of the appendix (see Rule 30(b)).

NOTES OF ADVISORY COMMITTEE ON RULES—1970 AMENDMENT

The time prescribed by Rule 31(a) for preparing briefs—40 days to the appellant, 30 days to the appellee—is well within the time that must ordinarily elapse in most circuits before an appeal can be reached for consideration. In those circuits, the time prescribed by the Rule should not be disturbed. But if a court of appeals maintains a current calendar, that is, if an appeal can be heard as soon as the briefs have been filed, or if the practice of the court permits the submission of appeals for preliminary consideration as soon as the briefs have been filed, the court should be free to prescribe shorter periods in the interest of expediting decision.

NOTES OF ADVISORY COMMITTEE ON RULES—1986 AMENDMENT

The amendments to Rules 31(a) and (c) are technical. No substantive change is intended.

NOTES OF ADVISORY COMMITTEE ON RULES—1994 AMENDMENT

Subdivision (b). The amendment allows a court of appeals to require the filing of a greater, as well as a lesser, number of copies of briefs. The amendment also allows the required number to be prescribed by local rule as well as by order in a particular case.

COMMITTEE NOTES ON RULES—1998 AMENDMENT

The language and organization of the rule are amended to make the rule more easily understood. In addition to changes made to improve the understanding, the Advisory Committee has changed language to make style and terminology consistent throughout the appellate rules. These changes are intended to be stylistic only; a substantive change is made, however, in subdivision (b).

Subdivision (a). Paragraph (a)(2) explicitly authorizes a court of appeals to shorten a briefing schedule if the court routinely considers cases on the merits promptly after the briefs are filed. Extensions of the briefing schedule, by order, are permitted under the general provisions of Rule 26(b).

Subdivision (b). The current rule says that a party who is permitted to file "typewritten ribbon and carbon copies of the brief" need only file an original and three copies of the brief. The quoted language, in conjunction with current rule 24(c), means that a party allowed to proceed in forma pauperis need not file 25 copies of the brief. Two changes are made in this subdivision. First, it is anachronistic to refer to a party who is allowed to file a typewritten brief as if that would distinguish the party from all other parties; any party is permitted to file a typewritten brief. The amended rule states directly that it applies to a party permitted to proceed in forma pauperis. Second, the amended rule does not generally permit parties who are represented by counsel to file the lesser number of briefs. Inexpensive methods of copying are generally available. Unless it would impose hardship, in which case a motion to file a lesser number should be filed, a represented party must file the usual number of briefs.

COMMITTEE NOTES ON RULES—2002 AMENDMENT
Subdivision (b). In requiring that two copies of each brief "must be served on counsel for each separately represented party," Rule 31(b) may be read to imply that copies of briefs need not be served on unrepresented parties. The Rule has been amended to clarify that briefs must be served on all parties, including those who are not represented by counsel.

Changes Made After Publication and Comments. No changes were made to the text of the proposed amendment or to the Committee Note.

COMMITTEE NOTES ON RULES—2009 AMENDMENT
Subdivision (a)(1). Subdivision (a)(1) formerly required that the appellant's reply brief be served "at least 3 days before argument, unless the court, for good cause, allows a later filing." Under former Rule 26(a), "3 days" could mean as many as 5 or even 6 days. See the Note to Rule 26. Under revised Rule 26(a), intermediate weekends and holidays are counted. Changing "3 days" to "7 days" alters the period accordingly. Under revised Rule 26(a), when a period ends on a weekend or holiday, one must continue to count in the same direction until the next day that is not a weekend or holiday; the choice of the 7-day period for subdivision (a)(1) will minimize such occurrences.

COMMITTEE NOTES ON RULES—2018 AMENDMENT
Subdivision (a)(1) is revised to extend the period for filing a reply brief from 14 days to 21 days. Before the elimination of the "three-day rule" in Rule 26(c), attorneys were accustomed to a period of 17 days within which to file a reply brief, and the committee concluded that shortening the period from 17 days to 14 days could adversely affect the preparation of useful reply briefs. Because time periods are best measured in increments of 7 days, the period is extended to 21 days.

Rule 32. Form of Briefs, Appendices, and Other Papers

(a) Form of a Brief.

(1) Reproduction.

(A) A brief may be reproduced by any process that yields a clear black image on light paper. The paper must be opaque and unglazed. Only one side of the paper may be used.

(B) Text must be reproduced with a clarity that equals or exceeds the output of a laser printer.

(C) Photographs, illustrations, and tables may be reproduced by any method that results in a good copy of the original; a glossy finish is acceptable if the original is glossy.

(2) Cover. Except for filings by unrepresented parties, the cover of the appellant's brief must be blue; the appellee's, red; an intervenor's or amicus curiae's, green; any reply brief, gray; and any supplemental brief, tan. The front cover of a brief must contain:

(A) the number of the case centered at the top;

(B) the name of the court;

(C) the title of the case (see Rule 12(a));

(D) the nature of the proceeding (e.g., Appeal, Petition for Review) and the name of the court, agency, or board below;

(E) the title of the brief, identifying the party or parties for whom the brief is filed; and

(F) the name, office address, and telephone number of counsel representing the party for whom the brief is filed.

(3) Binding. The brief must be bound in any manner that is secure, does not obscure the text, and permits the brief to lie reasonably flat when open.

(4) Paper Size, Line Spacing, and Margins. The brief must be on 8½ by 11 inch paper. The text must be double-spaced, but quotations more than two lines long may be indented and single-spaced. Headings and footnotes may be single-spaced. Margins must be at least one inch on all four sides. Page numbers may be placed in the margins, but no text may appear there.

(5) Typeface. Either a proportionally spaced or a monospaced face may be used.

(A) A proportionally spaced face must include serifs, but sans-serif type may be used in headings and captions. A proportionally spaced face must be 14-point or larger.

(B) A monospaced face may not contain more than 10½ characters per inch.

(6) Type Styles. A brief must be set in a plain, roman style, although italics or boldface may be used for emphasis. Case names must be italicized or underlined.

(7) Length.

(A) Page Limitation. A principal brief may not exceed 30 pages, or a reply brief 15 pages, unless it complies with Rule 32(a)(7)(B).

(B) Type-Volume Limitation.

(i) A principal brief is acceptable if it:
  • contains no more than 13,000 words; or
  • uses a monospaced face and contains no more than 1,300 lines of text.

(ii) A reply brief is acceptable if it contains no more than half of the type volume specified in Rule 32(a)(7)(B)(i).

(b) Form of an Appendix. An appendix must comply with Rule 32(a)(1), (2), (3), and (4), with the following exceptions:

(1) The cover of a separately bound appendix must be white.

(2) An appendix may include a legible photocopy of any document found in the record or of a printed judicial or agency decision.

241

(3) When necessary to facilitate inclusion of odd-sized documents such as technical drawings, an appendix may be a size other than 8½ by 11 inches, and need not lie reasonably flat when opened.

(c) Form of Other Papers.

(1) Motion. The form of a motion is governed by Rule 27(d).

(2) Other Papers. Any other paper, including a petition for panel rehearing and a petition for hearing or rehearing en banc, and any response to such a petition, must be reproduced in the manner prescribed by Rule 32(a), with the following exceptions:

(A) A cover is not necessary if the caption and signature page of the paper together contain the information required by Rule 32(a)(2). If a cover is used, it must be white.

(B) Rule 32(a)(7) does not apply.

(d) Signature. Every brief, motion, or other paper filed with the court must be signed by the party filing the paper or, if the party is represented, by one of the party's attorneys.

(e) Local Variation. Every court of appeals must accept documents that comply with the form requirements of this rule and the length limits set by these rules. By local rule or order in a particular case, a court of appeals may accept documents that do not meet all the form requirements of this rule or the length limits set by these rules.

(f) Items Excluded from Length. In computing any length limit, headings, footnotes, and quotations count toward the limit but the following items do not:

- cover page;
- disclosure statement;
- table of contents;
- table of citations;
- statement regarding oral argument;
- addendum containing statutes, rules, or regulations;
- certificate of counsel;
- signature block;
- proof of service; and
- any item specifically excluded by these rules or by local rule.

(g) Certificate of Compliance.

(1) Briefs and Papers That Require a Certificate. A brief submitted under Rules 28.1(e)(2), 29(b)(4), or 32(a)(7)(B)—and a paper submitted under Rules 5(c)(1), 21(d)(1), 27(d)(2)(A), 27(d)(2)(C), 35(b)(2)(A), or 40(b)(1)—must include a certificate by the attorney, or an unrepresented party, that the document complies with the type-volume limitation. The person preparing the certificate may rely on the word or line count of the word-processing system used to prepare the document. The certificate must state the number of words—or the number of lines of monospaced type—in the document.

(2) Acceptable Form. Form 6 in the Appendix of Forms meets the requirements for a certificate of compliance.

(As amended Apr. 24, 1998, eff. Dec. 1, 1998; Apr. 29, 2002, eff. Dec. 1, 2002; Apr. 25, 2005, eff. Dec. 1, 2005; Apr. 28, 2016, eff. Dec. 1, 2016; Apr. 25, 2019, eff. Dec. 1, 2019.)

NOTES OF ADVISORY COMMITTEE ON RULES—1967

Only two methods of printing are now generally recognized by the circuits—standard typographic printing and the offset duplicating process (multilith). A third, mimeographing, is permitted in the Fifth Circuit. The District of Columbia, Ninth, and Tenth Circuits permit records to be reproduced by copying processes. The Committee feels that recent and impending advances in the arts of duplicating and copying warrant experimentation with less costly forms of reproduction than those now generally authorized. The proposed rule permits, in effect, the use of any process other than the carbon copy process which produces a clean, readable page. What constitutes such is left in first instance to the parties and ultimately to the court to determine. The final sentence of the first paragraph of subdivision (a) is added to allow the use of multilith, mimeograph, or other forms of copies of the reporter's original transcript whenever such are available.

COMMITTEE NOTES ON RULES—1998 AMENDMENT

In addition to amending Rule 32 to conform to uniform drafting standards, several substantive amendments are made. The Advisory Committee had been working on substantive amendments to Rule 32 for some time prior to completion of this larger project.

Subdivison (a). Form of a Brief.

Paragraph (a)(1). Reproduction.

The rule permits the use of "light" paper, not just "white" paper. Cream and buff colored paper, including recycled paper, are acceptable. The rule permits printing on only one side of the paper. Although some argue that paper could be saved by allowing double-sided printing, others argue that in order to preserve legibility a heavier weight paper would be needed, resulting in little, if any, paper saving. In addition, the blank sides of a brief are commonly used by judges and their clerks for making notes about the case.

Because photocopying is inexpensive and widely available and because use of carbon paper is now very rare, all references to the use of carbon copies have been deleted.

The rule requires that the text be reproduced with a clarity that equals or exceeds the output of a laser printer. That means that the method used must have a print resolution of 300 dots per inch (dpi) or more. This will ensure the legibility of the brief. A brief produced by a typewriter or a daisy wheel printer, as well as one produced by a laser printer, has a print resolution of 300 dpi or more. But a brief produced by a dot-matrix printer, fax machine, or portable printer that uses heat or dye transfer methods does not. Some ink jet printers are 300 dpi or more, but some are 216 dpi and would not be sufficient.

Photographs, illustrations, and tables may be reproduced by any method that results in a good copy.

Paragraph (a)(2). Cover.

The rule requires that the number of the case be centered at the top of the front cover of a brief. This will aid in identification of the brief. The idea was drawn from a local rule. The rule also requires that the title of the brief identify the party or parties on whose behalf the brief is filed. When there are multiple appellants or appellees, the information is necessary to the court. If, however, the brief is filed on behalf of all appellants or appellees, it may so indicate. Further, it may be possible to identify the class of parties on whose behalf the brief is filed. Otherwise, it may be necessary to name each party. The rule also requires that attorney's telephone numbers appear on the front cover of a brief or appendix.

Paragraph (a)(3). Binding.

The rule requires a brief to be bound in any manner that is secure, does not obscure the text, and that permits the brief to lie reasonably flat when open. Many judges and most court employees do much of their work at computer keyboards and a brief that lies flat when open is significantly more convenient. One circuit already has such a requirement and another states a preference for it. While a spiral binding would comply with this requirement, it is not intended to be the exclusive method of binding. Stapling a brief at the upper left-hand corner also satisfies this requirement as long as it is sufficiently secure.

Paragraph (a)(4). Paper Size, Line Spacing, and Margins.

The provisions for pamphlet-size briefs are deleted because their use is so rare. If a circuit wishes to authorize their use, it has authority to do so under subdivision (d) of this rule.

Paragraph (a)(5). Typeface.

This paragraph and the next one, governing type style, are new. The existing rule simply states that a brief produced by the standard typographic process must be printed in at least 11 point type, or if produced in any other manner, the lines of text must be double spaced. Today few briefs are produced by commercial printers or by typewriters; most are produced on and printed by computer. The availability of computer fonts in a variety of sizes and styles has given rise to local rules limiting type styles. The Advisory Committee believes that some standards are needed both to ensure that all litigants have an equal opportunity to present their material and to ensure that the briefs are easily legible.

With regard to typeface there are two options: proportionally-spaced typeface or monospaced typeface.

A proportionally-spaced typeface gives a different amount of horizontal space to characters depending upon the width of the character. A capital "M" is given more horizontal space than a lower case "i." The rule requires that a proportionally-spaced typeface have serifs. Serifs are small horizontal or vertical strokes at the ends of the lines that make up the letters and numbers. Studies have shown that long passages of serif type are easier to read and comprehend than long passages of sans-serif type. The rule accordingly limits the principal sections of submissions to serif type, although sans-serif type may be used in headings and captions. This is the same approach magazines, newspapers, and commercial printers take. Look at a professionally printed brief; you will find sans-serif type confined to captions, if it is used at all. The next line shows two characters enlarged for detail. The first has serifs, the second does not.

Y Y

So that the type is easily legible, the rule requires a minimum type size of 14 points for proportionally-spaced typeface.

A monospaced typeface is one in which all characters have the same advance width. That means that each character is given the same horizontal space on the line. A wide letter such as a capital "M" and a narrow letter such as a lower case "i" are given the same space. Most typewriters produce mono-spaced type, and most computers also can do so using fonts with names such as "Courier."

This sentence is in a proportionally spaced font; as you can see, the m and i have different widths.

This sentence is in a monospaced font; as you can see, the m and i have the same width.

The rule requires use of a monospaced typeface that produces no more than 10½ characters per inch. A standard typewriter with pica type produces a monospaced typeface with 10 characters per inch (cpi). That is the ideal monospaced typeface. The rule permits up to 10½ cpi because some computer software programs contain monospaced fonts that purport to produce 10 cpi but that in fact produce slightly more than 10 cpi. In order to avoid the need to reprint a brief produced in good faith reliance upon such a program, the rule permits a bit of leeway. A monospace typeface with no more than 10 cpi is preferred.

Paragraph (a)(6). Type Styles.

The rule requires use of plain roman, that is not italic or script, type. Italics and boldface may be used for emphasis. Italicizing case names is preferred but underlining may be used.

Paragraph (a)(7). Type-Volume Limitation.

Subparagraph (a)(7)(A) contains a safe-harbor provision. A principal brief that does not exceed 30 pages complies with the type-volume limitation without further question or certification. A reply brief that does not exceed 15 pages is similarly treated. The current limit is 50 pages but that limit was established when most briefs were produced on typewriters. The widespread use of personal computers has made a multitude of printing options available to practitioners. Use of a proportional typeface alone can greatly increase the amount of material per page as compared with use of a monospace typeface. Even though the rule requires use of 14-point proportional type, there is great variation in the x-height of different 14-point typefaces. Selection of a typeface with a small x-height increases the amount of text per page. Computers also make possible fine gradations in spacing between lines and tight tracking between letters and words. All of this, and more, have made the 50-page limit virtually meaningless. Establishing a safe-harbor of 50 pages would permit a person who makes use of the multitude of printing "tricks" available with most personal computers to file a brief far longer than the "old" 50-page brief. Therefore, as to those briefs not subject to any other volume control than a page limit, a 30-page limit is imposed.

The limits in subparagraph (B) approximate the current 50-page limit and compliance with them is easy even for a person without a personal computer. The aim of these provisions is to create a level playing field. The rule gives every party an equal opportunity to make arguments, without permitting those with the best in-house typesetting an opportunity to expand their submissions.

The length can be determined either by counting words or lines. That is, the length of a brief is determined not by the number of pages but by the number of words or lines in the brief. This gives every party the same opportunity to present an argument without regard to the typeface used and eliminates any incentive to use footnotes or typographical "tricks" to squeeze more material onto a page.

The word counting method can be used with any typeface.

A monospaced brief can meet the volume limitation by using the word or a line count. If the line counting method is used, the number of lines may not exceed 1,300—26 lines per page in a 50-page brief. The number of lines is easily counted manually. Line counting is not sufficient if a proportionally spaced typeface is used, because the amount of material per line can vary widely.

A brief using the type-volume limitations in subparagraph (B) must include a certificate by the attorney, or party proceeding pro se, that the brief complies with the limitation. The rule permits the person preparing the certification to rely upon the word or line count of the word-processing system used to prepare the brief.

Currently, Rule 28(g) governs the length of a brief. Rule 28(g) begins with the words "[e]xcept by permission of the court," signaling that a party may file a motion to exceed the limits established in the rule. The absence of similar language in Rule 32 does not mean that the Advisory Committee intends to prohibit motions to deviate from the requirements of the rule. The Advisory Committee does not believe that any such language is needed to authorize such a motion.
Subdivision (b). Form of an Appendix.

The provisions governing the form of a brief generally apply to an appendix. The rule recognizes, however, that an appendix is usually produced by photocopying existing documents. The rule requires that the photocopies be legible.

The rule permits inclusion not only of documents from the record but also copies of a printed judicial or agency decision. If a decision that is part of the record in the case has been published, it is helpful to provide a copy of the published decision in place of a copy of the decision from the record.
Subdivision (c). Form of Other Papers.

The old rule required a petition for rehearing to be produced in the same manner as a brief or appendix. The new rule also requires that a petition for rehearing en banc and a response to either a petition for panel rehearing or a petition for rehearing en banc be prepared in the same manner. But the length limitations of paragraph (a)(7) do not apply to those documents and a cover is not required if all the information needed by the court to properly identify the document and the parties is included in the caption or signature page.

Existing subdivision (b) states that other papers may be produced in like manner, or "they may be typewritten upon opaque, unglazed paper 8½ by 11 inches in size." The quoted language is deleted but that method of preparing documents is not eliminated because (a)(5)(B) permits use of standard pica type. The only change is that the new rule now specifies margins for typewritten documents.
Subdivision (d). Local Variation.

A brief that complies with the national rule should be acceptable in every court. Local rules may move in one direction only; they may authorize noncompliance with certain of the national norms. For example, a court that wishes to do so may authorize printing of briefs on both sides of the paper, or the use of smaller type size or sans-serif proportional type. A local rule may not, however, impose requirements that are not in the national rule.

COMMITTEE NOTES ON RULES—2002 AMENDMENT

Subdivision (a)(2). On occasion, a court may permit or order the parties to file supplemental briefs addressing an issue that was not addressed—or adequately addressed—in the principal briefs. Rule 32(a)(2) has been amended to require that tan covers be used on such supplemental briefs. The amendment is intended to promote uniformity in federal appellate practice. At present, the local rules of the circuit courts conflict. See, e.g., D.C. Cir. R. 28(g) (requiring yellow covers on supplemental briefs); 11th Cir. R. 32, I.O.P. 1 (requiring white covers on supplemental briefs).

Changes Made After Publication and Comments. No changes were made to the text of the proposed amendment or to the Committee Note.

Subdivision (a)(7)(C). If the principal brief of a party exceeds 30 pages, or if the reply brief of a party exceeds 15 pages, Rule 32(a)(7)(C) provides that the party or the party's attorney must certify that the brief complies with the type-volume limitation of Rule 32(a)(7)(B). Rule 32(a)(7)(C) has been amended to refer to Form 6 (which has been added to the Appendix of Forms) and to provide that a party or attorney who uses Form 6 has complied with Rule 32(a)(7)(C). No court may provide to the contrary, in its local rules or otherwise.

Form 6 requests not only the information mandated by Rule 32(a)(7)(C), but also information that will assist courts in enforcing the typeface requirements of Rule 32(a)(5) and the type style requirements of Rule 32(a)(6). Parties and attorneys are not required to use Form 6, but they are encouraged to do so.

Subdivision (c)(2)(A). Under Rule 32(c)(2)(A), a cover is not required on a petition for panel rehearing, petition for hearing or rehearing en banc, answer to a petition for panel rehearing, response to a petition for hearing or rehearing en banc, or any other paper. Rule 32(d) makes it clear that no court can require that a cover be used on any of these papers. However, nothing prohibits a court from providing in its local rules that if a cover on one of these papers is "voluntarily" used, it must be a particular color. Several circuits have adopted such local rules. See, e.g., Fed. Cir. R. 35(c) (requiring yellow covers on petitions for hearing or rehearing en banc and brown covers on responses to such petitions); Fed. Cir. R. 40(a) (requiring yellow covers on petitions for panel rehearing and brown covers on answers to such petitions); 7th Cir. R. 28 (requiring blue covers on petitions for rehearing filed by appellants or answers to such petitions, and requiring red covers on petitions for rehearing filed by appellees or answers to such petitions); 9th Cir. R. 40-1 (requiring blue covers on petitions for panel rehearing filed by appellants and red covers on answers to such petitions, and requiring red covers on petitions for panel rehearing filed by appellees and blue covers on answers to such petitions); 11th Cir. R. 35-6 (requiring white covers on petitions for hearing or rehearing en banc).

These conflicting local rules create a hardship for counsel who practice in more than one circuit. For that reason, Rule 32(c)(2)(A) has been amended to provide that if a party chooses to use a cover on a paper that is not required to have one, that cover must be white. The amendment is intended to preempt all local rulemaking on the subject of cover colors and thereby promote uniformity in federal appellate practice.

Changes Made After Publication and Comments. No changes were made to the text of the proposed amendment or to the Committee Note.

Subdivisions (d) and (e). Former subdivision (d) has been redesignated as subdivision (e), and a new subdivision (d) has been added. The new subdivision (d) requires that every brief, motion, or other paper filed with the court be signed by the attorney or unrepresented party who files it, much as Fed. R. Civ. P. 11(a) imposes a signature requirement on papers filed in district court. Only the original copy of every paper must be signed. An appendix filed with the court does not have to be signed at all.

By requiring a signature, subdivision (d) ensures that a readily identifiable attorney or party takes responsibility for every paper. The courts of appeals already have authority to sanction attorneys and parties who file papers that contain misleading or frivolous assertions, see, e.g., 28 U.S.C. §1912, Fed. R. App. P. 38 & 46(b)(1)(B), and thus subdivision (d) has not been amended to incorporate provisions similar to those found in Fed. R. Civ. P. 11(b) and 11(c).

Changes Made After Publication and Comments. No changes were made to the text of the proposed amendment. A line was added to the Committee Note to clarify that only the original copy of a paper needs to be signed.

COMMITTEE NOTES ON RULES—2005 AMENDMENT

Subdivision (a)(7)(C). Rule 32(a)(7)(C) has been amended to add cross-references to new Rule 28.1, which governs briefs filed in cases involving cross-appeals. Rule 28.1(e)(2) prescribes type-volume limitations that apply to such briefs, and Rule 28.1(e)(3) requires parties to certify compliance with those type-volume limitations under Rule 32(a)(7)(C).

COMMITTEE NOTES ON RULES—2016 AMENDMENT

When Rule 32(a)(7)(B)'s type-volume limits for briefs were adopted in 1998, the word limits were based on an estimate of 280 words per page. In the course of adopting word limits for the length limits in Rules 5, 21, 27, 35, and 40, and responding to concern about the length of briefs, the Committee has reevaluated the conversion ratio (from pages to words) and decided to apply a conversion ratio of 260 words per page. Rules 28.1 and 32(a)(7)(B) are amended to reduce the word limits accordingly.

In a complex case, a party may need to file a brief that exceeds the type-volume limitations specified in these rules, such as to include unusually voluminous information explaining relevant background or legal provisions or to respond to multiple briefs by opposing parties or amici. The Committee expects that courts will accommodate those situations by granting leave to exceed the type-volume limitations as appropriate.

Subdivision (e) is amended to make clear a court's ability (by local rule or order in a case) to increase the length limits for briefs and other documents. Subdivision (e) already established this authority as to the length limits in Rule 32(a)(7); the amendment makes clear that this authority extends to all length limits in the Appellate Rules.

A new subdivision (f) is added to set out a global list of items excluded from length computations, and the list of exclusions in former subdivision (a)(7)(B)(iii) is deleted. The certificate-of-compliance provision formerly in Rule 32(a)(7)(C) is relocated to a new Rule 32(g) and now applies to filings under all type-volume limits (other than Rule 28(j)'s word limit)—including the new word limits in Rules 5, 21, 27, 29, 35, and 40. Conforming amendments are made to Form 6.

COMMITTEE NOTES ON RULES—2019 AMENDMENT

The phrase "corporate disclosure statement" is changed to "disclosure statement" to reflect the revision of Rule 26.1. The other amendment to subdivision (f) does not change the substance of the current rule, but removes the articles before each item because a document will not always include these items.

Rule 32.1. Citing Judicial Dispositions

(a) Citation Permitted. A court may not prohibit or restrict the citation of federal judicial opinions, orders, judgments, or other written dispositions that have been:

(i) designated as "unpublished," "not for publication," "non-precedential," "not precedent," or the like; and

(ii) issued on or after January 1, 2007.

(b) Copies Required. If a party cites a federal judicial opinion, order, judgment, or other written disposition that is not available in a publicly accessible electronic database, the party must file and serve a copy of that opinion, order, judgment, or disposition with the brief or other paper in which it is cited.

(As added Apr. 12, 2006, eff. Dec. 1, 2006.)

COMMITTEE NOTES ON RULES—2006

Rule 32.1 is a new rule addressing the citation of judicial opinions, orders, judgments, or other written dispositions that have been designated by a federal court as "unpublished," "not for publication," "non-precedential," "not precedent," or the like. This Committee Note will refer to these dispositions collectively as "unpublished" opinions.

Rule 32.1 is extremely limited. It does not require any court to issue an unpublished opinion or forbid any court from doing so. It does not dictate the circumstances under which a court may choose to designate an opinion as "unpublished" or specify the procedure that a court must follow in making that determination. It says nothing about what effect a court must give to one of its unpublished opinions or to the unpublished opinions of another court. Rule 32.1 addresses only the citation of federal judicial dispositions that have been designated as "unpublished" or "non-precedential"—whether or not those dispositions have been published in some way or are precedential in some sense.

Subdivision (a). Every court of appeals has allowed unpublished opinions to be cited in some circumstances, such as to support a contention of issue preclusion or claim preclusion. But the circuits have differed dramatically with respect to the restrictions that they have placed on the citation of unpublished opinions for their persuasive value. Some circuits have freely permitted such citation, others have discouraged it but permitted it in limited circumstances, and still others have forbidden it altogether.

Rule 32.1(a) is intended to replace these inconsistent standards with one uniform rule. Under Rule 32.1(a), a court of appeals may not prohibit a party from citing an unpublished opinion of a federal court for its persuasive value or for any other reason. In addition, under Rule 32.1(a), a court may not place any restriction on the citation of such opinions. For example, a court may not instruct parties that the citation of unpublished opinions is discouraged, nor may a court forbid parties to cite unpublished opinions when a published opinion addresses the same issue.

Rule 32.1(a) applies only to unpublished opinions issued on or after January 1, 2007. The citation of unpublished opinions issued before January 1, 2007, will continue to be governed by the local rules of the circuits.

Subdivision (b). Under Rule 32.1(b), a party who cites an opinion of a federal court must provide a copy of that opinion to the court of appeals and to the other parties, unless that opinion is available in a publicly accessible electronic database—such as a commercial database maintained by a legal research service or a database maintained by a court. A party who is required under Rule 32.1(b) to provide a copy of an opinion must file and serve the copy with the brief or other paper in which the opinion is cited. Rule 32.1(b) applies to all unpublished opinions, regardless of when they were issued.

Changes Made After Publication and Comment. (At its June 15–16, 2005, meeting, the Standing Rules Committee with the advisory committee chair's concurrence agreed to delete sections of the Committee Note, which provided background information on the justification of the proposal.) The changes made by the Advisory Committee after publication are described in my May 14, 2004 report to the Standing Committee. At its April 2005 meeting, the Advisory Committee directed that two additional changes be made.

First, the Committee decided to add "federal" before "judicial opinions" in subdivision (a) and before "judicial opinion" in subdivision (b) to make clear that Rule 32.1 applies only to the unpublished opinions of federal courts. Conforming changes were made to the Committee Note. These changes address the concern of some state court judges—conveyed by Chief Justice Wells at the June 2004 Standing Committee meeting—that Rule 32.1 might have an impact on state law.

Second, the Committee decided to insert into the Committee Note references to the studies conducted by the Federal Judicial Center ("FJC") and the Administrative Office ("AO"). (The studies are described below. [Omitted]) These references make clear that the arguments of Rule 32.1's opponents were taken seriously and studied carefully, but ultimately rejected because they were unsupported by or, in some instances, actually refuted by the best available empirical evidence.

Rule 33. Appeal Conferences

The court may direct the attorneys—and, when appropriate, the parties—to participate in one or more conferences to address any matter that may aid in disposing of the proceedings, including simplifying the issues and discussing settlement. A judge or other person designated by the court may preside over the conference, which may be conducted in person or by telephone. Before a settlement conference, the attorneys must consult with their clients and obtain as much authority as feasible to settle the case. The court may, as a result of the conference, enter an order controlling the course of the proceedings or implementing any settlement agreement.

(As amended Apr. 29, 1994, eff. Dec. 1, 1994; Apr. 24, 1998, eff. Dec. 1, 1998.)

NOTES OF ADVISORY COMMITTEE ON RULES—1967

The uniform rule for review or enforcement of orders of administrative agencies, boards, commissions or officers (see the general note following Rule 15) authorizes a prehearing conference in agency review proceedings. The same considerations which make a prehearing conference desirable in such proceedings may be present in certain cases on appeal from the district courts. The proposed rule is based upon subdivision 11 of the present uniform rule for review of agency orders.

NOTES OF ADVISORY COMMITTEE ON RULES—1994 AMENDMENT

Rule 33 has been entirely rewritten. The new rule makes several changes.

The caption of the rule has been changed from "Prehearing Conference" to "Appeal Conferences" to reflect the fact that occasionally a conference is held after oral argument.

The rule permits the court to require the parties to attend the conference in appropriate cases. The Committee does not contemplate that attendance of the parties will become routine, but in certain instances the parties' presence can be useful. The language of the rule is broad enough to allow a court to determine that an executive or employee (other than the general counsel) of a corporation or government agency with authority regarding the matter at issue, constitutes "the party."

The rule includes the possibility of settlement among the possible conference topics.

The rule recognizes that conferences are often held by telephone.

The rule allows a judge or other person designated by the court to preside over a conference. A number of local rules permit persons other than judges to preside over conferences. 1st Cir. R. 47.5; 6th Cir. R. 18; 8th Cir. R. 33A; 9th Cir. R. 33–1; and 10th Cir. R. 33.

The rule requires an attorney to consult with his or her client before a settlement conference and obtain as much authority as feasible to settle the case. An attorney can never settle a case without his or her client's consent. Certain entities, especially government entities, have particular difficulty obtaining authority to settle a case. The rule requires counsel to obtain only as much authority "as feasible."

COMMITTEE NOTES ON RULES—1998 AMENDMENT

The language of the rule is amended to make the rule more easily understood. In addition to changes made to improve the understanding, the Advisory Committee has changed language to make style and terminology consistent throughout the appellate rules. These changes are intended to be stylistic only.

Rule 34. Oral Argument

(a) In General.

(1) Party's Statement. Any party may file, or a court may require by local rule, a statement explaining why oral argument should, or need not, be permitted.

(2) Standards. Oral argument must be allowed in every case unless a panel of three judges who have examined the briefs and record unanimously agrees that oral argument is unnecessary for any of the following reasons:

(A) the appeal is frivolous;

(B) the dispositive issue or issues have been authoritatively decided; or

(C) the facts and legal arguments are adequately presented in the briefs and record, and the decisional process would not be significantly aided by oral argument.

(b) Notice of Argument; Postponement. The clerk must advise all parties whether oral argument will be scheduled, and, if so, the date, time, and place for it, and the time allowed for each side. A motion to postpone the argument or to allow longer argument must be filed reasonably in advance of the hearing date.

(c) Order and Contents of Argument. The appellant opens and concludes the argument. Counsel must not read at length from briefs, records, or authorities.

(d) Cross-Appeals and Separate Appeals. If there is a cross-appeal, Rule 28.1(b) determines which party is the appellant and which is the appellee for purposes of oral argument. Unless the court directs otherwise, a cross-appeal or separate appeal must be argued when the initial appeal is argued. Separate parties should avoid duplicative argument.

(e) Nonappearance of a Party. If the appellee fails to appear for argument, the court must hear appellant's argument. If the appellant fails to appear for argument, the court may hear the appellee's argument. If neither party appears, the case will be decided on the briefs, unless the court orders otherwise.

(f) Submission on Briefs. The parties may agree to submit a case for decision on the briefs, but the court may direct that the case be argued.

(g) Use of Physical Exhibits at Argument; Removal. Counsel intending to use physical exhibits other than documents at the argument must arrange to place them in the courtroom on the day of the argument before the court convenes. After the argument, counsel must remove the exhibits from the courtroom, unless the court directs otherwise. The clerk may destroy or dispose of the exhibits if counsel does not reclaim them within a reasonable time after the clerk gives notice to remove them.

(As amended Apr. 1, 1979, eff. Aug. 1, 1979; Mar. 10, 1986, eff. July 1, 1986; Apr. 30, 1991, eff. Dec. 1, 1991; Apr. 22, 1993, eff. Dec. 1, 1993; Apr. 24, 1998, eff. Dec. 1, 1998; Apr. 25, 2005, eff. Dec. 1, 2005.)

NOTES OF ADVISORY COMMITTEE ON RULES—1967

A majority of circuits now limit oral argument to thirty minutes for each side, with the provision that additional time may be made available upon request. The Committee is of the view that thirty minutes to each side is sufficient in most cases, but that where additional time is necessary it should be freely granted on a proper showing of cause therefor. It further feels that the matter of time should be left ultimately to each court of appeals, subject to the spirit of the rule that a reasonable time should be allowed for argument. The term "side" is used to indicate that the time allowed by the rule is afforded to opposing interests rather than to individual parties. Thus if multiple appellants or appellees have a common interest, they constitute only a single side. If counsel for multiple parties who constitute a single side feel that additional time is necessary, they may request it. In other particulars this rule follows the usual practice among the circuits. See 3d Cir. Rule 31; 6th Cir. Rule 20; 10th Cir. Rule 23.

NOTES OF ADVISORY COMMITTEE ON RULES—1979 AMENDMENT

The proposed amendment, patterned after the recommendations in the Report of the Commission on Revision of the Federal Court Appellate System, Structure and Internal Procedures: Recommendations for Change, 1975, created by Public Law 489 of the 92nd Cong. 2nd Sess., 86 Stat. 807, sets forth general principles and minimum standards to be observed in formulating any local rule.

NOTES OF ADVISORY COMMITTEE ON RULES—1986 AMENDMENT

The amendments to Rules 34(a) and (e) are technical. No substantive change is intended.

NOTES OF ADVISORY COMMITTEE ON RULES—1991 AMENDMENT

Subdivision (d). The amendment of subdivision (d) conforms this rule with the amendment of Rule 28(h).

NOTES OF ADVISORY COMMITTEE ON RULES—1993 AMENDMENT

Subdivision (c). The amendment deletes the requirement that the opening argument must include a fair statement of the case. The Committee proposed the change because in some circuits the court does not want appellants to give such statements. In those circuits, the rule is not followed and is misleading. Nevertheless, the Committee does not want the deletion of the requirement to indicate disapproval of the practice. Those circuits that desire a statement of the case may continue the practice.

COMMITTEE NOTES ON RULES—1998 AMENDMENT

The language of the rule is amended to make the rule more easily understood. In addition to changes made to improve the understanding, the Advisory Committee has changed language to make style and terminology consistent throughout the appellate rules. These changes are intended to be stylistic only. Substantive changes are made in subdivision (a).

Subdivision (a). Currently subdivision (a) says that oral argument must be permitted unless, applying a local rule, a panel of three judges unanimously agrees that oral argument is not necessary. Rule 34 then outlines the criteria to be used to determine whether oral argument is needed and requires any local rule to "conform substantially" to the "minimum standard[s]" established in the national rule. The amendments omit the local rule requirement and make the criteria applicable by force of the national rule. The local rule is an unnecessary instrument.

Paragraph (a)(2) states that one reason for deciding that oral argument is unnecessary is that the dispositive issue has been authoritatively decided. The amended language no longer states that the issue must have been "recently" decided. The Advisory Committee does not intend any substantive change, but thinks that the use of "recently" may be misleading.

Subdivision (d). A cross-reference to Rule 28(h) has been substituted for a reiteration of the provisions of Rule 28(h).

COMMITTEE NOTES ON RULES—2005 AMENDMENT

Subdivision (d). A cross-reference in subdivision (d) has been changed to reflect the fact that, as part of an effort to collect within one rule all provisions regarding briefing in cases involving cross-appeals, former Rule 28(h) has been abrogated and its contents moved to new Rule 28.1(b).

Rule 35. En Banc Determination

(a) When Hearing or Rehearing En Banc May Be Ordered. A majority of the circuit judges who are in regular active service and who are not disqualified may order that an appeal or other proceeding be heard or reheard by the court of appeals en banc. An en banc hearing or rehearing is not favored and ordinarily will not be ordered unless:

(1) en banc consideration is necessary to secure or maintain uniformity of the court's decisions; or

(2) the proceeding involves a question of exceptional importance.

(b) Petition for Hearing or Rehearing En Banc. A party may petition for a hearing or rehearing en banc.

(1) The petition must begin with a statement that either:

(A) the panel decision conflicts with a decision of the United States Supreme Court or of the court to which the petition is addressed (with citation to the conflicting case or cases) and consideration by the full court is therefore necessary to secure and maintain uniformity of the court's decisions; or

(B) the proceeding involves one or more questions of exceptional importance, each of which must be concisely stated; for example, a petition may assert that a proceeding presents a question of exceptional importance if it involves an issue on which the panel decision conflicts with the authoritative decisions of other United States Courts of Appeals that have addressed the issue.

(2) Except by the court's permission:

(A) a petition for an en banc hearing or rehearing produced using a computer must not exceed 3,900 words; and

(B) a handwritten or typewritten petition for an en banc hearing or rehearing must not exceed 15 pages.

(3) For purposes of the limits in Rule 35(b)(2), if a party files both a petition for panel rehearing and a petition for rehearing en banc, they are considered a single document even if they are filed separately, unless separate filing is required by local rule.

(c) Time for Petition for Hearing or Rehearing En Banc. A petition that an appeal be heard initially en banc must be filed by the date when the appellee's brief is due. A petition for a rehearing en banc must be filed within the time prescribed by Rule 40 for filing a petition for rehearing.

(d) Number of Copies. The number of copies to be filed must be prescribed by local rule and may be altered by order in a particular case.

(e) Response. No response may be filed to a petition for an en banc consideration unless the court orders a response.

(f) Call for a Vote. A vote need not be taken to determine whether the case will be heard or reheard en banc unless a judge calls for a vote.

(As amended Apr. 1, 1979, eff. Aug. 1, 1979; Apr. 29, 1994, eff. Dec. 1, 1994; Apr. 24, 1998, eff. Dec. 1, 1998; Apr. 25, 2005, eff. Dec. 1, 2005; Apr. 28, 2016, eff. Dec. 1, 2016.)

NOTES OF ADVISORY COMMITTEE ON RULES—1967

Statutory authority for in banc hearings is found in 28 U.S.C. §46(c). The proposed rule is responsive to the Supreme Court's view in Western Pacific Ry. Corp. v. Western Pacific Ry. Co., 345 U.S. 247, 73 S.Ct. 656, 97 L.Ed. 986 (1953), that litigants should be free to suggest that a particular case is appropriate for consideration by all the judges of a court of appeals. The rule is addressed to the procedure whereby a party may suggest the appropriateness of convening the court in banc. It does not affect the power of a court of appeals to initiate in banc hearings sua sponte.

The provision that a vote will not be taken as a result of the suggestion of the party unless requested by a judge of the court in regular active service or by a judge who was a member of the panel that rendered a decision sought to be reheard is intended to make it clear that a suggestion of a party as such does not require any action by the court. See Western Pacific Ry. Corp. v. Western Pacific Ry. Co., supra, 345 U.S. at 262, 73 S.Ct. 656. The rule merely authorizes a suggestion, imposes a time limit on suggestions for rehearings in banc, and provides that suggestions will be directed to the judges of the court in regular active service.

In practice, the suggestion of a party that a case be reheard in banc is frequently contained in a petition for rehearing, commonly styled "petition for rehearing in banc." Such a petition is in fact merely a petition for a rehearing, with a suggestion that the case be reheard in banc. Since no response to the suggestion, as distinguished from the petition for rehearing, is required, the panel which heard the case may quite properly dispose of the petition without reference to the suggestion. In such a case the fact that no response has been made to the suggestion does not affect the finality of the judgment or the issuance of the mandate, and the final sentence of the rule expressly so provides.

Under the present rule there is no specific provision for a response to a suggestion that an appeal be heard in banc. This has led to some uncertainty as to whether such a response may be filed. The proposed amendment would resolve this uncertainty.

While the present rule provides a time limit for suggestions for rehearing in banc, it does not deal with the timing of a request that the appeal be heard in banc initially. The proposed amendment fills this gap as well, providing that the suggestion must be made by the date of which the appellee's brief is filed.

Provision is made for circulating the suggestions to members of the panel despite the fact that senior judges on the panel would not be entitled to vote on whether a suggestion will be granted.

Subdivision (d). Subdivision (d) is added; it authorizes the courts of appeals to prescribe the number of copies of suggestions for hearing or rehearing in banc that must be filed. Because the number of copies needed depends directly upon the number of judges in the circuit, local rules are the best vehicle for setting the required number of copies.

The language and organization of the rule are amended to make the rule more easily understood. In addition to changes made to improve the understanding, the Advisory Committee has changed language to make style and terminology consistent throughout the appellate rules. These changes are intended to be stylistic only.

Several substantive changes are made in this rule, however.

One of the purposes of the substantive amendments is to treat a request for a rehearing en banc like a petition for panel rehearing so that a request for a rehearing en banc will suspend the finality of the court of appeals' judgment and delay the running of the period for filing a petition for writ of certiorari. Companion amendments are made to Rule 41.

Subdivision (a). The title of this subdivision is changed from "when hearing or rehearing in banc will be ordered" to "When Hearing or Rehearing En Banc May Be Ordered." The change emphasizes the discretion a court has with regard to granting en banc review.

Subdivision (b). The term "petition" for rehearing en banc is substituted for the term "suggestion" for rehearing en banc. The terminology change reflects the Committee's intent to treat similarly a petition for panel rehearing and a request for a rehearing en banc. The terminology change also delays the running of the time for filing a petition for a writ of certiorari because Sup. Ct. R. 13.3 says:

if a petition for rehearing is timely filed in the lower court by any party, the time to file the petition for a writ of certiorari for all parties . . . runs from the date of the denial of the petition for rehearing or, if the petition for rehearing is granted, the subsequent entry of judgment.

The amendments also require each petition for en banc consideration to begin with a statement concisely demonstrating that the case meets the usual criteria for en banc consideration. It is the Committee's hope that requiring such a statement will cause the drafter of a petition to focus on the narrow grounds that support en banc consideration and to realize that a petition should not be filed unless the case meets those rigid standards.

Intercircuit conflict is cited as one reason for asserting that a proceeding involves a question of "exceptional importance." Intercircuit conflicts create problems. When the circuits construe the same federal law differently, parties' rights and duties depend upon where a case is litigated. Given the increase in the number of cases decided by the federal courts and the limitation on the number of cases the Supreme Court can hear, conflicts between the circuits may remain unresolved by the Supreme Court for an extended period of time. The existence of an intercircuit conflict often generates additional litigation in the other circuits as well as in the circuits that are already in conflict. Although an en banc proceeding will not necessarily prevent intercircuit conflicts, an en banc proceeding provides a safeguard against unnecessary intercircuit conflicts.

Some circuits have had rules or internal operating procedures that recognize a conflict with another circuit as a legitimate basis for granting a rehearing en banc. An intercircuit conflict may present a question of "exceptional importance" because of the costs that intercircuit conflicts impose on the system as a whole, in addition to the significance of the issues involved. It is not, however, the Committee's intent to make the granting of a hearing or rehearing en banc mandatory whenever there is an intercircuit conflict.

The amendment states that "a petition may assert that a proceeding presents a question of exceptional importance if it involves an issue on which the panel decision conflicts with the authoritative decisions of every other United States Court of Appeals that has addressed the issue." [The Supreme Court revised the proposed amendment to Rule 35(b)(1)(B) by deleting "every" before "other United States Court of Appeals".] That language contemplates two situations in which a rehearing en banc may be appropriate. The first is when a panel decision creates a conflict. A panel decision creates a conflict when it conflicts with the decisions of all other circuits that have considered the issue. If a panel decision simply joins one side of an already existing conflict, a rehearing en banc may not be as important because it cannot avoid the conflict. The second situation that may be a strong candidate for a rehearing en banc is one in which the circuit persists in a conflict created by a pre-existing decision of the same circuit and no other circuits have joined on that side of the conflict. The amendment states that the conflict must be with an "authoritative" decision of another circuit. "Authoritative" is used rather than "published" because in some circuits unpublished opinions may be treated as authoritative.

Counsel are reminded that their duty is fully discharged without filing a petition for rehearing en banc unless the case meets the rigid standards of subdivision (a) of this rule and even then the granting of a petition is entirely within the court's discretion.

Paragraph (2) of this subdivision establishes a maximum length for a petition. Fifteen pages is the length currently used in several circuits. Each request for en banc consideration must be studied by every active judge of the court and is a serious call on limited judicial resources. The extraordinary nature of the issue or the threat to uniformity of the court's decision can be established in most cases in less than fifteen pages. A court may shorten the maximum length on a case by case basis but the rule does not permit a circuit to shorten the length by local rule. The Committee has retained page limits rather than using word or line counts similar to those in amended Rule 32 because there has not been a serious enough problem to justify importing the word and line-count and typeface requirements that are applicable to briefs into other contexts.

Paragraph (3), although similar to (2), is separate because it deals with those instances in which a party files both a petition for rehearing en banc under this rule and a petition for panel rehearing under Rule 40.

To improve the clarity of the rule, the material dealing with filing a response to a petition and with voting on a petition have been moved to new subdivisions (e) and (f).

Subdivision (c). Two changes are made in this subdivision. First, the sentence stating that a request for a rehearing en banc does not affect the finality of the judgment or stay the issuance of the mandate is deleted. Second, the language permitting a party to include a request for rehearing en banc in a petition for panel rehearing is deleted. The Committee believes that those circuits that want to require two separate documents should have the option to do so.

Subdivision (e). This is a new subdivision. The substance of the subdivision, however, was drawn from former subdivision (b). The only changes are stylistic; no substantive changes are intended.

Subdivision (f). This is a new subdivision. The substance of the subdivision, however, was drawn from former subdivision (b).

Because of the discretionary nature of the en banc procedure, the filing of a suggestion for rehearing en banc has not required a vote; a vote is taken only when requested by a judge. It is not the Committee's intent to change the discretionary nature of the procedure or to require a vote on a petition for rehearing en banc. The rule continues, therefore, to provide that a court is not obligated to vote on such petitions. It is necessary, however, that each court develop a procedure for disposing of such petitions because they will suspend the finality of the court's judgment and toll the time for filing a petition for certiorari.

Former subdivision (b) contained language directing the clerk to distribute a "suggestion" to certain judges and indicating which judges may call for a vote. New subdivision (f) does not address those issues because they deal with internal court procedures.

COMMITTEE NOTES ON RULES—2005 AMENDMENT

Subdivision (a). Two national standards—28 U.S.C. §46(c) and Rule 35(a)—provide that a hearing or rehearing en banc may be ordered by "a majority of the circuit judges who are in regular active service." Although these standards apply to all of the courts of appeals, the circuits are deeply divided over the interpretation of this language when one or more active judges are disqualified.

The Supreme Court has never addressed this issue. In Shenker v. Baltimore & Ohio R.R. Co., 374 U.S. 1 (1963), the Court rejected a petitioner's claim that his rights under §46(c) had been violated when the Third Circuit refused to rehear his case en banc. The Third Circuit had 8 active judges at the time; 4 voted in favor of rehearing the case, 2 against, and 2 abstained. No judge was disqualified. The Supreme Court ruled against the petitioner, holding, in essence, that §46(c) did not provide a cause of action, but instead simply gave litigants "the right to know the administrative machinery that will be followed and the right to suggest that the en banc procedure be set in motion in his case." Id. at 5. Shenker did stress that a court of appeals has broad discretion in establishing internal procedures to handle requests for rehearings—or, as Shenker put it, " 'to devise its own administrative machinery to provide the means whereby a majority may order such a hearing.' " Id. (quoting Western Pac. R.R. Corp. v. Western Pac. R.R. Co., 345 U.S. 247, 250 (1953) (emphasis added)). But Shenker did not address what is meant by "a majority" in §46(c) (or Rule 35(a), which did not yet exist)—and Shenker certainly did not suggest that the phrase should have different meanings in different circuits.

In interpreting that phrase, 7 of the courts of appeals follow the "absolute majority" approach. See Marie Leary, Defining the "Majority" Vote Requirement in Federal Rule of Appellate Procedure 35(a) for Rehearings En Banc in the United States Courts of Appeals 8 tbl.1 (Federal Judicial Center 2002). Under this approach, disqualified judges are counted in the base in calculating whether a majority of judges have voted to hear a case en banc. Thus, in a circuit with 12 active judges, 7 must vote to hear a case en banc. If 5 of the 12 active judges are disqualified, all 7 non-disqualified judges must vote to hear the case en banc. The votes of 6 of the 7 non-disqualified judges are not enough, as 6 is not a majority of 12.

Six of the courts of appeals follow the "case majority" approach. Id. Under this approach, disqualified judges are not counted in the base in calculating whether a majority of judges have voted to hear a case en banc. Thus, in a case in which 5 of a circuit's 12 active judges are disqualified, only 4 judges (a majority of the 7 non-disqualified judges) must vote to hear a case en banc. (The First and Third Circuits explicitly qualify the case majority approach by providing that a case cannot be heard en banc unless a majority of all active judges—disqualified and non-disqualified—are eligible to participate.)

Rule 35(a) has been amended to adopt the case majority approach as a uniform national interpretation of §46(c). The federal rules of practice and procedure exist to "maintain consistency," which Congress has equated with "promot[ing] the interest of justice." 28 U.S.C. §2073(b). The courts of appeals should not follow two inconsistent approaches in deciding whether sufficient votes exist to hear a case en banc, especially when there is a governing statute and governing rule that apply to all circuits and that use identical terms, and especially when there is nothing about the local conditions of each circuit that justifies conflicting approaches.

The case majority approach represents the better interpretation of the phrase "the circuit judges . . . in regular active service" in the first sentence of §46(c). The second sentence of §46(c)—which defines which judges are eligible to participate in a case being heard or reheard en banc—uses the similar expression "all circuit judges in regular active service." It is clear that "all circuit judges in regular active service" in the second sentence does not include disqualified judges, as disqualified judges clearly cannot participate in a case being heard or reheard en banc. Therefore, assuming that two nearly identical phrases appearing in adjacent sentences in a statute should be interpreted in the same way, the best reading of "the circuit judges . . . in regular active service" in the first sentence of §46(c) is that it, too, does not include disqualified judges.

This interpretation of §46(c) is bolstered by the fact that the case majority approach has at least two major advantages over the absolute majority approach:

First, under the absolute majority approach, a disqualified judge is, as a practical matter, counted as voting against hearing a case en banc. This defeats the purpose of recusal. To the extent possible, the disqualification of a judge should not result in the equivalent of a vote for or against hearing a case en banc.

Second, the absolute majority approach can leave the en banc court helpless to overturn a panel decision with which almost all of the circuit's active judges disagree. For example, in a case in which 5 of a circuit's 12 active judges are disqualified, the case cannot be heard en banc even if 6 of the 7 non-disqualified judges strongly disagree with the panel opinion. This permits one active judge—perhaps sitting on a panel with a visiting judge—effectively to control circuit precedent, even over the objection of all of his or her colleagues. See Gulf Power Co. v. FCC, 226 F.3d 1220, 1222–23 (11th Cir. 2000) (Carnes, J., concerning the denial of reh'g en banc), rev'd sub nom. National Cable & Telecomm. Ass'n, Inc. v. Gulf Power Co., 534 U.S. 327 (2002). Even though the en banc court may, in a future case, be able to correct an erroneous legal interpretation, the en banc court will never be able to correct the injustice inflicted by the panel on the parties to the case. Morever [sic], it may take many years before sufficient non-disqualified judges can be mustered to overturn the panel's erroneous legal interpretation. In the meantime, the lower courts of the circuit must apply—and the citizens of the circuit must conform their behavior to—an interpretation of the law that almost all of the circuit's active judges believe is incorrect.

The amendment to Rule 35(a) is not meant to alter or affect the quorum requirement of 28 U.S.C. §46(d). In particular, the amendment is not intended to foreclose the possibility that §46(d) might be read to require that more than half of all circuit judges in regular active service be eligible to participate in order for the court to hear or rehear a case en banc.

Changes Made After Publication and Comments. No changes were made to the text of the proposed amendment. The Committee Note was modified in three respects. First, the Note was changed to put more emphasis on the fact that the case majority rule is the best interpretation of §46(c). Second, the Note now clarifies that nothing in the proposed amendment is intended to foreclose courts from interpreting 28 U.S.C. §46(d) to provide that a case cannot be heard or reheard en banc unless a majority of all judges in regular active service—disqualified or not—are eligible to participate. Finally, a couple of arguments made by supporters of the amendment to Rule 35(a) were incorporated into the Note.

COMMITTEE NOTES ON RULES—2016 AMENDMENT

The page limits previously employed in Rules 5, 21, 27, 35, and 40 have been largely overtaken by changes in technology. For papers produced using a computer, those page limits are now replaced by word limits. The word limits were derived from the current page limits using the assumption that one page is equivalent to 260 words. Papers produced using a computer must include the certificate of compliance required by Rule 32(g); Form 6 in the Appendix of Forms suffices to meet that requirement. Page limits are retained for papers prepared without the aid of a computer (i.e., handwritten or typewritten papers). For both the word limit and the page limit, the calculation excludes any items listed in Rule 32(f).

Rule 36. Entry of Judgment; Notice

(a) Entry. A judgment is entered when it is noted on the docket. The clerk must prepare, sign, and enter the judgment:
  (1) after receiving the court's opinion—but if settlement of the judgment's form is required, after final settlement; or
  (2) if a judgment is rendered without an opinion, as the court instructs.

(b) Notice. On the date when judgment is entered, the clerk must serve on all parties a copy of the opinion—or the judgment, if no opinion was written—and a notice of the date when the judgment was entered.

(As amended Apr. 24, 1998, eff. Dec. 1, 1998; Apr. 29, 2002, eff. Dec. 1, 2002.)

NOTES OF ADVISORY COMMITTEE ON RULES—1967

This is the typical rule. See 1st Cir. Rule 29; 3rd Cir. Rule 32; 6th Cir. Rule 21. At present, uncertainty exists as to the date of entry of judgment when the opinion directs subsequent settlement of the precise terms of the judgment, a common practice in cases involving enforcement of agency orders. See Stern and Gressman, Supreme Court Practice, p. 203 (3d Ed., 1962). The principle of finality suggests that in such cases entry of judgment should be delayed until approval of the judgment in final form.

COMMITTEE NOTES ON RULES—1998 AMENDMENT

The language and organization of the rule are amended to make the rule more easily understood. In addition to changes made to improve the understanding, the Advisory Committee has changed language to make style and terminology consistent throughout the appellate rules. These changes are intended to be stylistic only.

COMMITTEE NOTES ON RULES—2002 AMENDMENT

Subdivision (b). Subdivision (b) has been amended so that the clerk may use electronic means to serve a copy of the opinion or judgment or to serve notice of the date when judgment was entered upon parties who have consented to such service.

Changes Made After Publication and Comments. No changes were made to the text of the proposed amendment or to the Committee Note.

Rule 37. Interest on Judgment

(a) When the Court Affirms. Unless the law provides otherwise, if a money judgment in a civil case is affirmed, whatever interest is allowed by law is payable from the date when the district court's judgment was entered.
(b) When the Court Reverses. If the court modifies or reverses a judgment with a direction that a money judgment be entered in the district court, the mandate must contain instructions about the allowance of interest.

(As amended Apr. 24, 1998, eff. Dec. 1, 1998.)

NOTES OF ADVISORY COMMITTEE ON RULES—1967

The first sentence makes it clear that if a money judgment is affirmed in the court of appeals, the interest which attaches to money judgments by force of law (see 28 U.S.C. §1961 and §2411) upon their initial entry is payable as if no appeal had been taken, whether or not the mandate makes mention of interest. There has been some confusion on this point. See Blair v. Durham, 139 F.2d 260 (6th Cir., 1943) and cases cited therein.

In reversing or modifying the judgment of the district court, the court of appeals may direct the entry of a money judgment, as, for example, when the court of appeals reverses a judgment notwithstanding the verdict and directs entry of judgment on the verdict. In such a case the question may arise as to whether interest is to run from the date of entry of the judgment directed by the court of appeals or from the date on which the judgment would have been entered in the district court except for the erroneous ruling corrected on appeal. In Briggs v. Pennsylvania R. Co., 334 U.S. 304, 68 S.Ct. 1039, 92 L.Ed. 1403 (1948), the Court held that where the mandate of the court of appeals directed entry of judgment upon a verdict but made no mention of interest from the date of the verdict to the date of the entry of the judgment directed by the mandate, the district court was powerless to add such interest. The second sentence of the proposed rule is a reminder to the court, the clerk and counsel of the Briggs rule. Since the rule directs that the matter of interest be disposed of by the mandate, in cases where interest is simply overlooked, a party who conceives himself entitled to interest from a date other than the date of entry of judgment in accordance with the mandate should be entitled to seek recall of the mandate for determination of the question.

COMMITTEE NOTES ON RULES—1998 AMENDMENT

The language and organization of the rule are amended to make the rule more easily understood. In addition to changes made to improve the understanding, the Advisory Committee has changed language to make style and terminology consistent throughout the appellate rules. These changes are intended to be stylistic only.

Rule 38. Frivolous Appeal—Damages and Costs

If a court of appeals determines that an appeal is frivolous, it may, after a separately filed motion or notice from the court and reasonable opportunity to respond, award just damages and single or double costs to the appellee.

(As amended Apr. 29, 1994, eff. Dec. 1, 1994; Apr. 24, 1998, eff. Dec. 1, 1998.)

NOTES OF ADVISORY COMMITTEE ON RULES—1967

Compare 28 U.S.C. §1912. While both the statute and the usual rule on the subject by courts of appeals (Fourth Circuit Rule 20 is a typical rule) speak of "damages for delay," the courts of appeals quite properly allow damages, attorney's fees and other expenses incurred by an appellee if the appeal is frivolous without requiring a showing that the appeal resulted in delay. See Dunscombe v. Sayle, 340 F.2d 311 (5th Cir., 1965), cert. den., 382 U.S. 814, 86 S.Ct. 32, 15 L.Ed.2d 62 (1965); Lowe v. Willacy, 239 F.2d 179 (9th Cir., 1956); Griffith Wellpoint Corp. v. Munro-Langstroth, Inc., 269 F.2d 64 (1st Cir., 1959); Ginsburg v. Stern, 295 F.2d 698 (3d Cir., 1961). The subjects of interest and damages are separately regulated, contrary to the present practice of combining the two (see Fourth Circuit Rule 20) to make it clear that the awards are distinct and independent. Interest is provided for by law; damages are awarded by the court in its discretion in the case of a frivolous appeal as a matter of justice to the appellee and as a penalty against the appellant.

NOTES OF ADVISORY COMMITTEE ON RULES—1994 AMENDMENT

The amendment requires that before a court of appeals may impose sanctions, the person to be sanctioned must have notice and an opportunity to respond. The amendment reflects the basic principle enunciated in the Supreme Court's opinion in Roadway Express, Inc. v. Piper, 447 U.S. 752, 767 (1980), that notice and opportunity to respond must precede the imposition of sanctions. A separately filed motion requesting sanctions constitutes notice. A statement inserted in a party's brief that the party moves for sanctions is not sufficient notice. Requests in briefs for sanctions have become so commonplace that it is unrealistic to expect careful responses to such requests without any indication that the court is actually contemplating such measures. Only a motion, the purpose of which is to request sanctions, is sufficient. If there is no such motion filed, notice must come from the court. The form of notice from the court and of the opportunity for comment purposely are left to the court's discretion.

COMMITTEE NOTES ON RULES—1998 AMENDMENT

Only the caption of this rule has been amended. The changes are intended to be stylistic only.

Rule 39. Costs

(a) Against Whom Assessed. The following rules apply unless the law provides or the court orders otherwise:
(1) if an appeal is dismissed, costs are taxed against the appellant, unless the parties agree otherwise;
(2) if a judgment is affirmed, costs are taxed against the appellant;
(3) if a judgment is reversed, costs are taxed against the appellee;
(4) if a judgment is affirmed in part, reversed in part, modified, or vacated, costs are taxed only as the court orders.

(b) Costs For and Against the United States. Costs for or against the United States, its agency, or officer will be assessed under Rule 39(a) only if authorized by law.
(c) Costs of Copies. Each court of appeals must, by local rule, fix the maximum rate for taxing the cost of producing necessary copies of a brief or appendix, or copies of records authorized by Rule 30(f). The rate must not exceed that generally charged for such work in the area where the clerk's office is located and should encourage economical methods of copying.
(d) Bill of Costs: Objections; Insertion in Mandate.
(1) A party who wants costs taxed must—within 14 days after entry of judgment—file with the circuit clerk and serve an itemized and verified bill of costs.
(2) Objections must be filed within 14 days after service of the bill of costs, unless the court extends the time.
(3) The clerk must prepare and certify an itemized statement of costs for insertion in the mandate, but issuance of the mandate must not be delayed for taxing costs. If the mandate issues before costs are finally determined, the district clerk must—upon the circuit clerk's request—add the statement of costs, or any amendment of it, to the mandate.

(e) Costs on Appeal Taxable in the District Court. The following costs on appeal are taxable in the district court for the benefit of the party entitled to costs under this rule:
(1) the preparation and transmission of the record;
(2) the reporter's transcript, if needed to determine the appeal;
(3) premiums paid for a bond or other security to preserve rights pending appeal; and
(4) the fee for filing the notice of appeal.

(As amended Apr. 30, 1979, eff. Aug. 1, 1979; Mar. 10, 1986, eff. July 1, 1986; Apr. 24, 1998, eff. Dec. 1, 1998; Mar. 26, 2009, eff. Dec. 1, 2009; Apr. 26, 2018, eff. Dec. 1, 2018; Apr. 25, 2019, eff. Dec. 1, 2019.)

NOTES ON ADVISORY COMMITTEE ON RULES—1967

Subdivision (a). Statutory authorization for taxation of costs is found in 28 U.S.C. §1920. The provisions of this subdivision follow the usual practice in the circuits. A few statutes contain specific provisions in derogation of these general provisions. (See 28 U.S.C. §1928, which forbids the award of costs to a successful plaintiff in a patent infringement action under the circumstances described by the statute). These statutes are controlling in cases to which they apply.

Subdivision (b). The rules of the courts of appeals at present commonly deny costs to the United States except as allowance may be directed by statute. Those rules were promulgated at a time when the United States was generally invulnerable to an award of costs against it, and they appear to be based on the view that if the United States is not subject to costs if it loses, it ought not be entitled to recover costs if it wins.

The number of cases affected by such rules has been greatly reduced by the Act of July 18, 1966, 80 Stat. 308 (1 U.S. Code Cong. & Ad. News, p. 349 (1966), 89th Cong., 2d Sess., which amended 28 U.S.C. §2412, the former general bar to the award of costs against the United States. Section 2412 as amended generally places the United States on the same footing as private parties with respect to the award of costs in civil cases. But the United States continues to enjoy immunity from costs in certain cases. By its terms amended section 2412 authorizes an award of costs against the United States only in civil actions, and it excepts from its general authorization of an award of costs against the United States cases which are "otherwise specifically provided (for) by statute." Furthermore, the Act of July 18, 1966, supra, provides that the amendments of section 2412 which it effects shall apply only to actions filed subsequent to the date of its enactment. The second clause continues in effect, for these and all other cases in which the United States enjoys immunity from costs, the presently prevailing rule that the United States may recover costs as the prevailing party only if it would have suffered them as the losing party.

Subdivision (c). While only five circuits (D.C. Cir. Rule 20(d); 1st Cir. Rule 31(4); 3d Cir. Rule 35(4); 4th Cir. Rule 21(4); 9th Cir. Rule 25, as amended June 2, 1967) presently tax the cost of printing briefs, the proposed rule makes the cost taxable in keeping with the principle of this rule that all cost items expended in the prosecution of a proceeding should be borne by the unsuccessful party.

Subdivision (e). The costs described in this subdivision are costs of the appeal and, as such, are within the undertaking of the appeal bond. They are made taxable in the district court for general convenience. Taxation of the cost of the reporter's transcript is specifically authorized by 28 U.S.C. §1920, but in the absence of a rule some district courts have held themselves without authority to tax the cost (Perlman v. Feldmann, 116 F.Supp. 102 (D.Conn., 1953); Firtag v. Gendleman, 152 F.Supp. 226 (D.D.C., 1957); Todd Atlantic Shipyards Corps. v. The Southport, 100 F.Supp. 763 (E.D.S.C., 1951). Provision for taxation of the cost of premiums paid for supersedeas bonds is common in the local rules of district courts and the practice is established in the Second, Seventh, and Ninth Circuits. Berner v. British Commonwealth Pacific Air Lines, Ltd., 362 F.2d 799 (2d Cir. 1966); Land Oberoesterreich v. Gude, 93 F.2d 292 (2d Cir., 1937); In re Northern Ind. Oil Co., 192 F.2d 139 (7th Cir., 1951); Lunn v. F. W. Woolworth, 210 F.2d 159 (9th Cir., 1954).

NOTES OF ADVISORY COMMITTEE ON RULES—1979 AMENDMENT

Subdivision (c). The proposed amendment would permit variations among the circuits in regulating the maximum rates taxable as costs for printing or otherwise reproducing briefs, appendices, and copies of records authorized by Rule 30(f). The present rule has had a different effect in different circuits depending upon the size of the circuit, the location of the clerk's office, and the location of other cities. As a consequence there was a growing sense that strict adherence to the rule produces some unfairness in some of the circuits and the matter should be made subject to local rule.

Subdivision (d). The present rule makes no provision for objections to a bill of costs. The proposed amendment would allow 10 days for such objections. Cf. Rule 54(d) of the F.R.C.P. It provides further that the mandate shall not be delayed for taxation of costs.

NOTES OF ADVISORY COMMITTEE ON RULES—1986 AMENDMENT

The amendment to subdivision (c) is intended to increase the degree of control exercised by the courts of appeals over rates for printing and copying recoverable as costs. It further requires the courts of appeals to encourage cost-consciousness by requiring that, in fixing the rate, the court consider the most economical methods of printing and copying.

The amendment to subdivision (d) is technical. No substantive change is intended.

COMMITTEE NOTES ON RULES—1998 AMENDMENT

The language and organization of the rule are amended to make the rule more easily understood. In addition to changes made to improve the understanding, the Advisory Committee has changed language to make style and terminology consistent throughout the appellate rules. These changes are intended to be stylistic only. All references to the cost of "printing" have been deleted from subdivision (c) because commercial printing is so rarely used for preparation of documents filed with a court of appeals.

COMMITTEE NOTES ON RULES—2009 AMENDMENT

Subdivision (d)(2). The time set in the former rule at 10 days has been revised to 14 days. See the Note to Rule 26.

COMMITTEE NOTES ON RULES—2018 AMENDMENT

The amendment of subdivision (e)(3) conforms this rule with the amendment of Federal Rule of Civil Procedure 62. Rule 62 formerly required a party to provide a "supersedeas bond" to obtain a stay of the judgment and proceedings to enforce the judgment. As amended, Rule 62(b) allows a party to obtain a stay by providing a "bond or other security."

COMMITTEE NOTES ON RULES—2019 AMENDMENT

In subdivision (d)(1) the words "with proof of service" are deleted and replaced with "and serve" to conform with amendments to Rule 25(d) regarding when proof of service or acknowledgement of service is required for filed papers.

Rule 40. Petition for Panel Rehearing

(a) Time to File; Contents; Answer; Action by the Court if Granted.

(1) Time. Unless the time is shortened or extended by order or local rule, a petition for panel rehearing may be filed within 14 days after entry of judgment. But in a civil case, unless an order shortens or extends the time, the petition may be filed by any party within 45 days after entry of judgment if one of the parties is:

(A) the United States;

(B) a United States agency;

(C) a United States officer or employee sued in an official capacity; or

(D) a current or former United States officer or employee sued in an individual capacity for an act or omission occurring in connection with duties performed on the United States' behalf—including all instances in which the United States represents that person when the court of appeals' judgment is entered or files the petition for that person.

(2) Contents. The petition must state with particularity each point of law or fact that the petitioner believes the court has overlooked or misapprehended and must argue in support of the petition. Oral argument is not permitted.

(3) Answer. Unless the court requests, no answer to a petition for panel rehearing is permitted. But ordinarily rehearing will not be granted in the absence of such a request.

(4) Action by the Court. If a petition for panel rehearing is granted, the court may do any of the following:

(A) make a final disposition of the case without reargument;

(B) restore the case to the calendar for reargument or resubmission; or

(C) issue any other appropriate order.

(b) Form of Petition; Length. The petition must comply in form with Rule 32. Copies must be served and filed as Rule 31 prescribes. Except by the court's permission:

(1) a petition for panel rehearing produced using a computer must not exceed 3,900 words; and

(2) a handwritten or typewritten petition for panel rehearing must not exceed 15 pages.

(As amended Apr. 30, 1979, eff. Aug. 1, 1979; Apr. 29, 1994, eff. Dec. 1, 1994; Apr. 24, 1998, eff. Dec. 1, 1998; Apr. 26, 2011, eff. Dec. 1, 2011; Apr. 28, 2016, eff. Dec. 1, 2016.)

NOTES OF ADVISORY COMMITTEE ON RULES—1967

This is the usual rule among the circuits, except that the express prohibition against filing a reply to the petition is found only in the rules of the Fourth, Sixth and Eighth Circuits (it is also contained in Supreme Court Rule 58(3)). It is included to save time and expense to the party victorious on appeal. In the very rare instances in which a reply is useful, the court will ask for it.

NOTES OF ADVISORY COMMITTEE ON RULES—1979 AMENDMENT

Subdivision (a). The Standing Committee added to the first sentence of Rule 40(a) the words "or by local rule," to conform to current practice in the circuits. The Standing Committee believes the change noncontroversial.

Subdivision (b). The proposed amendment would eliminate the distinction drawn in the present rule between printed briefs and those duplicated from typewritten pages in fixing their maximum length. See Note to Rule 28. Since petitions for rehearing must be prepared in a short time, making typographic printing less likely, the maximum number of pages is fixed at 15, the figure used in the present rule for petitions duplicated by means other than typographic printing.

NOTES OF ADVISORY COMMITTEE ON RULES—1994 AMENDMENT

Subdivision (a). The amendment lengthens the time for filing a petition for rehearing from 14 to 45 days in civil cases involving the United States or its agencies or officers. It has no effect upon the time for filing in criminal cases. The amendment makes nation-wide the current practice in the District of Columbia and the Tenth Circuits, see D.C. Cir. R. 15(a), 10th Cir. R. 40.3. This amendment, analogous to the provision in Rule 4(a) extending the time for filing a notice of appeal in cases involving the United States, recognizes that the Solicitor General needs time to conduct a thorough review of the merits of a case before requesting a rehearing. In a case in which a court of appeals believes it necessary to restrict the time for filing a rehearing petition, the amendment provides that the court may do so by order. Although the first sentence of Rule 40 permits a court of appeals to shorten or lengthen the usual 14 day filing period by order or by local rule, the sentence governing appeals in civil cases involving the United States purposely limits a court's power to alter the 45 day period to orders in specific cases. If a court of appeals could adopt a local rule shortening the time for filing a petition for rehearing in all cases involving the United States, the purpose of the amendment would be defeated.

COMMITTEE NOTES ON RULES—1998 AMENDMENT

The language and organization of the rule are amended to make the rule more easily understood. In addition to changes made to improve the understanding, the Advisory Committee has changed language to make style and terminology consistent throughout the appellate rules. These changes are intended to be stylistic only.

COMMITTEE NOTES ON RULES—2011 AMENDMENT

Subdivision (a)(1). Rule 40(a)(1) has been amended to make clear that the 45-day period to file a petition for panel rehearing applies in cases in which an officer or employee of the United States is sued in an individual capacity for acts or omissions occurring in connection with duties performed on behalf of the United States. (A concurrent amendment to Rule 4(a)(1)(B) makes clear that the 60-day period to file an appeal also applies in such cases.) In such cases, the Solicitor General needs adequate time to review the merits of the panel decision and decide whether to seek rehearing, just as the Solicitor General does when an appeal involves the United States, a United States agency, or a United States officer or employee sued in an official capacity.

To promote clarity of application, the amendment to Rule 40(a)(1) includes safe harbor provisions that parties can readily apply and rely upon. Under new subdivision 40(a)(1)(D), a case automatically qualifies for the 45-day period if (1) a legal officer of the United States has appeared in the case, in an official capacity, as counsel for the current or former officer or employee and has not withdrawn the appearance at the time of the entry of the court of appeals' judgment that is the subject of the petition or (2) a legal officer of the United States appears on the petition as counsel, in an official capacity, for the current or former officer or employee. There will be cases that do not fall within either safe harbor but that qualify for the longer petition period. An example would be a case in which a federal employee is sued in an individual capacity for an act occurring in connection with federal duties and the United States does not represent the employee either when the court of appeals' judgment is entered or when the petition is filed but the United States pays for private counsel for the employee.

Changes Made After Publication and Comment. The Committee made two changes to the proposal after publication and comment.

First, the Committee inserted the words "current or former" before "United States officer or employee." This insertion causes the text of the proposed Rule to diverge slightly from that of Civil Rules 4(i)(3) and 12(a)(3), which refer simply to "a United States officer or employee [etc.]." This divergence, though, is only stylistic. The 2000 Committee Notes to Civil Rules 4(i)(3) and 12(a)(3) make clear that those rules are intended to encompass former as well as current officers or employees.

Second, the Committee added, at the end of Rule 40(a)(1)(D), the following new language: "—including all instances in which the United States represents that person when the court of appeals' judgment is entered or files the petition for that person." During the public comment period, concerns were raised that a party might rely on the longer period for filing the petition, only to risk the petition being held untimely by a court that later concluded that the relevant act or omission had not actually occurred in connection with federal duties. The Committee decided to respond to this concern by adding two safe harbor provisions. These provisions make clear that the longer period applies in any ease where the United States either represents the officer or employee at the time of entry of the relevant judgment or files the petition on the officer or employee's behalf.

COMMITTEE NOTES ON RULES—2016 AMENDMENT

The page limits previously employed in Rules 5, 21, 27, 35, and 40 have been largely overtaken by changes in technology. For papers produced using a computer, those page limits are now replaced by word limits. The word limits were derived from the current page limits using the assumption that one page is equivalent to 260 words. Papers produced using a computer must include the certificate of compliance required by Rule 32(g); Form 6 in the Appendix of Forms suffices to meet that requirement. Page limits are retained for papers prepared without the aid of a computer (i.e., handwritten or typewritten papers). For both the word limit and the page limit, the calculation excludes any items listed in Rule 32(f).

Rule 41. Mandate: Contents; Issuance and Effective Date; Stay

(a) Contents. Unless the court directs that a formal mandate issue, the mandate consists of a certified copy of the judgment, a copy of the court's opinion, if any, and any direction about costs.

(b) When Issued. The court's mandate must issue 7 days after the time to file a petition for rehearing expires, or 7 days after entry of an order denying a timely petition for panel rehearing, petition for rehearing en banc, or motion for stay of mandate, whichever is later. The court may shorten or extend the time by order.

(c) Effective Date. The mandate is effective when issued.

(d) Staying the Mandate Pending a Petition for Certiorari.

(1) Motion to Stay. A party may move to stay the mandate pending the filing of a petition for a writ of certiorari in the Supreme Court. The motion must be served on all parties and must show that the petition would present a substantial question and that there is good cause for a stay.

(2) Duration of Stay; Extensions. The stay must not exceed 90 days, unless:

(A) the period is extended for good cause; or

(B) the party who obtained the stay notifies the circuit clerk in writing within the period of the stay:

(i) that the time for filing a petition has been extended, in which case the stay continues for the extended period; or

(ii) that the petition has been filed, in which case the stay continues until the Supreme Court's final disposition.

(3) Security. The court may require a bond or other security as a condition to granting or continuing a stay of the mandate.

(4) Issuance of Mandate. The court of appeals must issue the mandate immediately on receiving a copy of a Supreme Court order denying the petition, unless extraordinary circumstances exist.

(As amended Apr. 29, 1994, eff. Dec. 1, 1994; Apr. 24, 1998, eff. Dec. 1, 1998; Apr. 29, 2002, eff. Dec. 1, 2002; Mar. 26, 2009, eff. Dec. 1, 2009; Apr. 26, 2018, eff. Dec. 1, 2018.)

NOTES OF ADVISORY COMMITTEE ON RULES——1967

The proposed rule follows the rule or practice in a majority of circuits by which copies of the opinion and the judgment serve in lieu of a formal mandate in the ordinary case. Compare Supreme Court Rule 59. Although 28 U.S.C. §2101(c) permits a writ of certiorari to be filed within 90 days after entry of judgment, seven of the eight circuits which now regulate the matter of stays pending application for certiorari limit the initial stay of the mandate to the 30-day period provided in the proposed rule. Compare D.C. Cir. Rule 27(e).

NOTES OF ADVISORY COMMITTEE ON RULES——1994 AMENDMENT

Subdivision (a). The amendment conforms Rule 41(a) to the amendment made to Rule 40(a). The amendment keys the time for issuance of the mandate to the expiration of the time for filing a petition for rehearing, unless such a petition is filed in which case the mandate issues 7 days after the entry of the order denying the petition. Because the amendment to Rule 40(a) lengthens the time for filing a petition for rehearing in civil cases involving the United States from 14 to 45 days, the rule requiring the mandate to issue 21 days after the entry of judgment would cause the mandate to issue while the government is still considering requesting a rehearing. Therefore, the amendment generally requires the mandate to issue 7 days after the expiration of the time for filing a petition for rehearing.

Subdivision (b). The amendment requires a party who files a motion requesting a stay of mandate to file, at the same time, proof of service on all other parties. The old rule required the party to give notice to the other parties; the amendment merely requires the party to provide the court with evidence of having done so.

The amendment also states that the motion must show that a petition for certiorari would present a substantial question and that there is good cause for a stay. The amendment is intended to alert the parties to the fact that a stay of mandate is not granted automatically and to the type of showing that needs to be made. The Supreme Court has established conditions that must be met before it will stay a mandate. See Robert L. Stern et al., Supreme Court Practice §17.19 (6th ed. 1986).

COMMITTEE NOTES ON RULES——1998 AMENDMENT

The language and organization of the rule are amended to make the rule more easily understood. In addition to changes made to improve the understanding, the Advisory Committee has changed language to make style and terminology consistent throughout the appellate rules. These changes are intended to be stylistic only.

Several substantive changes are made in this rule, however.

Subdivision (b). The existing rule provides that the mandate issues 7 days after the time to file a petition for panel rehearing expires unless such a petition is timely filed. If the petition is denied, the mandate issues 7 days after entry of the order denying the petition. Those provisions are retained but the amendments further provide that if a timely petition for rehearing en banc or motion for stay of mandate is filed, the mandate does not issue until 7 days after entry of an order denying the last of all such requests. If a petition for rehearing or a petition for rehearing en banc is granted, the court enters a new judgment after the rehearing and the mandate issues within the normal time after entry of that judgment.

Subdivision (c). Subdivision (c) is new. It provides that the mandate is effective when the court issues it. A court of appeals' judgment or order is not final until issuance of the mandate; at that time the parties' obligations become fixed. This amendment is intended to make it clear that the mandate is effective upon issuance and that its effectiveness is not delayed until receipt of the mandate by the trial court or agency, or until the trial court or agency acts upon it. This amendment is consistent with the current understanding. Unless the court orders that the mandate issue earlier than provided in the rule, the parties can easily calculate the anticipated date of issuance and verify issuance with the clerk's office. In those instances in which the court orders earlier issuance of the mandate, the entry of the order on the docket alerts the parties to that fact.

Subdivision (d). Amended paragraph (1) provides that the filing of a petition for panel rehearing, a petition for rehearing en banc or a motion for a stay of mandate pending petition to the Supreme Court for a writ of certiorari stays the issuance of the mandate until the court disposes of the petition or motion. The provision that a petition for rehearing en banc stays the mandate is a companion to the amendment of Rule 35 that deletes the language stating that a request for a rehearing en banc does not affect the finality of the judgment or stay the issuance of the mandate. The Committee's objective is to treat a request for a rehearing en banc like a petition for panel rehearing so that a request for a rehearing en banc will suspend the finality of the court of appeals' judgment and delay the running of the period for filing a petition for writ of certiorari. Because the filing of a petition for rehearing en banc will stay the mandate, a court of appeals will need to take final action on the petition but the procedure for doing so is left to local practice.

Paragraph (1) also provides that the filing of a motion for a stay of mandate pending petition to the Supreme Court for a writ of certiorari stays the mandate until the court disposes of the motion. If the court denies the motion, the court must issue the mandate 7 days after entering the order denying the motion. If the court grants the motion, the mandate is stayed according to the terms of the order granting the stay. Delaying issuance of the mandate eliminates the need to

254

recall the mandate if the motion for a stay is granted. If, however, the court believes that it would be inappropriate to delay issuance of the mandate until disposition of the motion for a stay, the court may order that the mandate issue immediately.

Paragraph (2). The amendment changes the maximum period for a stay of mandate, absent the court of appeals granting an extension for cause, to 90 days. The presumptive 30-day period was adopted when a party had to file a petition for a writ of certiorari in criminal cases within 30 days after entry of judgment. Supreme Court Rule 13.1 now provides that a party has 90 days after entry of judgment by a court of appeals to file a petition for a writ of certiorari whether the case is civil or criminal.

The amendment does not require a court of appeals to grant a stay of mandate that is coextensive with the period granted for filing a petition for a writ of certiorari. The granting of a stay and the length of the stay remain within the discretion of the court of appeals. The amendment means only that a 90-day stay may be granted without a need to show cause for a stay longer than 30 days.

Subparagraph (C) is not new; it has been moved from the end of the rule to this position.

COMMITTEE NOTES ON RULES—2002 AMENDMENT

Subdivision (b). Subdivision (b) directs that the mandate of a court must issue 7 days after the time to file a petition for rehearing expires or 7 days after the court denies a timely petition for panel rehearing, petition for rehearing en banc, or motion for stay of mandate, whichever is later. Intermediate Saturdays, Sundays, and legal holidays are counted in computing that 7-day deadline, which means that, except when the 7-day deadline ends on a weekend or legal holiday, the mandate issues exactly one week after the triggering event.

Fed. R. App. P. 26(a)(2) has been amended to provide that, in computing any period of time, one should "[e]xclude intermediate Saturdays, Sundays, and legal holidays when the period is less than 11 days, unless stated in calendar days." This change in the method of computing deadlines means that 7-day deadlines (such as that in subdivision (b)) have been lengthened as a practical matter. Under the new computation method, a mandate would never issue sooner than 9 actual days after a triggering event, and legal holidays could extend that period to as much as 13 days.

Delaying mandates for 9 or more days would introduce significant and unwarranted delay into appellate proceedings. For that reason, subdivision (b) has been amended to require that mandates issue 7 calendar days after a triggering event.

Changes Made After Publication and Comments. No changes were made to the text of the proposed amendment or to the Committee Note.

COMMITTEE NOTES ON RULES—2009 AMENDMENT

Under former Rule 26(a), short periods that span weekends or holidays were computed without counting those weekends or holidays. To specify that a period should be calculated by counting all intermediate days, including weekends or holidays, the Rules used the term "calendar days." Rule 26(a) now takes a "days-are-days" approach under which all intermediate days are counted, no matter how short the period. Accordingly, "7 calendar days" in subdivision (b) is amended to read simply "7 days."

Changes Made After Publication and Comment. The Appellate Rules Committee made only one change to Rule 26(a) after publication and comment: Because the Committee is seeking permission to publish for comment a proposed new Rule 1(b) that would adopt a FRAP-wide definition of the term "state," the Committee decided to delete from Rule 26(a)(6)(B) the following parenthetical sentence: "(In this rule, 'state' includes the District of Columbia and any United States commonwealth, territory, or possession.)" That change required the corresponding deletion—from the Note to Rule 26(a)(6)—of part of the final sentence (the deleted portion read ", and defines the term 'state'—for purposes of subdivision (a)(6)—to include the District of Columbia and any commonwealth, territory or possession of the United States. Thus, for purposes of subdivision (a)(6)'s definition of 'legal holiday,' 'state' includes the District of Columbia, Guam, American Samoa, the U.S. Virgin Islands, the Commonwealth of Puerto Rico, and the Commonwealth of the Northern Mariana Islands.")

The Appellate Rules Committee made one change to its proposed amendments concerning Appellate Rules deadlines. Based on comments received with respect to the timing for motions that toll the time for taking a civil appeal, the Committee changed the cutoff time in Rule 4(a)(4)(A)(vi) to 28 days (rather than to 30 days as in the published proposal). The published proposal's choice of 30 days had been designed to accord with the proposed amendments published by the Civil Rules Committee, which would have extended the deadline for tolling motions to 30 days. Because 30 days is also the time period set by Appellate Rule 4 and by 28 U.S.C. §2107 for taking a civil appeal (when the United States and its officers or agencies are not parties), commentators pointed out that adopting 30 days as the cutoff for filing tolling motions would sometimes place would-be appellants in an awkward position: If the deadline for making a tolling motion falls on the same day as the deadline for filing a notice of appeal, then in a case involving multiple parties on one side, a litigant who wishes to appeal may not know, when filing the notice of appeal, whether a tolling motion will be filed; such a timing system can be expected to produce instances when appeals are filed, only to go into abeyance while the tolling motion is resolved.

By the time of the Appellate Rules Committee's April 2008 meeting, the Civil Rules Committee had discussed this issue and had determined that the best resolution would be to extend the deadline for tolling motions to 28 days rather than 30 days. The choice of a 28-day deadline responds to the concerns of those who feel that the current 10-day deadlines are much too short, but also takes into account the problem of the 30-day appeal deadline. As described in the draft minutes of the Committee's April meeting, Committee members carefully discussed the relevant concerns and determined, by a vote of 7 to 1, to assent to the 28-day time period for tolling motions and to change the cutoff time in Rule 4(a)(4)(A)(vi) to 28 days.

The Standing Committee changed Rule 26(a)(6) to exclude state holidays from the definition of "legal holiday" for purposes of computing backward-counted periods; conforming changes were made to the Committee Note.

COMMITTEE NOTES ON RULES—2018 AMENDMENT

Subdivision (b). Subdivision (b) is revised to clarify that an order is required for a stay of the mandate.

Before 1998, the rule referred to a court's ability to shorten or enlarge the time for the mandate's issuance "by order." The phrase "by order" was deleted as part of the 1998 restyling of the rule. Though the change appears to have been intended as merely stylistic, it has caused uncertainty concerning whether a court of appeals can stay its mandate through mere inaction or whether such a stay requires an order. There are good reasons to require an affirmative act by the court. Litigants—particularly those not well versed in appellate procedure—may overlook the need to check that the court of appeals has issued its mandate in due course after handing down a decision. And, in Bell v. Thompson, 545 U.S. 794, 804 (2005), the lack of notice of a stay was one of the factors that contributed to the Court's holding that staying the mandate was an abuse of discretion. Requiring stays of the mandate to be accomplished by court order will provide notice to litigants and can also facilitate review of the stay.

255

Subdivision (d). Three changes are made in subdivision (d).

Subdivision (d)(1)——which formerly addressed stays of the mandate upon the timely filing of a motion to stay the mandate or a petition for panel or en banc rehearing——has been deleted and the rest of subdivision (d) has been renumbered and renamed accordingly. In instances where such a petition or motion is timely filed, subdivision (b) sets the presumptive date for issuance of the mandate at 7 days after entry of an order denying the petition or motion. Thus, it seems redundant to state (as subdivision (d)(1) did) that timely filing of such a petition or motion stays the mandate until disposition of the petition or motion. The deletion of subdivision (d)(1) is intended to streamline the rule; no substantive change is intended.

Under the new subdivision (d)(2)(B), if the court of appeals issues a stay of the mandate for a party to file a petition for certiorari, and a Justice of the Supreme Court subsequently extends the time for filing the petition, the stay automatically continues for the extended period.

Subdivision (d)(4)——i.e., former subdivision (d)(2)(D)——is amended to specify that a mandate stayed pending a petition for certiorari must issue immediately once the court of appeals receives a copy of the Supreme Court's order denying certiorari, unless the court of appeals finds that extraordinary circumstances justify a further stay. Without deciding whether the prior version of Rule 41 provided authority for a further stay of the mandate after denial of certiorari, the Supreme Court ruled that any such authority could be exercised only in "extraordinary circumstances." Ryan v. Schad, 570 U.S. 521, 525 (2013) (per curiam). The amendment to subdivision (d)(4) makes explicit that the court may stay the mandate after the denial of certiorari, and also makes explicit that such a stay is permissible only in extraordinary circumstances. Such a stay cannot occur through mere inaction but rather requires an order.

The reference in prior subdivision (d)(2)(D) to the filing of a copy of the Supreme Court's order is replaced by a reference to the court of appeals' receipt of a copy of the Supreme Court's order. The filing of the copy and its receipt by the court of appeals amount to the same thing (cf. Rule 25(a)(2)(A)(i), setting a general rule that "filing is not timely unless the clerk receives the papers within the time fixed for filing"), but "on receiving a copy" is more specific and, hence, clearer.

Rule 42. Voluntary Dismissal

(a) Dismissal in the District Court. Before an appeal has been docketed by the circuit clerk, the district court may dismiss the appeal on the filing of a stipulation signed by all parties or on the appellant's motion with notice to all parties.

(b) Dismissal in the Court of Appeals. The circuit clerk may dismiss a docketed appeal if the parties file a signed dismissal agreement specifying how costs are to be paid and pay any fees that are due. But no mandate or other process may issue without a court order. An appeal may be dismissed on the appellant's motion on terms agreed to by the parties or fixed by the court.

(As amended Apr. 24, 1998, eff. Dec. 1, 1998.)

NOTES OF ADVISORY COMMITTEE ON RULES——1967

Subdivision (a). This subdivision is derived from FRCP 73(a) without change of substance.

Subdivision (b). The first sentence is a common provision in present circuit rules. The second sentence is added. Compare Supreme Court Rule 60.

COMMITTEE NOTES ON RULES——1998 AMENDMENT

The language of the rule is amended to make the rule more easily understood. In addition to changes made to improve the understanding, the Advisory Committee has changed language to make style and terminology consistent throughout the appellate rules. These changes are intended to be stylistic only.

Rule 43. Substitution of Parties

(a) Death of a Party.

(1) After Notice of Appeal Is Filed. If a party dies after a notice of appeal has been filed or while a proceeding is pending in the court of appeals, the decedent's personal representative may be substituted as a party on motion filed with the circuit clerk by the representative or by any party. A party's motion must be served on the representative in accordance with Rule 25. If the decedent has no representative, any party may suggest the death on the record, and the court of appeals may then direct appropriate proceedings.

(2) Before Notice of Appeal Is Filed——Potential Appellant. If a party entitled to appeal dies before filing a notice of appeal, the decedent's personal representative——or, if there is no personal representative, the decedent's attorney of record——may file a notice of appeal within the time prescribed by these rules. After the notice of appeal is filed, substitution must be in accordance with Rule 43(a)(1).

(3) Before Notice of Appeal Is Filed——Potential Appellee. If a party against whom an appeal may be taken dies after entry of a judgment or order in the district court, but before a notice of appeal is filed, an appellant may proceed as if the death had not occurred. After the notice of appeal is filed, substitution must be in accordance with Rule 43(a)(1).

(b) Substitution for a Reason Other Than Death. If a party needs to be substituted for any reason other than death, the procedure prescribed in Rule 43(a) applies.

(c) Public Officer: Identification; Substitution.

(1) Identification of Party. A public officer who is a party to an appeal or other proceeding in an official capacity may be described as a party by the public officer's official title rather than by name. But the court may require the public officer's name to be added.

(2) Automatic Substitution of Officeholder. When a public officer who is a party to an appeal or other proceeding in an official capacity dies, resigns, or otherwise ceases to hold office, the action does not abate. The public officer's successor is automatically substituted as a party. Proceedings following the substitution are to be in the name of the substituted party, but any misnomer that does not affect the substantial rights of the parties may be disregarded. An order of substitution may be entered at any time, but failure to enter an order does not affect the substitution.

(As amended Mar. 10, 1986, eff. July 1, 1986; Apr. 24, 1998, eff. Dec. 1, 1998.)

NOTES OF ADVISORY COMMITTEE ON RULES——1967

Subdivision (a). The first three sentences described a procedure similar to the rule on substitution in civil actions in the district court. See FRCP 25(a). The fourth sentence expressly authorizes an appeal to be taken against one who has died after the entry of judgment. Compare FRCP 73(b), which impliedly authorizes such an appeal.

The sixth sentence authorizes an attorney of record for the deceased to take an appeal on behalf of successors in interest if the deceased has no representative. At present, if a party entitled to appeal dies before the notice of appeal is filed, the appeal can presumably be taken only by his legal representative and must be taken within the time ordinarily prescribed. 13 Cyclopedia of Federal Procedure (3d Ed.) §63.21. The states commonly make special provisions for the event of the death of a party entitled to appeal, usually by extending the time otherwise prescribed. Rules of Civil Procedure for Superior Courts of Arizona, Rule 73(t), 16 A.R.S.; New Jersey Rev. Rules 1:3—3; New York Civil Practice Law and Rules, Sec. 1022; Wisconsin Statutes Ann. 274.01(2). The provision in the proposed rule is derived from California Code of Civil Procedure, Sec. 941.

Subdivision (c). This subdivision is derived from FRCP 25(d) and Supreme Court Rule 48, with appropriate changes.

NOTES OF ADVISORY COMMITTEE ON RULES—1986 AMENDMENT

The amendments to Rules 43(a) and (c) are technical. No substantive change is intended.

COMMITTEE NOTES ON RULES—1998 AMENDMENT

The language and organization of the rule are amended to make the rule more easily understood. In addition to changes made to improve the understanding, the Advisory Committee has changed language to make style and terminology consistent throughout the appellate rules. These changes are intended to be stylistic only.

Rule 44. Case Involving a Constitutional Question When the United States or the Relevant State is Not a Party

(a) Constitutional Challenge to Federal Statute. If a party questions the constitutionality of an Act of Congress in a proceeding in which the United States or its agency, officer, or employee is not a party in an official capacity, the questioning party must give written notice to the circuit clerk immediately upon the filing of the record or as soon as the question is raised in the court of appeals. The clerk must then certify that fact to the Attorney General.

(b) Constitutional Challenge to State Statute. If a party questions the constitutionality of a statute of a State in a proceeding in which that State or its agency, officer, or employee is not a party in an official capacity, the questioning party must give written notice to the circuit clerk immediately upon the filing of the record or as soon as the question is raised in the court of appeals. The clerk must then certify that fact to the attorney general of the State.

(As amended Apr. 24, 1998, eff. Dec. 1, 1998; Apr. 29, 2002, eff. Dec. 1, 2002.)

NOTES OF ADVISORY COMMITTEE ON RULES—1967

This rule is now found in the rules of a majority of the circuits. It is in response to the Act of August 24, 1937 (28 U.S.C. §2403), which requires all courts of the United States to advise the Attorney General of the existence of an action or proceeding of the kind described in the rule.

COMMITTEE NOTES ON RULES—1998 AMENDMENT

The language of the rule is amended to make the rule more easily understood. In addition to changes made to improve the understanding, the Advisory Committee has changed language to make style and terminology consistent throughout the appellate rules. These changes are intended to be stylistic only.

COMMITTEE NOTES ON RULES—2002 AMENDMENT

Rule 44 requires that a party who "questions the constitutionality of an Act of Congress" in a proceeding in which the United States is not a party must provide written notice of that challenge to the clerk. Rule 44 is designed to implement 28 U.S.C. §2403(a), which states that: "In any action, suit or proceeding in a court of the United States to which the United States or any agency, officer or employee thereof is not a party, wherein the constitutionality of any Act of Congress affecting the public interest is drawn in question, the court shall certify such fact to the Attorney General, and shall permit the United States to intervene . . . for argument on the question of constitutionality."

The subsequent section of the statute—§2403(b)—contains virtually identical language imposing upon the courts the duty to notify the attorney general of a state of a constitutional challenge to any statute of that state. But §2403(b), unlike §2403(a), was not implemented in Rule 44.

Rule 44 has been amended to correct this omission. The text of former Rule 44 regarding constitutional challenges to federal statutes now appears as Rule 44(a), while new language regarding constitutional challenges to state statutes now appears as Rule 44(b).

Changes Made After Publication and Comments. No changes were made to the text of the proposed amendment or to the Committee Note.

Rule 45. Clerk's Duties

(a) General Provisions.

(1) Qualifications. The circuit clerk must take the oath and post any bond required by law. Neither the clerk nor any deputy clerk may practice as an attorney or counselor in any court while in office.

(2) When Court Is Open. The court of appeals is always open for filing any paper, issuing and returning process, making a motion, and entering an order. The clerk's office with the clerk or a deputy in attendance must be open during business hours on all days except Saturdays, Sundays, and legal holidays. A court may provide by local rule or by order that the clerk's office be open for specified hours on Saturdays or on legal holidays other than New Year's Day, Martin Luther King, Jr.'s Birthday, Washington's Birthday, Memorial Day, Independence Day, Labor Day, Columbus Day, Veterans' Day, Thanksgiving Day, and Christmas Day.

(b) Records.

(1) The Docket. The circuit clerk must maintain a docket and an index of all docketed cases in the manner prescribed by the Director of the Administrative Office of the United States Courts. The clerk must record all papers filed with the clerk and all process, orders, and judgments.

(2) Calendar. Under the court's direction, the clerk must prepare a calendar of cases awaiting argument. In placing cases on the calendar for argument, the clerk must give preference to appeals in criminal cases and to other proceedings and appeals entitled to preference by law.

(3) Other Records. The clerk must keep other books and records required by the Director of the Administrative Office of the United States Courts, with the approval of the Judicial Conference of the United States, or by the court.

(c) Notice of an Order or Judgment. Upon the entry of an order or judgment, the circuit clerk must immediately serve a notice of entry on each party, with a copy of any opinion, and must note the date of service on the docket. Service on a party represented by counsel must be made on counsel.

(d) Custody of Records and Papers. The circuit clerk has custody of the court's records and papers. Unless the court orders or instructs otherwise, the clerk must not permit an original record or paper to be taken from the clerk's office. Upon disposition of the case, original papers constituting the record on appeal or review must be returned to the court or agency from which they were received. The clerk must preserve a copy of any brief, appendix, or other paper that has been filed.

(As amended Mar. 1, 1971, eff. July 1, 1971; Mar. 10, 1986, eff. July 1, 1986; Apr. 24, 1998, eff. Dec. 1, 1998; Apr. 29, 2002, eff. Dec. 1, 2002; Apr. 25, 2005, eff. Dec. 1, 2005.)

The duties imposed upon clerks of the courts of appeals by this rule are those imposed by rule or practice in a majority of the circuits. The second sentence of subdivision (a) authorizing the closing of the clerk's office on Saturday and non-national legal holidays follows a similar provision respecting the district court clerk's office found in FRCP 77(c) and in FRCrP 56.

The amendment adds Columbus Day to the list of legal holidays. See the Note accompanying the amendment of Rule 26(a).

The amendment to Rule 45(b) permits the courts of appeals to maintain computerized dockets. The Committee believes that the Administrative Office of the United States Courts ought to have maximum flexibility in prescribing the format of this docket in order to ensure a smooth transition from manual to automated systems and subsequent adaptation to technological improvements.

The amendments to Rules 45(a) and (d) are technical. No substantive change is intended. The Birthday of Martin Luther King, Jr. has been added to the list of national holidays.

The language and organization of the rule are amended to make the rule more easily understood. In addition to changes made to improve the understanding, the Advisory Committee has changed language to make style and terminology consistent throughout the appellate rules. These changes are intended to be stylistic only.

Subdivision (c). Subdivision (c) has been amended so that the clerk may use electronic means to serve notice of entry of an order or judgment upon parties who have consented to such service.

Changes Made After Publication and Comments. No changes were made to the text of the proposed amendment or to the Committee Note.

Subdivision (a)(2). Rule 45(a)(2) has been amended to refer to the third Monday in February as "Washington's Birthday." A federal statute officially designates the holiday as "Washington's Birthday," reflecting the desire of Congress specially to honor the first president of the United States. See 5 U.S.C. §6103(a). During the 1998 restyling of the Federal Rules of Appellate Procedure, references to "Washington's Birthday" were mistakenly changed to "Presidents' Day." The amendment corrects that error.

Changes Made After Publication and Comments. No changes were made to the text of the proposed amendment or to the Committee Note.

Rule 46. Attorneys

(a) Admission to the Bar.

(1) Eligibility. An attorney is eligible for admission to the bar of a court of appeals if that attorney is of good moral and professional character and is admitted to practice before the Supreme Court of the United States, the highest court of a state, another United States court of appeals, or a United States district court (including the district courts for Guam, the Northern Mariana Islands, and the Virgin Islands).

(2) Application. An applicant must file an application for admission, on a form approved by the court that contains the applicant's personal statement showing eligibility for membership. The applicant must subscribe to the following oath or affirmation:

"I, _____, do solemnly swear [or affirm] that I will conduct myself as an attorney and counselor of this court, uprightly and according to law; and that I will support the Constitution of the United States."

(3) Admission Procedures. On written or oral motion of a member of the court's bar, the court will act on the application. An applicant may be admitted by oral motion in open court. But, unless the court orders otherwise, an applicant need not appear before the court to be admitted. Upon admission, an applicant must pay the clerk the fee prescribed by local rule or court order.

(b) Suspension or Disbarment.

(1) Standard. A member of the court's bar is subject to suspension or disbarment by the court if the member:

(A) has been suspended or disbarred from practice in any other court; or

(B) is guilty of conduct unbecoming a member of the court's bar.

(2) Procedure. The member must be given an opportunity to show good cause, within the time prescribed by the court, why the member should not be suspended or disbarred.

(3) Order. The court must enter an appropriate order after the member responds and a hearing is held, if requested, or after the time prescribed for a response expires, if no response is made.

(c) Discipline. A court of appeals may discipline an attorney who practices before it for conduct unbecoming a member of the bar or for failure to comply with any court rule. First, however, the court must afford the attorney reasonable notice, an opportunity to show cause to the contrary, and, if requested, a hearing.

(As amended Mar. 10, 1986, eff. July 1, 1986; Apr. 24, 1998, eff. Dec. 1, 1998.)

Subdivision (a). The basic requirement of membership in the bar of the Supreme Court, or of the highest court of a state, or in another court of appeals or a district court is found, with minor variations, in the rules of ten circuits. The only other requirement in those circuits is that the applicant be of good moral and professional character. In the District of Columbia Circuit applicants other than members of the District of Columbia District bar or the Supreme Court bar must claim membership in the bar of the highest court of a state, territory or possession for three years prior to application for admission (D.C. Cir. Rule 7). Members of the District of Columbia District bar and the Supreme Court bar again excepted, applicants for admission to the District of Columbia Circuit bar must meet precisely defined prelaw and law school study requirements (D.C. Cir. Rule 7½).

A few circuits now require that application for admission be made by oral motion by a sponsor member in open court. The proposed rule permits both the application and the motion by the sponsor member to be in writing, and permits action on the motion without the appearance of the applicant or the sponsor, unless the court otherwise orders.

Subdivision (b). The provision respecting suspension or disbarment is uniform. Third Circuit Rule 8(3) is typical.

Subdivision (c). At present only Fourth Circuit Rule 36 contains an equivalent provision. The purpose of this provision is to make explicit the power of a court of appeals to impose sanctions less serious than suspension or disbarment for the breach of rules. It also affords some measure of control over attorneys who are not members of the bar of the court. Several circuits permit a non-member attorney to file briefs and motions, membership being required only at the time of oral argument. And several circuits permit argument pro hac vice by non-member attorneys.

NOTES OF ADVISORY COMMITTEE ON RULES——1986 AMENDMENT

The amendments to Rules 46(a) and (b) are technical. No substantive change is intended.

COMMITTEE NOTES ON RULES——1998 AMENDMENT

The language and organization of the rule are amended to make the rule more easily understood. In addition to changes made to improve the understanding, the Advisory Committee has changed language to make style and terminology consistent throughout the appellate rules. These changes are intended to be stylistic only.

Rule 47. Local Rules by Courts of Appeals

(a) Local Rules.

(1) Each court of appeals acting by a majority of its judges in regular active service may, after giving appropriate public notice and opportunity for comment, make and amend rules governing its practice. A generally applicable direction to parties or lawyers regarding practice before a court must be in a local rule rather than an internal operating procedure or standing order. A local rule must be consistent with—but not duplicative of—Acts of Congress and rules adopted under 28 U.S.C. §2072 and must conform to any uniform numbering system prescribed by the Judicial Conference of the United States. Each circuit clerk must send the Administrative Office of the United States Courts a copy of each local rule and internal operating procedure when it is promulgated or amended.

(2) A local rule imposing a requirement of form must not be enforced in a manner that causes a party to lose rights because of a nonwillful failure to comply with the requirement.

(b) Procedure When There Is No Controlling Law. A court of appeals may regulate practice in a particular case in any manner consistent with federal law, these rules, and local rules of the circuit. No sanction or other disadvantage may be imposed for noncompliance with any requirement not in federal law, federal rules, or the local circuit rules unless the alleged violator has been furnished in the particular case with actual notice of the requirement.

(As amended Apr. 27, 1995, eff. Dec. 1, 1995; Apr. 24, 1998, eff. Dec. 1, 1998.)

NOTES OF ADVISORY COMMITTEE ON RULES——1967

This rule continues the authority now vested in individual courts of appeals by 28 U.S.C. §2071 to make rules consistent with rules of practice and procedure promulgated by the Supreme Court.

NOTES OF ADVISORY COMMITTEE ON RULES——1995 AMENDMENT

Subdivision (a). This rule is amended to require that a generally applicable direction regarding practice before a court of appeals must be in a local rule rather than an internal operating procedure or some other general directive. It is the intent of this rule that a local rule may not bar any practice that these rules explicitly or implicitly permit. Subdivision (b) allows a court of appeals to regulate practice in an individual case by entry of an order in the case. The amendment also reflects the requirement that local rules be consistent not only with the national rules but also with Acts of Congress. The amendment also states that local rules should not repeat national rules and Acts of Congress.

The amendment also requires that the numbering of local rules conform with any uniform numbering system that may be prescribed by the Judicial Conference. Lack of uniform numbering might create unnecessary traps for counsel and litigants. A uniform numbering system would make it easier for an increasingly national bar and for litigants to locate a local rule that applies to a particular procedural issue.

Paragraph (2) is new. Its aim is to protect against loss of rights in the enforcement of local rules relating to matters of form. The proscription of paragraph (2) is narrowly drawn—covering only violations that are not willful and only those involving local rules directed to matters of form. It does not limit the court's power to impose substantive penalties upon a party if it or its attorney stubbornly or repeatedly violates a local rule, even one involving merely a matter of form. Nor does it affect the court's power to enforce local rules that involve more than mere matters of form.

Subdivision (b). This rule provides flexibility to the court in regulating practice in a particular case when there is no controlling law. Specifically, it permits the court to regulate practice in any manner consistent with Acts of Congress, with rules adopted under 28 U.S.C. §2072, and with the circuit's local rules.

The amendment to this rule disapproves imposing any sanction or other disadvantage on a person for noncompliance with such a directive, unless the alleged violator has been furnished in a particular case with actual notice of the requirement. There should be no adverse consequence to a party or attorney for violating special requirements relating to practice before a particular court unless the party or attorney has actual notice of those requirements.

COMMITTEE NOTES ON RULES——1998 AMENDMENT

The language of the rule is amended to make the rule more easily understood. In addition to changes made to improve the understanding, the Advisory Committee has changed language to make style and terminology consistent throughout the appellate rules. These changes are intended to be stylistic only.

Rule 48. Masters

(a) Appointment; Powers. A court of appeals may appoint a special master to hold hearings, if necessary, and to recommend factual findings and disposition in matters ancillary to proceedings in the court. Unless the order referring a matter to a master specifies or limits the master's powers, those powers include, but are not limited to, the following:

(1) regulating all aspects of a hearing;

(2) taking all appropriate action for the efficient performance of the master's duties under the order;

259

(3) requiring the production of evidence on all matters embraced in the reference; and

(4) administering oaths and examining witnesses and parties.

(b) Compensation. If the master is not a judge or court employee, the court must determine the master's compensation and whether the cost is to be charged to any party.

(As amended Apr. 29, 1994, eff. Dec. 1, 1994; Apr. 24, 1998, eff. Dec. 1, 1998.)

NOTES OF ADVISORY COMMITTEE ON RULES—1994 AMENDMENT

The text of the existing Rule 48 concerning the title was moved to Rule 1.

This new Rule 48 authorizes a court of appeals to appoint a special master to make recommendations concerning ancillary matters. The courts of appeals have long used masters in contempt proceedings where the issue is compliance with an enforcement order. See Polish National Alliance v. NLRB, 159 F.2d 38 (7th Cir. 1946), NLRB v. Arcade-Sunshine Co., 132 F.2d 8 (D.C. Cir. 1942); NLRB v. Remington Rand, Inc., 130 F.2d 919 (2d Cir. 1942). There are other instances when the question before a court of appeals requires a factual determination. An application for fees or eligibility for Criminal Justice Act status on appeal are examples.

Ordinarily when a factual issue is unresolved, a court of appeals remands the case to the district court or agency that originally heard the case. It is not the Committee's intent to alter that practice. However, when factual issues arise in the first instance in the court of appeals, such as fees for representation on appeal, it would be useful to have authority to refer such determinations to a master for a recommendation.

COMMITTEE NOTES ON RULES—1998 AMENDMENT

The language and organization of the rule are amended to make the rule more easily understood. In addition to changes made to improve the understanding, the Advisory Committee has changed language to make style and terminology consistent throughout the appellate rules. These changes are intended to be stylistic only.

APPENDIX OF FORMS

Form 1. Notice of Appeal to a Court of Appeals From a Judgment or Order of a District Court

United States District Court for the _____ District of _____

File Number _____

A.B., Plaintiff

v.

}Notice of Appeal

C. D., Defendant

Notice is hereby given that _____(here name all parties taking the appeal)_____, (plaintiffs) (defendants) in the above named case,* hereby appeal to the United States Court of Appeals for the _____ Circuit (from the final judgment) (from an order (describing it)) entered in this action on the _____ day of _____, 20__.

(S)_____

ATTORNEY FOR _____

ADDRESS: _____

[Note to inmate filers: If you are an inmate confined in an institution and you seek the timing benefit of Fed. R. App. P. 4(c)(1), complete Form 7 (Declaration of Inmate Filing) and file that declaration along with this Notice of Appeal.]

* See Rule 3(c) for permissible ways of identifying appellants.

(As amended Apr. 22, 1993, eff. Dec. 1, 1993; Mar. 27, 2003, eff. Dec. 1, 2003; Apr. 28, 2016, eff. Dec. 1, 2016.)

Form 2. Notice of Appeal to a Court of Appeals From a Decision of the United States Tax Court

UNITED STATES TAX COURT

Washington, D.C.

A.B., Petitioner

v.

Commissioner of

}Docket No._____

Internal Revenue,

Respondent

Notice of Appeal

Notice is hereby given that _____(here name all parties taking the appeal) *_____ hereby appeal to the United States Court of Appeals for the _____ Circuit from (that part of) the decision of this court entered in the above captioned proceeding on the _____ day of _____, 20__ (relating to _____).

(S)_____

COUNSEL FOR _____

ADDRESS: _____

* See Rule 3(c) for permissible ways of identifying appellants.
(As amended Apr. 22, 1993, eff. Dec. 1, 1993; Mar. 27, 2003, eff. Dec. 1, 2003.)

Form 3. Petition for Review of Order of an Agency, Board, Commission or Officer

United States Court of Appeals
for the _____ Circuit

A.B., Petitioner
   v.
XYZ Commission,
}Petition for Review
Respondent

_____(here name all parties bringing the petition) *_____ hereby petition the court for review of the Order of the XYZ Commission (describe the order)
entered on _____, 20__.
(S)_____,
ATTORNEY FOR PETITIONERS
ADDRESS:_____
* See Rule 15.
(As amended Apr. 22, 1993, eff. Dec. 1, 1993; Mar. 27, 2003, eff. Dec. 1, 2003.)

Form 4. Affidavit Accompanying Motion for Permission to Appeal In Forma Pauperis

UNITED STATES DISTRICT COURT

for the

<_____> DISTRICT OF <_____>

\<Name(s) of plaintiff(s)\>,	)	
	)	
Plaintiff(s)	)	
	)	
v.	)	
	)	Case No. \<Number\>
\<Name(s) of defendant(s)\>,	)	
	)	
Defendant(s)	)	
	)	

AFFIDAVIT ACCOMPANYING MOTION
FOR PERMISSION TO APPEAL IN FORMA PAUPERIS

Affidavit in Support of Motion	Instructions
I swear or affirm under penalty of perjury that, because of my poverty, I cannot prepay the docket fees of my appeal or post a bond for them. I believe I am entitled to redress. I swear or affirm under penalty of perjury under United States laws that my answers on this form are true and correct. (28 U.S.C. § 1746; 18 U.S.C. § 1621.)	Complete all questions in this application and then sign it. Do not leave any blanks: if the answer to a question is "0," "none," or "not applicable (N/A)," write in that response. If you need more space to answer a question or to explain your answer, attach a separate sheet of paper identified with your name, your case's docket number, and the question number.

Signed: _____   Date: _____

My issues on appeal are:

1.   *For both you and your spouse estimate the average amount of money received from each of the following sources during the past 12 months. Adjust any amount that was received weekly, biweekly, quarterly, semiannually, or annually to show the monthly rate. Use gross amounts, that is, amounts before any deductions for taxes or otherwise.*

Income source	Average monthly amount during the past 12 months		Amount expected next month	
	You	Spouse	You	Spouse
Employment	$	$	$	$
Self-employment	$	$	$	$
Income from real property (such as rental income)	$	$	$	$
Interest and dividends	$	$	$	$
Gifts	$	$	$	$
Alimony	$	$	$	$
Child support	$	$	$	$
Retirement (such as social security, pensions, annuities, insurance)	$	$	$	$
Disability (such as social security, insurance payments)	$	$	$	$
Unemployment payments	$	$	$	$
Public-assistance (such as welfare)	$	$	$	$
Other (specify):	$	$	$	$
Total monthly income:	$	$	$	$

2. *List your employment history for the past two years, most recent employer first. (Gross monthly pay is before taxes or other deductions.)*

Employer	Address	Dates of employment	Gross monthly pay
			$
			$
			$

3. *List your spouse's employment history for the past two years, most recent employer first. (Gross monthly pay is before taxes or other deductions.)*

Employer	Address	Dates of employment	Gross monthly pay
			$
			$
			$

4. *How much cash do you and your spouse have? $_____*

Below, state any money you or your spouse have in bank accounts or in any other financial institution.

Financial Institution	Type of Account	Amount you have	Amount your spouse has
		$	$
		$	$
		$	$

If you are a prisoner seeking to appeal a judgment in a civil action or proceeding, you must attach a statement certified by the appropriate institutional officer showing all receipts, expenditures, and balances during the last six months in your institutional accounts. If you have multiple accounts, perhaps because you have been in multiple institutions, attach one certified statement of each account.

5. *List the assets, and their values, which you own or your spouse owns. Do not list clothing and ordinary household furnishings.*

Home	Other real estate	Motor vehicle #1
(Value) $	(Value) $	(Value) $
		Make and year:
		Model:
		Registration #:

Motor vehicle #2	Other assets	Other assets
(Value) $	(Value) $	(Value) $
Make and year:		
Model:		
Registration #:		

6. *State every person, business, or organization owing you or your spouse money, and the amount owed.*

Person owing you or your spouse money	Amount owed to you	Amount owed to your spouse
	$	$
	$	$
	$	$
	$	$

7. *State the persons who rely on you or your spouse for support.*

Name [or, if under 18, initials only]	Relationship	Age

8. *Estimate the average monthly expenses of you and your family. Show separately the amounts paid by your spouse. Adjust any payments that are made weekly, biweekly, quarterly, semiannually, or annually to show the monthly rate.*

	You	Your Spouse
Rent or home-mortgage payment (include lot rented for mobile home) 　　Are real estate taxes included?　　[ ] Yes [ ] No 　　Is property insurance included?　　[ ] Yes [ ] No	$	$

Utilities (electricity, heating fuel, water, sewer, and telephone)	$	$
Home maintenance (repairs and upkeep)	$	$
Food	$	$
Clothing	$	$
Laundry and dry-cleaning	$	$
Medical and dental expenses	$	$
Transportation (not including motor vehicle payments)	$	$
Recreation, entertainment, newspapers, magazines, etc.	$	$
Insurance (not deducted from wages or included in mortgage payments)		
Homeowner's or renter's:	$	$
Life:	$	$
Health:	$	$
Motor vehicle:	$	$
Other:	$	$
Taxes (not deducted from wages or included in mortgage payments) (specify):	$	$
Installment payments		
Motor Vehicle:	$	$
Credit card (name):	$	$
Department store (name):	$	$
Other:	$	$
Alimony, maintenance, and support paid to others	$	$
Regular expenses for operation of business, profession, or farm (attach detailed statement)	$	$
Other (specify):	$	$
Total monthly expenses:	$	$

9. *Do you expect any major changes to your monthly income or expenses or in your assets or liabilities during the next 12 months?*

    [ ] Yes [ ] No   If yes, describe on an attached sheet.

10. *Have you spent — or will you be spending — any money for expenses or attorney fees in connection with this lawsuit?* [ ] Yes [ ] No

    If yes, how much? $ _____

11. *Provide any other information that will help explain why you cannot pay the docket fees for your appeal.*

12. *State the city and state of your legal residence.*

    Your daytime phone number: (___) _____

    Your age: _____ *Your years of schooling:* _____
    (As amended Apr. 24, 1998, eff. Dec. 1, 1998; Apr. 28, 2010, eff. Dec. 1, 2010; Apr. 16, 2013, eff. Dec. 1, 2013; Apr. 26, 2018, eff. Dec. 1, 2018.)

    COMMITTEE NOTES ON RULES—2010 AMENDMENT
    Changes Made After Publication and Comment. No changes were made after publication and comment.

    COMMITTEE NOTES ON RULES—2013 AMENDMENT
    Changes Made After Publication and Comment. No changes were made after publication and comment.

Form 5. Notice of Appeal to a Court of Appeals From a Judgment or Order of a District Court or a Bankruptcy Appellate Panel
    United States District Court for the _____
    District of _____

In re

_____,
        Debtor

_____,   File No. _____
        Plaintiff
            v.

_____,
        Defendant

Notice of Appeal to United States Court of Appeals for the _____ Circuit

_____, the plaintiff [or defendant or other party] appeals to the United States Court of Appeals for the _____ Circuit from the final judgment [or order or decree] of the district court for the district of _____ [or bankruptcy appellate panel of the _____ circuit], entered in this case on _____, 20_____ [here describe the judgment, order, or decree] _____

The parties to the judgment [or order or decree] appealed from and the names and addresses of their respective attorneys are as follows:

DATED _____

SIGNED _____

ATTORNEY FOR APPELLANT

ADDRESS: _____

_____

[Note to inmate filers: If you are an inmate confined in an institution and you seek the timing benefit of Fed. R. App. P. 4(c)(1), complete Form 7 (Declaration of Inmate Filing) and file that declaration along with this Notice of Appeal.]

(As added Apr. 25, 1989, eff. Dec. 1, 1989; amended Mar. 27, 2003, eff. Dec. 1, 2003; Apr. 28, 2016, eff. Dec. 1, 2016.)

FORM 6

Form 6. Certificate of Compliance With Type-Volume Limit

Certificate of Compliance With Type-Volume Limit,
Typeface Requirements, and Type-Style Requirements

1.   This document complies with [the type-volume limit of Fed. R. App. P. [*insert Rule citation; e.g., 32(a)(7)(B)*]] [the word limit of Fed. R. App. P. [*insert Rule citation; e.g., 5(c)(1)*]] because, excluding the parts of the document exempted by Fed. R. App. P. 32(f) [and [*insert applicable Rule citation, if any*]]:

☐   this document contains [*state the number of*] words, **or**

☐   this brief uses a monospaced typeface and contains [*state the number of*] lines of text.

2.   This document complies with the typeface requirements of Fed. R. App. P. 32(a)(5) and the type-style requirements of Fed. R. App. P. 32(a)(6) because:

☐   this document has been prepared in a proportionally spaced typeface using [*state name and version of word-processing program*] in [*state font size and name of type style*], **or**

☐   this document has been prepared in a monospaced typeface using [*state name and version of word-processing program*] with [*state number of characters per inch and name of type style*].

(s)_____

Attorney for _____

Dated:

(As added Apr. 29, 2002, eff. Dec. 1, 2002; amended Apr. 28, 2016, eff. Dec. 1, 2016.)

COMMITTEE NOTES ON RULES—2002

Form 7. Declaration of Inmate Filing

_____

[insert name of court; for example,
United States District Court for the District of Minnesota]

A.B., Plaintiff
v.
}Case No._____
C.D., Defendant

I am an inmate confined in an institution. Today, _____ [insert date], I am depositing the _____ [insert title of document; for example, "notice of appeal"] in this case in the institution's internal mail system. First-class postage is being prepaid either by me or by the institution on my behalf.
I declare under penalty of perjury that the foregoing is true and correct (see 28 U.S.C. §1746; 18 U.S.C. §1621).
Sign your name here_____
Signed on _____[insert date]

[Note to inmate filers: If your institution has a system designed for legal mail, you must use that system in order to receive the timing benefit of Fed. R. App. P. 4(c)(1) or Fed. R. App. P. 25(a)(2)(A)(iii).]
(As added Apr. 28, 2016, eff. Dec. 1, 2016; amended Apr. 26, 2018, eff. Dec. 1, 2018.)

APPENDIX

[SEE COURT SITE FOR CURRENT FORMS]

(As added Apr. 28, 2016, eff. Dec. 1, 2016.)

LENGTH LIMITS

Appendix: Length Limits Stated in the Federal Rules of Appellate Procedure is set out in the order of the Supreme Court amending the Federal Rules of Appellate Procedure, April 28, 2016, available at the Supreme Court website.

Made in the USA
Middletown, DE
22 September 2020